THE LETTERS OF
RALPH WALDO EMERSON

Concord
Aug. 4 1861

My dear Cabot,

I was very
glad yesterday to hear
from you, & on such high
matters. The war—though
from such despicable
beginnings, has assumed
such huge proportions,
that it threatens to engulf
us all—no preoccupation
can exclude it, & no
hermitage hide us—

We must all go to the next ↑Club↓, & there is not a special agreement?

Facsimile Page of Letter to James Elliot Cabot
August 4, 1861

THE LETTERS OF
RALPH WALDO
EMERSON

IN SIX VOLUMES

EDITED BY

RALPH L. RUSK
**PROFESSOR OF ENGLISH IN
COLUMBIA UNIVERSITY**

VOLUME FIVE

NEW YORK AND LONDON
COLUMBIA UNIVERSITY PRESS

Copyright 1939

RALPH WALDO EMERSON MEMORIAL ASSOCIATION

First printing 1939
Second printing 1966

PUBLICATION OF THIS WORK WAS MADE POSSIBLE
THROUGH THE AID OF THE ALBERT H. WIGGIN FUND

Printed in the United States of America

THE LETTERS OF
RALPH WALDO EMERSON
1856–1867

1 8 5 6

To Hermann Raster, Rock Island? January 1, and Dixon, Illinois, January 4, 1856 [1]

Concord Massachusetts
1 January 1856

Dear Sir,

You shall excuse, if you can, my extreme tardiness in replying to your note, which I received in November, but, at a moment so crowded with correspondence & other duties, that I was forced to lay aside for the time all letters not imperative.

If it is not yet too late for Dr Elze's purpose, you shall say to him, that he is entirely at liberty to make what use he will of any books of mine, in Germany, or in Europe *out of England;* for, in England, some of my books have been copyrighted, or at any rate the forms have been been gone through of taking copyright. Nowhere else in Europe have I given to any publisher any title in writings of mine.

Dr Elze honors me by his design, & I wish him success in the whole undertaking.

You mention " Representative Men " & the " Essays " as the works he wishes to comprise in his edition. Of the Essays, there are two Series, First, & Second, each making one volume. But I would suggest that my knowledge of the circulation of these books would lead me to print in

1. MS owned by Mr. W. T. H. Howe; ph. in CUL. For Emerson's whereabouts on Jan. 1, *cf.* Dec. 30, 1855. That the letter must have been addressed to Hermann Raster, editor of a German paper in New York, is clear from his letter to Emerson, New York, Nov. 4, 1855, in which he explained that his friend Dr. Karl Elze, of Dessau, Germany, wished authorization to publish *Representative Men* and *Essays* in a series of standard American authors. If Emerson wished, no copy of the reprint would ever be sold in England or the United States. A few words by way of introduction were desired. *Representative Men* duly appeared as the twenty-second volume of *Dürr's Collection of Standard American Authors,* edited by William E. Drugulin. It bore the imprint of Alphons Dürr, Leipsic, 1856. Friedrich Karl Elze had later some reputation as a literary critic and as professor of the English language and literature at Halle. Raster is mentioned in Faust, II, 369, as one of the " forty-eighters " who made their mark in journalism.

his collection also the little independent book called " Nature," which was first published separately, & is now included in the volume of " Miscellanies."

Respectfully,
R. W. Emerson

Dixon [2] Illinois 4 January
1856
Dear Sir, I have seized on a journey a few moments to make the above slow reparation for my neglect, but thought it fit to date it from my usual residence.

R. W. E.

To Lidian Emerson, Dixon, Illinois, January 3, 1856 [3]

Dixon, Ill.
[1]3 January — 56[1]

Dear Lidian,

[II]A cold raw country this, & plenty of night travelling and arriving at 4 in the morning, to take the last & worst bed in the tavern. Advancing day brings mercy & favor to me, but not the sleep.[II] But I suppose this rough riding will not last long. I was yesterday at Lasalle [4] and at 12.10 P. M. took the train for Dixon,[5] the [III]mercury at 15 below zero.[III] The pinch of all this is the impossibility of sending out of such circumstance the last sheets [6] which the printers are waiting for. [IV]But I pick up some materials as I go for my chapter of the Anglo American, if I should wish to finish that. I hope you are not so cold and not so hard riders at home. I find well disposed kindly people among these sinewy farmers of the north; but in all that is called cultivation they are only ten years old, so that there is plenty of non-adaptation & yawning gulfs never bridged in this ambitious lyceum system they are trying to import. Their real interest is in prices, & sections & quarter sections of swamp lands.[IV] I go tomorrow to Freeport,[7] and, if you have sent me

2. See Jan. 3, 1856.

3. MS owned by RWEMA; ph. in CUL. Excerpts I–IV are in Cabot, II, 567–568.

4. The MS memorandum book for 1856 gives Jan. 2 to La Salle.

5. A paper called " the *Dixon Telegraph* " (quoted in the *Freeport Weekly Bulletin* of Jan. 24, 1856) noted that Emerson read his lecture on " Beauty " and described his style as " most miserable."

6. Of *English Traits,* which did not include a chapter on the Anglo-American.

7. The *Freeport Weekly Journal,* Jan. 10, 1856, reports the reading of " Beauty " on Jan. 4 before the Young Men's Association of the little Illinois town. The reporter thought that for intellectual quality this was " vastly superior to any lecture we have yet had," but that there was none of the magnetism important in popular oratory.

any letters, shall find them there. Mr H H. Taylor there is my general committee for ten or eleven towns.[8] You must send the children to Aunt Mary,[9] as they go by, with a pear, & go to see her yourself, & invite her to dine. I will send you a hundred dollars the first time I come to a town with a broker's office in it. Dear love to my girls & boy. W.

To Lidian Emerson, Galena, Illinois, January 5, 1856 [10]

> De Soto House
> Galena, Illinois
> 5 January 1856

Dear Lidian,

I send you a draft of $150.00 which you must endorse, & give to Mr Cheney, and he will give you the amount, and you must pay your most important bills in whole or in part. I have Ellen's letter on persons & pears [11] If George Bradford comes again, tell him I gave his " Life of Voltaire " [12] back to Mrs Ripley. But here is an important message. You must by yourself or by Ellen look over my files of letters of 1855 (all, I believe, or chiefly in the second drawer of the bureau in the red room) & find the *name of my correspondent of the Exeter N. H. Lyceum;* and then of the *Harvard,* Mass. Lyceum (the last I believe is

———————— Babcock) I want his whole name — and send me not the letters but these two names; to *care* of *John C. Vaughan,* Esq. Chicago, Illinois at once. For I suppose I must excuse myself to these two Lyceums,[13] &, unfortunately, I have left their letters at home. Tis just possible, — not probable, — that the letters may not be in the drawer, but on the top of cabinet in the study. From Boston a letter can come in two days to Chicago, as I did, 1035 miles. If you see the Davises, you

8. *Cf.* Jan. 13, 1856, to Taylor. There were probably a number of letters to this correspondent of which I have no trace.

9. Mary Moody Emerson seems to have remained in Concord, though not in the Emerson home, during the rest of the winter and the following spring (see June 2, 1856).

10. MS owned by RWEMA; ph. in CUL. A lengthy account of Emerson's lecture before the Young Men's Association of Galena on Jan. 5 appeared in the *Galena Daily Advertiser* of Jan. 8, 1856. The subject was reported as " the influence, civilization and power of England." The audience were given, said the reporter, " a literary treat of the highest character."

11. Dated Dec. 29 and 30, 1855.

12. Probably Eugène Noël's *Voltaire,* Paris, 1855, which Emerson told Carlyle (Aug. 22, 1856) of having read.

13. The MS memorandum book for 1856 shows that Exeter was at one time set down for Jan. 30 and Harvard for Jan. 29.

can say that I saw Charles Davis, Jr. here at Dixon, in good health & hope, on Thursday. Tis bitter cold but tonight I am very comfortably housed, & so, have a good Sunday before me. Tell the children dear that I have brought Vaughan, not John C. but Henry, in my trunk, & have read sweet verses in him, mindful also of them.[14] Affectionately,

W. —

And until you hear further, tis safest to send to me, care of John C. Vaughan, Esq.

Chicago Illinois

To Lidian Emerson, Belvidere, Illinois, January 8, 1856 [15]

Belvedere Illinois

8 Jan.ʸ 1856

Dear Lidian

Mercury below zero 22° and this the twelfth day of the cold snap. Winter in Illinois has a long whip. To cuddle into bed is the only refuge in these towns. I do not know but I must omit my lecture tonight in Elgin [16] on account of my private cold, as well as the public one. The cruel kindness of a gentleman at Galena carried me out in a bitter cold sleigh jaunt on the river to see the lead mines. I not suspecting the 5 miles, thinking it 3, it turned out seven; & last night I could hardly speak. One petty misfortune causes me a deal of trouble, — those shirts are not measured rightly, & will not button. Arriving late in the evening, tis a vexation to find your shirt was made for a smaller neck. And I do not stay long enough anywhere to get my wardrobe in order. From Galena I sent you by mail a letter [17] containing a draft for $150. I trust you received it two mails before this. My present address is Tremont House Chicago, and till the 20 Jan. you may safely address me there. Afterwards 21, 22, write to care of J. Hutcheson, Esq. Columbus, Ohio, where I shall be on the 24th.[18] Afterwards keep your letters at home where I hope to be about 30 Jan. I will send you another draft probably in a few days. Affectionately, W.

14. Perhaps the copy of Vaughan was one Emerson had received as a gift just before he left home for the West.

15. MS owned by RWEMA; ph. in CUL. *The Belvidere Standard* of Jan. 15, 1856, praised Emerson's " Beauty," read on Jan. 7, and reprinted what was said to be an account of the lecturer from a phrenological journal.

16. The time is the same recorded for Elgin in the MS memorandum book for this year.

17. Of Jan. 5, 1856.

18. See Jan. 14 following.

To Lidian Emerson, Chicago, January 13 and 14, 1856 [19]

> Tremont House
> Chicago, Sunday 13
> Jan.ʸ
> 1856

Dear Lidian,

I came here last night very glad to be in warm comfortable quarters again, after my cold fortnight's adventures on the prairie. I have seen some very good people, & have had some experiences useful if I were younger. I was glad to get this morning if it were only an envelope from you, with the account of good health of the children. For the Bacon MSS. I had no intention they should be forwarded to the Putnam people, without my expressed leave. I told you where they were, meaning that they shd. go to them, if you received a letter from Miss B. to me deciding to send them to Putnam. I had dissuaded her from doing so. I shall now write to W. E. on the subject.

I hope you have heard from me, especially at Galena,[20] whence I sent you a draft, & from Belvedere,[21] (I think) I asked you to look up the name of my *Exeter* & of my *Harvard* correspondents in the file of letters in the bureau drawer where you found Miss Bacon's papers. The safest address to me now will be, *Care of G. H. Wyman, Esq. Cleveland, Ohio.* where I shall be on the 23ᵈ [22] I think I may be at home on the 30th, but probably enough not till a day or two later. But I have not yet received the letters that will determine me. The worst effect of the bitter cold of the last week, which reached 28 and 29 degrees below zero, where I was, has been to prevent me altogether from ending my book, & sending home the sheets to P. & S.; which will have pestered Henry Thoreau, very likely, with vain expectation, as I begged him to look after them. You have had great snows; we have none. Edward's skating is spoiled, but Ediths " Christie Johnstone " [23] is in great request. I enclose to

19. MS owned by RWEMA; ph. in CUL. The MS memorandum book for 1856 gives Jan. 13 (Sunday) to Chicago, but I have no proof of a lecture there at this time. That the main business of these days in Chicago was work toward the completion of *English Traits* is clear from the letter of Jan. 24, 1857. According to the memorandum book, however, there were some lectures at other towns, beginning on Jan. 16 at Galesburg, Ill. Then, apparently, Emerson was in Chicago again just before setting out for Cleveland (cf. the first letter of Feb. 10, 1856).

　20. Jan. 5, 1856.
　21. Jan. 8, 1856.
　22. See Jan. 14, 1856.
　23. Cf. June 19, 1855.

you a draft for $150. drawn on John E. Thayer & Co [24] by Geo Smith [25] which you will endorse by writing pay to Mr Cheney cash.ʳ & Mr C. will pay it. to you Dear love to the children.

Affectionately,
W.

I had to keep this letter one day longer for my draft
14 Jan.ʸ

To Henry H. Taylor, Chicago, January 13, 1856

[Taylor, Freeport, Ill., Jan. 18, 1856, acknowledges this letter "of Tremont House," Jan. 13, and tells of forwarding mail to Emerson.]

To William Emerson, Chicago, January 14, 1856 [26]

Tremont House
Chicago, 14 Jan 1856

Dear William,

Since you have so kindly interested yourself in my duties to Miss Bacon,[27] I must trouble you once more. Lidian has sent the MSS to you. I left them in her charge to await the arrival of a letter from Miss B. in London, to say whether she would print them in Putnam, or, as I advised, in a separate book. I could not tell, besides, whether $55 which you reported as their price for the first livraison, was good pay, until I could count the pages. When I found it made 17 pp., I tho't the compensation totally inadequate. She ought to have 8 dollars a page, if that is their best price; and I wrote Mr Olmstead to that effect, I believe, from this place, a fortnight ago.[28] But Parke Godwin, whom I met here,[29] thought it would be best for her book to publish it first in Putnam, & promised to talk with Mr O. & obtain better terms. So that

24. The *Boston Directory* lists Jos. E. Thayer of Thayer & Co.

25. A George P. Smith was, at least a little earlier, a clerk in the Exchange Bank (*The Chicago City Directory*, 1855).

26. MS owned by HCL; ph. in CUL.

27. *Cf.* a note on July 31, 1855. William Emerson, Dec. 21, 1855 (MS owned by Dr. Haven Emerson), tells of conversations and correspondence with Olmstead (or Olmsted) about Delia Bacon's MS. The editor of *Putnam's* was in doubt about the wisdom of using Miss Bacon's article at all, but would be willing to examine a further instalment of it. If the new material proved acceptable, he would publish part of it in February. For the January article he would allow $55. I am uncertain whether he was the D. H. Olmstead of Dec. 11, 1856.

28. Dec. 30? 1855.

29. See Dec. 30, 1855.

now the sheets are sent to him, without my leave, I incline to let him print the next chapter for February,[30] *but no more* until he or I shall hear from Miss Bacon. So please to tell him, & recover from his custody the third & fourth chapters, & keep them for me, and oblige, as always,

Your affectionate brother,

Waldo —

My address for a week will be *Cleveland* care of G. H. Wyman, Esq where I shall be on 23ᵈ Jan.[31] or *Columbus,* Ohio, *Care of Jos. Hutcheson,* Esq. where I shall be on the 24ᵗʰ [32]

To Abel Adams, Boston, February 8, 1856 [33]

Boston, Friday, P. M

My dear friend,

I am sorry to find that Mr Dexter [34] is in Vermont and a gentleman in the Vermont Central Office said that Mr D's clerk Mr Tuckerman had just informed some one " that he did not know when he would return." This looks very bad for my information, now too when I am going away, & when days may be precious.

I do not know but the best way to relieve you & me of all uncertainty

30. " William Shakespeare and his Plays; an Inquiry Concerning them " had been printed, unsigned, in *Putnam's Monthly Magazine* for Jan., 1856; but no further instalments appeared.

31. This lecture of Jan. 23 was " Beauty " once more, and it won the profound attention, it was said, of the most intellectual audience of the season sponsored by the Library Association. The old debate as to Emerson's style of oratory took a favorable turn. His delivery, said the reporter, was most pleasing, though there were no theatrical flourishes, no pulpit affectations, no oratorical displays. (*Cleveland Daily Plain Dealer,* Jan. 23 and 24, 1856.) George H. Wyman is listed as a lawyer in *Spear, Denison, & Co.'s Cleveland City Directory,* 1856.

32. " Beauty " was again read at Deshler's Hall in Columbus, before the Atheneum, on Jan. 24. The local critic did not fail to find objections to Emerson's manner — too bad, he thought, that one who possessed so many of the graces of mind should not study somewhat the graces of attitude. Emerson's delivery seemed careless. Yet his would " long be remembered as the finest lecture ever delivered at the Atheneum." (*Daily Ohio State Journal,* Jan. 24 and 25, 1856.) Joseph Hutcheson, according to the *Columbus Business Directory,* 1855, was cashier of a bank.

33. MS owned by RWEMA; ph. in CUL. The date is fixed by the reference to the trip to Maine and by comparison with Feb. 23, 1856, to Adams.

34. *Cf.* Feb. 23, 1856, to Adams. The *Boston Directory,* 1856, shows that George M. Dexter was vice-president of the Vermont & Canada R. R. Co., at 108 State St., and that J. Francis Tuckerman was at the same address. Dexter was doubtless the George Minot Dexter who had entered Harvard with Emerson (MS *Records of the College Faculty,* IX, 121–122, in HCL) .

& vexation, will be to send the V. & C. scrip to your broker, & instruct him to get the most he can for it. I must go home this P. M. & shall probably come down on Sunday P. M. to the American House to take the Monday morn⁵ train for Portland.[35] So that I fear I shall not be within reach of your counsel, which I much want.

Affectionately,
R. W. Emerson.

Mr Adams.

To William Emerson, Concord, February 10, 1856 [36]

Concord 10 Feb.

Dear William,

  I received your letter at Chicago [37] & would gladly have promised, as you bade me, to stop at N. Y. on my way home; but I found the travelling so uncertain, that it would not do for me to make any new engagements before me for many days. — Well if I could keep those I had. Still I meant to indulge myself, if I could. On the whole, I managed to keep most of my days but in spite of every endeavor was thrown out by what seemed slight hindrances from making the right connections on the last days and came home by shortest ways to repair my failures. We are all well here now, though my journeying is not ended. I go tomorrow to Maine; [38] next week to Berkshire.[39] Thanks, thanks, for your attentions to Miss Bacons affair. I have the letter of Dix & Edwards in reply.[40] Love to Susan and to all the house.

Waldo

35. See the first letter of Feb. 10, 1856.

36. MS owned by HCL; ph. in CUL. The year is fixed by evidence cited below.

37. *Cf.* the letter of Jan. 13 and 14, 1856. William Emerson had written, Jan. 19, 1856, asking his brother to spend a night in New York on the way home from the West (MS owned by Dr. Haven Emerson).

38. The MS memorandum book for this year gives Feb. 11 to Hallowell (but as a doubtful appointment), the 12th to Gardiner, the 13th to Bath, the 14th to Bangor, and the 15th to Belfast.

39. Feb. 18–21 was set down for "Berkshire," without further explanation, *ibid.*

40. For the Bacon matter, *cf.* Jan. 14, 1856. Dix & Edwards, the new publishers of *Putnam's Monthly Magazine* since its sale by Putnam, wrote from New York, Jan. 24, 1856, inclosing a copy of a letter they had sent Delia Bacon under date of Jan. 20. They represented to her that a reading of what were intended to be the second, third, and fourth instalments of her paper in the magazine had convinced them that Emerson was right in advising that the work be published in book form. After putting the second instalment into type for the February number, they had changed their minds, but would still be glad to print one of the later chapters.

To WILLIAM EMERSON, CONCORD, FEBRUARY 10, 1856 [41]

Concord
10 Feb.ʸ
1856

Dear William,

Our good friend & pastor, Rev. Mr Frost,[42] is about sailing for the West Indies, as you may have heard, for the benefit of his health. He will probably wish to visit several points in the islands; and it occurs to me that, if Mr Sidney Mason is in New York, I shall be glad to ask, through you, his interest in Mr F.'s behalf, to give him a letter to his house, if, as I believe, he still has a commercial house, in St Johns. Tell him, that Mr Frost is a very worthy & very highly esteemed clergyman, pastor of the church here, for ten or fifteen years, & a man of excellent social & civil qualities, for whose health & prosperity all good men here are interested; and, if he can introduce him to any good persons in St Johns or St Thomas', it will be a kindness which we shall all thank him for. I think he means to go to Santa Cruz & to Cuba, also. Mr Prichard is already interested for Mr F. & will take charge of any letter you may obtain for him.

Affectionately
Your brother
Waldo —

Wᵐ Emerson, Esq.

To ABEL ADAMS, BOSTON, FEBRUARY 23, 1856 [43]

Harvard Club Rooms [44]
49 Tremont Street

My dear friend,

I have seen Mr Whitmore [45] today, & he very kindly ran over

41. MS owned by HCL; ph. in CUL.

42. Barzillai Frost is mentioned in earlier letters, as is Mason, the West India merchant who had befriended Emerson's brothers Edward and Charles when they were in Porto Rico. Frost, according to *Memoirs of Members of the Social Circle*, 3d series, p. 56, went to the West Indies in Feb., 1856, and was compelled to voyage there again the following winter. A broadside entitled *To the First Church and Parish of Concord* and dated Sept. 13, 1857, declares his resignation on account of ill health, after a pastorate of nearly twenty-one years. Mason appeared in *Trow's New York City Directory* for 1855–1856.

43. MS owned by RWEMA; ph. in CUL. The date, from the endorsement, apparently in the hand of Abel Adams, fits the subject matter of the letter.

44. Charles W. Eliot had sent Emerson a printed circular dated July 10, 1855, suggesting the establishment of a Harvard Club in Boston.

45. C. O. Whitmore was a director of the Vermont Central (*Boston Directory*, 1856).

the main points of the Vermont story & his statement was certainly a good argument for holding the stock of V. & Canada. Mr Dexter [46] was not to be found: his office closed: Mr Bartlett [47] too was absent for the day. On the whole, it seemed imprudent & even violent to persist to sell against such statements and I told Sam. G. W. that I should keep it, which he, on the whole, approved, though I fancy he keeps his first opinion. Still he does not pretend to have examined the history or present state of this complicated affair, and, as he says, tis only a balance of opinions. But I have read the Report, and added Mr Whitmore's to all the weight of testimony you gave me; so I shall sleep very securely, for the present, until you send me some new facts.

Tell Abby, that Edith " found it was not so bad as she thought, and that it was not bad at all " to stay all night! Ever your bounden,

R. W. Emerson.

To Sarah? Rotch? Arnold, Concord, February 23, 1856 [48]

Concord
23 Feb.ʸ 1856

Dear Mrs Arnold,

My wife begs me to take the pen for her, to thank you for your kind note, since I have told her that I am quite unable to keep the hours which you say must be to meet the Lyceum. It happens unfortunately, that I cannot be in Boston on Thursday morning earlier than ten o'clock, which is too late for your first train. Mrs Emerson is so much interested to go, that she thinks that she shall make strength, & that I must break through incompatibilities, to this good end. So you must still let her keep this pleasant picture of a visit to you floating before her until some happier day when all the bars vanish. With Mrs E.s and my own kind regards to Mr and to Miss Arnold,

I am yours respectfully,
R. W. Emerson

46. See Feb. 8, 1856.

47. Doubtless the Sidney Bartlett of July 5, 1859.

48. MS owned by Mr. Thomas F. Madigan; ph. in CUL. The MS memorandum book for 1856 gives Thursday, Feb. 28, to New Bedford. A diary entry, apparently written on the following day, recalls a conversation at New Bedford with a Mr. Arnold (*Journals*, IX, 15) who may have been, I conjecture, the husband of Emerson's correspondent. It is probable that he was James Arnold, the able and cultured merchant who had married Sarah, daughter of William Rotch, Jr. (*cf.* Daniel Ricketson, *New Bedford of the Past*, pp. 41, 152, and 155; and *The Diary of Samuel Rodman*, ed. Z. W. Pease, n. d. [1927?], p. 327).

To Abel Adams, Concord, March 4, 1856 [49]

Concord
4 March 1856

My dear friend,

Here is Mr Chapman's letter. Pray say, whether you think Mr M.'s proposition reasonable, & should be accepted by me, though inconvenient.

Yours ever,
R. W. Emerson

Mr Adams.

To R. A. Chapman, Concord? March c. 10? 1856

[The first of two letters to Chapman mentioned in Mar. 24, 1856, to Adams.]

To Susan Bridge Jackson, Concord, March 17, 1856 [50]

Concord, 17 March,
1856

Dear Susan,

Do not you wish to let your boys come & spend a fortnight or more, as their vacation may be, with us at election, or in June. In that case, I wish to propose an exchange, & you shall take Edith next Friday for three days, for one of them; &, when she comes home, Edward three days, for the other. That is precisely the bargain I wish to make. Ellen has been tempting Edith to come to see or do some things with her, & Mrs Hillard [51] has invited Edith to come; but I do not quite like to have her stay there But Edith is bent on going, & I have no peace, nor shall have, until I have arranged it, and Edward means to have his clash of swords & shields with Johnnie, immediately on her return. For, their vacation begins Thursday morning. I grudge to allow either of them to

49. MS owned by RWEMA; ph. in CUL. For Chapman and Mills, see Oct. 3, 1855, and *cf.* Mar. 24, 1856, to Adams.

50. MS owned by RWEMA; ph. in CUL.

51. Apparently the wife of the noted lawyer George Stillman Hillard. Ellen Emerson was, it seems, living in the Hillard home while she attended Agassiz's school. At any rate, a letter dated Boston, Feb. 6, 1856, signed by Geo. S. Hillard, inclosed a quarterly bill and reported that the family liked Ellen. Probably she had gone to the Hillards' the preceding fall or winter, as Susan T. Hillard, Boston, Sept. 15, endorsed 1855, had reminded Emerson of his wish to have his daughter stay with " us " during the winter. For the Agassiz school, see June 2, 1856.

go into your crowded house, & can only, on the promise of a fair exchange.

I have a half dollar for you to send to Signor Gajani,[52] as I found the
hall cost but 3.00 & I had reserved 3.50, but as this will not go so well by
mail I keep it today. I write in default of my dame who is quite prostrate.

Your affectionate brother
Waldo Emerson

Mrs Susan B Jackson

TO ARTHUR HUGH CLOUGH, CONCORD, MARCH 18, 1856

[MS owned by Mr. Arthur Clough; ph. in CUL. Printed in *Emerson-Clough
Letters.*]

TO WILLIAM EMERSON, CONCORD, MARCH 18, 1856 [53]

Concord 18 March
1856

Dear William,

I am not sure that you have ever met Mr Sanborn, who is quite
too important a person to old as well as to young Concord,[54] than that
you should have missed him if you were both here at the same time. So
I shall charge him to call on you now that he is going to New York,[55] &
he will bear commendations of all of us to Susan. Edith & Eddy bring
me daily news from school that Mr Loring wishes to sell his house without delay, & wishes that Uncle William would buy it. The " Home Jour-

52. Doubtless the Roman who gave, at Concord, on Mar. 5, 1856, a " highly interesting Lecture " on the ill-starred republican movement of 1848–1849 but whose name
remained a mystery to the local recorder of the event (MS records of the Concord
Lyceum, owned by the Concord Free Public Library) . Susan Bridge Jackson, Mar. 31
(MS endorsed 1856 in Emerson's hand) , said she sent a copy of Gajani's book at his
request and asked Emerson and his wife to tea the following Thursday with Gajani
and Scherb. The " Fourth Thousand " of *The Roman Exile,* " by Guglielmo Gajani,
Professor of Civil and Canon Law, and Representative of the People in the Roman
Constituent Assembly in the Year 1849," was published at Boston, 1856. L. H. Angier,
Concord, Apr. 8, 1856, thanked Emerson for a copy of this book. *Cf.* a letter of
May 6 following.

53. MS owned by HCL; ph. in CUL.

54. *Cf.* June 12, 1855.

55. William Emerson, Mar. 30, 1856, tells of Sanborn's coming (MS owned by Dr.
Haven Emerson) .

nal," which Edith appropriates, gives us constant friendly notice of you in the lack of all letters.

Affectionately —
Waldo

To R. A. Chapman, Concord? March c. 22? 1856

[The second of two letters to Chapman mentioned in Mar. 24, 1856, to Adams.]

To Abel Adams, Concord, March 24, 1856 [56]

Concord, 24 March 1856

My dear friend,

I hope the troublesome complaint has quite left you before this. It was very clumsy in me to misdirect my letter.[57] When no answer came, I imagined that writing was forbidden you — for I presently heard by Ellen of your illness, — and I wrote to Mr Chapman,[58] that I was unfortunately left without advice when I much needed it, & must now rely on his good judgment; that it would be inconvenient to me to wait a year, but if he thought the request reasonable of Mr Mills, he must grant it. I have not heard from him since, but on receiving your note, the other day, I wrote immediately to Mr C. saying, that, in the contingency that the affair was not yet settled, I had this further matter to put into my case, &c. I have not any reply.

I have been requested by some young men to repeat some of my country lectures in town,[59] they undertaking to relieve me of all care in the matter, of advertising, &c. so I could not choose but consent. I enclose my cards, if Abby should happen to be in town on a Thursday night.

I am willing to believe that your hemorrhage is a good friend, but only once in a great while. Affectionately,

Mr Adams.   R. W. E.

56. MS owned by RWEMA; ph. in CUL.
57. Probably of Mar. 4, 1856, where Chapman and Mills appear.
58. Mar. c. 10? 1856.
59. This course at the Freeman Place Chapel was announced in the *Boston Daily Advertiser*, Mar. 14 and Mar. 27–May 1, 1856 (title of the first lecture from *Boston Evening Transcript*, Mar. 25): " English Civilization," Mar. 27; " France," Apr. 3; " Beauty," 9; " Signs of the Times," 17; " Poetry," 24; " The Scholar," May 1. The announcements made it clear that these lectures were old ones but had not been read in Boston. One of the young men who instigated the course was apparently W. R. Alger (see Apr. 7, 1856).

To Amos Bronson Alcott, Concord, March 24, 1856 [60]

Concord 24 March
1856

[My dear] friend,

I have heard that you are in Eastern Massachusetts which I hardly believe, as I have not seen you. I am to read some of my country lectures over in Boston, &, at the risk of doing the ridiculous, enclose my cards.

Yours,

Mr Alcott.

To Arthur Buckminster Fuller, Concord, March 24, 1856 [61]

Concord 24 March
Mass.tts 1856

Dear Sir,

I have to thank you for your kind new gift, "At Home & Abroad," [62] whose principal value to me, like that of the preceding selection, is the proof it gives of the demand for these books, & so, of the growing esteem in which your sister's name & character are held. I have read so much & so faithfully from her flowing pen, long since, that I can hardly hope to find any thing quite new to me now. But I am very glad to see that you have preserved Landor's verses to her memory, which were the tribute she would have most fancied.

I use the occasion of this note to enclose a card to some Lectures I have been asked to read in town, [63] if you should chance to be at leisure on any Thursday Evening.

Your obliged servant —
R. W. Emerson

Rev. Mr Fuller.

60. MS owned by Mr. F. W. Pratt; ph. in CUL. All but the tips of a few letters of the bracketed words were cut away, no doubt for the sake of the signature, which must have been written on the opposite side of the sheet but is now lacking. For the lectures, *cf.* the letter of the same date to Adams.

61. MS owned by HCL; ph. in CUL.

62. This book by Margaret Fuller, edited by her brother Arthur, was published on Mar. 27 (*Boston Evening Transcript*, Mar. 25 and 27, 1856). Landor's verses " On the Death of M. Ossoli and his Wife, Margaret Fuller," notable for high praise of Margaret Fuller's husband, appeared on pp. 464–465. *Woman in the Nineteenth Century*, 1855, had been edited by the same brother.

63. See the letter of the same date to Adams.

To William Rounseville Alger, Concord, March 25, 1856?

[MS listed in C. F. Libbie & Co., Nov. 15–17, 1905, where no year is given. That this may have been written shortly before the letter of Apr. 7, 1856, in relation to Emerson's lectures mentioned there, is, I think, a not unreasonable conjecture, for which, however, there is no proof.]

To Oliver Wendell Holmes, Concord, March, 1856 [64]

Concord March 1856

My dear Sir,

I am very sensible of the kindness which dictates your note I have not seen a true report of your speech,[65] & confess to have drawn my sad thoughts about it from the comments of the journals I am relieved to know that they misreported you and the more they misre-

I divide

ported or the wider you are from their notion of you, the better I shall be

men as aspirants & desperants   vast

pleased. A scholar needs not be cynical to feel that the ~~great~~ multitude

the rich   their

~~of men~~ are almost on all fours; that <u>wealth</u> always votes after ~~its~~ fears that cities churches colleges all go for the quadruped interest, and it is against this coalition that the pathetically small minority of disengaged or thinking men stand for the ideal right, for man as he should be, &, (what is essential to any sane maintenance of his own right) for the right of ~~all~~ every other as for his own. When masses then as cities or

things as they are,

churches go for ~~commodity~~ we take no note of it, we expected as much. We leave them to the laws of repression, to the checks nature puts on

as,

beasts of prey, ∧ mutual destruction, blind staggers, delirium tremens, or whatever else, but when a scholar, (or disengaged man,) seems to

throw himself on the dark   from the aspirants side

~~go for the quadruped~~ a cry of grief is heard exactly proportioned in its

64. MS owned by RWEMA; ph. in CUL. The first sheet of this rough draft is endorsed in Emerson's hand: " Draught of letter to Dr Holmes." I have kept the canceled passages and have shown the interlinear emendations.

65. The *Boston Daily Advertiser* of Dec. 22, 1855, had reported the celebration by the New England Society of New York on Dec. 21. Holmes, as the orator of the occasion, created a sensation when, according to the newspaper, he " denounced the abolitionists of New England in good round terms, as ' traitors to the Union.' "

intensity to his believed spiritual rank. Of course, this must be so, and you might well complain if, on their misapprehension of your meaning, they had not exclaimed. It would have been a poor compliment to your fame, if every humblest aspirant had not showed sorrow & anger at the first rumor that such a leader were lost.

[66] The ~~cry~~ ^{cant} of Union like the cant of extending the area of liberty by th annexing Texas & Mexico is too transparent ~~for any body to believe~~ its most impudent repeater to hope to deceive you And for the Union with Slavery no manly person will suffer a day to go by without discrediting disintegrating & finally exploding it. ~~Union~~ the " union " they talk of, is dead & rotten, the real union, that is, the will to ~~remain~~ keep & renew union, is like the will to keep & renew life, & this alone gives any tension to the dead letter & if when we have broken every ^{several}∧ inch of the old wooden hoop will still hold us staunch

You see I am not giving weight to your disgust at the narrowness & ferocity of their virtue for they know that the side is right & it is leading them out of low estate into manhood & culture [67]

To WILLIAM EMERSON, CONCORD, APRIL 5, 1856 [68]

Concord, 5 April, 1856.

Dear William,

Your letter should have been answered on the instant, such an acclamation of joy broke out from the young people. at the reading of your Arabian invitation,[69] and each one of the invited multitude thought that, at least, he or she should go. But it does not look very probable that either Lidian who sends her special & kindest thanks, nor I, nor Edith, can easily go from home in the summer. But I under-

66. What follows is on a separate sheet of a different size and may possibly be a fragment of a separate letter, though I think not.

67. This final sentence was written up side down on the same sheet with the preceding part of the letter. Between the lines appear, entirely detached, Emerson's complimentary close and signature:

" With constant regards
" of R. W. E."

68. MS owned by HCL; ph. in CUL.

69. William Emerson, Mar. 30, 1856 (MS owned by Dr. Haven Emerson), invited his brother and all his family to spend a month in Staten Island during the following summer.

stand that Ellen manifests the best will to go if she can & see her pleasant home, & Edward has the best will to accompany her; so that, if
there should be a few days, — any few days, — in August when you are
likely to be all at home, tis probable that Concord will appear by a
small delegation. But before that time, you yourself, I hope, & Susan
will be " stepping northward," [70] and will cheer our house & all the better if some of the young people are with you

I had ended I supposed my winter & winter like trips, when some
young men in Boston begged me to repeat there such lectures as had
never been read there and if I would do this they would relieve me of all
trouble of advertising; & engaging a hall; &c & would secure my interest
in the matter, &c. So I allowed them to announce six lectures, and have
read two.[71] Very good houses, and in April. The poor delayed book
thinks it no harm to wait longer; indeed, it has got used to it.

For Miss Bacon's MSS.[72] I think they had better come back to me by
the first safe means. Whenever the early vols. of Mme Sand's autobiography [73] come back to me from the Miss Prichard's or other ladies who
hold them, I mean to send them home to you with those I have the
Home Journal punctually reports your love & care. Dear love to Susan
& to the boys Affectionately, Waldo.

To WILLIAM ROUNSEVILLE ALGER, CONCORD, APRIL 7, 1856 [74]

Concord 7 April 1856

My dear Sir,

   I find it necessary to adjourn my " Signs of the Times," a
little, and therefore shall read this week the lecture on " Beauty." [75] I
will write to Mr Woodman today, & say so.[76] My wife & some other

70. An allusion, doubtless, to Wordsworth's " Stepping Westward."
71. *Cf.* the letters of Mar. 24, 1856. William Emerson had written in his letter of
Mar. 30, cited above: " I picture you to myself, pursued by lecture committees on the
one hand, & a pack of printers' devils on the other, and hardly knowing which way to
turn. Is it not so? Or have you escaped from the fangs of the pursuing hounds, and
settled yourself in scholarly repose within reach of the Walden echoes? "
72. *Cf.* the first letter of Feb. 10, 1856. William Emerson had asked in his letter of
Mar. 30 whether he should keep the Bacon MSS then in his possession.
73. *Cf.* Sept. 24, 1855, and May 6, 1857.
74. MS owned by the Henry E. Huntington Library; ph. in CUL. For Alger, *cf.* a
note on Mar. 24, 1856, to Adams. A copy of Alger's *The Poetry of the East*, 1856, is still
in the Emerson library at the Antiquarian House.
75. See a note on Mar. 24, 1856, to Adams.
76. I have found no proof of the letter, though it was doubtless written. Woodman

ladies assured me, last week, that the Chapel was not light enough. Can it be made brighter, — not the pulpit, of course, but the house? I understand it to be indispensable to ladies to know who is there. One thing more — has the sexton any chairs or stools that he can permit to be carried into the aisles by such as come too late to find good seats otherwise? If he has, let him make them accessible. I am assuming that your surprising audiences continue. I am manifestly under good overseers. Yours,

R. W. Emerson

Rev. Mr Alger.

To Leonard Bacon, Concord, April 25, 1856

[Printed in Theodore Bacon, pp. 162–163.]

To Arthur Hugh Clough, Concord, May 5, 1856

[MS owned by Mr. Arthur Clough; ph. in CUL. Printed in *Emerson-Clough Letters.*]

To Jane Carlyle, Concord? May? c. 5? 1856

[Mentioned in May 6, 1856, to Carlyle; an introduction for Anna Barker Ward.]

To Coventry Patmore, Concord? May? c. 5? 1856

[Patmore acknowledged this letter soon after he received it, apparently some months after it was written:

" British Museum.
" September 30. 1856

" My dear Mr Emerson,
  " I take the opportunity offered by Mrs Ward's return to America to convey to you my sincere thanks for the kind and encouraging letter presented to me by that lady yesterday afternoon, and for the truly charming introduction to your friend. I had the pleasure of shewing Mrs Ward over the Museum, and I assure you that her expressions of satisfaction with my Poem gave me more immediate pleasure than I have received from any other source in connexion with that work. I have in me enough of the spirit of Mr Felix Vaughan to feel a very lively delight at any expressions of approval from women generally, but one

---

was, I conjecture, the Horatio Woodman then active in founding the Saturday Club (*cf. The Early Years of the Saturday Club,* pp. 12 ff. and 124 ff.) . Like Alger, he was presumably one of the " young men " who sponsored Emerson's Boston lectures of this spring.

could not talk for an hour with your friend without discovering that there were better reasons than one's idiosyncratic fondness for female commendation to justify pride in *her* approval.

" I have never been more surprised than by hearing of the success of my book in America. In England it has created little or no reputation, except among a few of the best readers. Tennyson, Carlyle, Ruskin, Browning, and a few others of that order speak of the poem in a way which leaves little doubt in my mind of it's making an impression here after a course of years. Meantime, it is an expense to me to print it, so little do the public make of it; and Messrs Ticknor & Field have little chance of seeing the rest of the work unless they send me over such a share of the profits as may enable me to continue the time-absorbing labour of production. If however they, or unforeseen success in England, enable me to suspend my Edinburgh reviewing and other such work, so as to complete this darling labour of my life, I trust that you will find that you have not seen the best of the work yet. I regard these two first volumes as little more than a prelude to the whole poem.

" I have to thank you for your present of your last book, which I and my wife have read with unusual pleasure. I fear we English are getting more flattery just now than is good for us. Your book and Montalembert's, coming out close together, are enough to turn our heads.

" I suppose you hear sometimes from the literary friends you made here. If not you may like to know that Mr Carlyle is near the conclusion of a great work on Frederick II, and that Mr Tennyson has really begun and written nearly a volume of the long promised poem, or rather series of poems, on Arthur.

" My wife desires to be kindly remembered to you.

" Believe me very sincerely yours,

" Coventry Patmore.

" R. W. Emerson, Esq."]

To Thomas Carlyle, Concord, May 6, 1856

[MS owned by RWEMA; printed in *C–E Corr.*, 1883, with the omission of the names of Mrs. Ward and the Barings. The *New-York Daily Tribune* of May 9, 1856, lists Mrs. S. G. Ward among the passengers who had sailed in the " Arabia " from Boston for Liverpool.]

To Charles Thomas Jackson, Concord, May 6, 1856

[MS listed and partly quoted in John Grant, Nov., 1937, where the letter is described as " to ' My Dear Brother,' enclosing £10 borrowed and asking money to be given to Susan ' received for one of Mr Gajani's (?) books.' " For conclusive evidence of the identity of Emerson's correspondent, and for Gajani, see Mar. 17, 1856. Jackson was Emerson's brother-in-law.]

To HENRY WADSWORTH LONGFELLOW, CONCORD, MAY 10, 1856 [77]

Concord
10 May 1856

Dear Longfellow,

Will you please pay into the hands of Sam. G. Ward, State Street, say as soon as 1 June, your promised subscription of fifty dollars to the Alcott fund,[78] & look for no reward as the immortals do.

Ever yours,
R. W. Emerson.

H. W. Longfellow.

I heard with terror of the accident to your son, but learned on inquiry, that bad as it was, twas less bad than the first report gave it; yet I shrink to name it.[79]

To JOHN HOWLAND THOMPSON, CONCORD? MAY 13, 1856

[Thompson, Chicago, Sept. 16, 1856, says he wrote last spring an invitation to lecture for the Young Men's Association in Chicago and duly received Emerson's letter of May 13, deferring an answer till autumn; he now hopes for a definite acceptance. *Cf.* Oct.? *c.* 1? 1856, to him. According to *Case & Co.'s Chicago City Directory for the Year Ending June First, 1857,* p. xix, Thompson, an attorney, was corresponding secretary of the Young Men's Association.]

To WILLIAM EMERSON, CONCORD, JUNE 2, 1856 [80]

Concord, 2 June —
1856

Dear William,

I am, as so often, guilty of silence, which is ungrateful in every sense. The days have not yet arrived, which, for years I have believed were only a few months distant, when I should be free of enforced tasks, & able to meet my natural duties as they rose. Well, by & by they may yet come. Meantime, I have acknowledged nothing, I believe, of all your kind tho'ts & deeds. The " Home-Journal " touches me like a coal

77. MS owned by the Trustees of the Longfellow House, Cambridge; ph. in CUL.
78. *Cf.* the letters of Apr. 30, and June 13 and 29, 1855. The letter of July 13, 1859, to Lowell, shows that the campaign for funds continued for some years, and also that it originated in a conversation between Emerson and Longfellow.
79. Longfellow recorded the accident in his MS diary (at the Longfellow House, Cambridge) under date of Apr. 10, 1856: " A dreadful accident happened to Charley to-day. The bursting of a gun has shockingly mangled his left hand."
80. MS owned by HCL; ph. in CUL.

of fire every week from N. Y. Friendly invitations & messages find short answers or none. And we idle dumb people fancy tis because *we* are so crowded with duties! Then, where to begin when I begin? My course of Lectures in Boston [81] was pleasant & well-paid. I think I received $770. as my share, and I wanted it so much, that it was quickly spent. Since then, I have taken up again those weary refractory concluding chapters of the little English book,[82] and the chapter of " Eng. Literature " is in the printer's hands. " Stonehenge " goes next, & then probably a chapter called " Result," or else, a kind of Personal Narrative, as a basket of remainders. But what times are these, & how they make our studies impertinent, & even ourselves the same! I am looking into the map to see where I shall go with my children when Boston & Massachusetts surrender to the slave-trade.[83] If the Free States do not obtain the government next fall, which our experience does not entitle us to hope, nothing seems left, but to form at once a Northern Union, & break the old. Your Chancellor King was an excellent " Voice of New York." [84] I hope the hands will be even with it.

But what to tell you of us. Aunt Mary has been inhabiting Mrs Clark's parlor all winter,[85] & is now going, perhaps today, to Wayland, — to seek her fortune. We are all as well as usual. Ellen has had thus far a prosperous year at the Cambridge school.[86] We are talking, as we have talked for more than a year, of transprting the whole cage, young

81. See the letters of Mar. 24, 1856.

82. A letter of June 23, 1856, tells of the completion of *English Traits*, after many years of delay.

83. On May 26, 1856, Emerson had delivered, in Concord, his speech inspired by the assault on Sumner (*Cent. Ed.*, XI) . *Cf.* also Mar., 1856, for Emerson's tense feeling about slavery. The philosopher was being forced into political activity in spite of his old conviction that his chief duty was still to be philosopher and not politician. On May 31 of the same year George Stevens wrote from Lowell, Mass., a notification that Emerson had been appointed an alternate delegate to the first national nominating convention of the Republican Party, to be held in Philadelphia on June 17. Whittier wrote from Amesbury, June 13, that Governor Boutwell could not attend the convention at Philadelphia and urged Emerson to go in Boutwell's place. " A thousand thanks," wrote Whittier, " for the speech at the Concord meeting! "

84. *The Evening Post*, May 31, 1856, reported, under the caption " The Voice of New York " the speech of President Charles King of Columbia College at a great meeting held at the Tabernacle to denounce the assault on Sumner.

85. *Cf.* Jan. 3, 1856.

86. *Cf.* a note on Mar. 17, 1856. That the school was Agassiz's is clear from Oct. 1, 1855; from various letters from Agassiz to Emerson; and from William Emerson, June 29, 1856 (MS owned by Dr. Haven Emerson) . Agassiz, in order to eke out his inadequate income, was forced to keep this school for " young ladies " from 1855 to 1863 (Elizabeth Cary Agassiz, *Louis Agassiz*, 1886, II, 526–530) .

birds & old, for a week to Pigeon Cove.[87] Rev. Mr Bartol, an old *habitué* there, negociated for us, & has made some kind of cavity, I believe, where we can nest, and the nidification is 15 July — Ellen not meaning, for all that, to lose her visit to Staten Island — in August, is it not? The original charm of the Pigeon Cove, is, magnificent seabeach, which my young things have never seen. Bulkeley has just paid his " election visit," as usual, & has written a letter which I enclose. Mr Hoar's bill, which I paid, was only 27.45 for the year ending 13 April. Dear love to Susan & to the boys, one, two, three, who are constant topics of conversation here.

Waldo.

To DELIA SALTER BACON, CONCORD, JUNE 23, 1856

[MS owned by Miss Jessie Bacon; printed in Theodore Bacon, pp. 191–195.]

To WILLIAM EMERSON, CONCORD, JUNE 23, 1856 [88]

Concord 23 June

Dear William,

I had your letter on the loss of Miss Bacon's MSS.[89] Wo the while! I have written to her in full.[90] I have not sent you any money for Abel Adams has sent me none and I have been unable to go to him to put him in mind. I go Saturday. My book is ended at last, a week ago.[91] I am to be sure, at court, yesterday & today, defending me a piece of woodland against a claimant under an old deed new found; but my warrantors defend me. Still I do not wish to be beat, & the boys in town reciting at second hand the legal complaint, say, " Mr E is to be tried for stealing Charles Bartlett's wood." [92] Tis a strange turn of the tables, for I am always complaining that he steals mine, which he does, tree by tree, the rogue.

So you see my plight is bad.

Waldo.

87. *Cf.* Aug. 6, 1855, and *Journals*, IX, 54–55.

88. MS owned by HCL; ph. in CUL. The year 1856, supplied in William Emerson's hand, is obviously correct.

89. William Emerson, June 11, 1856, reported that he had committed the Bacon MSS to Sophy Ripley, who was to take them to Concord, but that she had lost them on her way from his house to the ferry.

90. June 23, 1856, to Delia Bacon.

91. For publication, see Aug. 7, 1856.

92. A letter of July 1, 1858, and note explain the history and final settlement of this suit.

To Benjamin Peirce, Concord, June 25, 1856 [93]

Concord —
Wednesday.

Dear Sir,

      I will come to you with great good will on Friday, at 4 o'clock.

Yours, with great regard,

R. W. Emerson

Professor Pierce.

To Emily Mervine Drury, Concord? July? 3? 1856?

[A telegraphic letter mentioned in July 3, 1856?]

To Emily Mervine Drury, Concord and Boston, July 3, 1856? [94]

Concord 3 July
Thursday morn[g]

My dear friend,

      Your telegraphic word did not come to me until nearly sunset and your note arrived presently after. I replied at once by telegraph that I would come to Boston this morn but when I read your note I fear you will be at Nahant. Is it not in your power to come to Concord tomorrow & spend the day, if I shall not succeed in finding you today. I am entirely at liberty on Friday except that I ought to be in Concord, on account of a sort of town festival

Well now here in Boston I find you have gone. Come be good & come to Concord tomorrow train leaving Boston at $7\frac{1}{2}$ A M.

Ever yours,

R W Emerson

Mrs Drury.

93. MS owned by the Wellesley College Library; ph. in CUL. Peirce, whose name is misspelled, had written from Cambridge, June 24, 1856, asking Emerson to dine with him and Agassiz and a few other friends on the following Friday at four o'clock. This fixes the date of Emerson's reply.

94. MS owned by the Marietta College Library; ph. in CUL. The date " 1856 or 1857 " has been supplied. July 3 fell on Thursday in 1856, which, so far as I know, may well be the correct year.

Another manuscript owned by the Marietta College Library (ph. in CUL) is a copy, in the hand of Mr. Willis E. Hall, of an incomplete letter, apparently from Emerson to Mrs. Drury and dated Concord, Feb. 10, 1856. The writer mentions his failure to reach Canandaigua and suggests the possibility that Mrs. Drury might make a visit to Concord when she comes to Boston.

To Lucy D. Henry, Concord? July c. 13? 1856

[Lucy D. Henry, Cub Creek Post Office, Charlotte County, Va., July 1, 1856, asked that Emerson correspond with her, giving her one hour a week. She wrote again, apparently on July 17 of the same year, complaining of the restraint of the note she had received from him and discussing her reading, about which he had, it seems, made some suggestion.]

To Joseph H. Bragdon, Concord? July? c. 14? 1856

[Bragdon, Newburyport, Mass., July, 1856, in a printed circular, asked for a lecture and inquired as to date, subject, and fee. Emerson's endorsement shows that he answered he would come on Dec. 12.]

To C. R. Tomlinson, Concord? July? c. 14? 1856

[Tomlinson, Paterson, N. J., July 21, 1856, acknowledged this letter and accepted Emerson's terms, $40 for one lecture; for the time, he preferred some Thursday in December or January, but, if notified soon, would accept Emerson's choice.]

To William Emerson, Concord, July 23, 1856 [95]

Concord, 23 July, 1856

Dear William,

Allow me to introduce to you my townsman & neighbor, Charles Goodnow, Esq. Counsellor at law, who wishes to see you on some matter of business. Let him also tell you that he left Concord in its very handsomest coat of green, & with the promise of the best crop, & let him advise you to come & see it for yourself, & those who dwell therein. Yours affectionately,

Waldo E.

William Emerson, Esq.

To Delia Salter Bacon, Concord, July 28, 1856 [96]

Concord, 28 July, 1856.

My dear Miss Bacon,

My late heavy letter to you, heavy with East wind & all kinds of bad tidings seems to have been met & crossed by your courageous epistle bearing good omens which always exist for the brave. I am

95. MS owned by HCL; ph. in CUL.
96. MS owned by Mr. W. T. H. Howe; ph. in CUL. Miss Jessie Bacon owns a copy (ph. in CUL) which, she informs me, was made by Rose Hawthorne Lathrop.

heartily glad that Mr Hawthorne has seen your MSS. He is a valuable
independent critic & good hearted.[97] The words you quote from him
are worthy of him. In my judgment, the right solution of all the present
knots would be that you should come home & take the affair of publishing into your proper hands, with all the advantage that acting & con-
versing directly with all parties concerned would give. You would not
then be annoyed & hurt by contradictory advice and would probably
gain by rejecting all advice. I am sad to think what you will say & feel
about the loss of those MS chapters.[98] I try to assure myself that you
have perfect copies. For the new letter you have enclosed in mine I have
sent it to Dix & Edwards; [99] but I have availed myself of the sort of discretionary power you gave me, to erase 8 or 10 lines at the end of the
postscript. A friend of your studies has sent me $50.[100] which I under-
stand is a mite offered to the love of Shakspeare & of you, but with strict
injunctions on me to withhold the name. So I enclose it in the form of a
bill of Exchange for £10 You may be sure it comes from a heart full of
tendernness & respect.

With best wishes & hopes,
Ever yours,
R. W. Emerson

Miss D. S. Bacon.

To Marshall M. Strong, Concord? August 4, 1856

[Strong, Boston, Aug. 4, 1856, said he would like to come to Concord; he had
noted Oriental sources Emerson had used, and he wanted Emerson to suggest
further Oriental reading for him. Strong, Aug. 10, 1856, said he had found
Emerson's friendly note of the 4th upon his return to Boston and would visit
Concord later; he also sought to interest Emerson in his studies in the philosophy of crime. Cf. Feb. 12, 1860.]

To Benjamin Peirce, Concord? August c. 6? 1856

[Peirce, Function Grove, Cambridge, Aug. 10, 1856, accepted Emerson's invitation to dinner the following Saturday.]

97. Hawthorne's attempts to aid Delia Bacon are recorded in *The Works*, n. d.
(c. 1891) , VII, 129–143, and VIII, 334–336.

98. *Cf.* the letters of June 23, 1856, one of which is described in the opening sentence of this paragraph.

99. Emerson probably wrote a letter to accompany the one he forwarded, but I
have no proof.

100. That Eliza Buckminster Lee sent Emerson money for Delia Bacon at this
time and asked that it be given anonymously is shown by Mrs. Lee's letters from
Brookline, Mass., July 4 and 30, 1856.

To Thomas Carlyle, Concord? August? *c.* 6? 1856

[Acknowledged in Carlyle, Aug. 28, 1856 (*C–E Corr.*).]

To James Elliot Cabot, Concord, August 7, 1856 [101]

Concord, 7 Augt 1856

Dear Cabot,

I am afraid you will never lend me any more books, since I keep them so long. The reason is, they are so good, that I cannot bear to give them up; and my eyes, in the last year, are bad servants, and I read little or slowly. The Edda is excellent with its strength & surprises, & tis wonderful that it has been allowed to sleep till within twenty years.[102] The apprehensive, like the creative mood, must have long periods. And I must think so too in regard to all this Oriental wisdom so newly imported into the West. Dcheladeddin Mewlana & Ferideddin Attar were deep men who knew as much of the soul & ethics as any Greek or Englishman, and yet our libraries have been stuffed with dull books of third-rate writers. It does not lessen the wonder that Tholuck's book is dated 1825,[103] & Von Hammer's 1818.[104] I knew pretty well the " Mystical " parts, as we rudely call them, in Von Hammer and am surprised he left such admirable things for T. to glean. But my special interest & thanks are moved by the traces of your own pencil through Tholuck, & the character of the notes. I admire the hints of this retentive man who only seems to have a right to speak, & wonder when he will break the long silence of these rare studies. Is not the fifth & the ninth year complete? [105] And is it pride, or, is it a grander aim than our poor America allows that keeps him dumb? I believe the best, but meantime, I think you should read occasionally to private classes, as learned pro-

101. MS owned by Professor Philip Cabot; ph. in CUL.

102. Versions of both *Eddas* are still in the Emerson library at the Antiquarian House — *Icelandic Poetry, or the Edda of Saemund Translated into English Verse*, put forth by the Amos Cottle of Byronic fame at Bristol in 1797; and George Webbe Dasent's translation, *The Prose or Younger Edda*, 1842. Apparently Emerson supposed that Dasent's was the first English translation of the prose *Edda*.

103. F. A. G. Tholuck's *Blüthensammlung aus der morgenländischen Mystik*, Berlin, 1825, contains selections from Mewlana Dschelaleddin and Feridoddin Attar — so the names are spelled by Tholuck.

104. Joseph von Hammer's *Geschichte der schönen Redekünste Persiens*, Vienna, 1818, still in the Emerson library at the Antiquarian House. For Emerson's interest in Hammer-Purgstall, see also the letters of Nov. 2, 1847, and Sept. 26, 1855.

105. *Leviticus*, 19:25, fixes the fifth year as that in which the fruits, theretofore forbidden, should be eaten. Probably Emerson's ninth year is that mentioned *ibid.*, 25:22.

fessors do, parts & results of your proceeding studies, and I wish heartily to be admitted of the class.

Ever yours,
R. W. Emerson.

J. E. Cabot, Esq.
I ordered Phillips Sampson, & Co. to send you a copy of my little English book,[106] which I hope they have done.

To Moses Dresser Phillips, Concord, August 9, 1856 [107]

Concord —
9 August 1856

Dear Sir,

Certainly, if Mr Routledge will take the trouble of of forwarding the presentation copies to their addresses in England, I will not call in the aid of Mr Chapman: my reason for applying to him being only that he probably knows the present address of a few persons on the list who may have changed their address. But I wish you would ask Mr Routledge's kind & particular attention to the matter. Where the parties are at a distance from London I am anxious that the books should not be sent to them in an expensive way, but if it can be found that they have any place of deposit in London, left there; or, if sent on expense, the expense prepaid, & charged to me: Especially, Miss Martineau; Dr Brown; Mr Gill; Mr Scott; & Mr Ireland. I have written the addresses to the best of my knowledge but that of Mr W. E. Foster [108] I do not feel certain of. He lived, when I knew him, at Rawdon, near Leeds; is a manufacturer, & the author of a pamphlet on William Penn, in reply to Macaulay. I enclose a corrected list of them all.

Respectfully,
R. W. Emerson

Mr Phillips.
" From the Author " should be written on each.[109]

106. *English Traits* was published on Aug. 6 (*Boston Daily Advertiser*, Aug. 5 and 6, 1856).

107. MS owned by Wellesley College Library; ph. in CUL. Moses D. Phillips was the senior partner of Phillips, Sampson & Co., publishers of *English Traits* (*Boston Directory*, 1856, and *Boston Evening Transcript*, Aug. 22, 1859). George Routledge was the founder of the firm of G. Routledge & Co., publishers of the London edition of *English Traits*, 1856.

108. That is, Forster; the letter of Jan. 8 and 12, 1848, tells of Emerson's meeting with him. Forster's pamphlet is mentioned in July 28, 1851.

109. Among the acknowledgments Emerson received from England perhaps none

To WILLIAM EMERSON, CONCORD, AUGUST 12, 1856 [110]

Concord, 12 Aug. 1856

Dear William,

I send my children, but I send nothing else, not even the long promised account from my dispersive leger. You must have faith more than Christian, — such verily as Mahomet demanded. My little book [111] has always promised to make a little money; and it will yet, I am told; but yesterday when I went to Boston the bookseller treated me to the beautifullest fair words, & not a cent: " he will prepare his account in a few days." " Seventeen hundred copies had gone in four days," which is well, since I had forbidden all their puffing advertisements. The poor book has long been a bore & an obstruction to me; 'tis time it should be something else.

You see I have availed myself of your permission in your letter to withhold a settlement with you to a more convenient day. I was never so balked of money as in the last two years what with railroads & other matters. Vt. & Canada are never better Nor will Abel Adams let me sell the shares for half. And my Rutland Bond, (which is good I am assured

---

was of greater interest than that from Hawthorne, who was not wholly pleased with the flattering picture of England as the most successful of modern nations:

" Liverpool, Sept 10th 1856.

" My dear Emerson,

" I thank you for your book, which reached me a week or two ago, just as I was about starting on a journey to London; so I made it my travelling companion, and compared it all the way with the England actually before my eyes.

" Undoubtedly, these are the truest pages that have yet been written, about this country. Some of them seem to me absolutely true; — as regards others, the truth has not been made apparent to me by my own observations. If I had time — and a higher opinion of my own fitness — I should be glad to write notes on the book.

" I am afraid it will please the English only too well; for you give them credit for the possession, in very large measure, of all the qualities that they value, or pride themselves upon; and they never will comprehend that what you deny is far greater and higher than what you concede. In fact, you deny them only what they would be ashamed of, if they possessed it.

" But perhaps I am no fair judge of Englishmen, just now. Individually, they suit me well; it is very comfortable to live among them. But yet I am not unconscious of a certain malevolence and hostility in my own breast, such as a man must necessarily feel, who lives in England without melting entirely into the mass of Englishmen. I must confess to have sympathized with Russia more than England, in the late war; and nothing has given me quite so much pleasure, since I left home, as the stoop which I saw in every Englishman's shoulders, after the settlement of the Enlistment question.

" Sincerely yours, Nathl Hawthorne."

110. MS owned by HCL; ph. in CUL.
111. *English Traits.*

for $1100. & more,) I understand, is now to yield money or money's worth in October. So, if the convenient day does not come soon I mean to force it. Ellen & Edward depart in confidence that they are to bring home Haven with them; Haven, at least; (which is much;) but Charlie, & William, and their father & mother also: — so the young people here, — their wish being father to their thought, — believe; and the old people here are of the same creed. Dear love to Susan.

                                                        Waldo.

To Mary Preston Stearns, Concord, August 19, 1856 [112]

                                        Concord, 19 August,
                                                        1856

My dear Mrs Stearns,
        Eddie is at New York spending a fortnight with his cousins. I do not think he will be at home sooner than seven or eight days hence. He bears Frank in very high regard, and, I am sure, will be well content to make him another visit. If a week from next Saturday is open for Frank, perhaps Edward will come on that day. At all events, as soon as he returns, he shall answer for himself, or I will, & we will settle on the new day.
        Mrs Emerson sends you her kind regards.
                                                Yours,
                                                R. W. Emerson.

To Ellen Emerson, Concord, August 20, 1856 [113]

                                        Concord —
                                        20 August, 1856

Dear Ellen,
        You thought 5. would bring you home,[114] but I enclose $10. to exclude accidents.
        We were all glad to read your letter to Edith today, & to hear also from Uncle William that Haven will come with you. Draw out of Aunt Susan, if you can, a promise to come with you or after you.
        Did I tell you to ask Wᵐ Jr. if he received his copy of " Eng. Traits." It was sent with his father's to Francis' bookstore.

112. MS owned by Mr. F. R. Fraprie; ph. in CUL. For Mrs. Stearns, *cf.* Jan. 8, 1855, to her. She had written from Medford, Mass., Aug. 17, 1856, inviting Emerson's son to visit her son Frank on the following Saturday.
113. MS owned by RWEMA; ph. in CUL.
114. From New York; *cf.* Aug. 12, 1856.

Edith sent you Alice Hooper's letter for *you* to answer. I have a letter from Mr Sanborn at Oscaloosa, Iowa, on his way to Gen. Lane's camp,[115] dated 13 August. He intended returning home after the 23ᵈ

Tell Uncle William I had a letter from Mr Sumner yesterday, dated 16ᵗʰ Aug., announcing his convalescence, & that he had ridden out on horseback three times with good result.[116]

Papa.

over

Mrs Brown has looked at her letter again & finds only the name of Mr Staunton 25 William Street,[117] son of Mr John Staunton, of London, late of N. Y.

To Thomas Carlyle, Concord, August 22, 1856

[Printed in Conway, *Autobiography*, II, 412–413. Carlyle wrote this reply:

" Kinloch Luichart
" Dingwall, N. B. 16 Septr 1856

" Dear Emerson,

"Your second Letter finds me up here, aloft among the Highland mountains (a Hunting seat of Lord Ashburton's) whither I have been tossed out of my snug Border solitude, — not in good hour. The mountains and Lakes are very beautiful; but the storms, in this equinoctial time, are already very loud, and I can do nothing with Deer, not even eat them. — In a fortnight hence I hope to be back at Chelsea; but in the meantime will answer your magnanimous Bibliopolical Proposal (yours or Sampson's thro' you, is all one, in the haste I am in — just waiting for the ' Skye Mail ' which passes once in two days) , — some word of answer or acknowledgement, not to lose more time than we can help.

"I say then that the Project of Mm. Phillips Sampson & Cᵒ, so far as I in my ignorance can judge of it, seems very rational, and that, once in London, I will make further investigation into the practical particulars, and prepare myself to say Yes or No when the time comes for that finality. Meanwhile let Mm Phˢ & Sⁿ do one thing as preliminary, Tell me *how much,* in current money, they will give for a cast of those potential Stereotypes, to the extent of 2, 4, 6 or as many *thousands* as they wᵈ like to purchase at once; — *how much per thousand,* in fact? For it would not be convenient to *sell* the Stereotypes otherwise, I think; — and I suppose there are ways of making certain that the use of them should be *restricted* to the thousands covenanted for, & that the Plates could be put under

115. In his *Recollections*, I, 52 ff., Sanborn tells the story of his tour of inspection as agent of the Massachusetts State Kanzas Committee. Probably he received some letters from Emerson at this time, as a statement in *The Personality of Emerson*, p. 87, implies.

116. Sumner, Cresson, Pa., Aug. 16, 1856, told also of his pleasure in such passages from *English Traits* as he had seen in the newspapers.

117. *Trow's New York City Directory* for 1856–1857 gives a slightly different spelling but the same address — John Stanton, Jr., 25 William St.

lock and key till wanted again. Once knowing what the value per thousand from Messrs Sampson will be, and what the cost in London to myself as preliminary, I shall know the whole matter, and be able to pronounce some decision or other — — I am much ashamed to trouble *you* with this matter; but what can I do at the present stage of it.

" Your Book is to be here tomorrow by post. You shall hear soon all the faults I have against it. An Irish Newspaper (the *Nation*) brought me some notice of it the other day, wh^h somewhat raises my interest. A *medicinal* intention, then, on the Author's part? God knows there was hardly ever such a Hospital of Lepers. More power to such a Doctor, if that is his part!

" Adieu, dear Friend, there is the Skye mail. Yours ever T. Carlyle "]

To WILLIAM H. RICHARDSON, CONCORD? AUGUST? *c.* 25? 1856

[Richardson, Philadelphia, Sept. 4, 1856, says Emerson's reply encouraged him to hope for a lecture before the People's Literary Institute; the Institute would be willing to pay $120 for two lectures, Jan. 2 and 9.]

To AUSTIN ADAMS, CONCORD, AUGUST 26, 1856

[MS owned by the Historical, Memorial and Art Department of Iowa; printed in *The Iowa Journal of History and Politics,* XXV, 240–241 (Apr., 1927), where the place and date are given only in the introductory comment.]

To WILLIAM SWINTON, CONCORD, AUGUST 26, 1856

[MS listed in Anderson Galleries, Feb. 26–Mar. 1, 1918, where it is described as referring to a translation made and sent to Emerson by Swinton and as praising the book itself but not criticizing the translation. This letter is an answer to Swinton, New York, Aug. 21, 1856, announcing that he sends a copy of his version of Rousseau (*The Confessions*), telling of his debt to Emerson, and offering to do research work for him in the Astor Library. Swinton also mentions Whitman, whom he knows well and sees often and who, he says, is " to bring us a new sheaf of ' Leaves,' in a day or so."]

To FRANCIS H. UNDERWOOD, CONCORD, AUGUST 26, 1856

[Printed in Bliss Perry, *Park-Street Papers,* 1908, p. 232.]

To WILLIAM EMERSON, CONCORD, SEPTEMBER 2, 1856 [118]

Concord —
2 September 1856

Dear William,

Our children returned in high spirits, very proud & happy to have been made much of by their friends, & strong with Haven at

118. MS owned by HCL; ph. in CUL.

their side, a great day for Edith, & for Edith's papa & mamma. With all their tidings & bringings, & they were not few, — they brought Papa also a famous fairing from New York & Uncle William, in the shape of the goodly proof-print which now adorns my sitting room We shall keep it there till we have learned all we can, & have showed all that we learn to our neighbors. Haven's visit has been all one holiday in this house, he is very highly prized by us all, & I trust you will forgive the urgency with which the children three have pressed him to stay over one day, to be manager of Ediths fancy ball, or sociable, or drop-in, as it is variously termed. The main argument to shake his homeward tendencies that was relied on, was, that only by staying could he see Aunt Elizabeth, &, of course, Haven's Father & Mother would thank them for their zeal. My young people have great penitence that Charlie was not pointedly entreated to come also at this time, & all the more now that we at Concord make out that there was nothing in the way, & he might have come as well as not. I tell them, the loss is all ours, & Charlie has had a cloud & a distraction the less to his bright days. I must say a word to the notes you sent me on " English Traits." [119] p. 113 Fauriel the Belgian biographer of Wellington represents him as such a dear stupid good creature, that he chose to consider himself responsible for the army debts, & would not stir abroad for fear of bailiffs; which I call the family-man carried to the sublime. On p. 212, I find no difficulty For p. 103, I own *solidarity* is not yet a good English word; but Fourier & Socialism have made it so common in French books, that it has become inevitable in English. But it means responsibleness, as when Alfred divided his people into Hundreds, & each Hundred responsible for a crime committed by any man belonging to it. — I spelled sirloin, but my " corrector " printed *s*urloin, & I rarely defy him.

The book prospers well enough. After selling 3000, they have a new edition of 2000, which goes off fast enough, I believe, but my publishers, I think, know with whom they deal, and I cannot get the first line of an account from them, though you may remember that my contract with them requires them to pay me my 20 per cent *on the day of publication.*

119. William Emerson, Aug. 19, 1856 (MS owned by Dr. Haven Emerson) : " I cannot but echo Geo. Ripley's surprize at your suffering the printers to use so poor a type. On page 113, I am posed for the sequitur in W.'s not being able to stir abroad, &c. On p. 212, the sentence beginning ' English wealth ' is not a little embarrassing to me. As to ' responsibleness ' on page 103, I suppose it is only a misprint for ' responsiveness,' & ' surloin ' for ' sirloin,' page forgotten. Thus have I emptied my critical budget, & I will only add that Susan & I have been very much interested and entertained in the perusal of the book, to which we wish all success."

They have promised however an early communication.[120] Lidian sends her love to Susan, & says, she would gladly accept her kind instances if she could. I wish I heard of firmer health in both of you. And why should William Junior be invalid. Tell him I think it not only lamentable, but absurd.

Your affectionate brother
Waldo.

To WILLIAM HOWLAND, CONCORD, SEPTEMBER 4, 1856 [121]

Concord, Mass^{tts}
4 September, 1856

Dear Sir,

It will give me pleasure to come to Lynn, and, as you leave me so wide a margin to choose in, I will say, Friday, 26 December. You do not say what day of the week you prefer. If it is indifferent, you shall hold me engaged for the day I have named.

Respectfully,
R. W. Emerson

Mr Howland.

To JOHN BACKUP, CONCORD? SEPTEMBER? c. 6? 1856

[Backup, Roxbury, Mass., Sept. 4 (endorsed 1856), asked permission to list Emerson as a lecturer in the course at Roxbury beginning in November. Emerson answered " Yes," according to his notation on Backup's letter.]

To CHARLES KING NEWCOMB, CONCORD? SEPTEMBER? c. 6? 1856 [122]

Dear Charles,

Your kind & characteristic letter thanking me for the use of the book which you have not read [123] was received with great

120. Moses D. Phillips, Boston, Sept. 30, 1856, inclosed a " note for balance " and said he would send the account and write more particulars on the following day.

121. MS owned by Goodspeed's Book Shop; ph. in CUL. William Howland, Lynn, Mass., Sept. 5, 1856, replied that he had intended to name Wednesday as the preferred day and suggested any Wednesday in December except Dec. 3. Emerson actually read " Life " before the Lynn Library Association on Wednesday, Dec. 10 (*Lynn Weekly Reporter*, Dec. 13, 1856) .

122. MS owned by RWEMA; ph. in CUL. This fragmentary rough draft in Emerson's hand bears the notation by Edward Waldo Emerson: " perhaps to Mr Newcomb. E. W. E." This conjecture is, I think, undoubtedly correct, as is shown by evidence cited below.

123. Newcomb, Providence, Sept. 2, 1856, thanks Emerson for *English Traits* and

sensibility. O certainly we must shun excitement & night air & lamp smoke Perhaps the Austrians are right in trammeling the Press,[124] which is elsewhere the occasion of whole atmosphere of talk & some insanity and Talleyrand you remember found nonsense extremely refreshing.[125]

To Samuel Gray Ward, Concord? September 12, 1856

[Partly printed in *The Early Years of the Saturday Club*, p. 16. Emerson remarks that he always pays — for his dinner at the Club — through Woodman. The following letter (MS owned by Goodspeed's Book Shop; ph. in CUL) refers to the same club and may have been written to Woodman, I conjecture. The year could have been 1856 or later.
" My dear Sir,
        " Please energize at Parkers that we may have a sufficient table set at first, for the last club lost nearly an hour. And I suppose the club will be large as I have 3 guests.
                                                                      " R. W. E."
The photostat does not show the endorsement, according to which, it seems, this note once belonged to James T. Fields (see Goodspeed's Book Shop, catalogue 274, p. 45). It is barely possible that Fields was the person addressed. If so, the date is later than 1856.]

To C. R. Tomlinson, Concord? September 15, 1856

[Tomlinson, Paterson, N. J., Sept. 17, 1856, notes that Emerson's letter of the 15th suggests a day in January for his lecture; this day is acceptable.]

To Edwin S. Wells, Concord? September 15, 1856

[According to Wells, Chicago, Sept. 27, 1856, Emerson told of his plan to lecture at Columbus, O., Jan. 19 and 20 and said he would come to Chicago Wednesday, Jan. 22. But Wednesday was Jan. 21, said Wells, and Emerson could not arrive by that time if he kept his second engagement in Columbus. Wells urged that Emerson be in Chicago on the 21st. *Cf.* the note on Oct. 1, 1856.]

-----

goes on to discuss the subject of that book, but says that he is perhaps now writing what Emerson has already written. Newcomb wrote again, Sept. 11, apologizing because, in acknowledging Emerson's book, he was so stupid as not to explain that he seized the first opportunity of making the acknowledgment before he had time to open the leaves. It is possible, of course, that the present letter followed Newcomb's second one.

124. This remark could, of course, have been made at almost any time between 1848 and 1860, but would have been most appropriate perhaps during the régime of Lieut.-Gen. Kempen.

125. This is the sentiment of a sufficiently well-known but anonymous rimed saying. In *The Conduct of Life* (*Cent. Ed.*, VI, 269) , it is again attributed to Talleyrand.

To ————————, CONCORD, SEPTEMBER 15, 1856

[MS listed and partly quoted in Merwin-Clayton Sales Co., Feb. 13, 1906; mentions the fact that Ward, who was Emerson's guest " at our last sitting," wishes to come again; and suggests that, if he asks it, the financial mysteries of the club be explained to him. Apparently the letter was addressed to some member of what presently took definite form as the Saturday Club (*cf.* Sept. 12, 1856), and probably to Horatio Woodman (*cf.* a note on Apr. 7, 1856) .]

To ARTHUR BUCKMINSTER FULLER, CONCORD, SEPTEMBER 17, 1856 [126]

Concord 17 Sept. 1856

Dear Sir,

I am much to blame for delaying so long my reply to your note,[127] and yet not so blameworthy as you may imagine.

I am not at all acquainted with any printed articles of Margaret's out of the Dial, & Tribune, & her Books. I have a little MS. *brochure* of her poems,[128] which is at your service, — & I am not sure what pages in it have been once printed. I will leave it, when I next go to town, with your brother Richard. I am under the impression that some of the pieces are in the " Dial "; and my " Dial " is still, I believe, with your brother R. These are poems full of life & character, but were strictly occasional, & there is no record known to me of the occasions. They will interest those who knew her, in the degree in which they knew her; but I am not sure that this very implication in her life, and the absence, almost the scorn of poetic finish in the pieces, may not so far disqualify them for the bulk of readers. At all events, I will send them. Yours respectfully,

R. W. Emerson

Rev. Arthur Fuller.

To ———————— DERMOT, CONCORD, SEPTEMBER 23, 1856

[MS listed in Anderson Galleries, Feb. 1–3, 1926; described as containing an offer to come to Blackstone for $20. *Cf.* J. C. Hobbs, Blackstone, Mass., July 21, 1856, asking whether Emerson could lecture before the Blackstone Literary Association the coming season.]

126. MS owned by HCL; ph. in CUL.

127. Arthur B. Fuller, Boston, Aug. 14, 1856, tells of his intention of preparing another volume of his sister's writings and asks whether Emerson can supply a list of her publications outside *The Dial* and the *Tribune*.

128. Some of Margaret Fuller's poems had been printed in earlier posthumous volumes, but the largest number, probably including some or all from the MS Emer-

To H. T. Helm, Concord? October 1, 1856

[Acknowledged in Helm, Chicago, Oct. 6, 1856. Helm regretted complications that had arisen — two lyceums in Chicago were attempting to engage Emerson for the same date. Helm and Wells represented the Metropolitan Literary Union; Thompson, the Young Men's Association. For Emerson's lecture for the latter organization, see Jan. 24, 1857. *Case & Co.'s Chicago City Directory for the Year Ending June First, 1857* lists H. T. Helm as an attorney at 3 Metropolitan Hall and E. S. Wells, dealer in boots and shoes, "under" Metropolitan Hall; but I find no mention of the Metropolitan Literary Union. For Thompson, see May 13, 1856. For Wells, see also Oct. 27, 1859, note.]

To William? H.? Fish, Concord, October *c.* 1? 1856

[MS listed in Anderson Galleries, May 24, 1911, where it is described as to "Mr. Fish," Concord, Oct., 1856, and as "making an appointment." Presumably it is in answer to William H. Fish, McLean, N. Y., Sept. 23, 1856, asking Emerson to lecture at Cortlandville, N. Y.]

To John Howland Thompson, Concord? October? *c.* 1? 1856

[Thompson, Chicago, Oct. 6, 1856, said Emerson's letter had arrived. Thompson also told of a communication from Wells, of the rival lyceum, about Emerson's schedule in Chicago.]

To John Winship, Concord? October? *c.* 1? 1856

[Winship, South Reading, Mass.? Oct., 1856, says Nov. 13, the evening Emerson has proposed, will be satisfactory. The MS memorandum book for 1856 gives the same date to South Reading, but does not indicate the state.]

To James Russell Lowell, Concord, October 3, 1856

[MS listed and partly quoted in John Heise Autographs, catalogue 2467. Emerson asks Lowell to dinner on the following Saturday, when Agassiz and others will also come; he says he sends this letter to Underwood, as he hears Lowell will come to town today. It is not clear whether Emerson wrote to Underwood at the same time. *Cf.* Oct. 7, 1856.]

To James Russell Lowell, Concord, October 7, 1856 [129]

Concord 7 Oct 1856

My dear Lowell

    I sent you a note on Saturday [130] which I fear might not have

---

son mentions, were to appear in *Life Without and Life Within*, n. d. (c. 1859). The "little MS. *brochure*" may have contained the poems mentioned in her letter of Nov. 17, 1844 (see a note on Dec. 3 of that year).

    129. MS owned by HCL; ph. in CUL.

    130. Apparently the letter of Friday, Oct. 3, 1856.

reached you as it was enclosed to Mr Underwood.[131] Its message was to pray you to come & dine with me on Saturday next when Agassiz & Ward & a few good men are to come. We will dine at $2\frac{1}{2}$ o clock, & the awkward 11 o'c train which stirs the bile of Concord daily, — will yet this time give us the chance of showing you our gay bushes, & perhaps even the river. I rely on your goodness.

Yours ever,
R. W. Emerson.

J. R. Lowell.

To W. L. Ropes, Concord? October? c. 7? 1856

[Ropes, Wrentham, Mass., Oct. 3, 1856, asked whether Emerson could name a day for a lecture; Emerson's endorsement shows he named Dec. 26.]

To James Russell Lowell, Concord, October 8, 1856 [132]

Concord Wednesday
8 Oct.^r

Dear Lowell,

I have written you two notes to ask you to come & dine with me here next Saturday Now I have to ask you to come to me at Parker's [133] Boston at the same hour. My daughter Ellen who is grown important to my housekeeping is untimely sick for these few days, & my wife is little better; &, though they may both be well again suddenly, I think it safe to alter the *venue*. I do not know that I shall succeed in bringing Thoreau to the city, but the others whom you were to meet I will bring. So I rely on you.

R. W. Emerson.

Professor [134] Lowell.

To Samuel Longfellow? Concord, October 14, 1856 [135]

Concord, Oct. 14, 1856.

My Dear Sir,

Could I give a series of five lectures on five successive days, say, beginning on Monday, 24 November? or is that inadmissible, & must the

131. See the note on Oct. 3, 1856.

132. MS owned by HCL; ph. in CUL. This pretty definitely follows the letters of Oct. 3 and 7, 1856; and Oct. 8 fell on Wednesday in that year.

133. The Parker House is listed in the *Boston Directory*, 1856.

134. Lowell had recently returned from abroad, ready to take up his duties as Longfellow's successor.

135. MS owned by the New York Public Library; ph. in CUL. It seems altogether

evenings alternate? At least it would be practicable to put four into a week & so to read 5 or 6 lectures in 8 or 10 days. I had left the space between 21 Nov^r & 10 Decr open, with another view, &, if you still think it desireable, I can attempt this. Perhaps *Five* Lectures is the safer announcement. I ought to receive not less than $50. for each lecture. You see therefore your dangers. Be dissuaded in time from any rash undertakings. If you ask for my subjects, I have a new lecture not quite ready, which I call " Conduct of Life." Of those which I read in Boston, last winter,[136] two with bad names turned out to be successful enough 1. " Poetry," &, 2. " The Scholar." Perhaps we can mend the names. Then I have a chapter on France, or French traits, with which I like to reward the young people for good behaviour at the foregoing metaphysical lessons and one called the Anglo American, which is a pendant to that. But if I prosper in my present writings for a week or two, I hope to bring you something different & better, — if I come. With kindest regards to Col M'Kay,[137] whom I wish to see, I must go to my brother. Yours constantly,

R. W. Emerson

To MONCURE DANIEL CONWAY, CONCORD, OCTOBER 16, 1856

[Partly printed in Conway, *Autobiography*, I, 243.]

To WILLIAM ROUNSEVILLE ALGER, CONCORD, OCTOBER 19, 1856

[MS owned by the Yale University Library; printed in *The Journal of English and Germanic Philology*, XXVI, 483–484 (Oct., 1927).]

---

probable that the person addressed was Samuel Longfellow (brother of the poet), who had then been for some years pastor of the Second Society in Brooklyn. At any rate William Emerson wrote, Dec. 12, 1856 (MS owned by Dr. Haven Emerson): " Mr Frothingham told me some days ago that he expected you at Jersey City for one evening when you came to read a course at Brooklyn, but that Mr Longfellow's illness had prevented him (Mr L.) from coming to a perfect understanding with you as to when you would come. This morning, however, I encountered Col. McKay, who said that Mr Longfellow had been expecting a letter from you for some time in answer to one he had written you . . ." The letter of Dec. 11, 1856, shows that the Brooklyn course was abandoned.

136. See a note on Mar. 24, 1856, to Adams.

137. No doubt the same Col. James McKaye who had written from 82 Broadway, Feb. 3, 1855, inviting Emerson to be his guest. *Trow's New York City Directory* for 1856–1857 shows that this McKaye's home was in Brooklyn.

To William Emerson, Concord, October 27, 1856 [138]

Concord —
27 October, 1856.

Dear William,

If you can remember the name of your too silent brother, who shrinks over this paper to think how rarely he writes to New York you must make the best apologies for him you can. If you will have yourself elected secretary of the Staten Island Lyceum for a month or so, & guess from the correspondence it entails what quantity of letters he has to write who corresponds with fifty Lyceums, you will learn much mercy. But I am now to say what all in this house & I also can no longer wait for the Governor's proclamation [139] to say that we wish to persuade you & Susan & the boys three to come & eat your Thanksgiving pie in Concord; & we will promise you the thankfullest young eyes & old eyes for your reward and the best company out of the house that we can find in Concord to aid you to forget the majesties of New York for a few days. We will give you good room, for Mrs Brown's house is vacated for the time to add to ours. & Mrs Ripley & Sophy, &, between whiles, Aunt Elizabeth, shall shine upon you. Tell Susan, if she could see the entreaty in the faces of her three young friends near me she would not wait to be asked twice. So listen & come.

Your brother
Waldo —

To Octavius Brooks Frothingham, Concord? c. October? 1856

[Frothingham, n. d., thanks Emerson for his note just received and asks whether he can come the last week of November or the second week in December. Emerson endorsed " 1856 " and " 25 Nov? or 10 Dec." Frothingham, Jersey City, Nov. 14, 1856, explains the necessity of altering the schedule of lectures in his course; Wendell Phillips, he says, seems to insist on Nov. 26. Frothingham asks whether Emerson expected to come to Jersey City week after next. It seems possible that the present letter is that of Oct. 27, 1856, which is listed, without the name of the person addressed, in C. F. Libbie & Co., May 9–10, 1911.]

138. MS owned by HCL; ph. in CUL.
139. Governor Gardner's proclamation was dated Oct. 29 (see a note on Dec. 11, 1856).

To H. Lambert, Concord? November *c.* 4? 1856

[Lambert, West Newton, Mass., Nov. 3, 1856, asked for a lecture on Nov. 17. The endorsement shows Emerson answered he would come then.]

To Edwin Percy Whipple, Concord? November? *c.* 9? 1856

[Whipple, Boston, Nov. 11, 1856, says he will come to Concord to lecture on Dec. 10, as Emerson requests. I am uncertain whether Emerson's invitation is the letter to Whipple listed in *Catalogue of Autograph Letters . . . Donated to the Mississippi Valley Sanitary Fair, and to be Sold . . . October 7th and 8th, 1864,* where it is dated simply 1856. Whipple writes again, Nov. 30, 1856, asking that his evening at Concord be changed.]

To A.? M.? Ide, Concord, November 13, 1856

[MS listed in Anderson Galleries, Jan. 14–15, 1925, where it is described as relating to an appointment. I conjecture that the Ide addressed may have been A. M. Ide, who wrote from Taunton, Mass., Nov. 26, 1863, about a lecture and, Apr. 5, 1864, about returning a book to Emerson.]

To James Elliot Cabot, Concord, November 18, 1856 [140]

Concord Nov 18 1856

My dear Cabot,

Thanks for the kind suggestion or provocation you are pleased to send. I often amuse myself with ideal classes, like all dreaming professors, & fancy what sleeping eloquence & added power they would call out. But if the classes came, tis likely the powers would not. I was quickly informed of that luckless slip about Marathon,[141] & could hardly believe it. Yet why not? I often make them; & great is the oblivion of audiences: in a fortnight, they suffer me to come & make new ones. Do not fail to let me see the Icelander, that is, if it is done into good German,[142] — me first, & Thoreau afterwards, who reads less in books lately, & more in nature, though it happens at this moment, he is at Marcus Spring's New Jersey Colony, surveying farms & I believe lecturing to the colonists.[143] I meant to send you some time ago Wilkinsons

140. MS owned by Professor Philip Cabot; ph. in CUL.
141. Perhaps in a lecture Cabot had heard Emerson read.
142. Possibly the *Eyrbyggja Saga* mentioned in Apr. 13, 1857.
143. Thoreau had arrived at Eagleswood, Perth Amboy, late in October; and on Nov. 25 he was home again in Concord. During his month abroad he surveyed, lectured, set out an orchard and vineyard, and, most important of all, went in company with Alcott to call on Walt Whitman in Brooklyn. (*The Writings,* VI, 286–291, and XV, 134–139.)

tract on the stereoscope,[144] but it went out of sight. I think I can send it by tomorrow's mail. It need not be returned.

Yours ever,
R W Emerson

To Frederic Frothingham, Concord, November 19, 1856 [145]

$$\left.\begin{array}{l}\text{Concord}\\\text{Mass}\end{array}\right\}\ 19\ \text{Nov}.^r\ 1856$$

Dear Sir,

I received & lost your first letter, & looked for it much in vain. I am sorry to say that your new letter does not find me in the power or hardly the mood to attempt what you wish. I am the more sorry, because I think this is not the first or the second time that your friends & the friends of freedom at Portland have honored me with this request. Still, I have no choice, but must wait until I can say something to the purpose.

Respectfully,
Mr Frothingham.   R W Emerson

To R. A. Chapman, Concord? November? c. 20? 1856

[Mentioned in Dec. 15, 1856.]

To Charles? F.? Smith, Concord, November 27, 1856

[MS listed and partly quoted in Goodspeed's Book Shop, catalogue 174; Emerson says he is to be in Ohio almost to the end of January. For the possibility that the Smith addressed is Charles F. Smith, of Charlestown, Mass., *cf.* Nov. 8, 1853, and Oct. 15, 1862, both to him.]

To D. H. Olmstead, Concord? November? 1856

[In Dec. 11, 1856, Emerson says he has been corresponding occasionally with Olmstead. *Cf.* also Dec.? *c.* 5? 1856.]

144. J. J. G. Wilkinson's pseudonymous *Painting with Both Hands; or the Adoption of the Principle of the Stereoscope in Art.*

145. MS owned by the Syracuse Public Library; ph. in CUL. The envelope is addressed to Frederic Frothingham at Portland, Me. This was apparently the " Frederick " Frothingham who became, about this time, the pastor of the Second Unitarian Society in Portland (William Willis, *The History of Portland,* 2d ed., 1865, p. 672) .

To WILLIAM EMERSON, CONCORD, DECEMBER 1, 1856 [146]

Concord Dec 1

Dear William,

      I see that Bulkeley in this letter which he wrote here & leaves open with me quite ignores his whereabout & whomwithal. But he is in good health & as peaceful as now for years he has been. He has spent four days with us & has just gone home. All that is unpromising in his condition is the illness of Mrs Hoar who I fear will not live long, &, I doubt, this may break up the family & lose B. his home. We grieved old & young at the absence of you old & young at our feast.[147] Mrs Ripley Phebe Sophy & Geo Bradford came as usual. Love to Susan and to the 3 youths.

W.

To THOMAS STARR KING, CONCORD, DECEMBER 2, 1856

[Acknowledged in King, Boston, Dec. 17, 1856; King said he had no Wednesdays or Thursdays left till the middle of March. Emerson probably wrote again, for King, Dec. 22, 1856, once more discussed the possibility of lecturing in Concord.]

To D. H. OLMSTEAD, CONCORD? DECEMBER? c. 5? 1856

[See the note on Nov.? 1856.]

To JOHN MURRAY FORBES, CONCORD, DECEMBER 8, 1856 [148]

Concord
Dec. 8, 1856.

My dear Sir,

      I thought I had shut myself quite out of Milton Lyceum, by a vigorous exertion of will, when I found myself one day face to face with one of your Curators. To be sure, tis quite another matter to be summoned thither *via* your house. But I do not think I can come even with that bribe; at least, not at the time you propose. I have several contingent promises floating at present which will one or the other be

146. MS owned by HCL; ph. in CUL. The year is from William Emerson's endorsement.

147. In a letter of Oct. 27, 1856, Emerson had invited his brother's family to Concord for Thanksgiving.

148. MS owned by RWEMA; ph. in CUL. Forbes had written from Milton, Mass., Dec. 4, 1856, to ask whether Emerson could lecture there on Feb. 13; he also told of his sister Margaret's ill health and desire to see Emerson again.

pretty sure to absorb the week you have indicated: And on the whole, for the present, I think this must be left uncertain & you may if you will keep the door ajar that I may hereafter send you word that I wish to come in, if there still is room. For any " promise," that you intimate, I do not recall it.

I am very sorry for what you say of your sister's ill health. I heartily wish I knew how to be a neighbor to a lady so excellent. My wife sends to her her kindest salutations.

With great regard,
Yours,
R W Emerson.

J. M. Forbes, Esq.

To George Sumner, Concord, December 8, 1856 [149]

Concord, 8 Decr 1856

Dear Sir,

You must remember that we are relying on you for a lecture in our Lyceum. Will you fix a Wednesday in February, when you can come, & much oblige

Yours gratefully,
R. W. Emerson

Mr Sumner.

To William Emerson, Concord, December 11, 1856 [150]

Concord 11 Decr 1856

Dear William,

Tis high time you should begin to receive your own again. So I enclose to you the whole payment 101.94,[151] of 7 December, on T. Gilberts note. The payment is 120.00; from which I deduct 18.06, to pay the interest due, as usual, to Estate of R. Haskins. I have made some feeble attempts once & again to collect the items of my account against you. But I must beg you, I find, to send me the date of the last account of Bulkeley's expenses which I rendered: So you will be less

149. MS owned by Mr. Owen D. Young; ph. in CUL. According to the MS records of the Concord Lyceum (in the Concord Free Public Library) , George Sumner lectured on " France," Friday, Feb. 13, 1857, but had hardly begun when " the cry of Fire Started up his audience, the flames from which . . . could be seen from the Hall " and " The gentlemen generally withdrew, leaving a select audience of Ladies . . ."

150. MS owned by HCL; ph. in CUL.

151. The upper third of the first leaf, which is missing, doubtless contained only an order for this sum.

likely to have my charges repeated. I find now as so often that tis very far from Concord to New York after several spasmodic endeavors we have both made to make them nearer. I tried to make some covenant with my Brooklyn friends [152] to come & spend a fortnight in your region; but the Governors perversely conspired to appoint the Thanksgivings on different weeks,[153] & baulked my good meanings. Of course, I refused my vote to Governor Gardner. Now I am to fly through N. Y. about 7 or 8 Jan.ʸ to Philadelphia [154] & am corresponding occasionally with D H Olmstead [155] about some appointment in N. Y. which is not yet fixed. We are all as well as usual. The fine skating keeps Edward & Edith in good red faces & even Ellen at last has bought skates & carried them to Cambridge today, on challenge of Ida Agassiz to skate with her. We have met with a serious loss in Mr Sanborn's determination to accept the office of Secretary of the State Committee of Kanzas Relief,[156] until April next. He has put young Abbott of Boston, a Sophomore in Cambridge, in his place here; but I fear it will take him long to fill it: and perhaps Sanborn will not return. I have not heard lately of William's (Jr) health. That he is well again, & his father & his mother, & his brothers, I heartily hope. Affectionately,

Waldo.

To Abel Adams, Concord, December 15, 1856 [157]

Concord, 15 Dec. 1856.

My dear friend,

I received your note with its enclosed cheque for $120., as a very good bird. I enclose to you Mr Chapman's last letter, received nearly a month ago. I wrote him in reply [158] what his letter seemed to

152. *Cf.* Oct. 14, 1856.

153. Nov. 20 in New York and 27 in Massachusetts (*New-York Weekly Times,* Nov. 22, and *Boston Daily Advertiser,* Oct. 31, 1856) .

154. See Jan. 13, 1857.

155. Letters of Nov.? and Dec.? *c.* 5? 1856. Dwight H. Olmstead was listed as a lawyer in *Trow's New York City Directory* for the year ending May 1, 1857.

156. An earlier advertisement of this organization had urged contributions to help the cause of antislavery settlers in the Territory (*Boston Daily Advertiser,* Aug. 20, 1856) . Sanborn had already served as secretary of the Middlesex Kanzas Committee (*ibid.,* Oct. 21, 1856) . In *Recollections,* I, 73, he tells how he turned over his Concord school to Francis Abbot and became secretary and general agent of the State Committee in Dec., 1856.

157. MS owned by RWEMA; ph. in CUL.

158. Nov.? *c.* 20? 1856. For Chapman and Mills, see Oct. 3, 1855, and Mar. 24, 1856, to Adams. For Dexter, see Feb. 8, 1856.

wish that I should say, namely, that I believed I must not entertain Mr Mills's proposition, as I had other uses for the money, which had long been waiting for it. But I have not heard from him again. I saw Mr Dexter in the street, a few days ago. He told me he had written me a letter & asked for my proxy, to carry to Montpelier to the meeting of the V. & C. Road Company. So I went into an office, & signed a " proxy." I did this without hesitation, remembering your favorable opinion respecting him. If for any cause he does not represent the like interests with mine in the matter, I suppose I can yet recall it.

I am sorry to write; I wish to come to you; but the Lyceum is a terrible tyrant with long arms that reach from Chicago & Milwaukie [159] to Concord, and a hundred hands, each of which writes me a letter that I must answer. As usual, I never mean to leave home another winter. With kindest remembrance to Mrs Adams, to Abby, & to Mrs A. L. — and I wish I might hear better news of Abby L.

Yours faithfully,
R. W. Emerson.

Mr Adams.

To John Murray Forbes, Concord, December 16, 1856 [160]

Concord, 16 Dec.ʳ 1856

My dear Sir,

      It seems as if things should give way to such an invitation as you send me,[161] with many branches, & fruit on them all. But they will not. Friday, there is a kind of Club, which I am bound to attend. Saturday, I am to dine with Sam. G. Ward, by an invitation of some standing, too; so that I must lose Miss Sedgwick, — which I very much regret, — & postpone my visit to Milton to a day when there shall be a better consent of stars. Ellen, too, whom you are so kind as to include in your invitation, would have even renounced Mr Agassiz & Miss Ida for one day, to see Miss Sedgwick at your house. With kindest remembrance to Mrs Forbes, Yours faithfully,

R. W. Emerson.

Mr Forbes.

159. For Chicago, see Jan. 24, 1857; apparently there was no lecture in Milwaukee this winter.

160. MS owned by RWEMA; ph. in CUL.

161. Forbes, Milton, Mass., Dec. 11, 1856, said he would see the directors of the lyceum and try to keep the door open till February; meantime he wished Emerson and Ellen to come for a visit on Dec. 19 or 20, when Miss Sedgwick would be a guest.

To Daniel Ricketson, Concord, December 19, 1856 [162]

Concord, 19 Dec.ʳ 1856.

My dear Sir,

It will give me much pleasure to come & see you on Monday, that is, if the laws of time & space, which are known to be a little stingy & tyrannical, allow. I fear I cannot come to N. B. until the P. M. & must be in Boston again the next day at 4 P. M. when our Concord train departs. If between those limits I can manage to spend a night with you without annoying a quiet family, I will gladly do so. But, otherwise, you must come & give me an hour at Parker's (is it not?) Hotel, where I will first go. I am very sorry, but I can find no young companion for this march, on that day.

Yours gratefully,

R. W. Emerson.

Mr Ricketson.

To Octavius Brooks Frothingham, Concord? December c. 24, 1856

[Frothingham, Jersey City, Dec. 22, 1856, is still concerned about a lecture date for Emerson and now proposes an evening " this week " or any day in the week of Jan. 24 or in the two succeeding weeks. Frothingham, Dec. 26, 1856, mentions Emerson's note and accepts Feb. 13, though Emerson has made it clear that he may not be able to come even then.]

To Charles Sumner, Concord? December 26, 1856? [163]

Friday Morⁿᵍ
26 Dec.

Dear Sumner,

I heartily wish you will make it possible to see your face tomorrow at our Club, at 2½ o'clock, Saturday; at Parker's, School St. There is very much to learn of you. Yours

R. W. Emerson

162. MS owned by Miss Edith Guerrier; ph. in CUL. The envelope is addressed to Daniel Ricketson at New Bedford. The MS memorandum book for 1856 gives Monday, Dec. 22, to that place. According to *New Bedford,* 1889, p. 75, the Parker House, leading hotel of the town, had been opened in 1841.

163. MS owned by RWEMA; ph. in CUL. The year 1856, added in another hand, is very probably correct. After the founding of the Saturday Club and before Sumner's death, Dec. 26 fell on Friday in that year, in 1862, and in 1873. Sumner became a member of the club in 1862, but the present note seems to imply that he was not yet

To William Emerson, Concord, December 29, 1856 [164]

Concord 29 Dec 1856

Dear William,

I have only received your letters, one, two, three, I believe, since I wrote, but I am too little in my library to write so many. The magical box, with surcoat of brown paper, arrived safely; but a suspicion instantly arose, from its form & general appearance, among our three young tyrants, that there was somewhat dangerous within it; & they strictly forbade its being opened until New Years day, when there is a solemn breakfast, as I understand, & the hour is thought auspicious, & repellent of danger. So you shall hear again from us, if any crisis should occur.

With love to Susan & to the boys.

Affectionately,
Waldo.

To William Emerson, Concord, December 30, 1856 [165]

Concord, 30 Dec. 1856.

Dear William,

I am charged to send the love & best wishes of us all at home to you all at home. I send a little box for New Year's token: the trencher is for Susan: the Beaumont & F. for William, Jr. the Horace for Haven: & the bookslide & inkhorn for Charles's table. With the dear love of our boy & girls.

Lidian thanks Susan for her kind plans, but dares not promise a visit this winter. Yet perhaps I will persuade her when the right day comes. Waldo.

To ———— Wise, Concord, December 31, 1856

[MS listed in Hodgson & Co., July 24, 1935; described as referring to a " journey of lectures."]

---

a member. Just recovering from the assault made upon him in the Senate chamber, he was received with acclaim by his Boston friends in Nov., 1856; on Dec. 24 he dined with Longfellow (Samuel Longfellow, *Life*, n. d. [c. 1891], II, 323–324). Sumner's note dated simply " Saturday " in which he says, " I must forgo the opportunity you kindly give me " may, I believe, belong to Dec. 27, 1856, and be an answer to the present letter.

164. MS owned by HCL; ph. in CUL.
165. MS owned by HCL; ph. in CUL.

To ——————, Concord? 1856

[Partly quoted in *The Index,* June 14, 1883, p. 594, where it is dated only as to year. An introductory note explains that the letter is " to a lady " and that it refers to a recent volume of poems by B. W. Ball. Emerson says he is returning the book, comments upon its charm and power, and recalls a pleasant walk with its author many years earlier.]

To Horatio Woodman, Concord, *c.* 1856?

[MS listed in George D. Smith, n. d., where the date is given as about 1852; described as to " Mr. Woodman," accepting an invitation to a club meeting and notifying him that Emerson will bring a guest. This description suggests, however, a date during the formative period of the Saturday Club. For Woodman and that club, see a note on Apr. 7, 1856. *Cf.* also letters of Sept. 12 and 15 of the same year.]

1857

TO RICHARD HENRY DANA, JR., CONCORD, JANUARY 1, 1857 [1]

Concord, 1 Jan.
1857

My dear Sir,

I know nothing of the letter of which you write, & know of no suit, & have not written to you. Perhaps it is from my cousin, Wm Ralph Emerson,[2] of Boston, nephew of Geo. B. E.?

Yours, with the best hopes & wishes of the day,

R. W. Emerson.

Mr Dana.

TO ABEL ADAMS, CONCORD, JANUARY 2, 1857 [3]

Concord, 2 Jan. 1857

My dear friend,

I send you Mr Chapman's last letter as I sent you the previous one to keep you informed of the little story [4] & mainly that you may advise me if you find I am pressing Mr Mills too hardly. Of course, I prefer mild methods to harsh ones, & if you find this " execution " & so forth unreasonable, I wish to give Mr M. whatever indulgence is proper. He has never written to me.

With the best wishes for the new year to you, & to Mrs Adams, & to all your house,

Yours affectionately,
R. W. Emerson

Mr Adams.

1. MS owned by the Richard H. Dana Estate; ph. in CUL.

2. William Ralph Emerson is duly listed in *The Ipswich Emersons*, p. 227, as a nephew of George B. Emerson, mentioned frequently in earlier letters. According to the *Boston Directory*, 1857, he was a member of Preston & Emerson, architects and builders. For his part in the rebuilding of the Concord home some fifteen years later, see Sept. 13, 1872.

3. MS owned by RWEMA; ph. in CUL.

4. *Cf.* Dec. 15, 1856, and earlier letters.

To ———, CONCORD, JANUARY 5, 1857 [5]

Concord —
5 January 1857

Dear Sir,

I am afraid I shall hardly be able to recall to your thought,
'tis so long ago, that I was to send you the Bhagvat, when it came into
my hands: and I should fear to send it now, only that I remember you
were to come under a sort of covenant not to read any copy but mine.
With hope of better speed in the new year, I remain

Yours, with great regard,

R. W. Emerson

To EDITH EMERSON, BOSTON, JANUARY 7, 1857 [6]

American House
Wednesday

Dear Edith,

I hear from home that there are letters on the way for you,
& that the whole household are well. I enclose a couple of dollars, on
remembering that you are to get home from Boston, as well as Portsmouth, on Friday.

Papa.

To LIDIAN EMERSON, BUFFALO, JANUARY 13, 1857 [7]

American House
Buffalo 13 Jan

Dear Lidian

I came hither safely from Philadelphia [8] where I had a very

5. MS owned by Mr. William H. M. Adams; ph. in CUL. The name of the person
addressed is unknown, but the lower part of the second leaf is missing, and a single
stroke of the pen still visible indicates that Emerson probably wrote the name there.
As for the evidence afforded by mention of the *Bhagavadgita*, unfortunately the lending of that book was a habit with Emerson.

6. MS owned by RWEMA; ph. in CUL. The date Jan. 7, 1857, supplied in another
hand, is correct. That day was Wednesday, and Edith Emerson wrote to her father
from Concord, Jan. 11 (endorsed 1857 by her father) : " I received your letter enclosing two dollars on Thursday." For her visit at Portsmouth, N. H., see the letter of
Jan. 16, 1857, to her. Emerson probably spent the night of Jan. 7 in Boston in order
to catch an early train to New York on the 8th (*cf.* Jan. 13 following) .

7. MS owned by RWEMA; ph. in CUL. The year is fixed by evidence cited below.
Emerson's lecture before the Young Men's Association on Jan. 13, 1857, is announced
in the *Buffalo Commercial Advertiser* of that date.

8. The *Public Ledger*, Jan. 9, 1857, announced that Emerson would lecture on
" The Conduct of Life " before the People's Literary Institute that evening.

pleasant visit, seeing Furness, S Bradford, the Randolphs,[9] & other friends, then a tedious ride of 350 miles brot me here, where I have found Mr Tracy [10] who is almost as rare a talker as Mr Alcott Mrs Drury of Canandaigua & several other good people Tonight after lecture I am to ride 70 miles by way of inducing sleep & appetite [11] & in a day or two I will send you some new word we will hope better. Here I have received today the letters you enveloped At N. Y.[12] I saw William I & II at the Astor House but nothing of the rest of their household. Love to the children I hope Edith did not be pinched with cold at P.[13] The cold began & ended with the limits for her visit. Tell [14]

To Moncure Daniel Conway, Syracuse, New York, January 16, 1857 [15]

Syracuse, 16 Jan.ʸ 1857

My dear Sir,

I have your note, which causes me no little uneasiness, when I see you working so earnestly & efficiently in my behalf, whilst I am hardly prepared to meet the claims you are creating for me. I fear I was inconsiderate in not reckoning my means more exactly in the hasty conversation in Concord about lectures, & that I counted eggs hatched & not quite hatched, for what seemed to me so improbable a contingency as a *course* in Cincinnati.[16] My chapter on " Memory," the most matured in my studies of " Intellect," is not yet presentable. An essay which I call " Days," which may yet deserve the Hesiodic title of " Works & Days," is not yet presentable. At this moment, after I shall

9. Philip Randolph appears in earlier and later letters. *Cf.* the note on July *c.* 20? 1851. His cousin Richard Randolph was also, at least within a few years, an occasional correspondent of Emerson's.

10. For Albert H. Tracy, see *Journals*, IX, 64–67. He is listed in *The Commercial Advertiser Directory for the City of Buffalo*, for 1857, as Tracey, an attorney. On Sept. 18 (or 10?), 1856, he had written from Buffalo in praise of *English Traits*. Emerson later wished to bring Tracy and Alcott together (see Nov. 2, 1857).

11. Ellen Emerson, Concord, Jan. 17, 1857, said her father's first letter came on the 16th and that she hoped the seventy miles gave sleep and appetite.

12. *Cf.* the note on Jan. 7, 1857. The MS memorandum book for this year has no New York entry but gives Jan. 8 to Paterson, N. J., where Emerson probably lectured.

13. See Jan. 16, 1857, to Edith Emerson.

14. The letter was apparently unfinished; the fourth page is blank. But *cf.* a note on Jan. 17, 1857.

15. MS owned by Mrs. Mildred Conway Sawyer; ph. in CUL. The *Syracuse Daily Journal* of Jan. 17, 1857, reported that Emerson read " Objects of Life " before the Franklin Institute on the 16th.

16. For the Cincinnati course and Conway's valiant aid, see Jan. 29, 1857.

have read my lecture on " Life " to the Mercantile Library, I shall only
have two more with me. which I care to read at C., one " on Beauty,"
& one " on Poetry." A third, " the Scholar," which was an address at
Amherst,[17] did very well at Boston, last spring, & might pass at C. and
" France."; but I think, that, unless the project can be postponed until
April, so that I can go home & prepare for it, it had better be dropped.
I am sorry to meet your kind zeal for me so very ill; but though one or
two additional lectures were spoken of, I did not look beyond that, and
I believed before this, that the scheme was out of your mind, for indeed
you have enough to do, &, as I learn & read, are doing it well. Shall we
not say, then, that Mr E. who does not mean to read in many places another winter, may yet come, *then,* to Cincinnati as he will to Philadelphia & to Boston? Or, if you think the late spring of this year will serve,
I will come.

Yours gratefully,
R. W. Emerson

Rev Mr Conway.

To Edith Emerson, Syracuse, New York, January 16, 1857 [18]

Syracuse N. Y.
16 January

Dear Edith, Here is a rude copy from memory of Thomson's description
of the nightingale's song, which is sometimes called the finest passage
in the " Seasons." You have Thomson among Grandmama's books. If
you cannot find it, you may find the poem in my big *Hazlitt's British
Poets* a thick *8vo* vol. bound in boards, & rather shabby, high up on my
shelves,

> Oft when returning with her loaded bill,
> The astonished mother finds her vacant nest
> By the hard hand of unrelenting clowns
> Robbed, — to the ground the vain provision falls,
> Her pinions ruffle, & low-drooping scarce
> Can bear the mourner to the poplar grove,

17. See Aug. 6, 1855, and, for Boston, a note on Mar. 24, 1856, to Adams.

18. MS owned by Mrs. Ward I. Gregg; ph. in CUL. Edith Emerson wrote, Concord, Jan. 11 (endorsed 1857), that she got safely home from Portsmouth on Friday;
next week was the week for poetry and she wished to know what she should read. The
passage Emerson quotes from Thomson in the present letter is very nearly accurate,
and it is probable that he remembered it from the time when he copied it into his
quotation book, in 1820 or 1821 (*cf. Journals,* I, 89). These lines, 717–728 in " Spring,"
were in William Hazlitt's *Select British Poets,* London, 1824, p. 410.

Where, all abandoned to despair, she sings
Her sorrows thro' the night and, on the bough
Sole sitting, still at every dying fall
Takes up again the lamentable strain
Of winding wo, till wide around the woods
Sigh to her song, & with her wail resound.

If you prefer rhyme, you can read the "Destruction of Sennacherib,"
out of the "Hebrew Melodies," which you will find in my "Byrons
Works," — also a thick shabby volume in the same shelves. I am glad
to hear of your pleasant visit in Portsmouth, & particularly pleased that
you did not overstay the Friday.

Papa.

To Charles Stetson, Syracuse, New York, January 16, 1857 [19]

Syracuse N. Y.
16 January 1857

My dear Sir,

I found last night at Rochester your very kind note. I am
very heartily obliged by your friendly invitation: but my visit to Cincinnati notwithstanding my best endeavors to the contrary, promises
at present to be but a flying one, and I cannot think of giving Mrs Stetson, of whose goodness I have the best remembrances, the annoyance
of a traveller's arrival & departure at uncivil railroad hours. in her
peaceful home. But I do not mean that my visit shall be so short as to
hinder me from paying my personal respects to her & to yourself.

With grateful regards,
Yours,

Mr Stetson.

R. W. Emerson.

To the Editor of *Putnam's Monthly Magazine*, Syracuse? New York?
January? *c.* 16? 1857

[MS listed in William Evarts Benjamin, Sept., 1896, where it is dated only as
to year and is described as introducing Edwin Morton. For Emerson's meeting
with Edwin Morton at Syracuse, N. Y., see Jan. 17, 1857. For Emerson at Syracuse, see also the letters of Jan. 16, 1857.]

19. MS owned by CUL; ph. in CUL. For the projected course in Cincinnati, *cf.*
the letter of the same date to Conway. Conway, who had much to do with arrangements for these lectures, has recorded Emerson's special enjoyment of a dinner given
by Charles Stetson (*Autobiography*, I, 283). Mrs. Stetson was Rebecca Vose, whom
Emerson had found on his first visit to the West (see May 28, 1850, and Ellen F.
Vose, *Robert Vose and his Descendants*, 1932, p. 184).

To LIDIAN EMERSON, SYRACUSE? NEW YORK? JANUARY 17, 1857 [20]

Horace Greeley came with me from Syracuse to Rochester, on Thursday P. M. to hear me, as he said. But the restless man likes to be going, he had missed his own appointment for that night, & wherever he comes, he is accosted by scores & watched by more, — which he knows & enjoys. His entrance into a tavern, much more into a lecture hall, awakens gratulating shouts, and I could scarcely keep the people quiet to hear my abstractions, they were so furious to shout Greeley! Greeley! [21] Catch me carrying Greeley into my lecture again! After we got him well home however to the tavern, where we took a parlour with two little bed chambers opening into it, he was very quiet good company for a little while before bed; but he rose at 6, lit the candles, & scribbled political paragraphs to send away to the Tribune. He is an admirable editor, but I had as lief travel with an Express man or with Barnum.

At Buffalo, did I tell you? I found Mrs Drury; at Syracuse, Miss Laura Fay of St Albans, Vt. sister of Zina Fay.[22] And there too was Edwin Morton & his pupil young Smith. But there are no compensations for the waste & discomfort of this journeying, & the stultification of brain which it causes. I must find better ways to live.

17 Jan

20. MS owned by RWEMA; ph. in CUL. This sheet, which could have been addressed to no one but Lidian Emerson, I think, was probably sent with another sheet — most probably as part of a letter from Syracuse on the 17th, containing money (see Jan. 29, 1857), but possibly with the fragmentary letter written at Buffalo on Jan. 13. Jan. 19 following refers to a letter from Buffalo which had apparently been slow in reaching Concord; and Ellen Emerson wrote, Jan. 22, 1857, that one to her mother had arrived from Buffalo on the 21st. On the other hand, Ellen may have referred to a letter now lost. The year of the present letter is fixed by evidence cited below.

21. The *Rochester Daily American*, Jan. 16, 1857, reports Emerson's lecture on "Conduct of Life" before the Athenæum and Mechanic's Association on Jan. 15. The large audience was held "with a sort of fascination" by the "intensely Emersonian" performance. But there were accidents. Twice during the lecture the gas lights caused trouble. "During the first darkness, a few lamps were obtained and placed upon the platform, and the audience called for Hon. Horace Greeley, who occupied a seat on the platform, being casually in town. Mr. Greeley rose in the darkness and spoke a few words . . . When the gas was re-lighted, Mr. Emerson resumed and spoke till the next interruption, which was brief. After which he concluded his lecture."

22. Zina Fay had first written to Emerson from St. Albans, Vt., Oct. 5, 1856, when she knew him only through *English Traits*.

To Lidian Emerson, Columbus, Ohio, January 19, 1857 [23]

Columbus, Ohio
19 January 1857

Dear Lidian,

I am sorry to have made you uneasy by not writing. I did not know that I did not; but I believe I have sat still nowhere until at Buffalo, & I think I must have written thence.[24] However, I have had all your letters, at B. at Syracuse, & at Rochester, & now three new ones here. I am sorry Plymouth pays no better, & I found a pencil scratch that " the house wanted coats of paint, which would cost 45." I suppose you must write Mr Jackson word that it must be done. I hope Court Street did its duty in these times. You send me no word from Springfield.[25] tis time to hear again. If you are pinched, I will send you a draft on Phillips & Sampson, who are, I believe, my debtors. Yes, surely, let Manon draw the wood home, if Dolly cannot; but I told James [26] he might go to Billings & get another horse to put with Dolly, which might be better, provided the snow is not deep, as keeping Dolly in work, & Billings, I suppose, has a farm-working horse. I should like well to have dined with Mrs Hooper. I am grieved at the rogue Morton's success [27] with his crocodile tears, but must think that few people can be so silly as Mr Lawrence. But I also hope Edith did not go to play a part at Aunt Susan's.[28] By no means. Love to the children

W.

To Lidian Emerson, Chicago, January 22? 1857

[Mentioned in the letters of Jan. 24 and 29, 1857.]

23. MS owned by RWEMA; ph. in CUL. The lectures before the Atheneum at Columbus were " The Conduct of Life," Jan. 19, and " Poetry," 20 (*Daily Ohio State Journal*, Jan. 19–21, 1857).

24. Jan. 13, 1857. For Syracuse and Rochester, see the letters of Jan. 16 and 17 of this year.

25. That is, from the Mills affair, mentioned in a number of earlier letters.

26. Burke, no doubt.

27. The Morton-Jackson controversy is mentioned in many earlier letters. For later developments, see Mar. 1, 1863, and Apr. 18, 1864, to Boutwell.

28. At Susan Bridge Jackson's.

To Lidian Emerson, Chicago, January 24, 1857 [29]

Tremont House
Chicago
24 January '57

Dear Lidian,

With this you ought to receive another letter [30] enclosing a draft from the Marine Bank of Chicago on the Metropolitan Bank of N. Y. for $130. — Pay first the $98. or 99. due on my tax, to Mr Holbrook.[31] I have not yet found here any letters from you though I still hope for such, as the mails are some days in arrears here on account of snow. The winter is nearly as savage in the West as was the last to the great annoyance of me & of all travellers & of the people themselves who have heretofore found this climate milder much than ours. I go hence tomorrow night to Cincinnati, where it seems, I am expected to give a course after my lecture to the Mercantile Library.[32] If I consent, I shall either have to return home first or else set Ellen on a rummaging in the lower regions of the library to find certain MSS. to be sent thither by Express. So she must not accept any invitations to long visits in Cambridge. She can tell Mr Agassiz if she have opportunity that a book [33] I brought with me is an immense comfort to a wayworn traveller & I believe is read with more zest in taverns on the prairie, than it will be by those who read it luxuriously in their libraries at home. I have imparted glimpses of it to but one ardent scholar on the way, & to him as under lock & key, and to his great joy. I have found very kind reception here in Chicago — beside the warmth sleep & comfort which I always find in this excellent hotel, where, last winter, I worked on " English Traits." [34] Two or three very agreeable persons I find here; among others, tell

29. MS owned by RWEMA; ph. in CUL. Though there is no signature, the text is presumably complete. *The Chicago Daily Journal,* Jan. 22, 1857, announced that Emerson would lecture on " The Conduct of Life " before the Y. M. A. that evening. *Cf.* the note on Oct. 1, 1856.

30. Jan. 22? 1857.

31. Joseph Holbrook was the town treasurer (*Reports of the Selectmen, and Other Officers, of the Town of Concord,* 1857) .

32. See Jan. 29 ff., 1857.

33. Probably Agassiz's *Contributions to the Natural History of the United States* (Vols. I and II, 1857) , mentioned in May 17, 1858, to Clough. Apparently Emerson had some of the MS or proof sheets, as it seems that no part of the work had yet been published (*cf.* Jules Marcou's contradictory statements in *Life, Letters, and Works of Louis Agassiz,* 1896, II, 63, 67, and 291, and *Journals,* IX, 80) .

34. See the letter of Jan. 13 and 14, 1856.

Henry T., Mr Wiley,[35] who remains loyal to him, & who, to be sure, invited me to a ride on the prairie; but I told him I had ridden on the prairie to my heart's content. I advised him to invite Mr T. to a summer expedition with him to the Yellow Stone River, which, I told him, I doubted not Henry would like; & Wiley will, I think, propose something like that to him. Love to Ellen, to Edith, to Edward, & warmer weather be to you, than is to me. Greeley was here yesterday,[36] & went with me as far as Waukegan,[37] on his way to Kenosha to lecture. I at W. & thence back, this morn. He said that the chief use of lecturing was to teach humility.

To LIDIAN EMERSON, CINCINNATI, JANUARY 27, 1857

[Telegram mentioned in the letters of Jan. 29 and 31 and Feb. 3, 1857.]

To LIDIAN EMERSON, CLEVELAND, JANUARY 29, 1857 [38]

> Angier House
> Cleveland, 29 Jan
> '57

Dear Lidian,

At Cincinnati,[39] I had letters with Ellen's; here tonight, I find yours of last Saturday. You do not say that you have either of my money letters though one went from Syracuse [40] the day I left S. & an-

35. For B. B. Wiley's enthusiasm for Thoreau, see Feb. 23, 1863, which, like a number of other later letters, is addressed to Wiley.

36. *The Chicago Daily Journal*, Jan. 23, 1857, noted that both Greeley and Emerson were at the Tremont House.

37. According to the MS memorandum book for 1857, Emerson was to be — and doubtless to lecture — at Waukegan, Ill., on Jan. 23.

38. MS owned by RWEMA; ph. in CUL. The *Cleveland Daily Plain Dealer*, Jan. 29, 1857, announced that Emerson would lecture before the Young Men's Library Association that evening; according to the MS memorandum book for that year, the subject was " Conduct of Life."

39. The story of Emerson's lectures in Cincinnati is pretty fully told in the *Daily Cincinnati Gazette*, Jan. 27-Feb. 6, 1857. On Jan. 27 he read " The Conduct of Life " to the Young Men's Mercantile Library Association. Four days later he began a series of lectures at the Unitarian Church under Conway's direction: he read " Beauty," Jan. 31; " Poetry," Feb. 2; " Works and Days " (never before delivered, said the paper) , 4; " The Scholar," 6. In Conway's *Autobiography*, I, 282-285, there is some interesting comment on the lecture course and on a talk which Emerson gave to the children on Sunday morning. There is also some confusion of dates.

40. Probably a part of Jan. 17, 1857, now lost; *cf.* a note on that letter.

other from Chicago last Thursday [41] which you must have ere this.
From Cincinnati I sent you my telegraph [42] to send the Amherst-
Williamstown Discourse, " the Scholar " — which message I hope arrived, & is in act of being performed on your part, since it ought to
reach me by next Wednesday to be of good use.[43] I very reluctantly decided to stay at Cincinnati, having many times in heart turned my face
homeward not wishing to trust the prairie any more. But Conway had
worked so hard for me,[44] & filled the papers with paragraphs & persuaded so many people that they ought to be glad to listen, that it
seemed perverse, when the days were really at my disposal, not to stay.
The last three days too have brought such a blessed change in the
weather, from the bitter climate which made all riding & especially night
riding dangerous, & would not let me cure a cold, to these halcyon days
makes the forest through which I ride a hundred miles together, gay &
vernal, that I fancied I could get right again without absolute rest
which was becoming necessary. Love to all the children. As my plans
are now, I do not leave Cin^l for home till Saturday morning, Feb. 7 &
with good hap, which is a little rare on Feby roads, should not reach
home till Monday night, or Tuesday, and on Tuesday I am due at
Charlestown [45] So I will hope the South wind will blow. You can safely
write to me [at Burnet House, Cin.^{l} Ohio][46] until Tuesday night. How
touching is poor Mr Reuben Hoar's letter! Tell Ellen I was relieved to
hear she did not suffer in the bitter cold night of her ride to Mr Longfellow's,[47] & yet I think the cold you speak of nursing was caught then.
I hate that Mr Ward should be sick. He was never sick before, that I
know, since his Illinois journey 17 years ago. Lake Erie before my windows today is a brilliant ice field as far as I can see, and, I think, is

41. Letter of Jan. 22? 1857.

42. Jan. 27, 1857.

43. According to the MS memorandum book for 1857, Emerson received at 2 p.m.
on Feb. 3 " the concio ad clerum for which I sent to Concord last Tues." As we have
seen, he read this lecture on Feb. 6. For his reading of the same lecture at Williamstown and at Amherst, see Aug. 8, 1854, and Aug. 6, 1855.

44. Cf. Jan. 16, 1857, to Conway.

45. On his way home Emerson was detained by a flood at Albany and failed to deliver his lecture which the Mishawum Association had announced for Feb. 10 (The
City Advertiser, Charlestown, Mass., Feb. 11, 1857) . He probably telegraphed on Feb.
9 or 10 to John F. Ayer, the secretary, who signed a newspaper announcement for the
Association.

46. The square brackets seem to be Emerson's own and are, at any rate, the means
he frequently employs for setting off such information.

47. Doubtless the Twelfth Night party of which Longfellow tells in his diary
entry of Jan. 6, 1857 (Samuel Longfellow, Life, n. d. [c. 1891], II, 325) .

frozen twelve or fifteen miles from the shore. The boys skate. Tomorrow to Cincinnati again.[48]

To Lidian Emerson, Cincinnati, January 31, 1857 [49]

> Burnet House
> Cincinnati
> 31 January 1857

Dear Lidian

Here again from Sandusky & Cleveland; [50] but the fates mean I shall travel by night, which I hate, & which hates me. Yesterday, at Columbus, on arriving from Cleveland, we were told the Cin! train had just gone, & we must wait from 1.30 till 9 P. M. for the next train; & so rode all night, & arrived here at 6 o'clock morning. The only alleviation was the meeting in the evening a remarkable man, Mr Corry,[51] active in Ohio politics, & a brilliant talker full of talent & character, &, as he ranks as a democrat, & affects to represent Young America, inspires some hope for that Sodom in which he lives. He has been to visit Buchanan, with intent to inspire him with honest American policy, &, at least, to warn him to come out from the rottenness of Douglas & Pierce. His account of his visit was like the visits of George Fox & Penn to Cromwell & Charles II.[52] The fine weather remains here & diminishes my homesickness. I hope you have as good, after the rigors you tell of a week ago. I sit hoping that my telegraph [53] reached you, & set you on a timely search of the lower regions of the library, & that you have sent my Lecture.

Mr Conway has taken a deal of pains for my benefit here & certainly made me up a very respectable class. I beg you will bear it in mind for his benefit hereafter. Who do you think called upon me yesterday, among the rest, but Mr Joseph Ladd?[54] He said he only came to make a

48. The letter ends, without signature, near the bottom of the eighth page.

49. MS owned by RWEMA; ph. in CUL.

50. The MS memorandum book for 1857 seems to show that Emerson read " Beauty " at Sandusky, O., on Jan. 28. For Cleveland, see Jan. 29, 1857.

51. Perhaps William Corry, a member of the Ohio legislature (cf. *Quarterly Publication of the Historical and Philosophical Society of Ohio*, IX, 67). But according to Conway (*Autobiography*, I, 283), Emerson became acquainted at this time with Thomas Corwin, the former senator from Ohio, and was particularly pleased with him. Possibly he wrote " Corry " for " Corwin." Neither Corry nor Corwin, however, seems to be quite accurately described here.

52. For Emerson's interest in the life of Fox, cf. Feb. 17, 1835.

53. Of Jan. 27, 1857.

54. *Cf.* letters written in Dec., 1852.

moments call but would see me again so, of course, no allusion to the past was made, but I told him all he wished to know of eastern cousins & friends & we parted " with all the honors." Last night I had Ellen's letter of the 22ᵈ which assures me that you had my letters of Buffalo & Syracuse,[55] & tells very good household stories of icehouses & Eddy's school recitations, & Edith's reading.[56] Well, I am glad Edward chose his own piece, & spoke it his own way. Now I will give him a piece which I know is a good one, namely, " the horse that brought the good news to Ghent from Aix." [57] He knows the poem; but it is admirable for declamation. Papa.

To Ellen Emerson, Cincinnati, February 3, 1857 [58]

Burnet House
Cincinnati
Feb. 3

Dear Ellen,

Your parcel containing the MS.[59] & letters, arrived at my door today at noon, some hours less than a week since I sent forth my electrical dove [60] for this leaf. Tis a very gratifying result & should re-assure travellers. I suppose the message was not sent over the wires to Boston, until Wednesday morn, as it was 10 'o'clock at night, or after, when I carried my note to the office here. But I do not like to hear that you are still sick & with jaundice. What have you done, or not done, to suffer so? Ask the doctor mainly after the causes. The malady is rare, & I never heard of it in my blood, & though your mother once suffered, I had not known that it was in her family. Let us never hear of it more. I was glad of your last letter, & of this, bating the jaundice. I do not know what mishaps I told your mother from Columbus,[61] that I should have

55. The letters of Jan. 13, 16, and, perhaps, 17, 1857.

56. Ellen Emerson had also told, in her letter of Jan. 22, 1857, how Thoreau helped the children make some experiments on the passage of light and air through snow. For Edith's reading, cf. Jan. 16, 1857, to her.

57. Browning's " How they Brought the Good News from Ghent to Aix " was now old enough to be pretty well known.

58. MS owned by RWEMA; ph. in CUL.

59. Of " The Scholar "; see Jan. 29, 1857.

60. Telegram of Jan. 27, 1857. The dove and leaf are doubtless from *Genesis*, 8:8–11.

61. Apparently Emerson thought he was answering comment on his letter of Jan. 19, 1857, which Ellen does, indeed, mention in her letter of Jan. 28 of this year — unless her reference there is to another letter from Columbus, now lost.

been given up for lost so suddenly. I have coughed along through this country as the travelling public will, but not worse; & rely on seeing you all, say next Tuesday

Papa.

I am expecting Mr J. Longworth,[62] who is to carry me out to his house to pass the night.

To William Emerson, Concord, February 25, 1857 [63]

Concord
25 February, 1857

Dear William,

[1]Please send me your draft for the hundred dollars which you were having put into English that is Boston [64] for me, first deducting all losses by bad bills then by exchange & lastly by any special charge you may have lying against me.[1] I have not yet adventured on " that Account." [65]

I am sitting here well & suddenly recovered from a a sudden & pretty serious attack which lasted two or three days, from Measles, — so Dr B. called it, — fancying my skin marbled, &c. Be it what it might, once is enough for one of these dismal fellows, & I desire no more acquaintance with the like. The rest of us are all well & so be it with you! Affectionately

Waldo E

To Mark Trafton, Concord? February? c. 25? 1857

[Stephen Higginson, Boston, Mar. 11, 1857, says he received Emerson's note recommending his son Frank to Trafton. The note was not forwarded till this day for fear it might not reach Trafton, but meantime the desired appointment has been secured. Trafton was a member of Congress from Massachusetts, 1855–1857. Francis John Higginson was appointed to the U. S. Naval Academy from Massachusetts in 1857.]

62. The Longworths of Cincinnati appear in earlier letters.

63. MS owned by HCL; ph. in CUL. Excerpt I is in *The Numismatist*, XLVI, 689 (Nov., 1933). The last digit in the date line is very carelessly written, and the year is given in another hand as " 1859? " But I believe the figure in question is pretty definitely " 7 " and several canceled engagements noted in the MS memorandum book about this time seem to confirm this reading, though their evidence is doubtful.

64. Apparently the implication is that Boston money was " English " — that is, dependable. There is a discussion of this point in T. O. Mabbott's " Numismatic References of Three American Writers," *The Numismatist* for Nov., 1933.

65. *Cf.* May 6, 1857.

To Benjamin Peter Hunt, Concord, February 28, 1857 [66]

Concord, Mass^{tts}

28 Feb. 1857.

My dear Sir,

    I find, on my return home, a pillar of coffee standing in my hall, enclosed in certain bagging & wrappings, superscribed very distinctly with my name, & described when it arrived as coming from you. Judge Hoar is the principal witness that there is no error or chance in the matter, but that it was wilfully & persistently sent to me by a gentleman of extraordinary tenacity of purpose. Nothing is left for me but to say that the precious bag is well & safely received, not only for the eminent merits of the sender, but for its own good sake.

    But I must reflect on you as on a man having one of the best memories I ever knew. It would please me well, however, to make a little nearer comparison of notes in that kind, & know if really the much-tried much-practised man have kept the impress of those hours which as a boy he knew how to make delicious to an older reader & lover of the same books & thoughts that pleased himself.[67] Why, when you were here, did you not give me a chance to see you? You have for many years pleased yourself with serving me. You cannot serve me so well as by making an experiment or two, until we shall succeed in having 'a solid season,' as the Quakers say. I know very well that I have your *Histoire de Hayti*.[68] And am in perpetuity Yours gratefully,

R. W. Emerson.

B. P. Hunt, Esq.

To Theodore Parker, Concord, March 2, 1857 [69]

Concord 2 March

1857

Dear Parker,

    We depend on you in this town, & at this house, for Wednes-

66. MS owned by Mr. Owen D. Young; ph. in CUL.

67. For Hunt as Emerson's pupil at Chelmsford, Mass., see a note on Dec. *c.* 20? 1825. Some account of Hunt shortly after the time of the present letter is given in Furness, Sept. 14, 1859 (*Records of a Lifelong Friendship*, p. 116).

68. Probably Thomas Madiou the Younger, *Histoire d'Haiti*, 3 vols., 1847–1848.

69. MS owned by RWEMA; ph. in CUL. According to the MS records of the Concord Lyceum (in the Concord Free Public Library), Parker lectured there on Wednesday, Mar. 4, 1857.

day night. Meantime, Mrs Ripley begged me to ask you to drink tea
with her before Lecture.

Ever yours,
R. W. Emerson

To Evert Augustus Duyckinck, Concord, March 5, 1857

[MS owned by the New York Public Library; ph. in CUL. Reproduced in facsimile in *The Bookman*, New York, XVII, 331 (June, 1903).]

To Thomas? Earle, Concord, March 7, 1857 [70]

Concord
7 March 1857

Dear Sir,

     I will endeavor to come to Worcester on Thursday Ev$^{\underline{g}}$
March 26th

Respectfully,
R. W. Emerson

Mr Earle.

To John Murray Forbes, Concord, March 7, 1857? [71]

Concord, March 7.

My dear Sir,

     I will come to you with great pleasure, next Wednesday,[72]
& by the 3 o'clock train, which connects well with our down train at
1.30.[73] The pertinacity of your Lyceum [74] does me so much honor, that

---

70. MS owned by Goodspeed's Book Shop; ph. in CUL. A notice of the Worcester
Lyceum and Library Association in *The Worcester Almanac . . . for 1857*, p. 85, gives
Thomas Earle as secretary. The MS memorandum book for 1857 duly gives Mar. 26
to Worcester, though there seems to be no evidence in the *Worcester Daily Transcript* or *The Worcester Daily Spy* of a lecture by Emerson; Capt. John Brown was to
appear on the 25th and John Weiss on the 26th.

71. MS owned by RWEMA; ph. in CUL. The date " '56? " added in an unknown
hand, is, I believe, an error. Evidence cited below makes 1857 very probable.

72. Pretty obviously for a visit, with the matter of a lecture at Milton still unsettled.
For the lecture, see the letters of Mar. 12 and 16 following.

73. In both 1856 and 1857 there was a train from Concord to Boston at 1:30 on the
Fitchburg road, and a train from Boston for Neponset at 3 on the Old Colony &
Fall River road (*Boston Daily Advertiser*, Mar. 8, 1856, and Mar. 7, 1857).

74. *Cf.* Dec. 8, 1856, to Forbes, and a note on Dec. 16, 1856.

I do not see how I can resist any longer any evening they can choose to appoint when I shall be disengaged.[75]

> Yours, with kindest regard,
> R. W. Emerson

Mr Forbes.

To JOHN MURRAY FORBES, CONCORD, MARCH? 7? 1857? [76]

> Concord
> Saturday P. M.

My dear Sir,

  I have your second note. I am very sorry that I am engaged on Wednesday 18th; [77] but I shall write this hour,[78] & endeavor to free myself, and shall come to Milton if I can. Yours ever,

Mr Forbes.   R. W. Emerson

To PETER KAUFMANN, CONCORD, MARCH 9, 1857 [79]

> Concord, 9 March, 1857.

My dear Sir,

  You will think me very ungrateful in my slow acknowl- edgment of your letter, which breathes such enthusiastic good will: but I am slow to write letters, and, at the time when I had your sheet, dwell-

75. See later letters of this month to Forbes.

76. MS owned by RWEMA; ph. in CUL. Mar. 18 fell on Wednesday in 1857 and this note may well have been written on the same day with that just preceding.

77. The MS memorandum book for 1857 gives Mar. 18 to Gloucester, Mass.

78. Probably a letter was written at this time which I have not found.

79. MS owned by Miss Mary E. Herbst; ph. in CUL. Kaufmann had written from Canton, O., Feb. 23, 1857, that he had only recently had the great good fortune to be- come acquainted with four volumes of Emerson. Now, he said, he had more than half finished a lengthy epistle designed for Concord. No doubt Whitman and others revered Emerson, but Kaufmann, as he testified in this letter, bore him love such as God alone could barely surpass. In reply to the present letter, Kaufmann wrote again, Mar. 16 following: He had noted in reading Emerson's letter published in *Leaves of Grass* that that strong book had caused Emerson to desire to see its author. He ventured to hope that his own forthcoming communication — the long epistle promised in his first letter — would inspire a like desire. An occasion for a meeting might soon occur, for he expected to make a journey to New York. On the 24th of the same month Emerson, moved no doubt by the unmistakable vigor both of Kauf- mann's interest and of his style, wrote his tentative acceptance of the proposal for an interview.

ing in such a cold aphelion of trifles & tasks, that I had no right to entertain any spark of generosity & heroism, but must wait until I were
worthier & happier. Besides, do you know that you run huge risks in
venturing that great warm heart of yours against my congelations of
nearly fifty four years? I dare not be responsible for the hurts you would
suffer in my churlish solitude. I must defend you from myself I am
happy in the heroic tone in which you speak of your duty to the Country. We, & that third & that fourth person, though he were a son of God,
must keep & show our loyalty to each other & to ideas, by our truth to
the poor betrayed imbruted America, infested by rogues & hypocrites.
In our corners, in days of routine & unfit society, we will speak plain
truth & affirm the old laws, heard or not heard, secure that thus we
acquit ourselves, & that our voices will reach unto & cheer our distant
friends, who will find them on the same key with their own. This is all
I dare say, on this cold day of obstruction with me; for I will not have
your gifts of youth & genius profaned. And when the Muses are nearer,
& the Virtues which are their Mothers, I may be prompted to write you
again.

> Meantime, Yours gratefully,
> R. W. Emerson

Mr Kaufmann.

To John Murray Forbes, Boston, March 12, 1857? [80]

> Boston, Thursday Eve.
> 12 March

My dear Sir,

      I find my correspondents so slow & intractable & such ab-
surd difficulties intervene, that I must give up, with much regret, the
brave holiday you offer me on Wednesday.[81] For the Lyceum, if Wednesday 25th will serve them, I will come on that day.[82]

> Yours,
> R. W. Emerson.

Mr Forbes.

80. MS owned by RWEMA; ph. in CUL. For the year, Mar. 12 fell on Thursday
in 1857, 1863, 1868, and 1874. Evidence cited below indicates 1857.
81. Cf. Mar.? 7? 1857?
82. The MS memorandum book for 1857 gives Mar. 25 to Milton.

To John Murray Forbes, Concord, March 16, 1857? [83]

Concord
16 March

My dear Sir,

No there is yet no such good rest for me or mine as your house. I am to return to Concord on Thursday, by the early train, with a guest, and must therefore spend the night in town. My wife thanks Mrs Forbes for her friendly thought.

There can be no doubt about our Fitchburg hours. For several years, the first train, in summer as in winter, has left Boston at 7.30 A. M. I will not fail, however, to make the inquiry. Yours faithfully,

R. W. Emerson

Mr Forbes.

To ———————, Concord, March 19, 1857

[MS listed and partly quoted in Thomas F. Madigan, Oct., 1936, where the name of the person addressed is not given. Emerson says he has no objection " to your use of the verses you mention." He suggests that a poem on old wine, old books, and old friends, claimed by R. H. Messinger, and Whittier's " Ichabod " should be reprinted in the collection his correspondent is preparing. He also says that if he is in New York before the book is completed he will wish " to intercede for many things." It seems possible that this letter was to John Williamson Palmer, whose *Folk Songs,* New York, 1861, included two poems by Emerson and some stanzas entitled " Give me the Old," attributed to Robert Hinckley Messinger, but no " Ichabod."]

To Peter Kaufmann, Concord, March 24, 1857 [84]

Concord 24 March
1857

My dear Sir,

Your letter is in every way entitled to a faithful reply, and to an immediate one, — and yet I am so slow. Whilst I am waiting ac-

---

83. MS owned by RWEMA; ph. in CUL. The year 1857 has been added in another hand. The return from Milton to Concord on Thursday, Mar. 26, suggests, but does not prove, that this letter follows that of Mar. 12, 1857? which names Mar. 25 as a day when Emerson could lecture at Milton. The Fitchburg train mentioned here is scheduled in the *Boston Daily Advertiser* of Mar. 16, 1857.

84. MS owned by Miss Mary E. Herbst; ph. in CUL. This is an answer to Kaufmann's letter of the 16th of the same month (see the note on Mar. 9, 1857). Kaufmann acknowledged the present letter on Mar. 29, but had meantime written on the 26th that his visit to New York would probably fall between the 10th and 18th of May.

cording to my bad habit, for these vivacious ingredients which you throw into the pot to crystallize in due order, that I may well know what to say, I will not baulk your expectation wholly, but inform you, that I have this, & shall await the larger letter you promise me. Meantime I must add, that I know not what to do with this vast exaggeration which temperament, or solitude, or, is it theory, — gives to your personal estimates. You & I, no doubt, are clever ingenious men, as the world goes; but, in the next street, unknown to you or to me, is probably or possibly a better man than either of us, as the chances of life every now & then convince us. Nature is a terrible leveller, & never bestows a fine talent, but she lames you with numb palsy on the other side. So that one is often fain to look upon his faculty as an indemnification for his cavernous defects.

For the kind invitation which you give, — it has strong attractions, but requires perhaps more courage than I have, to accept. I am not sure that I can, — that I am not tied fast at home; — but, if you will send me the date & the place of your visit in New York, I will keep it before me, till I learn if I have liberty. Meantime, be sure that this time I have read your letter with care. With kindest respect,

Mr Kaufmann.   R. W. Emerson

To ——————, CONCORD? MARCH 30, 1857

[MS listed and partly quoted in Thomas F. Madigan, Sept.–Oct., 1912; Emerson suggests that a subscription of $15 which he originally intended for " the Lyceum " might be appropriated to John Brown of Kansas instead. Emerson had, it is said, contributed $50 to the Kansas fund in May, 1856; and in Mar., 1857, Brown was in Concord (Sanborn, *Recollections*, I, 105 and 108).]

TO ABEL ADAMS, CONCORD, APRIL 6, 1857 [85]

Concord
6 April 1857

My dear friend,

I enclose to you Mr Chapman's [86] last letter that you may see that your kind care & watchfulness of that Rutland Bond came to a good issue. I remember your discovery of the peculiarity of the paper as a draft and your heed to the notarial forms, which, I suppose, were essential to its value. The amount is swelled, I believe, by one or two unpaid coupons, which were attached to the Bond.

85. MS owned by RWEMA; ph. in CUL.
86. *Cf.* Jan. 2, 1857, and earlier letters. Apparently Emerson wrote more than once to Chapman about this time.

If you will not come & see me, I must certainly come & see you, & that soon, for new advices, & as ever, to thank you. Meantime my wife desires kindest remembrances, with mine, to all your house.

Yours affectionately,
R. W. Emerson.

Abel Adams.

TO SARAH SWAIN FORBES, CONCORD, APRIL 6, 1857 [87]

Concord
6 April, 1857.

My dear Mrs Forbes,

I believe I was to send you the true title of the Hindoo book which I admired so much when I read it last summer, the " Upanishads." [88] So I have set it down at full from my memorandum. Tis a little book that you must send to London for. I roll up Maria Lowell's Poems,[89] containing the miniature from Page's head of her. You thought you should like to see the book. It ought to have gone a week ago, & was in my hands for that purpose, when I was suddenly called from home. But I have still a very happy remembrance of my visit to your house,[90] & therefore cannot think it late. My wife was delighted with her flowers.

With best regards,
R. W. Emerson.

Mrs Forbes.

TO JAMES ELLIOT CABOT, CONCORD, APRIL 13, 1857 [91]

Concord
13 April 1857

Dear Cabot,

My list was so short that it did not seem worth bringing you. I had marked down some important books, which, on new ex-

87. MS owned by RWEMA; ph. in CUL.

88. Doubtless Emerson means Roër's translation alluded to in Apr. 13, 1857. Quotations which Emerson cites simply as from " Upanishad," with some of the stanzas of his own " Brahma," appear, as the present letter would lead one to expect, in the *Journals* of the preceding summer (IX, 56–57).

89. *The Poems of Maria Lowell*, Cambridge, privately printed, 1855. Cheney's drawing from William Page's portrait of Maria White Lowell, there used as a frontispiece, is more easily accessible in H. E. Scudder, I, opposite p. 360.

90. *Cf.* Mar. 16, 1857?

91. MS owned by Professor Philip Cabot; ph. in CUL.

amination I found had been added to the library.[92] But I send you the few I named. Taylor's Translations [93] have had so few readers in England that they have been very cheap in the shops; yet we have many readers in this country to whom they would be precious. Bohn's Plato, of course, has superseded Taylor's; but those which I have marked, I should not like to spare. I am daily expecting when Bohn shall announce a translation of *Plutarch's Morals;* [94] meantime, we must have the old one. I am sorry, I cannot even give you the name of the translator of Sadi's Gulistan.[95] My copy, to my great regret, has been lost for years. It is the same edit^n as that in the College Library; & much preferable to a much ornamented recent English book,[96] which was probably a new translation. Thoreau has the Upanishads, which English Cholmondeley gave him.[97] Tis an inestimable little book, — good enough to make me hesitate to put it into a library —

I neither like to send home nor to keep the Eyribiggia Saga; [98] but today a little less to send it home, so being so deep in sin, shall plunge a little further. Continue to forgive Yours gratefully,

R. W. Emerson

Mr Cabot.

92. It seems probable that the list here mentioned was intended for the library of the Boston Athenæum, for which, according to *The Early Years of the Saturday Club,* p. 264, Cabot did much advisory work.

93. A number of Thomas Taylor's translations from Plato and the Neoplatonic writers, as well as Bohn's Plato, apparently, are mentioned in earlier letters.

94. William W. Goodwin's edition of *Plutarch's Morals,* with an introduction by Emerson himself, was more than ten years earlier than Bohn's edition (*cf.* Aug. 10, 1870, to Ellen Emerson).

95. See a note on Oct. 10? 1843. An 1808 reprint of Francis Gladwin's translation is among the books in the Emerson House, at Concord. A copy of the American edition of 1865, *The Gulistan or Rose Garden,* tr. Gladwin, with an essay by James Ross and a preface by Emerson, is in the Emerson library at the Antiquarian House.

96. There are numerous ornamental editions.

97. Doubtless Vol. XV of *Bibliotheca Indica; a Collection of Oriental Works . . . Translated from the Original Sanscrit. By Dr. E. Roër. Calcutta . . . 1853.* The copy still in the Emerson library at the Antiquarian House is inscribed: " Henry D. Thoreau from Thomas Cholmondeley R. W. Emerson from Henry D. Thoreau." The volume is of special interest as one of the sources of " Brahma " (*cf.* Christy, pp. 167–168) . This poem was published in the first number of *The Atlantic,* only a few months after the present letter was written.

98. See Nov. 18, 1856.

To Theodore Parker, Concord, April 20, 1857? [99]

Concord
20 April

Dear Parker,

You are magnanimous & maximanimous, but you must. lie still & get ready for a journey to the mountains, or a voyage to the islands, as soon as there is fine weather again & not bother yourself about who comes & goes in the interim to the Music Hall, or about our delicate nerves. I mean to try the plunge.

Yours ever,
R. W. E.

To James Elliot Cabot, Concord, c. April? 1857 [100]

Concord, Saturday

My dear Cabot,

I give you all joy of the welcome news your note brought me, last evening. Nothing can be more seriously or deeply gratifying that we mortals know, than these new days of a connection which all good omens attend. I must think him happy who seeks & finds in wise daylight the mate whom the most of mankind grope for in the dark, & fatally mis-find. In your instance, I read a well-founded joy, which the following years shall raise & enlarge. Beautiful are the gates to a road on which all that is most real & grave in human lot lies. Woman brings us so much good, that I think the right condition of the union is, when the man is conscious that it is very much which he offers; — too happy almost, when fate allows that the counterpart is as variously, more sweetly gifted. It is so little that I know of your friend, — & yet how much we know of each other at the first glance, — & on this ground of

99. MS owned by RWEMA; ph. in CUL. For the year, I believe this to be the letter to which Parker dictated an answer dated Apr. 25, 1857. Parker's letter, which was to be delivered by a messenger who would conduct Emerson to the Music Hall, contained information about the order of exercises at the Hall. O. B. Frothingham, *Theodore Parker*, 1874, 491–493, tells of Parker's collapse in Mar., 1857, and quotes his statement of Apr. 7, 1857, that, in more than three weeks, he had written but one letter with his own hand.

100. MS owned by Professor Philip Cabot; ph. in CUL. The date "spring 1857" has been added, apparently in the hand of James Elliot Cabot. The present letter pretty clearly relates to the engagement of Cabot to Elizabeth Dwight. According to the *Boston Daily Advertiser*, Oct. 7, 1857, they were married at King's Chapel on Sept. 28 of this year.

divination I send you most assured greetings. I shall use the privilege you give me to make that brief acquaintance better with every opportunity. I shall be in town on the first days of the week, and hope to see Miss Dwight, to whom I beg you to offer my sincere congratulations.

Yours faithfully,
R. W. Emerson

To Peter Kaufmann, Concord, May 3, 1857 [101]

Concord, 3 May, 1857.

My dear Sir,

      I received your letter of the 29 March, which had every claim to an instant reply. And yet it is not my daily tasks, — though I have abundance of writing, & reading, & going, — that I can charge my slowness upon. But your letters are such in amount & in quality that it would not be a compliment to answer in haste. Indeed, I often think of friendship, & all high relations, that they are *time*ous & secular things, hating hurry & despatch. And now I have, the night before the last, your promised manuscript [102] in perfect order as it came from your hands. I read yesterday the entire biography, and with less care glanced at the concluding pages. It is little to say that the story is full of interest & encouragement, & bears the stamp of truth throughout. I look, of course, sharply to the power, & joyfully to the faith evinced. I am glad to see how this Franklin-like [103] ability has been working all this while so effectually in Ohio; — glad at heart to see it combined with what is better than Franklin ever knew. — But I am not yet ready — I am far from ready yet — to give you my inference from the whole.[104] — Meantime, I must needs value at a very high rate the noble covenant you offer me; — but you seem to forget in in your large faith the immense odds

101. MS owned by Miss Mary E. Herbst; ph. in CUL. *Cf.* the letters of Mar. 9 and 24 of this year.

102. On Apr. 27 Kaufmann had written to announce that this epistle of eighty pages was on its way by express and to supply a key to its meaning. The lengthy manuscript, described on its first page as " commenced in January 1857, concluded on April 26th," contains a history of its author's life — a section for each year over a long period ending with his discovery of Emerson — together with an exposition of philosophical views.

103. See the note on May 14 following.

104. Apparently Emerson was never ready with a final estimate. It must have been this enormous letter to which he referred in Feb., 1874 (*Journals*, IX, 93), as " the singular Diary Kaufmann sent me many years ago " — he grieved that he had neglected it so long.

that in actual nature exist against any two parties understanding one another. I am very sure of shocking by my imbecility so formidable a performer as yourself; and I have long since learned, that, in regard to friendship, the first & second parties are degraded as it were into witnesses, merely; it is the invisible Third Party that comes in thither also as chief & only agent. However, of this, as of all the rest, more in future: — I write now only to say, that I have your papers; and to add, that my present wish is to be in New York, if I can arrange it, about the 15th May, where I will try to meet you. I have your address, & my brother Wm Emerson, 10 Wall Street, will tell you if I am in town; [105] but I shall probably send you a line, a few days hence. With great respect,

R. W. Emerson

To William Emerson, Concord, May 6, 1857 [106]

Concord, May 6

Dear William

I heard with great pleasure — by Haven's letter, I believe, — that you & Susan were coming to see us in May. I trust nothing will prevent you from putting your design into act. But the children say, it was " about the fifteenth "; and thereon I may have somewhat to say. My long design of making some effectual repairs of my roof [107] to keep the rain off the heads of my family & guests, is, at last, to begin to take effect tomorrow morning, if the sun shines; if not, the next day: and I suppose it will be a fortnight before the house is in order. Meantime, I have almost promised certain parties that I will be in New York some day in May, & the last letter from them seemed to fix the 16th as the right one.[108] So that I propose that you shall, if you have no fixed day at Portsmouth or Boston, set your watch a few days slower, & say the 20th or 19th, & then I shall have the comfort of accompanying you to Concord. But the young people here, as the old, will give you a double

105. See May 6 following.

106. MS owned by HCL; ph. in CUL. William Emerson's annotation shows he answered on May 7, 1857, the year indicated by evidence cited below.

107. The MS *Autobiography* says the roof was raised and the house repaired in May of this year. William Emerson, July 6, 1857 (MS owned by Dr. Haven Emerson), mentions the incompleteness of his brother's roof and tells of the return of members of his own family from Concord and Portsmouth.

108. *Cf.* the earlier letters to Peter Kaufmann, who is mentioned below, and see May 14 following.

welcome for every one of the young people there you shall add to your party. We are pretty well: Ellen very busy with her sewing-machine, though a little febrile in habit, & staying from school. I have your " account " fairly on foot last night, & shall send or bring it. Affectionately,

Waldo

To my consternation I uncovered in a deep crypt in my cabinet, a few days since, 7 or 8 livraisons of your *Life* of *Mme Sand*,[109] which I had fondly believed restored long ago. It will come, if I come.

If a Mr Kaufmann from Ohio comes to your office, on any day, asking for me, please entertain him kindly, & say, that you are expecting me in N. Y. I will write you soon more exactly of my when & where.

To James Elliot Cabot, Concord, May 8, 1857 [110]

Concord May 8

Dear Cabot

Here is Clough's letter,[111] which I think it safest to send you entire, not only as a memorandum to bring a notice to the Athenaeum Committee,[112] but also for the notice of Faraday's Lecture, which may interest you, if you have not already read a report of it. There is, I believe, a full report of the Lecture itself in the (London) " Mechanics' Magazine." [113]

Yours ever,
R W Emerson

109. *Cf.* Apr. 5, 1856.

110. MS owned by Professor Philip Cabot; ph. in CUL. Evidence cited below shows that the year was 1857.

111. Clough wrote from London, Mar. 23 (1857), of Faraday's " remarkable lecture at the Royal Institution about 3 weeks ago . . . on Conservation of Forces " and of Woolner's bust of Tennyson, which ought, he said, to be bought in America (*Emerson-Clough Letters*).

112. Probably for the notice of the bust of Tennyson. For Emerson's interest in " the library " about this time, *cf.* Apr. 13, 1857, also to Cabot.

113. Faraday's lecture of Feb. 27, 1857, is reported fully in *The Mechanics' Magazine* for Mar. 28 and Apr. 4, 1857. In the following July or August Emerson copied passages into his *Journals* (IX, 106–107). Many years later, when his memory was failing, he seemed to believe that he had heard Faraday deliver this lecture (see Aug. 16, 1877).

To William Emerson, Concord, May 12, 1857 [114]

Concord, 12 May
1857.

Dear William,

I am hardly ready to say what I will do. Our building [115] has seriously outrun my first plan, & may keep me at home, to answer questions relating to it, for some days. Then my correspondent whom it was a point with me to see in N. Y. is not to arrive there quite so early as he expected. But I still mean to come, & am now to settle with carpenter & slater when it shall be. A furnished & crowded house is a tender thing when the roof is off, & the new roof will not on for a few days in fickle May weather. But I think we shall be weather proof by Saturday night, if only it will shine so long. After that, we can hammer & dovetail & plaster & paint & paper at leisure, & laugh at rain.

But one thing seems sure, of all the fine things you propose to me, that I cannot go to the Falls or to Canada, with you & Susan, at present; which I much regret, as I like such things as well as when a boy.

So I write today only to say, that I will write tomorrow or next day,[116] as quickly as it appears out of the medley what I shall do. So you shall wait with all charity.

Affectionately,
Waldo

To ————————, Concord, May 12, 1857

[MS listed and partly quoted in Merwin-Clayton Sales Co., Nov. 20–21, 1911, where it is described as relating to the founding of *The Atlantic*. Emerson says he has not spoken of " it " to any person except Whipple. *Cf.* May 17, 1857,

114. MS owned by HCL; ph. in CUL.

115. *Cf.* May 6, 1857, where the correspondent Emerson was to meet in New York is also mentioned. Entries of May 9 and 10, 1857, in Alcott's MS diary (owned by Mr. F. W. Pratt) throw some light on the more ambitious designs. On the 9th Alcott arrived in Concord, and on Sunday the 10th his creative imagination was once more at work on his friend's behalf: " I sit in the Summer House, and walk about the grounds, plotting improvements, with Emerson, of his Estate — the scite for a woodhouse which he intends building, the lines for his paths — Mrs. Emerson and the children, approving or dissenting . . ." The summer house, an earlier monument to Alcott's architectural genius, was, he wrote, still the chief attraction of the grounds; but its thatching was dishevelled, and he now suggested that Emerson should train grapevines over it, " thus making a mystic arbour for a poet's pleasance . . . a bower for contemplation; or for entertaining the Muses, or any company he lists."

116. Probably Emerson wrote such a letter, of which, however, I have no further evidence.

which is to Lowell. But I think that the present letter was more probably to Underwood or to Phillips. A letter of May 12, n. y., to Underwood, listed in American Art Association, Nov. 5-6, 1923, may possibly be the same; in it Emerson says he hopes to be present at a meeting. Under date of May 16, 1857, in the MS *Autobiography,* the first meeting of a " Magazine Club " is noted.]

To Peter Kaufmann, Concord, May 14, 1857 [117]

Concord, 14 May

My dear Sir,

You have taken such a world of kind pains for me, and you offer me such alliances, that I think I cannot do less than make the journey to New York, which I should not otherwise make at this time. I happen to be building some addition to my house in these days, but my brother in N. Y. is coming to Concord with his family, & I will bring him home with me. I shall probably take a room at the Saint Denis House, Broadway, and I shall probably arrive there about 5 or 6 o clock P. M. on Monday, 18th instant. Tis possible, I may go out (after leaving my baggage there,) to Staten Island, to pass the night with my brother. In that case, I shall be at the St Denis again, the next morning, at 10. But if you choose to meet me at the St Denis, on the arrival of the P. M. train from Boston, I will spend that night in N. Y.

Faithfully,

Mr Kaufmann.   R. W. Emerson

To James Russell Lowell, Concord, May 17, 1857 [118]

Concord

17 May, Eve.ᵍ

Dear Lowell,

I am sorry to find that I must be in New York tomorrow night,[119] & for a day or two; probably returning on Thursday; — so I

117. MS owned by Miss Mary E. Herbst; ph. in CUL. Kaufmann, after a lengthy preliminary correspondence, had written on the 4th of this month, urging once more a meeting in New York. Emerson recorded the meeting in his entry of May 19 (*Journals,* IX, 93) , appraising the Ohioan as " another Benjamin Franklin "; and on June 17 following Kaufmann wrote again from Canton, recalling " the well spent hours " of " our late reunion in New York," and was satisfied, he said, that Emerson was the man he had judged him to be from his writings.

118. MS owned by Mr. Oliver R. Barrett; ph. in CUL. The year is fixed by evidence cited below.

119. See May 14, 1857.

shall miss the Tuesday dinner,[120] which, failure of mine in these beginnings & embryonic aims at association, is to be regretted. You will please
let me be strictly held as a subscriber, this time, as Mr Phillips is our
guest. And you shall be sure of my vote in any thing that goes to secure
an honest wise & witty journal. My confidence in success is, however,
based mainly on your accepting the responsibility of editor, with as
much and as various aid as you please.

Yours faithfully,
R. W. Emerson.

To Samuel Gray Ward, Concord, May 18, 1857?[121]

Concord
18 May

My dear friend,

I send you M. Boucher[122] again, with Edward's thanks, &
mine. I also send you the promised old copy of the " Vita Nuova," which
should have come sooner, but I found its coat quite too bad, & had to
find it a new one more worthy of your hands.

Ever yours,
R. W. E.

Mr Ward.

To William Emerson, Concord? May 22, 1857

[Acknowledged in William Emerson, May 25, 1857. William recalls the details
of his and Folsom's complete payment, in 1853, of their debt to Emerson. The
present letter doubtless asked for these details.]

To Francis H. Underwood, Concord? June 1, 1857

[Moses D. Phillips wrote, Boston, June 2, 1857, that Underwood had handed
him Emerson's " note of yesterday " and had said he wished a letter to Patmore;
Underwood, he said, would sail the following day. I am uncertain whether the
present letter is the same partly quoted in John Townsend Trowbridge, *My
Own Story*, 1903, p. 245; it is possible that the letter there quoted was written
June 2 or 3 as a result of Phillips's request on behalf of Underwood.]

120. For Moses D. Phillips's own account of the dinner he had recently given to
Emerson, Lowell, and other friends of the nascent *Atlantic*, and for his mention of
their invitation to him to meet them again on May 20 — the dinner here referred to
— see H. E. Scudder, I, 410–411.

121. MS owned by HCL; ph. in CUL. The year 1857, endorsed, apparently by
Ward, is probably correct.

122. Doubtless one of the volumes of Jacques Boucher de Perthes, *Antiquités
celtiques et antédiluviennes,* of which the twelfth volume was published at Paris in
1857.

To Amos Bronson Alcott, Concord, June 9, 1857 [123]

Concord 9 June 1857.

My dear friend,

Will you have the goodness to send me a note of the day when you were born; and, if you have it, of the year when you came to Boston to reside; and the year when you came to Concord to reside. I have had the temerity to promise a biographical paragraph, — only one paragraph, — to some New-York Biographical Dictionary on the subject of you. Better, much better, if you come yourself. But I want the dates presently.

Yours faithfully,
R. W. Emerson.

Mr Alcott.

To William Henry Furness, Concord, June 9, 1857

[MS owned by Mr. Horace Howard Furness Jayne; printed in *Records of a Lifelong Friendship,* pp. 113–114.]

To William Emerson, Boston, June 11, 1857 [124]

Boston, 11 June, 1857.

Dear William,

I have made a sad botch of my draft,[125] whicch accompanies this, for One hundred & two dollars, which you will please credit me with on our account. We are making some progress at home, with masons carpenters & plumbers, but they make noise & dirt.[126] I hope to show you shortly their completed work. When will William return? & when will you & Susan come?

Affectionately,
Waldo.

In Harvard Clubroom

123. MS owned by Mr. F. W. Pratt; ph. in CUL. This is a copy which Alcott made in his diary under date of June 10, 1857, where he noted that Emerson was to prepare the sketch " for Appleton's New York Biographical Dictionary to be edited by George Ripley and Charles A. Dana." For publication of *The New American Cyclopædia,* as this work was called, see notes on Apr. 22, 1858, and May 4, 1860, to William Emerson. Emerson's article on Alcott duly appeared.

124. MS owned by HCL; ph. in CUL. The number of the day of the month is blurred, but my reading corresponds with the endorsement.

125. In a wide margin Emerson began but did not complete a draft for money to be paid to his brother.

126. *Cf.* May 6, 1857.

To Theodore Parker, Concord, June 29, 1857 [127]

> Concord, June 29.
> 1857.

Dear Parker,

A fortnight ago this sumptuous looking Archaic volume of Tauler [128] came to me without any accompanying message — nothing to guess from, except the excellent hands that bore it, & the unmistakeable character in which my name was written within — as to the sender of the book. What should induce you or other divine organ to enrich me with this virtuous book, does not in any manner appear. But it would have been impertinent to have stood cavilling with the angels at the doorstep, so I sat thankfully down to hear what they had to say. I read on the evening on which I received it all that Kingsley had to say, & the whole biography so quaint & monastic & *A Kempian:* The Sermons themselves were not quite so easy reading; & my wife, who believes that women have the first right in all religious books, has been charmed with the Saint, & has carried him to her own reading-closet. When he returns to me, I shall finish my studies of him. I write now only to make you sure that this high-looking deodand did not swerve, but truly came to me, if I did not get over my surprise to write sooner & say so. I did not read so docilely, however, as not to discover, that, whilst the Man is quite right in rating the Master, the man lays himself very open to criticism in his own dogmatism. I send back Mr Dennys's & Miss Beechers letters.

> Ever your bounden
> R. W. Emerson

To John Murray Forbes, Concord, August 4, 1857 [129]

> Concord
> Tuesday 4 August

My dear Sir,

I am charmed with your invitation.[130] I believe I never go

---

127. MS owned by RWEMA; ph. in CUL.

128. In spite of the epithet "Archaic" and the fact that Johann Tauler's works had been in print for centuries, the volume Emerson had received from Parker must have been *The History and Life of the Reverend Doctor John Tauler of Strasbourg; with Twenty-five of his Sermons,* tr. Susanna Winkworth, with a preface by Charles Kingsley, London, 1857.

129. MS owned by Miss Anne Forbes; ph. in CUL. The year 1857, added in another hand, fits the evidence cited below; and Aug. 4 fell on Tuesday in that year.

130. Forbes, Naushon Island, Mass., Aug. 2, 1857, asked Emerson to bring his wife

abroad, but it is not every day or every summer that one has a summons to Naushon. But, first, I cannot go next week, as my children have sent for a company of fine girls, & I am bound to see that they do not fall into the river or get lost in the woods. But the week after, I think, I shall come if I dare; on Tuesday, you say, and you add " to Friday "; but no I shall not in a year muster resolution to stay in one house so long as that. Well, let me please myself at least with the intention to come & see you & your woods & sea, on Tuesday (18th) & certainly by New Bedford. And if any mischance threaten to hinder me, I will send you word. With kindest remembrance to Mrs Forbes,

Yours, R. W. Emerson

My wife & daughter are in Boston, or I doubt they would insist to come.

To Cyrus Augustus Bartol, Concord, August 14, 1857 [131]

Concord, 14 Aug^t.

1857

My dear friend,

I am glad to think of you as sitting again on your broad slabs of granite by the sea, & presiding, — for the benefit of all comers, — over those perfumed berry pastures. And my children, in the hot days, praise Pigeon Cove,[132] by their hearty wishes to be there again: but neither old man nor young women can always or very often do as they would, and it does not look now as if we could make any family visit to your shore, nor dare I promise today so much as a private one from myself to your large invitation. I have been repairing & enlarging my house, ever since May,[133] until last Monday night, when the workmen left us. And it has cost me & all of us as much time, with much less joy, as if we had been sauntering on all the beaches & in all berry bearing mountains. You have been in the White Hills, I have heard, which even your Swiss experiences will not make contemptible, — which Nature never is.

Your extraordinary question on my antiquities of thirty years ago,[134]

<hr />

and daughter for a visit on Tuesday or Friday of the following week; he gave the time of trains to New Bedford and suggested a sail on his yacht " Azalea." Naushon Island, the Forbes estate off Woods Hole, on the way to Martha's Vineyard and Nantucket, reappears in many letters. Emerson's later impression of Forbes as the squire of Naushon is recorded in *Journals*, X, 72–75.

131. MS owned by RWEMA; ph. in CUL.

132. *Cf.* the letters of Aug. 6, 1855, and June 2, 1856.

133. *Cf.* May 6, 1857, and later letters.

134. Miss Margaret A. Sullivan informs me that the present letter accompanied Emerson's sermon on the Lord's Supper, the MS of which Emerson gave to Bartol;

has made all this delay in my reply. I have explored the old nooks, &
am resolved to smother you with a share of the same dust which I encountered: so I send you the *ipsissima verba* to which you refer, — all
yellow, — and infirm as old, I dare say, without daring to look. If you
have courage, you can read the sermon; but, I doubt, a page of it will
suffice. As you hint, it was a sad matter to me, who have quite too much
sympathy to be a right reformer.

Ellen & Edith were hindered by those same repairs which I mentioned,
from negociating for a visit from Lizzie Bartol in the early days of the
vacation as they had arranged. They wish you to tell her from them
that in all this long time they are far from forgetting her promise to
come & see them, and they wish she would fix an early day that suits
her, to try if they cannot keep her from homesickness for seven entire
days. The present time is the best time and they propose it shall be, —
say, Monday 24th instant; which, they think, will have given her time
for a bath in the sea, after climbing the mountains; & now she will be
ready to endure better the very very gentle life of our meadows.

To this prayer of Ellen & Edith Mrs Emerson & I add our strong
wishes. With kindest remembrances from me & from all our household
to Mrs Bartol,

Yours faithfully,
R. W. Emerson

To ————————, CONCORD, AUGUST 31, 1857

[MS listed and partly quoted in John Heise, catalogue 63 (1912); Emerson
accepts an invitation to New Bedford. The MS memorandum book for this
year indicates that he lectured at that town on Dec. 22.]

To JOSIAH PHILLIPS QUINCY, CONCORD, SEPTEMBER 1, 1857 [135]

Concord
Tuesday 1 Sept. 1857

My dear Sir,

Did you not signify a good-will to come & see me in the
fields, some day? I persuade myself that you did, — if it were only by

---

that in Apr., 1920, Elizabeth H. Bartol gave both the MS sermon and this letter to
Edith Emerson Forbes; and that in Apr., 1933, both sermon and letter came once
more to light.

135. MS owned by Mr. M. A. DeWolfe Howe; ph. in CUL. Quincy, son of Emerson's college classmate, was, some twenty years earlier, the "youthful prophet" of
Alcott's school who is praised in *Journals*, IV, 69. There were further letters to him in
later years. *Cf.* especially Jan. 23 and 25, 1861.

force of my own wish to push a little farther a conversation only begun. To give the benevolence I impute to you a chance, I will entreat you to spend next Sunday, 6th, with me. If tis a fair day, I can show you our woods & hills; and if it rains, I am sure, we shall not be quite without resources. If that day happens not to be free to you, perhaps you will come out on Saturday, in the 11 o'clock train, & dine with me, & we will have a long afternoon before the evening train at 7, to the city. If neither of these days suit you, I hope you will propose one of your own. With kindest regards, to your Father & Mother

Yours with great esteem,
R. W. Emerson

Josiah Quincy 3d

To Abby Larkin Adams, Concord, September 23, 1857 [136]

Concord
23 September
Wednesday

Dear Abby,

So long as you have been coming to Concord & have never come! You will never find the way. You must get out your Gazetteer, & map, & road-guide, or you will stray into New-Hampshire. But I was to tell you when the carpenters were gone. They never fairly left me until last week, and Mr & Mrs Watson of Plymouth [137] were here for a few days. What do you say to next Tuesday? It is a kind of holiday here, when we are bound to put away our books, & show our corn & squashes to the county. And I am writing to Miss Mattie Griffith, a brilliant young lady from Kentucky, of whom perhaps you know something, as she is or was with Mrs Follen,[138] to ask her to come & see us on that day. Will you try to leave your fine things & landscape, & come & do penance a few days in the meadows? It may do you a world of good, teaching patience & humbleness, & how the farmers live. Ellen & Edith will diligently instruct you in the politics of Mr Sanborn's School,[139] &

136. MS owned by RWEMA; ph. in CUL. Sept. 23 fell on Wednesday in 1857, the year clearly indicated by evidence cited below. For the repairing of the house, cf. May 6, 1857, and later letters. The departure of the workmen recorded in Aug. 14 must have been premature.

137. There were several Watsons at Plymouth, Mass., but the reference is doubtless to B. Marston Watson and his wife.

138. Before Emerson's letter reached Brookline, however, Mattie Griffith had gone (see the note on Sept. 23? 1857).

139. Cf. June 12, 1855.

of Mr Frost's Church, of the boat-club, & of the " drop-ins." [140] And Mrs Emerson sends her love, & begs you to come, & has much to ask & to tell. A train leaves Boston at 11 o'clock A. M. and I will have man & horse for you at the Depot here. If you cannot come on that day, what first day will you come & see your affectionate Uncle

R. W. Emerson

With kindest remembrances to your Uncle & Aunt.

To Mattie Griffith, Concord? September 23? 1857

[Mattie Griffith, Brookline, Mass., Sept. 11, 1857, said she had hoped to make Emerson another visit for further discussion of problems of the age. In Sept. 23 following, Emerson said he was writing to this " brilliant young lady from Kentucky." She wrote again, Philadelphia, Oct. 10, 1857, that until a few days ago, she had not received his letter directed to her at Brookline; had she received it in time, she would have accepted his invitation.]

To ——————, Concord? September c. 24, 1857

[In Sept. 24, 1857, to Bigelow, Emerson says he has " just been writing . . . to some correspondents farther west."]

To ——————, Concord? September c. 24, 1857

[See the preceding note.]

To Henry H. Bigelow, Concord, September 24, 1857 [141]

Concord
24 Sept. 1857

Dear Sir,

I am flattered by the kindness of your last note & have tried to make it practicable to me to go to Cleveland But, at present, it seems quite out of question, & that I must stay near home. And I have just been writing this decision to some correspondents farther west.

If later in the season I shall find more freedom, I shall presume on the friendly welcome you offer me, to re-open the correspondence, & ask you to find me a day.

With great regard, yours

Mr Bigelow.

R. W. Emerson

140. *Cf.* Sept. 2, 1856.

141. MS owned by the Drexel Institute; ph. in CUL. Henry H. Bigelow appears in *Boyd's Cleveland City Directory*, 1857, as an accountant and notary public and as corresponding secretary of the Cleveland Library Association.

To FRANCIS H. UNDERWOOD, CONCORD, SEPTEMBER 24, 1857

[MS listed in Thomas F. Madigan, Sept. 8, 1926; printed in Bliss Perry, p. 245.]

To ABBY LARKIN ADAMS, CONCORD, OCTOBER 1, 1857 [142]

Concord
Thursday 1 Oct.ʳ

Dear Abby,

It was very ill of you to be ill on Tuesday. You shall never hope to see better apples, pears, or yearling calves, than we had to show you. But now what day? Let it be Wednesday next and begin your strokes of persuasion early to bear on your Uncle & Aunt, for we shall set our hearts on seeing them here to dine on that day. And if they will not stay, & make me a visit, you shall. Elizabeth Hoar, who has been absent a month, will be at home, I believe, very soon. Will you come at 11 o'c in the train? At any rate, on that day we will not dine till 2. So with kindest remembrance from all of us to your Uncle & Aunt,

Yours affectionately,
R. W. Emerson

To JAMES THOMAS FIELDS, CONCORD, OCTOBER 9, 1857 [143]

Concord, 9 Oct. 1857

Dear Sir,

I return with thanks the book you were kind enough to lend me I have kept it too long, — you must forgive me.

Have you not a copy, *one* copy of Mr Smiths pamphlet, A Letter to Lord Ellesmere, I believe, about Shakspeare [144] — If you can procure me that, I wish to buy it. If not buyable, can you tell me where I can borrow it? & greatly oblige

Your obliged servᵗ
R. W. Emerson

Mr Fields.

142. MS owned by RWEMA; ph. in CUL. Oct. 1 fell on Thursday in 1857, and this letter pretty clearly followed that of Sept. 23 in that year, which had proposed Tuesday for a visit from Abby Adams.

143. MS owned by the Henry E. Huntington Library; ph. in CUL.

144. William Henry Smith, *Was Lord Bacon the Author of Shakespeare's Plays? A Letter to Lord Ellesmere*, London, 1856. Caroline H. Dall, Boston, Dec. 6, 1857, said she had learned that Emerson had a copy of the English volume of a certain Smith who had stolen or borrowed Miss Bacon's hypothesis and facts.

To William? V.? K.? Lansing, Concord, October 10, 1857 [145]

Concord 10 Oct[r]

Mass   1857

Dear Sir,

I have decided not to go westward this winter,[146] and I shall lose the opportunity you kindly offer me of visiting Rochester.

Respectfully,

R. W. Emerson

Mr Lansing.

To Caroline Sturgis Tappan, Concord, October 13, 1857 [147]

Concord Oct. 13' 1857

Dear Caroline,

You will never write me again, I have been so ungrateful, I who value every line & word from you, or about you. Perhaps 'tis my too much writing in youth that makes it so repulsive now in these old days. What to tell you now that I have begun — you that are in the land of wine & oil,[148] of us in the land of meal? Italy cannot excel the banks of glory wh. sun & mist paint in these very days on the forest by lake & river. But the Muses are as reticent as Nature is flamboyant, & no fireeyed child has yet been born. 'Tis strange that the relations of your old friends here remain unchanged to the world of letters & society, I mean, that those who held of the Imagination & believed that the necessities of the New World would presently evoke the mystic Power, & we should not pass away without hearing the Choral Hymns of a new age & adequate to Nature, still find colleges & books as cramp & sterile as ever, & our discontent keeps us in the selfsame suspicious relation to beauties & elegant society. We are all the worse that you, & those who are like you, if any such there be, as there are not, — but persons of positive quality, & capacious of beauty — desert us, & abdicate their

145. MS owned by the Rochester Historical Society, Rochester, N. Y.; ph. in CUL. The *Rochester Daily Union Annual City Directory,* 1859, shows that William V. K. Lansing, a bookkeeper at a lumber office, was then president of the Rochester Atheneum & Mechanics Association.

146. *Cf.* Sept. 24, 1857, to Bigelow.

147. MS owned by RWEMA; ph. in CUL. This is a copy made by Cabot, who describes the letter as " unsent."

148. A postponement of Caroline Tappan's voyage to Europe is mentioned in July 9, 1855. Apparently she was abroad when the present letter was written, and in July 10, 1859, there is mention of her recent travel in Germany.

power at home. Why not a mind as wise & deep & subtle as your Browning, with his trained talent? Why can we not breed a lyric man as exquisite as Tennyson; or such a Burke-like *longanimity* as E. Browning (whom you mention in interesting positions, but do not describe to me) ? Our wild Whitman, with real inspiration but choked by Titanic abdomen, & Delia Bacon, with genius, but mad, & clinging like a tortoise to English soil, are the sole producers that America has yielded in ten years. Is all the granite & forest & prarie & superfoetation of millions to no richer result? If I were writing to any other than you, I should render my wonted homage to the gods for my two gossips, Alcott & Henry T., whose existence I impute to America for righteousness, though they miss the fame of your praise. Charles Newcomb, too, proves the rich possibilities in the soil, tho' his result is zero. So does Ellery. But who cares? As soon as we walk out of doors Nature transcends all poets so far, that a little more or less skill in whistling is of no account. Out of doors we lose the lust of performance, & are content to pass silent, & see others pass silent, into the depths' of a Universe so resonant & beaming. But you will dispense with my whims, wh. you know, for a few grains of history. There is nothing very marked in our neighbourhood, which keeps its old routinary trot. I suffered ann [149]

TO CHARLES MACKAY, CONCORD, OCTOBER 26, 1857 [150]

Concord —
Monday, 26 Oct^r

My dear Sir,

I receive the news of your arrival,[151] & Mr Hawthorn's note,[152] with much pleasure. I am engaged to be absent from home two

149. Emerson may have ended abruptly here, but the fact that the extant sheet is completely filled makes it seem probable that a part of the copy has been lost. The " a " of the last word may be a capital. An unpublished passage in the diaries, belonging presumably to 1859, broadens the census of American genius, declaring that Whitman and Delia Bacon were the sole producers " until Wendell Holmes's gay genius, in a dozen years " and adding, as an afterthought, " Here is Lowell also " (typescript *Journals* for 1859–1860) .

150. MS owned by Mr. W. T. H. Howe; ph. in CUL.

151. The *Boston Evening Transcript*, Oct. 23, 1857, announced: " CHARLES MACKAY, the popular English Lyrist, whose songs have encircled the world, arrived in Boston this morning. We understand he intends giving three lectures on Songs, National, Historical and Popular, during his stay in the country."

152. Hawthorne had written:

or three days of this week but do not mean to be hindered from at least the pleasure of calling on you in town, & we will find a day that suits you to come out into the country. Meantime, I will beg you to keep next Saturday disengaged, & you shall dine with me at our Club,[153] which holds Longfellow, Agassiz, Lowell, & other good men. I will see you before that.

Yours, with respect & kind regard,

R. W. Emerson.

Dr Mackay.

To Emily Mervine Drury, Concord, November 2, 1857 [154]

Concord, 2 November
1857

My dear Mrs Drury,

I know I am a very bad correspondent, & that you have good reason to complain of me, but I shall not let Mr Alcott leave home without a line to you, as I have always promised you that he should come to you some day. He is going to Syracuse, & means to stop in Buffalo, & may reach Cincinnati before he returns; [155] and I wish you would give him a home in Canandaigua for a day, on his way, that you may see him & talk with him. Ask him all the brave questions which you or I cannot answer,

---

" Liverpool, Sept. 24th 1857.
" My dear Emerson,

" I have not often (if indeed ever) sent any body to you with a letter of introduction; so that you would pardon me even for introducing a common man; and I know you will thank me for being the medium of making Dr. Mackay known to you. Will you be kind enough to show him Thoreau, and Ellery Channing, and any other queer and notable people who may, by this time, have taken up their abode in Concord?

" I have resigned my Consulate, but instead of drawing homeward, am going farther than ever from my old cottage and sand-hill. In fact, I have continually seen so many of my countrymen (more than ever before in my life) that I feel as if I were now only on the point of first coming abroad.

" Truly yours,
" Nath' Hawthorne.
" R. W. Emerson."

153. The Saturday Club was now well established.
154. MS owned by Mr. W. T. H. Howe; ph. in CUL.
155. Louisa May Alcott wrote in her journal for Nov., 1857: " Father goes West, taking Grandma home "; and in the following January she noted his return (*Louisa May Alcott*, ed. Cheney, p. 96) . An earlier, but unsuccessful, attempt to bring Alcott to Mrs. Drury's is mentioned in Nov. 23, 1853.

& see how he will deal with them. I think I am giving you a great privilege, for which you will thank me, in sending him to you. Give my kind regards to Mr Drury, & tell him, that, if he is out of the mood of law & politics, & in the mood of Sinnamahonig,[156] he will find much to interest him in our philosopher. If Mr Daggett [157] is in town, tis all the better, & I think you will be able to summon an evening circle for conversation. No tea, no party, I pray you, — but ask any intelligent sincere people you know to come & talk with him, in an evening, & he will readily propose a subject, & open it at leisure. I shall give Mr Alcott a note to Mr Tracy [158] at Buffalo & if I had your brother in law's address, I should write to him. Your friend,

R. W. Emerson.

To William? Frederick? Poole, Concord, November 3, 1857

[MS listed and partly quoted in Maggs Bros., catalogue 511, 1928. This letter introduces Dr. Charles Mackay, of London. I conjecture that Poole, whose full name is not given in the catalogue, was William Frederick Poole, then and for years afterward librarian of the Boston Athenæum and still remembered as compiler of the index to periodical literature.]

To Thomas Carlyle, Concord, November 4, 1857 [159]

Concord —
4 November, 1857.

My dear Carlyle,

The bearer, Mr John C. King, is a sculptor of good fame among us for his portrait busts, and has resided in this country for many years. He is a countryman of of yours, & is now on his way to England, & is ambitious to make a cast of your head. You shall tell him whether he shall have that success. He is favorably known to some of your friends, having taken, I believe, a bust of Webster, for the late Lord

156. The spelling is doubtful but is certainly incorrect. Sinnamahoning, summer retreat of the Drurys, appears in earlier letters.

157. Probably Oliver E. Daggett, for many years pastor of the Congregational Church at Canandaigua (cf. Caroline Richards, *Village Life in America*, 1912, p. 18 and opposite p. 111).

158. For Albert H. Tracy, whom Emerson thought something of an Alcott, see a note on Jan. 13, 1857.

159. MS owned by HCL; ph. in CUL. John Crookshanks King was a native of Ayrshire but had long resided in the United States. Among his best-known busts are those of Webster and Emerson. A picture of the latter bust is to be found in *The Critic*, XLII, 429 (May, 1903), and elsewhere.

Ashburton. He has lately made, under difficult circumstances, a successful bust in marble of a venerable townsman & friend of mine, Mr Samuel Hoar.[160] Ever yours affectionately,

R. W. Emerson.

Thomas Carlyle, Esq.

To ——————————, CONCORD, NOVEMBER 20, 1857

[MS listed in C. F. Libbie & Co., Jan. 27–28, 1914, where it is described as a business letter.]

TO FRANCIS H. UNDERWOOD, CONCORD, NOVEMBER 21, 1857

[MS owned by CUL; ph. in CUL. Printed in Bliss Perry, pp. 253–254. I am uncertain whether this is the letter of the same date listed, without name of correspondent, in C. F. Libbie & Co., Dec. 11–12, 1916.]

TO FRANCIS H. UNDERWOOD, CONCORD? DECEMBER? c. 1? 1857

[MS listed and partly quoted in Goodspeed's Book Shop, catalogue 169, where it is dated only as to year. Emerson says he sends the first instalment of "Books." In Nov. 21 preceding he had written that he could send nothing for *The Atlantic* sooner than the end of the month. For the second instalment, see Dec.? 3? 1857.]

TO FRANCIS H. UNDERWOOD, CONCORD? DECEMBER? 3? 1857 [161]

Thursday

Mr Underwood
     Dear Sir,

         I send you the second instalment of "Books," & there must be as many as 20 to 25 pages behind, to go tomorrow. In these dangerous conditions, please send word at once whether you want the whole piece, or prefer to divide it, & keep the conclusion for the next number. What follows is "Favorites," "Vocabularies," "Imaginative,"

160. Hoar had died on Nov. 2 of the preceding year.
161. MS owned by Mr. Alwin J. Scheuer; ph. in CUL. For the date, this follows the letter of Dec.? c. 1? 1857, and "Books" was printed in *The Atlantic* of Jan., 1858. A review of this number appeared in the *Boston Daily Advertiser* of Dec. 23, 1857. No advertisement of it seems to have appeared in that paper until Dec. 28, though the notice then inserted was dated Dec. 22. On the whole, the evidence cited points to Dec. 3 — or possibly 10 — as the Thursday of Emerson's date line. In the printed article the divisions were not kept. Underwood was "The Editor who was never the Editor" of Bliss Perry's *Park-Street Papers.*

and " Bibles," with a peroration. — If it is all to go now, I will cut out some pages.

Yours,

R. W. Emerson

To William Rounseville Alger, Concord, December 4, 1857 [162]

Concord

4 December 1857.

My dear Sir,

I am happy to know that you are coming to Concord, next Thursday evening.[163] It will give my wife & me great pleasure if you will spend the night at our house, & we will do our best to keep you from the cold, & from the Hotel.

With great regard,

Yours,

R. W. Emerson.

Rev. Mr Alger.

To Mary Moody Emerson, Concord, December 10, 1857 [164]

Concord Dec 10 1857

Dear Aunt,

I am always meaning to take up that dropt thread of old correspondence, but the oppressive miscellany of my *business-letters,* — so to call them, has long ago destroyed almost all inclination to write. Carlyle, Helps, Caroline Tappan, and all the rest of my correspondents I have allowed to go. Yet I wish to be written to by you, & I prize every syllable of your records. And it occurs today, that Elizabeth,[165] devoted to her sick Sister at Cambridge, may cease for the time to write,[166] &

162. MS owned by the Henry E. Huntington Library; ph. in CUL. The " 7 " has been heavily written over " 6."

163. According to the MS records of the Concord Lyceum (in the Concord Free Public Library), Alger actually appeared on Wednesday, Dec. 9, 1857, and his subject was " Chivalry." Some other lectures of the same season were given on Thursday, and this fact may explain Emerson's error. The same records show that Emerson served as a curator of the Lyceum during the season of 1857–1858.

164. MS owned by RWEMA; ph. in CUL.

165. Probably Elizabeth Hoar, whose sister, Sarah Hoar Storer, is mentioned in a number of earlier letters.

166. Mary Moody Emerson had written from Cummington, Mass., Mar. 17, 1857, that she heard from Elizabeth often.

that I for the day will take her place. We live much as we are wont, that is, in the poor ways that have no glitter, & no result to tell you of, but the children are good & the foolish parents can see faith & hope reappearing in the young with no less vigor for all the bankruptcies of all the progenitors. Mrs Ripley came here on Thanksgiving Day, her first going abroad, radiant as ever, & not suffering afterwards, I learn. The hard times [167] & their terrible social effect have given everybody a start, & made people in the street thoughtful to the verge of revolution Their " solid men of Boston " New York, & London, the hitherto unquestionable *goods*, whatever else might be, or might not be, — are rotten straw, & the obscurest creature that is honest, & lives within compass, is grown an object of respect. If the seriousness & the new respect would only last! In politics, too, men begin to believe there may be a Providence after all. I sent you, a month ago, the first number of the *Atlantic*.[168] Today, I send you the second, by mail. Lidian sends her love, & Ellen, who is important at home.

Affectionately, Waldo E.

To Francis H. Underwood, Concord, December 18, 1857

[MS owned by CUL; ph. in CUL. Printed in Bliss Perry, p. 254.]

To William Emerson, Concord, December 30, 1857 [169]

Concord
30 December

Dear William,

Tis dangerous to think of what spaces of time are coming to separate our letters in a correspondence that was once tolerably active. I know not when I have written or read a letter from you. Well it will correct itself soon as the leisure that is due to both of us shall at last arrive. Ellery Channing chides me sometimes for being as busy as a shoemaker. But here is the New Year just upon us and my young people carried me to Boston in their chains and by their advice & consent for I am as obedient as old age is wont, I send a Gulistan [170] to William

167. The panic of 1857 had begun in August.
168. The first number, for Nov., 1857, contained some of Emerson's best verses. The second had only a little of his prose.
169. MS owned by HCL; ph. in CUL. The " 30 " was written over " 29."
170. *Cf.* Apr. 13, 1857.

Selden [171] to Haven & a microscope to Charles with the love & joy & wishes of the New Year from us all to the good brave boys. Give my dear love to Susan & tell her that the Antislavery Fair Ladies [172] have won from some European virtuoso a facsimile in bronze of St Peters bell with all the Apostles for her table. Ellen is afraid she has tied its tongue so tight, that she will not find its sweet voice. These same chatting girls sit by, & I can only learn that Ellen would know if William Jr. has worn out his pincushion. I hoped to be in N. Y. soon for I was to go to Brooklyn, but I hear nothing lately, & infer that their plan has failed. I am to go to Philadelphia 2ᵈ February.[173]

Affectionately your brother
Waldo.

To William? Cadwell, Concord, December 30? 1857

[Mentioned in Jan. 6, 1858. The only person of that name listed in *The New Bedford Directory*, 1856, was William Cadwell, apothecary.]

To Henry Whitney Bellows, Concord? 1857

[See the following note.]

To Henry Whitney Bellows, Concord, 1857

[MS listed in Goodspeed's Book Shop, Nov., 1936, where it is dated only as to year and is described as " apologizing for ' an unintelligible billet from me sometime about a fortnight ago.' "]

To Daniel Ricketson, Concord? 1857

[MS listed in Goodspeed's Book Shop, Oct., 1920.]

To Louis Agassiz, Concord? 1857?

[Printed without date in *The National Magazine*, V, 52 (Oct., 1896), where a part of the letter is also reproduced in facsimile — it is difficult to believe that Emerson's spelling of Agassiz's name is here correctly given. For the date, the mention of Humboldt's award of a decoration to Jackson, which occurred in 1857 (*ibid.*, p. 53), as recent points to that year.]

171. The gift may have been the second edition of *The Table-talk of John Selden,* ed. Singer, published at London in 1856.

172. The twenty-fourth National Anti-slavery Bazaar opened in Boston on Dec. 17 and was to close on Dec. 26 (*Boston Daily Advertiser,* Dec. 15–24, 1857).

173. See Jan. 18, 1858.

1858

To John Murray Forbes, Concord, January 3, 1858 [1]

Concord, 3 Jan.ʸ
Sunday Night

My dear Sir,

Miss Barrett [2] is well contented to receive Malcolm. [3] Storrow H. [4] has not returned, but she has a letter from him to say that he comes back alone tomorrow; so that she presumes his consent. Mr Sanborn is still absent, but I will see him in the morning. I learn that new scholars are coming; but the school is not yet full. So we shall all be glad to see Malcolm on Tuesday.

With all kind regards,
R. W. Emerson

Mr Forbes.

To Daniel Ricketson, Concord, January 6, 1858 [5]

Concord, 6 Janʸ 1858

My dear Sir,

When I was at New Bedford I did not see the Treasurer of the Lyceum. A week ago, I wrote to Mr Cadwell the Secretary who had invited me to the Lyceum asking him to request the Treasurer to remit to me Fifty dollars, which the Lyceum had offered me for a lec-

1. MS owned by RWEMA; ph. in CUL. Jan. 3 fell on Sunday in 1858, the year of the endorsement.
2. Apparently a teacher in Sanborn's school, which is mentioned in earlier letters.
3. For J. Malcolm Forbes, son of Emerson's correspondent, see *Letters and Recollections of John Murray Forbes, passim.*
4. Doubtless Samuel Storrow Higginson, who graduated from Harvard in 1863. He reappears in July 21, 1859.
5. MS owned by Dr. Curtis Hidden Page; ph. in CUL. The envelope is addressed to Daniel Ricketson at New Bedford.

ture: [6] but I hear nothing from either party, & I fear that Mr Cadwell may not be in town, & so the message not transmitted. Will you have the goodness to look into this matter, and if there be any reason to me unknown why this money should not be paid, inform me of it,[7] & oblige

Yours gratefully,

R. W. Emerson

Mr Ricketson

To Daniel Ricketson, Concord, January 10, 1858 [8]

Concord
10 Jany 1858

My dear Sir,

I received safely, last night, your note & its enclosure, which I found, too, you had been at the kind trouble to register. I am heartily obliged to you for your goodness in looking so tenderly after my little affair.[9] It happened to be important to me at this moment, & I did not wish to have made any mistake. Mr Thoreau met your New Bedford Rev. Mr Thomas,[10] at my house, last evening. The naturalist was in the perfect spirits habitual to him, and the minister courteous as ever, &, as it happened, cognisant of the Cape, & of Henry's travels thereon. I am bound to be specially sensible of Henry Ts merits, as he has just now by better surveying quite innocently made 60 rods of woodland for me, & left the adjacent lot, which he was measuring,[11] larger than the deed gave it. Theres a surveyor for you!

With kindest regards to your family, & to Ellery Channing,

Yours ever,

R. W. Emerson

6. The MS memorandum book for 1857 gives Dec. 22 to New Bedford. Benjamin Rodman wrote Emerson on Dec. 9, 1857, asking him as a guest when he should come to New Bedford on the 22d.

7. *Cf.* Jan. 10 following.

8. MS owned by Mr. W. T. H. Howe; ph. in CUL. The envelope now with this letter is addressed to Ricketson, at New Bedford, and bears a Concord postmark dated Jan. 11.

9. See Jan. 6, 1858.

10. Moses G. Thomas was resident at New Bedford, without a charge (*The Yearbook of the Unitarian Congregational Churches, for 1858*). For his earlier acquaintance with Emerson, see Oct. 10, 1828.

11. Thoreau was frequently busy surveying in Dec., 1857, and Jan., 1858. On Jan. 1 he wrote that he had lately been surveying the Walden woods so extensively and so minutely that he now saw them mapped in his mind's eye as so many men's woodlots (*The Writings*, XVI, 233).

To WILLIAM HENRY FURNESS, CONCORD, JANUARY 15, 1858

[MS owned by Mr. Horace Howard Furness Jayne; printed in *Records of a Lifelong Friendship*, p. 115.]

To HENRY WADSWORTH LONGFELLOW, CONCORD, JANUARY 15, 1858 [12]

Concord 15 January
1858

Dear Longfellow,

This is to introduce to you Horace Day, Esq. a gentleman much esteemed in New Haven, which is his home. Mr Day is Librarian of the Institute at N. H.[13] which corresponds to the Mercantile Library Association in Boston, & other cities; and he wishes to consult you on behalf of his association.

Yours faithfully,
R. W. Emerson

H. W. Longfellow, Esq.

To ABEL ADAMS, CONCORD, JANUARY 18, 1858 [14]

Concord, 18 Jany 1858

My dear friend,

I am sorry the Mad River Road [15] will not pay, and I shall always think the worse of these railroad-men that they have given you in these your honored fireside days so much vexation. Thank you for giving me the information, as tis best to know. But I have not confided in them, since you or others told me the road was in a bad way. I must patch up my housekeeping, then, with a course of lectures in Boston,[16] next month, and try to live without the Corporations. I find it hard to get a free day, this winter, though almost all my work is at home, — or I should have come out to see you & yours, & to know of Abby, who, I heard, was quite ill since I saw her. But she is better & best again, before

12. MS owned by the Trustees of the Longfellow House, Cambridge; ph. in CUL.

13. Day duly appears in *Benham's New Haven Directory*, 1857, as librarian of the Young Men's Institute. In the MS memorandum book for 1857, Dec. 17 is given to New Haven. Day does not seem to be mentioned in Longfellow's MS diary (at the Longfellow House, Cambridge) for the latter half of Jan., 1858.

14. MS owned by RWEMA; ph. in CUL.

15. The Mad River & Lake Erie is mentioned in earlier letters; *cf.* also Feb. 24, 1858. This and the Vermont & Canada seem to have been Adams's most unfortunate guesses as Emerson's financial adviser.

16. See Mar. 2, 1858.

this. And Mrs Adams I trust is well. Perhaps I shall not come till I return from Philadelphia, where I am to be 1 February.[17]

Yours affectionately,

R. W. Emerson

Abel Adams.

To CHARLES SUMNER, CONCORD, JANUARY 19, 1858 [18]

Concord

19 January 1858

Dear Sumner,

I have been growing so rich within the last few days in additions to my library, that tis quite time to signify my sense of the benefit to my benefactor, whose name I find franking the parcels, & giving them a direction to me. I am now possessed of the 3 volumes of the " Japan Expedition " [19] in 4to.; and of the 4 vols. of the " Explorations of R R Route from Missisippi to the Pacific," [20] in 4to; with all the rich illustrations of these Reports, added to their intrinsic interest. Then I have The Military Report on th Camels; [21] & Mr [E]spy's Report; [22] with other volumes on " Finances," [23] & " Patents," [24] which, if I cannot use, I will try to find an owner or a user for. But as I look at these, I can see

17. The testimony of both the MS memorandum book for 1858 and the Philadelphia papers goes to show that Emerson's first lecture was set for Feb. 2, not 1. The *North American and United States Gazette,* Jan. 30–Feb. 3, announced Emerson, without subject, before the People's Literary Institute on Feb. 2, and as reading " Works and Days," for the benefit of the Union Temporary Home, on Feb. 3.

18. MS owned by RWEMA; ph. in CUL. There is a slight mutilation, and the portions of the text in square brackets are conjectural.

19. Francis L. Hawks, *Narrative of the Expedition of an American Squadron to the Chinese Seas and Japan . . . under the Command of Commodore M. C. Perry,* 1856. At least one of the three volumes is in the Emerson library at the Antiquarian House.

20. These volumes of *Reports of Explorations and Surveys,* all concerned with the route of the proposed railroad to the Pacific, were published by the Government over a period of years. *Cf.* Feb. 27, 1861.

21. *Report of the Secretary of War . . . respecting the Purchase of Camels for the Purposes of Military Transportation,* 1857 (Senate Ex. Doc. 62, 34th Cong., 3d Sess.).

22. Probably James Pollard Espy's fourth meteorological report, published at Washington, 1857 (Senate Ex. Doc. 65, 34th Cong., 3d Sess.). For Emerson's acquaintance with Espy, see the letter from Washington, Jan. 14, 1843.

23. Probably a report of the Secretary of the Treasury.

24. The *Report of the Commissioner of Patents* for 1857, for example, comprised entirely separate parts — one devoted to agriculture, another, in three volumes, to arts and manufactures. The reports for 1857 bear the imprint date 1858, and I am uncertain whether they are the ones Emerson had received.

behind them older messengers of the same kind, & behind them others, to count the years of your Senatorship by. Well, these are good [tok]ens & a good calendar to reckon upon., We shall reckon much American history by the years of your consulship. For every reason, & for the best public & private good, may they be many, & the last days the best! So prays your friend,

R. W. Emerson —

Hon. Charles Sumner.

To Harrison Gray Otis Blake, Concord, January 24, 1858 [25]

Concord —
24 January, 1858

My dear Blake,

I have been out of town since I had your note, or it should have had an earlier reply. I am glad that my pledge, which I supposed was quite forgotten, is yet to avail me a visit to you & your friends. But I think since this project of ours seems to affect great slowness & secularity of realization, that we will indulge it, & not cramp its large proportions by any premature speed of completion! I believe it is settled that I am to read some lectures in Boston, in the end of February, and, as these will require special care, I shall prefer to come to Worcester & spend a day with you, immediately after them, to coming before. Say so for me to your friends & mine.

Affectionately,
R. W. Emerson

H. G. O. Blake.

To Mary Moody Emerson, Concord, January 27, 1858 [26]

Concord
27 January, 1858

My dear Aunt,

I often wonder that in so many traditions as I heard in my youth, from you chiefly, of my ancestors, I should never have heard, or never distinctly understood who was your greatgrandfather, that is, who was the father of Joseph Emerson of Malden? Please to answer me at

25. MS owned by CUL; ph. in CUL. *Cf.* the letters of Mar. 2 and Apr. 8 following.
26. MS owned by RWEMA; ph. in CUL. Excerpt I is in Cabot, I, 54.

once, if you know. I am very little given to genealogy, which is wont, like an epidemic fever, to attack all persons who have past fifty years, but sometimes, after lying latent for years, a natural question like this comes again & again with force to mind, in the very last times when it can be answered. For as I look up & down in my kindred, there is not another than you in the world, I suppose, who can answer it. And do not take this stirring of the blood as any change of direction. ᴵI abide in my old turret, — or if you will, — coop or tub of observation, & mean to keep my eyes open, whether any thing offers to be observed, or not.ᴵ Every day is by no means sure to bring its reasonable hour, and I have often to remember Niebuhr's discovery that his power of divination had departed from him,[27] and to repeat to [28]

To William Emerson, Concord, February 12, 1858 [29]

Concord, 12 Feb.ʸ·
1858

Dear William,

I safely received the letter & draft for $40. which I duly neglected to acknowledge, my pen having grown rusty & almost refusing to write. At home,[30] I found Lidian still in bed, as I had left her, & though she has since been on her feet & abroad, she is still a poor prisoner there the most of the day. She heartily thanks Susan for her kind thoughts & invitation: I found letters at home from Aunt Mary, who lives near Charlotte Cleveland at Ashfield. By the way, I will tell you, for William Junior's benefit & your own, what she told me. I wrote [31] to ask her, who was the father of Rev Joseph Emerson of Malden, our great grandfather? She replies, " Edward Emerson,[32] Esq. of Newburyport, who lies buried in Malden. His wife lies beside him, or did," &c I know not how it happened that I never asked this question before of Aunt Mary or else

27. Emerson had recorded this more fully in *Journals* for 1855 (VIII, 524). *Cf. The Life and Letters*, tr. Winkworth, New York, 1852, pp. 34–35.

28. The letter must have been continued on a second sheet, which I have not found.

29. MS owned by HCL; ph. in CUL.

30. For the lectures in Philadelphia early in February, see Jan. 18, 1858. The MS memorandum book for this year shows engagements at Chicopee, Mass., Feb. 9, and Springfield, Feb. 10.

31. Jan. 27, 1858.

32. According to Cabot, I, 8–9, this Edward Emerson was of Newbury, not of Newburyport.

never received the answer. She is now the only person living I suppose who could answer it authoritatively. Has William Jr. the fact set down so in his pedigree?

Yesterday, I called on Dr & Mrs Dewey, Mary & Kate, who are in a good boarding-house in Otis Place. I went to see George B. E. and spent an hour with him & Mrs E. He has had a very satisfying tour, and now comes back to the State Board of Education [33]

Affectionately,
Waldo

To Leonard Bacon, Concord, February 18, 1858

[Printed in Theodore Bacon, p. 312.]

To Abel Adams, Concord, February 24, 1858 [34]

Concord
24 Feb.^y

My dear friend,

Will it be too much trouble to you to send me a description of my " Mad River & Lake Erie Bonds," namely, the year of issue, &c? Sam. G. Ward has a friend, who is acquainting himself with the affairs of that Corporation, for his own & others' benefit; & Mr Ward thinks I had better let him inquire also into the character & prospects of these, at the same time.

I long to come to your house, but am a prisoner, for the present. [35]

Ever yours,
R. W. Emerson

Mr Abel Adams.

To Leonard Bacon, Concord, February 25, 1858

[Printed in Theodore Bacon, p. 313.]

33. G. B. Emerson makes some references to the Massachusetts board of education and to a trip to Europe in his *Reminiscences of an Old Teacher*, pp. 96–100.

34. MS owned by RWEMA; ph. in CUL. The date is fixed by Adams's reply, Jamaica Plain, Feb. 25, 1858, stating that Emerson's Mad River & Lake Erie bonds were dated Feb. 1, 1851, were due Feb. 1, 1866, and belonged to a series of one thousand. Adams believed in the " eventual goodness " of these bonds but feared it would be necessary to wait for a part of the interest.

35. Emerson was doubtless preparing his lectures for the course he was about to begin in Boston; see Mar. 2, 1858.

To Horatio Woodman, Concord, March 1, 1858?

[MS listed, without year, and partly quoted in American Art Association, Apr. 28 and 29, 1924. Emerson says that, on reflection, he is of Woodman's opinion: it is better to dispose of the two miscellaneous topics at the beginning of the course and then proceed to the connected lectures; he really wishes to win the attention of good heads to the attractive side of intellectual science. For the year, it should be noted that the first two subjects of the Boston course commencing Mar. 3, 1858, were "miscellaneous" and that the remaining ones were connected and were on "intellectual science" (see a note on Mar. 2 following).]

To James Thomas Fields, Concord, March 2, 1858 [36]

Concord 2 March
Tuesday Evening

My dear Sir,

I have just received your note bringing me unexpected but most hospitable invitation. You have my kindest thanks, but I am a confirmed tavern-goer, to that extent, that I can seldom enter a private house where a public one is open, and indeed had already declined other invitations for these coming Wednesdays,[37] when your kind note arrived.

Yours with great regard,
R. W. Emerson

Mr Fields.

To William Rounseville Alger, Concord, March 4, 1858

[MS listed and partly quoted in Merwin-Clayton Sales Co., Nov. 27–28, 1905; since Alger persists in his "hospitable design," Emerson chooses the following Wednesday.]

36. MS owned by Mr. Oliver R. Barrett; ph. in CUL. Of the years during Emerson's acquaintance with Fields when Mar. 2 fell on Tuesday, only 1858 fits the Wednesday lectures.

37. The *Boston Evening Transcript*, Mar. 3–Apr. 7, 1858, announced these Wednesday lectures at the Freeman Place Chapel on the days of delivery and the topics and dates are confirmed by the MS memorandum book for this year: " Country Life," Mar. 3; " Works and Days," 10; " Powers of the Mind," 17; " The Natural Method of Mental Philosophy," 24; " Memory," 31; " Self-possession," Apr. 7. The same paper for Apr. 8 praised the lecturer and his audience and rated the course a success " in the fullest meaning of the term."

To Frederic Henry Hedge, Concord, March 12, 1858? [38]

Concord 12 March

Dear Hedge,

　　　　I ought to have told you already that I read the paper on Youth [39] the same night I saw you, and with real interest. It reports private & genuine experiences of somebody with simplicity & just confidence & inspires in the reader the wish for more revelations. I shall look up the paper you mentioned on Hebrew Poetry.[40] Meantime I will soon find another time to look over this MS. again; and if I find there what I read out of it on Wednesday, I will send it to Lowell with my best advice.

Ever yours,

Dr Hedge.   R. W. Emerson

To Thomas Wentworth Higginson, Concord, April 8, 1858 [41]

Concord
8 April
1858

My dear Sir,

　　　　I should like to come to Worcester very well, but it is not so easy for me as if the Worcester & Nashua trains [42] had an earlier evening hour. Now I cannot go without great loss of time, which I am still such an unthrift as to reckon narrowly. Great men, I believe, make their own, & do not watch their watches. Then I had rather not read on Sunday. But, if you say so, I will come *any day of next week*, that you will name, &, by the Boston train, and read one lecture, say, " Natural Method of Mental Philosophy," and you shall pay my expenses, and if it

38. MS owned by RWEMA; ph. in CUL. The date is 1858 if my conjectures regarding the articles cited below are correct.

39. This I believe to be the " Youth " published in *The Atlantic* for Sept., 1858, without the author's name but credited in *The Atlantic Index*, 1889, to J. Albee. The article is transcendental in tone. John Albee appears elsewhere in the correspondence as a young disciple of Emerson.

40. This seems to refer to a paper already in print — almost certainly to " Hebrew Poetry," in *The Christian Examiner* for Jan., 1858. This article appeared anonymously, but *Poole's Index* credits it to John Albee. Like " Youth," it is much in the Emersonian vein.

41. MS owned by Goodspeed's Book Shop; ph. in CUL.

42. *Cf.* Mar. 17, 1849.

turns out that there can be a paying audience, & especially if they wish to hear more lectures, I can easily arrange it to come again; if not you & my other friends shall be harmless. I will, at the same visit, offer my private reading of " Works & Days " to Miss Buttman & Mr Blake. Will you not say this to Blake, & send me word what day.[43]

Yours faithfully,
R. W. Emerson

T. W. Higginson.

To William Emerson, Concord, April 15, 1858 [44]

Concord.
15 April
Thursday

Dear William,

I am afraid I am losing my natural & valued rights, which I could ill spare, of knowing & dealing with you & yours as with me & mine. For I was taken by surprise the other day with the intelligence that William was betrothed,[45] and now I am told that you & Susan have a new daughter [46] who has leaped into life looking thirteen years old, — and all this without the leave of me. I must positively come & spend a fortnight with you, or I shall lose all my avuncular rights. You might in charity give me an early whisper of the affairs at Helvellyn, before I read them in the Journal of Commerce. Meantime, I confess to great unworthiness, I have written no letters, & I have failed to reach the Island when I was at N. Y. But I had nothing to tell, & had gathered no new daughters. And now I will make haste to tell you that Helen Haven is

43. *Cf.* letters of Apr. 15, 1858, to Higginson and Blake. *The Worcester Daily Spy* of the 15th announced that Emerson would lecture at Mechanics' Hall on the 16th, " by invitation of some friends in this city," but did not name the subject. On Apr. 23 Emerson lectured at Brinley Hall on " The Analogies of Nature to the Processes of the Mind " after a different topic had been announced (*ibid.*, Apr. 22–24, 1858) .

44. MS owned by HCL; ph. in CUL.

45. William Emerson wrote from Helvellyn, his Staten Island home, on Apr. 17, 1858, that the announcement of the engagement had been withheld for a time because his son was not yet admitted to the bar (MS owned by Dr. Haven Emerson) . The marriage of William Emerson, Jr., to Sarah H. Gibbons occurred on Nov. 25, 1863 (*The New-York Times*, Nov. 27, 1863) :

46. William Emerson explained, in his letter cited above, that the " new daughter " was Emily Jenks, a daughter of Susan Haven Emerson's cousin Prudence Haven Jenks, who had recently died, leaving the child, less than fourteen years of age, under his guardianship.

here on a visit to Edith Emerson. She came with her sister Mary H. to spend a week, but was taken ill with measles, and her father came to see her, & has taken Mary home. Helen is bright & cheerful, & appears to be doing very well. She is a dear little girl, & I don't think it will do her any harm to be sick in Edith's chamber instead of her own. I finished just now my six lectures in Boston [47] four of which were new & on topics of Mental Philosophy. We had the best houses that could be. Affectionately,

Waldo

Give my love to Susan, to whom this letter is also written.

To Thomas Wentworth Higginson, Concord? April 15, 1858

[A telegram mentioned in Apr. 15, 1858, to Blake as just sent.]

To Harrison Gray Otis Blake, Concord, April 15, 1858

[MS listed and partly quoted in American Art Association, Nov. 24–25, 1924; quoted at greater length in Ernest Dressel North, Apr., 1909. Emerson tells of his correspondence with Higginson about a choice of lectures for Worcester, and says he has just now telegraphed him, promising to bring " Country Life " and some other lectures so that a final choice can be made at the last minute.]

To Edwin Percy Whipple, Concord, April 22, 1858

[MS listed and partly quoted in C. F. Libbie & Co., Apr. 7–8, 1903; Emerson incloses a letter from C. C. Felton which, he says, he at first thought to be praise of his own article but later found to be praise of " your article, not mine." *The Atlantic* for Apr., 1858, contains Emerson's " Persian Poetry " and Whipple's review of *The New American Cyclopædia*.]

To Abby Larkin Adams, Concord, April 26, 1858 [48]

Concord
26 April 1858

Dear Abby,

Do you not remember that, long ago, you were to bring Dr Hedge to your house to dine, & I was to fix the day when I was to come, & be of the party? Well, time brings everything round, & I, mindful of

47. See Mar. 2, 1858. In the MS the close and signature are set off from the preceding sentence by an irregular line.
48. MS owned by RWEMA; ph. in CUL.

your good designs, invited Dr Hedge to dine with your Uncle on the Tuesday after the 1 May, that is, on Tuesday 4th May,[49] when I mean to come with him; but I am to spend the night at his house. Now, if this scheme falls on a day which for any cause will not suit you, or your Uncle & Aunt, you will please send me a line at once. Wednesday 5th or Thursday 6th will, I believe, please Dr H. & me quite as well; or a later day shall, if you desire it. I write to Dr H. the day first named, (4th;) and we shall keep it, unless you contradict me.

   With love to all your house, Yours,

                                                    R. W. Emerson

Miss Abby L. Adams.

To FREDERIC HENRY HEDGE, CONCORD, APRIL 26, 1858 [50]

                                                    Concord
                                                    April 26, 1858

Dear Hedge,

          I write to Abby Adams today that you & I will come, by my invitation, to dine with her Uncle on Tuesday 4 May; and, that if she knows any lett or hindrance to the design, she shall inform me at once. You also, for your part, take notice, that is Tuesday; & if you do not like that day, say to me Wednesday, or Thursday, & I will change it at once: but, to the best of my remembrance, you said, that, though Tuesday was your Cambridge day, it would serve. I suppose the hour is 2.30 P. M.

                                          In good hope, faithfully yours
                                                    R. W. Emerson

Dr Hedge.

To HENRY STEPHENS RANDALL, CONCORD, APRIL 28, 1858

[MS listed and partly quoted in American Art Association, Apr. 28 and 29, 1924; Emerson mentions the arrival, apparently in his care, of the four volumes of E. B. O'Callaghan's documentary history of New York and adds that Thoreau, whose study now seems to be divided equally between natural and civil history, has received these books. The letter also reports praise of Randall's own work, *The Life of Thomas Jefferson*. Emerson says he may soon have something to write of his own impressions of that biography.]

---

49. The MS memorandum book for 1858 gives that day to Jamaica Plain. Frederic Henry Hedge was now a pastor in Brookline, as well as a professor in Harvard.
50. MS owned by RWEMA; ph. in CUL.

To Mary Moody Emerson, Concord, May 2, 1858 [51]

Concord
May 2, 1858

Dear Aunt,

We all hear with great interest that you will come, as you ought, to your old home & people, and Lidian sends you her best love & respect, & with me desires that you will come at the first day & hour your convenience will allow, to our house. Your chamber & bed are ready, & the young people also will eagerly welcome your arrival. Come this time, & try to stay, and domesticate yourself for good with this dull household of ours. We will all try to defend you from the common enemy — Time & its noise & fracas, — & bring to you the common friend, Peace & Good-will. Elizabeth, of course, is on the lookout for a a boarding place, but do you come & stay here, with your own, & let the strangers alone.[52] Love from us all to Charlotte,[53] — and will not she bring Mr Cleveland now, on his way to Boston, to make the promised visit?

Your affectionate
Waldo E.

To George Bancroft, Concord? May? c. 10? 1858

[Partly printed in Howe, *The Life and Letters of George Bancroft*, II, 107, where it is described as written " in 1858." Vol. VII of Bancroft's *A History of the United States*, the book which Emerson praised in this letter, was advertised in *The New-York Times*, May 5, 1858, as just published in Boston. Whatever the date of the letter, it was, I think, very probably earlier than July 1, 1858, when Emerson tells of his invitation to visit Bancroft at Newport, R. I.]

To Henrietta Crosby Ingersoll, Concord, May 11, 1858 [54]

Concord
11 May 1858

Dear Madam,

I have just recovered your note, which I had mislaid — I believe in some special care to keep it in sight, — as I chanced to be much hindered when it arrived. It will give me much pleasure to keep the day

51. MS owned by RWEMA; ph. in CUL.

52. The letters of Oct. 18 and 25, 1858, show that Mary Moody Emerson was for some time a boarder in Concord but not in the Emerson home.

53. Cleveland.

54. MS owned by the Library of Congress; ph. in CUL. The middle third of the second leaf is missing. It doubtless contained Emerson's signature and perhaps the

the ladies have assigned me, Thursday, 14 October, and you may rely on my coming, unless you shall hear from me in good time previously. Nor shall I forget that it is to be my privilege to visit Mrs Appleton in the evening.[55]

To Theodore Parker, Concord, May 14, 1858?[56]

Concord 14 May

My dear Parker,

Mr Stacy[57] is to learn today, I believe, whether you will come hither on Sunday, or not. Whatever day shall be fixed, we are depending on seeing you, at our house; & my wife begs me to write & ask, — which I also am fain to do, — that you will persuade Mrs Parker[58] to come up with you, & give us an opportunity of seeing her too. Let it be so, if you can.

Yours faithfully,
R W Emerson

Mr Parker.

To Thomas Carlyle, Concord, May 17, 1858

[MS owned by RWEMA; printed in *C–E Corr.*, 1883. This version seems to be a fragment of what was actually sent to Carlyle. Another MS, a rough, incomplete draft owned by RWEMA (ph. in CUL), contains much that has not been printed and is otherwise different from the printed version, which it seems to have preceded by a couple of days:

---

name of his correspondent. This letter is one of two from Emerson belonging to a group described in the *Handbook of Manuscripts in the Library of Congress*, 1918, p. 175, as " to Mrs. H. C. Ingersoll, of Washington, D. C., 1838–1886." According to Lillian Drake Avery, *A Genealogy of the Ingersoll Family*, 1926, p. 61, Henrietta Crosby was the wife of George Washington Ingersoll (1803–1860), who gained prominence as a lawyer at Bangor, Me., was a leading member of the House of Representatives, 1854–1855, and was elected attorney-general of Maine shortly before his death.

55. The MS memorandum book for 1858 has a canceled entry for Oct. 14: " Bangor Mrs Appleton Sec of Mrs G. W. Ingersoll." Bangor again appears in the entry of Oct. 28 for the same year, where it is not canceled.

56. MS owned by RWEMA; ph. in CUL. The date " 1858? " has been supplied in another hand, but I have no proof. The year seems at least possible, however, as Parker, his biographers show, partly regained his strength in 1858 and was active for a time before his long final illness.

57. The MS records of the Concord Lyceum (in the Concord Free Public Library) show that an A. Stacy — probably the Albert Stacy of earlier letters — was in Feb., 1858, a member of a committee to procure subscriptions. But Parker's coming apparently was to have nothing to do with the Lyceum. John Stacy may be meant.

58. Parker had married Lydia Cabot in 1837, and she survived him.

"Concord May 15 1858

"Dear Carlyle,

"I am afraid to go on any longer in this contumacy. There came to me a little while ago an agreeable gentleman, Mr Probym, with a letter from you, dated, to be sure, a year before. I gladly greeted the letter & the bearer, but found that he did not know you but one of your friends. He made himself very welcome to all who saw him, & I carried him to our Club where are Agassiz Longfellow Lowell & other good people

"But I thought I would no longer omit to ~~gather up & knit again our somewhat broken threads~~ weld the rusted wires, & see if the subtle stream would not speed again. Every week for months I have watched for the appearance of

                                                    since
Frederic, who does not appear. I am better ready for it, ~~as I chanced to read~~
                                                    ~~that~~
one or two books about Voltaire, Maupertuis, & company, fell in my way. Voltaire appeared to disadvantage in the Frederic business, but redeemed himself by the Abolitionist energy of his heroic interferences against fanaticism in his old age. Yet that will never happen which I wish to see, namely, that you should cull the result of privatest conviction a liber veritatis a few sentences a hint of the final moral you drew from so much penetrating inquest into past & present men and tell me that. All writing is necessitated to be exoteric and written to a ~~mortal~~ human *Should* instead of to the dreadful *Is*. And I say this to you because you are the bravest & truest of writers. Every writer is like a
                    partly   &
skater & must go ~~not quite~~ where he would, ~~but~~ partly where the skates carry
                                                    be blown
him; or like a sailor, who can only land where sails can ~~carry him.~~ The variations to be allowed for in the surveyors compass are nothing like so large as those that must be allowed for in every book And a friendship of old gentlemen who have got rid of so many illusions survived their ambition, & blushes, & passion for euphony, & superficial harmonies, and tenderness for their acci-
                    kept
dental literary stores, but have ~~retained~~ their entire curiosity & awe touching the problems of Man & Fate & the Cause of Causes A friendship of old gentlemen of this character is looking more comely & profitable than anything I have read of love. Such a dream flatters my incapacities for conversation for we can all play at monosyllables who cannot vie with panoramic pictorial exhal/atings. So if ever I hear that you have betrayed a symptom of age, that your back is bent a tenth of an inch from the perpendicular, ~~I may come in the first steamer~~ "]

TO ARTHUR HUGH CLOUGH, CONCORD, MAY 17, 1858

[MS owned by Mr. Arthur Clough; ph. in CUL. Printed in *Emerson-Clough Letters*. A rough draft dated May 15, 1858 (owned by RWEMA; ph. in CUL), contains nearly the same matter but with the paragraphs arranged in a different order.]

To ————————, CONCORD, MAY 21, 1858

[MS listed and partly quoted in C. F. Libbie & Co., Mar. 20–21, 1906; Emerson says that since good hearing makes the good speech he can guarantee in advance " any chapter that shall be read to your company especially in your house."]

To MARY? RUSSELL? WATSON, CONCORD, MAY 26, 1858

[MS listed and partly quoted in Anderson Galleries, Feb. 1–3, 1926, where the name of the person addressed is given merely as Miss Watson. In Goodspeed's Book Shop, Apr., 1907, the year is given as 1855, clearly an error. Anna Watson, who may have received the present letter, appears in Oct. 26, 1859. But as this relates to an article (on Channing's poems) which Emerson had found it inadvisable to recommend to *The Atlantic,* there is reason to suppose that the recipient was not a Miss Watson but Mrs. Mary Russell Watson, whose review of the *Waverley Novels* was published in *The Atlantic* for May, 1858, and two of whose compositions were printed in the same magazine for June and Sept., 1860, after long delay (see the note on *c.* May? 1860?).]

To ————————, CONCORD, MAY 26, 1858

[MS listed and partly quoted in C. F. Libbie & Co., Mar. 20–21, 1906; Emerson acknowledges an additional instalment of $4 from some lecture fund.]

To FRANCIS H. UNDERWOOD, CONCORD, JUNE 3, 1858 [59]

Concord

3 June 1858

Mr Underwood

Dear Sir,

Here are a couple of articles offered by their authors to the Atlantic. That on " Napoleon's Nemesis " comes from Cincinnati, & from a good head.[60] The other from a *Medicinae Doctor.* Please to keep them so marked that they may be reclaimed by their authors, if they do not suit your purpose.

I shall be able to send you a chapter pretty soon, I think, as I have found an old MS. that seems to admit of salvation.

Yours

R. W. Emerson

59. MS owned by the Henry E. Huntington Library; ph. in CUL.

60. This article was apparently not published in *The Atlantic.* I conjecture that Emerson's friend Goddard, the Cincinnatian mentioned in earlier letters, may have been the author. It is possible that the article by the doctor of medicine was published, but I cannot, at any rate, determine its identity.

Please say to Mr Wyman I wish the Atlantics bound in plain calf Wait till I come to town [61]

To ——————— ROSSMAN, CONCORD, JUNE 5, 1858

[MS listed in the American Autograph Shop, Oct., 1935; Emerson accepts honorary membership in the Kane Monument Association and permits the use of his name.]

To JAMES RUSSELL LOWELL, BOSTON, JUNE 22, 1858? [62]

> Boston Athenaeum
> 22 June

Dear Lowell,

I was setting forth an hour ago to find Mr Stillman [63] & yourself, as heads of the Adirondac party; but learning just now that Mr S. does not live in Cambridge, & that it was doubtful if you were at home, I shall check my social zeal till Saturday. I have only to propose Edward Hoar [64] as a member of the party. You do not know him: he was at Cambridge with Frank Lee, & his friend; & has been practising law & in a very Californian manner in California for the last 8 years, is a good naturalist or botanist,[65] & daily becoming better. We value him very highly at Concord & are in monthly fear lest he shall wander back again to the Pacific. He is a gentleman, & cannot, I am sure, be

61. The last sentence probably explains why the postscript was ineffectively canceled with a single stroke of the pen.

62. MS owned by HCL; ph. in CUL. The year is pretty definitely fixed by references to Edward Sherman Hoar and the Adirondack party. As 1858 was the year of the first encampment of the Adirondack Club, though Stillman and Lowell, with a small party, had made a preliminary exploration in 1857, the present letter could hardly have been earlier. On the other hand, Emerson says Hoar has practiced in California " for the last 8 years." This means that he did not return from California till the year of this letter. We know from letters of July 1 and 27 following that he was in Concord in 1858. The present letter could not, therefore, be later than that year.

63. Emerson must have known of William J. Stillman some years earlier as one of the editors of *The Crayon* (see May 8, 1855). Stillman wrote from Belmont, Mass., July 22 (MS endorsed 1858 by Emerson), that he was going ahead of the main party and would trust Lowell to give final instructions to the others; he also said Emerson could have his choice of a large assortment of guns, and so need bring none.

64. A Francis L. Lee graduated from Harvard in 1843, and Edward Hoar graduated in the following year.

65. See a note on Mar. 28, 1840, to Ruth Haskins Emerson. The accounts of the first encampment cited in a note on July 27, 1858, do not mention Edward Hoar, who evidently did not go, though his brother, Judge Hoar, was a member of the party. Edward Hoar, according to his daughter, had gone to California in 1849, to practice law, and returned, she thinks, in 1858.

troublesome to any campaigner. Is there any bar in the way? I know
you will be crowded with recruits.

Yours faithfully,

J. R. Lowell, Esq.   R W Emerson

To Gisela von Arnim, Concord, June 29, 1858

[MS owned by the Goethe- und Schiller-Archiv, Weimar. Printed in *The Atlantic*, XCI, 471 (Apr., 1903); reprinted in *Correspondence between Ralph Waldo Emerson and Herman Grimm*, ed. Frederick William Holls, 1903, pp. 27–28.]

To Herman Grimm, Concord, June 29, 1858

[MS owned by the Goethe- und Schiller-Archiv. Printed in *The Atlantic*, XCI, 470–471 (Apr., 1903); reprinted in *Correspondence*, pp. 23–24.]

To William Emerson, Concord, July 1, 1858 [66]

Concord 1 July

Dear William,

I had a letter many days ago, — or weeks, is it? — announcing
your safe arrival at home Every week comes the Home Journal as a
token; now & then a letter from Haven, or W^m Jr, to one of the house;
&, last night, came a letter & parcels for Lidian, which, — in her absence,
& the letter unread I divine to be the keeping of your promise to Bulkeley Lidian is gone to Lynn, Medford, & Brookline, but should return tonight. Here awaits her an invitation from Mrs Bancroft for Newport —
L & I to go thither on the 10th for a few days [67] — very charming invitation, but very hard to accept. Let the lady come home tonight & say what
she desires. I am keeping my leisures to spend in a mass at Adirondac in
August.[68] Agassiz promises me to go, & Dr Jeffries Wyman is a new re-
cruit; & Longfellow, tis said, will go.[69] You ask for the lawsuit, it went
for the enemy. and I have sat expectant for a fortnight, when the sheriffs

66. MS owned by HCL; ph. in CUL. The year is established by evidence cited
below.

67. The visit with the Bancrofts at Newport is recorded in July 15, 1858.

68. *Cf.* the letters of July 27 and Aug. 5 following.

69. Wyman and Agassiz went (*Journals*, IX, 158 ff.). Longfellow did not (Samuel
Longfellow, *Life*, n. d. [c. 1891], II, 363). It seems that Longfellow refused to go when
he was informed that Emerson would carry a gun. The version of the story which
states that Emerson had purchased a gun seems surprising in view of Stillman's offer
mentioned in a note on June 22, 1858? In his MS diary (at the Longfellow House,
Cambridge), Longfellow noted in August a favorable report of the expedition:
"Thursday. 19. Agassiz passes the evening with us. He is just back from the Adirondac delighted with the expedition and with the beauty of the country."

or messengers would summon me to pay whatever damages accrue.[70] But none has come, or perhaps my guarantors have intervened. I have been cutting a fine crop of clover in my heater piece,[71] & got it well wet: and now a better crop in my housefield; put it yesterday into the barn in best condition. Today my cow has dropped a little bullock in the pasture. Our fields are looking well on this cold July day, but regretting June. Thoreau, Edward Hoar, & Blake of Worcester set out today for a fortnight at the White Mountains,[72] with tents & provision. Thank Haven for sending me the history of the Aurora lines.[73] Love to the boys, & love to Susan. Ellen is in Boston, & Edith & Eddy at school. Affectionately,

Waldo

To ———————, Concord, July 1, 1858

[MS listed in American Autograph Shop, May, 1935, where it is described as relating to a lecture course.]

To Ellen Emerson, Concord, July 4, 1858? [74]

Concord
Fourth of July

Dear Ellen,

Your mother thinks she will not go to Boston on Monday So

70. In June 23, 1856, to his brother, Emerson tells of defending " a piece of woodland against a claimant under an old deed new found," but, he says, " my warrantors defend me." The *Boston Evening Transcript* of Apr. 20, 1857, repeated an account of the trial up to that time, with a similar explanation of the nature of the controversy: " The case, as we are informed, is simply this: Mr. Emerson bought a piece of woodland, and paid for it. After a long period, an *older deed* was discovered; and, under its shelter, a suit was instituted, nominally against him, but really against his warrantors, who undertake to maintain his title." The history of the suit is summarized in the MS records of the Court of Common Pleas of Middlesex County, volume beginning Mar., 1858: Charles Bartlett brought suit against Emerson in June, 1855, and, in an amended declaration of June 28, 1856, specified that since Dec. 1, 1854, Emerson had, with his servants, wagons, etc., entered Bartlett's land at various times and had torn up and damaged the soil and cut down trees to the value of $500. Emerson denied the charge and asserted that the land in question was his own. The suit was tried and retried. According to the final action, June 11, 1858, Emerson was directed to pay damages of $25 and costs amounting to several times as much.

71. *Cf.* the first letter of Feb. 13, 1847.

72. According to Thoreau (*The Writings*, XVII, 3–55), he actually started on July 2 and returned on the 19th. Edward Hoar and Thoreau began the journey together and did not join H. G. O. Blake until later.

73. Perhaps some work on the aurora borealis, such as the Smithsonian Institution's publications of 1856.

74. MS owned by RWEMA; ph. in CUL. The year 1858 has been added in another hand.

you shall not look for her. I yesterday engaged Dr Keep to receive her at 11 o'clock on Monday, & it is yet possible she may keep the appointment, — but wants to be at home on Monday. The cannon was found yesterday & is now to be presented with all the honors. Love to Edith. I fear Mrs Ward's sick nerves will be sadly wrung with a houseful of girls [75] in such forbidding weather.

Papa

Later. The cannon has been presented, & received with great joy, Johnnie assisting, & will soon speak for itself.

.   .   .   .   .[76]

surely recommend for honesty & capacity.[77]

To John Murray Forbes, Concord, July 8, 1858 [78]

Concord, 8 July, 1858

My dear Sir,

You surely did not suppose that such a card as an invitation of a whole family to Naushon, could be quietly received & answered by return of mail, like a summons to dinner. On the contrary, it produces a joyful consternation, as every body wants to go, & wants every other to go. At present, it seems quite too certain that I cannot go, as I am of a party bound to the Adirondac, on the 1 August, & we talk of 2, 3, or 4 weeks.[79]

My children are spiriting up their mother to accept the privilege of your woods & waters for a few days, and I think she will come with two of them, at least, on the day you indicate; or, if it promise to be impossible, you shall have an early intimation. Meantime, I am chagrined by being thrown out by this contretemps, & think of suing for a place on the Island as light house man, or gamekeeper, or fenceviewer, — especially the last, since the fence is the sea. With kindest regards from all in this house to all in yours,

R. W. Emerson

J. M. Forbes, Esq.

75. July 1, 1858, to William Emerson shows that Ellen was then in Boston.
76. The leaf has been partly cut away, and presumably more than half a page of the text is missing.
77. Apparently the letter ended here.
78. MS owned by RWEMA; ph. in CUL.
79. *Cf.* later letters of July and August.

To John Murray Forbes, Concord, July 15, 1858 [80]

Concord
15 July 1858

My dear Sir,

I returned home last night from Newport, — where my wife & I have spent a few days with the Bancrofts,[81] — to find your note, which else should have been at once answered. This very circumstance does not make the problem easier. Newport, Adirondac, Naushon, all in one summer, may well turn the brain of a better scholar. But as there is a very safe element in all these dissipations, I decide to accept your new proposition, & to come to you with my wife for a few days, on Tuesday, 3 September,[82] — and a couple of children if I cannot fight them off. Meantime we are all in great hope

Yours ever,
R. W. Emerson

Mr Forbes.

To ——————— Brainard, Concord, July 19, 1858 [83]

Concord —
19 July, 1858.

Dear Sir,

I think nothing can be done at present with Mr Rowse's sketch.[84] He left it imperfect six weeks ago, not being contented with its progress & intending, I believe, to try to mend it, after an interval, or to make a new one.

Yours respectfully,
R. W. Emerson

Mr Brainard.

80. MS owned by RWEMA; ph. in CUL.
81. *Cf.* July 1, 1858, to William Emerson.
82. That is, apparently, Aug. 3, though that date would have conflicted with the Adirondack scheme. For the change in plan, see July 25, 1858, to Forbes; and for Emerson's own visit to Naushon, see the letters of Aug. 26 and Sept. 18 following.
83. MS owned by HCL; ph. in CUL.
84. *Cf.* Jan. 14, 1859, and *Journals*, IX, 154. Reproductions of both the sketch and the finished crayon portrait are in the *New England Magazine*, n.s., XV, 456–457, where the date of the sketch is given as 1858. Reproductions of the portrait are fairly common.

To John Murray Forbes, Concord, July 25, 1858 [85]

Concord

July 25

My dear Sir,

It shall be as you say, & Edith & Edward shall come to Naushon on Tuesday 3 August, and the seniors shall console themselves with the hope of seeing you later. You should have had a prompter reply, but that I have been out of town.

With kindest regards to your household,

Yours,

R. W.. Emerson

Mr Forbes.

To Charles King Newcomb, Concord, July 25, 1858 [86]

Concord

25 July, 1858 —

Dear Charles,

It is very good of you to send me this invitation, which I should not resist, if I could accept. But I am going next week with a party to the Adirondac country,[87] to try our fortunes in the wilderness for two or three weeks: The bravest mean to stay four. And even beyond this northern visit I believe I am to go for a few days to Naushon,[88] which is nearer to you. So you see how ill I deserve your compliment of " leaving my labors."

I wish I could make you acquainted with Philip Randolph [89] of Philadelphia, who has bought a farm in the Narraganset country, & spends a part of every summer there. He is an upright sincere gentleman, with a love of truth, — working truth. With kind regards to your mother,

Yours affectionately,

R W Emerson

To ——————— Butman, Concord? July 27? 1858

[Mentioned in July 27, 1858.]

85. MS owned by RWEMA; ph. in CUL. Aug. 3 fell on Tuesday in 1858, the year which has been added to Emerson's date line in another hand and which fits the evidence of other letters of July, Aug., and Sept., 1858.

86. MS owned by the Concord Free Public Library; ph. in CUL.

87. Cf. other letters of July, Aug., and Sept., 1858.

88. See the letters of Aug. 26 and Sept. 18, 1858.

89. He appears in several earlier letters.

To Harrison Gray Otis Blake, Concord, July 27, 1858 [90]

Concord
27 July 1858

My dear Blake,

Tell that kind friend of mine who imagines herself not hospitable if her house is not always inhabited, & its doors always open, that I must be made of porcupine quills if I could question her bountiful good will. But I have just written to Miss Butman,[91] that I cannot come to Worcester at present, since our Adirondac party sets out on Monday Morning & promises to stay out 2, 3, or 4 weeks.[92] I have even, beyond that, some glimpse of a duty to carry my wife to Naushon, on the 31 August.[93] Will you & your friends not blot me out of remembrance, but let me join some future lily- or lake-party, when these present lilies [94] are faded? It must be so, & we will not always live in a hurry or a *contretemps.*

[95] I have heard not so much as I wished of your mountain journey [96] but both from Henry T. & Edward Hoar that it had its rewards.

Yours affectionately,

R. W. Emerson.

To Sarah? Sturgis? Shaw, Concord, July 30, 1858

[MS listed and partly quoted in Francis Edwards, Nov., 1920, where the name of the person addressed is given as " Mrs. Shaw "; includes Emerson's statement that no " valuable thought " or " good line of poetry " had yet come from " the new psychologists." It seems probable that the Mrs. Shaw of this letter was Sarah Sturgis Shaw, mother of the soldier Robert Gould Shaw (*cf.* Apr. 23, 1868).]

90. MS owned by Mr. W. T. H. Howe; ph. in CUL.

91. *Cf.* Apr. 8, 1858.

92. *Cf.* earlier letters and Aug. 5, 1858. The story of this first encampment of the Adirondack Club has been told by Stillman in *The Autobiography of a Journalist,* 1901, I, 239 ff.; by Emerson in *Journals,* IX, 159–161, and in his poem " The Adirondacs "; and by E. W. Emerson in *The Early Years of the Saturday Club,* pp. 169 ff., where Stillman's painting of the campers is reproduced.

93. *Cf.* Aug. 26, 1858.

94. *Cf.* Thomas Wentworth Higginson's " Water-lilies," first published in *The Atlantic* for Sept., 1858.

95. The remainder of the letter, including Emerson's name, is from a MS scrap in the hand of Blake, where it is followed by this explanation:

" May, 13, 1885. The above is a copy, just now made, of the remainder of this note, the original of which copy, I propose to send to Miss E. E. Kenyon. Date of the note 27 July 1858."

96. See July 1, 1858, to William Emerson.

To Henry Whitney Bellows, Concord, August 1, 1858

[MS listed in American Art Association, Mar. 10–11, 1924, and partly quoted there. Emerson commends Josephine Hosmer to friends of Bellows in Brooklyn.]

To Charles S. Farley, Concord? August 1, 1858

[Farley, Brooklyn, July 26, 1858, asks for " Country Life " or some other lecture for about the second week in January; Farley, Aug. 28, 1858, acknowledges Emerson's letter of the first and gives Jan. 11 as the date of the lecture.]

To Lidian? Emerson, Saranac, New York, August 5, 1858

[Ellen Emerson, Aug. 3–9, 1858 (under date of Aug. 9) , said her father's letter dated Saranac, Aug. 5, had arrived that morning.]

To John Murray Forbes, Concord, August 26, 1858 [97]

Concord
26 August 1858

My dear Sir,

Your island has such a fame in these parts, that my children [98] think one may well go to Adirondac by way of study & preparation for Naushon. My wife & Ellen refuse to go without me, or to let me go without them, and since the invitation is reckoned a command, you must take us all on Tuesday.

Mr Sanborn's term [99] begins on the 7th September.

With kind regards,
R. W. Emerson

Mr Forbes.

To William Stevens Robinson, Concord, September 9, 1858 [100]

Concord
9 Septr 1858

My dear Sir,

You scare me with your proposition, all friendly as it is meant. I have been drawn into this trap of a Cattle Show Speech, by

97. MS owned by RWEMA; ph. in CUL.
98. Cf. July 25, 1858, to Forbes, for a proposed visit to Naushon by two of Emerson's children.
99. For Forbes's interest in this school, cf. Jan. 3, 1858.
100. MS owned by the New York Historical Society; ph. in CUL.

neglecting to say *No* early enough; and have only consoled myself that it did not signify much what I should say to a few of my neighbors in the obscurity of our Town Hall. But, though ordinarily nervous enough about Reporters, it did not occur to me that the New York Tribune would be in the gallery.[101] I beseech you to banish from your mind a whim so absurd as the applying your telescope to our small things in Concord.

If there must be any reporting, — as I think there will not, — for all is shut up in a hall under a doorkeeper, you shall have any advantage I can give you. But I trust there will be none at all.

Yours with great regard,
R. W. Emerson

Mr Robinson.

To Sarah Swain Forbes, Concord, September 18, 1858 [102]

Concord
Friday Ev^g
18 September

My dear Mrs Forbes,

I am just come home from the city, where I had a great mortification. At Naushon,[103] I wrote some verses in your Island Book,[104] which seemed to me to belong well enough to your landscape. I am not sure that the first sketch of them did not originate at Naushon, a year ago. At any rate, when Lowell asked me for verses to print in the " Atlantic " seven or eight months ago, I gave him these with others to choose from.

101. For Robinson as correspondent of the *Tribune* from 1857 to 1861 and at intervals thereafter, see his " *Warrington* " *Pen-portraits*, ed. by his wife, 1877, *passim*. Emerson's fear of the press was not unfounded. The *Daily Evening Traveller*, of Boston, printed on Sept. 30, 1858, an account of the " Cattle Show at Concord " which included a fairly lengthy synopsis of Emerson's address. The " Address " as printed in *Transactions of the Middlesex Agricultural Society, for the Year 1858*, pp. 45–52, was described as " corrected from the Report in the Boston Courier." As for Robinson's own paper, the *New-York Daily Tribune* lived up to its reputation and printed, on Oct. 1 following, a full report of what it called " Farmers and Farming."

102. MS owned by RWEMA; ph. in CUL. Though Sept. 18 was Saturday in 1858, that year is proved by evidence cited below.

103. Probably in early September of this year; *cf.* Aug. 26, 1858.

104. The MS *Island Book*, a register and album for the use of visitors to Naushon, is described in *Letters and Recollections of John Murray Forbes*, I, 108. Mr. W. Cameron Forbes informs me that the book, begun in 1833, is now completing its seventh volume and that " Waldeinsamkeit " remains where Emerson wrote it.

He took the other pieces, & rejected this, I continuing to fancy this. Wishing yet to give my poor rhymes a chance with a selectest audience, I wrote them in your book. What was my vexation yesterday to find them printed in the Atlantic for October! [105] I went to Sub-Editor, whom I found on the ground, and asked how he had broken the rule " to send me a proof of every line of mine before printing "? He said, " he had found this & printed it when I was in the Adirondac "; [106] & appeared greatly pleased with his efficiency!

Will you please now with a sharp pair of scissors to cut the dishonored leaf clean out of the Book, I contracting to replace it with new &, I hope, better matter, at an early day. If I cannot find the rhymes at home, I do not know but I shall come by stealth & land at Naushon from a poacher's boat, & find my way to " Apollo " & " Briareus " [107] to hear what the beeches say.

Meantime, in great shame & tribulation, I am yours with better meaning

R. W. Emerson

Mrs Forbes.

To Thomas Carlyle, Concord, October 5, 1858 [108]

Concord

Oct. 5, 1858

Dear Carlyle,

If Elizabeth Hoar comes where you are,[109] I pray you to receive her as a lady of the highest worth. She is the friend of many excellent persons, yet an adorer of truth above all persons. You will find none who knows your genius better, yet the mould in which she was

105. This October number, in which, as Emerson says, " Waldeinsamkeit " was published, was announced for sale in the *Boston Daily Advertiser* of Sept. 18, 1858. It is clear, then, that the present letter follows close upon the discovery that the verses had been printed against his will.

106. See the letters of July 27 and Aug. 5, 1858.

107. " The gray old gods whom Chaos knew " are mentioned in " Waldeinsamkeit " as hiding in a watery nook of Naushon. According to family tradition, Apollo and Briareus were notable beech trees, and Apollo was the tallest tree on the Island. Mr. W. Cameron Forbes remembers Briareus, reaching up from a hollow called the Amphitheatre.

108. MS owned by RWEMA; ph. in CUL.

109. For Elizabeth Hoar's sailing for Europe, see a letter of Oct. 18 following. *Cf.* also Oct. 5, 1858, to Patmore, which names her brother and Miss Prichard as fellow passengers.

made will hardly allow the finest genius in the world to warp her. She has in her blood & family eminent claims to honor; & not less in herself. She should have been my sister, if my brother Charles had lived, & has been as my sister all my life. I hope Mrs Carlyle may see her, & think better of us New England people than her husband does. Ever yours,
T. Carlyle, Esq.   R. W. Emerson

To Coventry Patmore, Concord, October 5, 1858

[Printed in Basil Champneys, II, 382–383; introduces Elizabeth Hoar, as does the letter of the same date to Carlyle.]

To Gisela von Arnim, Concord? October? 5? 1858?

[Mentioned in July 10, 1859. For the probable date, cf. the letters of Oct. 5, 1858.]

To Richard Henry Stoddard, Concord, October 11, 1858 [110]

Concord
Oct. 11, 1858

My dear Sir,

I confess, I fancy it a little awkward to go to *writing* my verses for the press,[111] when printing answers the purpose so vastly better, but the kind manner in which you please to urge your request, leaves me no choice but to comply, and you see what I have made of it. You should have indicated the size & form of page which you preferred, and if my copy does not suit your page, I can try again, &, next time, with a quill, instead of steel, to which *aging* eyes have driven me.

I recognized at once your name with which & some of your verses I have long been familiar

With great regard,
Your obed^t servant,
R. W. Emerson.

Mr Stoddard.

110. MS owned by the Authors Club, New York; ph. in CUL.
111. According to a note formerly filed with a photostat of this letter in the New York Public Library, a Stoddard collection included a signed autograph transcript of " The Humble-bee."

To William Emerson, Concord, October 18, 1858 [112]

Concord
Oct 18 1858

Dear William,

By way of adventure, just to see what comes of it, to write a letter to Staten Island, I must try to send you our greetings & news. We believe you to be safe & sound, for a *Home Journal* comes duly to us with your beneficent superscription. Nay, a copy of the *N. Y. Express* came, in which, and in the *Tribune*, we read with great eyes the history of the Staten Island Revolution,[113] the Reign of Terror, the Burning of the Bastille, &c, not a little startled to find the Judge himself, that model citizen, father, & gentleman of the old school, an orator & ring-leader of the *bonnet rouge*. Well, there is much to say on both sides. No wonder you would be quit of your bad neighbors. We shall all be glad to have you. — But the manner of it — — I will not argue till I see you. We have been sending away Elizabeth H.[114] and hearing of her safe arrival at Halifax, & now she is in England; and now for a week or two we have been told that Susan was on the point of coming to Boston, had come, or should have come. But up to this moment, she comes not to Concord, nor sends us any word; so I firmly disbelieve the whole rumor. But I still hope it is an aurora of her coming. We shall be too glad to see her here. Edith goes down to school every day at Cambridge,[115] but is presently to live with Mrs Lowell for the winter. Ellen goes back as quietly to Mr Sanborn, as if she had never left the village; and Alice Jackson has come to stay with us this quarter, & attend the school " *Ancora imparo* " said Michel Angelo,[116] & so say these graduated maidens.

112. MS owned by HCL; ph. in CUL.

113. The *New-York Daily Tribune*, Sept. 3 and 4, 1858, tells how the people of Staten Island feared that yellow fever would spread from the quarantine station there to their homes, how the Board of Health at Castleton condemned the quarantine as a nuisance, and how a mob of Staten Islanders destroyed it. In the *New-York Evening Express* of Sept. 3 the same events inspired alarmist headlines: " Latest from Staten Island. Highly important. Tremendous Excitement. The Incendiaries again at Work. The Yellow Fever Panic. Another Destructive Conflagration. The Brick Row Burnt! The Marine Hospital All in Ruins! The Docks Destroyed! " And so forth.

114. The *Boston Daily Advertiser*, Oct. 7, 1858, shows that Miss E. Prichard, Miss E. Hoar, and Edward S. Hoar, of Concord, sailed for Liverpool on the " Niagara," Oct. 6.

115. To attend Agassiz's school; *cf*. Feb. 21, 1859. Both Agassiz's school and Mrs. Lowell are mentioned in earlier letters.

116. That is, " Anchora inparo." As the letter of July 8, 1840, shows, Emerson was acquainted with R. Duppa, where the anecdote appears on p. 174 and the design expressing the same sentiment is reproduced in an appendix.

Of Aunt Mary, I have had somewhat to write you since E. H. went away. Elizabeth found that Aunt was only willing to pay $3. for her board; [117] and when Mrs Wright refused to keep her for that sum, Elizabeth paid the difference without telling Aunt. Mrs Wright found that 4.00 was not enough, and at last Elizabeth paid $5., but for what time, I could not learn from her. Her payment ended on the 2ᵈ September. Since that I have paid at the same rate, and, as Elizabeth showed me that Aunt was now rich enough to be able to pay 4. per week, I shall let her pay so much, & divide the other dollar each week with you. The only difficulty that occurs to me, is, the explanation with her to be made that she is to pay 4.00 She is indignant when she is charged more than 3. But we outsiders all agreed that 5. was little enough for Mrs W. to charge.

I am trying to publish my " Conduct of Life," [118] this autumn or winter; but it is not yet ready. You must read a brilliant chapter on Caleb Cushing by Lowell in the new Atlantic; [119] wife & children all gone up for the night, or would severally send their best loves. Your brother

Waldo E.

To Peter Kaufmann, Concord, October 18, 1858 [120]

Concord Oct 18 1858

My dear Sir,

I received a few days ago your letter & book,[121] and was very glad to hear once more from you, & in so significant a manner. A book which a man of your depth has considerately written & published, I take for granted, is a piece of thorough work which can well wait for our whims & preoccupations to be past, & will approve itself good to all eyes as they come to it. But I should gladlier have had a book of results, in which you left us to divine the premises. And I am now & then looking about in the " Temple," to spy where you have lodged the few formulas which contain the whole, & for which all was written. I have

117. Mary Moody Emerson's intention to come to Concord some months earlier is noted in May 2, 1858.

118. The book was delayed for two years.

119. " A Sample of Consistency," in *The Atlantic* for Nov., 1858.

120. MS owned by Miss Mary E. Herbst; ph. in CUL. *Cf.* letters to Kaufmann of Mar.–May, 1857.

121. Kaufmann's *The Temple of Truth, or the Science of Ever-progressive Knowledge; containing the Foundation and Elements of a System for Arriving at Absolute Certainty in all Things,* Cincinnati and Canton, O., 1858. The book is anything but Emersonian in its formal and detailed definition and argument.

already come upon one or two of them, each of which is worth any twenty pages at least. When I have satisfied myself that I have found all that is for me in the book, I shall introduce it to the knowledge of some good readers in my neighborhood, & we will see what they can make of it. It is a great comfortt that it comes from a precise mind which uses language accurately; and that it marches with method; &, best of all, to a moral determination. For a loving aim glorifies a whole work. If I were younger, as I told you perhaps already, I should not let such a correspondence sleep as you so magnanimously begun, and did your part in; and I am always believing, that, if I once get certain tasks well off my mind, I shall recover a heart of youth again, & shall meet noble propositions & proposers nobly. Meantime you must indulge me, & hope the best for me, as you will.

With thanks & best wishes,
Your debtor,
R. W. Emerson

Mr Kaufmann.

To William H. Fish, Concord, October 22, 1858 [122]

Concord, 22 Oct 1858

My dear Sir

      I cannot quite settle it in my mind whether you have had any answer to your note of the summer? [123] — yea or nay, I cannot tell. If you had, it referred to a further writing, which it is quite time to make: if you had not, it is overtime now. Of course, I should like to go to Cortland, if I go into your region. And just now there is a little knot of propositions, which, if they can be combined, might untie well. I am to be at Albany on 13 Jan.ʸ. Might I not go thence, on the 14ᵗʰ to Auburn; on Saturday 15 to Cortland; & spend Sunday there, as you bade me: on Monday, 17ᵗʰ to Port Byron; on 18ᵗʰ to Batavia; & thence to Cleveland, for the 20th?

I accepted the invitation to Cleveland, long since, when I supposed it might be followed by letters which almost annually come from Buffalo

122. MS owned by Mr. Ernest Dressel North; ph. in CUL. Probably, as the final sentence suggests, Emerson wrote about the same time to other persons regarding lectures.

123. Fish replied from Cortland, N. Y., Oct. 25 following, that the present letter was the only one he had received in answer to his own of the last summer. All the lecture engagements listed below, except that for Port Byron, are mentioned in the letters of Jan., 1859.

& other cities on your central road; but, this year, my letters come rather from the south, than the west. Now please to answer me at once, out of your goodness, whether your people will pay me Thirty dollars for a Lyceum lecture on Saturday 15 Jan.ʸ If so, I will gladly bring you any *unprofessional* aid I can on Sunday 16ᵗʰ. And if the other parties to whom I write agree sufficiently, I will come to you on that day above named.

With great regard,
R. W. Emerson.

Rev Mr Fish.

To William Emerson, Concord, October 25, 1858 [124]

Concord
25 Oct. 1858

Dear William, It was only on Saturday mornᵍ I discovered this main portion of my letter to you fluttering among waste papers in my study & fancied that I had probably put into the envelope in lieu of it another fragment which I had once begun to you & then mislaid. But at all risks I put this now on its way. On my return on Saturday night from Brookline I found your letter & learned with consternation that I had passed by Susan to go to Abel Adams's; and a note also from Henry James, to invite me to spend Sunday with him in Boston. I have sent Edith today to Susan, to bring her home to us or to say when she wills that I shall come for her. There is much for her & for us to tell & to ask on all sides, & I trust she does not mean to hurry by us. Aunt Mary has just been packed up & carried to Boston to Mrs Cobb's, — a large part of Concord assisting; but will probably return tomorrow.

Affectionately, W.aldo

To George Field, Concord, November 15, 1858 [125]

Concord
15 Nov. 1858

Dear Sir,

I have let your note lie too long unanswered, in the wish to offer you a fixed day. But I have too many contingencies at this moment

---

124. MS owned by HCL; ph. in CUL. The inclosed " main portion of my letter " was perhaps one of the two sheets belonging to the first letter of Oct. 18, 1858.

125. MS owned by Mr. Winthrop B. Field; ph. in CUL. The MS memorandum

hanging to be able to name a time for visiting Athol. Perhaps in a few days I may be ready to propose a day.

I read with sorrow the sad loss you tell me of, & of which I had no hint before. I remember the engaging child, and, as far as I knew, with every promise of life. Life is deep & serious in view of such presence & absence.

With sympathy and respect, yours,

R. W. Emerson

Dr Field.

To HENRY JAMES, SR., CONCORD, NOVEMBER 15, 1858

[MS, incomplete, owned by Mr. Henry James; printed in R. B. Perry, I, 86.]

To ———— McCARTER, CONCORD, NOVEMBER 23, 1858

[MS listed in Newark Galleries, Dec. 10, 1931; Emerson offers to sell some recently purchased land.]

To WILLIAM EMERSON, CONCORD, NOVEMBER 26, 1858 [126]

Concord
Nov 26 1858

Dear William,

I was instructed some days ago to write to you & thank Susan for the bundle of blackberries, which arrived in perfect order, during (& this was the point of emphasis in the instructions) the absence of Lidian in Boston, & so failed to secure her instant acknowledgment. She sends her love & thanks to Susan.

Your umbrella came safely to me from the conductor, & I will bring it to you. So also your copy of my head shall come by me if Mr Prichard will not take charge of it.

The next important point is, that Aunt Mary fully intends to go with me to N. Y., arriving there on the P. M. of 15th December, on her way to

---

book for 1857 indicates that Emerson had lectured at Athol, Mass., on Dec. 15 of that year. I have no evidence that he returned as a result of the request alluded to in the present letter. Field was a physician at Athol (*The Massachusetts Register* for 1857 and later). A letter of July 25, 1859, is also to him. According to the *Harvard Alumni Bulletin*, Jan. 15, 1931, there was a third letter to the same correspondent.

126. MS owned by HCL; ph. in CUL.

Williamsburg.[127] I go to Hartford on the 14th: [128] we shall spend the night there, & take the next days train to N. Y. Your letter has just arrived containing the important announcement very welcome to me on this occasion, that you are in Lamartine Place. You shall have your aunt & brother for guests that night, it seems pretty certain. On the 16th I go to Philadelphia.[129] I should have said, on the 15th I speak at Brooklyn,[130] — 16th at Phila.; 17th probably back to N. Y., & home. Then again I am to be at Brooklyn on the 11 January: [131] and, as I have no engagement on the 12th I shall probably stay in the city that day & go to Albany on the 13th Jany [132] We had a very good day yesterday with our usual company, Mrs Ripley & family, Dr Jackson & family, G. P Bradford Mr Wainwright, Mr Channing, &c.

Ever affectionately, Waldo E

I see that I also go to Baltimore for Tuesday 4 Jany [133] and so shall probably be in N. Y. on my return on 6th Jan

I had an invitation lately from Prof. J J Mapes, of Mechanics Institute, 18 & 20 Fourth Avenue,[134] inviting me to read one or two Lectures at the Cooper Institute, & requesting terms &c. Since my reply expressing willingness, but also with a willingness to receive a hundred dollars, I have not heard from him. If you know the man or the Association, I should like to suggest to them that I shall be in N. Y. at liberty on the 12th Jan.y [135] and if they are of a condition to higgle for prices, I will listen to reason when I am in N. Y. without going for their sake. &c. &c. Yet tis never desireable to me to speak in the city, until the courts will issue an injunction on the Tribune office & others.

127. She was to spend most of her remaining years at Williamsburg, L. I.

128. In spite of bad weather, a large audience came to hear " The Law of Success " at Hartford, Conn., on Dec. 14 (*Hartford Daily Post,* Dec. 14 and 15, 1858) .

129. The *Public Ledger,* Dec. 16, 1858, announced " The Law of Success " for that evening.

130. I have found no newspaper notice of this lecture, but the MS memorandum book for 1858 gives Dec. 15 to Brooklyn.

131. Emerson read " Country Life " before the Brooklyn Mercantile Library on Jan. 11 (*New-York Daily Tribune,* Jan. 11 and 12, 1859) .

132. See Jan. 13, 1859.

133. See Jan. 2, 1859.

134. *Trow's New York City Directory . . . For the Year Ending May 1, 1860* shows that James J. Mapes was editor of a farm periodical and president of the Mechanics' Institute, 20 Fourth Ave.

135. Apparently Emerson read no lecture at the Cooper Institute at that time.

To Abel Adams, Concord, December 13, 1858 [136]

> Concord
> Dec 13 Monday

My dear friend,

     If you have not sent me Gilberts interest, will you please make it payable to J. M. Cheney, cashier, Concord, Mass$_{tts}^{tts}$; as I am setting out, this morning, for N. Y. & Philadelphia, to be gone a few days. Mr Dixwell,[137] on Saturday, gave me good accounts of you all.

  With love to all your household,

> Ever yours affectionately
> R. W. Emerson

Mr Adams.

To John S. Tyler, Concord, December 18, 1858

[MS listed in Chicago Book & Art Auctions, Dec. 15, 1931; Emerson accepts an invitation to the celebration of the Burns centenary on condition that he can get released from a speaking engagement. John S. Tyler, as president of the Boston Burns Club, signed the account of the celebration, containing Emerson's speech, reprinted from the *Boston Daily Advertiser* in *Littell's Living Age,* Mar. 19, 1859.]

To Jessie White Mario, Concord? December 19? 1858

[Mentioned in Dec. 19, 1858, to William Emerson. Mme Meriton Mario, better known as Jessie White, was a lecturer on Italian liberalism; she came to America in Nov., 1858 (Howard R. Marraro, *American Opinion on the Unification of Italy,* 1932, p. 218).]

To William Emerson, Concord, December 19, 1858 [138]

> Concord
> 19 Decr 1858

Dear William,

     May I give you the trouble to forward this enclosed letter to Madame Mario. I have mislaid her note & address but the bookshop

136. MS owned by RWEMA; ph. in CUL. Dec. 13 fell on Monday in 1858, the year endorsed, apparently in the hand of Abel Adams; and the same year is confirmed by the reference to the trip to New York and Philadelphia (*cf.* the letters of Nov. 26 and Dec. 19, 1858, to William Emerson).

137. Presumably John J. Dixwell, president of a Boston bank, whose residence, according to the *Boston Directory,* 1858, was in West Roxbury. *Cf.* Aug. 19? 1870.

138. MS owned by HCL; ph. in CUL.

which sells her tickets in N. Y. will certainly know it. I am sorry to give
you the annoy. I go tomorrow morning to Hamilton & Toronto.[139] I
had an easy & pleasant passage enough home [140] in the Stonington-boat
train excepting the odious hour of its arrival in Boston on the coldest
of mornings at 4.30 The captain of the boat, instructed by Mr Bovee,
was extremely kind. All at home well. My short visit at your house makes
me wish to go again.

                                                          Waldo E

To Francis H. Underwood, Concord, December 19, 1858 [141]

                                                        Concord
                                                        Dec 19 1858
My dear Sir,

        I ought to have sent you this MS., of which I spoke to you be-
fore, but, in going to Philadelphia, forgot it. It was left with me by
C. G. Ripley, Esq. who recᵈ it of the author Mr Collins,[142] on shipboard.
If not received by you he desires I see that it may be sent to the N. Y.
Times. I am going westward a little while,[143] & so pray your kind atten-
tion to this circumstance

                                                      Respectfully,
                                                      R. W. Emerson
Mr Underwood.

To John S. Tyler? Concord, December 27, 1858

[MS listed, without the name of the person addressed, in C. F. Libbie & Co.,
Apr. 26 and 27, 1904; described there as " in reference to the Burns Festival."
Cf. Dec. 18, 1858.]

    139. I am indebted to Mr. Carl F. Klinck for newspaper notices of these Canadian
lectures of Emerson's. *The Daily Spectator and Journal of Commerce,* of Hamilton,
Dec. 23, 1858, announced " Works and Days " for the benefit of the Mercantile
Library Association on that evening. *The Leader,* Toronto, Dec. 18, had stated that
Emerson would read " The Law of Success " under the auspices of the Ontario
Literary Society on the 22d of that month.
    140. For Emerson's recent visit to New York, cf. Dec. 13, 1858.
    141. MS owned by HCL; ph. in CUL.
    142. Probably William Wilkie Collins. His earlier interest in *The Atlantic* and
his willingness to contribute to it are shown in his letter of Dec. 30, 1857, to Under-
wood (Bliss Perry, p. 250). Apparently, however, nothing by Collins was printed
in *The Atlantic* and there seems to have been nothing over his signature in *The
New-York Times* for a month or more after this letter was written.
    143. Cf. the letters of Jan., 1859.

To William Emerson, Concord, December 31, 1858 [144]

Concord
31 Dec[r] 1858

Dear William,

Tis not even yet quite certain whom I am to bring along with me to your house. Edith is resolute to go; but the bad weather inflames her throat, & Ellen has been resolute that her mother should go; but the day & hour of departure are making it very improbable. So please do not look for us until we come. Meantime, with the best love & hope of tomorrow, there should go with this note a copy of Burns for Haven to read on the Twenty fifth January; [145] and a pencil for Charles; and I am almost sorry that William has grown quite too great than that we should dare send him any tokens. So we will put in an emblematic blank book. What multitudes of fair pages he is to fill! & how well! There is a little prism for Emily [146] with rainbows. The year goes out in storm, but the old sun is always behind. With dear love from all of us to all of you, Affectionately,

Waldo E.

To Francis H. Underwood? Concord? 1858

[MS listed and partly quoted in C. F. Libbie & Co., May 1, 1912, where it is described as relating to a contribution to *The Atlantic*. " Here," Emerson says, " is a first installment." Several contributions by him were published by that magazine in 1858.]

To Anna Jackson Lowell, Concord? c. 1858?

[A fragment is quoted in *Memoirs of Members of the Social Circle in Concord*, 2d series, 2d part, p. 175 (same page in *Emerson in Concord*). As the letter relates to the discontent of young Charles Russell Lowell, the most plausible date would be about 1858, when he was in his early twenties. He was born in 1835, and during the years 1861–1864 he served as an officer in the Union army, dying of his wounds on Oct. 20, 1864 (*Harvard Memorial Biographies*, 1866, I, 296).]

144. MS owned by HCL; ph. in CUL.
145. The centenary of Burns's birth and the day of Emerson's speech at the Burns dinner in Boston (*cf.* Dec. 18, 1858).
146. For Emily Jenks, see Apr. 15, 1858, to William Emerson.

1859

To WILLIAM EMERSON, BOSTON, JANUARY 2, 1859 [1]

American House.
Boston. Sunday
2 Jan.

Dear William,

Edith was quite too unwell, yesterday, with inflamed throat,[2] to come with me, & most reluctantly postponed her visit to the 11th.[3] Lidian had found lions in the way, &, to Ellen's great displeasure, had postponed her visit already to the 11th You may *then* look for an incursion of small & great.

I am advised that tis better to set off for N. Y. by tonight's mail-train, at 6.30 P. M.[4] But I am a little in the dark where I shall alight in N. Y. at 3 A. M.!! Perhaps I shall find tis best to go forward at once to Phila. & Baltimore.[5] So do not look for me, (if I do not come to Lamartine Place,) until the 5th — or 6th

Ever affectionately,
Waldo E

To ELLEN EMERSON, BOSTON, JANUARY 10, 1859 [6]

American House
10 January

Dear Ellen,

It seems Iphianassa is Lucretius's synonym for Iphigenia [7] —

1. MS owned by HCL; ph. in CUL. Jan. 2 fell on Sunday in 1859, the year clearly indicated by the evidence cited below.

2. *Cf.* Dec. 31, 1858.

3. See Jan. 13, 1859.

4. This hour of departure is given for the "New York Sunday Mail Train" in the *Boston Daily Advertiser,* Jan. 3, 1859.

5. The *Baltimore American,* Jan. 4, 1859, announced the "Law of Success" before the Mercantile Library Association that evening.

6. MS owned by RWEMA; ph. in CUL. The year is fixed by evidence cited below.

7. In *De Rerum Natura,* Book I, ll. 62–93.

did you hear Mr Sanborn's account of it last night So the lady was well-advised.

I inclose for Mrs Brown her dividend from B. & Providence Railroad, 24.00 — Mr Cheney will pay the cheque. I have paid Bigelow & Kennard.[8]

I *believe* I left you 25. (Jewetts money & 5.) to pay on Walcott & Holdens a/c; and the other \$20. should go to Reynolds & Derby, on theirs. You will find their bills in the *"Unpaid"* file. I will send you money by Edith for the Kimball & Wight, & more afterwards. I have paid Mr Jewett. I shall be at Albany 13 [9] (Care of Mercantile Lib.y Assoc.)

Cortland, N. Y. 15

(Care Rev. W. H. Fish.) [10]

Batavia, N. Y. 18th care W. G. Bryan [11]

Cleveland, Ohio, 20th M. L. Assocn [12]

Ann Arbor, Michigan,[13] Richd. Beardsley 21st

And letters may be sent to Cortland N. Y. or Cleveland Ohio, best.

If you can find President Wheeler's [14] letter, which I think may be in your mother's work table in her chamber, — it is not on my study table, which I searched, — you had better enclose it to *George M. Barnard Esq Commercial Wharf, Boston,* with these words, " My father on leaving home for a journey of a fortnight requested me to enclose this note from President Wheeler, to you."

Ellen E — ".

And so, with love to all, Goodbye,

Papa.

8. The *Boston Directory,* 1859, shows that Bigelow Bros. & Kennard were jewellers.

9. See Jan. 13, 1859.

10. The lecture of the 15th, " The Law of Success," was mentioned in *The Republican Banner,* Cortland Village, N. Y., Jan. 19, 1859, and was reported more fully *ibid.,* Feb. 9 following. For Fish, see Oct. 22, 1858.

11. According to an announcement in the *Genesee Weekly Democrat,* Batavia, N. Y., Jan. 8, 1859, signed by William G. Bryan and others, Emerson was to read " Town and Country " on Jan. 18.

12. This lecture of Jan. 20 before the Cleveland Library Association inspired an unfriendly report in the *Cleveland Daily Plain Dealer* of the following day. Emerson, said the writer, was a man of massive intellect but no lecturer — ". . . we had quite as lief see a perpendicular coffin behind a lecture-desk as Emerson. The one would amuse us as much as the other. Mr. Emerson is not the man to talk to the people of the West about the ' Law of Success.' "

13. The MS memorandum book for 1859 gives Jan. 21 to Ann Arbor, but I have found no notice in the local papers.

14. Perhaps John Wheeler, president of the University of Vermont until about ten years before this date and still closely associated with that institution in 1859.

To Ellen Emerson, Albany, New York, January 13, 1859 [15]

Albany

13 January

Dear Ellen,

      Tell mamma I left Edith very well in N. Y.[16] this morning preparing to go to the opera [17] this evening, with her Uncle & Cousin William. Yesterday I called on Mr & Mrs Bancroft. Mrs B. engaged me to let Edith come & dine with her on Sunday at 5 o'c, and Sandie Bliss should see her home, which proposition pleases Baby E: & she will go. Mr Bancroft carried me to Mr Astor's house to see Powers's California, a superb statue which has just arrived.[18] Mrs Edmund Quincy we found in the train to N. Y. and as she returns in the beginning of the week I proposed to put Edith under her protection. But Aunt Susan & the cousins plead for her stay until Thursday week when Mr Howland [19] will carry to Boston, & I left a contingent permission if as good an opportunity should not occur earlier. On arriving here, this P. M. my black bag does not appear, though I hold my baggage check for it. Luckily, the bag contains nothing but my toilette articles & no MSS. The Officials promise to find it yet. I hope, by this time, Mr A. Jackson has enabled you to pay G. Hosmer B. Hastings &c. &c.

Papa.

J. Brown, and Walcott, & Reynolds.[20]

I sent you 15. by Phebe R.[21]

15. MS owned by RWEMA; ph. in CUL. Evidence cited below and the Albany date line fix the year. The *Albany Evening Journal*, Jan. 13, 1859, announced " Town and Country " for the Young Men's Association that evening, and reported, on the following day, that there had not been room for all who came to hear.

16. For Edith's plan to come to New York on Jan. 11, see Jan. 2, 1859. Her return home is mentioned in Feb. 2 following. Emerson himself had read " Country Life " at the Brooklyn Mercantile Library on the 11th (*New-York Daily Tribune*, Jan. 11–12, 1859) .

17. Mlle Piccolomini was to make her farewell appearance in *La Traviata* this night (*New-York Daily Tribune*, Jan. 13, 1859) .

18. Hiram Powers's " California," dated 1858, was given by William B. Astor to the Metropolitan in 1872 (*The Metropolitan Museum of Art Catalogue of Sculpture*, 1908, p. 32) . At the present time this figure stands, as if placed by some one aware that Emerson had praised it, near Daniel Chester French's bronze bust of the Concord seer.

19. Perhaps the Francis Howland of Aug. 12, 1850. He is listed as a merchant in *Trow's* for 1859–1860.

20. This reminder, probably of further debts to be paid, was added above the date line.

21. Ripley, no doubt.

To Edith Emerson, Auburn, New York, January 14, 1859 [22]

Auburn

14 January

Dear Edith,

You must remember to ask your Uncle William if the Rowse head [23] came safely, for, if it is tumbled, we can perhaps manage to send him another. I hope you will be able to make a call on Aunt Mary & Mrs Parsons.[24] You were will [25] not forget to give Mary [26] a half dollar from me, and you must add a quarter for yourself, if you like.

I am almost tempted to say, since there is no mamma nor Ellen, that, if it is a cold day when you go to Mrs Bancroft,[27] you should not go drest in such summery shortness, if you have winter sleeves, for it makes one feel that you must be cold. A happy ride home to you on the earliest day though I like well that you should enjoy the excellent friends of 29th Street.

Papa.

To William Emerson, Concord, February 2, 1859 [28]

Concord

2 February, 1859

Dear William,

Have the Masons still a house at Porto Rico? [29] I do not remember whether I did not hear that Mr John Mason was established at Philadelphia In the uncertainty, I will say, that, if they still retain their old foothold, I wish to commend Theodore Parker to their good offices, if he should, during the winter, land on that island. He sails this week

22. MS owned by RWEMA; ph. in CUL. The year 1859, added by another hand, is clearly correct. Emerson had left his daughter in New York the day before (cf. Jan. 13, 1859). His reading of " The Law of Success " on Jan. 14 is recorded in the *Auburn Daily Advertiser,* Jan. 14–15, 1859.

23. Cf. July 19, 1858.

24. Hannah Haskins Parsons.

25. The change in structure occurs at the beginning of a page.

26. Possibly a servant, but the reference is not clear.

27. Cf. Jan. 13, 1859.

28. MS owned by HCL; ph. in CUL.

29. William Emerson replied, Feb. 4, 1859 (MS owned by Dr. Haven Emerson), that he had learned the name of Sidney Mason's successor, and that Sanborn had called and told of the plans of Parker and his party.

from N. Y. to Sta. Cruz *via* New Providence, in the English steamer. Mrs Parker, Hannah Stevenson, & Dr S. G. Howe, perhaps also Mrs Howe, will go with him, and, though he is badly broken, he has some good chances for rallying, & is a man to make the most of those he has.[30] Mr Sanborn will go with him to New York. If Mr Mason is at St Johns, tell him from me, that Mr P. is one of the costliest jewels of New England and that every good man is interested in his safekeeping. I trouble you thus, for I have never seen either of the Masons.

Edith came back wonderfully enriched by all her N. Y. experiences,[31] & has been feeding her sister & brother ever since with the same. Charles's wit is especially famed now in Concord. Dear love to all your house.

Waldo E

To Margaret P. Forbes, Concord? February 14, 1859

[Partly printed in *Journals,* IX, 170–171.]

To Edith Emerson, Concord, February 21, 1859 [32]

Concord, 21 Feby 1859

Dear Edith,

I enclose 38.00 Mr Agassiz's bill is 37.50 You will bring me back the bill receipted.

Papa.

To James Russell Lowell, Boston, February 27, 1859? [33]

American House
Boston, 27 Feb.^y.

Dear Lowell,

Miss Peabody wishes to read to a class she has in Boston

30. All the persons named sailed on the " Karnak," which cleared from New York for Havana and Nassau, apparently on the 9th (*The New York Herald,* Feb. 9, 1859).

31. *Cf.* the letters of Jan. 13 and 14, 1859.

32. MS owned by RWEMA; ph. in CUL. For Edith Emerson's attendance at Agassiz's school, see Oct. 18, 1858, to William and Feb. 15, 1864. A later term of this " School for Young Ladies " is announced in the *Boston Daily Advertiser,* July 7, 1859.

33. MS owned by HCL; ph. in CUL. The year offers some difficulty. Lowell's endorsement gives 1858; but this may have been written long after the letter was received, and I believe it is an error. Feb. 27 fell on Sunday in 1859, but not in 1858.

tomorrow (Monday) afternoon, her Essay on "*Primeval History,*" [34] which I sent to you once for the "Atlantic," & which was declined. Is it possible that it can be recovered, & at such short notice, & sent in to Phillips & Sampson's to be called for by her say at 2 o'c or 3 — P. M. tomorrow? If it can be, without spoiling you of an hour, pray send it by omnibus man, & we will gladly pay all charges. I was to have seen you at the Club, but you were too wise to come.

One more matter; please take notice, that we took no action yesterday on ballot for Cabot, but mean to ballot for him on the next Club day.

Ever yours,

R. W. Emerson.

Mr Lowell.

To Charles Eliot Norton, Concord, March 10, 1859 [35]

Concord

10 March

My dear Sir,

I thank you for your kind thoughtfulness in this notice duly given.[36] I wish I could make use of it today. — I cannot, nor yet for weeks, I fear: but before the course ends, I hope to hear the Professor, — which I have never done, — from his chair. I like to know his hours, even if I cannot use them.

I can find nothing to hold me in a London book, "Man & his dwelling," which the English journals discuss; [37] nor are their books very

---

Twice in the course of the present letter Emerson fixes the day as Sunday, the day of the week he was least likely to mistake; and the reference at the end to a meeting of the Saturday Club "yesterday" is especially noteworthy. An even stronger argument for 1859 is the allusion to Cabot, which exactly fits letters of Mar. 22 and 23, 1859.

34. Elizabeth Peabody may have used this paper in preparing some passages in her *Universal History*, New York, 1859.

35. MS owned by HCL; ph. in CUL. The year 1859, added in another hand, fits the evidence cited below, though so far as the month is concerned, April would be somewhat more plausible than March.

36. I have seen no letter from Norton that seems to contain the notice alluded to — apparently a notice of a course of lectures by Lowell at Harvard. Lowell's name has been written in another hand between the lines after the word "Professor."

37. James Hinton's *Man and his Dwelling-place* had been published anonymously on Feb. 17 of this year (*The Times*, London, Feb. 17, 1859) . Possibly the notices Emerson saw were in, or quoted from, English newspapers. Apparently few reviews on either side of the Atlantic paid much attention to the book, though there was something in *The Athenæum* for Mar. 5, 1859, and much in *Fraser's* for the following June.

often as good as their criticism; which is reversing Gray's rule.[38] My
Jamblichus,[39] — I am afraid I have never told you, — sits safe, & looks
encouragingly down from my shelf. — I am the more your debtor,
Mr Norton.   R. W. Emerson

TO JAMES I. WYER, CONCORD, MARCH 18, 1859 [40]

Concord
18 March 1859

My dear Sir,

When I saw you in the Fitchburg train,[41] I promised to send
you any information I might procure respecting the " Scientific School."
I saw Mr Agassiz shortly afterwards, who me that the chemical Professor
charged $75. for each of the two college terms,[42] and there were no
scholarships or abatements. I hoped that I might yet have seen Professor
Horsford, & so delayed writing; but I have been, & am too much occupied to go to Cambridge, & have not met him. I inquired of Dr C. T.
Jackson, what he tho't would be the value of a Chemical Course to your
son? he said, a year's course will make all chemical reading (in Agricultural or other books) intelligible to him, but will not make him a practical chemist, which requires much more time. I was a little daunted at
finding the rate of instruction so costly; that of the Zoologic Course is
much less. I think, Mr Agassiz said $50. a term. The expenses of the
chem. laboratory are great. Having so little to communicate, I did not
write; & now, having learned no more, only write to keep my word.
With my love to Mrs Wyer & kind regards to your family, Your cousin,
Mr Wyer.   R. W. Emerson

38. Gray thought " even a bad verse as good a thing or better than the best observation that ever was made upon it," as Emerson might have read in William Mason's
badly garbled selections from the letters in *The Poems of Mr. Gray*, York, 1775, p. 257.
39. *Cf.* Mar. 25? 1841.
40. MS owned by Mr. Malcolm G. Wyer; ph. in CUL. I am indebted to Dr. James
I. Wyer for information regarding his grandfather, the recipient of the present letter,
who had married Emerson's cousin Hannah Haskins Ladd in 1839. Their son, here
mentioned as a prospective student, was born in 1842 and was named for his father.
41. The MS memorandum book for 1859 notes " J. I. Wyer " under date of Feb. 26.
42. According to *A Catalogue . . . of Harvard University, for . . . 1858–1859*,
1859, p. 74, the fees in the chemical course were $50 a term for instruction and an
equal amount for laboratory apparatus and supplies. Horsford was dean of the Lawrence Scientific School. The " me " of the preceding line begins a page in the MS.

To Edith Emerson, Concord? March 22, 1859 [43]

22 March.

Dear Edith,

I send you a card to my lecture, having none by me of the other color. I shall be at the American House tomorrow. [44] Your mother will not try to go. Ellen seems to have made Mr Forbes believe, I am to be in Boston on Sunday. Of course, I shall not be.

Papa.

To Henry Wadsworth Longfellow, Concord, March 22, 1859 [45]

Dear Longfellow,

Please bear it in mind, that the name of J. E. Cabot is to be balloted for at our next Club. I believe I was charged to remind you.

Yours faithfully,

R. W. Emerson

Concord 22 March 1859

To ———————, Concord, March 22, 1859

[MS listed in C. F. Libbie & Co., Feb. 25–26, 1909. This, I conjecture, may be the same letter listed and partly quoted in Goodspeed's Book Shop, Jan., 1910, where it is dated only as to year but is described as asking " My Dear Professor " to see that the name of J. E. Cabot is balloted for at the next club. For the date, *cf.* the letters of Mar. 22 (to Longfellow) and 23, 1859. The person addressed might be any of the Harvard professors in the Saturday Club except Longfellow and Lowell — Agassiz, Felton, Holmes, or Peirce.]

43. MS owned by RWEMA; ph. in CUL. The year 1859, added in another hand, is doubtless correct.

44. For Emerson's Boston course beginning Mar. 23, 1859, see a note on Apr. 4 following.

45. MS owned by the Trustees of the Longfellow House, Cambridge; ph. in CUL. In his MS diary (also at the Longfellow House) , Longfellow records the club dinner of " Saturday 26 " but makes no mention of the voting. For Cabot's election, see Nov. 28, 1860, which explains the long delay.

To James Russell Lowell, Concord? March 23, 1859 [46]

Dear Lowell,

        Please bear in mind that the name of J. E. Cabot is to be balloted for at our next Club. We had no quorum in February,[47]

                        Yours,

                        R. W. Emerson

23 March

To Edith Emerson, Concord? April 2, 1859 [48]

                        Saturday, 2 April

Dear Edith,

        Ellen asks me to say this morning that Mr Sanborn & your Mother & Ellen mean to come to Mrs Lowell's [49] on Tuesday Evening. You must thank Mrs Lowell from me for my invitation; I am very sorry not to see what would interest me so much.

        Your Mother persuaded Ellen that there was a letter for her due on Thursday, which Ellen has been looking for — ever since. But I think you had not sent one.

                        Papa —

Here is your knife waiting.

To Elbridge G. Dudley, Concord, April 4, 1859 [50]

                        Concord

                        4 April 1859

My dear Sir,

        I have just learned from Mr Sanborn, that you are expecting me at the Music Hall, next Sunday. I cannot come. Indeed, I had a few words with you one night lately at the Freeman P. Chapel, & I said, I

---

    46. MS owned by HCL; ph. in CUL. Comparison with Mar. 22, 1859, to Longfellow, a fully dated letter, fixes the year.

    47. *Cf.* Feb. 27, 1859?

    48. MS owned by RWEMA; ph. in CUL. Apr. 2 fell on Saturday in 1859, and Edith Emerson attended Agassiz's school during the one term 1858–1859 (*cf.* Feb. 21, 1859).

    49. During her days at Agassiz's school, Edith lived with Anna Jackson Lowell. Mrs. Lowell wrote to Emerson, Cambridge, June (1859), that she did not wish to make any charge for the last few weeks, as Edith had been absent often and was very welcome in the house anyhow.

    50. MS owned by Goodspeed's Book Shop; ph. in CUL. Dudley had much later correspondence with Emerson in regard to addresses to the congregation that Parker had shepherded before his health was finally broken. The *Boston Directory*, 1859, lists Dudley as a counselor.

could not come whilst these lectures [51] were going on, & I understood you to reply, — ' Certainly, we will not expect you until they are ended.' — In fact, I am quite occupied during the week with the preparation of these, which are new, and my eyes do not allow me many hours in a day. You must do without me until the 27th April, &, if necessary, I will come to the Music Hall on the first day of May.[52]

But I am truly sorry if you have been relying on me for the next Sunday, which was never fixed, (I think we talked of 2d or 3d Sunday,) and which I tho't you acquiesced in giving up.

Yours respectfully,
R. W. Emerson

Mr Dudley.

To EDITH EMERSON, CONCORD, APRIL 4? 1859 [53]

Concord Monday
April 5

Dear Edith,

I am sorry to say, that Ellen cannot come to Cambridge, as she hoped, on Tuesday. She has exerted herself so much on her " Committee " duties, the past fortnight, as to lose much sleep & food, for she did not come home to dinner on several days, & now for two days, she has been quite down sick. So give her love to Mrs Lowell, & tell her not to expect her, which is a huge disappointment to Ellen. Last night, your mother had given up thought of going, but Ellen, who feels better today, thinks she shall be well enough by tomorrow to need no care, so that she thinks she shall persuade Mamma to go. I will write you a note, by this afternoon's mail, with her decision, for she is not awake. I hope you had a note by Mr Lowell on Saturday.[54]

Papa.

No, Alice tells me that she meant fully, last night, to go, & leave Ellen with her, Alice.[55]

51. Emerson's lectures at Freeman Place Chapel and (the last three) at the Boston Music Hall were announced by the *Boston Evening Transcript* on the days of delivery as follows: " The Law of Success," Mar. 23, 1859; " Originality," 30; " Clubs," Apr. 6; " Art and Criticism," 13; " Manners," 20; " Morals," 26.

52. The MS memorandum book gives that day to the Music Hall, but I have found no other evidence.

53. MS owned by RWEMA; ph. in CUL. The letter obviously belongs to the same year with that of Apr. 2, 1859. Monday, however, would have been Apr. 4, not 5; and Emerson would more easily have mistaken 4 for 5 than Tuesday for Monday.

54. Letter of Apr. 2, 1859, no doubt.

55. The Alice with whom Lidian Emerson was to leave Ellen may have been

To Edwin Percy Whipple, Concord, April 16? 1859?

[MS listed and partly quoted in C. F. Libbie & Co., Apr. 7–8, 1903, where it is dated simply Apr. 16; Emerson says he is too well pleased to know he has fallen into such good hands and promises to make out a list of the dates Whipple may want. It is apparently the same letter listed in Anderson Galleries, Mar. 31–Apr. 2, 1919, where it is said to have been written on Apr. 18 but is described as promising a list of dates. I conjecture that Whipple was gathering material for an article on Emerson; and perhaps the letter of Apr. 22, 1859, relates to the same project.]

To Edwin Percy Whipple, Concord, April 22, 1859

[MS listed and partly quoted in C. F. Libbie & Co., Apr. 7–8, 1903; Emerson says he is the eighth consecutive clergyman in a line reaching back to Peter Bulkeley and asks whether it was not time that he should bolt, for the necessity of change.]

To Mary Preston Stearns, Concord, April 27, 1859 [56]

Concord, Wednesday
27 April

My dear Mrs Stearns,

A day or two after I saw you in town, Frank surprised me, one morning, with a perfect heliotrope "for me,' he said, "from his mother." I made him say it over again to be sure of the fact, and there stood the flower without fault, all leaves & blooms, & filling the air of the house with perfume. I thought I would sit down in the afternoon & write you my thanks for the gift, — but I was whirled off by Mr Thoreau, who is planting a woodlot for me, & there was no writing. Next day came the inevitable work of the lecture, & would have no end, & all duties & honesties had to wait for the *theory* of duties. Now I have come home in peace to enjoy my beautiful flower, — but, is it in wrath for not postponing the whole world to its claims, — some leaves have withered. What to do? My wife is in Boston — I can't ride to Medford; — dare not experiment alone. I shall now take it in arms & carry it across the street

---

"Alice the sempstress" of Aug. 11, 1859. Whether she was Alice Jackson, who was much at Concord and who appears in Apr. 13, 1860, I am uncertain.

56. MS owned by Mr. F. R. Fraprie; ph. in CUL. The year 1859, added in another hand, was the only year in which Apr. 27 fell on Wednesday after the beginning of Emerson's acquaintance with the Stearns family and before the death of Thoreau. Thoreau records, Apr. 19–21, 1859, his setting pines "in R. W. E.'s Wyman lot" (*The Writings*, XVIII, 152–155).

to Mrs Brown who is wise in house-plants She shall deal with it, & give me lessons. Meantime, I beg you to accept my hearty thanks, & you shall hear of its health again. Yours faithfully,

R. W. Emerson

To ——————, Concord, April 27? 1859 [57]

Concord
27 April 1859

My dear friend,

Home again this afternoon I take the first moment I have had to thank you for your note, which I received a week ago tonight, — the lithographs only this morning. I am so glad of a note from you, that I need not tell you the afflictions of a very unskilful poor country gentleman, who undertakes at the same time to plant woodlots in his pasture, & write a lecture for the town, &, between the two, does not sleep o' nights. He has, for one thing, to write no letters, though he have notes from those he wishes would write more, & though they send him fountain-girls & parks in moonlight. But now, as then, I am very glad to be made partaker of your Newport visit; & these tokens from the painter himself, or, as you say, from Mrs H., I set a high value on. Whatever comes from William Hunt I think important, & shall often look at attentively: but now, I think the three first pictures which he bro't me before, the best. Yet I fancy I see what he prizes in the new ones, & both of these landscapes — shall I call them? — speak well enough. It is by no means indifferent to me, that Eddie, my boy, who is a great lover of pictures, grants very distinct praise of them. Will you not send my special thanks to your friends, when you write to them, — if I should delay my note. Or send me word if you think they would like to hear from me. Of course, though, I must write. I have " Rumour " Mrs Mary Shaw's copy, which she told me I might keep, & perhaps I shall. Shall I send it

57. MS owned by Mrs. Gorham Brooks; ph. in CUL. The day of the month is not clearly written and might be 21 rather than 27. The person addressed may, I conjecture, be Margaret P. Forbes, to whom, some two months before, Emerson had returned an earlier novel by Elizabeth Sara Sheppard, the author of *Rumour*, 1858 (*cf.* Feb. 14, 1859). The planting of a woodlot is mentioned in the letter of Apr. 27. The lecture for the town may be that promised conditionally in Apr. 4 preceding. Hunt's series of six lithographs, including " Girl at the Fountain " and " Deer in the Moonlight," is recorded in Helen M. Knowlton, *Art-life of William Morris Hunt*, 1899, p. 37. For Edward Waldo Emerson's visit to Hunt's studio at Newport and the artist's gift to him of some of these lithographs, see *The Early Years of the Saturday Club*, p. 467.

to you I ran thro' one volume. but the second stopped me by something disagreeable.

Ever yours,
R. W. Emerson

To THOMAS CARLYLE, CONCORD, MAY 1, 1859

[Incompletely printed in Ireland, *In Memoriam*, pp. 71–72, and in his *Ralph Waldo Emerson*, pp. 182–184. Ireland's fragments were reprinted in *C–E Corr.*, 1883. The presumably complete text was published in *C–E Corr.*, 1886. The fragmentary version contained in an unpublished entry of the diaries for 1859–1860 has, however, one variant sentence worthy of note: " School girls fill their folio sheets each day, & eyes so wary & much-omitting & which have learned to shut on so much are gathering an hourly harvest " (typescript *Journals*). Emerson wrote this letter in reply to Carlyle's of a few weeks earlier:

" Chelsea, London, 9 April, 1859

" Dear Emerson, — Long months ago there was sent off for you a copy of *Friedrich* of Prussia, two big red volumes (for wh^h Chapman the Publisher had found some ' safe swift ' vehickle) ; and *now* I have reason to fear they are still loitering somewhere, or at least have long loitered: sorrow on them! This is to say: If you have not *yet* got them, address a line to ' Saml F. Flower Esq, Librarian of Antiquarian Society *Worcester* Mass.' (forty miles from you, they say) ; and that will at once bring them. In the Devil's name! —

" I never in my life was so near choked; swimming in this mother of Dead Dogs, and a long spell of it still ahead! I profoundly *pity myself* (if no one else does) . You shall hear of me again if I survive; — but really that is getting beyond a joke with me; and I ought to hold my peace (even to you) and swim what I can.

" Your little Touch of Human Speech on *Burns* was charming; had got into the Papers here (and been clipt out by me) before y^r copy came; — and has gone far & wide since: Neuberg was to give it me in German from the *Allgemeine Zeitung;* but lost the leaf. — — Adieu, my Friend; very dear to me, tho' dumb.

" T. Carlyle (in such haste as seldom was) — "]

To ANNA BARKER WARD, CONCORD, MAY 5, 1859 [58]

Concord, 5 May, 1859.

My dear Anna,

       I cannot let these ugly chasms of time & space, & long disuse of speech or pen, bereave me of the right once conceded & prized to call you thus; though your children there,. & mine here, are growing up & skilful already to weigh the fine scruples of address. What if you go

58. MS owned by HCL; ph. in CUL. Excerpts I–III were printed in *Memoirs of Members of the Social Circle*, 2d series, 2d part, p. 257 (same page in *Emerson in Concord*) , from a draft in the MS *Journals*. For the Wards in Europe a year earlier and

away, & stay away, & try to hide yourself farther away from me in seclusions of opinion — you have ever been to me an endeared & enshrined person, beaming a generous & happy influence, & I must ever hold life richer for you, even when I do not say so. Then here is ever, if you are gone, the admirable Sam Ward, loyal, high-hearted, & sure; — without professions, but himself that which professions say, — and we look in his house for you! And here are these dear children. Tom I see almost daily, a boy whose innocence has not left him; I fancy sometimes that

---

for Mrs. Ward's conversion to Catholicism, see May 17, 1858, to Clough. Apparently Mrs. Ward had since remained abroad. Their children Thomas Wren Ward, Lydia von Hoffmann, and Elizabeth de Schönberg are named in Ward's will, signed Jan. 15, 1903, and filed on Nov. 18, 1907 (MS in Office of Register of Wills, Washington, D. C.). In the same document is the name of Ward's grandson Ward Thoron, son, I believe, of the Annie mentioned in the present letter (*cf.* July 10, 1868).

The draft mentioned above differs so widely from the text of the completed letter that I print it here (from typescript *Journals* for 1859–1860):

" I must lament the chance-wind that has made a foreigner of you, — whirled you from the forehead of the morning into the mediaevals, again. We can ill spare you, & there is none to supply your place, in the little society that I know. I suppose, to your taste for historic splendor, & poetic & mannered style, the old forms of your race looked cold & wanting, Well, to some natures, manner is so much, & Wordsworth said to me, ' yes, but the matter comes out of the manner,' — that we must try to resign you, whilst the spell lasts, to your own pleasure. If every body is unhappy about it, you must accept that cordial tribute to your genius, that we are unhappy unless you are happy in our way. To me, the difference of churches looks so frivolous, that I cannot easily give the deference that civility should, to one or another. To old eyes, how supremely unimportant the form, under which we celebrate the justice, love, & truth, the attributes of the Deity & the soul! A priest, as we know him, is a hat & coat, of whom or of which very little can be said: Usually an Irishman, though he comes to you from Rome."

I add here, from the typescript *Journals* (*O P Gulistan,* dated 1848, but containing matter belonging to various years) a fragment of a letter to " Anna " — apparently Anna B. Ward — which, to judge from its tone and from its reference to the calendar, may well have been written later in this month but could, so far as I know, be a part of *c.* 1855? or of some other letter I have not found:

" The faults of youth will not wash out, no nor the merits, & creeping time convinces ever the more of the insignificance of us & the irresistible bias. Still this is only science We must forever hold our companions responsible, or they are not companions, but stall-fed I think as we grow older, we decease as individuals & like an audience who hear stirring music, & only join emphatically in the chorus. So we volunteer no opinions, despair of guiding people, but are confirmed in our perception that Nature is ' all right, & that we have a good understanding with it We must shine to a few brothers as palms or pines or roses do, from their convenient nature, but tis almost chemistry at last, though a metachemistry. Here comes out around me at this moment the new June — the leaves say June, though the calendar says May — and we must needs hail our young relatives again, tho' with something of the gravity of adult sons & daughters receiving a late-born brother or sister. Nature herself seems a little ashamed of a law so monotonous, billions of summers & now the old game again without a new bract or sepal "

his deafness was some angelic guard to defend his ear from vulgarity &
vice. He is a darling of the young people, who all prize in him this in-
fantile purity & grace. Ellen, who is no sentimentalist, says he is always
picturesque, & the tones & play of his voice give no hint of infirmity. Of
Lily too, I hear frequent praises from Edith & Ellen. They say she has
made great steps lately, & is the loveliest guardian to Bessie. I should
not think it prudent to let you overhear my children prate about yours,
if you were not already setting your face homeward. Else, it were a stave
of the *Ranz des vaches*, & you could not stay where you are, even with
Annie to hold you. I grieve whenever I hear that you still suffer — But
what an alterative will this coming home be! Nothing should resist it!
You have suffered so bravely & so long — that you ought to reckon securely on that self-limiting rule of all distempers. *They* wear out, & usually much faster than we. Home & solitude, husband & children shall
heal you, and the silent benedictions of a wide neighborhood of friends
shall not be wanting.

Some day — a good while hence, you will perhaps tell me — I know
how perfectly you can, — of these journeys & abidings; possibly, too, of
the passages of religious experience, of which I have heard remotely.
Yet ^Ito me the difference^I between church & church ^{II}looks so frivolous,
that I cannot easily give the^{II} deference which a sympathetic civility
holds due ^{III}to one or another. To old eyes, how supremely unimportant the form under which we celebrate the Justice, Love, & Truth, —
the attributes of the Deity & the Soul!^{III} And how the few strokes of
character of the few persons " capable of virtue," we have seen (as Jona.
Phillips said of Dr C.) [59] reduce all we made so much of! Farewell now,
& peace & joy & possession present & endless be yours!

Affectionately,[60]

To Rebecca Duncan, Concord, May 6, 1859 [61]

Concord
6 May, 1859.

My dear Miss Duncan,

I enclose Mr Allingham's verses [62] which my daughter has
copied for you, & I hope you will like them as well as I do. Thanks for

59. Channing, no doubt.
60. The lower edge of the leaf, doubtless containing the signature, has been cut
away.
61. MS owned by Goodspeed's Book Shop; ph. in CUL.
62. A MS copy of William Allingham's " The Touchstone " is still with the letter.

the friendliest invitation which you renew to me to come to your sister's house.[63] I was always a slow visiter, but I shall keep your courtesy as a pleasant hope before me. —

With kind regards,

R. W. Emerson

Miss Duncan.

To James Elliot Cabot, Concord, May 10, 1859 [64]

Concord

10 May 1859

Tuesday Ev.ᵍ

My dear Cabot,

[1]I send back the book with thanks and as I said with some wonder at your interest in it. I sometimes think that you & your coevals missed much that I & mine found: for Calvinism was still robust & effective on life & character in all the people who surrounded my childhood, & gave a deep religious tinge to manners & conversation. I doubt the race is now extinct, & certainly no sentiment has taken its place on the new generation, — none as pervasive & controlling. But they were a high tragic school, & found much of their own belief in the grander traits of the Greek mythology, — Nemesis, the Fates, & the Eumenides, and, I am sure, would have raised an eyebrow at this pistareen Providence of Robert Huntington & now of George Muller.[65] There is piety here, but tis pulled down steadily into the pantry & the shoe-closet, till we are distressed for a breath of fresh air. Who would dare to be shut up with such as these from year to year? Certainly there is a philosophic interest & question here that well deserves attention, — the success, namely, to which he challenges scrutiny, through all these years, God coming precisely in the mode he is called for, & to the hour & minute.[66] But this narrative would not quite stand cross examination[1] — Yet I found one wise page where he insists on his Bible as food. Yet far be it from me to cavil. Thanks & & greetings rather, & on account of this

63. Rebecca Duncan's sister was the wife of Elbridge G. Dudley (see Sept. 21, 1860).

64. MS owned by Professor Philip Cabot; ph. in CUL. Excerpt I is in Cabot, II, 418.

65. The author of *The Life of Trust: being a Narrative of the Lord's Dealings with George Müller,* Boston, 1861; and it was, I conjecture, an earlier edition of this book that was returned. Cabot, II, 417–418, explains why it was sent to Emerson.

66. Müller believed in the practical application of prayer to temporal ends.

book, or rather on what is the core of this book. I send back also at last
the old Sagas [67] with penitence! Yours faithfully,

R. W. E.

To Caroline Sturgis Tappan, Concord, May 13, 1859

[Incompletely printed in Holmes, *Ralph Waldo Emerson*, 1885, pp. 225–227,
where the name of the correspondent is not given. A "scrap copy" — apparently part of a rough draft — of this letter was transcribed by Emerson some
years later in his *Journals* (X, 142–143). *Cf.* July 10, 1859, for Mrs. Tappan's
travels in Germany and for mention of the present letter.]

To William Emerson, Concord, May 23, 1859 [68]

Concord
23 May 1859

Dear William,

I have your letter, which I found on going to City Sat. P. M.
and am just returned. I will immediately go to Mary Simmons, who is
Aunt's Treasurer here, & to whom Ezra Ripley remits his receipts. I will
also endeavor to put myself right very soon on your account, or take
steps in that direction. Thanks for your too liberal apologies made for
me. But I never get out of my coils. Let us hope that I can. I saw in
town Dr Cheever [69] by chance, & he told me that he is looking for Susan's
arrival in Boston. Let it be so, & the soonest; for Concord is shining in
the sun, at last, and our young people are immensely talkative & entertaining lately, & tis time that Aunts & Uncles & Cousins should come to
see us & them. With dear love to Susan & the boys,

Yours affectionately,
Waldo E.

P. S. I have just been to Mrs Simmons. She says she has 62. & a fraction
belonging to Aunt M. in her hands. Ezra paid her $45 in March: she
found $15. in Aunt's box: & Ezra sent her some money in Feb. of which
she had sent $20. only to Aunt's order. Ezra has not yet sent the 40. of
May, but she will ask him for it. I received of her $60.00, which I
enclose.

67. *Cf.* the letters of Nov. 18, 1856, and Apr. 13, 1857.
68. MS owned by HCL; ph. in CUL.
69. Probably the David W. Cheever, physician, listed in the *Boston Directory*,
1859, who was, it seems, a nephew of Susan Haven Emerson (Josiah Adams, p. 33).

To Convers Francis, Concord, May 25, 1859?[70]

Concord 25 May

My dear Sir,

I am sorry I cannot give you the name of the author of " Transcendentalism." [71] Soon after it was published, I remember, I was told it was Mr Henry Winsor, a gentleman with whom I had some acquaintance. But, on meeting him one day, he utterly denied it, and seemed surprised at the imputation. If I ever heard afterwards, who wrote it, I have forgotten it, as indeed the little book itself has left no memory with me but of its name.

Yours faithfully,
R. W. Emerson

Dr Francis.

To L. Macfarland and others, Concord, May 26, 1859[72]

Concord
26 May 1859

Gentlemen,

I regret that it will not be in my power, to accept the friendly invitation with which you have honored me, to the Dinner of the Massachusetts & of the Boston Homoeopathic Medical Societies, on Thursday next, at Faneuil Hall.[73] Apart from some private engagements which next week hold me strictly at home, I must plead my extreme disinclination, rarely overcome, to venture into public festivals, in excuse of my failing to avail myself of the privilege you offer me.

70. MS owned by the Pierpont Morgan Library; ph. in CUL. The year 1859 has been added in another hand, but I have no further evidence of that date.

71. Perhaps *An Essay on Transcendentalism,* published anonymously, 1842, and reviewed in *The Dial* for Jan., 1843. Lindsay Swift, *Brook Farm,* 1900, p. 12, says the little book " is attributed " to Charles M. Ellis.

72. MS owned by Mr. Thomas F. Madigan; ph. in CUL. L. Macfarland, Milton Fuller, David Thayer, Christian F. Geist, and I. Tisdale Talbot are all listed as physicians in the *Boston Directory,* 1859.

73. It seems that the managers of the " Homœopathic Festival " made a serious effort to dignify the occasion. The dinner was held in Faneuil Hall, Longfellow was present, and a letter from William Cullen Bryant was read *(Boston Evening Transcript,* June 3, 1859) .

With high respect for the members & for the aims of the societies, I remain, gentlemen, gratefully & respectfully,

Your obedient servant,
R. W. Emerson.

L Macfarland, M D
Milton Fuller, M. D.
David Thayer M. D.
C. F. Geist, M. D.
I. T. Talbot M. D.

To William Emerson, Concord, May 27, 1859 [74]

Concord
Friday Evening
May 27, 1859

Dear William

Mrs Reuben Hoar has just come from Littleton to tell me that Bulkeley died this morning, at 7 o'clock.[75] I am not sure that I sent you any details of his illness in the end of the winter. He had, about the end of February, a sort of fit, which Dr Bartlett, as well as the Littleton physician, thought apoplectic, though of short duration, and after that was feeble & lost flesh. I went to see him, & sent Doctor Bartlett afterwards with Lidian; & Ellen & Edward have visited him lately But he had now got out of doors again, & resumed work a little, & yesterday was abroad, appearing comfortable. This morning he did not come down at his usual hour, Mr H. spoke with him once & again, and Mrs Hoar went to call him, and asked him if he would not come down to breakfast. He appeared surprised to know that it was past the hour, but would not come down; and when she went up again, he was speechless, & soon dead. It seems that only on Wednesday he was dressing himself to come to Concord to visit us, as has always been his practice on " Election Day," but Mr Hoar thought him not quite strong enough & dissuaded him. I am very sorry tonight that I have not seen him again in this week, or the last, as I had hoped to do. It seems, he said, this morning, to Mr Hoar, that he thanked him & Mrs H. for their kindness to him. (Mrs Hoar arrived at our house, when I was in the village, & waited long to see me, and I only met her, on my return, already setting forth on her way back. She had given Lidian her account of his last days. I have

75. MS owned by HCL; ph. in CUL.

75. The *Boston Evening Transcript*, May 30, 1859, announced the death, at Littleton, Mass., May 27, of Robert Bulkeley Emerson, aged 52.

agreed with her, that I will send the sexton to Littleton, early on Sunday morning, to bring the body hither, & that the funeral shall take place on Sunday P M at 4 o'clock from this house. Mr & Mrs Hoar signify their wish to attend it. They have been very kind & tender to him, especially through all this illness.

It is very sorrowful, but the sorrow is in the life & not in the death. In the last few years he has never seemed to enjoy life, and I am very happy to hear of this singular piece of sanity, this premonition of approaching death which led to the thanking Mr Hoar.

On consideration of the short time, I have not thought it necessary to telegraph you; as indeed there was scarcely time before our office was shut. You would not easily arrive at the funeral, if it were praticable at so sudden a call. I will write you again presently

Affectionately,

Waldo E

I ought to have said that Dr Bartlett, when he visited him, said, there was congestion of the brain, & that it might end in apoplexy, or, more probably, in idiocy. The event agrees with his belief. — [76]

To William Emerson, Concord, May 30, 1859 [77]

Concord

30 May 1859

Dear William,

You will have received my letter of Friday night.[78] Yesterday morning, at 9 o'clock, Bulkeley's body was brought to my house by our sexton, Mr Melvin, in a herse. His face was not much changed by death, but sadly changed by life from the comely boy I can well remember. His expression was now however calm & peaceful and all the rites seemed to have been duly paid. The body was contained in a handsome black walnut coffin, & the silver plate inscribed with his name & age. Mr Thoreau kindly undertook the charge of the funeral and Rev Mr Reynolds [79] to whom I had explained what I thought necessary, & whom Lidian visited afterwards lest he should not do justice to Bulkeley's virtues, officiated. Mr & Mrs Reuben Hoar came from L. Mr Alcott, Judge Hoar, Dr Bartlett, and Mrs Ripley's family, & others, were present. The bearers were,

76. The final paragraph was written on a separate half sheet, but undoubtedly belongs to this letter.

77. MS owned by HCL; ph. in CUL.

78. May 27, 1859.

79. Grindall Reynolds had succeeded Frost as pastor of the First Church in Concord on July 8, 1858 (*Memoirs of Members of the Social Circle*, 3d series, p. 245).

Mr Cheney, Mr Prichard, Mr Edmund Hosmer, Mr Moore, Mr Stow, Mr Eaton, Mr Staples, & Mr Stacy. The afternoon was warm & breezy half in sun half in shade and it did not seem so odious to be laid down there under the oak trees in as perfect an innocency as was Bulkeleys, as to live corrupt & corrupting with thousands. What a happiness, that, with his infirmities, he was clean of all vices!

I told you, I believe, that he died at 7 o'clock on Friday. I have learned that he did not die till about 2 P. M. Did I tell you that he thanked Mr & Mrs Hoar on that morning for all their kind care. I have promised to go to Littleton on Thursday, if it is a good day, & settle the few debts that have accrued, — to his Doctor, and some costs of his sickness, & of the funeral. In some conversation, a month ago, with Mr Hoar, I told him, he must charge me with his board since his sickness at some re-munerating rate for the very considerable increase of trouble he has given. They had given him their parlor for his chamber, & Mr Hoar did for some time sleep in the same room, to help him at night, if needed, &c. &c. Mr H. replied, — No, that he should charge the same board as before, & that we might make him any additional allowance that we thought fit for these services. In these circumstances, I shall do the best I can, and, on my return, I will make my report. Lidian will probably go with me. We think Mr & Mrs Hoar (you know she is a second wife married I think within two years) have behaved with uniform kindness & good sense to him & to us. Bulkeley has a deposit in the Savings Bank here, of which I believe the principal is nearly $50. and the interest is to be added. He has put into it Susan's New Years gifts for a long time; &, Mrs Hoar told me, he meant to bring one of last January, when he should have come on " Election Day."

I should have said above, that the body was deposited as was Mother's, in a brick vault, in my lot, in Sleepy Hollow.

Affectionately,

Waldo E

To William Emerson, Concord, June 2, 1859 [80]

Concord

June 2, 1859.

Dear William,

Please write & sign an order, (to be also signed by me,) on John M. Cheney, Cashier of Middlesex Institution for Savings, for Forty

80. MS owned by HCL; ph. in CUL.

six dollars deposited by Bulkeley in the Bank, & such interest as may have accrued.

I have your letter, and one or two letters of yours beside, to which answers shall come.

You will have seen what good speech Dr Holmes made at our Morphy dinner.[81] I was four times solicited to go, but remained contumacious, partly through the circumstances, partly through reason; though I share the curiosity & admiration he excites. William & Pell,[82] I hope have done their duty by him. I was to have gone to Littleton today, but have been compelled to postpone it till tomorrow; &, last night, Mr Forbes invites me to meet Mr Cobden at Milton [83] tomorrow, which I should like to do.

Your island ought to shine in these days, & Susan to be strong, in in spite of the complainings I have heard of. Helen Haven spent a day here much to the pleasure of all.

Waldo E

To William Emerson, Concord, June 8, 1859 [84]

Concord
8 June 1859

Dear William,

I learned from Mr Cheney, that, on the 1 June 1860, is made the dividend of the surplus earnings of 5 years, so that Bulkeley's little deposit will draw better interest by letting it lie a a year, than it will probably in our hands. So I return your order [85] for the present. I went on Friday to Littleton, & settled his affairs there. Mr Hoar was at first disposed to receive the usual annual payment for board, & leave to

81. Oliver Wendell Holmes's address at the dinner of May 31 in honor of Paul Morphy, chess champion of the world, was printed in the *Boston Daily Advertiser*, June 1, 1859. Lowell and Longfellow were present; Lowell read a poem suitable to the occasion.

82. Possibly William Emerson, Jr., and his friend attended one of the Morphy celebrations held in New York about this time and reported in the *New-York Daily Tribune*, May 14 and 27, 1859. *Trow's New York City Directory* for the year ending May 1, 1860, lists both young Emerson and a William Cruger Pell as lawyers, though not at the same address.

83. For Emerson's account of Cobden at Milton, see Sanborn, *The Personality of Emerson*, p. 123. Cobden was in the United States during the early months of 1859 on behalf of the English shareholders in an American railroad.

84. MS owned by HCL; ph. in CUL.

85. *Cf.* June 2, 1859.

us the discretionary allowance for his care & expenses since his last sickness began. But I thought it best he should make his own terms, which he did thus; 9 weeks at $5. = 45.

               9 weeks at 2.$ 18.

               9 weeks at $1.   9.

.   .   .   .   .[86]

I will endeavor that Ellen, who is the best accountant in the house, shall presently make this account of Bulkeley's dues to this world complete, since we shall never have the sad comfort of paying money for him more.

As far as I am yet advised by your letters, my share of Aunt Mary's extra charges is $\frac{1}{2}$ of $41.82 or 20.91. I will enclose in this letter 30. to be set to my credit on that account.

On Monday, Ellen & I will probably make our exploratory visit to Waterford, and as my summer plans depend a good deal on that contingency, I will write you again, when the result of our visit appears.

With love to Susan, & to the heroic youths.

Waldo E.

To WILLIAM EMERSON, CONCORD, JUNE 16, 1859 [87]

Concord 16 June
1859

Dear William

Last Friday, 10th June, I mailed to you a letter [88] containing an account in part of Bulkeley's expenses at Littleton, & of my settlement with Mr Hoar, & others, and also enclosing to you $30.00, on my account, for Aunt Mary. I have no reply from you & as you are so punctual (though I am not) I fear that my letter has not reached you. It was a double letter & I put two stamps on it. If it have not come to you will you make inquiries & send me word.

I have just been making a journey to Waterford, with Ellen, whereof you must not speak to Aunt Mary or to those who will tell her. We arrived there at 1 o'clock on Tuesday & left it at 9 o'clock the next day, & found time in those 18 hours to see the beautiful little town pretty thoroughly for our purposes. We found two or three houses, either of which

86. I have omitted here about two MS pages containing further details of the expenses on Bulkeley's account and some comment relating to these expenses.

87. MS owned by HCL; ph. in CUL.

88. Apparently the letter of June 8, 1859, which, according to William Emerson's notation, was delivered on June 11 and was answered on the 16th.

we can rent for 6 weeks, the furnished house at $25 per month; the un-
furnished, at $12. Ellen means to carry through her project of a vacation
of independence. We shall see, & shall tell you more presently.

Waldo E

TO JAMES RUSSELL LOWELL, CONCORD, JUNE 17, 1859 [89]

Concord

17 June 1859

Dear Lowell,

     I send you an offering to the "Atlantic" of three papers,
which are sent to me without the author's name, though I fancy I know
it. They are from a lady who shows character & sprightliness, and I think
very favorably of the pieces. They might be called, "Letters to Estelle."
The second piece, the "Arm Chair," the friend who brought them
seemed to wish to withdraw, fearing, as I suppose, that it might tell the
lady's secret near her home, as the old man is evidently a portrait. But I
told him, I thought the piece needful to give variety to the whole contribution, and he was satisfied with a few alterations in pencil. I hope
you may like the MSS. as well as I do, though the writer spells like a
Prussian princess, & will give Mr Underwood some trouble. One name
must be corrected from "Romany Rye."

     I read in the journals that Thackeray is to edit a "Monthly" in Lon-
don,[90] in the style of yours.

Yours faithfully,

R. W. Emerson

Mr Lowell.

TO ———— YOUNG, CONCORD? JUNE c. 20? 1859

[Mentioned in June 20, 1859.]

TO ———— TRUE, CONCORD? JUNE 20? 1859

[Mentioned in June 20, 1859.]

89. MS owned by HCL; ph. in CUL. The lady whose name Emerson fancied he
knew was, it seems, Mary Russell Watson, said to have been Thoreau's "Maiden in
the East" (cf. The Writings, VI, 329). One of her letters to "Estelle" appeared in
The Atlantic for June, 1860, under the title of "The Humming-bird." The "second
piece" must have been that printed in the same magazine for Sept., 1860, as "The
Great Arm-chair" (cf. the note on c. May? 1860?).

90. The Cornhill Magazine began publication with the number for Jan., 1860.

To —————— HOUGHTON, CONCORD, JUNE 20, 1859 [91]

Concord⎱ 20 June
Mass. ⎰ 1859

Dear Mrs Houghton,

We incline to take Mrs True's house, if she is willing to rent it on easy terms. I send a letter to Mr True, explaining my wishes in the matter. I have also written to Mrs Young. I think not to write to Mr Danly, until I hear from Mr True in reply. Our plan is, to come to Waterford, if we can, about the 16 July.

Mrs Emerson will be much obliged to you, if you will let the ticks she sent, be filled with oat straw.

Yours respectfully,
R. W. Emerson.

To WILLIAM EMERSON, CONCORD, JUNE 21, 1859 [92]

Concord
21 June 1859

Dear William

I have your letter. I am sorry you should allow Aunt Mary to dictate to you I am accustomed to say to her, when I hold any moneys of hers, "You shall have all you want to pay any bill, but nothing to keep by you; I will keep it till you need it." For her heedlessness is extreme: she loses her money on the first occasion; & then taxes all her intimate friends with the theft. I thought I had told you how important it is, that you should be firm with her. I think, Gore Ripley & I are the only persons who understand this. I sent you details on the account of Bulkeley at Littleton, but have not yet received some of those that belong in Concord. But I do not wish, as you intimate, that you should remit money for your part; I rather wish to keep down my debt to you, which I have allowed to increase, when I meant to diminish it.

We shall go to Waterford, probably 16 July. Dr Jackson & his family talk of taking our house for the 6 weeks. I send you in reference to a private note of yours, a note which Lidian had from Miss Peabody's brother. but do not know its value. Should I have better light shall im-

91. MS owned by Scripps College Library; ph. in CUL. The exploratory visit to Waterford which resulted in the present letter is mentioned in June 16, 1859. July 17 following explains why the projected vacation had to be abandoned.

92. MS owned by HCL; ph. in CUL.

part it. Do any of your house know Elmira Flint, of Concord now a widow by name of Mrs Small. I think very favorably of her, in the same view,

Yours, Waldo

To ABEL ADAMS, CONCORD, JUNE 24, 1859 [93]

Concord
24 June 1859

My dear friend,

. . . . .

formant than I. I did not attempt to give you any further account of it, than that . . . went to your house.

I am really anxious that you should know all the facts, — then I shall entirely give my proxy with yours, & shall be too happy to have no opinion to form; but I fancied on reading your note, that you might not have heard the strongest part of the Committee's story.

Yours affectionately,
R. W. Emerson

Mr Adams.

To CYRUS AUGUSTUS BARTOL, CONCORD, JULY 1, 1859? [94]

Concord
1 July Friday

My dear Bartol,

How are you to spend the Fourth My wife & daughters begin to despair of ever seeing you & your family in Concord unless by the violence of invitation But we think you are still in town & might be generous & come spend next Monday, day & night, with us & see " the splendor in the grass," [95] & our prize regatta on the river, and I know

93. MS owned by the Carlyle's House Memorial Trust; ph. in CUL. The lower two-thirds of the first leaf is missing, and the points indicate the resulting gaps in the text. The letter seems to relate to a meeting of the stockholders of the troublesome Vermont & Canada. *Cf.* the letters of July 5 and 15, 1859.

94. MS owned by the Library of Sarah Lawrence College; ph. in CUL. July 1 fell on Friday in 1853, 1859, and 1864, during the years when Edward could have acted as boatman and when Edith was still at home. As Edward was born in 1844, the most probable year would be 1859. Whether the Bartols came is not clear, but in July 15, 1859, Emerson mentions " the crowded holiday " of that month. For Bartol at Pigeon Cove, Mass., *cf.* June 2, 1856, and other earlier letters.

95. Wordsworth's " Ode Intimations of Immortality," l. 179, not quite exactly quoted.

not what remarkable teaparty in the P. M: which will furnish Lizzie with matter for her next week's theme. But really Concord is in its best cap & shoes; &, if the day is good, we shall vie with the dingles behind Pigeon Cove. Be brave, I entreat you, & persuade my friends, Mrs Bartol & Lizzie to come. Edward is a boatman bold, & will be proud to show Lizzie the beauties of the North Branch. Ellen & Edith, as well as Mrs Emerson, join in this request.

Yours affectionately,
R. W. Emerson

C. A. Bartol.

TO JOHN MURRAY FORBES, CONCORD, JULY 4, 1859 [96]

Concord 4 July

My dear Sir,

You are bent on stirring a mutiny in my young troop, — what with your Faerieland. of Naushon. But a little campaign in Maine is a plan which my girls have made of themselves and I am willing they should stand by it, & try it, though it will cost them this summer the loss of the island visit they so prize. For we go to Maine on the 15 July,[97] & to stay for six weeks. I wish they may find somewhat in Maine to console them for missing your drives & walks & waters — and I must lose the beechen enchantments to say nothing of my " swordfishing," & my brilliant shooting!

And yet the Maine solitude has its good side, & I shall let Ellen explain it some time to Mrs Forbes. Meantime, Mrs Emerson joins me in warmest thanks to you & Mrs F. for this large invitation, & so, you may be sure, do my young people.

We are very happy in having Mary [98] here these pleasant days though they contrive that I shall rarely have a glimpse of her. I saw her dancing very gracefully tonight in the Town Hall.

Yours faithfully,
R W Emerson

J. M. Forbes.

96. MS owned by RWEMA; ph. in CUL. The mention of the plan for a vacation in Maine fixes the year.

97. *Cf.* June 21, 1859. A few days after the present letter was written Emerson had a fall on Wachusett, and the " campaign in Maine " was out of the question (*cf.* the letters of July 15 and 17 following) .

98. Doubtless Forbes's daughter, later Mrs. H. S. Russell (see *Letters and Recollections of John Murray Forbes*, I, 188 *et passim*) .

To Sidney Bartlett, Concord, July 5, 1859 [99]

Concord 5 July 1859

Sidney Bartlett, Esq.
    Dear Sir,
        My friend Mr Abel Adams informs me that you propose to attend the meeting of the V. & Canada Railroad to be held soon; &, at his suggestion, I have hastened to write the above lines, in case you should see any need for the use of these votes. I am very happy to put myself in so good hands; but it occurs to me that I may not have put my wishes in proper form. If there be need of it, you will have the goodness to send me the proper form to sign.

               With great respect & regard, yours,
                     R. W. Emerson

To Herman Grimm, Concord, July 9, 1859

[MS owned by the Goethe- und Schiller-Archiv. Printed in *The Atlantic*, XCI, 471–472 (Apr., 1903); reprinted in *Correspondence between Ralph Waldo Emerson and Herman Grimm*, pp. 31–35.]

To Gisela von Arnim, Concord, July 10, 1859

[MS owned by the Goethe- und Schiller-Archiv. Printed in *The Atlantic*, XCI, 472–474, and in *Correspondence*, pp. 39–44. This is a reply to a letter received in Concord some six months earlier. Ellen Emerson, writing to Gisela von Arnim, June 28, 1860, told of the reception of that letter and gave, in her German script — which I transliterate without any other change — an account of what was partly, no doubt, the characteristic procedure when the Berlin mail arrived. " Es war im Januar 1859," she reported, " während mein Vater im Westen war (das heisst in den Westlichen Staaten) wie gewöhnlich zu jener Jahreszeit, um Vorlesungen zu halten (und wenn er verreist ist so öffne ich alle seine Briefe) dass mein Bruder und ich eines Nachmittags auf die Post gingen und das grosse viereckige Couvert fanden mit der von Herman Grim̱ geschriebenen Aufschrift, die bei uns lange bekannt und gern gesehen war. Wir haben es freudig nach Hause gebracht und ich habe's schnell aufgemacht. Es war nicht die Handschrift des Herrn Grimm sondern die einer Frau. ' O Mutter, Gisela von Arnim hat an den Vater geschrieben — und alles auf Deutsch und ich werde es ihm lesen müssen ' schrie ich schon ehe ich den Brief heraus zog. Und zuerst habe ich den Anfang gesucht, und dann das Ende. Da hab' ich Ihren Namen ' Gisela Arnim ' gefunden, und ihn meiner Mutter

99. MS owned by the Library of the University of Pennsylvania; ph. in CUL. Both Sidney Bartlett and Sidney Bartlett, Jr., are listed in the *Boston Directory*, 1859, as counselors. *Cf.* July 15, 1859.

und meinem Bruder als ein Gegenstand von grossem Interesse gezeigt. Sie aber haben ihn nicht lesen können, denn ich war damals die Einzige in der Familie welche die Deutsche Handschrift lesen konnte. War es nicht glücklich dass ich den Brief lesen konnte? Denn sonst hätte der Vater weit gehen müssen um den Inhalt zu lernen. Ida, die Tochter des Professors Agassiz, ist meine Freundin und hat mich Deutsch mit solcher Liebe und Begeisterung gelehrt, dass jedes Deutsche Wort meinen Ohren süss klingt, und alles Deutsches etwas Anziehendes für mich hat. Ich konnte die Handschrift der Ida sehr leicht lesen, und ich hatte eine andre zu sehen gewünscht um zu wissen ob ich alle lesen konnte. Da hatte ich Ihren Brief Allen ausser mir unlasbar, interessant nur anzusehen; da er von der Hand Bettines Tochter geschrieben war. Ich fing begierig an zu lesen aber fand die neue Handschrift eine grössere Schwierigkeit als ich erwartet hatte, so dass ich nur zwei oder drei Seiten gelesen hatte, als der Vater heimkehrte. Der Morgen seiner Rückkehr ist immer von der ganzen Familie im Study (so nennen wir die Arbeitsstube des Vaters) zugebracht, und Alles was sich während seine Abwesenheit sich begeben hat wird auf beiden Seiten erzählt. Eine freudige gesprächige Zeit und diessmal die erste Neuigkeit welche er hörte war dass ihm ein Brief von Ihnen gekommen sey. Das machte ihm Freude und er war begierig ihn zu hören — sah mit Erstaunen dass er auf Deutsch geschrieben war, und indem er die Bogen entfaltete fand er die Blumen die Sie schickten. Er betrachtete sie, und sagte mir das ich Acht geben solle, damit sie nicht gebrochen werden. Dann, als wir und alle im Study eingerichtet hatten, hab' ich die Seiten, die ich schon übersetzt hatte, vorgelesen. Und es wurde von der Familie mit solchem Interesse angehört, dass ich auch die ich jedes Wort liebte vollkomen befriedigt war. Denselben Tag hab' ich noch zwei Seiten übersetzt. Ich ging jeden Tag in die Schule und habe auch imer viele Geschäfte; darum bedurf es den ganzen Winter, den Brief zu enträthseln, war er auch mein beständiger Gesellschafter. Einige Seiten waren so schwer, dass ich Sie sechs und siebenmal übergehen musste ehe ich die wichtigen Worte finden konnte. . . . Endlich im April hab' ich zur letzten Seite gelangen, und dann hab ich ihn fast auswendig gewusst. Es blieben Sätze aber hier und da die mich ganz verworren und ich bat den Vater mir zu erlauben den Brief zur Ida Agassiz zu bringen . . ." (MS owned by the Goethe- und Schiller-Archiv.)]

To William Emerson, Concord, July 13, 1859 [100]

Concord

July 13. 1859

Dear William,

    I enclose you fifty dollars, of ninety one which Mrs Simmons paid me yesterday, for Aunt Mary,[101] & which I detained thinking it best to pay you here: but on second thoughts think it best to run the risk of

100. MS owned by HCL; ph. in CUL.

101. *Cf.* May 23, 1859, for Mary Ripley Simmons as Mary Moody Emerson's treasurer.

your having left N. Y. & send you what Aunt Marys debts may have made important to you to receive.

Charles made us a very pleasant visit of a few days, & went to Boston yesterday.[102] I look steadily for your. arrival.

Yours,
Waldo E.

Wm Emerson Esq

To James Russell Lowell, Concord, July 13, 1859 [103]

Concord
13 July 1859

My dear Lowell,

I have threatened you from time to time with springing on you the subscription paper of what Mr Ward's clerk calls a little magniloquently the Alcott Fund, I dare not say, prophetically. It was set on foot more than two years ago,[104] & took its first shape as I think in a conversation between Longfellow & me at Longfellow's house, when I was describing the genius & the wants of the man, & querying whether some moderate annuity might not be gathered for him, from his friends. Longfellow said, Every body shall give him one day: he would give him a poem, fifty dollars; I should give him a lecture,'s value; Whipple, Parker, Phillips, should give as much: and your name was relied on by both of us for a poem also. I proceeded at once to obtain such promises as I could,[105] and, as his nearest neighbor, led the subscription. Theo-

102. William Emerson, July 15, 1859 (MS owned by Dr. Haven Emerson), tells of his son's arrival in New York, from Concord, on the 14th.

103. MS owned by HCL; ph. in CUL.

104. It had been much longer. *Cf.* May 10, 1856, and, for the earlier history of the fund, the letters of June 13 and 29, 1855.

105. In Alcott's MS diary (owned by Mr. F. W. Pratt) there is entered under date of May 10, 1857, this note by Alcott with the list of subscriptions penciled in Emerson's hand:

"Of subscriptions to the Life-Annuity, there have been paid in, he tells me, to Sam. G. Ward, and by him invested, awaiting additions, the following sums, by him pencilled for my reference and keeping: thus — from —

Longfellow	50.
T S King	50.
Cheney	50.
W. Phillips	50.
T Davis	100.
F Beck	40.
C F Hovey	10.
H D Thoreau	1.
Emerson	100."

dore Parker promised his part, Starr King, Whipple, Phillips, Woodman, Thomas Davis of Providence. Mr Apthorp said, he could obtain me certain names, & I was told of friends at New Bedford, & Hingham; so that I began to hope for an annuity of $100. But the Kansas claim [106] drained some of our friends, & others failed us from other reasons, so that my real issue is now, as follows; T. Davis $100, R. W. E. $100. T. S. King 50. H. W. Longfellow 50. W. Phillips 50 H. Woodman 50. Mr & Mrs S. Cheney 50. F. Beck 40. C. F. Hovey $10. H D Thoreau $1.00 One or two promises more I still confide in, particularly of a Mr Locke, who told me he had great expectations before him, & who is much Mr A's friend. The money collected is in Sam. G. Ward's hands, & draws interest; — & Ward also intimated his good-will to add to it. If now you are not dangerously drawn upon by the wants, that always go in swarms, & if you believe, as I, that among the things that go to make up the world, there must be one Capuchin or divine mendicant, & that Alcott is he, — then you shall, at your own time, send your gift for him to S. G. Ward.[107]

Mr Alcott knows that some such fruit was forming, but that he was never to hold it in his hands, & only bite an annual berry —

Yours faithfully,
R. W. Emerson.

James R. Lowell.

To Abel Adams, Concord, July 15, 1859 [108]

Concord
15 July, 1859.

My dear friend,

I observed by your note that you expected to see me on Sunday 3 July; but when I made the slow discovery that the 4th of July followed the third, & that I could not go to Brookline without staying over till the middle of the crowded holiday,[109] I gave it up; & found

106. Cf. Dec. 11, 1856.

107. Lowell replied, Newport, R. I., July 18, 1859, that he would pay his $50 in September; he thought there should be a place for the navel-contemplating Brahmin in a private university and was glad to pay his tuition fee. This letter of Lowell's is printed in *New Letters*, p. 97, and the suggestion is made (p. 96) that it relates to some project for the appointment of an Oriental professor at Harvard. But in the light of Emerson's letter, it is clear that Lowell's university was only a figure of speech. Cf. also July 25, 1859, to Lowell.

108. MS owned by RWEMA; ph. in CUL.

109. Cf. July 1, 1859?

that a milk-train would carry me home on Sunday Night. And I was sure you would not look for me.

I received your second note about V. & C. road; & accordingly sent my proxy to Mr Bartlett.[110]

Today, I have a note from Mr C. C. Jewett,[111] informing me that Mr Gilbert wishes to pay his notes to the Estate of Mr Ralph Haskins, &, with the rest, that which I hold; & would be glad to do so next Monday. I believe that you have the note in your keeping, for me. I am sorry that he wishes to pay it, as we must find a new investment for the money. . Can you send it, on Monday, to me in Boston at *Phillips Sampson & Co's,*[112] Winter Street? or, if it is already in Boston, send me a line (to P. S. & Co) how I shall come upon the paper. Add any suggestion that occurs to you that I should know, Or tell me, if you know, what I should do with the money to place it as well as now. It is not all mine, as I re-pay to the Haskins Estate $36.12 out of the $240. every year.

I met with an unlucky fall, the other day, in coming down Wachusett, in Princeton, & sprained my foot, which has made me a prisoner to my chair, for some days, & is likely to hold me for more.[113] But my affairs will send me to Boston, I think, Monday, & I can ride about, without harm. But it looks badly for my Waterford plan.[114]

With love to all your family,

Yours faithfully,
R W Emerson

Abel Adams.

To William Emerson, Concord, July 17, 1859[115]

Concord 17 July
Sunday.

Dear William,

   I looked for you, all yesterday & the day before, and, last night, came your note.

110. In July 5, 1859.

111. *Cf.* Dec. 20, 1852, to Lidian Emerson.

112. The endorsement of this letter includes the following record, apparently in Adams's hand:

" Sent the note & Mortgage to Phillips Sampson Co July 18."

113. There are allusions to this accident in many letters from this time till early in 1860.

114. *Cf.* the letters of June 16 and 21, 1859.

115. MS owned by HCL; ph. in CUL. July 17 fell on Sunday in 1859, the year fixed by the reference to the sprained foot and the abandoned scheme for a vacation at Waterford.

My sprain has only one serious consequence, that it keeps us all at home: for the wife & children, as we had arranged it, cannot well go to Waterford, without me, — as we had rented our house — for one thing; and Dr Barrett, on being consulted, said, that sprains, in the majority of cases, required absolute rest of 6 weeks, &, in the minority of cases, of 3 weeks. Well, on such terms, my own chamber where my tools are, is better than the Waterford chamber, where they are not. And it becomes easiest to stay where we are: so do not delay a day to come & see me. There are plenty of good reasons to keep us at home, when once we are looking that way, though I mean to gratify Ellen & Edith hereafter with Waterford, if I can. Besides, they mean to make something of the next weeks in the way they wished to use them in Maine — for household work, tho', tis said, it is not as easy to d[o][116] here. We all had much pleasure in Charles's little visit, & most in the excellent news he brought, that he will come to Cambridge.[117] Let not that steel grow cold on the anvil, for an instant. This letter will hardly get to you I fear before your departure, but think it best to send it still. Ever yours

                                                        Waldo E
I keep the balance of Aunt Mary's money for your coming.

To WILLIAM EMERSON, CONCORD, JULY 18, 1859 [118]

                                        Concord 18 July, 1859
Dear William,

        I wrote you yesterday a letter to N. Y. which may not reach you, to say, that I am not at Waterford, nor likely soon to be, — but at home, in the sure hope of seeing you there.

                                        Affectionately,
                                            Waldo —

To ABEL ADAMS, CONCORD, JULY 20, 1859 [119]

                                        Concord
                                        20 July 1859
My dear friend,

        It was very kind in you to send my paper to town, by horse &

116. The word is partly blotted out.
117. Cf. July 21, 1859.
118. MS owned by Mr. Edward Waldo Forbes; ph. in CUL.
119. MS owned by RWEMA; ph. in CUL.

man, like a state despatch; & it did not lessen Mr Jewett's [120] regret when
he hastened to tell me that he had written that morning to Concord to
tell me that Mr Charles Francis Adams, who was, I believe, to furnish
the money, & take the papers, had not decided to take them all. Well,
I told him that I had no desire to be paid, as I believed the investment
perfectly secure; and he promised to send me word again presently,
when the other parties had made up their minds. So after riding about
town & doing my errands I brought my paper home with me to await
Mr Gilberts conclusion. Did I tell you that Sam G. Ward has taken Edward, with Tom W., up into the Adirondac. My foot mends by means of
a tight bandage. With kind remembrance to all of you.

Yours ever, R. W. Emerson

TO WILLIAM EMERSON, CONCORD, JULY 21, 1859 [121]

Concord 21 July 1859

Dear William,

After watching every train these two days past, I have
Charles's letter, that you have been ill, & will not come. I am very sorry
for the effect, & for the cause. Especially I regret it, after the news in
Charles s letter, that neither will he come. There is in this house a deep
regret that you decide so, after what Charles told me of his College.[122]
And I, who had some suspicion that his going alone to Cambridge
might expose him to some discouragements that he could have better
faced if he had gone with backers, depended on your coming, to talk
the thing out fully. Now I entreat you to give this matter your best consideration. Let Charles enter the Freshman Class. It is a fine looking
class of 120 young men, *older* than any class that has entered: 17 is
the age of the majority. Twentyfive boys perfectly fitted enter from the

120. See July 15, 1859, both for Jewett and for the lame foot.
121. MS owned by HCL; ph. in CUL.
122. What the difficulty was is not clear, but this seems to have been a period of
declining standards of scholarship at Columbia. According to the testimony of the
exceptionally well-informed authority whom Emerson had cited in his letter of July
14, 1852, Columbia dropped from her place " far in advance of the New England
colleges and *a fortiori* of all others in the country " in the 1830's to a far lower standard in the 1850's (Charles Astor Bristed, *Five Years in an English University*, 1852,
I, 8, and II, 89–90; and 3d ed., 1873, p. 454) . Charles Emerson, who had matriculated
in the class of 1862, actually transferred to Harvard in 1859, when he was enrolled in
the freshman class.

Boston Latin School. I know not how many from Mr Dixwell's.[123] The two Higginsons,[124] whom Charles has seen, both excellent fellows, enter. I am sure Charles will find mates & rivals, &, I hope, kings for competitors. What if he has gone through the course at Columbia? It will only permit him to be a better & more thoroughly-grounded scholar, & allow him time for Plutarch & Gibbon, or whatever subsidiary studies. For preparation, he ought to come back on Monday morning to Cambridge, & put himself under the care of James Lowell, or of James Thayer, each of whom "crams men for examination." Lidian, & Ellen & Edith entreat me to say, that we shall be at home here joyfully, for the six weeks, & he can take a season ticket, & go down every day to Cambridge to recite, as Edith has done for the last school term. We are proposing now that Edward shall go next year; in that case, you will see a strong motive we have to find Charles there — But I think it far better for C., after his own account of Colᵃ College. Indeed when C. told me what his purpose was, I was too glad of it to think it necessary to inquire very much into his plans. But, by all means, persuade him to come at once, & enter Freshman. Storrow Higginson has no chum, & if C wishes, I will write to him, that he shall not engage one, until he hears from Charles.

My second business is this. Mr Jewett [125] writes me that Mr T. Gilbert the responsible partner (not signer) of the mortgage note which R. Haskins conveyed to Mother, wishes to pay that note. Rather, he wishes it assigned to Charles Francis Adams, who will pay it. You remember the face of the note was 4000. Mr Haskins owed Mother $3400. She, therefore, or we, gave a note for 600. There is a fraction in the amounts, & I pay Estate of R. H. $18.06 semi-annually, & receive from Gilbert 120.00 Now, on our account, yours & mine, I believe this mortgage note is or was in a process of becoming mine; by my releasing to you a note of Eatons for $1000. and by charging me with the balance say $700. as due from me to you. But I think no paper of assignment to me has been made, & correspondent note from me? What then is necessary to do in order to assign this mortgage note to C. F. Adams? Does it not need your signature? Must I send the note, & papers with it to you? As I looked at the paper this morning, I thought it best by all means to be paid. For

123. Doubtless Epes S. Dixwell's private Latin school in Boston (*Boston Directory*, 1858).

124. Francis Lee Higginson and Samuel Storrow Higginson both belonged to the class of 1863.

125. *Cf.* the letters of July 15 and 20, 1859. Gilbert and Sears appear in many earlier letters.

Sears, the signer, failed; & I do not see Gilberts name on it. And the relation to the Haskins Estate, & the arrangement between you & me, complicate it further, so that it should not go so loaded to new heirs. Perhaps I will send it to you by the next mail, (though I hate to risk such a thing on its travels,) unless I see Mr Brooks [126] tonight. Affectionately,

Waldo

To George Field, Concord, July 25, 1859

[MS owned by Mr. Stearns Morse; printed by him in " An Emerson Letter," *Harvard Alumni Bulletin,* Jan. 15, 1931. As late as Dec. 30, 1859, Dr. Field wrote Emerson, from Boston, some advice about the lame foot mentioned in the present letter. A genealogical note preserved by the family, as Mr. Winthrop B. Field informs me, indicates that Dr. Field removed from Athol, Mass., to Boston about 1859, a year and a half before his death. *Cf.* a letter of Nov. 15, 1858.]

To John Murray Forbes, Concord, July 25, 1859 [127]

Concord
25 July 1859

My dear Sir,

Your persistent courtesy had certainly a right to an earlier word in reply.

It looks very much as if I should be " too bad " to go to Naushon; not but that my foolish foot will or should be walking, but it will have many steps now omitted to take in other directions.

But I think that Mrs Emerson & Edith will not be able to resist the invitation you send them, and that by the 8 August, if the heavens smile, they will be very happy to visit you in your island.

But before the 8 August, are not you promised to the Adirondac Party? [128] Your presence was made one of the inducements to the Excursion, in the meeting I attended.

Yours faithfully,
R. W. Emerson

Mr Forbes.

126. Doubtless the George M. Brooks of Nov. 19, 1853, to William Emerson, and earlier letters.

127. MS owned by RWEMA; ph. in CUL.

128. Lowell, in his letter of July 18, 1859, had urged Emerson, in spite of his accident on Wachusett, not to give up the Adirondacks.

To James Russell Lowell, Concord, July 25, 1859 [129]

Concord
25 July, 1859.

My dear Lowell,

I join you in giving Mr Gray [130] leave to withdraw Mr Howe's name, for the reason, that, in the present state of the tribe & the wigwam, one member should not ask more than one guest. I approve all the other names. Why are no boys offered us? Last year, three or four were on fire to go. Sam. Ward has taken mine, as well as his own, along with Stillman,[131] & has thus made my reasons for going one less. But if my absurd foot will heal itself, I am not without appetite, and, I thought at one time, a degree of necessity, of going. At all hours, the invitation has a kind of mountain echo [132] in it. You are excellent in coming to the help of Alcott so frankly,[133] & all the more, that I always reckon you only a three-quarters-believer in this Gautama. But you will help him to live to justify himself entirely to your eyes. For the Holmes' Birthday, — yes, of course. But can we not combine with it a welcome to Hawthorne, by inviting him to it? Longfellow particularly wishes that he should be fêted on his return, & he sails from Liverpool, on 13 or 15ᵗʰ August.[134]

For the Atlantic article, I have it honestly before me, but you cannot rely on it for September,[135] with your rates of speed. Ever yours,

J. R Lowell.   R. W. Emerson

129. MS owned by HCL; ph. in CUL. This apparently answers Lowell's letter of the 18th, already cited, and a later one from the same correspondent, doubtless containing a list of persons proposed for invitation by the Adirondack Club — a list Lowell had promised in his letter of the 18th.

130. I am uncertain whether this was the younger Horace Gray, who afterwards became a member of the Saturday Club (cf. *Later Years of the Saturday Club*, 1927, pp. 49 ff.) . Howe is also hard to identify, as it seems improbable that the reference is to Dr. Estes Howe, who had earlier belonged to the Club or at least gone with the members on their summer outing, and who had married the sister of Lowell's first wife.

131. Stillman records this fact in his account of the third excursion of the Club (*The Autobiography*, I, 289) .

132. Emerson's correspondent doubtless knew the Wordsworthian flavor of this (" Yes, it was the Mountain Echo ") .

133. See July 13, 1859, to Lowell.

134. Hawthorne changed his plans and did not return till the following year; but there was a dinner on Aug. 29 in honor of Holmes's fiftieth birthday, and the speech which Emerson apparently made on that occasion is printed in *Journals*, IX, 226–229.

135. In his letter of July 18 Lowell had urged Emerson to have his " essay " ready for *The Atlantic* for the following September. Emerson, however, published no further prose in that magazine until a year later. For his substitution of a poem for the prose he was unable to supply, see Oct. *c.* 15? 1859.

To William Emerson, Concord, July 26, 1859 [136]

Concord, 26 July 1859

Dear William,

I hope tonight may bring me your answer on the subject of the mortgage note for which Mr Gilbert waits. On Saturday eve^g, Mr Simmons [137] was here to bind my foot — the beneficent amateur that he is, — and I told him, I would consult him professionally about the methods of making the desired assignment. He said, it was not necessary, what I had feared, — to send the note & mortgage back & forth; but that I could send you a description of the paper, which would serve your purposes to draw up a joint assignment, which you could sign, & send to me to sign. I enclose to you his *description of the paper.*

I have not hastened to forward this, thinking that your letter might offer other views. Last night, Mr S. sends me the note which I enclose also, of his second thoughts on the matter. You will remember, I am not sole executor.

I have to write my letter before yours arrives, or there will be no time for the night's mail. If you think I shall want these forms again, you must reinclose them.

Meantime, I hope Charles is on his way to Concord & Cambridge, & the papers can well wait his arrival.[138]

Affectionately,
Waldo E

To William Emerson, Concord, August 1, 1859 [139]

Concord,
1 August, 1859

Dear William,
Mr Simmons sends me the accompanying assignment to send to you for your signature. I infer that you must have called on him, & he was

---

136. MS owned by HCL; ph. in CUL.

137. For Charles Francis Simmons, doubtless the person meant, see Sept. 5, 1855, to William Emerson and Aug. 1, 1859. This Simmons wrote a number of letters to Emerson in 1859–1860, advising him regarding the prospect of collecting royalties from the assignees of the bankrupt firm of Phillips, Sampson & Co. He was listed as a counselor in the *Boston Directory*, 1859.

138. Charles Emerson's presence at Cambridge is alluded to in Aug. 11, 1859.

139. MS owned by HCL; ph. in CUL.

deceived by brown locks & unsnowed beard to believe you the younger brother, & has given me seniority in the instrument.

I forwarded to Wall Street a letter which arrived here for you.

Perhaps you had better return this paper directly to Mr S. in Boston.

> G. F. Simmons [140] Esq
> > Railroad Exchange
> > > Court St
> > > > Boston

I thought of much to say to you, as soon as you were gone.

Affectionately,

Waldo E

To John Murray Forbes, Concord, August 6, 1859 [141]

Concord

6 Augt Saturday

My dear Sir,

My wife & Edith elect the yacht on Monday for their transport,[142] and will leave Boston at 11'o clock. For the question of living *all summer* at Prospero's Island,[143] Mrs Emerson imputes to herself immense self command that she can say, No; for, I believe she has promises or duties at Plymouth, which will lead her there, after a week.

I am glad you will go to Adirondac; which my boy has just seen [144] with great contentment. I fear I cannot hope to go to Naushon or to Ambersand.[145]

Yours ever,

R. W. Emerson.

Mr Forbes.

140. Emerson doubtless means C. F. Simmons; *cf.* a note on July 26, 1859.

141. MS owned by Mr. Elliot Forbes; ph. in CUL. Evidence cited below shows that the year was 1859, when Aug. 6 fell on Saturday.

142. Their plan to go to Naushon on Aug. 8 is mentioned in July 25, 1859, to Forbes, where there is also something about Forbes's projected trip with the Adirondack Club.

143. In Shakespeare's *The Tempest;* Emerson lavished, in various letters, a wealth of literary and mythological allusions and epithets on Naushon.

144. *Cf.* July 25, 1859, to Lowell.

145. That is, Ampersand, between Lake Placid and the Follensby Pond of the Adirondack Club.

To Samuel Gray Ward, Concord, August 10, 1859? [146]

Concord. 10 Aug^t

My dear friend,

You sent me $8 for 7. I am so glad to get a note from you, that I do not grudge my blunders, if they extort one. But I don't trust you, for all your diligent figures, & believe that E's blanket is quite too cheap.[147] Anna's letter is very welcome to me. She is always a porphyrogenet,[148] and her handwriting palatial. She writes with confidence in her physician & his treatment. But for her church,[149] she shares the exaltation shall I say? which belongs to all new converts in the dogmatic churches, & which gives so much pleasure that it would be cruel to check it if we could, — which we cannot. The high way to deal with her is to accept the total pretension of the Roman Church, & urge her through the whole rococo to the sentiment of Fenelon & A Kempis in its cloister, — which burns backward the whole church to foul smoke. But who is good enough to deal with converts so? She was born for dignity, but I would not see her an abbess. Her own house, her children, & her husband's claims to daily & lifelong respect & confidence, are the best electuary. But I hope she is already getting well, — then she will get well of this also.

Ever yours,
R. W. Emerson

S. G. Ward.

To William Emerson, Concord, August 11, 1859 [150]

Concord
11 August, 1859

Dear William

Thank Mr Calvert [151] very kindly whenever you write to him for his thoughtfulness of me. I do not think there is any disloca-

146. MS owned by HCL; ph. in CUL. The year 1859, supplied in another hand, is probably correct.

147. For Edward Emerson's recent trip to the Adirondacks with Ward, see July 25, 1859, to Lowell.

148. That is, porphyrogenite. The English form of the word seems still to be somewhat unsettled, but Emerson's version is apparently not justified by usage.

149. Cf. May 5, 1859.

150. MS owned by HCL; ph. in CUL.

151. Doubtless the George Henry Calvert of earlier letters.

tion,[152] or it would give me more pain: it only is slow to cure: and two days ago, when I unbound it, & let it remain loose, it swelled again, in a couple of hours, so that I tied it up again.

Our house is almost empty. Ellen & Edith heroically made bread & pudding last week, and, this week, Lidian & Edith are gone to Naushon, & Ellen makes bread & performs other mysteries quite alone for the sustentation of Edward & me. James, & Alice the sempstress,[153] are the only other inhabitants.

Mr Simmons received safely your document,[154] but, I believe, Mr Adams is not in town, so that the conclusion is not yet.

We have not yet seen Charles & hardly expect it at present Mr Charles Lowell I saw, & he said that James said, C. would easily enter, but must drill for it.[155] We will have him one of these days. With love to Susan & to the boys. Thanks for the Central Park.[156] Edward & I have mastered it.

Waldo E

To Edith Emerson, Concord, August 17, 1859 [157]

Concord 17 Aug^t

Dear Edith

Mamma says you want a piece which I send but you need only ask Mr F. to please break you a dollar bill that you might have a penny to put into a fish's mouth if you should meet a saint on the south beach, & he should request you to do so. I am sure, Mr F. in these circumstances, would be swift to aid you.[158] Mamma came yesterday, but Ellen refused to kiss her until she promised to go to Secconnet.[159] Look for " Seacliff " [160] which your mother says, Mr F. took in hand in helping her to the boat, but which she does not remember seeing again. Ed-

152. *Cf.* July 15, 1859, and later letters.
153. *Cf.* a note on Apr. 4? 1859.
154. *Cf.* Aug. 1, 1859.
155. See July 21, 1859.
156. Perhaps *A Pocket Map & Visitor's Guide to the Central Park, in the City of New-York,* 1859, or some similar publication.
157. MS owned by Mrs. William B. Bowers II; ph. in CUL. The year is fixed by evidence cited below.
158. For the visit of Edith Emerson and her mother to Naushon, see the letters of Aug. 6, 11, and 20, 1859.
159. Apparently Sakonnet (or Seaconnet) Point, R. I
160. John W. De Forest's *Seacliff or the Mystery of the Westervelts* was published at Boston in 1859.

ward went this morning an hour ago with knapsack & staff, & Ned Bart-lett to Wachusett,[161] 31 miles.

Papa.

To WILLIAM EMERSON, CONCORD, AUGUST 20, 1859 [162]

Concord
20 August

Dear William,

I enclose $41. balance of the sum received for Aunt Mary of Mary Simmons,[163] & which you should have taken of me here. On the hint of your Calvert letter,[164] I took my foot to Dr Henry J. Bigelow in Boston, an expert in bones who pronounced that there was no disloca-tion, & gave advice. Every new doctor contradicts the last. Dr B. said, "a splint & absolute rest." Dr Russell,[165] who carried me to him, said, " rest," yes, but " splint " no! — and when I got home, Dr Bartlett said, ' go & walk, or you never will.' — Clear, isn't it? Meantime yester-day my hand was numb & would not write. Dr Bartlett said, throw away that crutch which deadens the nerve, & so one lives between fires. Lidian has come back from Naushon & Edith should come tonight.[166] Edward walked to Wachusett on Wednesday, with Ned Bartlett, camped out thereon one night, & in a wood, another, & returned last night, each campaigner having spent one dollar in three days.

Charles walked up — , last Sunday morning, from Cambridge,[167] & spent the day with us, to the great pleasure of the family, & walked back Monday.

Love to Susan, & boys twain

Waldo

To FRANCIS H. UNDERWOOD, CONCORD, AUGUST 31, 1859

[MS listed in American Art Association Anderson Galleries, Nov. 30, 1931.]

161. See Aug. 20, 1859.
162. MS owned by HCL; ph. in CUL. The date is clear from William Emerson's notation and from evidence cited below.
163. *Cf.* May 23, 1859.
164. *Cf.* Aug. 11, 1859.
165. Both George and Le Baron Russell are listed as physicians in the *Boston Directory*, 1859. The sprained ankle is mentioned in several earlier letters of 1859.
166. For the Naushon visit and the trip to Wachusett mentioned below, *cf.* Aug. 17, 1859.
167. For Charles Emerson at Harvard, see a note on July 21, 1859.

To WILLIAM EMERSON, CONCORD, SEPTEMBER 8, 1859 [168]

Concord
8 September, '59

Dear William,

Where is Haven? You promised him for the early days of September. Charles entered Cambridge; [169] Camp Massachusetts came to Concord; but Haven has not appeared. His cousins & Uncles have kept a good hope, but the noisy Muster which has filled all the region with stir & alarm,[170] will have gone, I fear, before he arrives. Well, there are as good days & better ahead, which we shall gladly share with him, and I hope he will not disappoint us.

I have had so many frets lately that I am asserting all the claims of Mr Crump in the comedy.[171] My two cows, which had been all summer at pasture in New Hampshire, strayed, on the return, & are not found. A windy day strewed the ground with my unripe pears. My saint of an Irishman [172] has had a *spree* on a most unfitting time. More grave disaster I find in the loss of Mr Phillips, my publisher, and the loss & inconvenience that comes therefrom may be greater to me than I know.[173]

168. MS owned by HCL; ph. in CUL.

169. *Cf.* a note on July 21, 1859.

170. An account of the beginning of the brief encampment of several military units about two miles west of Concord village was given in " Camp Massachusetts," *Boston Daily Advertiser*, Sept. 7, 1859. It seems to have been a gala affair. According to the reporter, the " pocket pistol " circulated freely and was " a very popular ' arm ' in camp." Endicott & Co., New York lithographers, recorded the more martial aspect of the occasion in their large print entitled " Review of the Mass. Volunteer Militia, at Concord, Sept 9th, 1859," a copy of which still hangs in the Concord Free Public Library.

171. The allusion is not clear, though Emerson wrote much the same thing in an entry of Sept., 1859, in *Journals* (IX, 230–231). An attempt has been made to explain the " Mr. Crump " in chapter ix of *English Traits* as an allusion to the story of the American who offered to pay Macaulay $500 if he could introduce the name of Crump into the history he was writing (see *Notes and Queries*, May 25, 1912). Macaulay's story, which dates from 1852, and which is told in G. O. Trevelyan, *The Life and Letters*, New York, 1876, II, 176, does not, however, seem to be a very probable source for Emerson's " Mr Crump in the comedy."

172. Probably James Burke; *cf.* Sept. 16, 1859.

173. Moses D. Phillips died on Aug. 20, only a few weeks after the death of Charles Sampson, another member of the firm (*Boston Evening Transcript*, Aug. 22, 1859). Emerson's fears were well founded, for within two days after the present letter was written the badly disorganized publishing house announced suspension of payment, and presently there were meetings of the creditors (*ibid.*, Sept. 12 and 28, 1859). For Emerson's indecision regarding the choice of a new publisher, *cf.* Oct. *c.* 15? 1859.

After getting over my sprain, ten days ago, so as to walk pretty far, I overwalked, & now have been sitting again But I hope to surmount some of my afflictions yet, & am ever affectionately

Yours,

R. W. E.

To CHARLES H. DALTON, CONCORD? SEPTEMBER? *c.* 15? 1859

[Mentioned in Sept. 19, 1859.]

To ELLEN EMERSON, BOSTON, SEPTEMBER 16, 1859 [174]

Boston

Sept. 16 '59

Dear Ellen,

Write to Ida Agassiz & to Mrs Lowell, at once, — an easy task, because you can content yourself with quoting Mrs Cheney's letter.[175]

Thanks for the cornucopiae basket, — but you might have sent my black valise, which I left at home. As your Mother did not send Froude's England,[176] I suppose Mr Channing had taken it. Thanks for the story of the Declamation. My orators did not shine much. Edward is bound to make that speech bring an echo. If I had asked for anything more than you have sent, it would have been one of my great coats, say, the old snuff colored velvet collared one that hangs in the entry, & my gaiters which are in the Study, under the sofa. But if Aunt Elizabeth comes on Wednesday, I may easily come home on that day at 12. If James has any more apples, Wright had better take them.

Papa.

174. MS owned by RWEMA; ph. in CUL.

175. Ellen Emerson's letter endorsed Sept., 1859, inclosed one from Mrs. Cheney and asked advice as to what to write to Ida and to Mrs. Lowell. The same letter from Ellen told of the "speaking yesterday."

176. The first volumes of Froude's *History of England* had been published in 1856.

To ELLEN EMERSON, BOSTON? SEPTEMBER 19, 1859[177]

Monday 19 Sept.

Dear Ellen, I am sorry not to write you something exact, but until the offending foot[178] behaves better, I decide on nothing. Doctor Hewitt[179] blames it as " loose," & as having tendency to tedious inflammation. I spare it, & walk less & less, in short, only to his house & back. But I think to come home on Tuesday or Wednesday as I ought to keep my word, & go on Thursday to Chelmsford celebration.[180] I wrote to Mr Dalton, I would go thither if he would bring Mr Hunt from Philadelphia there. He replies that he will. But I wish to be sure. Tell mamma, my hand is very well, it thanks her. I hope Edith will stop here as she passes home tomorrow — but you sent no pattern for her, which you say you do. Glad of the home news; and hope Edward & you will take the hint which Frank Higginson gave him in his call the other evening, " Why does n't Chapin[181] go into society? " I wish you may by this time have a full staff — of cook, chambermaid, &c. Do not yet put off Aunt Elizabeth's day,[182] for I wish by all means to come, if it is prudent, and will decide in the morning tomorrow.[183]

To CHARLES H. DALTON? CONCORD? SEPTEMBER c. 20, 1859

[See a note on Sept. 19, 1859.]

177. MS owned by RWEMA; ph. in CUL. Sept. 19 fell on Monday in 1859, the year fixed by the evidence cited below and by a letter from Ellen Emerson dated Sept. 17, 1859.

178. Cf. numerous earlier letters.

179. Cf. Dec. 1, 1829. The Massachusetts Register . . . for the Year 1859, p. 116, lists S. C. Hewett among Boston physicians who were not members of the regular medical societies.

180. The Boston Daily Advertiser, Sept. 24, 1859, tells of the dedication, on Sept. 22, of the Chelmsford monument to Revolutionary soldiers. Charles H. Dalton is named as chairman of the committee on arrangements. The paper does not print the letters from Emerson and Benjamin P. Hunt which were read. According to Wilson Waters, p. 591, both wrote that ill health prevented their attendance. The notes which Emerson made apparently in preparation for a speech on this occasion are printed in Journals, IX, 235–237. Cf. also Sept. c. 20, 1859.

181. Possibly the Edward Chapin who entered Harvard in 1860 and who appeared in the annual catalogues through the first three years of the course, but apparently did not graduate.

182. Cf. Sept. 16, 1859. Ellen had written on Sept. 17 that if her father was not to be home she must ask " Aunt Lizzy " — Elizabeth Hoar — to change the day.

183. The letter ends without signature, though with ample space for it. But the MS is probably complete and was doubtless sent. It bears what seems to be a contemporary endorsement.

To William Henry Furness, Concord, September 22, 1859

[MS, incomplete, owned by Mr. Horace Howard Furness Jayne; printed in
Records of a Lifelong Friendship, pp. 119–120.]

To Elbridge G. Dudley, Concord, September 29, 1859 [184]

Concord —
29 Sept' 1859

My dear Sir,

　　　　You shall, if you please, entitle my lecture, " Natural & Moral
Beauty." [185]

I believe I was bound to send you a precise answer to your friendly
invitation before this. Please tell Mrs Dudley that I mean to tax her
goodness on Saturday Eve. & Sunday, & to an older guest than she invited; for my sprain remains obstinate, & makes me seventy at least in
my walk, if not in my conversation.

Our Saturday evening train will not bring me to your house till
after 8 P. M.

With great regard,
R. W. Emerson

Mr Dudley.
　(over.

I receive with thanks the ticket to the " Fraternity Lectures." [186]

To ———————————, Concord, September 30, 1859

[MS listed in C. F. Libbie & Co., June 21, 1911.]

184. MS owned by the Abernethy Library, Middlebury College; ph. in CUL.

185. This was duly announced as the subject of Emerson's lecture before Theodore
Parker's old congregation at the Music Hall on Sunday morning, Oct. 2 (*Boston
Evening Transcript*, Oct. 1, 1859).

186. The opening night of the second series of " Fraternity Lectures " — under the
auspices of the Fraternity of the Twenty-eighth Congregational Society (Parker's) —
was to be Oct. 4; on that occasion Rufus Leighton, Jr., was to read a poem and Wendell
Phillips was to make an address (*Boston Daily Advertiser*, Oct. 4, 1859). Emerson
himself appeared as lecturer in this course on Nov. 8 following (*ibid.*, Nov. 8, 1859).
For Leighton, *cf.* Aug. 20, 1861.

To Anna Barker Ward, Concord, October 4, 1859 [187]

Concord
4 October, 1859 —

My dear friend,

A bright hour brought all our young people home last night, Tom [188] inclusive, with such joyful accounts of their visit. May the power to radiate happiness in such large measure never depart from you! Ellen's contentment & narratives — I overheard — far into the night. And they all give me very favorable assurances — of your health — shall I say? well, if not precisely of that, then of a certain glory or super health, which I confide has natural foundations as well as moral — The children brought also beautiful tokens for themselves & for Lidian & me, from you, rich & rare & making each of us proud to be so remembered, & by you, & in such places.[189] I leave the receivers to render each their thanks to you. And when I have seen my " prisoner's " face for a few hours or days more, I trust to reach to its last meaning.[190] I have only time in this hurried moment to say, that we are heartily glad to know that you can & will come here, & it must be whilst the crimson leaves are still over us. I shall see Miss Barrett [191] about Tom & write you presently.

Affectionately yours,
R. W. Emerson

Messages of love & gratitude to you come down from my wifes chamber, & there is no more space!

To William Henry Furness, Concord, October 6, 1859

[MS owned by Mr. Horace Howard Furness Jayne; printed in *Records of a Lifelong Friendship*, pp. 123–124.]

To Daniel Ricketson, Concord, October 11, 1859

[MS listed and partly quoted in American Art Association, Nov. 24–25, 1924; acknowledges a copy of Ricketson's *The History of New Bedford* (1858) and

187. MS owned by HCL; ph. in CUL. Though her name does not appear, Mrs. Ward is pretty obviously the person addressed.
188. Thomas Wren Ward; *cf.* May 5, 1859.
189. Apparently Mrs. Ward had brought back gifts from Europe.
190. In *Journals*, IX, 244 (Oct.? 1859), Emerson records his conversation with his friend " who has just joined the Church of Rome."
191. Perhaps the Miss Barrett mentioned in Jan. 3, 1858.

adds that Emerson and others were anxious that Thoreau should make a successful appearance at the Music Hall in Boston the preceding Sunday. In his journal, Thoreau noted for Oct. 9: " Read a lecture to Theodore Parker's society " (*The Writings*, XVIII, 374) .]

To ——————————, CONCORD, OCTOBER 14, 1859

[MS listed in C. F. Libbie & Co., Feb. 3–5, 1892.]

To JAMES RUSSELL LOWELL, CONCORD, OCTOBER *c.* 15? 1859 [192]

Private)

Concord
October 1859

Dear Lowell,

Just before your note, Bartlett [193] came here, with a double purpose; in both points a friendly one, so far as I was concerned: 1. he wished to justify himself for his suspicions formerly expressed touching P. S. & Co. by telling me of a fraud which they had committed on him, & which he had just detected by examining their books in the hands of the assignees, and which certainly was gross enough: and, 2. he wished to advise me to make Little & Brown my publishers.

I judge by your note that he had not conversed with you. I wish he had, for I think all his informations of some importance to you; but especially for my sake, because I should like your opinion on his showing of the advantage of publishing by L. & B.

It is very easy for me to fall into the hands of Ticknor & Co., whom you recommend; the gravitation is plainly that way. It will require will, which I hate to exert, to go elsewhere. So, if you see him, say I told you he advised me to go to L. & B. & please ask him why? I ought to decide tomorrow, today, this hour perhaps, for the sake of having a printers devil to spur the sides of my lazy intent.[194] I only wish to know if you will say Ticknor, in full view of L. & B.[195]

192. MS owned by HCL; ph. in CUL. This letter clearly precedes that of Oct. 23, 1859, to William Emerson and seems to be answered by Lowell's of Oct. 21, cited below.

193. Probably John Bartlett.

194. Doubtless an echo of Shakespeare's *Macbeth*, I, vii.

195. Lowell wrote, Oct. 21, 1859 (H. E. Scudder, I, 451–452) , emphatically recommending Ticknor & Fields. Emerson was doubtless thinking of *The Conduct of Life*, though that book was not actually published for more than a year.

I send you a poem for the December Atlantic,[196] in despair of having presentable prose, — which both of us would prefer. But do not let the Magazine stop. I will really work for it, rather, & so will we all.

Ever yours,

Mr Lowell.   R. W. Emerson.

I hope to mend the poem in printing.

To ——————, CONCORD, OCTOBER 20, 1859

[MS listed in Merwin-Clayton Sales Co., Nov. 12–16, 1906, where it is described as relating to engagements for lectures in the West.]

To WILLIAM EMERSON, CONCORD, OCTOBER 23, 1859 [197]

Concord
23 October

Dear William,

   I have elected Ticknor & Fields as my publishers,[198] & now only wait the return of the Assignees' Account to put it in their hands & allow them to make the best bargain they can with the assigneees for the sheets, as suggested in Mr Simmons' letter.[199] So, if you have not sent them, please let them come by the next mail. Ticknor said, he would secure to me my full copyright on them. I finished the " Song of Nature," stimulated by your favorable opinion, by writing six more quatrains, & sent it to Lowell.,[200] who has it, he says, already in print. It shall be mended, I hope, when the proof comes to me. We are all very well, in spite of the sad Harpers Ferry business, which interests us all who had Brown for our guest twice. And the story of " bushels of letters " [201] naturally alarmed some of his friends in Boston. He is a true hero, but lost his head there.

Affectionately
Waldo. —

196. *Cf.* Oct. 23, 1859, to William Emerson. The " Song of Nature " did not appear till the following January.

197. MS owned by HCL; ph. in CUL.

198. *Cf.* Oct. *c.* 15? 1859.

199. *Cf.* a note on July 26, 1859.

200. See Oct. *c.* 15? 1859.

201. The " Harpers Ferry business " was reported in the *Boston Daily Advertiser* of Oct. 18, 1859; and it was stated *ibid.*, Oct. 21 following, that John Brown had admitted correspondence with persons at the North and that he had numerous sympathizers in all the free states. The *Boston Evening Transcript* of Oct. 20 reported that captured papers showed many friends were well informed of his movements.

To Franklin Benjamin Sanborn, Concord? October 23, 1859

[Printed, apparently incompletely, in Sanborn, *Recollections*, I, 196, where it is dated only "Sunday Night." This is Emerson's answer to Sanborn's letter of Oct. 22, 1859 (see a note on Oct. 26 following). Oct. 23 fell on Sunday in 1859.]

To Samuel Gray Ward, Concord? October? c. 24? 1859

[Partly printed in *Journals*, IX, 242. The letter relates to John Brown and must have been written some time after he was captured at Harper's Ferry (Oct. 18) and before he was executed (Dec. 2). It seems probable that the date is earlier than that of his conviction of treason and murder (Oct. 31).]

To Sarah Swain Forbes, Concord, October 26, 1859 [202]

Concord
26 October

Dear Mrs Forbes,

We have been all a good deal uneasy about Mr Sanborn's absence, just at this time.[203] But he conferred with no one here, so there was nothing to be said, and he has accustomed his School to short absences of himself, so that no one was surprised. Whatever was the occasion of his absence, I have a note this morning indicating that he is on his way home, & I suppose he will be here tonight.

Our children are delighted with hearing from Anna Watson that Mary [204] was coming to Concord; which they couple with another brilliant hope they have for the school from another side.

The school was never in such good condition & hope as now: the new teacher, Miss Waterman,[205] is a perfect success. So that we are very happy in your sympathy & good meanings toward it & Mr Sanborn.

For Captain Brown, he is a hero of romance, & seems to have made

202. MS owned by RWEMA; ph. in CUL.

203. The whole episode of Sanborn's first flight from Concord to escape arrest as a supporter of John Brown is told in *Recollections*, I, 187–196. On Oct. 22, 1859, he had written from Boston, apologizing for his sudden disappearance and expressing the hope that his school might go on in other hands. Emerson's urgent request seems to have brought him back to Concord a few days later. But he was forced to retire to Canada a second time a few months later (see Jan. 24, 1860).

204. Mr. W. Cameron Forbes informs me that Anna Watson, afterward Mrs. William J. Ladd, was the daughter of Sarah Swain Forbes's twin sister and attended school in Concord; *cf.* also *The Ladd Family*, pp. 240–241. Mary was doubtless Mary Forbes, daughter of Sarah Swain Forbes and later the wife of Henry S. Russell.

205. *Cf.* Sanborn, *Recollections*, I, 194.

this fatal blunder only to bring out his virtues. I must hope for his escape to the last moment.

With kindest regards,
R. W. Emerson

To Penoyer L. Sherman, Concord? October 27, 1859

[Edwin S. Wells, Chicago, Nov. 3, 1859, acknowledged this letter " to Mr. Sherman " and said they relied upon Emerson for Feb. 6. The MS memorandum book for 1860 notes the Chicago lecture and several names, including those of Sherman and Wells, under date of Feb. 6. *Cf.* the letter of Feb. 10, 1860. *D. B. Cooke & Co.'s Directory of Chicago,* 1858, lists Wells as proprietor of Metropolitan Hall and Sherman as a lawyer.]

To Edith Emerson, Boston, October 30, 1859? [206]

Boston 30 Oct
10 o'c

Dear Edith

      Mother & Ellen have not come down today. So you had better make your way to Concord by the driest way you can find, and not come to Boston. If it should happen to be fairer weather at 1 o'clock, I will take a turn by the Revere House at 1.30, & stop at Dr Jackson's But tis safest for you not to wander far from roofs today.

Papa.

To Julia Ward Howe, Concord, November? *c.* 1? 1859

[Described by Julia Ward Howe in a letter of Nov. 6, 1859, as about " the last number of my Cuba " (Laura E. Richards and Maud Howe Elliott, I, 177). The final instalment of " A Trip to Cuba " was printed in *The Atlantic* for that month.]

To James Russell Lowell, Concord, November 2, 1859

[MS listed in John Heise Autographs, catalogue 2468; described there as about a visit to Lowell on the ensuing Saturday.]

To Joseph Gilbert, Concord, November 3, 1859

[MS owned by Miss Margaret Gillum; printed by Leslie H. Meeks in the *Indiana Magazine of History,* XXIX, 90 (June, 1933).]

206. MS owned by RWEMA; ph. in CUL. The year 1859, added in another hand, would seem to be at least a reasonable guess.

To ————————, CONCORD, NOVEMBER 3, 1859

[MS listed in C. F. Libbie & Co., Feb. 3–5, 1892, where it is vaguely described as relating to the publication of Emerson's writings.]

TO FRANKLIN BENJAMIN SANBORN, BOSTON, NOVEMBER 9, 1859

[MS listed and partly quoted in C. F. Libbie & Co., Apr. 23, 1918; printed, with date line given informally, in Sanborn, *Recollections*, I, 199–200.]

TO MONCURE DANIEL CONWAY, CONCORD? NOVEMBER *c.* 13, 1859

[Acknowledged by Conway:

"Cin. Nov. 16. 1859.

" My dear Mr. Emerson,

"Your kind letter came this morning, and after a rather discouraging one from Higginson was indeed a cordial. Very long has this revival of the Dial been my dream: I feel as if it were a hilt for which my hand has long been aching. You need not fear that my purpose will fail: it will never fail. The Dial will be a Western Institution, able to pay for it's contributions, in two years from this.

" I intend to preserve several features of the Old Dial; but one that will interest me most will be the Ethnological Scriptures, of which, now that I have the Redekunste & the Bhagavat Geeta, I can make a pretty fair collection; and to which I invite you & Mr. Thoreau to send on sentences whenever you find them. I shall republish some of the best of those in the Dial.

" I wish you to permit me at some time to publish the beautiful and sacred verses which you once gave me and which have so long been in my treasury, —

' Spin the ball! I reel, I burn.'

I believe it has not been published, — though I recited it at our Club here once.

" What do you think of our printing on the title-page as a motto, the Inscription on the Dial in the *Jardin des Plantes:* Horas non numero nisi serenas? — As giving the Idea that our Dial marks the more sane and lucid intervals of men. I wish much your opinion of this — & ask it even at the risk of being voted a bore.

" I wish you would not call it 'loading' Spofford and myself, to get up a series of Lectures for you — a work on our part so utterly selfish. Levis amoris labor.

" I am sorry that you will not abandon your hotel rule: I shᵈ hope to give you all the privacy and independence you could wish here, — but, though I hope you will agree to let us get up the 'series,' and also that you will order yͬ omnibus to drive to 114 *Hopkins* St (a name which shᵈ remind you that a man shᵈ be willing to be damned for the glory of God,) I will not urge anything that would render your visit less free and pleasant to you. I feel now that I am *cut* by Bellows, King & Co. in their visits to the Mercantile out here, that I deserve charitable visitation from the heretics. Starr King has recently behaved in a very shabby way out here, acting with a timidity of which I did not suppose him capable.

"Can you tell me anything of a book called 'The Divine Drama,' or its author?

"Yours,
"M. D. Conway.

"R. W. Emerson."]

To Lydia Maria Child, Concord, November 23, 1859 [207]

Concord
23 Nov? 1859

Dear Mrs Child,

Forgive me for my slow answers; the Lyceum & some accidents make a multitude of letters [208] for me in these weeks, which aggravate the distemper of slow writing. Thanks thanks for your letter to Captain Brown: — and his reply [209] will stand instead of all letters to you. I cherish to the last, hope for his brave life. He is one of those on whom miracles wait. I do not much think I shall go to Boston on the 2ᵈ December.[210] We are talking of a little ceremony here, which Thoreau has projected, for that day. If I change my mind, I will write you word in season.

Yours gratefully,
R. W. Emerson

Mrs Child.

To ——————————, Concord? December? c. 5? 1859

[The letter to some person at Sterling, Mass., mentioned in Dec. 19, 1859, to Blake.]

207. MS owned by Mr. W. T. H. Howe; ph. in CUL.

208. Apparently a number of such letters were written which I have not found. On the back of a letter of Nov. 3, 1859, from E. S. Wells of Chicago, Emerson wrote two rough outlines of his projected Western tour, duplicating each other to a considerable extent but including eighteen different towns and cities in Indiana, Illinois, Michigan, and Wisconsin. Some of these places — for example, Terre Haute — he apparently dropped.

209. Mrs. Child's letter of Oct. 26, 1859, to John Brown, expressing her sympathy with him and her wish to be his nurse, is printed, with his reply, in *Letters of Lydia Maria Child*, 4th ed., 1884, pp. 118–120.

210. Emerson had already spoken at the meeting held in Boston on Nov. 18 for the relief of Brown's family, and his "Remarks" is printed in *Cent. Ed.*, XI. The John Brown meeting of Dec. 2 in Boston is reported in the *Boston Daily Advertiser*, Dec. 3, 1859; but Emerson was busy on that day at Concord, in a similar meeting (see *Journals*, IX, 253, and James Redpath, *Echoes of Harper's Ferry*, 1860, pp. 437-454). Thoreau had an important part in the Concord meeting.

To THADDEUS HYATT, CONCORD? DECEMBER? *c.* 7? 1859
[Mentioned in Dec. 12, 1859.]

To WILLIAM EMERSON, BOSTON, DECEMBER 12, 1859 [211]

American House
Boston 12 Dec[r]

Dear William

I have waited two or three days to answer your question [212] precisely. A Mr Hyatt of N. Y. a good Brownist, but not I think a very judicious person solicits me daily by mail & telegraph to come to Brown Relief Meeting with Beecher, Phillips, & Cheever.[213] I answered, I can come 15th or 17th provided, those three named persons will come: not else. Now Beecher will not. I therefore say to him, today by telegraph,[214] I will not. For I have no sufficient readiness to go to N. Y. on matter of my own & could only at this moment venture to join what is already strong. So tell Mr Spring, or I will write him, that I shall not probably come at present But if I come or when I come I will gladly negociate with him. But the rest tomorrow [215]

To STEPHEN G. BENEDICT, CONCORD, DECEMBER 13, 1859 [216]

Concord, 13 Dec[r]
1859.

Dear Sir,

You shall hold me engaged to you for 8th February. I see you write me *Rev[d]*, to which I have no title. Do not advertise me so.

Respectfully,
R. W. Emerson

211. MS owned by HCL; ph. in CUL. The year 1859, supplied by William Emerson, is obviously correct.

212. William Emerson, Dec. 7, 1859 (MS owned by Dr. Haven Emerson) : " I wish you would let me know when I can expect to see you this way." This letter inclosed one from Marcus Spring, apparently requesting a lecture.

213. Thaddeus Hyatt's letter of Dec. 9, 1859, was one of the several communications referred to. Hyatt explained that Thursday would be better than Saturday even if Beecher had to be left out — Phillips, Cheever, and Emerson would be enough to fill the house anyhow. Dec. 14, 1859, records further developments.

214. But it does not seem quite certain that this telegram was sent.

215. Here the letter breaks off, without signature and with part of p. 3 and all of p. 4 left blank.

216. MS owned by the State Historical Society of Wisconsin; ph. in CUL. The

To William Emerson, Concord, December 14, 1859 [217]

Concord

14 Dec 59

Dear William,

I had hardly sent away my note to you yesterday,[218] when Wendell Phillips came here to entreat me to go to N. Y., in spite of Mr Hyatts maladministration. Fresh from North Elba,[219] he had such wishes & hopes for his poor people, that I even put myself in his hands, & he is to telegraph me away again to Mr Hyatt & his company. But I believe it is for Saturday now. I shall arrange, if I go,[220] to be put in some hotel in the vicinity of the Cooper Institute, and, if it be Saturday, will try to come out & dine with you on Sunday.

Affectionately,

Waldo E.

If you should see us advertised for Saturday, I could go to Mr Spring Monday, if that wd. would suit him For prices my price abroad is $50. but I suppose $30. would do at Eagleswood.[221]

To Harrison Gray Otis Blake, Concord, December 19, 1859 [222]

Concord

19 Dec[r]

My dear Sir,

I wrote to Sterling [223] immediately on receiving your first note. After many days their answer came, — it seems my letter was a

---

address, S. G. Benedict, Madison, Wis., has been added opposite the signature, in another hand. Probably Emerson wrote the name of his correspondent in a corner of the MS which has been cut away. For both Benedict and the lecture at Madison, see also Feb. 10, 1860.

217. MS owned by HCL; ph. in CUL.

218. Apparently the letter of Dec. 12, 1859, which William Emerson marked " Rec'd Dec[r] 14/59." It relates to Hyatt and the proposed " Brownist " meeting in New York, as well as to Spring's proposal.

219. The New York village where John Brown was buried on Dec. 8, 1859.

220. The meeting was shifted back to Thursday, the 15th. Wendell Phillips wrote an undated letter, postmarked Dec. 14, 1859, saying he had just heard from Hyatt that it was too late to change the evening; so, Phillips said, he would have to go to New York on the following day and face three thousand people who would wish to see Emerson instead. The meeting of the 15th at the Cooper Institute, with Phillips's address, is reported in the *New-York Daily Tribune*, Dec. 16, 1859.

221. For this community near Perth Amboy, N. J., see Nov. 18, 1856.

222. MS owned by Mr. Abel Cary Thomas; ph. in CUL. The year is fixed by evidence cited below.

223. Dec.? *c.* 5? 1859.

week in the transit, — & it is is settled that I am to go there next Thursday Evening.[224] They did not ask for my subject — I shall probably read one of my last spring lectures,[225] " Manners "; or " Success."

Ever yours,
R. W. Emerson

Mr Blake.

To Elbridge G. Dudley, Concord, December 19, 1859 [226]

Concord
19 December, 1859

Dear Sir,

I will try to come to Music Hall next Sunday, if Dr Furness does not. If you hear from him that he will come, please send me early word On Friday morning I will send you a title for announcement. And I think to accept, this time, the hospitalities which your ladies so persistently offer me.

With great regard,
R. W. Emerson —

Mr Dudley.

To William Henry Furness, Concord, December 23, 1859

[MS owned by Mr. Horace Howard Furness Jayne; printed in *Records of a Lifelong Friendship*, p. 127.]

To William Emerson, Concord, December 30, 1859 [227]

Concord, 30 Dec.

Dear William,

I have just come home from two days absence & find your letter, & unfailing wonder-box.[228] I sympathize in your parental priva-

224. The *Worcester Daily Spy*, Dec. 23, 1859, reports the lecture at Sterling, Mass., on the 22d; many people traveled from Worcester, perhaps twelve or fifteen miles away, to hear Emerson.

225. Listed in a note on Apr. 4, 1859.

226. MS owned by Dr. Frederic Ives Carpenter; ph. in CUL. The letter of Dec. 23, 1859, shows that Furness was expected in Boston by the 29th. But the *Boston Evening Transcript*, Dec. 24, 1859, announced that Emerson would lecture on " Conversation " before Parker's Society at the Music Hall on the morning of the 25th.

227. MS owned by HCL; ph. in CUL. Evidence cited below fixes the year.

228. The box of gifts was announced in William Emerson, Dec. 28, 1859 (MS owned by Dr. Haven Emerson) .

tions alluded to in a former letter,[229] but not less real now, but tis the common lot of parents, &, if it were not, they would have more reason to complain. Who wants sons & daughters such that the world will allow him to keep them to himself? Charles is a great favorite at Cambridge, as well as at Concord, only he seems a little of the Bolingbroke [230] persuasion, & keeps himself from the gazer's eyes. There is much glee here that he will come tomorrow Dear love to Susan, whom I shall not see so early in the winter as I hoped. My N. Y. plans have not fruited.[231] I send today a book to Haven the mate of an old one he has, and must write the end of my letter when light comes —

In twilight yours
Waldo.

To ———————, CONCORD? DECEMBER? 1859?

[MS listed and partly quoted in C. F. Libbie & Co., May 9–10, 1911; described as accompanying notes of the John Brown speech of Dec., 1859, sent for publication in John S. Dwight's journal (where, however, nothing of the sort seems to have appeared). For Emerson's speeches on John Brown, see notes on Nov. 23, 1859, and on Jan. 2, 1860, to Rantoul.]

229. A letter dated Dec. 7, 1859 (owned by Dr. Haven Emerson) complains that all of the three sons have left home — " & ye have taken Charley away."
230. The king, in Shakespeare's *I Henry IV*, III, ii.
231. Probably a scheme in which Marcus Spring had a part (*cf.* Dec. 14, 1859).

1860

To Wendell Phillips, Concord, January 1, 1860

[MS listed in American Art Association, Mar. 10–11, 1924, where it is described as an attempt to straighten out an appointment. For the occasion of the letter and for what was apparently Phillips's answer, see a note on Jan. 2, 1860, to Rantoul.]

To William Henry Furness, Concord? January? *c.* 1? 1860?

[MS owned by Mr. Horace Howard Furness Jayne; printed, without place or date, in *Records of a Lifelong Friendship,* p. 172. The reference to Emerson's plan to attend a " Brown Meeting " at Salem on Thursday or Friday pretty definitely fixes the date, which, however, might be late Dec., 1859, rather than early Jan., 1860 (*cf.* especially Jan. 2, 1860, to Rantoul). The present letter seems to be referred to in Jan. 14, 1860.]

To Charles Eliot Norton, Concord, January 2, 1860 [1]

Concord
2 January 1860

My dear Sir,

Your beautiful Christmas gift [2] came to my eyes only in the last hour of the year, and as musical & deep-meaning as its chimes when bells did chime at that season. Tis a compliment to the race, — a book upon Dante, — & brings us all to our best thoughts. And loyalty & nobleness are better shown in this choice & in the treatment of the matter, than in praises of the virtues. I thank you for myself, & in behalf of many retired readers who will enjoy this homage done both inwardly & outwardly to the old deep serious genius, on whom love & taste are so well bestowed. I shall use my early leisure in good readings of it.

1. MS owned by HCL; ph. in CUL.
2. A copy of Norton's *The New Life of Dante. An Essay, with Translations,* printed at Cambridge, 1859, is still in Emerson's library at the Antiquarian House.

I thank you for Fauriel — the new; It reminds me that tis quite time to restore the prior volumes. They shall come soon.[3]

Very gratefully
Yours,
R. W. Emerson —

Mr Norton.

To Robert Samuel Rantoul, Concord, January 2, 1860 [4]

Concord
Monday Mor^{ng}
2 Jan^y

Dear Sir,

    I slipped your note into my pocket half read, for later consideration On my return home that night I could not find it. My belief is that you fixed Friday.[5] Can you not telegraph me. if it be so. It has become desireable to me to be free on Thursday night. Yet I shall not make myself so until I hear from you. Yours,

R. W. Emerson

Mr Rantoul.

3. See Mar. 10, 1860.

4. MS owned by the Providence Athenæum; ph. in CUL. Evidence cited below shows that the year was 1860, when Jan. 2 fell on Monday.

5. Apparently in answer to the letter of Jan. 1, Wendell Phillips wrote, Jan. 3, 1860, that Rantoul had " fixed on *Friday* next for us to come to Salem " and that he and Clarke would aid Emerson. The *Salem Gazette,* Jan. 3 and 6, 1860, announced that the meeting for the aid of the relief fund for the destitute families of John Brown and his associates had been postponed to Friday, Jan. 6. The event was reported *ibid.,* Jan. 10 following: James Freeman Clarke, Emerson, and Wendell Phillips were the speakers; and R. S. Rantoul read letters from John A. Andrew, Jacob Manning, and Whittier. A fund of about $100 was raised. Sanborn, two months later, wrote to Emerson, advising that the whole of the address at Salem be published:

" Concord, Tuesday Evening
" March 6<u>th</u> '60

" My dear Sir;

    " On reading the Salem speech it seems to me so pertinent and good that I should not know what to omit, but were it left to me should print the whole. The only question in my mind would be whether you might not rather print it yourself in some magazine or book, and so it might not be advisable to give it to Mr Redpath. Your synopsis of the life of Brown seems of no less value than before the book of Redpath appeared; and your criticism of the *man* is so apt an answer to such censures as that in the last Atlantic that I would fain see it soon printed.

    " But before copying it I will wait for any farther instructions from you

" Yours truly
" F. B. Sanborn "

Emerson's speech was duly printed in Redpath's *Echoes of Harper's Ferry,* pp. 119–122, and is to be found in *Cent. Ed.,* XI.

To ————————, CONCORD, JANUARY 12, 1860

[MS listed in Maggs Bros., 1898.]

To WILLIAM HENRY FURNESS, CONCORD, JANUARY 14, 1860

[MS owned by Mr. Horace Howard Furness Jayne; printed in *Records of a Lifelong Friendship,* pp. 130–131.]

To ABEL ADAMS, CONCORD, JANUARY 16, 1860 [6]

> Concord
> 16 Jan.ʸ 1860

My dear friend,

My lame foot,[7] — which now mends so far at least as to bear a good deal of use without being worse the next day, — has made me an aged man for these last months, or I should have come to see you once & again. This afternoon, I go to New York, on my way to the West,[8] and shall probably be absent a month. I wish not to leave a mortgage-note in my tinderbox at home, and therefore shall carry it to town to-day, & leave it enclosed to your address, at the Globe Bank. Will you please take care of it, and, which is a main point, let Mr Coverly,[9] State Street, the signer, be instructed to pay the interest, due in February & August, at the Bank; which, I suppose, will be the most convenient arrangement for him. This note I had made, when Mr Gilbert insisted on paying his. I make no apology for pestering you with this affair, for I count it only a continuation of the old one with which you kindly charged yourself. I trust, on my return, to walk bodily up your hill, & thank you. Dear love to your inmates!

> Yours affectionately,

Mr Adams.   R. W. Emerson.

If I send only one paper, it is because the other is still, since August, in the Register's Office, for record.

6. MS owned by RWEMA; ph. in CUL.

7. This lameness is mentioned in many letters of the latter half of 1859.

8. *Cf.* letters of Jan. 21 and later, 1860.

9. Samuel Coverly is listed as a broker of State St. in the *Boston Directory,* 1859. C. F. Simmons, Boston, Feb. 28, 1860, inclosed " Sam'l Coverly's mortgage."

To H. O. Houghton and Company, Boston? January 16, 1860 [10]

Mess Houghton & Co
  Gent.

       Please print from my plates five hundred copies " Essays, second Series " for Ticknor & Fields [11]

               Yours &c

Jany 16. 1860   R. Waldo Emerson

To Ellen Emerson, Utica, New York, January 20, 1860

[Mentioned in the letters of Jan. 24 and 29, 1860.]

To Emily Mervine Drury, Utica, New York, January 21, 1860 [12]

            Utica 21st Jan. 1860

My dear friend,

      I ought to have written you long ago., to say that I cannot come to Canandaigua, as I had gladly have done,[13] on the day you invite me. I am engaged to be at Batavia on the 25th instant; [14] and at Rochester on the 26th instant; [15] then at Toronto; & so westward.

  But you intimate that may be at Rochester, which I strongly hope Here I am in Utica,[16] yet my foot is not strong enough for walking & I fear that I shall not even find my way to fathers house —

  10. MS owned by CUL; ph. in CUL. Only the signature is in Emerson's hand. I conjecture that the rest of the note was written, perhaps from Emerson's dictation, by some member or clerk of the firm of Ticknor & Fields.

  11. The second series duly reappeared with the imprint " Boston: Ticknor and Fields. MDCCCLX."

  12. MS owned by CUL; ph. in CUL. This is a copy, in pencil, made by Emily Mervine Drury in her notebook, where she introduced the text thus: " To Rev Mr Taylor I give a letter from Mr Emerson as he is a lover of Mr E.

  " the copy of the letter is below."

The omission of two pronouns which must have been in the original and the incomplete transcription of other words mar this text. The date is clearly given as Jan. 21; but the geography of Emerson's lecture appointments, discussed below, seems to offer some ground for doubt as to its correctness.

  13. Perhaps the phrase has been altered by the copyist.

  14. For Emerson's lecture at Batavia on the 25th, see Jan. 24, 1860.

  15. See Jan. 29, 1860.

  16. Apparently Emerson did not lecture at this time, for the MS memorandum book marks Jan. 20 " Pt Byron? " leaves Jan. 21 blank, and gives Jan. 22 to Rochester; and I have found no notice in the Utica papers. Now, according to the MS memorandum book, Emerson was at Hamilton, N. Y., on the 19th, and he might very well have spent some time in Utica the following day on his way to Port Byron to lecture that night. Once at Port Byron, he would hardly have turned eastward again to Utica before going on to Rochester for his lecture of the 22d. But the Port Byron appoint-

Mr Beecher whom I met the other day, had much good to say & think of you & claims to be a cousin of your husbands.[17]

Do not fail to let me see you if it be possible, for I have not seen a reasonable person to talk with for many days & I wish to hear of all the reasonable persons whom you have seen & all the good book you have read, & better yet, all the good solitudes & solitary thought you have known —

I shall go to the Eagle Hotel [18] Is not that a good one? & perhaps if you cannot come you will let me hear from you there.

With kindes regards,
R W Emerson

Mrs Drury

To Ellen Emerson, Buffalo, January 24, 1860 [19]

American House.
Buffalo, 24 Jan^y.

Dear Ellen, You are excellent with your letters, your own I mean, and also with your faithful despatches, which all arrived, — those at Lima,[20] last night; — those to Buffalo,[21] today. You need not seal the *proofs*,[22] which subjects them to letter postage, but merely roll them in a paper as the printers do, writing "*proof*" outside. Then a cent will carry them far. But here come more letters; for Mr Bryan of Batavia [23] has just bro't me his package to Buffalo. Never Papa could so well afford to go

---

ment is marked as uncertain, and I have not been able to find conclusive evidence regarding it; so it is possible that Emerson remained at Utica from the 20th to the 21st or even the 22d. That he was at Utica on the 20th is pretty clear from the letter of that date.

17. Miss Mildred R. Mervine informs me that it was Emerson who introduced Henry Ward Beecher to Mrs. Drury.

18. The MS memorandum book for 1860 has this entry for Jan. 22: "Rochester Eagle Hotel Worship."

19. MS owned by RWEMA; ph. in CUL. The year is fixed by evidence cited below.

20. The MS memorandum book for 1860 gives Jan. 23 to Lima, N. Y., and notes that the lecture was "Manners."

21. Emerson read "Manners" before the Young Men's Association at St. James Hall on the 24th (*Buffalo Commercial Advertiser*, Jan. 25, 1860).

22. *Cf.* Jan. 16, 1860, to H. O. Houghton & Co.; but it seems hardly probable that the reference here is to the new printing of the second series of *Essays*. There are several other possibilities.

23. Emerson's reading of "Manners" at Batavia, N. Y., on the 25th, is noted in two papers of that town, *The Daily Republican Advocate*, Jan. 25, and *The Genesee County Herald*, Jan. 28, 1860. William G. Bryan wrote from Batavia on Feb. 1 following, inclosing a draft for $50, the fee for "Manners." For Bryan, see May 30, 1862.

from home, since you can & will send me such spritely Chronicles. The account of the School readings leaves nothing to be desired. And the story of the school & the schoolmaster is getting a painful interest in your last details,[24] and I am sorry to be absent just now.

I decided not to send back the Fauriels & brot one volume with me. But if you have sent one to Mr Norton, there is no harm.[25] I mean to send you a hundred dollars in this note. I sent you $100. last Friday, from Utica,[26] which, I hope, arrived. I shall not send you any more for a week, for I must send 200. to the Atlantic Bank to pay my note, before 5 Feby You need not be uneasy about my foot, which likes railroad riding all day very well, the lazy dog. But I make it go when I dismount anywhere. It is doing well enough. I have read Frank Nash's paper [27] & am glad that he is doing such things. Edith is good with her story of the school which ended too soon, & she might have sent me Edward's poem. Well for the boy that he is to read with Aunt Elizabeth H. Love to Mamma, who will not wish any letter from me now that you can relieve both of us of the annoy of accounts. Let her tell James, that I remember him every day, & depend entirely on him. I go to Batavia tomorrow. I enclose 10.00 & a draft for $90. on N. Y. payable to Mr Cheney who will give you the money for it. Papa.

To Ellen Emerson, Detroit, January 29, 1860 [28]

Russell House,
Detroit, Sunday
29 Jan

Dear Ellen,
          Here from Toronto,[29] on my way to Toledo [30] tomorrow,

24. Ellen had written, Jan. 19 and 20, 1860, of Sanborn's intention to leave Concord the following week and said that she had told him of her own plan to go to Cambridge. Sanborn's difficulties in connection with the John Brown episode are alluded to in other letters. *Cf.* especially Jan. 29, 1860.

25. See Mar. 10, 1860. Ellen had written in her letter of the 19th and 20th that Norton's book had gone.

26. In the letter of Jan. 20, 1860.

27. Frank Nash, Boston, Jan. 17 (1860), told of an article on the late king of Naples which he wished to submit to *The Atlantic* after Emerson had read and criticized it. Apparently, however, Nash published nothing in that magazine.

28. MS owned by RWEMA; ph. in CUL. The date is obviously 1860, and Jan. 29 fell on Sunday in that year. Apparently there was no lecture at Detroit at this time.

29. Mr. Carl F. Klinck informs me that Emerson's " Manners and Morals," read before the Ontario Literary Society on Jan. 27, 1860, was recorded by two Toronto

but to be here again on the 18 Feb.ʸ ³¹ I had a bountiful supply of letters, as I already acknowledged, at Buffalo. None at Rochester. I hope you have my two *valuable* letters from Utica & Buffalo. each enclosing $100. At Toronto yesterday a very agreeable visit as the last year. A company of young men so intelligent well-mannered & cordial, tis a happiness to meet. They gave me a drama " Saul," written by a Canadian,³² which I have been reading, & which has real merit. They also stuffed into my pocket Tennyson's new poem " Sea-dreams," in " Harper's Weekly," ³³ which I read on my way. At Toronto, I found a letter from Mr Sanborn, which explained his plans as far as he could.³⁴ Tis a calamity for the

---

papers the following day. *The Globe* said the lecture was heard with the most rapt attention and *The Leader* praised it generously. The same lecture is listed in the MS memorandum book for this year. J. D. Edgar, Toronto, Jan. 28, 1860, wrote Emerson his thanks.

30. Emerson read " Manners " before the " Y. M. A." on Jan. 30; every sentence, said the reporter, was " a living thought " and the speaker's intellectual power, freely exercised, became " absolutely painful " (*Daily Toledo Blade,* Jan. 31, 1860) .

31. See the letter of that date.

32. Charles Heavysege's *Saul,* apparently first published at Montreal in 1857, was praised in *The North British Review,* Aug., 1858, as " indubitably one of the most remarkable English poems ever written out of Great Britain." The copy reviewed " was given to the writer of the present article by Mr Nathaniel Hawthorne, to whose recommendation of this, to him and to us, unknown Canadian poet, our readers and English literature generally are beholden for their first introduction to a most curious work."

33. For Jan. 28, 1860.

34. Sanborn wrote:

" Montreal Jan'y 24ᵗʰ 1860

" My dear Sir;

" You have no doubt heard before this by your letters from home that I was summoned by the Marshall the same day you left Concord. Today I should have been in Washington to answer the summons, but am here instead. I have sent to the Committee declining to comply with their summons from an apprehension of personal danger, but offering to testify in Mass. This was at the suggestion of Messrs Keyes and Andrew, and I hope will not place me in a false position — for it is not the personal risk that keeps me away — What notice the Senate will take of this paper you may perhaps know before this reaches you —

" From this place I shall quietly watch the issue, and act accordingly — I left Concord yesterday morning (Monday) at 7 1/2; leaving my school in charge of Miss Hoar and Miss Elizabeth Ripley in addition to the other teachers. Miss Jackson also teaches half a dozen small classes — Should I not return before Feb 8ᵗʰ Mr Whittemore a graduate of 1857 and now teaching in Mr Dixwell's school — a cousin of the Mansfields — will probably take my place, and I either stay here or go across the water —

" I came here against my own inclination, which was to remain in Concord until the end of this week, and then not to leave the state; but my family and many friends were so anxious about my safety that I took an earlier start — to avoid the possibility of an arrest. It was generally thought I was going to Washington; nor do half a dozen

present to Concord & to him. On the 8ᵗʰ Feb.ʸ it seems, Mr Whittemore
will take his place at the school. Tis an unlucky coincidence that you
should quit the sinking boat just now ³⁵ Perhaps you will like to postpone Cambridge for ten days, signifying to Ida ³⁶ your good intention
still. If your staying, as is very likely, can decide some good girls to stay,
I think you had better give up Cambridge, till the next term. But you
can see truly on the spot. As you will probably know by your own climate, I have had the gentlest weather, & no chance yet, tell Alice, to
unfold my " *scarf,*" (is it?) or, tell Mother, my " down." At Toronto it
must needs suddenly snow & empty the streets of all women so that I
could not see a girl's fur cap. I went to a furrier's shop & hastily got a
couple of what he assured me were the best skating caps worn but
I know not if I can get them home safe, & much doubt their availabil-
ity: but you can give them to young things, if you do not like them. Love
to Mamma & Edith & Edward. Papa.

To Lidian Emerson, Lafayette, Indiana, February 5, 1860 ³⁷

Lafayette Indiana
5 February, 1860

Dear Lidian,

Ellen says you wish for letters: tis a surprising anachronism
— be sure, — that you should fancy that an old gentleman plodding

---

persons now know my whereabouts. Which will be a secret until the Committee has
acted on my request — I am at the St Lawrence Hotel and shall be for the present —
I saw your family on Sunday, except Ellen and Edward, who were at Milton. Mr
Channing is a very serviceable friend in my absence.

" I send this to you at a venture but hope it may reach you at Toronto, where I
hear you are to be on the 27ᵗʰ Not knowing your address I send to the Lyceum
Committee —

" The presence of Realf at Washington makes it still more undesirable that I
should go there. I wait with curiosity to see what he will say, and how much will be
believed, and how Wilson will answer his statements —

" I hope you are well and do not find your journey too wearisome. I am almost
tempted to go to Toronto and hear you, but shall be obliged to wait here for letters, I
suppose — If I stay long in Canada I shall go and investigate the condition of the
fugitives about Chatham and at St Catherine's —

" I am always with respect

" Very truly yours
" F. B Sanborn

" Mr Emerson "

35. *Cf.* a note on Jan. 24, 1860.
36. Agassiz.
37. MS owned by RWEMA; ph. in CUL. Emerson lectured at Lafayette, Ind., on
Feb. 4, according to the *Lafayette Daily Journal*, Feb. 4 and 6, 1860. The newspaper

through this prairie mud, on such dingy errands, too, should be capable of letters. They are for idle young people, & from such. Praise rather my good manners which would save you wearisome details, & turn them on Ellen, who is willing & ought to learn them. She is a darling of a correspondent too, & has kept me in letters at each step of my march. I have had a much easier western trip thus far, than ever before, partly owing to the fine weather, which has been almost unbroken. My foot, which admires railroad cars, rewards their rest by strength & almost friskiness, on each arrival.[38] I walk much without a cane. I fear I shall not even reach home on the 21 or 22ᵈ, as I have designed; as it will probably cost me a day or two to repair a failure of mine at Zanesville,[39] and I must write today to Cambridgeport where I am due on 21ˢᵗ [40] to pray for release. I hope all goes as well at home as usual, & with yourself — I have not yet been able to obtain Darwin's book which I had depended on as a road book You must read it, — " Darwin on Species." [41] It has not arrived in these dark lands. I shall send Ellen money from Chicago.[42] Dear love to my darlings!

Waldo E

To William Emerson, Lafayette, Indiana, February 5? 1860

[William Emerson, Mar. 4, 1860 (MS owned by Dr. Haven Emerson) : " I had a few lines from you dated at LaFayette."]

paid only the slightest attention to the event, but the MS memorandum book for 1860 gives " Conduct of Life " as the subject.

38. The accident is mentioned in July 15, 1859, and in many later letters.

39. See Feb. 21, 1860.

40. In the MS memorandum book for this year Cambridgeport is entered under Feb. 21 but is canceled.

41. *On the Origin of Species* had been published Nov. 24, 1859. Emerson, who had been for many years an interested spectator of the march of science and a student of earlier speculations on evolution, must have been deeply stirred by Darwin's great book. It was presumably about Feb. 2 or 3, 1860, that he discussed the momentous discovery to the delight of Conway (*Autobiography*, I, 282; and MS memorandum book for this year). A little later, apparently in May or June, Emerson noted Agassiz's insistence on permanent species, with Thoreau's clever remark (*Journals*, IX, 270) ; and this entry, though it does not mention Darwin, is surely an echo of the debate his book had aroused. Nine years later, in a letter of Mar. 16, 1869, Emerson refers to his reading of Darwin but without specific comment. And in Jan. 9, 1872, he tells of " a valuable conversation . . . on the present aspects of science, Darwin, Agassiz, &c." Agassiz, with his unswerving disbelief in the theory of evolution, must have loomed large on the horizon. But in such works as *The Conduct of Life*, published late in 1860, and *Letters and Social Aims*, which first appeared in 1875, Emerson definitely shows his allegiance to the general notion of evolution, in one case, curiously enough, naming Agassiz and Darwin together (*Cent. Ed.*, VI, 165, and VIII, 7) .

42. Sent in the letter of Feb. *c.* 7, 1860.

To ———————, LAFAYETTE? INDIANA? FEBRUARY 5? 1860

[This letter to somebody at Cambridgeport, Mass., about a lecture there, is mentioned in the letters of Feb. 5 and 10, 1860.]

To LIDIAN EMERSON, CHICAGO, FEBRUARY c. 7, 1860

[Described in Edith Emerson, Feb. 10 (endorsed 1860), as a letter to her mother with a check, from Chicago, received that morning. Described by Ellen Emerson, Feb. 11, 13, and 14, 1860, as "The Chicago letter to Mother" received the preceding Friday (Feb. 10). Alluded to in Feb. 10, 1860, where Emerson says, "I hope you have today the $100 draft I sent you from Chicago."]

To STEPHEN G. BENEDICT, ROCKFORD? ILLINOIS? FEBRUARY 8, 1860

[Mentioned in Feb. 10, 1860.]

To ELLEN EMERSON, MILWAUKEE, FEBRUARY 9? 1860

[First of the two letters from Milwaukee mentioned in Feb. 12, 1860, as containing money. Apparently it was this letter which, according to Ellen Emerson, Feb. 11, 13, and 14, 1860, arrived from Milwaukee on the 14th and contained $100.]

To ELLEN EMERSON, MILWAUKEE, FEBRUARY 10, 1860 [43]

Newhall House
Milwaukie
10 Feb.^y

Dear Ellen, Good visit to Chicago,[44] barring one circumstance that from Lafayette [45] I had to charter a special train to carry me 90 miles to Michigan City, in fault of any other means to reach Chicago in time. Saw Mr Wiley at Chicago Mr Thoreau's friend [46] who attended me like a friendly shadow. Thence to Rockford [47] good time; & thence to Madison, where I had telegraphed the Secretary " I come tonight, but doubt-

43. MS owned by RWEMA; ph. in CUL. The year is obviously 1860. Apparently "Success" was the Milwaukee lecture of Feb. 9 (*Milwaukee Daily Sentinel*, Feb. 9 and 10, 1860).

44. A large audience heard Emerson read "Manners" under the auspices of the Young Men's Association on Feb. 6 (*The Daily Chicago Times*, Feb. 5 and 8, 1860).

45. *Cf.* Feb. 5, 1860.

46. See Jan. 24, 1857.

47. *The Rockford Republican*, Feb. 9, 1860, reported the reading of "Manners" before the Young Men's Association on the 7th.

ful of my voice"; [48] for a wet nightshirt from the Chicago laundry had
choked my lungs. But all the way in the cars I sucked " Browns troches,"
and only awed my Wisconsin senate (for all the legislature was at
Madison,) with a rich[er][49] orotund than they had heard. I found there
my Mr Strong of Racine who once dined with us two years ago, & he
came with me here yesterday & will accompany me to Racine.[50] Here is
a magnificent hotel the best by far in all the West & my windows look
out on Lake Michigan. At Madison I looked through all the halls of
the University & the Historical Society under friendly guidance [51] Last
night, I had your letters of 6th & 7th and I hope you have today the $100
draft I sent you from Chicago.[52] But you must not give away any money
to G. L Emersons or the like whilst so many honest claims are unanswered. I do not wish to send you any more money than is indispensable,
as I must bring home means to pay a large debt at Concord Bank, or a
part of it. I cannot it seems come home to meet the Cambridgeport lecture 21st as I must stop & go to Zanesville on that day, and have so written our Cambridgeport, and I suppose it m[ay][53] take 2 or 2½ days thence
to Concord — I am very happy in James's message & in his staying from
the party Give him my love & reliance.

Dear love to Mamma, Edith & Edward who must write to Detroit to
Papa. I enclose $10.00

To BENJAMIN B. WILEY, RACINE, WISCONSIN, FEBRUARY 10? 1860

[Wiley, Chicago, July 22, 1862, recalls Emerson's letter of " Some two years
ago " from Racine " in regard to your preaching for the College." For Emerson
at Racine on Feb. 10, 1860, see the letter of Feb. 12. Whether the " preaching "
was at Racine College at that time, I do not know.]

48. Telegraphic letter of Feb. 8. *The Wisconsin Daily Patriot* of that date announced that Benedict had received that afternoon a telegram in which Emerson
promised to be on hand early in the evening. As a matter of fact, however, there was
a delay caused by " a change of time in the arrival of the freight train," and the lecture on " Manners " was tardily begun (*ibid.*, Feb. 9, 1860).

49. Part of the word is badly blotted and is illegible.

50. See Feb. 12, 1860.

51. Benedict was a curator of the Society (see *Publications of the State Historical
Society of Wisconsin, Collections*, XXI, 37, and *Report and Collections*, V, 32).

52. Feb. c. 7, 1860.

53. Badly blotted. A part of the final paragraph runs over the margin to the
opposite page and is set off with irregular lines.

To Ellen Emerson, Chicago, February 12, 1860 [54]

                                    Tremont House
                                    Chicago 12 Feb.ʸ
Dear Ellen,

   I hope you had a letter from me at Chicago, & two from Milwaukee; each of the three containing money.

  You wrote me faithfully to Milwaukee, &, in spite of Ellen Washburn, I mean to find news at Niles [55] tomorrow night. A very good visit to the Badgers of Wisconsin, especially at Racine, at the house of my friend Mr Strong.[56] He came with me thence to Kenosha,[57] & all this day by carriage to this place 55 miles, which proved necessary in order to go hence tomorrow morning to Niles. We are always looking out on this great green sea, dappled with ice, and lined along the horizon with a brilliant streak, as if the eye reached to an icy shore beyond; but of course no land can be seen. I look into schools & colleges, when I go by them, & heard a girl in the High School at Racine, read Willis's Hagar,[58] with taste & truth. A town here always indicates that there is a river or at least some ravine which runs down to the Lake, & makes the beginning of a harbor. Then they drive piles, & run out a pier, & a steamboat can load or discharge. At Racine, was a little stream called Root River, by translating the Indian name; so they called the town Racine. I read gladly your pencil note that Mrs Ripley & Sophy are well again; and, ere this, I hope your friend Miss Waterman is healed.

  I am very sorry for my promised detention at Zanesville, on account of my printers [59] as well as my home. Tell mamma Mr & Mrs Strong wish her to come with me, next winter. Please let my foot alone, — it is very well, it thanks you.

                                    Papa.

  54. MS owned by RWEMA; ph. in CUL. The year 1860, which has been supplied, is clearly correct.

  55. See the letter of Feb. 13 and 17, 1860.

  56. The *Racine Daily Journal,* Feb. 10, 1860, announced " Manners " for that evening. In *The Racine Journal-News,* Sept. 10, 1921, there is a sketch of Marshall M. Strong with some vague references to his friendship with Emerson. According to *The Racine City Directory . . . 1858,* Strong was a member of a law firm. *Cf.* Aug. 4, 1856.

  57. The MS memorandum book for 1860 gives " Manners " for Kenosha, Wis., Feb. 11.

  58. In *The Sacred Poems,* 1844.

  59. *Cf.* Jan. 24, 1860.

To Edith Emerson, Niles, Michigan, February 13, and Marshall, Michigan, February 17, 1860 [60]

Niles Michigan
¹13 February¹—

Edith, Edith, you should have sent me a few poor lines here,[61] that I should not miss Ellen's bounteous letter. You wrote me the beginning of one, & stopped. And where is Edward's supplemental pen, which Ellen commanded? I am here on the St Josephs River, or St Joe, as the people, the Michiganders call it, so calling it, & so themselves. Tis a full strong river & a rare blessing in a prairie country ᴵᴵI had travelled all the day before through Wisconsin, with horses, & we could not for long distances find water for them: The wells were dry, &, the people said, they had no water but snow for the house. The cattle were driven a mile or more to the Lake.

Marshall,[62] 17ᵗʰ ᴵᴵ You are a good girl, & have sent me two good letters, & made all amends. ᴵᴵᴵAt Kalamazoo a good visit; & made intimate acquaintance with a College, wherein I found many personal friends, though unknown to me. & one Emerson was an established authority. Even a professor or two came along with me to Marshall, to hear another lecture. My chief adventure was the necessity of riding in a buggy 48 miles to Grand Rapids; [63] then, after lecture, 20 more, on the return, &, the next morning, getting back to Kalamazoo, in time for the train hither at 12. So I saw Michigan & its forest, and the Wolverines, pretty thoroughly.ᴵᴵᴵ You know a Michigan man is a wolverine; a Wisconsiner

60. MS owned by Miss Pauline Forbes; ph. in CUL. Excerpts I–III are in Cabot, II, 568–569. The lecture engagements mentioned fix the year.

61. *The Niles Democratic Republican* of Feb. 11, 1860, announced that Emerson would read " Success " before the Young Men's Society on the 13th.

62. The MS memorandum book for 1860 gives Feb. 14 to Kalamazoo (" Manners ") and Feb. 16 to Marshall (" Conduct of Life ") . The entry for Kalamazoo lists the names of several persons, including Holden, Anderson, Olney, and Dr. and Mrs. Stone. These five were doubtless the L. E. Holden, Edward Anderson, Edward Olney, and J. A. B. Stone and his wife who appeared in S. Haskell, *Historical Sketch of Kalamazoo College*, 1864, pp. 8–9, as members of the faculty; and these were, I conjecture, among the " personal friends " in the college wherein " one Emerson was an established authority."

63. Mr. Samuel H. Ranck has sent me a copy of the report of the lecture of Feb. 15, 1860, printed in the *Grand Rapids Daily Eagle* of the following day. The newspaper critic found " Manners " a great disappointment, chiefly, it seems, because of Emerson's way of reading it.

a badger; Illinoian a sucker; an Indianaan a hoosier; a Missourian, a puke; [64] Iowan a hawkeye; and Ohioan a buckeye. The people are rough grisly Esaus,[65] full of dirty strength. Every forcible man came from New York or New England, for all the country was settled since 1834. Very good schools however in all the large towns, & in every town, schools.

Well, you send me much news to think of, of home & school. What can be the matter with Alice? [66] I grieve to read it. Mr S.'s return was timely you have all behaved well & Ellen is as energetic as a wolverine & could build a town. Papa.

It was a bright thought to send me Tom Brown [67] I read it at once. Thank you, & my dear boy.

To Ellen Emerson, Detroit, February 18, 1860 [68]

Russell House —
Detroit, 18 Feb. 1860

Why, you are a dear excellent Ellen, with all your letters & doings, but, in the first place, you have done an absurd thing to throw a draft for $50. into the western forest, when it had safely arrived at your hands. I doubt we shall not see it again. You should have locked it up as the means to go to Cambridge,[69] if you so decided. I shall now begin to write letters about it,[70] with faint hope.

For the school, I hesitate. If your staying gives, as it must, a certain feeling of stability, girls & boys will stay, who will otherwise grow rest-

64. This word has been canceled and " Pike " substituted, but apparently not by Emerson himself.

65. *Genesis*, 27:11–23.

66. Several letters from Ellen and Edith Emerson in Jan. and Feb., 1860, mention this Alice and her illness at a time when she was just beginning to teach again in the school which Sanborn had almost abandoned because of his being in danger of arrest as a confederate of John Brown. I am uncertain of her identity, but it seems probable that she was Alice Jackson, who is mentioned with Sanborn in Apr. 13, 1860.

67. Doubtless *Tom Brown's School-days,* published several years earlier. The final sentences, in the margins of p. 1, are separated by irregular lines from each other and from the heading.

68. MS owned by RWEMA; ph. in CUL. *The Detroit Daily Tribune,* Feb. 20, 1860, reported Emerson's reading of " Manners and Morals " before the Young Men's Society on the 18th. According to the letter of Feb. 19, 1860, there was an extra lecture on Sunday.

69. Ellen's return to Agassiz's school is mentioned in Apr. 25, 1860.

70. Perhaps no such letters were written, as the draft arrived an hour or so later (see Feb. 19, 1860) .

less, & go. I think you had better wait till my return, which will be on
Thursday or Friday.

On looking at my letters, I find I had your letter of Feb. 4ᵗʰ but no
draft came with it, & I am not even sure that I received it at Madison,
for I have destroyed the envelope. I write at once to Mr Benedict, and
also to Mr Bryan.[71] I think I have received all your letters though I
have not been still long enough at any place to write of them. I did go to
Toledo,[72] & found a letter there. I shall be at Zanesville on Tuesday.[73]

But I think I must not finish this note today. Papa.
Whenever you inclose money in a letter, say so. I have not received Mrs
Leonards [74] letter.

To Ellen and Edith Emerson, Detroit, February 19, 1860 [75]

Russell House
Detroit, 19 Febʸ
1860

Dear Ellen & Edith,

An hour after my chiding letter [76] had gone, yesterday
afternoon, arrived your letters, forwarded from Madison to Racine, &
thence to this place. The draft of Mr Bryan [77] was safe, & all the news
of caps & schools & masquerades came rejoicing to the daylight & me.
As I had had news of parties & theatricals before, I did not know but
you had referred to them in what you said of a masquerade letter:
Now I ask pardon of your Carnival, for having so disparaged it. Well
it was very gay & I ought to find an audience here to read your letters
to, which are quite as interesting as the New Boy at Stiles' at least to
all who have a Concord key. I do not despair of finding a good ear yet,
for I am to drink tea this evening with Mrs Clarke, Sophys Cousin, &

71. For Benedict and Bryan, for whom the letters were intended, see especially
Dec. 13, 1859, and Jan. 24, 1860.

72. *Cf.* Jan. 29, 1860.

73. See Feb. 21, 1860.

74. Mrs. Leonard was doubtless Charlotte Farnham Leonard, Emerson's cousin,
mentioned in Dec. 4, 1828. She had written to Emerson on Feb. 3, 1860, from Madison
(Ind.? or Wis.?) , assuring him that if her health permitted she would certainly meet
him, and recalling some of his early verse.

75. MS owned by RWEMA; ph. in CUL.

76. Of Feb. 18, 1860.

77. Ellen Emerson had written, Feb. 3 and 4, 1860, of receiving a letter from
W. G. Bryan inclosing a draft for $50. Bryan's letter is cited in a note on Jan. 24, 1860.

will find if she is deserving. Here too is Mr Rice, & John Hosmer,[78] — whom I have seen last night. I am sorry you are so poor & fear by your account that I cannot do much for the Concord Bank. I grieve that Alice [79] is so ill, & you give me no opinion of Dr Bartlett. I have had two letters from Mr Sanborn,[80] but have not written to him, as it seemed doubtful if a letter would reach him. Today finds me quite at ease, laid up in a most comforting hotel, with all my present tasks done, excepting the Zanesville episode. Mr Rice, however, has, it seems, taken some half word of consent of mine for ground to advertise this morning that I will read a lecture tonight at the Unitarian Church.[81] The Masquerade, as you tell it, was a success, and I like best in it the fact that you invent your own costumes. You do not say what numbers came in undress. And that is the " but " in such a party, that to boys & girls at a boarding school, it must be a vexation that they cannot provide a dress; or an expense, if they do. So you must be brave & discountenance such enterprizes again. For Mrs Lowell's party,[82] there is no such danger. Of that you do not tell, — I suppose it had not met. Mr Sanborn must have left town on the new action at Washington.[83] But I hope, from the present aspect of the affair, that the agitation will soon end, & he return.

You have had cold weather; I mild, until the last few days, & tell mamma, I have not yet unpinned her comforter; and only worn my scarf on my ride to Grand Rapids,[84] where it was welcome. Love to Edward, whose letter still miscarries badly. I hope James gets the newspaper every night, & Sundays.

Papa

78. Cf. Feb. 1, 1854. *Johnston's Detroit City Directory*, 1861, lists R. N. Rice as superintendent of the Michigan Central Railroad and Hosmer as a school inspector and as freight agent of the same railroad.

79. Cf. Feb. 13 and 17, 1860.

80. One is printed in a note on Jan. 29, 1860.

81. I am uncertain whether it was at this or at one of his other lectures in Detroit that Emerson, introduced by John Hosmer, told the audience of his pleasure in being thus presented by " the son of my old neighbor in Concord " (Mary Hosmer Brown, *Memories of Concord*, n. d. [c. 1926], p. 40) .

82. Ellen had written in her letter of Jan. 28, 1860, that Mrs Lowell — doubtless Anna Jackson Lowell — was to have a Dickens party and that Edith was to go as Dolly Varden.

83. Sanborn tells in *Recollections*, I, 206–207, of this new flight to Canada after the Senate had, on Feb. 16, voted his arrest.

84. See the letter of Feb. 13 and 17, 1860.

To James Elliot Cabot, Zanesville, Ohio, February 21, 1860 [85]

Zanesville Ohio
21 February, 1860

My dear Cabot,

Your note was forwarded to me from home, many days ago, but I have hardly had more time for a letter than the engineer on the locomotive. I enquired long since of Ticknor & Fields whether anything could be done for Carlyle's book? [86] & they replied, on learning that the Harpers had published the two earlier volumes, " Nothing, unless the Harpers themselves will pay something for it." This seemed equivalent to " le mort, sans phrase." [87] so reckless is the selfishness of those people. I once tried hard to make them give Dr Carlyle something for an early copy of his translation of Dante, & could only get 10 or 20 copies of their reprint.[88] Yet it is not wise to refuse the forlorn hope of asking a pirate's mercy for a friend; and I will ask them by letter [89] to please be good, & not eat him up skin & hair. I will, unless you know any person in New York who might accomplish something with them by interview, face to face. I once established some correspondence between Phillips & Sampson, & Carlyle — when they were able to fight the Harpers for him, but, for I know not what reason, he was very churlish & Scottish & suspicious,[90] & would not treat for this very book. Please send me a word to Concord, where I shall be in two or three days, signifying your assent, & I will write to these booksellers. What is the date promised for the coming of the sheets?

Yours,
R. W Emerson

J. E. Cabot, Esq.

85. MS owned by Professor Philip Cabot; ph. in CUL. Emerson's plan to lecture at Zanesville is mentioned in several earlier letters. According to the MS memorandum book for this year, he read " Manners " there on Feb. 21 and " Conduct of Life " on the following day.

86. The *History of Friedrich II.*, no doubt; some volumes had long since appeared.

87. For the famous apocryphal saying of Sieyès, which Emerson slightly misquotes, *cf.* Nov. 5, 1843.

88. See Aug. 16, 1848, and later letters.

89. The letter was probably written, but I have no proof.

90. *Cf.* Carlyle's letters of Aug. 28 and Dec. 2, 1856 (*C–E Corr.*) .

To James Elliot Cabot, Concord, March 1, 1860 [91]

> Concord 1 March
> 1860

Dear Cabot,

It is really important to apprize Carlyle of this statement of the Harpers.[92] When I attempted, at his instance, I believe, to make a bargain for his " Cromwell " (I think it was,) with Wiley & Putnam, they met me with the like information, that they had bought of Chapman & Hall advance sheets.[93] Carlyle was enraged at the news, & descended on his publishers, & brought them at once to penitence & promises. These books ought to be worth to him much more than any former ones.; & his pen can be so vengeful, that I think even our obtuse reprobates of Cliff Street may be reached by the fear of him.

I shall be glad to be bid to write to them in this cause.

> Yours,
> R. W. Emerson

Mr Cabot.

To Abel Adams, Concord? March? 1? 1860

[Adams, Boston, Mar. 2, 1860, says that, on his way to Boston, he received Emerson's note and was glad to hear of his return to Massachusetts in good condition.]

To Brown and Taggard, Concord? March? c. 1? 1860

[O. W. Wight to Brown & Taggard, New York, Mar. 9, 1860, acknowledges their letter of Mar. 8, " containing copy of Mr. Emerson's letter." Wight says he has sketched a letter to Carlyle, telling what he is doing with Carlyle's essays, but will now address his explanation to Emerson instead. Brown & Taggard wrote Emerson, Mar. 14, 1860, inclosing the letter of the 9th from Wight, who, they explained, was having Carlyle's essays stereotyped for publication by them. Cf. the letters of Apr. 16, May 21, and May? c. 21? 1860. Orlando Williams Wight edited or translated a number of books; for his activity in republishing standard works, see especially J. C. Derby, p. 276.]

91. MS owned by Professor Philip Cabot; ph. in CUL.
92. Apparently the Harpers had advertised an American edition of the *History of Friedrich II.* (*cf.* Feb. 21, 1860) .
93. Letters of 1845–1846 tell this story; *cf.* especially Jan. 27, 1846.

To Richard Randolph, Concord? March 6, 1860

[Acknowledged in Randolph, Philadelphia, Mar. 15, 1860. Randolph notes Emerson's invitation to call upon him at his Philadelphia quarters. For Emerson's discovery that his repute as a sympathizer with John Brown would prevent the projected engagement in Philadelphia, *cf.* Mar. 20. Philip P. Randolph, Philadelphia, May 8, 1860, told of a letter which his cousin Richard had received from Emerson — perhaps that of Mar. 6 or a later one.]

To Charles Eliot Norton, Concord, March 10, 1860 [94]

> Concord, 10 March,
> 1860 —

My dear Sir,

      I return with my thanks Vol. 1. of Fauriel on Romaic Poetry which you were so good as to send me from the College Library.[95] I do not know but you have had some fears for its safety. When I left home for the West, I took this volume with me, & left Vol. II. on my table. I had tied up your Fauriels [96] in a parcel to be despatched to you. My daughter, finding this Vol. II. outside, fancied that it had been forgotten, & sent it with your books.[97]

About the time of the arrival of your books, Mr Felton sent me his translations of some few of these poems.[98] But he did not seem to be aware that Margaret Fuller had translated the same pieces in the old Dial.[99] Goethe had already rendered them in German, on the first appearance of Fauriel. But I shall be glad to have a good English book made out of this.

> Yours gratefully,
> R. W. Emerson.

Mr Norton.

94. MS owned by HCL; ph. in CUL. This, by an unknown hand, appears at the end of the letter: " The beginning of acquaintance with C. E. N." If this means Norton's acquaintance with Emerson, it is apparently an error. *Cf.*, for example, Sept. 4, 1852, where Emerson writes to Norton of his desire for " new opportunities of establishing my acquaintance with yourself."

95. *Chants populaires de la Grèce moderne,* tr. and ed. C. Fauriel, Paris, Vols. I (1824) and II (1825), still in HCL, was received by that library in 1856.

96. Apparently the volumes referred to in Jan. 2, 1860, to Norton, as " Fauriel — the new." I conjecture that these were one of Fauriel's posthumous works and, in view of Norton's special interest in Dante at this time, most probably *Dante et les origines de la langue et de la littérature italiennes,* 2 vols., 1854.

97. See Jan. 24, 1860.

98. Cornelius Conway Felton, Jan. 12, 1860, said he was inclosing some specimens of Klephtic ballads in translation; he said he had already printed eight or ten such pieces in some selections for his students and that he thought of publishing a volume.

99. For the article in *The Dial* and for Goethe's translations, see the letters of Aug. 22 and Oct. 5, 1842.

To William W. Badger, Concord? March 15, 1860

[Badger, New York, Mar. 17, 1860, acknowledged this "note" and accepted Emerson's terms and subject for Mar. 23. Badger explained that the lecture, under the auspices of the Young Men's Christian Union, would be given at Chapin's church instead of the Cooper Union because Emerson had not fully accepted the terms offered.]

To William Davis Ticknor, Concord, March 16, 1860

[MS listed and partly quoted in American Art Association, Apr. 28 and 29, 1924. Emerson sends a preliminary form of his table of contents, doubtless for *The Conduct of Life,* published in the following December.]

To William Emerson, Concord, March 20, 1860 [100]

Concord
Tuesday, March 20.

Dear William,

    Ever since I had your note, which contained matters of much interest to all of us, I have been too ridiculously busy to write a note. First, Lidian charged me to write you at once that she grieved that Helvellyn was going to the stranger [101] & she could not see it first but Dr Furness had come to tell me that there was no room for me in Philadelphia to which he & his friends had invited me, — no room since John Brown.[102] But L. had already found before that she had not strength to go & then the tasks, &c. — but *that* I cannot go into. I have just learned that I am to go to N. Y. for a lecture on Friday night,[103] & may go to arrive on Friday morn? I shall see you so, & will therefore only now add that we are delighted that William is in his right place.[104] Well & best in every way we look at it. We never hear any but kindest words about Charles, whom Ellen & Edith sometimes see, but I never.

  Dear love to Susan & congratulation on these old but good news. Waldo E.

100. MS owned by HCL; ph. in CUL. Evidence cited below shows that the year was 1860, when Mar. 20 fell on Tuesday.

101. William Emerson, Mar. 4, 1860 (MS owned by Dr. Haven Emerson) , said he had leased Helvellyn, his Staten Island home, for three years from the first of May and that he and his family would board in town.

102. Brown had been executed on Dec. 2, 1859. Two weeks later an antislavery meeting in Philadelphia was marked by considerable disorders (*Public Ledger,* Dec. 16, 1859) . Emerson was already so closely identified with the Brownist sympathizers that his appearance in Philadelphia at this time might have caused further trouble.

103. See Mar. 23, 1860.

104. William Emerson, in his letter of Mar. 4, cited above, said that his son had accepted the invitation of the firm of Emerson & Prichard and had taken a desk in their office.

To WILLIAM EMERSON, NEW YORK, MARCH 23, 1860 [105]

Astor House
Friday Night

Dear William,

Mr MacAdam my President of the "Xn Union," & Mr Badger, had not made up their evening accounts; [106] & so I bade them call on you; & you will please receive my fee for me, & deduct from it 5.00 which Haven lent me, as I found myself short, having spent too much money in Boston, on my way. Then you shall please remit the balance to me. I told you the basis; that I was to be secured first in receiving $50. & my expenses from & to Concord; which may be called $13. when reduced to the lowest point. And, after that, I am to receive any excess of profits over that sum & less than $100. But I think the audience will not yield much excess.

Mr Bovee carried me, after lecture, to the Athenaeum,[107] & made a very pleasant evening for me. But I am sorry not to see Susan.

Affectionately,
W. Emerson, Esq.   Waldo E

To HENRY WHITNEY BELLOWS, NEW YORK, MARCH? 23? 1860? [108]

Astor House
Friday

My dear Bellows,

I received last night your friendly note, friendly & hospitable as always, but great are my demerits on these journeys & I am not worthy to come under private roofs, much more those of the sons of

105. MS owned by HCL; ph. in CUL. The date is from William Emerson's notation and is supported by evidence cited below. Mar. 23 fell on Friday in 1860.

106. According to *Trow's New York City Directory* for the year ending May 1, 1860, Richard Warren was actually the president. For arrangements with William W. Badger for the lecture, see Mar. 15, 1860. The announcement that Emerson would read "Manners" before the Young Men's Christian Union on Mar. 23, 1860, was printed in *The New York Herald* of that date, over the name of Badger, the chairman of the lecture committee.

107. For a lecture by Emerson at the Athenæum some weeks later, see a note on May 8, 1860; for Bovee, *cf.* especially Mar. 21, 1861.

108. MS owned by Mr. Robert P. Bellows and Mrs. Thorndike Howe Endicott; ph. in CUL. I have no satisfactory proof of the date. If, as I conjecture, the last sentence refers to a gift by Bellows to the "Alcott Fund," this letter must be later than that of July 13, 1859, to Lowell, where Bellows does not appear in Emerson's list of contributors. Friday, Mar. 23, 1860, seems a possible date, as Emerson, we know, was at the Astor House on that day.

light.[109] The railroad hours, which I obey, are quite too uncivil, — not to mention my private incapabilities. But if, in some summer day, when you are in Massachusetts, you will come & spend a day with me in Concord, I will make some covenant with you for a day not of railroads.

Yours, with special gratitude also for your eminent goodness to Alcott,

R. W. Emerson

To WILLIAM EMERSON, CONCORD, MARCH 25, 1860 [110]

Concord 25 March
1860

Dear William,

Mr Badger,[111] whom I requested to carry his money to you, has sent it to me this morning, $75.00; so I enclose to you $10.50, in acknowledgment of 5.00 borrowed of Haven; & 5.50, my bill at the Astor, for which I gave a draft on you. I was careless, and on Friday night found but 6.00 in my pocket, & I pounced upon Haven.

Miss Prichard, to my great regret, did not appear on Saturday morning, at the Depot. I found company, less agreeable, however, all the way to Worcester. At home I found Charles but we fancy he does not like Concord very well, for he was inexorably resolved to walk to Cambridge next morning at 6.30, & went. He looks very well, & seemed to have liked his Dickens Party [112] heartily.

I am sorry to find I bro't home a parcel, — a night-shirt I think it is, — belonging to you, & which Lidian had charged me to deliver. I have a note from Mrs Wm M. Jackson of Brooklyn, this morning, informing me that Miss Sarah Ripley has married Mr Jewett,[113] who has built a fine house, & furnished it finely, for her, in New Jersey. & Mrs J. says, that all parties are well pleased.

Affectionately,
Waldo E.

To ————————, CONCORD, APRIL 5, 1860

[MS listed in C. F. Libbie & Co., Mar. 7, 1919.]

109. Perhaps the phrase is from the fourth stanza of Shelley's " Adonais."
110. MS owned by HCL; ph. in CUL.
111. For Badger and the New York lecture, see Mar. 23, 1860.
112. Cf. a note on Feb. 19, 1860. It is not clear whether the same Dickens party is referred to here.
113. Cf. a note on Dec. 15, 1830.

To William Emerson, Concord, April 9, 1860 [114]

Concord

9 April

Dear William

Miss Anna Jones sent me word that she wished to see me & w^d come to Concord but I met her accidentally & agreed to visit her at her house which I did on Saturday. She had been unhappy in hearing that you would not come to her May Day; but I told her that I found you inclined to do so. Did you not say to me that you were content to come. She is at all events pushing her inquiries & correspondence to find her " girls," who are now strangely hidden under masks & behind fences — some inaccessible not of age of distance Western or European, but of age, disease & the impassable Styx But here is my friend talking in the room & I cannot finish my letter but was to ask you on part of Miss Jones whether you remember a Miss Goff? & who & where is she, if such was? And Miss Cushing? And Miss Holley? what was her married name & is she living? [115]

The rest of the questions tomorrow. Charles left us this morning after spending Sunday. Edward still sick [116] but the symptoms meliorating.

Love to Susan & boys, Waldo E

To John Murray Forbes, Concord, April 11, 1860 [117]

Concord, 11 April. 1860

My dear Mr Forbes,

You shall thank Mr Weiss [118] for me, for his kind thought in sending me tickets. I shall use them, if I can, allured also by the house door at Milton, which seems to be ever nailed open. I am charged by my

114. MS owned by HCL; ph. in CUL. The year is fixed by several letters of Apr. and May, 1860, about the reunion. The women named here and in later letters about that event were, nearly forty years earlier, " the fair-haired daughters of this raw city " against whom Emerson had assisted his " venerable brother " to " lift the truncheon," as he said in his letter of Mar. 12, 1822.

115. William Emerson, Apr. 10 and 11, 1860 (MS owned by Dr. Haven Emerson) , said that these three had risen above or below his horizon.

116. *Cf.* the following letters.

117. MS owned by RWEMA; ph. in CUL.

118. Perhaps John Weiss was to lecture at Milton, Mass. For Forbes's friendly relations with him, *cf. Letters and Recollections.*

wife & children three to acknowledge Mrs Forbes's box, — or shall I say, treasury of gifts, to Edward. — My wife thinks the *cellar* door at Milton must also be nailed back. It was very thoughtful & kind in Mrs F. who lives to be thoughtful & kind. Yesterday, when these arrived, was Edward's first day of mending, &, though the mending shows very little yet in his face or comfort, the Doctor today advises beef tea, which we hear as the best omen.

Sanborn seems quite clear headed, & to be also well advised. Last night, we had an intimation here that the sergeant at arms would reach Boston at midnight, & wd. come with force here this morning. Concord waked early, but McNair did not arrive in Boston — Sanborn is in his school all day. He is technically in custody of the deputy sheriff here, & means to have his Habeas Corpus sued before the Supreme Court, whenever arrested.[119] He means to resist the arrest also. Yet, I believe, he thinks the matter now stands so well, that he would not much regret going to Washington. I am sorry that Gov. Banks is in New York, & the Attorney General also. It is believed that Judge Shaw is not inclined to sustain the pretension of the Senate. Ever yours,

R. W. Emerson

Edward prays that I will express " his thankfulness & gratification " & say that " they always behave beautifully to him."

To WILLIAM EMERSON, CONCORD, APRIL 13, 1860 [120]

Concord
13 April 1860

Dear William,

Lidian is writing, I believe, her letter acknowledging the wonderful present that dazzled all the family out of their propriety, last night. You knew how to make two girls, Ellen & Edith, perfectly happy.

119. Sanborn's own account (*Recollections*, I, 208 ff.) gives considerable detail. Dunning R. McNair, sergeant-at-arms of the United States Senate, had sent one Silas Carleton to make the arrest on Apr. 3; but Carleton and his aides stirred up a hornets' nest in Concord and were glad to get away, leaving their prisoner nominally in the custody of local authorities. Sanborn was taken to Boston the next day and was formally discharged from Carleton's custody by Shaw, chief justice of the Supreme Judicial Court of Massachusetts. At the time of the present letter, Sanborn apparently feared rearrest, which, however, never occurred. The trial of Apr. 4, 1860, is recorded in Horace Gray, Jr., *Reports of Cases Argued and Determined in the Supreme Judicial Court of Massachusetts*, XV (1869), 399–403.

120. MS owned by HCL; ph. in CUL.

Papa was summoned on the instant to open the box; hammer, chisel, & screwdriver came as of their own accord. Alice Jackson [121] & Mr Sanborn stood by & assisted & watched every step of the process. Ellen & Edith held up every piece as it appeared, & the garden of Eden was not more admired. After their mother had seen all, Mrs Brown was sent for, & plates were carried up to Edward's bed. And, this morning, I was visited in my study by E & E with selected articles of superior splendor. I am afraid I shall be presently called upon to build a new china-closet for their storage, &, I know not but a drawing room for their adequate exhibition & use. You have been quite too short in your history of how they came to you,[122] & by what self denying ordinance [123] deserving heroic history, they came to us. Meantime, they arrived here in perfect safety.

You can well believe I have been uneasy enough about Edward. He still flames in the face with fever turns some hours of each day. But his symptoms are ever better, or with short interruption. Still, he is prostrate, & weak, & without food almost. Ellen & Edith have been exemplary nurses — I am sitting with him now whilst they are abroad.

I am glad to hear what you say concerning Aunt Mary's affairs; & concerning Miss Anna Jones, who names the hours of 3.30 till 6 o'clock P. M. on 1 May, for her party.[124]

Affectionately,
Waldo E

To Thomas Carlyle, Concord, April 16, 1860

[MS owned by RWEMA; printed incompletely in *C–E Corr.*, 1886.]

To William Emerson, Concord? April *c.* 19, 1860

[William Emerson, Apr. 23, 1860 (MS owned by Dr. Haven Emerson), says his brother's note was received on Friday (Apr. 20) and was sent at once to Bovee. For Bovee, see Mar. 23, 1860.]

121. Doubtless Alice Bridge Jackson, daughter of Lidian Emerson's brother (see *Genealogy of the John Bridge Family*, p. 322).

122. William Emerson, Apr. 10 and 11, 1860 (MS owned by Dr. Haven Emerson), explained that the set of breakfast china he was sending to Lidian Emerson had come to him as executor of a will.

123. The reference to the famous ordinance of Apr. 3, 1645, is a characteristic touch in a characteristic passage of Emersonian humorous exaggeration.

124. *Cf.* Apr. 9, 1860.

To Elbridge G. Dudley, Concord, April 20, 1860 [125]

Concord, 20 April, 1860

My dear Sir,

You shall, if you please, announce for my subject at the Music Hall, on Sunday,[126] " Education."

My wife has fully intended to accept Mrs Dudley's kind invitation to come with me to your house, next Saturday night. But my son Edward has been, for the last fortnight, prostrate with typhoid fever, &, though now recovering, mends so slowly as to require constant attention of his mother & sisters. Mrs Emerson, therefore, sends her thanks & best wishes to Mrs Dudley, and thinks, at present, that she shall not be able to accompany me. I am sorry, as I hoped to hear a very good dialogue or trialogue from the ladies. In the circumstances, I think I shall not be able to come to you, until after the morning service.

With kindest regards to your family,

Your friend & servant,
R. W. Emerson

Mr Dudley.

To William Emerson, Concord, April 25, 1860 [127]

Concord Wednesday
25 Apr

Dear William,

I have your note [128] & learn with some consternation what you say: William sick, & you hesitating to come. I trust heartily that William's attack is to pass off more lightly than the bad name you give it implies. For in these cases of the young & healthy, it is immensely tedious & disappointing. But you must not think of being nurse, or of being worker in the office on the first of May. Miss Jones & her friends have searched so far & wide for the scraps of steel that if you leave out now the part of Magnet we shall have no experiment. We have steadily

125. MS owned by Mr. W. T. H. Howe; ph. in CUL.

126. The *Boston Daily Journal*, Apr. 21, 1860, duly announced that Emerson would lecture at the Music Hall, by invitation of Parker's society, on the following Sunday morning, the 22d.

127. MS owned by HCL; ph. in CUL. The year is obviously 1860; *cf.* the several other letters about the reunion.

128. Of Apr. 23, 1860 (MS owned by Dr. Haven Emerson).

counted on your visit here, & Edward will I hope be sitting up to welcome you on Saturday. By no means can you disappoint us. But I must hasten to the post office or top the mail. Edward mends pretty steadily; & Ellen now goes to Agassiz again daily! [129]

Charles & Sally Gibbons [130] were here on Sunday, I alas! not.

Waldo E

To John Murray Forbes, Concord, April 28, 1860 [131]

Concord, 28 April,
1860

My dear Sir,

Is it possible that you have any room in your farm at Naushon, this summer, for a good Irishman? James Burke, who has lived with me for eight years past,[132] fancies himself this summer to need sea-air, & has been talking of going to Ireland on a visit, which, Dr Bartlett, who thinks him more spleeny than invalid, humored him in & encouraged. But his illness is soon over, & he thinks, will not return, if he could work a few months by the seaside, which, he remembers, was the only cure applied when he was, ten years ago, a mounted policeman in Ireland. James is a capable intelligent & faithful laborer, delights in horses, & perfect, I believe, in their care, takes care of the cows does all the ploughing digging, mowing, wood-chopping, &c of my farm (which includes a woodlot,) he never spares himself, & is a person of great virtues. He has no vice except a rare indulgence in drink, of which he is vastly ashamed, & thinks if I will only hide it, he shall never let it be known again. He thinks, if he can find work by the sea, he shall come back to me in the fall. Is it possible that you have employment for so many virtues & such a small disappearing vice? [133] Or can think of any good master for him? He is a bachelor, say, under 40 years. Ever gratefully yours,

R. W. Emerson

Mr Forbes.

129. *Cf.* the letters of Jan. 24 and 29, 1860.

130. Apparently Charles Emerson and the "Sally" Gibbons who was to become his brother William's wife.

131. MS owned by RWEMA; ph. in CUL.

132. *Cf.* Apr. 6, 1852, to William Emerson and many later letters.

133. Burke worked for Forbes for a time (*cf.* May 4, 1860, to Forbes, and later letters).

To WILLIAM EMERSON, CONCORD, MAY 2, 1860 [134]

Concord
2 May 1860

Dear William,

Your last letter was a grievous disappointment.[135] I had hoped surely that William would mend at once, & that you could come. I trust you can send me at once some better news of him. but none come tonight, for the mail I have waited for is now in. Edward has crept now for 32 days into something like safety & good assurance, & William should have a constitution as good. Send me early word. Charles was here yesterday (exhibition) [136] but had no word.

I went to the Ladies Party at Anna Jones's. Twenty or more appeared & it was a strange but altogether pleasing meeting in spite of all my apprehensions, for I tho't it a dangerous social experiment. I will write you presently more at large on it.[137] The most affectionate assurances & messages concerning & to yourself were pressed on me.[138] There was a charming bouquet for you and a gold ring attached marked Reunion, May 1, 1860 Mrs Torrey claimed to carry home the bouquet she being the first grandmother in the party & the ring was detached & I am to send it to you. Mrs Miles, Mrs Wigglesworth, *Mesdames* Pickering, Brown, Sever, Curtis, Grew, Williams, &c were there and in my speech [139] I made Academician like the eloge of my senior & principal which was well endorsed. Love to you & Susan, & health in your house!

Waldo

134. MS owned by HCL; ph. in CUL.

135. William Emerson, Apr. 28, 1860, said that, on account of ill health in his family, he had decided not to attend the reunion (MS owned by Dr. Haven Emerson).

136. Charles Emerson does not appear in the newspaper account as a participant in the "exhibition" at Harvard on May 1 (*Boston Daily Advertiser,* Apr. 30 and May 2, 1860). He apparently took advantage of his freedom to make a visit to Concord.

137. See May 4, 1860, to William Emerson.

138. The regard in which William Emerson was held by his former pupils is well illustrated in a letter which his brother Charles wrote to him on Apr. 23, 1829:

"Elizabeth Parsons . . . frequently made mention of you with great affection. Indeed it is wonderful the love your scholars all avow for their ancient master — Mrs. Torrey (Susan Tilden) says she desires nothing so much for her children as that they may have an instructer like Mr. Wm. Emerson. And I hear constantly the like expressions."

139. Partly printed in Cabot, I, 70–71.

To WILLIAM EMERSON, CONCORD, MAY 4, 1860 [140]

Concord, 4 May 1860

Dear William,

It was a joyful relief to hear from you yesterday the good news of William. You might have divined so much a day earlier, & have come where you were so much wanted! As I reckon, by memory, there must have been twenty ladies present. Most of them I knew at once But Mrs C. Brown I should not have deciphered into Isabella Tilden; nor Mrs Curtis into Isabella Stevenson; nor Mrs Williams into Miss Bangs; had I met them elsewhere. Miss Norwood is much altered. But Ann Carter has kept her beauty into her present stout figure and Mrs Miles is little changed, & Mrs Torry little. The party was altogether pleasant & affectionate, & dissipated all my hesitations Miss Jones Miss Joy & Miss Salisbury are lovely in their behavior. All were full of eager sympathy for you, & grief for your absence & its cause. At Miss Jones's request I read letters from Mrs Hassard & Mrs Livingston. Then I read yours. They all desired their sympathetic responses might be sent to you We went into the drawing room where a table was loaded with salads & sugars and I was then asked if I would speak — " No, not until the company sit." So they adjourned their banquet a little & I opened my mouth, & spake,[141] & made a biography of William Emerson, Esq. (which is at the service of the American Cyclopedia,) [142] then recorded my accession, & told what I remembered of the School. A cake was cut up in which was a ring. I did not hear who found it. Miss Jones bro't me a ring for you, (which I will send by letter, if you will risk it,) & another was given to me. I presume these gifts are hers. Mrs Austin (S Salisbury) did not come, being ill; Mrs Adams, being at Washington; Mrs Bowditch, because of her husband's illness, Miss Bryant because of her mother's death.

I could heartily have wished they should all have been there. It was entirely pleasant, & I stayed till 6½, losing my return train to Concord. I shall, in consequence of this party, renew my acquaintance with Ann

140. MS owned by HCL; ph. in CUL. For the reunion, *cf.* several earlier letters of April and May.

141. Emerson was probably thinking of *Daniel*, 10:16.

142. The sixteen volumes of *The New American Cyclopædia*, edited by George Ripley and Charles A. Dana, old Brook-Farmers, were in course of publication at this time.

Salisbury, Anna Jones, & Elizabeth Joy. And I am very sorry you should lose the occasion.

Edward is mending today a little faster in diet & sitting up. He has been slow enough, as he still spends all but all day in bed. Mrs Forbes invites him to Milton to get well. He dreams by night & thinks by day only of eating-houses. Love & congratulation to Susan & Haven — & to William sudden health!

Waldo E.

To John Murray Forbes, Concord, May 4, 1860 [143]

Concord, 4 May '60

My dear Sir,

When & where will you see James Burke. He was highly gratified, as I knew he would be, at learning that you could employ him [144] & will come to see you at Boston or at Milton whenever you require, to talk with you, & receive your commands. His plan has been to finish my planting before he went to Ireland; but, as I must fill his place immediately on his departure, I shall not detain him a day, to risk his not being wanted. I confide that you will find him an excellent workman.

Ever yours,
R. W. Emerson

Mr Forbes.

To Mary Howland Russell, Concord, May 7, 1860 [145]

Concord — 7 May 1860

My dear Miss Russell

Lidian, who cannot be convinced but that your interest in

143. MS owned by RWEMA; ph. in CUL.

144. *Cf.* Apr. 28, 1860. Forbes wrote, May 5, 1860, suggesting that Burke come to Milton as soon as Emerson could spare him.

145. MS owned by Mr. Edward Waldo Forbes; ph. in CUL. This MS copy, not in Emerson's hand, appears on the back of p. 252 in a typewritten volume entitled *Letters of R. Waldo Emerson* and containing numerous letters selected by Edith Emerson Forbes. Excerpt I is in *Records of a Lifelong Friendship*, p. 132. Edward Emerson's illness is mentioned frequently during both April and May. Mary Howland Russell appears in the correspondence of earlier years (see especially Mar. 2, 1835, and July 3, 1837, to Ruth Haskins Emerson). According to Stockwell, p. 61, she died in 1862, within less than two years after Emerson had recommended the curative virtues of Philadelphia and of his friend Furness.

her boy's health must bear some proportion to her own, entreats me to assure you that he is mending, and promising to get well, though slowly.

You see the dangers of the fame of a good heart, namely, that when you go abroad for rest and change of air, you are to be followed by histories of all the colds and fevers of all your friends. Lidian fortifies herself however on some imprudence of a kind inquiry sent from yourself, perhaps from Philadelphia. Edward is really better after being really sick, and though wasted almost to the bones, and, as yet, spending all but an hour of the day in bed, yet has a better face and rallying spirits. We shall try to defend him from any relapse.

¹I heartily wish to hear that you find the climate of Philadelphia kinder and gladder than ours in Massachusetts for the late weeks, and healing and inspiring to yourself. I delight in that city and reckon it a good hospital. William Furness (senior of course) has a face like a benediction, and a speech like a benefaction, and his stories more curative than the Phila. Faculty of Medicine. I entreat you to put yourself under his treatment,¹ and at all events to bring back new strength in June. For is not the time coming, long foretold, when we are all to check our hurry, and put up our tasks, and enjoy a piece of serene social afternoon. I think I have much to say to you; and how not to hear?

Yours affectionately
R. W. Emerson —

Miss (Mary H.) ¹⁴⁶ Russell

To John Murray Forbes, Concord, May 8, 1860 ¹⁴⁷

Concord, 8 May,
1860 —

My dear Sir,

James will come,¹⁴⁸ but perhaps not till next Monday Morning. He is not quite ready himself, & I am forced to go to New York tomorrow,¹⁴⁹ & have not quite settled on his substitute. If I can see my way & his, a little clearer in the course of today, I will perhaps

146. The parenthesis was doubtless supplied by the copyist.

147. MS owned by RWEMA; ph. in CUL.

148. *Cf.* May 4, 1860, to Forbes.

149. William Emerson, May 1, 1860 (MS owned by Dr. Haven Emerson), told in some detail of the arrangements made for his brother to lecture at the Athenæum in New York on the 10th of that month. I have found no newspaper account, but there is a clear reference to such a lecture in the letter of May 28.

write you more exactly tonight.[150] I have apprised him of the substance of everything you have said on the affair.

Edward rallies much yesterday & today.

Yours ever,

R. W. Emerson

Mr Forbes.

To James Elliot Cabot, Concord, May 21, 1860[151]

Concord

21 May

1860

My dear Cabot,

I have a letter from Carlyle,[152] containing a message to you, — which, in spite of very suppressible passages, I decide to send to you entire, that you may precisely have his meaning. I think, at the best, it is not quite clear & right. If the part relating to Harpers could be published, or if he would write a printable letter on that head, I think it would be easy to find an adventurous publisher, like Thayer & Eldridge, who print the John Brown books,[153] or Brown & Taggard, who have just printed his own " Miscellanies," [154] who, armed with such a diploma, could well & safely brave the Harpers, &, by means of a subscription-list, publish the two coming volumes of " Friedrich," exactly to match their edition of the two first volumes. All Carlyle's innumerable friends, & the lovers of fair play generally, would certainly buy the Author s edition and the Harpers would be fought down, to the great comfort of the public. I will write so to Mr Wight,[155] who is the proprietor of the Brown & Taggard edition, & who has promised Carlyle half profits.

Ever yours,

R. W. Emerson —

Mr Cabot.

150. I have no proof of such a letter.

151. MS owned by Professor Philip Cabot; ph. in CUL.

152. Apparently the letter of Apr. 30, 1860, incompletely printed in *C–E Corr.*

153. Thayer & Eldridge printed James Redpath's *Echoes of Harper's Ferry* and *The Public Life of Capt. John Brown,* the latter with a dedication to Wendell Phillips, Emerson, and Thoreau. The same publishers were courageous enough to sponsor a new edition of Whitman's *Leaves of Grass.*

154. *Critical and Miscellaneous Essays,* Boston, Brown & Taggard, 1860.

155. Letter of May? *c.* 21? 1860.

To Orlando Williams Wight, Concord? May? c. 21? 1860

[Wight, Rye, N. Y., June 3, 1860, says Emerson's note containing extracts from Carlyle's letter was duly received; comments at some length on Carlyle's relations with publishers; and states his own willingness to take the financial responsibility for republication of *The French Revolution* and divide profits with Carlyle. For the probable date, *cf.* May 21, 1860.]

To E. A. Silsbee, Concord? May? c. 21? 1860?

[Silsbee, Salem, Mass., May 28 (endorsed 1860), thanks Emerson for " the very elegant letter which you did me the honor to send me." Silsbee quotes a letter he had from Spencer the preceding February, in which the English philosopher asked about Emerson's attitude and hoped that, if favorable, it would be made known and so help Spencer. Spencer's letter had apparently accompanied a copy of the circular announcement of his projected work on synthetic philosophy.]

To William Emerson, Concord, May 28, 1860 [156]

Concord
28 May, 1860

Dear William,

It never occurred to me till yesterday that you might bring your horses with you here to your great comfort. A few shillings or a few dollars would make all the accommodation they want in my barn, & a ton of hay will supply their wants & my man Francis Buttrick will keep them in keeping my horse without any aid or trouble. So if you do not wish to sell them, bring them by all means.

The Athenaeum thro Mr Ashley have just written me a graceful letter & paid all their debts.[157]

With love, & expectation of you all,

Waldo E

To Mary Russell Watson, Concord? c. May? 1860?

[Mrs. Watson, Plymouth? Mass.? n. d. (endorsed 1860), thanked Emerson for his note and for the check he forwarded to her. She said the papers were so old a story that she had almost forgotten them. She had, however, no objection if Lowell still had a mind to print. Channing was good not to let them get

156. MS owned by HCL; ph. in CUL.
157. For Emerson's lecture before the Athenæum in New York, apparently on May 10, *cf.* May 8, 1860. L. Seymour Ashley duly appears in the *Charter and Constitution of the Athenæum Association, with a List of Members*, 1865, pp. 9 and 29.

into print a year ago. She mentioned the "Humming Bird" as one of the pieces. According to the index volume of *The Atlantic*, Mrs. Watson was the author of a review of the *Waverley Novels*, May, 1858; "The Humming-bird," June, 1860; and "The Great Arm-chair," Sept., 1860. The present letter pretty obviously belongs to some time in 1860 before "The Humming-bird" was published or to late 1859. *Cf.* also the letter of May 26, 1858 (to Mary? Russell? Watson), and June 17, 1859.]

To Charles D. B. Mills, Concord? June 2, 1860

[Mills, Syracuse, N. Y., June 26 (or 20?), 1860, acknowledges this letter and the return of a roll of his MSS with Emerson's approval. Mills thinks he can now give some additional items about Bruno — Giordano Bruno, no doubt. He had written years earlier, Oct. 16, 1856, to say he was returning the volumes of Bruno which Emerson had lent him.]

To Elbridge G. Dudley, Concord? June 6? 1860

[Mentioned in June 6, 1860, as just written. J. R. Manley, Boston, June 7 (endorsed 1860), says Dudley read to him that morning Emerson's note about Conway and others. Manley says he counts on "*remarks*" by Emerson at exercises in the Music Hall in honor of Parker. Emerson's address on that occasion is in *Cent. Ed.*, XI.]

To Moncure Daniel Conway, Concord, June 6, 1860 [158]

Concord, 6 June, 1860

My dear Sir,

When I shrink sometimes on the thought of your expectations & my abysmal non-performance, I try to assure myself that I never dared to make any exact promises, but only good intentions, to crystallize into act at a long day. Still whatever prudence or diffidence I may have used, I confess, [1]my dulness & incapacity at work has far exceeded any experience or any fear I had of it. It has cost me more time lately to do nothing, in many attempts to arrange & finish old MSS. for printing,[159] than ever I think before to do what I could best. For the scrap of paper that I was to send you, after Philadelphia, — Dr Furness, when he came here, told me, I was not to go.[160] Then I kept it to put into what will not admit anything peaceably, my "Religion" chapter, which has

158. MS owned by Mrs. Mildred Conway Sawyer; ph. in CUL. Excerpt I is in Conway, *Autobiography*, I, 312–313; parts of the same excerpt had already appeared in Conway, *Emerson at Home and Abroad*, pp. 14–15 and 181.

159. Probably in *The Conduct of Life*, published in the following December. The "'Religion' chapter" referred to below must have become the "Worship" of that book.

160. *Cf.* Mar. 20, 1860.

a very tender stomach, on which nothing will lie They say, the ostrich hatches her egg by standing off & looking at it, and that is my present secret of authorship. Not to do quite nothing for you, I long ago rolled up & addressed to you an ancient MS. Lecture called "Domestic Life," [161] & long ago you may be sure, familiar to Lyceums, but never printed except in newspaper reports. But I feared you would feel bound to print it, though I should have justified you if you had not printed a page.

For the question you now send me, all this is the answer. I have nothing to say of Parker. I know well what a calamity is the loss of his courage & patriotism to the country; but of his mind & genius, few are less accurately informed than I. It is for you & Sanborn & many excellent young men who stood in age & sensibility hearers & judges of all his discourse & action — for you to weigh & report. I have just written to his Society who have asked me to speak with Phillips, on the funeral occasion, that I must come to hear, not to speak; (though I shall not refuse to say a few words in honor.) My relations to him are quite accidental & our differences of method & working such as really required & honored all his catholicism & magnanimity to forgive in me. So I shall not write you an Essay: nor shall I in this mood, whilst I am hunted by printers (who do not nobly forgive as you do,) hope for reformation. But can you not, will not you come to Boston & speak to this occasion of eulogies of Parker?[1]

Yours, with very kind regards,

R. W. Emerson

Mr Conway.

To Herman Grimm, Concord, June 28, 1860 [162]

Concord

28 June 1860

My dear Sir,

Allow me to introduce to you my friend, Rev. Samuel Longfellow, of New York, who is parting for Europe, & means to pass through Berlin, on his tour. Mr Longfellow is highly valued among us for his accomplishments & his private worth. The name of his brother Henry, the poet, is probably not unknown to you.

161. Printed by Conway in *The Dial,* Cincinnati, Oct., 1860.

162. MS owned by the Goethe- und Schiller-Archiv; ph. in CUL. Samuel Longfellow was a passenger in the steamer " City of Washington," which sailed from New York for Liverpool, apparently on June 30 (*New-York Daily Tribune,* June 30 and July 2, 1860) . He had recently resigned his pastorate in Brooklyn.

I have charged him to bring me all the good news of you which he can gather.

Your affectionate servant,

R. W. Emerson

Herman Grimm.

To NATHANIEL HAWTHORNE, CONCORD, JUNE 29, 1860?

[MS listed and partly quoted in Merwin-Clayton Sales Co., Jan. 18, 1911, where the year 1862 is supplied; also in American Art Association, Nov. 5–6, 1923, where the date is given as Friday morning, June 29. Emerson says that his wife was charged last night to tell Hawthorne " that Judge Hoar invites you to dine with our club at Parker's tomorrow." Presumably the club was the Saturday Club; and during the only years — 1860–1864 — when Hawthorne was in America after its founding, June 29 was Friday only in 1860. We know from Samuel Longfellow's *Life* of his brother, n. d. (c. 1891), II, 405, that Hawthorne landed in this country on the 28th and attended the Saturday Club on the 30th. Meantime he seems to have been in his Concord home (Julian Hawthorne, II, 262), where, no doubt, Emerson's letter reached him.]

To EDITH EMERSON, CONCORD? JUNE? 1860 [163]

Dear Edith —

Why not a word of your patient [164] or yourself in five days? James Burke came here on Monday & has been at his brother's ever since looking very well in every other respect than his eye, which continues painful. He consults Dr Bartlett. He is very sorry, as I am, at the probability of forfeiting his place at Milton [165] which he has sense enough to know is the best he could hope for. He looks so well, however, that I have urged him to hasten back, & believe that his eyes will mend as soon as he is settled in it. I only hope that he will not be too late, & find his place filled. If it is not, tell Mr Forbes, that I trust he will come within a few days. And give my love to Mr & Mrs F.; & to Edward E. . Papa.

163. MS owned by RWEMA; ph. in CUL. A typed copy included in the volume *Letters of R. Waldo Emerson*, described in a note on May 7, 1860, is dated " June, 1860." Presumably this date was supplied by Edith Emerson Forbes and is, therefore, probably accurate.

164. Apparently Edward Emerson had gone to Milton in consequence of the invitation mentioned in the letter of May 4, 1860, to William Emerson, and his sister Edith was acting as his nurse.

165. For James Burke's prospective translation from Concord to Milton, see May 4, 1860, to Forbes.

To Abby Larkin Adams, Concord, July 23, 1860 [166]

Concord
23 July, Monday

Dear Abby,

Ellen who is always hinting that she will add herself to my party whenever I shall go to Brookline, thinks today that you will let us come tomorrow & spend a few hours. But if you have any other plans, you shall not break them for our uncertainties, &, if we do not find you, we shall hope to find your Uncle or your Aunt: — to whom, meantime, give my love.

Yours affectionately,
R. W. Emerson

Miss Abby Adams.

To Bryan Waller Procter, Concord, July 25, 1860

[MS listed and partly quoted in Anderson Galleries, Apr. 12–13, 1920; acknowledges Procter's many kindnesses when Emerson was in London and at other times.]

To Caroline Sturgis Tappan, Concord? July 30? 1860?

[Caroline Sturgis Tappan, Cotuit, Mass., July 31, n. y., said she was sorry that Emerson's note should come that day instead of himself. It may reasonably be conjectured that the visit to Cotuit mentioned in Aug. 6, 1860, followed this exchange of letters.]

To William Davis Ticknor, Concord, July, 1860 [167]

Concord July

Dear Sir,

I enclose a paper which had slipped out of the proofs I returned to you on Saturday. It is essential. But I find the printer must send me one more revise of that Worship chapter before final casting.

Yours
R. W. Emerson

Mr Ticknor

166. MS owned by RWEMA; ph. in CUL. The endorsement gives the date as 1860, when July 23 fell on Monday.

167. MS owned by CUL; ph. in CUL. It seems clear that the making of plates for the first edition of *The Conduct of Life* is referred to and that the date is therefore 1860. On Mar. 24, 1860, Ticknor & Fields had written that thirty-six pages of this book were already cast and had explained how the final casting would be held

To Franklin Benjamin Sanborn, Concord? July? *c.* 1860?

[MS listed and partly quoted in Anderson Auction Co., Jan. 24, 1908, where neither place nor date is given; requests that Edward be excused, as he is detained by haying. The conjectural date is plausible as being about a year before Edward finished his preparation for college and as falling within the years when Sanborn kept school in Concord.]

To Abel Adams, Concord, August 6, 1860 [168]

Concord
Aug. 6, 1860

My dear friend,

I hope no harm has befallen " Mad River & Lake Erie," that I hear nothing from you concerning the dividend, which, you told me ought to be paid about this time. Or, was I to to inquire at the office itself?

I went to Cotuit, last week, & spent a pair of beautiful days. Their little mimic port looks so like a picture before them, that I fancied it was a drop-scene which would be drawn up or down, & I should see nothing but pine woods again. But it lasted honest sea, whilst I stayed.

Love to all your house.

M[r Abel Adams]

To Benjamin H. Austin, Jr., Concord, August 29, 1860 [169]

Concord, 29 Aug.! 1860 —

Dear Sir,

I think it so highly probable that I shall go in winter a little farther westward than Buffalo, that I incline to accept your invitation, though with a little margin of contingency. If you will let me keep, say, the 15 Jan.ʸ open for me for the present, I will try to arrange what exist-

up until Emerson returned a second corrected proof of other pages. The " Worship chapter " was the sixth of the nine chapters published as *The Conduct of Life* in Dec., 1860.

168. MS owned by RWEMA; ph. in CUL. Doubtless Emerson's signature and the name of Abel Adams were written on the part of the third page which has been cut away. The reference to the railroad stock clearly indicates that the letter was to Adams.

169. MS owned by the Buffalo Public Library; ph. in CUL. The *Buffalo Commercial Advertiser,* Jan. 15, 1861, printed the announcement, signed by Benjamin H. Austin, Jr., that Emerson would lecture on " Clubs " before the Young Men's Association that evening. A not very favorable report of that lecture appeared *ibid.,* Jan. 16.

ing & what new engagements I may have, with a view to keeping that day for you. I should not like quite yet to announce a subject.

Respectfully,

R. W. Emerson

Mr Austin

To Elbridge G. Dudley, Concord, September 21, 1860[170]

Concord

21 September 1860

My dear Sir,

I have your note with its summons, & kind invitations. But I think I cannot come on the next Sunday. I am in a manner bound to my publishers to give them possession of all the *copy* of my book [171] by 1 October. I cannot quite keep the day, but must work for it, & shall end it, I hope, in the first days of the month. The second Sunday, or such day thereafter as you have vacant, I might come; [172] but could hardly, or not at all, do you justice, if I attempted the first. I am sorry if it is going to give you new trouble to find a substitute; but I see not how to help it.

With grateful remembrances from Mrs Emerson & myself to Mrs Dudley, and to Miss Duncan,[173]

Yours faithfully,

R. W. Emerson

Mr Dudley.

To Susan Haven Emerson, Concord, September 24? 1860? [174]

Concord

Tuesday, 24 Sept.

Dear Susan,

I tried seriously yesterday to persuade William to come to our house but he persisted to refuse. Today he has had a good deal of

170. MS owned by Mr. Abel Cary Thomas; ph. in CUL.

171. *The Conduct of Life.*

172. See Nov. 1, 1860, for what was probably Emerson's next appearance before Parker's old congregation at the Music Hall.

173. Rebecca Duncan, Boston, July 7, 1874, announcing the death of Mrs. Dudley, refers to her as " My sister." For Rebecca Duncan, *cf.* also Jan. 19, 1849, and later letters.

174. MS owned by HCL; ph. in CUL. The mention of Emily Jenks shows that the letter is not earlier than 1858; and, as " Edith is at school," it cannot be later than

acute pain on the left side, & keeps his bed, & Dr Bartlett has visited & blistered him. He is willing to come to us Lidian, & Ellen have been sitting with him. & if tomorrow is a fair day we shall hope to remove him. Ellen has been trying to find a nurse for him this P. M. without success. Emily Jenks [175] is with him now, & Galen Clark is to sleep in his room tonight. I have sent word to Haven that if he can come up & spend a day or two with him, he had better. Lidian thinks that if you feel able to come she is sure she can make you perfectly comfortable, and that you & William will feel both much easier than, if separated, to hear of symptoms, & fancy them worse. He needs much care, &, I fear, has not learned yet to spare & cosset himself. I am heartily grieved as we all are that he has not yet mended, as he promised. I should have mentioned already that Mr Clark is ill so that Mrs C.[176] is not free to take care of William [177] Lidian sends dear love to you; & Ellen also. Edith is at school.

Affectionately ever,
Your brother
Waldo

To Ida Agassiz, Concord? October? c. 1? 1860

[Ida Agassiz, Cambridge, Oct. 3, 1860, thanks Emerson for his " answer " and hopes he will go on with the projected reading and follow whatever method pleases him. *Cf.* Mar. *c.* 27, 1861.]

To H. J. Cross, Concord? October 8, 1860

[Acknowledged in Cross, Salem, Mass., Oct. 9, 1860. Cross, corresponding secretary of the Salem Lyceum, says he has put Emerson down for Dec. 19. The MS memorandum book for this year confirms the engagement.]

To Cornelia? Frances? Forbes, Concord? October 9? 1860

[C. Fanny Forbes, Milton, Mass., 9th (doubtless Oct. 9, 1860), thanked Emerson " for the note you were so kind in writing me " and for coming to Milton to see her; Emerson had evidently written, perhaps in answer to a note from her, about the death of a child. Cornelia Frances Forbes was the sister of J. M.

---

the early 1860's. During the years so bounded Sept. 24 fell on Tuesday only in 1861. But William Emerson, Jr., almost certainly the William of this letter, was not then in this country, and evidence cited below makes it very probable that the year was 1860.

175. *Cf.* Apr. 15, 1858, to William Emerson and Dec. 10, 1860.

176. Apparently the landlady of the William Emerson family during their long visits to Concord some five years earlier (*cf.* May 6, 1855, and later letters).

177. By Oct. 18, 1860, William Emerson, Jr., had returned safely to New York, as his letter of that date shows (MS owned by Dr. Haven Emerson). The kindness shown him at Concord had, he wrote, made illness almost a pleasure. *Cf.* also Dec. 10, 1860.

Forbes, who wrote from Milton, Oct. 14, 1860, that Emerson's note had comforted all his family. It seems probable that both Forbes and his sister referred to the same note, the occasion of which was evidently the death of his eldest daughter, Ellen, on Oct. 8 (*Boston Daily Advertiser*, Oct. 11, 1860).]

To ———————, Concord, October 16, 1860

[MS listed in C. F. Libbie & Co., Mar. 20–21, 1906, where it is described as regarding a lecture to be given to the teachers in Concord. *Cf.* Nov. 24, 1860?]

To Charles Sumner, Concord, October 30, 1860 [178]

Concord

30 October 1860

My dear Sumner,

I learn with great pleasure that it is settled that you shall come to Concord next week on Wednesday evening.[179] So I hasten to remind you that I depend on the happiness of receiving you at my house, for the night.

Yours faithfully,

R. W. Emerson

Mr Sumner.

To Elbridge G. Dudley, Concord, November 1, 1860 [180]

Concord

1 November

My dear Sir,

Tis high time I should answer your last note explicitly. I shall try to come to town on Saturday night. You shall, if you please, announce for my subject, " The Reformer." If Mrs Emerson is well enough to accompany me, I know she will be glad to accept Mrs Dudley's invitation, and I will send you word to that effect on Friday. If not I shall probably find it safer for my duties, to come to you on Sunday noon.[181]

With kindest regards to all your house,

R. W. Emerson.

Mr Dudley.

178. MS owned by RWEMA; ph. in CUL.

179. Sumner's lecture of Nov. 7, 1860, is recorded in the MS records of the Concord Lyceum (in Concord Free Public Library) and in *Journals*, IX, 286.

180. MS owned by Mr. Oliver R. Barrett; ph. in CUL.

181. The *Daily Evening Traveller*, Nov. 3, 1860, announced that Emerson would read " The Reformers " at the Music Hall on the morning of Sunday, Nov. 4. Cabot, II, 771, gives the subject as " Reform " and the date, wrongly I think, as Nov. 3.

To George Sewall Boutwell, Concord, November 5, 1860[182]

                                          Concord
                                5 November, Monday
My dear Sir,
         Our Saturday Club have invited Gov. Banks [183] to dine with
them at Parkers next Saturday at 3 o'clock, & he has accepted the invitation. Meantime whilst the Club invites no other guest, we have agreed
that each member may invite one. Will you give me the pleasure of your
company, on that occasion? I believe, you know all our members, & we
shall doubtless have a full company, who, I know, will be very glad to
meet you.
                                Yours, with great regard,
                                     R. W. Emerson
Mr Boutwell.

To James Elliot Cabot, Concord, November 5, 1860[184]

                                Concord 5 Novr 1860
My dear Cabot
         I received your note with great contentment. I learned last
night, that, after I left the club on the previous Saturday night, 27 Oct.
it was agreed that the club should hold an extraordinary session on
Saturday 10th Novr to invite Governor Banks to dine with us & each
member should have the privilege if he pleased, to invite one guest. I
am not sure that notice of this meeting has been sent you, as the committee will not have been informed of your acceptance of membership.[185] So I send this line, which can do no harm, praying you to attend,
if you can, on Saturday at 3 o clock: and, if you will, send notice of your

182. MS owned by the Massachusetts Historical Society; ph. in CUL. Nov. 5 fell
on Monday only in 1860 during the term of Nathaniel P. Banks as governor of Massachusetts, and the year is definitely proved by the letter of the same day to Cabot.
Boutwell tells in his *Reminiscences*, 1902, I, 248–249, how Emerson worked on his
behalf in the Concord Republican caucus of 1860, and how, after Boutwell's election
in 1862, Emerson supported him and wrote him " many letters." Some such letters
are noted later in the present volumes.
183. Banks was preparing to enter upon his brief term as an official of the Illinois
Central Railroad. The town of Waltham honored its departing citizen with a " complimentary levee " in its best style on Nov. 21 (*Waltham Sentinel*, Nov. 23, 1860),
and the Saturday Club may have honored him, likewise, because of his intended
departure.
184. MS owned by Professor Philip Cabot; ph. in CUL.
185. Apparently Cabot had not yet expressed his willingness to join the Saturday

intention to Horatio Woodman, who is to inform Mr Parker of the number of the company expected.

Ever yours,
R. W. Emerson

Mr Cabot.

To CHARLES ELIOT NORTON, CONCORD, NOVEMBER 8, 1860 [186]

Concord
8 November, 1860

My dear Sir,

      I have found, among my old pamphlets, four nos. of the Dial, namely, Nos. 9, 13, 15, & 16, all which I shall be most happy to send you, if you have not these already. I have visited Mr Alcott, who, it seems, has collected most of the Peabody remnants [187] also, & who can furnish you with one copy of every other number except the 5th, at the price of one dollar each number.

If you will send me the list of numbers wanting to your set, I can add to my own any that you wish from his collection, & will forward them to you.

With joy to you in the joy of the country,[188] ever yours,

R. W. Emerson

Mr Norton.

To JAMES THOMAS FIELDS, CONCORD? NOVEMBER 12, 1860? [189]

12 Nov

In looking over the " Contents," I can hardly find a fit one for your purpose; but I have one in mind that I think we may perhaps extort. I shall be in town tomorrow afternoon & will try to find you, or at least the *date*.

R. W. E.

Mr Fields.

Club and the Club had not yet formally elected him, at least not in a manner acceptable to him (see Nov. 28, 1860) .

186. MS owned by HCL; ph. in CUL.

187. For Elizabeth Peabody as publisher of *The Dial, cf.* Oct. 7, 1841, to William Emerson and later letters of that period.

188. Lincoln was elected on Nov. 6.

189. MS owned by HCL; ph. in CUL. The year is extremely uncertain. I conjecture that it may have been 1860, when, on Nov. 12, *The Conduct of Life* would have been within less than a month of its day of publication. As the letter is to Fields, it was in all probability not much earlier than 1860, though it may have been later.

To James Russell Lowell, Concord, November 14, 1860 [190]

My dear Lowell,

My riddle,[191] you see, is not very deep, & admits, like other riddles, of several solutions. Mine is, five national poets, Homer, Dante, Shakspeare, Swedenborg, & Goethe. A German can, if he will, interpret it, Bach, Mozart, Handel, Haydn, & Beethoven. If you choose to print it, I can put my solution into rhyme in another number. Ever yours,

R. W. Emerson

Mr Lowell.
Concord, Nov. 14, 1860.

To Charles Eliot Norton, Concord, November 17, 1860 [192]

Concord
17 Nov.ʳ 1860

My dear Sir,

Dante [193] arrived safely, & has been welcomed & examined with close attention by me, & a few other sympathizers. What a supernal figure! & how miraculously preserved through the times when Dante was unknown, to the times of the Appreciation! I heartily thank you for this fine drawing, which I shall hang up & study as one of the chief texts of history.

I find it is the same with Mrs Parkman's drawing.

I hesitate a little to send you W. E. C.'s poem,[194] when I find how un-

190. MS owned by RWEMA; ph. in CUL. Possibly this is the same as the letter of this date listed, without the name of the person addressed, in Thomas F. Madigan, Dec., 1911, though the description given there does not fit the present letter quite accurately.

191. " The Test " was published in *The Atlantic* for Jan., 1861. The " riddle " is explained by " Solution," which follows in the *Cent. Ed.*

192. MS owned by HCL; ph. in CUL.

193. This drawing was presumably one made from the famous fresco, very doubtfully attributed to Giotto, in the Bargello, where, not many years earlier, it had come to light from beneath a coat of whitewash. But the picture, if hitherto " miraculously preserved," suffered an evil fate in its " restoration." The copy of the " Giotto " Dante which still hangs in the Emerson House, at Concord, bears an inscription indicating that it was given by a friend, perhaps Sarah Clarke, about 1856; but this information is almost certainly erroneous. Norton's special interest in Dante, which appears in earlier letters, resulted, a few years later, in his book *On the Original Portraits of Dante*, 1865.

194. Doubtless *The Burial of John Brown*, which, according to *The Poets of Transcendentalism*, ed. Cooke, 1903, p. 313, was published in 1860.

pardonably negligent or capricious he has been in the delivery of his verses. It looks as if he had sent to the printer a bundle of notes roughly pencilled in the woods for his own use. A schoolboy could correct these pages. Yet the writer is a just & exact critic of poetry. Yet if a good walker, fond of birds & flowers, read the book for their sake, he will find the tokens of an original observer. But he is incapable of finish or even of correction.

Yours gratefully,
R. W. Emerson

Mr Norton.

The pamphlet [195] shall follow this note.

To Rebecca Duncan, Concord, November 24, 1860?

[Printed in the *Boston Evening Transcript*, July 12, 1897, p. 6, where the name of the correspondent is omitted and the date is merely Saturday, Nov. 24. Emerson's remark that a teachers' convention is to be held in Concord " next week " almost certainly refers to the convention of the Massachusetts State Teachers' Association held there on Nov. 26 and 27, 1860, at which Emerson himself was a speaker *(Boston Evening Transcript*, Nov. 28) ; and it should be noted that Nov. 24 fell on Saturday in that year. For Rebecca Duncan, *cf.* Sept. 21, 1860.]

To James Elliot Cabot, Concord, November 28, 1860 [196]

Concord —
28 Nov: 1860.

My dear Cabot,

You were yesterday elected unanimously a member of our Saturday Club. As I entreated your good will & consent to this action, a long time ago,[197] you will think there is somewhat more than Dutch length in our deliberations. Some misunderstanding chanced, one day, in our balloting, — but the odd circumstance was, that, from some supra-Castilian point of honor, with which the Club is afflicted, it became necessary to wait a year for the return of a member on the other side of the world. He came at last, and, in a full club, — and, I believe, all voting — we made our election. I entreat you to accede to our wishes, by coming loyally on the last Saturday of each month, at 3 o'clock, to our party. I have valued the Club for this, among my best reasons, that

195. It is difficult to say whether Emerson wrote an " s " at the end of this word. Presumably he refers to a copy of Channing's poem.

196. MS owned by Professor Philip Cabot; ph. in CUL.

197. *Cf.* letters of Mar. 22 and 23, 1859.

through it I was to get an interview now & then with you. I subjoin a list
of the members.[198]

Yours faithfully,
R. W. Emerson

J. E. Cabot, Esq.

over

 T. Appleton
  Agassiz
 J E Cabot
 R H Dana
  J S Dwight
  C Felton
J. M. Forbes
  Hawthorne
  Hoar
  Holmes
S. G. Howe
  Lowell
  Longfellow
  Pierce
  Ward
  Whipple
  Woodman

TO BESSIE PEDDER, CONCORD, NOVEMBER 29, 1860

[MS owned by the Yale University Library; printed in *The Journal of English and Germanic Philology*, XXVI, 477 (Oct., 1927).]

TO ——————————, CONCORD, DECEMBER 4, 1860

[MS listed in Merwin Sales Co., Mar. 17–18, 1914; described there as in reply to a proposal for a lecture tour.]

TO JAMES R. OSGOOD, CONCORD, DECEMBER 8, 1860

[MS listed and partly quoted in Anderson Auction Co., June 3, 1914; concerns a list of persons to whom copies of *The Conduct of Life* were to be sent.]

198. All in the list are duly recorded in *The Early Years of the Saturday Club.*

To WILLIAM EMERSON, CONCORD, DECEMBER 10, 1860 [199]

Concord, 10 Dec. 1860

Dear William,

I have just received your letter,[200] & hail the continued good news from William Junior, which are most welcome. It seems a happy circumstance that Charles can attend him just now, & good for both. I have never heard why Ballstoon was advised, but tis a great mitigation of the threatened exile of Minnesota: Yet can hardly be advised on the same grounds?

As for Charles's adventure [201] it is very hard to learn that we can teach our children nothing: that they must experiment for themselves: all the gold they get from us is counterfeit, and their own failures, which they will not make but once, are their benefactors, in the end. Charles is certainly showing a certain spirit & social power, which I rank high among the manly attributes, &, I suppose, he has reserves of character, which will not let these cost him too dear, But, I own, at first hearing, all my sympathies were with you & Susan.

I enclose Wm's draft, given me in July, for cash, & will beg you to credit me with the amount, on your account with me in Aunt Mary's affairs.

When I go to Boston tomorrow, I shall send a copy of " Conduct of Life " [202] to Aunt Mary, under cover to you. I am sorry to give you the trouble of it, but do not know how else to secure its arrival to her.

I am ashamed to think what a relief is the delivery from this so little book.

We are all well, except Lidian, who gets out of bed today to go to

199. MS owned by HCL; ph. in CUL.

200. William Emerson, Dec. 8, 1860 (MS owned by Dr. Haven Emerson). This letter shows that William Emerson, Jr., was at Ballston Spa, N. Y., for his health and that his brother Charles was there to serve as his nurse and to study under his direction.

201. See Apr. c. 7, 1861. Charles Emerson was in trouble with the college authorities because of his part in some hazing.

202. Published Dec. 8, 1860, according to the *Boston Daily Advertiser* of that date. I do not know on what authority Cooke, in his bibliography, gives the date as November. William Emerson received his copy on Dec. 8 — it was probably sent a day or two before publication (William Emerson, Dec. 8, cited above). Norton wrote to Clough, Dec. 11, 1860, that the book was published " a day or two since " and could not have appeared at a fitter time, as it confirmed moral principles and based them on eternal laws (*Letters of Charles Eliot Norton*, ed. Sara Norton and M. A. DeWolfe Howe, 1913, I, 215). The country was tense with the excitement which preceded the outbreak of the war.

Dr Keep in Boston. Ellen is staying with Mary Higginson in Boston. Edith & Edward begin school again today. Edith sees Emily, but she very rarely comes here. Dear love to Susan. Your affectionate brother Waldo

To Emily Mervine Drury, Concord? December? *c.* 10? 1860

[Mrs. Drury, Canandaigua, N. Y., Dec. 23, 1860, said she had long denied herself the pleasure of answering Emerson's " kind letter "; she noted his statement that he was to be in Rochester, N. Y., on Jan. 24 and in Buffalo on the 26th, and invited him to be the guest of her family on the 25th; she hoped the sprain no longer troubled him.

The Marietta College Library owns a copy (ph. in CUL) of what is described as an incomplete letter from Emerson to Mrs. Drury dated Concord, Wednesday, May 22, with " 1860–61 " supplied by Mrs. Drury. The year was pretty definitely 1861, when May 22 fell on Wednesday. There is mention of a proposed visit by Edward Waldo Emerson and Tom Ward to an officer — obviously William Mervine, Mrs. Drury's father — and his ship. On May 6, 1861, Mervine had been ordered to Boston; on the following day he was appointed flag officer of the Gulf Blockading Squadron; on the 22d of the same month he raised his flag on the " Mississippi "; and on the 27th he put to sea (*Official Records of the Union and Confederate Navies in the War of the Rebellion*, 1st series, XVI, 519–526 *passim*) . The final sentence in the copy indicates that Emerson had written a note of introduction to Mervine himself, presumably also dated May 22. There is some evidence of a letter to Ellen or Edith Emerson about the same time in regard to the proposed visit.]

To ————— Barnard, Concord, December 10, 1860? [203]

Concord
10 Dec. Monday

Dear Mrs Barnard,

It would give me great pleasure to come to you tomorrow, & to see Mr Yeatman again — after many years, — but I have promised to go to Mrs Doctor Jackson at the same hour, who, I believe, has invited some friends. I wish it were possible, — is it not? — that you & Mr Barnard & Mr Yeatman should come there. Mrs J. I know would rejoice. With great regard

Mrs Barnard.   R. W. Emerson

203. MS owned by the Minneapolis Public Library; ph. in CUL. The year is extremely doubtful; but Dec. 10, 1860, was Monday, and in the letter definitely so dated Emerson says he is to go to Boston on the 11th. So far as I know, the person addressed may have been the wife of George M. Barnard (*cf.* Aug. 15, 1831, and the *Boston Directory* for 1859–1860) .

To Charles Eliot Norton, Concord, December 25, 1860 [204]

Concord

25 December 1860

My dear Sir,

You are bent on making my cabinet of Dante complete with book, & picture, & cast.[205] I can only rejoice & admire. Yet these photographs [206] to the biography so satisfactory, & without one injurious line. His genius kept his body. These have disclosed an instant virtue in inspiring my young people with huge curiosity touching the history of the bust, which they are proceeding in all directions to satisfy. With renewed thanks, & the good wishes of the venerable day,

Yours faithfully,

R. W. Emerson

Mr Norton.

204. MS owned by HCL; ph. in CUL.

205. For book and picture, see letters of Jan. 2 and Nov. 17, 1860, both to Norton. Apparently Norton had now added a cast and photographs, though I have found nothing of the sort. I am not certain whether the cast was a replica of the mask later described in his book *On the Original Portraits of Dante* and reproduced in several photographic illustrations there. Richard T. Holbrook (*Portraits of Dante,* 1911, pp. 49–50) discredits Kirkup's " death mask," which Norton accepted as authentic.

206. The first page ends with this word. Part of the sentence seems to have been omitted in the transition to the following page.

1861

Astor House
N. Y. 6 Jan 1861

Dear Edith,

I enclose to you for your Aunt Brown her dividend from the Boston & Providence Railroad $35.00, which you will give her yourself, &, make a note of having paid it, on my Journal. I have also asked Uncle William to send you $80. with which you can begin to pay your bills, as, for example, Mr Stacy,[2] Ben. Hastings, & George Hosmer. Mr Cheney will give you cash for your Uncle's cheque. I saw Mr & Mrs Bancroft today & Mrs B. promises to call on Ellen whose address [at 260 Green St, near Eighth *Street*,][3] I gave her. I saw William Jr., too, who does not look strong, but much better & straighter than at Concord, & more himself. Aunt Susan was in bed, & looking quite feeble. I shall need to return here for Ellen, & to see Aunt Mary, &, Mr Bancroft insists, to dine with him. I go tomorrow morning at 7. westward.[4] I am not anticipating Ellen's chronicles, for she does not know that I saw Mrs B. In Boston I paid Mr Bates' bill & $50. on Warren's; so when I send you more money, as I may, Sumner, Chandler, Kimball, & 50. on Warrens account, are to be remembered. Tell mamma, that the trunk appears to hold all needed goods. I hope to hear at Cortland [5] how your Wednesday's ode & Edward's shall have gone.

Papa.

1. MS owned by RWEMA; ph. in CUL.

2. Edith Emerson, Jan. 9 (1861), said she had bought *Tom Brown's School-days* at Stacy's. *Cf.* Oct. 14, 1862.

3. The MS memorandum book for 1861 notes " Mrs Ludlow " at this address in the entry for Jan. 7. Emerson had probably brought Ellen to New York on his way westward. Apparently he did not lecture in New York at this time.

4. See the letters of Jan. 12, 1861.

5. The MS memorandum book gives Jan. 12 to Cortland, N. Y. Mrs. Byrl Jörgensen Kellogg informs me that *The Republican Banner* of that town printed in its issue of Jan. 16, 1861, praise of Emerson's lecture of the 12th and of his discourse on the following day, Sunday. According to the same paper for Jan. 9, the lecture was to be read before the Cortlandville Literary Association at the Stone Church.

To George Bancroft, Binghamton? New York, January 12, 1861

[Mentioned in the letter of the same date to Edith Emerson.]

To ———————, Binghamton? New York, January 12, 1861

[In the letter of the same date to his daughter, Emerson says, " I have just written to my correspondents westward . . ." It is not clear whether this means
more than one letter.]

To Edith Emerson, Binghamton, New York, January 12, 1861 [6]

Binghamton
Saturday 12 Jan[y]

Dear Edith,

You are a pearl of a correspondent I have a letter from
you every night at Elmira,[7] at Owego,[8] at Hornellsville, — all safe &
satisfactory but have not sat down anywhere with leisure to write. I
hope you received my note from the Astor House [9] containing your
Aunt's dividend, and ere this time, your Uncle William's remittance.
Today I must decide on the Western propositions. Sorry am I you
could not go to the Cabot Theatre,[10] which ought to show what is best
in private drama, though no " Comus " has yet been written for it. For
" Dorcas," I can do nothing with my imperfect memory of it. Glad you
can keep up your lessons, and administer at home.

Noon. I have just written to my correspondents westward [11] that I
will not go beyond Buffalo, & to Mr Bancroft [12] that I will dine with
him if he is disengaged on Thursday 17th so that I now expect to reach

6. MS owned by RWEMA; ph. in CUL. The references relating to Emerson's lecture schedule and other evidence cited below fix the year. The MS memorandum
book for 1861 lists " Hornellsville " for Jan. 11, with " Binghamton " written above
it in pencil. I am informed by Miss Helen G. Thacher that *The Hornellsville Tribune*
of Jan. 3 of this year announced Emerson's " Clubs " for the 11th.

7. " Clubs " was the lecture listed for Elmira, N. Y., Jan. 9 (MS memorandum
book for 1861).

8. Emerson wrote the word incompletely. " Classes of Men " was the subject for
Oswego, N. Y., on Jan. 10 (*ibid.*).

9. Of Jan. 6, 1861.

10. Edith told in her letter of Jan. 9 (1861) of invitations " to you and Ellen and
me, to some theatricals at the Cabot's theatre in Brookline," which she had had to
refuse.

11. See the second letter of Jan. 12, 1861.

12. Jan. 12, 1861, to Bancroft. Presumably there was a letter to Ellen of this same
date, but I have no further evidence.

home on the 18ᵗʰ at night. Of course, this is a little uncertain, but I shall write thus to Ellen.

Give my love to Edward, and, since Herman & Gisela & Emily Russell did not go to kindle the fire, I will hope that his Town did not.[13] Otherwise, he must make it famous as Troy town, by writing a poem out of it, like Homer. Tell mamma, I am furious to get home. Papa —

To Edward Bangs, Concord, January 18, 1861?[14]

Concord
18 January

My dear Sir,

I grieve to have missed your visit, — yours & Mrs Bangs's, and would gladly indemnify myself by carrying Ellen to your house to-night; but have just come home, this morning, from a journey, & must stay at home for a day or two.

I am very sorry to hear & slow to believe that your little boy can have any so grave complaint. My wife desires me to say that the name of the physician of whom she has had good accounts, is, Dr William Henry Munroe, of Chelsea. She means I believe to accompany this note with a little parcel of eider down, as some late experience leads her to believe that it is not just now to be found in the shops. I trust the little patient will soon be well.

With affectionate regards,
R. W. Emerson

Edward Bangs, Esq.

13. In her letter of Jan. 9, mentioned above, Edith said that Edward's composition, on which he had worked till midnight, was missing in the morning and that Katie was suspected of kindling the fire with it. The Grimms and Russell saved from the fire were, perhaps, letters from the persons named or papers belonging to them; but I am uncertain. A letter of Oct. 25, 1860, from Herman Grimm printed in *Correspondence*, told of his marriage to Gisela von Arnim. As it was not answered by Emerson till June 27 following, it may well be alluded to here.

14. MS owned by CUL; ph. in CUL. The year 1856, supplied in an unknown hand, is undoubtedly an error. On Jan. 18 of that year Emerson was still in the West, lecturing. But on the same day in 1861, if his plan was carried out, he returned home with Ellen from New York (see the letters of Jan. 6 and 12 preceding). The fact that he had arrived home in the morning instead of at night, as he had expected to do, is hardly a serious objection to the conjectural date. Finally, it should be added that Edward Bangs and Anne Hodgkinson were not married till Sept. 25, 1856, and their eldest son, Edward Appleton, probably the boy referred to here, was born June 26, 1860 (Dean Dudley, *History and Genealogy of the Bangs Family in America*, 1896, p. 264). Dr. Munroe is listed in *The Massachusetts Register, 1862*.

To Josiah Phillips Quincy, Concord, January 23 and 25, 1861 [15]

Concord, 23 Jan.ʸ 1861

My dear Sir,

My letter comes very tardily to tell you what good gifts you
sent me in your MSS. & in your letter. They found me very busy with
sundry tasks, before a journey, from which I have just returned. But I
carried my treasures with me, for such they are. I delight in talent, as
in the arts it has made — but " that strain I heard was of a higher mood,"
& gives me a better joy and opens a future. I share very heartily, whilst
I read, the austere & religious sentiment which prevades the poem, the
scorn of mean living, the aspiration, & the worship of truth. Perhaps
religion is yet too strong a word, — perhaps the character has not yet
arrived so high, has not cleared itself to that, but is resolutely dealing
with low enemies & dangers, listening to itself, & cheered haughtily by
comparing itself with these. Yet this heroism & stern self communion is
a germ of all grandeur, & we shall see the heights & celestial flowerings,
in due time.

25th I had written thus far, when a friend arrived here from New York,
who puts all *aside* where he comes, — has taken all hours whilst here,
gone to Boston with me, & still interferes a little with the earlier visions.
I am glad no printer has yet touched these sheets. Time enough for
him by & by. But I owe many delicious hours to unpublished records
of mind & heart. Their virginity charms, & perhaps I should not read
them if printed. If my ' farm ' were nearer to yours, I should try to show
you one or two such, long since confided to me, & which your poem &
letter again & again suggest & refresh in mind. The author of one of
them, if he is what he was, I think you should certainly know. But
though I wish this poem to lie in manuscript for a time, I heartily approve your design of continuing it & making it a canvas for new colors
& lines, as new experiences shall require. I have or shall have many little
matters of literary criticism to add, if it were going earlier to the public.

15. MS owned by Mr. M. A. DeWolfe Howe; ph. in CUL. For Quincy, *cf.* especially Sept. 1, 1857. In a letter dated Quincy, Mass., Dec. 30 (endorsed 1861, doubtless
the year of receipt, but not of writing) , he told of a manuscript he had sent, knowing
that Emerson would make no comment on it unless he wished to do so. Mary Miller
Quincy, Boston, Mar. 17, 1861, thanked Emerson for the encouraging letter he had
sent her son (presumably the present letter, though possibly a later one) . Young
Quincy had already published some dramatic poems, one of which, *Lyteria,* is mentioned in *Journals,* IX, 104–105. Emerson liked the poet better than the poem. Perhaps the imperious friend " from New York " was Henry James, Sr.

But its privacy & soliloquy deeply please & content me now. Not to keep this late note any longer, I must reserve what I have to say to your letter.

With kindest regards,
R. W. Emerson

Josiah P. Quincy.

TO ELBRIDGE G. DUDLEY, CONCORD, JANUARY 31, 1861 [16]

Concord
Thursday 31 Jan

My dear Sir,

You may be sure I have not forgotten my duties, no, nor my social hopes for Sunday. My wife sends her thankful salutations to Mrs Dudley & yourself, & would very gladly accept your friendly proposition, but she considers herself held at home by an engagement. Mr Alcott holds his class for conversation at our house, on Saturday Eve: and the more I go away, the more she must abide.

In this plight, I do not see that I can come to you till Sunday after lecture.

I think I will call my discourse, " Natural Religion." Perhaps it is needless to advertise it so. But you shall do as you choose.[17] Faithfully,
Mr Dudley.   R. W. Emerson

TO THOMAS CARLYLE, CONCORD, c. JANUARY? 1861?

[Incompletely printed in Ireland, *In Memoriam*, pp. 72–73, where it is dated simply 1861. The date is earlier than Mar. 4 of that year, as Buchanan is mentioned as President. Comparison with *Journals*, IX, 195–196 — an entry dated May? 1859 — suggests doubt as to the year. The letter and the entry in *Journals* show striking similarities, and at least part of the entry, referring to the death of Prescott, must belong to 1859.]

16. MS owned by Mr. Alwin J. Scheuer; ph. in CUL. Evidence cited below shows that the year was 1861, when Jan. 31 fell on Thursday. Apparently Alcott conducted a series of conversations in Concord this winter. Edith had written to her father on Jan. 13, 1861 (misdating her letter 1860), that she had attended Alcott's conversation of " Last night " — apparently Jan. 12. Emerson himself noted, Jan. 19 following, Alcott's conversation on " Health " as without inspiration (*Journals*, IX, 293).

17. The *Boston Evening Transcript*, Feb. 2, 1861, announced that Emerson would read " Natural Religion " before the Twenty-eighth Congregational Society (Parker's old congregation) at the Music Hall on Sunday morning, Feb. 3.

To J. G. SHERLIEN, CONCORD? FEBRUARY 6, 1861

[Acknowledged in Sherlien, Pittsburgh, Feb., 1861; apparently Emerson replied favorably to a request for permission to name a society after him — the Emerson Literary Society.]

To CHARLES SUMNER, CONCORD, FEBRUARY 27, 1861 [18]

Concord
27 February, 1861.

My dear Sumner,

Peace & prosperity adhere to your truth & firmness, as they ought! I am always consoled in the bad times by your fidelity. I happened to ask last night our village captain Barrett [19] if he was ready to march to Washington? he said, " Yes, that the great coats, haversacks, &c of his company had all been made, & the men had been all ready, if the Governor had ordered them ": " 2000 men were ready," &c. I hope it will not need, but the readiness is wholesome.

I have duly received the valued XII volume Part II, of the " Pacific Railroad Exploration," [20] and sundry other volumes of " Patent Office," [21] & " Chinese Correspondence," [22] sent by your orders to me, & several speeches, some very good ones, of divers patriots. Amid all this faithful care on your part, I fear, I have been so ungrateful as never to send you my little book published at New Years. [23] I shall be in town tomorrow, & if the bookseller confirms my misgiving, I shall make my tardy reparation.

May the Highest Wisdom & Strength keep & guide you, prays ever yours faithfully,

R. W. Emerson

Hon. Charles Sumner.

18. MS owned by RWEMA; ph. in CUL.

19. For Richard Barrett, see a note on Apr. 20, 1861.

20. Earlier volumes of this work are mentioned in Jan. 19, 1858. Vol. XII, Book II, was dated 1860.

21. Probably the three volumes of the report of the Commissioner of Patents for 1859, published in 1860 as Senate Ex. Docs. 11 and 12, 36th Cong., 1st Sess.

22. The correspondence and dispatches of American ministers to China published in 1860 as Senate Ex. Doc. 30, 36th Cong., 1st Sess.

23. Doubtless Emerson means *The Conduct of Life,* actually published early in the preceding December (see Dec. 10, 1860) .

To Charles Sumner, Concord, March 1, 1861 [24]

Concord
1 March, 1861

My dear Sumner

Mr Simeon Draper [25] of New York is, I believe, sending some recommendations to Washington in behalf of Mr Ralph Emerson, of Los Angeles, California, who is a candidate for one of three offices,[26]

1. Collector of the Port of San Pedro
2. Receiver in the Land Office
    3. Treasurer or Paymaster in the same

In behalf of Mr Emerson I can say that I knew him well in his youth, a fine graceful fellow, of excellent character. In business, in Porto Rico,[27] for a year or two, he learned Spanish thoroughly; in France, for several years with the Drapers, he learned French; &, I understand, he is also a good Italian. He has been many years in California, and some of his friends there have given me, with great good will, favorable testimonies to his character & ability. Possibly you have yourself seen him in Paris. He is a brother of George B. Emerson. If his nomination should ever come before you, I think you can rely on him as an amiable, accomplished, & worthy man.

With great regard,
Yours faithfully,
R. W. Emerson

Mr Sumner

To Christian? N.? Bovee, Concord, March 21, 1861

[MS listed and partly quoted in Anderson Galleries, Mar. 29–31, 1916, and in American Art Association, Mar. 3–4, 1925. Emerson welcomes Bovee and promises to meet him at Parker's as soon as the snow tempest is over; says the hour of dinner on Saturday is 2:15; and mentions a book of Leigh Hunt's which he does not know. Presumably this Bovee, whose initials are not given in the catalogues, was the Christian N. Bovee, New York lawyer and author, of Sept.? c. 28? 1862.]

To Frederick Goddard Tuckerman, Concord? March 25, 1861

[Mentioned and partly summarized in *Journals*, IX, 318. For the book of poems which Emerson acknowledged in this letter, see June 18, 1861.]

24. MS owned by RWEMA; ph. in CUL.
25. *Cf.* June 29 and July 5, 1833; and Dec. 3, 1850.
26. He seems not to have received any of these offices; but apparently he remained in California, where Emerson saw him many years later (see Apr. 27, 1871).
27. *Cf.* Apr. 20 and 23, 1831.

To IDA AGASSIZ, CONCORD? MARCH *c.* 27, 1861

[Mentioned in Mar. 27, 1861. *Cf.* also Oct.? *c.* 1? 1860.]

To EDITH EMERSON, CONCORD? MARCH 27, 1861 [28]

Wednesday Eve^g March

27 —

Dear Edith,

I have written to Miss Ida,[29] that I will hold a class meeting at Mrs Parkman's, on Saturday,[30] at 12, unless she knows it to be unsuitable on any account. So if you have any fancy to meet the ladies perhaps you will like to stay till Saturday at 4. On Tuesday, I go to New Bedford,[31] and perhaps I will ask Sibyl Farnham Lambard [32] to come on Wednesday the day of my return, & spend a pair of days here. Meantime you must write to Mrs Watson [33] what day you will arrive there. If you need to have the tooth taken out, go to Dr H. or I. or J. or K., but be sure that it ought to be taken. I inclose ten dollars.

Papa

To WILLIAM EMERSON, JR., CONCORD, MARCH 29, 1861

[MS listed and partly quoted in Bangs & Co., May 7 and 8, 1901. This is an answer to William Emerson, Jr., Farmington, N. Y., Mar. 24 (endorsed 1861; MS owned by Dr. Haven Emerson), in which young William asks his uncle for advice about the best translation of Plato for a gift, suggests that his cousin Edward Emerson go into the mountains for a year, and tells of his own improved health.]

28. MS owned by RWEMA; ph. in CUL. Mar. 27 fell on Wednesday in 1861, the year added in another hand and indicated by evidence cited below.

29. Mar. *c.* 27, 1861.

30. Emerson was at the Saturday Club on that day (*Journals*, IX, 320) and could easily have met the " class " at twelve before going to the Club, which usually assembled at three (*The Early Years*, pp. 19 and 22) . He seems to have had a series of " class " meetings during the spring. Ellen Emerson wrote, Dorchester, Mass., May 17, 1861, that, in accordance with his message, she was going to write to Ida that he would have the class in Boston on the 25th and proposed that on the two Saturdays following the 25th the meetings should be at Concord, that of June 8 to be a grand gala class with Alcott.

31. Mr. George H. Tripp informs me that the *Daily Evening Standard*, New Bedford, Apr. 2, 1861, announced Emerson's lecture on " Conversation " for that evening and that the same paper reported it the following day.

32. Emerson's cousin appears in a number of other letters, especially in early years.

33. Mary Russell Watson had written, Mar. 7, 1861, that Edith would be welcome whenever she wished to come and suggested what the rate should be by the week.

To Henry James, Sr., Concord, March 29, 1861

[MS owned by Mr. Henry James; printed in R. B. Perry, I, 92–93.]

To Mary Russell Watson, Concord, March? 1861?

[MS listed and partly quoted in Goodspeed's Book Shop, Sept., 1905, where no date is given; relates to the prospective visit of Emerson's daughter and expresses the hope that she will notify Mrs. Watson in advance of her "days of departure and arrival." For the probable date, *cf.* Mar. 27, 1861.]

To William Watson Goodwin, Concord? April *c.* 7, 1861

[Goodwin, Cambridge, Apr. 10, 1861, acknowledges receipt of Emerson's letter on the preceding Monday (Apr. 8); evidently Emerson had written in an attempt to help his nephew Charles Emerson out of difficulty with the Harvard authorities over some hazing (*cf.* Dec. 10, 1860).]

To Ellen Emerson, Concord? April *c.* 9? 1861

[Ellen Emerson, Dorchester, Mass., Apr. 10 and 11, 1861 (in the part written Apr. 10), acknowledges "your letter with the tickets." Probably the tickets were for her father's lectures in Boston (*cf.* a note on May 24, 1861).]

To Ellen Emerson, Concord? April 11, 1861

[Mentioned in Apr. 12, 1861.]

To Ellen Emerson, Concord, April 12, 1861 [34]

Concord

12 April

Dear Ellen,

Nothing has been done for Sophy.[35] Shut all your eyes, & think as hard as you can, & tell me what it must be: $25 is the mark, though it ought to be 50. Edw[d] had a happy vacation,[36] & appears to be well. I believe, he & Tom [37] have given over pre-engaging rooms, & mean to take their chance for rooms *in college,* after the Examination. I sent you in a letter yesterday $3.; and now $3. again, in this, but have heard

34. MS owned by RWEMA; ph. in CUL. The year is obviously 1861.

35. Ellen Emerson, Dorchester, Mass., Apr. 10 and 11, 1861, had asked whether any steps had been taken about "Sophy's present." The *Boston Daily Advertiser* of Apr. 27, 1861, reported the marriage of Sophia B. Ripley and James B. Thayer on the 24th of this month.

36. *Cf.* Mar. 29, 1861, to James.

37. Ward.

nothing of any such appeals as, you say, came by Alice & L. Concord is very well, it thanks you; though a gloom darkened all the valley on Monday night & Tuesday,[38] as you will have heard. You must remember that Aunt Elizabeth goes on the 17th, &, if you can safely, had better see her off at the steamer's wharf.[39] Mrs Brown is not so well today as heretofore. Mamma busy with Mrs Stearns & Company.

Papa.

Mamma asks, when to send a basket? & if you go to Mrs Forbes wishes to send her this circular.

To Thomas Carlyle, Concord, April 16, 1861 [40]

Concord, 16 April, 1861.

My dear Carlyle,

My friend — almost my sister, — Elizabeth Hoar, embarks again tomorrow for England.[41] She takes with her, her niece, to whom your climate has been recommended for health's sake. Miss Hoar did not see you when in London, last year [42] She called at your house, & saw Mrs Carlyle. You were away: I wish now she may be fortunate in seeing you also. You have not many readers with eyes so apprehensive & clear, & a moral verdict so unerring. I commend her a little proudly to your heroic regards, & to the kind counsels of my friend, Mrs Carlyle. Her brother, Judge Hoar, now of our Supreme Bench,[43] well remembers you, and Dr Jacobson, to whom you sent him at Oxford.[44]

. . . . .

To Arthur Hugh Clough, Concord, April 16, 1861

[MS owned by Mr. Arthur Clough; ph. in CUL. Printed in *Emerson-Clough Letters.*]

38. "Last evening" — perhaps Monday, Apr. 8 — "a note was discovered in the room of Miss Nelly Hunt, at the residence of Judge Hoar . . . bidding her friends a farewell . . . This morning . . . her body was found in the river" (Concord correspondence reprinted in the *Boston Evening Transcript,* Apr. 10, 1861).

39. Elizabeth Hoar and her party were passengers on the "America," which cleared for Liverpool on Apr. 16 (*Boston Daily Advertiser,* Apr. 17 and 18, 1861).

40. MS owned by RWEMA; ph. in CUL.

41. *Cf.* Apr. 12, 1861.

42. *Cf.* the letters of Oct. 5, 1858.

43. Of Massachusetts.

44. The remainder of the letter, except the name "T. Carlyle, Esq.," opposite Emerson's signature, is printed in *C–E Corr.,* 1883, where the date line and salutation also appear.

To Edith Emerson, Concord? April 20, 1861 [45]

ᴵDearᴵ Edith

ᴵᴵYou have heard that our village was all alive yesterday with the departure of our braves.[46] Judge Hoar made a speech to them at the Depot, Mr Reynolds made a prayer in the ring the cannon which was close by us making musical beats every minute to his prayer. And when the whistle of the train was heard, & George Prescott (the commander) who was an image of manly beauty, ordered his men to march, his wife stopped him & put down his sword to kiss him, & grief & pride ruled the hour. All the families were there. They left Concord 45 men, but on the way recruits implored to join them, &, when they reached Boston, they were 64.ᴵᴵ —

Papa

To James Thomas Fields, Concord, May 24, 1861 [47]

Concord
24 May 1861

Mr Fields,

Dear Sir,

"Blake's Poems," [48] & the English book "Faithful Forever," [49] have safely arrived.

I have also your "Ticket Account," & the draft it encloses for $124.$\frac{10}{100}$ dollars; and have to thank you & Mr Ticknor for your kind & careful

45. MS owned by Mr. David C. Forbes; ph. in CUL. Excerpts I–II are in Cabot, II, 601–602. The entire date has been supplied; the day of the month has been so written and rewritten that 20, 19, and 10 are all possible readings. But evidence cited below shows that Apr. 20 is correct.

46. On the afternoon of historic Apr. 19 the Concord company, "47 men, Captain Richard Barrett" arrived on the Boston Common, where great throngs had just cheered the company from Medford (*Boston Daily Advertiser*, Apr. 20, 1861). The departure from Concord is mentioned in a note in *Journals*, IX, 324. Barrett presently resigned, and the company went to Washington under Lieutenant George L. Prescott (*Memoirs of Members of the Social Circle*, 3d series, p. 171).

47. MS owned by Mr. James F. Clarke; ph. in CUL.

48. There seems to have been no new edition between that by Emerson's friend J. J. G. Wilkinson, in 1839, and D. G. Rossetti's in 1863 (Geoffrey Keynes, *A Bibliography of William Blake*, 1921, p. 261).

49. Ticknor & Fields published the American edition of Coventry Patmore's *Faithful for ever*, Boston, 1861.

attention to my little adventure,[50] which, in such unpropitious weeks, must be reckoned a success.

Yours gratefully,
R. W. Emerson

To Charles Sumner, Concord, June 17, 1861 [51]

Concord
17 June, 1861 —

My dear Sumner,

My cousin Ezra Ripley, Esq, son of our honoured Mrs Ripley whom you know, & himself long a valued member of the Middlesex Bar, living in East Cambridge, is now 3ᵈ Lieutenant of the East Cambridge Company of Volunteers now for many weeks in camp at Spy-Pond.[52] He is waiting orders to go to Washington, having already enlisted or declared his entire readiness to enlist for three years. But it appears that, on account of his age 36 [53] & on account of the Army rules which admit but two Lieutenants, he will drop into the ranks as a private, when his company joins the National Army. This circumstance has nowise changed his purpose or damped his ardor, for he is a determined patriot, and a man utterly unselfish. Meantime his friends think that a man of his education & abilities & character, who makes such costly sacrifices to his country, ought not to be thrown into the ranks but should have a commission from the United States.[54] And I write to say, that, if you know how to help him, you may safely assert that he is a man of noble sentiments & drawn now from his lucrative profession, only by his sense of public duty; that he has devoted himself now for these many weeks entirely to drill, & to lessons specially relating to his

50. Tickets for Emerson's course on " Life and Literature " were sold at the bookstore of Ticknor & Fields (*Boston Evening Transcript*, Apr. 2, 1861) . The *Transcript*, Apr. 9–May 15, 1861, announced the individual lectures — " Genius and Temperament," for Apr. 9; " Art," for 17; " Civilization at a Pinch," for 23; " Good Books," for May 1; " Poetry and Criticism in England and America," for 8; " Boston," for 15.

51. MS owned by RWEMA; ph. in CUL.

52. In a letter of this month Sarah Bradford Ripley tells how her son brought his company to Concord and to the Old Manse (*Worthy Women*, pp. 205–206) .

53. The number was probably inserted by Thayer; *cf.* June 17? 1861.

54. Sumner replied, Washington, July 1, 1861, that, as there were but few commissions to be had from the War Department, Ezra Ripley should apply to Governor Andrew for a place in a Massachusetts regiment. Ripley must have followed this advice, for he was commissioned first lieutenant of the 29th Massachusetts regiment on July 24 following (*Annual Report of the Adjutant-General, of the Commonwealth of Massachusetts* for 1862, pp. 306–307) ; he died almost exactly a year later (*ibid.* for 1863, pp. 782–783) .

duties as an officer; and, as I am assured by a competent witness, with
great success. Ezra Ripley will be loved & honored wherever he goes, for
he is the friend of the friendless, & urges every body's claims but his
own. I learn that he has just now secured a position on the Staff of one
of our State regiments for his own 4th lieutenant.

I do not know but I may be pressing on you matters that lie quite out
of your province. But, if not, I am very sure of my client whose merits
I have only begun to state.

Yours faithfully,
R. W. Emerson

Hon. Charles Sumner.

To James Bradley Thayer, Concord? June 17? 1861

[MS listed without date, and partly quoted, in Goodspeed's Book Shop, Nov.,
1935. Emerson inclosed a letter (of June 17, 1861) on behalf of Ezra Ripley,
which Thayer might forward to Sumner. In it, he said, he had left a blank in
which Thayer could, if he knew it, insert Ripley's age.]

To James Russell Lowell, Concord, June 18, 1861 [55]

Concord —
18 June, 1861.

Dear Lowell,

Fields thinks you have my copy of Tuckerman's Poems. If
so, will you please send them to T. & F. for me? For the poet, in sending
me his book, requested my attention to the " sonnets," which I have not
yet read: and it is time I should reply.[56]

Thanks for the most cheerful article on our politics which I have yet
seen.[57] Its wit, I hope, will smuggle it into Carolina, in spite of gun-
powder. If it must wait awhile, it will yet beguile the prison-hours of
the perverts one of these days.

Yours,
R. W. Emerson

J. R. Lowell, Esq.

To William Emerson, Concord? June c. 23, 1861

[William Emerson, June 25, 1861 (MS owned by Dr. Haven Emerson), says
that he was glad to see his brother's " handwriting again yesterday," and ex-

55. MS owned by HCL; ph. in CUL.

56. Emerson had already acknowledged the book in his letter of Mar. 25, 1861;
probably he wrote again.

57. Lowell's " The Pickens-and-Stealin's Rebellion " (*The Atlantic*, June, 1861)
confidently prophesied victory for the Union.

plains that his wife would have written at once had the college government come to any conclusion (cf. Apr. c. 7, 1861).]

To Herman Grimm, Concord, June 27, 1861

[MS owned by the Goethe- und Schiller-Archiv. Printed in *The Atlantic*, XCI, 475–477 (Apr., 1903); reprinted in *Correspondence between Ralph Waldo Emerson and Herman Grimm*. A rough draft owned by RWEMA (ph. in CUL) is dated June 26. It differs in many details from the 1903 version but contains nothing of importance that is not printed there.]

To Mary Moody Emerson, Concord, June 29, 1861 [58]

Concord June 29,
1861.

My dear Aunt,

Lidian is very uneasy that she has written no reply to one or two poetic messages, which you have directly or indirectly sent her, and I, who never write a letter except of necessity, must eagerly volunteer. If Death the Deliverer should not come to you with actual translation, as, the holy legends say, has sometimes befallen saints, but some bodily remainder should be found to bury, — be assured, that our little nook in Sleepy Hollow, in your native town, will be ready to receive & guard such deposit with all tender & honoring rites, & with what sympathy of stars & elements may be divined; — certainly, with a heed & pride of memory, in all the living who shall lay the dust there,[59] & revisit it. It does not now look probable that the foot of any slave-owner or slave-catcher will pollute that ground. Let us hope that the very South wind will come to us cleaner & purer of that taint, until it is sweet as the air of Maine Mountains. What a relief in the political convulsion, you must feel with us. The shame of living seems taken away, & to mature & old age the love of life will return, as we did not anticipate. Ever your affectionate & deeply obliged nephew,[60]

To Abel Adams, Concord, July 8, 1861 [61]

Concord
8 July, 1861 —

My dear friend,

I have eight shares Boston & Providence R R stock, of which

58. MS owned by RWEMA; ph. in CUL.
59. The promise was kept (cf. May 5, 1863).
60. A narrow strip below, which doubtless contained the signature, has been cut away.
61. MS owned by RWEMA; ph. in CUL.

you are keeping for me the certificates of, I believe, 5 or 6 shares. I wish to borrow some money, on their security, at the Concord Bank; & will give you the trouble to send me that scrip. I think the best way will be to send it to care of Mr Sprague, at the Globe Bank,[62] & I will call there for it.

I have been turning over daily the wonderful proposition [63] which you made to me at your house, and it shines brighter the more it is looked at. I told Edward, and he showed so much surprise & pleasure as if he knew all the importance of the benefit; although I have tried to protect him & his sisters from any feeling of poverty. Lidian & the girls appreciate the nobility of your design.

Edward is to be examined for College on Monday & Tuesday, 12 & 13 July.[64] On Wednesday, he goes, with Tom Ward, Julian Hawthorne, & five or six other boys to Monadnoc, to camp out for a week. Immediately on his return, I mean to bring him to see you, & I think my wife & daughters mean to hold Mrs Adams & Abby to their large invitation of the household. In that case, we will communicate with you first. Yours affectionately,

R. W. Emerson

I shall be in Boston on Thursday.

To EDWARD WALDO EMERSON, CONCORD, JULY 20, 1861

[MS owned by Mr. Raymond Emerson.]

To ABBY LARKIN ADAMS, CONCORD, JULY 22, 1861 [65]

Concord —
Monday, July 22 — 1861

Dear Abby,

Edward entered College, last Tuesday; [66] brought his papers home, that night, at 11.30; & set off with his party, seven boys, next morning for Monadnoc, where they were to camp out for a week. We

62. Charles Sprague was cashier of the Globe Bank (*The Boston Directory*, 1861).

63. Adams, generously repairing the losses which his advice on railroad securities had caused Emerson, paid for Edward's college course (*cf.* Sept. 22, 1867).

64. That is, July 15 and 16. For both college and Monadnock, see July 22, 1861, to Abby Adams.

65. MS owned by RWEMA; ph. in CUL.

66. Edward Waldo Emerson duly appears as a freshman in the Harvard catalogue for the first term of 1861–1862.

are looking for him again on Wednesday.[67] We are all thinking to come & spend a day with you presently; if you are all at home. I will venture to propose Friday next: but if you are to journey seaward or landward in these days, or if you have engagements for that day, please to send me word, & we will come later. With love to your Uncle, & Aunt, & yourself, from all of us,

Yours ever,
R. W. Emerson —

Miss Abby L. Adams —

To Edward Waldo Emerson, Concord? July 22, 1861

[This is a copy in *Letters of R. Waldo Emerson* (a typewritten volume owned by Mr. Edward Waldo Forbes) , p. 261. Apparently the original letter was dated merely as of Monday, July 22, without year.]

To James Russell Lowell? Concord? July 23, 1861

[MS listed, without the name of the person addressed, in *Catalogue of a Large Collection of Autographs . . . Donated to the Great Western Sanitary Fair, to be Sold . . . March 15th, 1864;* Lowell is named as the donor.]

To Abby Larkin Adams, Concord, July 24, 1861 [68]

Concord —
Wednesday

Dear Abby,

Thanks for your exact informations. We will then take the 12 o'c. horse-cars on Friday.[69] Edward came home yesterday, brown as a berry, from his mountain. Ellen & Edith say, they will very gladly stay with you till Monday. Everything shines with us but the Washington news.[70]

Yet, with the best hope,
R. W. Emerson

Miss Abby L. Adams.

67. *Cf.* the letters of July 8 and 24, 1861, for the Monadnock journey and for the proposed visit to the Adamses.

68. MS owned by RWEMA; ph. in CUL. The date is proved by the citations below.

69. For the visit and for Edward's trip to " his mountain," see July 22, 1861, to Abby Adams. The visit is also recorded in July 27, 1861.

70. July 21, 1861, was the day of the first Bull Run.

To William Emerson, Concord, July 27, 1861 [71]

Concord —
July 27, 1861 —

Dear William,

We were all in Boston yesterday, the whole family going, according to a promise of some standing, to visit Mr Adams at Jamaica Plain.[72] On our way back, we, that is, Edward & I, found the mare in her Boston stable,[73] & Edward rode her home, leaving Boston at $6\frac{1}{2}$ & arriving here at $9\frac{1}{2}$ o'c. He said she came very well to West Cambridge but after that seemed lame and towards the end of the journey it was hard for her to trot. This morning I brought Mr Tuttle to look at her, who at once said, she was badly shod on one of her forefeet; and, as Mr Hall the blacksmith is reckoned a very skilful shoer, I had both her fore shoes taken off, & better set, & have put her in the pasture, where her feet can be as wet as she likes. If this does not at once heal her, as Tuttle thinks it will, I am to have her foreshoes taken off for a time. In all other respects, she appears perfectly well, & a good beast. Edward likes her very well, & James, which is a great point, warmly approves her. I intend to take to the saddle, as soon as she is ready for it. May she be used in any other way, — as in the wagon?

We had a very pleasant visit at Mr A.'s, who had a particular wish to see Edward, whom he had not seen since he was a little boy. Mr A. is very much gratified, as well as I, that the Vermont Court has at last affirmed the rights of V^t & Canada R R., & the stock has risen to par. We rejoice that you are coming to us in August to encamp.

Waldo.

To James Elliot Cabot, Concord, August 4, 1861 [74]

Concord
Augt 4, 1861

My dear Cabot,

I was very glad yesterday to hear from you, & on such high

71. MS owned by HCL; ph. in CUL. The final sentence, which is concluded at the top of p. 1, is set off from the heading by irregular lines.

72. *Cf.* July 24, 1861.

73. Several letters from William Emerson in June and July, 1861 (owned by Dr. Haven Emerson), discuss plans for sending the mare Grace to Boston by express and thence to Concord.

74. MS owned by Professor Philip Cabot; ph. in CUL.

matters. The war, — though from such despicable beginnings, has assumed such huge proportions that it threatens to engulf us all — no preoccupation can exclude it, & no hermitage hide us — And yet, gulf as it is, the war with its defeats & uncertainties is immensely better than what we lately called the integrity of the Republic, as amputation is better than cancer. I think we are all agreed in this, and find it out by wondering why we are so pleased, though so beaten & so poor. No matter how low down, if not in false position. If the abundance of heaven only sends us a fair share of light & conscience, we shall redeem America for all its sinful years since the century began. At first sight, it looked only as a war of manners, showing that the southerner who owes to climate & slavery his suave, cool, & picturesque manners, is so impatient of ours, that he must fight us off. And we all admired them until a long experience only varying from bad to worse has shown us, I think finally, what a noxious reptile the green & gold thing was. Who was the French Madame who said of Talleyrand, " How can one help loving him he is so vicious? " But these spit such unmistakeable venom, that I think we are *desillusionnés* once for all. There is such frank confession in all they do, that they can have no secrets hereafter for us. Their detestation of Massachusetts is a chemical description of their substance, & if a state more lawful, honest, & cultivated were known to them, they would transfer to it this detestation. This *spiegato carattere* of our adversary makes our part & duty so easy. Their perversity is still forcing us into better position than we had taken. Their crimes force us into virtues to antagonize them and we are driven into principles by their abnegation of them. Ah if we dared think that our people would be simply good enough to take & hold this advantage to the end! — But there is no end to the views the crisis suggests, & day by day. You see I have only been following my own lead, without prying into your subtle hints of ulterior political effects. But one thing I hope, — that ' scholar ' & ' hermit ' will no longer be exempts, neither by the country's permission nor their own, from the public duty. The functionaries, as you rightly say, have failed. The statesmen are all at fault. The good heart & mind, out of all private corners, should speak & save.

I had a letter lately from Mrs Tappan, who encloses a patriotic plan of Virginia politics, written by her husband,[75] & really important, had

75. Lewis Tappan's pamphlet *The War: its Cause and Remedy* was dated from New York, May 14, 1861, and his *Immediate Emancipation: the Only Wise and Safe Mode* was dated from that city the 28th of the same month. Perhaps Emerson refers to some later publication.

it been earlier offered. I think it anticipated by what New Virginia has done.[76] Thanks for the account of the Scandinavian books,[77] which I shall look for at once. Josiah P. Quincy has just now come to see me. If you have opportunity I hope you will meet him. His instincts are the best. In the " Anti-Slavery Standard," he writes lately papers signed with a star *.[78] With new thanks for your letter,

Yours faithfully,
R. W. Emerson

We must all go to the next Club. Is there not a special agreement?

To Daniel Ross, Concord, August 8, 1861

[MS listed in Anderson Galleries, May 26–27, 1909, where it is described as apparently in reply to a request for Emerson's autograph.]

To Rufus Leighton, Jr.? Concord, August 20, 1861 [79]

Concord 20 August 1861

Dear Sir,

I think I shall not be able to attend the Friday Evening meeting at Allston Hall, to which you kindly invite me. It is always difficult to me to stay in the city overnight. And I do not know that I could add any facts of interest to the recollections of the occasion.

Yet Theodore Parkers mind was so lavishly given to the public welfare, that I can easily see how all the new & startling events in our politics may associate themselves with his memory.[80] In dark days & amidst

76. What is now the State of West Virginia was at this time taking steps to complete its separation from Virginia.

77. Apparently plural, but the ending is uncertain. It is possible that one such book was George Webbe Dasent's translation *The Story of Burnt Njal,* Edinburgh, 1861. This is noted, with some other titles, in the MS memorandum book for 1861 under the date Jan. 4, but it may have been written there much later, as the first pages of the book, not used for other purposes, might have served well for memoranda on books to be looked up; and in fact the space for Jan. 1–4 is entirely filled with jottings about books.

78. Articles signed with two asterisks and the letter " X " appear in the *National Anti-slavery Standard,* June 8 and 29 and July 6, 1861.

79. MS owned by Mr. Oliver R. Barrett; ph. in CUL. In spite of Emerson's spelling, I conjecture that the person addressed may have been the Rufus Leighton now known as one of Theodore Parker's editors. *Cf.* Leighton's verses mentioned in a note on Sept. 29, 1859, and published in *Poems Read at the Opening of the Fraternity Lectures 1858–1859,* 1859. Here Emerson himself had served as an example of great character (p. 54).

80. Parker had died May 10, 1860.

sinking men we miss his strength the more, and yet we cannot doubt his relief & joy in the present pronounced state of the Republic, over the so-called " integrity of the Republic," six months ago.

With kindest greetings to the friends in your meeting,

Yours respectfully,
R. W. Emerson

Mr Laighton

To Franklin Benjamin Sanborn, Concord, September 11, 1861

[MS listed in Anderson Galleries, Oct. 19–20, 1926, where it is described as a letter of appreciation for Sanborn's efforts as teacher of Emerson's children.]

To Moncure Daniel Conway and Ellen Dana Conway, Concord, October 6, 1861

[Printed in Conway, *Emerson at Home and Abroad,* pp. 15–16.]

To Abel Adams, Concord, October 8, 1861 [81]

Concord, 8 October.

My dear friend,

We are all very happy in the belief that you & Mrs Adams & Abby will come here on Saturday.[82] I hope today's rain will rain out, that you may see Concord in its best trim.

Will you have the goodness to bring with you one of my certificates of Atlantic Bank stock; say, the least in amount. The Bank surprised me by passing their dividend. So I went to town yesterday, & told them they must lend me $300., and I would bring them 4 shares as security, say, next Tuesday.

But if there is any kind of good weather, I shall see you on Saturday.

Ever yours,
R. W. Emerson

Mr Adams.

81. MS owned by RWEMA; ph. in CUL. The year is from the endorsement, apparently in Abel Adams's hand, and fits the evidence noted below.

82. The MS memorandum for 1861 has " Abel Adams & family " under Oct. 12.

To Elbridge G. Dudley, Concord, October 11, 1861 [83]

Concord —
11 October, 1861.

My dear Sir,

I must even accept this first day which you offer me, were it only to meet half way the persistent good will which your committee express toward me, and you shall therefore hold me engaged for a discourse on the last Sunday of this month.[84] But we will not at present make any promises beyond. Thanks thanks again for that ever open house of yours, & the welcome you send to my wife also! But she cannot go with me this time, and I mean to use the occasion to go out to a friend at Brookline, whom I have refused until now. But I mean to make a call on Mrs Dudley, & give account of myself. With kindest remembrance to her, & to Miss Rebecca,[85]

Yours faithfully,
R. W. Emerson.

Mr Dudley.

To William Emerson, Concord, November 6, 1861 [86]

Concord
6 Novr 1861

Dear William,

To skip all my penitences, and to hasten to make a new bridge over to you yonder — I report my household in usual good health except Edward, who, you may have heard showed himself so feeble when shut up in a college room & routine, that I have had him at home now for a fortnight & have almost decided to withdraw him altogether for this year & let him enter Freshman again next July. I talked with President Felton, & he acquiesced & will allow him to enter then without new examination. Tis a rude disappointment to all in this house, except Edward, who seems impatient to be fairly out, & fancies he shall be well & strong if he can join the Hudson's Bay Company, or cross the Plains to

83. MS owned by Mr. Abel Cary Thomas; ph. in CUL.
84. The *Boston Evening Transcript*, Oct. 26, 1861, announced that Emerson would address the Twenty-eighth Congregational Society at Music Hall on the following morning.
85. Duncan.
86. MS owned by HCL; ph. in CUL.

California,[87] or, at least, carry a chain on a railroad-survey, or go into a lumberer's gang in Maine His college career seemed the one thing assured, six weeks ago.

I learn that William will not return so soon as you have expected, but that he continues to send good accounts of his health. But if he stays two months, he ought to stay five.[88] Charles we hoped would be here at Thanksgiving nor do I understand why our festival being a week sooner than usual, should make a difference in his good intention. He may be sure he would be heartily welcomed. I read with great regret the altered news you sent me of Aunt Mary's health & state of mind. Our Dr Barrett has since received a letter from her which he was to keep profoundly secret from her family requesting him to procure board for her for the winter, at Mrs Clark's. I hope she is better & wiser, until the snows come & enforce patience. Ellen has lately discov [89] new sheaves of old letters of Aunt M.s which reinforce all ones respect & tenderness for her, of dates from 1811 to 1820, chiefly addressed to Mother.

But you have at present all the load of her charges which may easily be greatly inconvenient in these times. Of course you are charging me punctually with my part in the same, and, if you cannot easily forego payments in this year, you must send me word. I can always *force* myself to pay. But if you can still let the debt accumulate tis better for me. As soon as *V. & Canada* at last began to pay a dividend, the Atlantic Bank (alone among Boston Banks) omitted to pay its dividend in October. My books have no sale this year, and the Winter Lectures will for the most part, omit their dividends. I will not go into the dangerous matter of politics: yet have just read with great sympathy Count Gasparin's excellent book.[90]

What shall I do with the mare, Grace? She is no less lame, nor more, than when you saw her. She is very little used once in two or three days she bears the saddle, & rarely drags the wagon. Wetherbee would give no opinion. All observers say she has naturally bad feet, hoofs not high enough. But I can easily keep her this winter when I have added a little more room to my barn as I shall this week by removing the stairs of the

87. For the trip to California, see letters of Apr. 28 and later, 1862.

88. William Emerson, Jr., had gone, in May, 1861, to Curaçao, where he actually remained " many months " (*cf.* letters of Jan. 19 and May 26, 1862) .

89. Emerson failed to complete the word at the top of the following page.

90. *Les États-Unis en 1861*, Paris, 1861. In the third sentence following, the figures " 4 " and " 5 " have been written over the words " two " and " three " respectively, presumably by Emerson.

loft. I thot W^m would have returned & have seen her before winter.
And if I could not Edmund Hosmer said he would keep her cheaply.
Love to all

Waldo.

To John Murray Forbes, Concord, November 19, 1861 [91]

Concord

19 November, 1861.

My dear Mr Forbes,

I send you kindest thanks for your kind & active interest on
Edward's behalf. He saw Mr Shedd, liked his proposition very well, &
holds himself ready to go at his earliest command, which he is expecting,
perhaps on Friday.[92]

The boy came back from Milton in much better looks & plight than
he went thither, — thanks to Mrs Forbes, & William, & the young ladies.
I fear I must accuse your house of making their own houses distasteful
to a great many young & old ladies & gentlemen. We are all seriously interested in William's decision [93] which it seems he made without waiting for the better days & tidings of the last week. I believe all wise fathers
are coming to feel that they have no right to dissuade their sons from
this career. With affectionate regards to all your house,

Yours,

R. W. Emerson

Mr Forbes.

To William Emerson, Concord, December 6, 1861 [94]

Concord

6 December

Dear William,

I received your letter, & the enclosed account, which I have

91. MS owned by RWEMA; ph. in CUL.

92. For Edward's surveying Mt. Auburn lots with Shedd, see Dec. 6, 1861, to William Emerson.

93. William Hathaway Forbes was mustered in as second lieutenant in the
First Regiment of Cavalry, Massachusetts Volunteers, on Dec. 26, 1861; was made
first lieutenant in the same regiment on July 27, 1862; was transferred to the Second
Regiment of Cavalry, Massachusetts Volunteers, as captain, on Jan. 14, 1863; was
made major on May 12, 1863, and lieutenant-colonel on Oct. 21, 1864; and was
mustered out at the expiration of service on May 15, 1865 (*Record of the Massachusetts Volunteers*, 1868, I, 633–634 and 668–669).

94. MS owned by HCL; ph. in CUL. The year is shown by evidence cited below.

not examined, but will vouch for its correctness. You are to press its payment whenever you please, & I will please. I know not what to say of Aunt Mary, it is a piteous case for herself & for Mrs Parsons.[95] For the present, I hope Mrs P. will be able to hold on with her. If I can present the case in any proper way to the Farnhams, I shall.

Edward, for the last few days, is surveying Mount Auburn lots, with Mr Shedd,[96] & with good effect, apparently, to himself. All the rest of us are as well as usual. Give yourself no uneasiness about the mare Grace. She is very well in my stable, just now, and, if any need be, I can board her cheaply with Hosmer, and I will sell her if I can, consulting you thereon. We are all knitting socks & mittens for soldiers, writing patriotic lectures, & economizing with all our mights. No Christmas boxes, no New Years gift, this year to be offered by any honest party to any! Hereof take you also notice. My old neighbor, George Minott died & was buried this week.[97] Elizabeth Hoar is still at New Haven. I hate to hear that Susan is often an invalid. The news from William looks all favorable. Love to the boys, tho' C. is gone.

Waldo E.

To Moncure Daniel Conway, Concord, December 6, 1861 [98]

Concord
Friday Ev^g. 6 Dec^r

My dear Sir,

I learn by your letter received today, that you will read a lecture here tomorrow or Sunday Eve.^g [99] — I should think it courageous

---

95. William Emerson, Nov. 24, 1861 (MS owned by Dr. Haven Emerson), had told of Mary Moody Emerson's rapid decline and of Hannah Haskins Parsons's difficulty in caring for her.

96. *Cf.* Nov. 19, 1861.

97. Minott's serious illness is mentioned by Thoreau in a journal entry of July 19, 1860 (*The Writings,* XIX, 410).

98. MS owned by Mrs. Mildred Conway Sawyer; ph. in CUL. Dec. 6 fell on Friday in 1861, the year fixed by the evidence cited below.

99. Conway wrote from Cincinnati, Dec. 1 (MS endorsed 1861), that he was on the point of leaving for Boston to seek help in distributing *The Rejected Stone* among thousands of soldiers in the winter camps, and that he wished to raise some money at Concord by delivering there his lecture "The Death and Resurrection of Captain John Brown" on Saturday or Sunday, Dec. 7 or 8. Apparently the date was changed from December to January. It is clear from a letter Ellen Emerson wrote to her father on Jan. 29, 1862, that Conway had then recently lectured in Concord to an audience which filled the hall.

in you, & a full audience not to be warranted. But my wife thinks it worth trying, & has just named it to several persons. I think Sunday the better night, because full notice can be given on Sunday, and if you will come out tomorrow evening, my wife promises to make you comfortable in this house, whilst you stay in town, & to make your audience as large as she can. The same lady charges me to add, that she takes a warm interest in two of your children of which she knows, one that is named for her husband,[100] & the other " The Rejected Stone," [101] which she has carefully examined. But of both we shall have presently occasion to speak with you

With kind regards,

Mr Conway. R. W. Emerson

I shall see you, or if anything prevent, have a line from you tomorrow night, before advertising.

To Charles Eliot Norton, Concord, December 7? 1861? [102]

Concord
Saturday 5 Dec^r

My dear Norton,

    I return too slowly — for I was absent from home two days, — this sorrowful loving letter of Mrs Clough. I had received a note from her already, but mine is only a sketch of the story which she gives you in detail, & so well. It takes away much of the pain of the death [103] to learn how gently it came, & how tenderly watched. And I shall ever think more happily of my friend of a few months. Yet the news was a sad surprise. I had relied on his life, mainly, I believe, because his genius promised a large & long career, and my recollections of him are of a health which seemed vigorous & enduring.

  I have read the memoir in " the Spectator " [104] which is excellent, & inspired by friendship. Is it Matthew Arnold's? I think it should cer-

100. For Emerson Conway, see Oct. 6, 1861.

101. Conway's antislavery book *The Rejected Stone* was published, it seems, in Oct., 1861 (Conway, *Autobiography*, I, 342) .

102. MS owned by HCL; ph. in CUL. The date 1862 has been added, but evidence cited below points pretty clearly to 1861. Dec. 5 did not fall on Saturday in either year, but it is more probable that Emerson was right about the day of the week than that he gave the correct day of the month.

103. Clough had died at Florence, Nov. 13, 1861. *Cf.* the letter of Jan. 14, 1862.

104. Probably Emerson means " Arthur Hugh Clough. — In Memoriam," in *The Spectator* for the week ending Nov. 23, 1861.

tainly be reprinted in the book of " Poems," of which you speak,[105] as it
will give new value & interpretation to them.

I heartily thank you for so kindly sending me this precious letter.

Yours affectionately,
R. W. Emerson

Charles E. Norton, Esq.

To Charles Eliot Norton, Concord? 1861

[MS listed in Goodspeed's Book Shop, Mar.–Apr., 1923, where it is described
as regarding Rowse's head of Clough. *Cf.* Apr. 25, 1862.]

105. Apparently *The Poems of Arthur Hugh Clough,* with memoir by Norton,
which was to appear in 1862. For Emerson's receiving the copy Norton sent him, see
Oct. 30, 1862.

1862

To ——————————, Concord, January 6, 1862 [1]

Concord
6 January 1862

Dear Sir,

I was so careless in leaving your house, last night, as to forget to take my shawl, which, I suppose, was in my chamber. It is a thick grey shawl, & had a shawl-pin stuck in it. It is possible that it was left in the office on my arrival, as I remember you were kind enough to assist me in unpinning it. Will you have the goodness to give it to the driver of the Lowell & Framingham stage addressed to me, in Concord, & I will pay him for his trouble.

I am sorry to give you this inconvenience.

Respectfully,
R. W. Emerson

To Blanche Smith Clough, Concord, January 14, 1862

[MS owned by Mr. Arthur Clough; ph. in CUL. Printed in *Emerson-Clough Letters.*]

To Edward Bangs, Concord, January 19, 1862

[MS listed and partly quoted in Anderson Auction Co., Feb. 9–10, 1911; accepts an invitation " for the night." Bangs, Boston, Dec. 26, n. y., asks Emerson to stay at his house whenever he has occasion to do so.]

To William Emerson, Concord, January 19, 1862 [2]

Concord
19 January, 1862.

Dear William,

I am glad to have such cheerful looking news from William, and he is very kind to consult so thoughtfully for Edward, who is him-

1. MS at Longfellow's Wayside Inn, South Sudbury, Mass., owned by Mr. Henry Ford; a MS copy which I have made from the original is in CUL.
2. MS owned by HCL; ph. in CUL.

self very ready for this pleasant plan [3] But it does not offer any special advantage which he needs, and would cost too much for mere pleasure. Edward is gaining vigor, though not yet flesh. He has finished his task at Mount Auburn,[4] & now is doing a little chopping, every day in the woods. Work, or some journeying that involved a good deal of rude exercise, he seems to require. He has just heard of a proposed land journey to California [5] that interests him. But the times cripple his movements, as those of us all. I believe he is always dreaming of a commission in the cavalry, since William Forbes went away.[6] Our girls are counting the weeks till Charles's arrival here. And Ellen keeps us informed of her progress in negociations for Aunt Susan. I hope to see you, in passing, about the end of this month; for I have promised to be at Washington on the 31 January.[7] Lidian sends her special love to you & Susan, & thinks the only difficulty about " the arrangements " is the choice.

Affectionately,
Waldo E

To William Emerson, Concord, January 21, 1862 [8]

Concord
21 January 1862

Dear William,

You must give me a little longer day than 1 February, but I will instantly bestir myself & see what can be done to begin to pay my debts. [I] The 1 January has found me in quite as poor plight as the rest of the Americans. Not a penny from my books since last June, — which usually yield 5, or $600.00 a year: [I] The Atlantic Bank omitting its dividend: My Mad River & Lake Erie Bonds (Sandusky) which ought to pay $140. *per ann.* now for several years making no sign. Lidian's Plymouth House now for 3 years has paid nothing & still refuses. Her Court Street rents, which have grown important, are now withdrawn for the last year & a half & will not come to us again for a year & a half more, as they are paying a mortgage. [II] Then lastly, almost all income from lec-

3. William Emerson, Jan. 10, 1862 (MS owned by Dr. Haven Emerson) , reported his son's suggestion that Edward come out to Curaçao in the " Venus," the same bark in which William, Jr., himself had sailed thither " last May."

4. *Cf.* Dec. 6, 1861, to William Emerson.

5. Later letters of 1862 allude to the journey to California which Edward Emerson actually made.

6. *Cf.* Nov. 19, 1861.

7. See Feb. 5, 1862, to Ellen Emerson.

8. MS owned by HCL; ph. in CUL. Excerpts I–V are in Cabot, II, 612–613.

tures has quite ceased: so that your letter found me in a study how to pay 3, or 400.00 with $50.[II] My purpose now is to go to the Atlantic Bank & see if they will lend me what I want on the security of their own stock. For their shares are so reduced in the market, at present, that it would be unwise to sell them. This is my present dependence. For I have no stock which I should like to sell at present prices. [III]I have been trying to sell a woodlot[III] (the Saw-mill lot) [IV]at or near its appraisal, which would give me something more than $300. but the purchaser does not appear.[IV] Vt. & Canada pays its dividend, but not yet any back rent, so it sells for 100.,[9] tho' Abel Adams thinks it worth 150.

My fortunes must repair themselves by a new book, whenever books again sell; &, if things come right again, by the return to payment of the unpaying properties. [V]Meantime, we are all trying to be as unconsuming as candles under an extinguisher, and tis frightful to think how many rivals we have in distress & in economy. But far better that this grinding should go on bad & worse, than that we be driven by any impatience into a hasty peace, or any peace restoring the old rottenness.[V] I grieve that you have your largest load to bear at this worst time, & will try that you shall not also carry mine. But you had formerly spoken as if you were willing that mine should accumulate unpaid, as " an investment," you once said, " for your boys." So that, as I thought I saw an easier future for me ahead, I let the debt grow. At any rate, I will presently write again after I have made my visit to town, & tell you what I find.

I forgot to thank you for sending me an Island paper which contains nothing, however, of mine (about " Clubs ") ,[10] though it runs a little in the same historical direction. We are all as well as usual, & send joyful love to Susan & Haven.

Affectionately
Waldo E

To Ellen? Emerson, New York? January c. 27? 1862

[Ellen Emerson, Jan. 29, 1862: " Your letter has come with the 66.14." But the amount is not clearly legible.]

9. The *Boston Daily Advertiser*, Jan. 9, 1862, had reported the sale of ten shares of this road, which had long proved a serious disappointment to Emerson, at exactly 100.

10. William Emerson, Jan. 10, 1862 (MS owned by Dr. Haven Emerson) , said he was sending by mail a copy of the Richmond County paper containing something on clubs which he thought might possibly be a borrowing from his brother's lecture.

To Ellen Emerson, New York, February 5, 1862 [11]

St Denis Hotel
N. Y. 5 Feb. '62

Dear Ellen,

I have just received your second letter. I arrived from Washington [12] last night so late as to come here instead of 254 Fourth Avenue, as I wished. This morn⁸ find myself expected to lecture in Brooklyn on Friday [13] & decide to remain, writing instantly to Mr Dudley to settle with him the doubt whether I am to go to Music Hall next Sunday or the following. If it is next Sunday I shall go to Boston, on Saturday, & not home till Monday. And I think we will not meddle with a visit of the arts, in the city, until after my return home.

Thanks for all the good stories you tell me now & before. I enclose $10. I have a long story which deserves as faithful a chronicler as yourself. & ought to have had such a private secretary at Washington. I saw the President twice in his house; & everybody *but* Fremont He was not at home though Mrs F. kept us half an hour with assurances that he would be. I talked with Zagyoni [14] there. Love to each & all. Papa.

To Elbridge G. Dudley, New York, February 5, 1862 [15]

8 Wall Street
New York
5 February 1862

My dear Sir,

I am here on my return from Washington, & being much pressed to stay & read a lecture on Friday Evening,[16] I have consented,

11. MS owned by RWEMA; ph. in CUL.

12. The *Evening Star*, Jan. 31 and Feb. 1, 1862, records Emerson's lecture on " Nationality " before the Washington Lecture Association at the Smithsonian Institution on the 31st. The reporter gave a favorable account of the lecture but was somewhat unfriendly in his description of the lecturer — " very much a Yankee seer." Cabot, II, 786, gives the subject as " American Civilization." The story of Emerson's meetings with Lincoln and others at Washington during this very interesting visit is told in *Journals*, IX, 372–396.

13. *The Evening Post*, New York, Feb. 7, 1862, announced " American Civilization " at New Chapel, Brooklyn, that evening. *The Brooklyn City Directory* for 1862–1863 shows that New Chapel was the Unitarian church of which Samuel Longfellow, the poet's brother, was pastor. But *cf.* also Feb. 17, 1862.

14. According to Herbert Bashford and Harr Wagner, *A Man Unafraid*, n. d. (c. 1927), p. 385, the Hungarian Major Charles Zagonyi (for so the name is here spelled) commanded Frémont's bodyguard.

15. MS owned by Mr. Abel Cary Thomas; ph. in CUL.

16. *Cf.* the letter of Feb. 5 to Ellen Emerson.

but have suddenly been made uneasy by a doubt whether possibly I did not promise you to be at the Music Hall on the second Sunday of February. I hope not. But it is possible that it was so, & that you are relying on me. Please to make this clear to me at once by letter or Telegraph, *Yes* or *No*, to *William Emerson, Esq, No 8 Wall Street*, and I will come or not come, as you say. I hope it is a later day that you gave or can give me, as next, or some future Sunday. But rather than that you should have to suddenly provide an uncertain substitute, will come as I am, if it were so promised.[17]

Ever yours faithfully,
R. W. Emerson

I wish to give Mrs Dudley some of my Southern experiences.

To WILLIAM EMERSON, CONCORD, FEBRUARY 13, 1862 [18]

Concord
13 Feby 1862

Dear William,

I duly received, & ought instantly to have acknowledged, your note, containing the draft on the Metropolitan Bank for one hundred dollars.

But I found such a bundle of letters as well as of petty affairs at home to consider, that I waited, until, this morning, your new note & Mr Mills's make it proper to say that I have received no letter from Brooklyn.[19] Perhaps it has gone to Concord N. H.; which often happens to new correspondents: in that case, it will come surely back in another day. If it arrives tonight, I will send you word by tonight's mail to Boston.

Thanks, meantime, for your unceasing attention. I had a very pleasant journey home, finding Governor Andrew & Mrs A. & Gov. Boutwell, in my car. And the next day, (through much nocturnal diligence at the American House after my arrival) had a prosperous enough deliverance at the Music Hall.[20] I found at home that Ellen was away for a week in Cambridge & Boston, but for the rest all were in usual condi-

17. The *Boston Evening Transcript*, Feb. 8, 1862, announced that Emerson would appear at the Music Hall on Sunday, Feb. 9.

18. MS owned by HCL; ph. in CUL.

19. For the Brooklyn lecture, *cf.* Feb. 5, 1862, to Ellen Emerson and Feb. 17, 1862. The latter letter seems to indicate that Mills was the Swedenborgian James Mills.

20. See Feb. 5, 1862, to Dudley.

tion. Aunt Elizabeth spent yesterday with us. Charles Simmons is here at Mary Simmons's home from the army, where he was quartermaster (in 14ᵗʰ Massᵗᵗˢ) & in now broken health, is to go to Cuba, next Wednesday.[21] Love to Susan & Haven. Waldo E

To WILLIAM HENRY FURNESS, CONCORD, FEBRUARY 13, 1862

[MS owned by Mr. Horace Howard Furness Jayne; printed in *Records of a Lifelong Friendship*, pp. 135–136.]

To REBECCA DUNCAN, CONCORD? FEBRUARY 14, 1862

[MS listed and partly quoted in Goodspeed's Book Shop, Jan.–Mar., 1922, where it is dated only as to year. Printed incompletely in the *Boston Evening Transcript*, July 12, 1897, p. 6, where the author of the article " Theodore Parker's Bettine " has combined under one date a fragment of this letter of Feb. 14, 1862, and parts of a letter of May 15 of the same year, *q.v.* Neither the sales catalogue nor the newspaper article gives the name of this correspondent, which is, however, clear from evidence cited in a note on Jan. 19, 1849.]

To WILLIAM EMERSON, CONCORD, FEBRUARY 14, 1862 [22]

14 Feb

Dear William,

I doubt not that Mr Mills's commands will be fulfilled in good time, but, as you say the letter should have come, I think it proper to say, it has not arrived by this evening's mail.

We are all well who are at home, Ellen still in Boston. Waldo E

Friday, 5 P. M.

To CHARLES ELIOT NORTON, CONCORD, FEBRUARY 14, 1862

[MS owned by Mr. Arthur Clough; printed in *Emerson-Clough Letters.*]

21. Simmons was discharged from the 14th Regiment on Jan. 24, 1862, and he sailed for the West Indies on Feb. 25 following in a ship never heard from again (*Annual Report of the Adjutant-General of . . . Massachusetts* for 1862, pp. 156–157; and *Worthy Women*, p. 211) . For Simmons, *cf.* also a note on Sept. 5, 1855, to William Emerson.

22. MS owned by the Rev. George L. Paine; ph. in CUL. For the year *cf.* Feb. 13, 1862, to William Emerson, where Mills and the expected letter, as well as Ellen's visit to Cambridge and Boston, are mentioned. Feb. 14 fell on Friday in this year.

To William Emerson, Concord, February 17, 1862 [23]

Concord
17 Feb. Monday

Dear William,

I received on Saturday night W. P. Beale's draft for $50 for the Brooklyn Society.[24] So we will absolve Mr Mills, & again thank you. Ellen returns home tomorrow, so we hope then to be in perfect relations again with New York, besides that we are to receive Charles on Saturday.

Waldo E

To Cyrus Augustus Bartol, Concord, February 25, c. 1862?

[MS listed and partly quoted in American Art Association, Mar. 13–14, 1928, where no year is given; Emerson speaks of his lectures and of " an article for the Atlantic," and alludes to the slowness of the brain, become less impressionable with use and age. The year is highly conjectural, but could not be earlier than 1857, when *The Atlantic* was founded, nor, probably, later than the early 1870's, when Emerson practically ceased to lecture. He published little prose in *The Atlantic* after 1862, which was one of his most active years as contributor.]

To ——————— Parker, Concord, March 5, 1862 [25]

Concord
5 March 1862

I am very much gratified to hear once more from a valued correspondent, and who still puts me in debt by taking all my attempts in such good part. I have thought many times how I was to seek to recover the broken thread of last Spring, and make the best use of the clew. I shall

23. MS owned by Mr. Edward Waldo Forbes; ph. in CUL. The references to Mills, to Brooklyn, and to Ellen's absence from home fix the year as 1862, when Feb. 17 fell on Monday.

24. *Cf.* especially the letters of Feb. 5, 1862, to Ellen Emerson and Feb. 13, 1862, to William Emerson. The references to the " Brooklyn Society " and to Mills seem to show that Emerson had lectured in Brooklyn for the Brooklyn Society of the New Jerusalem, whose home was the Athenaeum, Atlantic and Clinton Sts., and whose leader was James Mills (*The Brooklyn City Directory for the Year Ending May 1st, 1862;* and Henry R. Stiles, 1870, III, 817) . I am uncertain whether the lecture for the " Society " was actually that given on Feb. 7 at New Chapel (Unitarian) , Clinton and Congress Sts.

25. MS owned by CUL; ph. in CUL. It seems possible that the letter was addressed to Lydia Cabot Parker, widow of Theodore Parker, but I have no proof. The Mrs. Bell whose genius had already won favor may well be the person of that name mentioned in Dec. 26, 1863, to Barlow. Mrs. Whitney was perhaps Adeline Train Whitney, of Milton, Mass., a writer of verse and fiction.

not fail to go to Mrs Mears tomorrow, since you tell me that you & your friends will be there, though I had not decided to go. If your Mrs Bell is my Mrs Bell, I have already a good faith in her genius. Mrs Whitney I have not seen, though I know her verses. You have given me too easy absolution, after piquing my curiosity & fear as to the " sealed pages," a year ago, in my book. I dared hope for new experience, new conviction, and that I was to be brought out of some capital error. So you still owe me a refutation. With grateful regard,

R. W. Emerson

Mrs Parker.

To William Emerson, Concord, March 22, 1862 [26]

Concord
22 March 1862

Dear William,

Your letter was duly communicated to Ellen & to Lidian the two high parties most interested as contractors in this Department. But all are interested. But I am sorry to say that Mrs Bigelow is somewhat disappointed. I was on a visit to Mr Thoreau when his mother told me that Mrs Brooks was quite unhappy that Mrs B. should disappointed of her boarders after she had made prospective arrangements for them & had been at expense for carpet or carpets, &c I denied the whole statement said that Ellen had in all the course of the affair said that Mrs Bigelow did not care to have boarders whilst Mrs Goodenow & Mrs Mann did, &c But when I told Ellen about it she said Yes Mrs Bigelow had expressed great regret to her, but made her promise not to repeat it. I told Ellen she was a goosey, & should have refused such a gag, & gone directly to you, or written. The snow has shut up Lidian in the house, & Ellen & Edith are in Cambridge. But you must authorize Lidian or Ellen to treat with Mrs B. on the matter, if (as L. thinks) Ellen had engaged you to her. I think if snow permit L. will go today & see Mrs B. & learn her story.

Affectionately
Waldo E

26. MS owned by HCL; ph. in CUL. William Emerson wrote, Mar. 30, 1862 (MS owned by Dr. Haven Emerson), acknowledging the present letter and explaining the negotiations he had carried on in Concord for lodging for his wife. Apparently, however, these negotiations came to nothing, for she lived, at least during some weeks of her Concord visit of the following summer, in her brother-in-law's home (see July 8, 1862, to William Emerson).

To CHARLES ELIOT NORTON, CONCORD, MARCH 28, 1862? [27]

                                        Concord
                                        28 March

My dear Norton,

    I send you hearty greetings on the happiness which your note an-
nounces.

    I can well believe the exalted report which has come to my ears of
your friend, though I have not yet the privilege to know her. But on
reading your note I have already built up for you a reality beyond romance, of happy days, which I shall not release either of you from making good. It is so seldom that the conditions for happiness meet! —
When they do, you have entered into bonds to the human race to find a
pure felicity.

                                        Ever yours,
                                        R. W. Emerson.

Charles E. Norton.

To JAMES THOMAS FIELDS, CONCORD? APRIL? *c.* 1? 1862

[MS owned by the Henry E. Huntington Library; ph. in CUL. Printed in
Harper's, LXVIII, 462 (Feb., 1884), and in Annie Fields, *Authors and Friends*,
p. 85. Both printings omit the salutation, " My dear Sir," and the complimentary close and signature, " Yours ever " and " R. W. E." The original, like the
printed texts, is without date. But as the letter relates to corrections in the
proof of " The Titmouse," which appeared in *The Atlantic* for May, 1862, I
conjecture that the date was about the beginning of April in that year.]

To CHARLES ELIOT NORTON, CONCORD, APRIL 25, 1862 [28]

                                        Concord
                                        25 April, 1862.

My dear Norton,

            I was in town yesterday, & found at Ticknor's the photo-
graph, if photograph it be, which your kindness has secured for me.
It is full of character, this thoughtful refined & virtuous face; but how

    27. MS owned by HCL; ph. in CUL. The year is probably 1862, as Norton married
Susan Ridley Sedgwick in May of that year after " a brief engagement " (see the
note on May 20, 1862).
    28. MS owned by HCL; ph. in CUL. The photograph was apparently of Clough,
whose recent death is mentioned in earlier letters.

strangely combined with this British neck & hindhead. In the living face was no suggestion of all this terrene force which secretly ministered to his talent & was subordinated & kept entirely out of sight by his commanding genius. And the expression of the whole head might belong to a saint. With new thanks to you for this new goodness,

Ever yours,
R. W. Emerson

Charles E. Norton.

To Abel Adams, Concord, April 28, 1862 [29]

Concord
Monday, 28 April —

My dear friend,

Edward did not begin his journey [30] on Friday, having received a letter from his correspondent at Minneapolis, Dr Anderson,[31] informing him that he had decided to go overland, & not by river, to Omaha, & should not arrive there before the 20th May; that Edward therefore need not leave home sooner than the 12th May, in order to meet him at Omaha. Edward, of course, does not like the delay, but means to avail himself of this leisure to ride over to Brookline & pay you a visit, — perhaps on Wednesday or Thursday — if James Burke will let him have the horse. Edward does not know how rarely a good boy finds such powerful friends as he has found in you; [32] yet he prizes his happiness at a very high rate, & your goodness is enriched to him by all the precious advantages with which his imagination has clothed this western romance of his.

I have seen Governor Cumming [33] again, whose opinion of the gen-

29. MS owned by RWEMA; ph. in CUL. Apr. 28 fell on Monday in 1862, which is obviously the correct year.

30. Later letters of this year show the progress of the journey across the plains to California. According to an unpublished passage in Emerson's diary for 1862–1863, Edward left Concord May 12 and arrived at Omaha May 19, at Ft. Kearney in June, at Ft. Laramie July 10, at Salt Lake City Aug. 9, at Sacramento Aug. 31, at San Francisco Sept. 5, at Panama Sept. 25, at New York Oct. 3, and at Concord Oct. 6 (typescript *Journals*).

31. Probably Dr. C. L. Anderson, whose name appears in a list of the physicians of Minneapolis in 1858 (*A Half Century of Minneapolis*, ed. Horace B. Hudson, 1908, p. 181).

32. *Cf.* July 8, 1861.

33. Alfred Cumming had served as superintendent of Indian affairs on the upper Missouri and (1857–1861) as governor of Utah Territory.

eral safety of the emigration route is not altered by the telegraph ru-
mours of the Indians. Edward Hoar (the Californian) [34] assures E. that
he will lose his dyspepsia, once for all, in his first day's ride.

Ever your affectionate
R. W. Emerson

Mr Adams.

To Harrison Gray Otis Blake, Concord, May 6, 1862

[MS listed and partly quoted in C. F. Libbie & Co., Jan. 27–28, 1914, where the
year is given as 1860; states that Henry Thoreau died " this morning " and announces the funeral for Friday. This may be the same letter which is quoted,
without date and without the name of the person addressed, in American Art
Association, Nov. 24–25, 1924. *Cf.* May 8 following.]

To James Thomas Fields, Concord, May 8, 1862 [35]

Concord
8 May, Thursday

My dear Sir,

[I]Come tomorrow & bring[I] Mrs Fields [II]to my house. We will give
you a very early dinner. Mr Channing is to write a hymn or dirge for
the funeral, which is to be from the church, at 3 o'clock. I am to make
an address, & probably Mr Alcott may say something.[II]

Yours,
R. W. Emerson

Mr Fields.

34. *Cf.* June 22, 1858?
35. MS owned by the Henry E. Huntington Library; ph. in CUL. Excerpts I–II
were printed in *Harper's*, LXVIII, 458 (Feb., 1884) , and in Annie Fields, *Authors and
Friends*, p. 70. The year is clear from the contents of the letter. Thoreau died at
Concord on May 6, 1862, and the funeral occurred there on May 9. " A brief ode,
written for the purpose by William Ellery Channing, was plaintively sung. Mr. Emerson read an address of considerable length . . .

" Mr. Alcot read some very appropriate passages from the writings of the deceased,
and the service closed with a prayer by the Rev. Mr. Reynolds. . . ." (*Boston Evening
Transcript*, May 10, 1862.)

Emerson's address, " with some additions," is now easily available in *Cent. Ed.*, X.
His obituary of Thoreau was printed in the *Boston Daily Advertiser*, May 8, 1862,
over the signature " E." and has been reprinted in Cooke, *A Bibliography*, pp. 120–
122. The " brief ode " by Channing was doubtless the poem " To Henry " printed in
Thoreau the Poet-naturalist (Sanborn's revised ed., p. 347) . A sonnet on Thoreau's
death, published in *The Monitor*, Concord, May 10, 1862, and reprinted, with corrections, on May 24 following, was, according to a note written on a copy of the
latter date now in the Concord Free Public Library, the work of Sanborn.

To Rebecca Duncan, Concord, May 15, 1862 [36]

Concord
15 May, 1862 —

My dear Miss Rebecca,

I am very slow to reply to your note, yet [I] the list you send me of the characters of " Charles Auchester " [37] looks probable in some points & may be true.[I] I am sorry I cannot give you for this goodness even the poor thanks of repeating the name which I once gave you; but my lips were not long since stringently sealed for days & weeks to come. [II] But I hope yet to give satisfactory account to you of this & other matters. Meantime, I remain with great regard, yours,

R. W. Emerson [II]

Miss Duncan.

To William Cabot Russel, Concord, May 15, 1862 [38]

Concord —
15 May, 1862 —

My dear Sir,

I share your satisfaction in the departure of the boys under such good auspices, mutually pleased with each other, & both anticipating happiness, instruction, & healthful training from the journey. Just before Edward set forward, I introduced him to a Mr Tappan of Denver, in Kansas,[39] a worthy young merchant of that place, who will accompany the boys so far, & thinks he can be useful to them in many ways. But he was not to leave Boston until 24 hours after Edward. So it was agreed between them that your son & Edward should wait the spare day at Niagara, & Mr T. gave Edward exact instructions to secure their rejoining each other on the train there. I was much relieved by learning from Mr Jackson,[40] at the Worcester Depot on Monday, that your son

36. MS owned by Mr. W. T. H. Howe; ph. in CUL. Excerpts I–II are erroneously printed as part of a letter dated Feb. 14, in the *Boston Evening Transcript*, July 12, 1897; see the note on Feb. 14, 1862, to the same correspondent.

37. See a note on Mar. 31, 1855.

38. MS owned by Mr. Oliver R. Barrett; ph. in CUL. William C. Russel is listed as a lawyer in *Trow's New York City Directory . . . Ending May 1, 1863*.

39. That is, in Colorado Territory, which, for a few years prior to Feb., 1861, had been included in Kansas Territory. George Tappan, of Denver, is named in an unpublished entry of a diary for 1862–1863 (typescript *Journals*).

40. A letter of June 3, 1862, shows that Cabot Russel was a grandson of Patrick Jackson, who died in 1847. I am uncertain what Jackson is meant here.

had not bought his railroad tickets, & would not until he reached Albany. Edward bought his under Mr Tappan's direction, & feared that Cabot might not keep the same route. I doubt not the boys will be very good friends on the way. I am sorry that Cabot will not go to San Francisco; for a capital object with Edward is to see the Mammoth Groves, one of which is at one day's or two days' distance from the city; the Yo Semite; & other points in California. Still, the day of return is important to both, & I do not wish Edward to risk an absence from Cambridge on the 1 October.

With great regard,

W. C. Russel. Esq.   R. W. Emerson

To EDWARD WALDO EMERSON, CONCORD, MAY 18, 1862

[MS owned by Mr. Raymond Emerson.]

To CHARLES ELIOT NORTON, CONCORD, MAY 20, 1862 [41]

Concord
20 May, Tuesday

My dear Norton,

With my respectful acknowledgments to your Mother, & my congratulations to her son, I shall be happy to obey her invitation & yours, on Wednesday Evening. The season and the better auspices that newly shine on the country, seem to second your Genius, & ring the bells.

Yours faithfully,
R. W. Emerson

Charles E. Norton, Esq.

To ——————, CONCORD, MAY? c. 20? 1862

[MS listed and partly quoted in Goodspeed's Book Shop, Nov., 1906, where it is dated only as to year; Emerson thanks the committee on the Unitarian Festival for the invitation sent by his correspondent. The Festival of this year was to be held in Boston on May 27 (*Boston Daily Advertiser*, May 12 and 26, 1862).]

41. MS owned by HCL; ph. in CUL. May 20 fell on Tuesday in 1862, and Norton married Susan Ridley Sedgwick on May 21 of that year (*Boston Daily Advertiser*, May 27, 1862; and *Letters of Charles Eliot Norton*, I, 224).

To Edward Waldo Emerson, Concord? May 22? 1862 [42]

Dear Edward, Use your best discretion at each stage of the journey, and, if you find that you have not strength enough for it, stop resolutely short, & find your way home again. But I hope you have not this to consider, but are a good little giant by this time. We wrote to you at Omaha, & at Ft. Kearney once before.[43] Papa.

To Charles Sumner, Concord, May 26, 1862 [44]

Concord —
26 May, 1862.

Dear Sumner,

My nephew, William Emerson, Jr. Esq, of New York, who has been spending many months in Curaçoa,[45] thinks it may interest you, if you have not seen it, to read the new law for the Emancipation of Slaves, which the Dutch Government has ordained for that Island, — & proposes to send you his translation of the Act.

Ever faithfully yours,
R. W. Emerson

Hon. Charles Sumner.

P. S:

Let me thankfully note the safe arrival of many valued Public Documents at my door. I believe my set of the " Pacific Railroad Exploration " is complete to the XII volume; [46] and the rich " Colorado Survey " [47] has come since. Thanks for the copies of your Speeches, — and for the Speeches themselves!

42. MS owned by Mr. Elliot Forbes; ph. in CUL. This is added as a postscript to a letter from Ellen Emerson to her brother dated Concord, May 22, 1862, and was probably written on that day.

43. One was doubtless the letter of May 18, 1862. It is not clear whether the other was from Emerson himself, but probably it was not.

44. MS owned by RWEMA; ph. in CUL.

45. For William Emerson, Jr., at Curaçao, or Curaçoa, *cf.* a letter of Jan. 19, 1862.

46. *Cf.* Feb. 27, 1861.

47. In Emerson's library at the Antiquarian House there is still a copy of *Report upon the Colorado River of the West, Explored in 1857 and 1858 by Lieutenant Joseph C. Ives,* 1861.

To Edward Waldo Emerson, Concord? May 26? 1862 [48]

Dear Edward, I have received from Mr Rob! Watson [49] for you a letter
of introduction to Mr Frederic Billings, of San Francisco, the best man,
he says, in California; [50] and for greater safety, I send it to Fort Laramie,
to the care of Col. Alexander.[51] Mr F.[52] is a lawyer, I believe, & lately a
partner of Gen. Halleck. We have not heard a word from you since
Niagara. Do not fail to find this letter at Fort L.

Papa.

To William G. Bryan, Concord, May 30, 1862 [53]

Concord
30 May 1862

[W].[54] G. Bryan, Esq.

My dear Sir,

      I am concerned to hear that your health is in any degree im-
paired but the remedy you propose to apply is to many & will be to you

48. MS owned by RWEMA; ph. in CUL. The year is clearly 1862. Emerson added
this note at the end of a letter from Ellen to her brother dated Monday, May 26, and
probably he wrote on that day.

49. Robert S. Watson is listed in *The Boston Directory*, 1862, as a treasurer at the
City Exchange. He was, I am informed, a brother-in-law of John Murray Forbes,
having married the twin sister of Sarah Swain Forbes; and he had spent some time
in California.

50. Frederick Billings had established himself as a lawyer in California in 1849,
and his firm came to be known as the best in San Francisco. Henry Wager Halleck,
his partner, had been an officer in the Mexican War.

51. Edmund Brooke Alexander was stationed at Ft. Laramie 1860–1862.

52. That is, F. B., no doubt — Frederick Billings.

53. MS owned by the Library of Congress; ph. in CUL. For Bryan, of Batavia,
N. Y., *cf.* Jan. 24, 1860. English born, he came to this country in early boyhood and
eventually won some repute as lawyer, orator, and scholar, but was known especially
for his defense of the rights of the Tonawanda Indians against a land company (see
the sketch of his life in George J. Bryan, *Biographies*, 1886, pp. 161–184). The *New
York Commercial Advertiser*, June 28, 1862, lists W. G. Bryan among the passengers
in the " Etna," bound for Liverpool.

54. The upper half of the left-hand margin of page 1 has been cut away, no doubt
because it contained the signature, so that Bryan's first initial and some other portions of the text, which I have supplied conjecturally as far as possible, in square
brackets, are badly mutilated or entirely missing. A fragment containing the words
" At all events, Yours," followed by Emerson's signature, has been pasted on page 2.
Apparently this curiously misplaced fragment was clipped from some other letter.

so delightful that I cannot [bring] myself to feel [any] deep anxiety for yo[ur] case.

But I am sorry to say, that, through my own fault purely, I have let fall all my English correspondence, which never was large, and now is ended, so that I have it not in my power to give letters of introduction, except in cases where a matter of business or of personal relation makes it imperative. This state of things is not owing solely to my indolence, but partly to the fact that my friends abroad very seldom sent friends to me, so that I could not well request kind offices of them. But I am persuaded you will find no difficulty in making useful & pleasant acquaintances in every part of England, — which is all alive to American politics, & which always values information & urbanity. With the best wishes for happy voyage & entire re[covery]

To Abel Adams, Concord, June 3, 1862 [55]

Concord —
3 June, Tuesday

My dear friend,

Ellen & Edith think you must be just as much interested in Edward's letter from the Platte River, as they are; & that if it is too small to be legible, why Cousin Abby can read it to you, which only recommends the sending to these absurd sisters; so I enclose the scrawl at all risks. His companion is Cabot Russell, son of Wm C. Russell of N. Y. (and a grandson of Patrick Jackson) who entered college in the same class with Edward, but is to enter Columbia College, N. Y. in September.[56] I hope to come in & see you some June day. With love to Mrs Adams and Abby, Ever yours,

Abel Adams.   R. W. Emerson

To Edward Waldo Emerson, Concord? June 3, 1862

[MS owned by Mr. Raymond Emerson.]

55. MS owned by RWEMA; ph. in CUL. The references to Edward's journey to the West fix the year.

56. Cabot Jackson Russel (as the name seems to have been properly spelled) entered Harvard in 1861, according to the catalogue of 1861–1862, but was not, so far as I can determine, a student at either Harvard or Columbia the following year. At all events he was soon sucked into the maelstrom of the war. On Mar. 23, 1863, he was commissioned first lieutenant; on May 11 of the same year he was promoted to be captain; on July 18 following, when he was still a boy of eighteen, he was killed in action. For William C. Russel, see May 15, 1862, to him.

To Edward Everett, Concord, June 11, 1862 [57]

Concord
11 June, 1862

Hon. Edward Everett.

Dear Sir,

I called at your house, a few weeks since, in company with Col. Henry Lee & Stephen M. Weld,[58] Esq., but learned that you were out of town. We were a committee representing certain non-resident tax-payers who wish to enjoy the benefit of the City Library. Will you have the goodness to appoint a day & hour, when you can, with convenience, give us a short conference on this matter, & receive our petition to the Trustees? [59] Any hour between 10 A. M. & 3 P. M. will, I believe, suit the convenience of the committee.

With great respect,
Your obedient servant,
R. W. Emerson

To Edward Waldo Emerson, Concord, June 12, 1862 [60]

Concord 12 June

My dear son,

I think all your letters have duly reached us excepting "one closed at Quincy," & all heartily welcomed by loving readers in this house, & around it. I write now only to say that I have told one or two boys to write you "to the care of Hon. W. H. Hooper." [61] Today I read in the Journal that he is at Washington. You must not the less inquire at his office or house for letters. Every thing in the journey interests us. If you can press your plants, you will find a name for each later. You ought to have carried an arrowhead in your pocket, to hold it up

57. MS owned by the Massachusetts Historical Society; ph. in CUL.

58. Doubtless the Stephen Minot Weld, of Jamaica Plain, whose son and namesake became a noted Boston manufacturer.

59. Everett, Washington, D. C., June 25, 1862, said he had just completed an extensive tour and so had only then received the present letter but would still appoint a day to meet Emerson's committee if the matter had not already been settled. He hoped to be home by July 5 and asked Emerson to write again. Cf. July 8, 1862, to Everett.

60. MS owned by Mr. Raymond Emerson; ph. in CUL. The year is proved by the references to Edward's Western travel and by further evidence cited below.

61. Among other notes relating to Edward's Western journey written at the end of the MS memorandum book for 1861 is this: "Hon W H Hooper, Utah." Hooper was a delegate to Congress from the Territory of Utah (Lanman, *Biographical Annals*, 1876).

to every Indian you meet, & have Mr Thoreau answered.[62] I saw yesterday a loon in Walden, but silent. In Mr Thoreau's MS. Journal, now
on my table, I read that he has heard its laughter on the pond in 1852.[63]
Hearken for them in Nebraska lakes. I dare not begin to tell you any of
our news, knowing that Ellen & Edith leave no thing untold. Mr Carlyle
has just sent me his 3d volume of " Frederic the Great," [64] and Mr
Matthew Arnold, his " Last Words on the Translation of Homer," [65]
the first the wittiest, & the last the most amiable of books. Our town is
still searched for troops. Captain Bowers has a commission & Mr Shep-
herd is his lieutenant [66] & Galen Hoar is one of his men. I have just
shaken hands with Cyrus Hosmer who has grown fat in prison.[67] His
comrades are not expected in town till tomorrow. Pray do not fall on
your head again. We hear gladly everything you write of your friend.[68]

R. W. Emerson

To William Emerson, Concord, July 8, 1862 [69]

Concord
8 July, 1862

Dear William,

    I have received through Susan your draft on Metropolitan
Bank, dated, (I believe), June 5, for thirty dollars, and now another
dated July for twenty four dollars, making together $54. which of course
pays nine weeks of board.[70] But as Susan was absent an entire week or
more, this amount settles the account until 10 July; without taking into

62. In the last days of his life, says Emerson in his biographical sketch, Thoreau
charged " a youth setting out for the Rocky Mountains " to find an Indian who could
tell the secret of the making of stone arrow-heads (*Cent. Ed.*, X, 473). The youth, as
the present letter shows, was Emerson's son.

63. *The Writings*, X, 379–381. Emerson was just now considering the possibility
of publishing the diaries Thoreau had left in MS (*cf. Journals*, IX, 430 ff.).

64. Tardily acknowledged in Dec. 8, 1862.

65. *On Translating Homer Last Words*, 1862. *Cf.* the note on Apr. *c.* 8? 1864.

66. According to the *Annual Report of the Adjutant-General . . . Massachusetts
. . . for the Year Ending December 31, 1862*, 1863, p. 326, Charles Bowers was actually
commissioned a captain and Edward O. Shepard a first lieutenant in the Thirty-
second Regiment of Massachusetts on June 16, 1862, some days after the date of the
present letter.

67. Cyrus Hosmer was listed in *The Massachusetts Register, 1862* as a sergeant in
Company " G " (Concord artillery) of the Fifth Regiment but as a prisoner at New
Orleans.

68. Probably young Russel, mentioned in earlier letters.

69. MS owned by HCL; ph. in CUL.

70. *Cf.* Mar. 22, 1862.

view that a canary should not pay the board of an eagle. But you will please take notice of that date. Ellen & Edith are gone today to Newport, where they are to spend a fortnight with Miss Clarke & with Mrs James.[71] I regret this on Susan's account, to whom I think Ellen knows how to make herself useful or agreeable at times. Edward is still on his way to Laramie and I fear that there, or at Salt Lake, he may be delayed by the late Indian alarms until his party find an Emigrant Escort (troops) or until the caravans of emigrants accumulate to a strength sufficient for their own protection. The worst for him, I trust, can not be more than overstaying his college date. The war drags on & drags us all into it, in some sort, by ourselves, our children, or our friends. Thus far I do not think it will have harmed you, and I hope it will not make more craving claims But the adult generation seems to have for the most part yielded the point that the juniors must on this matter take their own course. And when they prosper in it, how heartily we applaud them! Mrs Lowell says she gave up her boy [72] to the country at the first.

                                                    Affectionately
                                                         Waldo E.

We have all great satisfaction in Susan's society: great diffidence in our power to make her time pleasant.

To Edward Everett, Concord, July 8, 1862 [73]

                                          Concord, 8 July,
                                                    1862.

Dear Sir,

        If you will be good enough to name a time at which you will receive our committee on the subject of the City Library,[74] I think I may still rally my colleagues, notwithstanding the heat.

                                          With great regard,
                                               R. W. Emerson

Hon. Edward Everett.

71. For the visits at the homes of Sarah Clarke and of Henry James, Sr., cf. later letters of this month.

72. Captain James Jackson Lowell, of Cambridge, was listed in the *Boston Daily Advertiser,* July 7, 1862, as killed in battle near Richmond. The later official account says he was killed July 6, at Malvern Hill, Va. (*Record of the Massachusetts Volunteers,* 1870, p. 333) . Another version of the story has it that he died at Nelson's Farm, near Richmond, July 4, of a wound received at Glendale on June 30 (*Harvard Memorial Biographies,* I, 422) . He was the son of Charles Russell Lowell and Anna Cabot Jackson and was a nephew of James Russell Lowell.

73. MS owned by the Massachusetts Historical Society; ph. in CUL.

74. *Cf.* the letters of June 11 and July 10, 1862.

To Edward Everett, Concord, July 10, 1862 [75]

Concord
10 July, 1862.

My dear Sir,

I have notified the members of our committee that you will see them at 11 o'clock on Saturday next; in which good hope I remain Yours faithfully,

Hon. Mr Everett.   R. W. Emerson.

To Ellen Emerson, Concord, July 13, 1862 [76]

Concord
Sunday Night

Dear Ellen,

Your report is admirable of your soldiers, and tis a strange tragic interlude in a Newport summer. But it being there, I am glad you should meet it. Tell Edith, Frank H. made a pleasant call on me here, pleasant as roses. But I hope you will see my friend Miss Clarke, & make what acquaintance you can with her character, & her love of art & skill in it. She knows the Campagna by heart, & knows goodness also by heart.

Tell her that I have a manuscript Essay by Mr Cabot, on " the Relation of Art to Nature," which is a history of Art, & answers all the questions, & disposes of Ruskin, & much else, and which I think most instructive. I think he will presently print it in the Atlantic [77] and I am impatient that it should go to England & open their eyes as well as ours. I know not what Edith asks for ten cent stamps, for but I enclose them. I hardly know how to address Edward's letter [78] with security. Aunt Elizabeth pays Ellen what a compliment! She will write off the whole letter, before it goes, lest it be lost.

Papa.

75. MS owned by the Massachusetts Historical Society; ph. in CUL. Cf. July 8, 1862, to Everett.

76. MS owned by RWEMA; ph. in CUL. The date is fixed by comparison with the letters of July 8 (to William Emerson) and 16, 1862.

77. For the publication there of Cabot's essay " On the Relation of Art to Nature," see July 27, 1864.

78. Cf. July 16, 1862.

To Ellen Emerson, Concord, July 16, 1862 [79]

Concord, Wednesday
16 July

Dear Ellen,

We have tonight your Newport chronicle with full justice to all the heroes & heroines. and are glad that you & stereoscopes are invented, so that we need not travel any longer on our own feet. For the questions you ask, — Mr J. R. Lowell told me on Monday, that the message which came to Mrs Lowell that her son was alive on Wednesday Evening, came from Nelson's Landing, & without a name, but from a rebel source. He was struck on Monday, by a shell, & sent his father word, then, that " he was dressing his company at the moment " (by way of signifying to his father that he was perfectly cool.) The assurance that he was alive on Wednesday evening gives Dr Wyman much hope of life.[80] Miss Anna L.[81] you know has returned home safely. Aunt Susan went to Portsmouth on Monday & on that evening a letter from Charles was forwarded by me to her. I suppose you know that Sam Hoar was rejected yesterday at Cambridge. He is only 16, & can afford to wait & perhaps the check will be wholesome to him. But I think he should have considered his father & his Aunt Elizabeth who deserved no checks. For Edward, I decided to send your letter to Sacramento City, California, care of Orville D. Lambard,[82] Esq.; and I write to Salt Lake City saying that I have so sent it, and one or the other & perhaps both he will get. You speak of Edith's letter about Robby James,[83] but we have not received it. I hope my unvarying benefactress Mrs Bancroft will not refuse to shine on you also. Ask Miss Clarke if she has read Matthew Arnold's little tracts on Homer.[84] If any bundle goes to you I will put them in. Newport is a proud place, with such friends as you have seen.

Papa.

79. MS owned by RWEMA; ph. in CUL. July 16 fell on Wednesday in 1862, clearly the year of the letter.

80. See a note on July 8, 1862, to William Emerson.

81. Doubtless Anna Lowell.

82. Apparently the husband of Emerson's cousin Sibyl Farnham (cf. a note on May 24, 1831).

83. Robertson James, son of Henry James, Sr., had attended Sanborn's school in Concord. For this fact and for the Jameses at Newport, see The Early Years of the Saturday Club, p. 327.

84. The last of these is mentioned in June 12, 1862.

To Edward Waldo Emerson, Concord, July 17, 1862 [85]

Concord, 17 July, 1862.

Dear Edward,

I fear you have fewer letters than you look for, but we can very ill calculate your movements, and I decided yesterday to send an envelope containing long letters from Ellen & Edith at Newport to Sacramento, care of Orville D. Lambard. The girls are very happy at Newport, now with Miss Clarke & next week with Mrs James. You will be sorry to know that Sam Hoar was not admitted to college. He told Aunt Elizabeth, that he was sorry not to be in your class. You will have seen I suppose Army news, & learned that Capt. James Lowell was mortally wounded. He was left with the rebels & his fate is unknown here though Mrs Lowell received a message from some unknown rebel source that he was alive on Wednesday night, after the Monday when he was struck by the shell. This leaves a little hope. In Concord, we are to raise 22 men for the new forces, and I believe 8 have enlisted. At a Town-meeting we have agreed to pay $100. as a bounty to each recruit.

I am uneasy at hearing that the Indians infest the Plains, lest such a fact or the alarm of the report should cause a serious detention of your party. I am told that Governor Cumming [86] does not attach importance to these reports. But you will not wish to lose any days.

Our last letter from you is just before arriving at Fort Kearney, & Edith carried it to Newport to show it to Tom,[87] & I did not keep its date, but hope you are at Laramie ere now.

I think we have no domestic news for you. Haven is a medical cadet, & at present in the " Euterpe," a hospital ship, or boat in the James River.[88] Charles writes from the Seventh Regiment, in Baltimore,[89] in good spirits. Here at home all goes on as usual, & James B.[90] has been very well. Today we got in our best hay. Aunt Susan E. is for a week at Portsmouth. Mr Fay Barrett wishes to rent Mrs Brown's house. The

85. MS owned by Mr. Raymond Emerson; ph. in CUL. For most of the persons mentioned in this letter, cf. July 16, 1862.

86. Cf. Apr. 28, 1862.

87. Ward, no doubt.

88. Dr. Haven Emerson informs me that his father, a medical student at the College of Physicians and Surgeons, New York, served as a surgical dresser on the hospital boat on the James and later, after graduation, as a contract surgeon with the Army of the Potomac.

89. See Sept. 29, 1862.

90. Burke; cf. Apr. 28, 1862.

Jacksons [91] are to come to Mrs Clark's for the next month. Oscar & Eugenia are at the Flints'.[92] Your mother is quite as well as usual this summer. Julian Hawthorne, they told me yesterday, was badly poisoned, by dogwood probably. I believe the telegraph is in constant action between St Francisco & Boston. We have had news by it since the 4th. If therefore there is any important question to ask or news to tell, you must communicate so. I was very glad to hear that your health was good, & I doubt not the good effect of the journey. Send us word always how Russell [93] fares, as long as he remains with you Ellen met Mr Wetmore, his tutor, at Newport. There is very much that goes well in the country to compensate for war. Affectionately,

R. W. Emerson.

At San Francisco Mr T. S. King [94] will have letters for you.

To Ellen and Edith Emerson, Concord, July 22, 1862 [95]

Concord
Tuesday Morn^g
22 July

Dear Ellen & Edith,

What shall we do without you till Saturday? Old age will be twice dreary. Aunt Susan is still at Portsmouth, having wisely timed her absence, I suppose, till your return.[96] Mr Channing has brought Turners " Old Téméraire " to hang in Ellen's room for a time, till she gets acquainted with it. Mr Bradford Mr Hawthorne & Julian go or are gone to Mount Desert.[97] And we forbidden behold neither mountain nor sea nor the faces of Henry James or Samuel Ward or George Bancroft or Sarah Clarke nor of our children.[98] No letters from Edward. The last news touching Indians & mail routes, looks better. John Bancroft, you know was Charles Lowell's " genius," & Mrs Tappan's. Papa.

91. Charles T. Jackson and his family. The Oscar and Eugenia mentioned below were his children (Bridge, p. 326) .

92. Possibly the family of the J. Flint whose home, near the battle ground, is marked on Gleason's map in Thoreau, *The Writings*, XX, following 346.

93. *Cf.* June 3, 1862, to Adams for Cabot Jackson Russel.

94. *Cf. c.* Nov.? 1862?

95. MS owned by RWEMA; ph. in CUL. July 22 fell on Tuesday in 1862, clearly the year of this letter.

96. *Cf.* July 24? 1862.

97. *Cf.* Julian Hawthorne, II, 315–317.

98. Perhaps Emerson was thinking of *Paradise Lost,* III, 41 ff., or even of Coleridge's " This Lime-tree Bower my Prison."

To Edith Emerson, Concord, July 22, 1862 [99]

Concord
Tuesday night
July 22

Dear Edith,

Here is Edward's letter, which came this morning. All its news is good,, except his failing of news at Fort Kearney. One letter I remember, to which I had given that address,[100] Mr Keyes took the trouble to carry to Boston for me, & mail there, to make sure of being right with the Post Office. But his story of his health, & of Dr Anderson,[101] are satisfactory. But I think, if you have time, you must copy the letter, or it will be rubbed out before his boys can read it.

I am sorry you have such cold days at your seaside. You will be the less unwilling to come home. Miss Clarke has written me the kindest words of you both. My heart enlarges when I think of Mr James.

The papers announce that the mail-coach route from Salt Lake is changed, saving 140 miles, & safer from Indians. I suppose the emigrants will follow the new. But it has been discontinued until the 21 July & so our letters may have stood still somewhere.

Learn if you can whether Philip [102] or Emlyn [103] Randolph are living this summer at their Narraganset farm, opposite Newport. Learn any news about them. Emlyn R. was married two years ago, I think. And are you now with the Wards?

Papa.

To Ellen Emerson, Concord, July 24? 1862 [104]

Concord
Thursday P. M.

Dear Ellen,

I am just learning that you have not been to the Wards'.[105]

99. MS owned by RWEMA; ph. in CUL.

100. See May 22? 1862, for mention of the letter addressed to Ft. Kearney.

101. Cf. Apr. 28, 1862.

102. Philip Physick Randolph is mentioned in earlier letters; cf. also Dec.? c. 6? 1863.

103. Probably Emlen, which was, at any rate, a name belonging to the family: Philip Syng Physick and Elizabeth Emlen were the grandparents of Emerson's friends (cf. Nov. 15, 1867).

104. MS owned by RWEMA; ph. in CUL. The approximate date is shown by evidence cited below. It is, however, possible that the Thursday of this letter was July 31.

105. Cf. July 22, 1862, to Edith Emerson. Boyd's Newport City Directory, 1865, shows that Samuel G. Ward, of Boston, then had a house at Ocean Point.

I had supposed you were dividing this week between Mr James & Mr W.
Now yes, you can stay over Sunday if you wish but better come home as
soon as you can for Aunt Susan arrived today [106] & will be very dreary
with the old people.

Your mother says she sent you the wrong letter. Please Edith copy
Edward's letter [107] so that I may send it to Mr Adams.[108]

To Abel Adams, Concord, August 5, 1862 [109]

Concord —

5 August, 1862 —

My dear friend,

We were all so glad to hear from Edward at Fort Laramie, the
Gate of the Rocky Mountains, that I told Edith she must copy the letter [110] (which was written with pencil & hard to read,) & send it for
Abby to read to you, that you may know how he prospers. In a note
which came a day later to his friend Edward Bartlett, he says that he is
about to write to you. So perhaps you have heard from him.

I read in a N. Y. paper that every road from Oregon to Washington
Territory is filled with a solid column of emigrants going to the Salmon
River mines, — 600 to 1000 passing daily from Lewiston to Florence,[111]
— part of Edward's company are bound that way, — all forgetting us &
our war.

With love to all your house,

Yours,

R. W. Emerson

Mr Abel Adams.

106. *Cf.* July 22, 1862, to Ellen and Edith Emerson. A note on Sept. 12, 1862, indicates that Susan Haven Emerson paid board to her brother-in-law for the period
Aug. 7–Sept. 4 of that year, but it seems certain that the account there cited does not
cover the whole of her stay after her return from Portsmouth.

107. Probably the letter sent to Newport inclosed with July 22, 1862, to Edith
Emerson.

108. *Cf.* Aug. 5, 1862, which shows that the present letter could not be later than
Thursday, July 31, if it was actually written, as its date line indicates, on a Thursday.

109. MS owned by RWEMA; ph. in CUL.

110. See July 22 (to Edith Emerson) and July 24? 1862.

111. What is now Florence, Idaho, is near the Salmon River. Probably the Lewiston meant was the town, also in what is now Idaho, some distance northwest of
Florence. The *New York Commercial Advertiser*, July 25 and Aug. 6, 1862, has much
to say about the excitement in the mining regions of the Salmon and Powder Rivers
at this time; but Emerson apparently refers to some other paper.

To Edward Waldo Emerson, Concord? August *c.* 8, 1862

[Described in Aug. 19 following as of the 8th or 9th instant.]

To Abel Adams, Concord, August *c.* 10? 1862 [112]

Concord
August 1862

My dear friend,

I return with thanks Edward's letter which we have all read with much satisfaction as it gives details which he had not sent us. I am glad to read in the San Francisco news, that the new trains begin to arrive for Oregon & onward from Salt Lake. And it would look as if such a column of emigrants would be irrisistibly strong to keep the ways open against spiteful Mormons. Still I shall be glad to get a letter from the boy, next week, from Salt Lake.

Ever with love,
R. W. Emerson

Mr Abel Adams.

To Edward Waldo Emerson, Concord, August 19, 1862

[MS owned by Mr. Raymond Emerson.]

To William Emerson, Concord, September 12, 1862 [113]

Concord
Sept. 12 1862

Dear William,

I received your letter sent through Susan & its enclosed draft for fifty dollars and shall keep the accompanying "Account" [114] filed for my guidance. With thanks, ever,

Waldo E (over

We live in great comfort with your household. I am sorry that you should lose them: but if so, tis better that we knit friendship with them than that strangers should. Tis a daily joy to my young people. I think

112. MS owned by RWEMA; ph. in CUL. The date is obviously later than the sixth of the month, when Adams wrote, inclosing a letter he had received from Edward and returning the one sent to him in Aug. 5, 1862.

113. MS owned by HCL; ph. in CUL.

114. William Emerson, Sept. 3, 1862 (owned by Dr. Haven Emerson), contains an account of his indebtedness to his brother for board for himself and two members of his family, including charges for his wife from Aug. 7 to Sept. 4. Apparently she and one of her sons were still in Concord when the present letter was written.

that Edward may have sailed yesterday from San F.: if not, he will set out on the 21ˢᵗ But if, when he returns,[115] he shall insist, like his cousin, on going to the war, & to such a war! —

Affectionately,

W —

To ROBERT CASSIE WATERSTON, CONCORD, SEPTEMBER 23, 1862

[MS listed in Bangs & Co., May 7 and 8, 1901; presumably the same listed, without the name of the person addressed, in C. F. Libbie & Co., May 18, 1900, where it is also described as relating to lecture dates.]

To ELBRIDGE? G.? DUDLEY, CONCORD? SEPTEMBER 28, 1862

[MS listed and partly quoted in Goodspeed's Book Shop, n.d., No. 169; expressed pleasure in " the President's Proclamation " — the preliminary emancipation proclamation of Sept. 22, 1862.]

To CHRISTIAN NESTELL BOVEE, CONCORD? SEPTEMBER? c. 28? 1862

[Bovee, New York, Oct. 1, 1862, said he was glad that his books pleased Emerson, and especially that the note on the war found approval. There is some discussion of the Civil War in Bovee's *Intuitions and Summaries of Thought,* 1862, II, 198, where there is also an allusion to the author's conversation with " an accomplished essayist " in Boston, in Mar., 1861. Elsewhere Emerson is more than once quoted. For Bovee, see the obituary in *The American Author,* II, 394.]

To NATHANIEL PRENTISS BANKS, CONCORD, SEPTEMBER 29, 1862 [116]

Concord

September 29, 1862

My dear Sir,

I avail myself of an old claim of neighborhood to crave your regards & advice to a young soldier who wishes to make himself useful. Charles Emerson, the son of my brother Wm. Emerson Esq. of New York, left the present senior class in Harvard University to join the Seventh New York Regiment, when they marched to Baltimore, in May, & now that they have returned home, wishes to enter the Army. He is so firm to this purpose, & has such natural & acquired ability for it, that I do not feel like asking a favor so much as doing a service, when I

---

115. *Cf.* the letters of Oct. 4 and 14, 1862. The first conjecture regarding the date of departure from San Francisco was correct. Edward sailed from that port for Panama on Sept. 11 (typescript *Journals* for 1862–1863) .

116. MS owned by Mr. W. T. H. Howe; ph. in CUL.

seek a commission for him.[117] He has made diligent use of his recent opportunities to qualify him for his duties. — I hope he will be so fortunate as to see you, as I please myself that you will find a soldier made to your hand. Can you give him a word of advice how he shall best apply for admission to the Army?

With great respect,
R. W. Emerson

Major General Banks.

To Edwin McMasters Stanton, Concord? September? 29? 1862

[Mentioned in Oct. 4, 1862; probably written on the same day with that to Banks on the same subject. William Emerson, Oct. 18, 1862 (MS owned by Dr. Haven Emerson), says the letter was not presented, because, when Banks introduced Charles, Stanton, the Secretary of War, said briefly that the request (for a commission) could not be granted.]

To ———————, Concord? September? 29? 1862

[William Emerson, Oct. 2, 1862 (MS owned by Dr. Haven Emerson), tells how Charles returned to New York on Sept. 30 and set off for Washington on the following day, " armed with the letters you kindly gave him." As the letter to Stanton, though written, was not in Charles's hands at that time (see Oct. 4, 1862), there must have been a letter to some other official besides Banks.]

To Charles G. Loring, Concord? c. September? 1862

[Partly quoted in *Journals*, IX, 444. Apparently the entry belongs to c. Sept., 1862.]

To William Emerson, Concord, October 4, 1862 [118]

Oct 4. Concord.
1862

Dear William,

I have your letter with its tidings its account & its draft.[119] There

117. Charles Emerson had been enrolled as a private in the famous Seventh Regiment of the New York National Guard on May 25, 1862, and, like the rest of that regiment, was mustered out on Sept. 5 following. He was next mustered in, Oct. 22, 1862, as a second lieutenant in the 174th Regiment. He was later transferred to the 162d Regiment; became first lieutenant July 2, 1864; and was made captain Feb. 10, 1865 (these are the dates of the musters). He was discharged May 16, 1865. (Frederick Phisterer, *New York in the War of the Rebellion*, 3d ed., 1912, V, *passim*.) There are numerous references to his services in *The War of the Rebellion . . . Official Records*, 1902, 1st series, Vols. XXVI–XLI, showing that he was for some time on the staff of General Banks, to whom Emerson addressed this letter.

118. MS owned by HCL; ph. in CUL.

119. William Emerson, Oct. 2, 1862 (MS owned by Dr. Haven Emerson), inclosed

is an offset to the account which I have not the information at this moment to set down & will write again. But as you say Charles has gone to Washington, I think best to send forward at once the note I wrote him for Mr Stanton [120] that he may present it when he sees him I kept it meaning to clothe it with more authority from Sumner whom I thought I should then have seen within a day or two, but I have been held to my desk to write a paper for the Atlantic [121] this week & a discourse for Music Hall next week [122] & cannot go to town. If I can see Sumner on Monday & receive any good hint, I will forward it.

As for Edward, Edith is in chronic indignation at some writing of Ellen's to him advising him to stay in N. Y. " make a visit, & *do his shopping,*" so Edith says and desires me to write him & countermand & overrule all Ellen's too considerate & cool instructions. If the boy comes, pray let him omit *the shopping*: the most we can allow, is, that the boy stay over one train to see his Uncle, Aunt, & cousins, & then proceed on his journey hither.[123] Waldo E.

To WILLIAM EMERSON, CONCORD, OCTOBER 14, 1862 [124]

Concord —
Oct. 14, 1862 —

Dear William,

Thanks again for your kind care of my boy,[125] who must have looked badly enough on his disembarcation, since ten days have hardly accomplished much for his healing & fatting. But I do not know but the sudden return of dyspepsia, by the heat & imprisonment of the voyage, has operated to convince him that he is not a soldier, as he tho't himself when he left San Francisco; and he has yielded more to this experience

a check in payment for the board of his wife and two of his sons at his brother's home during September. The same letter shows that Charles Emerson returned to New York on Sept. 30 and started for Washington, D. C., on Oct. 1.

120. Probably on Sept. 29.

121. Apparently " The President's Proclamation," the only thing of Emerson's printed in *The Atlantic* for Nov., 1862. The preliminary proclamation of emancipation had been issued on Sept. 22.

122. It was duly announced that Emerson would appear at the Music Hall on Sunday morning, Oct. 12 (*Boston Evening Transcript,* Oct. 11, 1862) . Apparently he read the article he was preparing for *The Atlantic* (*cf.* Cabot, II, 788) .

123. For Edward Emerson's return, see Oct. 14, 1862. In his letter of Oct. 2, cited above, William Emerson had told of sending a note to be delivered to Edward before he landed, urging him to remain in New York for a day or two.

124. MS owned by HCL; ph. in CUL.

125. Edward had arrived in New York on Oct. 3 and in Concord on the 6th (see a note on Apr. 28, 1862) .

than to me, in consenting to go quietly to Cambridge,[126] for the present, there to put body & mind in such training as he can. He went this morning thither, with a view to see the President, make his arrangements, meaning to join the class next Monday, which, I believe, is the anniversary of his departure. When he came home last week, he took the earliest opportunity to convince me that his sole duty & necessity was to go to the war. And now he threatens that this *pis aller* of the college is only for the present, distemper.

I sent last week to you my letter for Charles to Mr Stanton,[127] finding myself far from Sumner. I have been once in Boston since, but failed to see him. I wait for good news of Charles, which seemed to be hinted in a letter to Ellen. I enclose 13.50, of which 7.50 please pay to Haven for the chairs; 1.00 to Charles being the sum Stacy [128] credits me with for a book of C.s; and 5.00 overpaid on Charles's board, as his last lonely week, the ladies were peremptory, was a visit. Affectionately,

Waldo E.

To Charles F. Smith, Concord, October 15, 1862 [129]

Concord

15 Oct

1862

Dear Sir,

I am sorry to have been so slow to answer your note. It will give me pleasure to come to your Lyceum and I can offer you Tuesday Evening, 9 December,[130] if that is open to you.

Respectfully,
R. W. Emerson

Mr C. F. Smith

126. He is listed as a member of the freshman class at Harvard in the catalogue for the first term of 1862–1863.

127. Sept.? 29? 1862.

128. For Stacy's lending library, or book store, some nine years earlier, see Thoreau, *The Writings*, XI, 41. *Cf.* also Jan. 6, 1861.

129. MS owned by Mr. Oliver R. Barrett; ph. in CUL. For Smith, *cf.* Nov. 8, 1853, to him.

130. The MS memorandum book for 1862, 1863, and 1864, notes " Perpetual Forces " for Charlestown, Dec. 9, 1862. The *Charlestown Advertiser*, Dec. 13 following, reports that " Cosmical Forces " was read before the Mishawum Literary Association on the 9th. The newspaper critic found evidence that, with the passing of time, Emerson's mysticism had abated somewhat and his diction had become clearer, but was offended by what he called a " fling at the church." According to the summary here printed, the lecturer counseled a strong assertion of man's moral nature as a remedy for the public profligacy.

To John Murray Forbes, Concord, October 16, 1862 [131]

Concord
Thursday, 16 Oct.ʳ 1862

My dear Mr Forbes,

I am heartily obliged to you, & your " young people," and, I am sure Edward will be, for this kindest interest shown in his behalf. I was disheartened to see him so wasted, on his return,[132] after uniform good reports of mended health & vigor on his route. But he has been gaining again, each day, since he came home, & promises better. If he were strong, I should find it not easy to persuade him to go to Cambridge. I find he left San Francisco under a cloud of bad news from Washington with a feeling that he ought to come home & go instantly to the war. And he set himself very seriously to convince me of this, presently after his arrival at home. I told him, this experience showed him how bad a soldier he was. If he went to the Potomac, he would figure in the hospital. Sleep, & a certain regular living, are essential to him. So that I propose he should go to Cambridge, under a self-denying ordinance, abjuring rank & prizes, & content to study only for knowledge, and devoting to cricket & the Gymnasium what time he needs. The boy has much fitness for the college, &, if he is ever to go, would like to go with his mates who are now there I am not sure it is a possible course for him and shall watch the experiment. If he cannot live there, but must live out of doors I shall then come & ask you if such good contingences as you suggest are all passed quite out of reach. Meantime, I delight in this kind thoughtfulness of yours. Edward is gone to Cambridge today to see the President. He shall come & give you, I hope, a better account of himself. With affectionate remembrances to your household,

Yours,
R. W Emerson

Mr Forbes.

———————

Yes, I mean to go to the next club.[133]

To Edward Waldo Emerson, Concord, October 24, 1862

[MS owned by Mr. Raymond Emerson. This letter inclosed a request to Dr. Peabody — presumably Andrew Preston Peabody, the acting president of Harvard — which was almost certainly from Emerson and in the form of a letter.]

131. MS owned by RWEMA; ph. in CUL.
132. Cf. Oct. 14, 1862.
133. Doubtless the Saturday Club, of which Forbes, like Emerson, was a member.

To Charles Eliot Norton, Concord, October 30, 1862 [134]

Concord —
30 October, 1862

My dear Norton,

I read the Poem [135] with great interest, — but I would not print it. It is a stroke of character, is the voice of a noble heart, & with such truth & articulateness, that it is the saddest and sincerest of odes. It should pass privately to all souls who are as much emancipated, & have learned how much history they can spare when they have been permitted a glance at the First Cause. But when it comes to the young public, it is a little rude. The affirmative part is short & vague, not an offset to the negative, & is said only that the poet may not say nothing. Meantime, the happiness of tender souls is assailed, whilst the dearest of all traditions is taken away, & nothing adequate is supplied: If the piece had shining poetic merits, it might be impossible not to publish it, in spite of its subject; but the sadness of the strain becomes really painful, & bereaves his genius of the splendor which charms me in the " Bothie." This was my first impression, as I read it immediately on the arrival of your letter, & I hold it still on a second reading today.

Let me at last thank you for the completed book [136] which you sent me, I know not how many weeks ago. I hold it affectionately. Clough does not, like most writers, separate his genius from himself, but every poem endears him to me. I should gladly have found every poem of the old series again. The new ones I have not yet exhausted. But the " Bothie " I like better than ever, & have tried it on my young people with entire success. I delight that the care of his works & his memory has fallen into such tender & judicious hands, as he well deserved.

Yours gratefully,
R. W. Emerson

C. E. Norton, Esq.
I have received Ernest Renan.[137] —

134. MS owned by HCL; ph. in CUL.

135. Apparently a poem of Clough's not included in the collection mentioned below but considered by Norton for publication at this time.

136. *The Poems of Arthur Hugh Clough. With a Memoir, by Charles Eliot Norton*, Boston, 1862.

137. In *Journals*, IX, 451 (Oct.? 1862), Emerson quotes from the essay on Cousin in Ernest Renan's *Essais de morale et de critique* a passage which appears on p. 62, not 63, in the 1859 edition.

To Horace Greeley, Concord? November *c.* 8, 1862

[Greeley, New York, Nov. 9, 1862, acknowledges " yours just received," which made it clear that no meeting with Emerson could be arranged for that week.]

To Elbridge G. Dudley, Concord, November 10, 1862 [138]

Concord
10 Novr 1862

My dear Sir,

I believe you have set me down for service at the Music Hall on Sunday 30th instant. I have just discovered that it follows immediately Thanksgiving week which would make it not easy for me to bring any useful lesson, for we have an annual gathering in this house, then, which turns me out of the library. I am ashamed to be so slow to put the facts together, when I remember that the time was chosen for my convenience. But I can go to no club in that week. Now can you not allow me to come on the first or second Sunday of December,[139] either of which I can keep, or rather can you not fill otherwise this 30th day, & I will take my chance for some following vacancy?

With kindest remembrances to your household,
Ever yours,
R. W. Emerson

Mr Dudley.

To Edward Waldo Emerson, Concord? November 10, 1862

[MS owned by Mr. Raymond Emerson.]

To Mary Preston Stearns, Concord, November 10, 1862 [140]

Concord
10 Novr Monday
1862

My dear Mrs Stearns,

My wife requests me to answer for her & myself your kind invitation. Thursday we cannot come nor Tuesday for the same reason

138. MS owned by Mr. Abel Cary Thomas; ph. in CUL.

139. The *Boston Evening Transcript*, Dec. 13, 1862, announces Emerson at the Music Hall on Sunday morning, Dec. 14. The MS memorandum book for 1862, 1863, and 1864 notes the engagement and gives " Health " as the subject. Cabot, II, 788, outlines this lecture.

140. MS owned by Mr. F. R. Fraprie; ph. in CUL.

that we have a lecture to write. But you have thoughtfully held out one day of grace more namely Wednesday that if it still proves a right day for you we shall find good for us. I find that I am engaged to be at Salem that evening [141] at 7.30 o'clock which would give me two or three hours at your house and Mrs Emerson should find me at Boston in the morning.

If this little programme though I regret the little cramp in its side seem to you practicable we shall keep it gladly.

With kindest regards,
R. W. Emerson

To Amory Dwight Mayo, Concord, November 12, 1862 [142]

Concord
12 Nov

Dear Sir

I can come easily on 5th *Jan* on my way to Toronto for the 6th; or on 9th *Jan*ᵛ, after Rochester where I am 8th.[143] If it must be in December, can come on the 26th; [144] not so well on another day. I call a new lecture I am writing for Boston " Perpetual Forces," but I suppose can easily write more fully on bad politics.

Hastily
but ever yours
R W Emerson

Rev A D Mayo

141. The *Salem Register*, Nov. 17, 1862, announced that Emerson would lecture before the Salem Lyceum on Wednesday, Nov. 19, at 7:30. The MS memorandum book for 1862, 1863, and 1864 gives " Perpetual Forces " as the subject.

142. MS owned by Mr. Walter R. Benjamin; ph. in CUL. Mayo, in earlier years pastor of the Independent Christian Church at Gloucester, Mass., and afterwards of a church in Cleveland, was now pastor of the Unitarian church at Albany, N. Y. Conway saw him there early in Jan., 1863 (*Autobiography,* I, 373) .

143. For the lectures at Toronto and Rochester, see Jan. 8, 1863.

144. For the lecture of Dec. 26 at Albany, see Dec. 24, 1862.

To ELBRIDGE G. DUDLEY, CONCORD, NOVEMBER 15, 1862 [145]

Concord
15 Nov[r] 1862

My dear Sir,

      I accept the new day you give at Music Hall; and I should be well content to accept for me & mine the summons for Tuesday Night, but it appears the plan is all arranged for Tuesday & Wednesday already otherwise.

      Mrs Emerson sends with mine, her affectionate acknowledgments to all of you.

Yours,
R. W. Emerson

To MARY PRESTON STEARNS, CONCORD, NOVEMBER 15 AND 17? 1862? [146]

Concord
15 Nov[r]

Dear Mrs Stearns

      I received the other day amid other conversation a verbal message from you by Mr Conway concerning Mrs E.'s & my visit to Medford this week.[147] Mr Conway added that you were coming up to Concord that afternoon & would speak for yourself. I have not seen him again but last night Mrs Conway told me that he wished me to write you on the point.

      In this twilight of Monday P M [148] I therefore try to make legible to you that Mrs Emerson is well pleased with the hope of passing Thursday Afternoon & Night with you & that I will come with her to dine & return to Concord that eve. If this is not according to the invitation you sent, perhaps you will send me word at Parkers Hotel on Tuesday.

With kindest regards,
R. W. Emerson

Mrs Stearns

    145. MS owned by Mr. Abel Cary Thomas; ph. in CUL. *Cf.* Nov. 10, 1862, to Dudley.

    146. MS owned by Mr. F. R. Fraprie; ph. in CUL. The date or dates almost certainly fall within the period of the Conways' residence in Concord, the only November of which was that of 1862 (*cf.* a note on Dec. 4, 1862).

    147. Apparently the verbal message answered the letter of Nov. 10, 1862, to Mrs. Stearns. Conway's frequent visits about this time to the Stearns home are noted in *The Life and Public Services of George Luther Stearns*, p. 274.

    148. This seems to show that the letter was completed on Nov. 17.

To Edward Waldo Emerson, Concord? November c. 15? 1862

[Mentioned in the following letter.]

To Edward Waldo Emerson, Concord, November 21, 1862 [149]

Concord, 21 Nov[r]

Dear Edward,

I hope you found your barrel of apples at Porter's Station though I have some misgiving that the note I wrote you to apprise you of its going did not reach you. Your parcel forwarded by Mr Ward from San Francisco has arrived at home, and Edith thinks you wish to open it yourself. I hope you may not find your rifle rusty. Your mother was to visit you today. R. W. E.

We expect her at 5 this P. M.)

To Thomas Starr King, Concord, c. November? 1862? [150]

My dear friend,

My boy brought back testimonies of your goodness which made all this house happy, & has fortified them since for many days that he stayed at home by new anecdotes, affirming that not only was Mr K. his benefactor in particulars & in totals, but he was the benefactor of all who had to do with him, & the salvation & future of California lay in his hands.[151]

We were glad for the boy who seemed to believe with a certain reli-

149. MS owned by RWEMA; ph. in CUL. The year, " 62," has been added, apparently in another hand; and the date is clearly shortly after Edward Emerson's return from California (cf. Oct. 14, 1862). The apples, it seems, were sent to Edward at college by way of Porter's Station, Cambridge.

150. MS owned by RWEMA; ph. in CUL. This is a rough draft, but I have not reproduced the few words that Emerson canceled. At the top of the first page he wrote " Letter to Rev. Starr King." The year 1862, added apparently by another hand, is very probably correct, as Emerson would naturally have written the letter soon after his son's return from California. The mention of the " many days that he stayed at home " shows, however, that the writing could hardly be earlier than late Oct. or Nov., 1862. For King in California, cf. July 17, 1862. He had written to Emerson, Sept. 9, 1862, of meeting Edward and had sent, at the same time, a photograph of what he said was the largest tree then standing in that state.

151. King, who had become pastor of a church in San Francisco, was an eloquent partisan of the Union and has been given chief credit for preventing the secession of California. He also took a particular interest in California's natural attractions and helped make them known.

gious fury in his ultramontane hero whom he sought so far & to whom
he had owed so much; — glad for ourselves as we had remembrances of
marked kindness from him to us many years old & glad for California
which had a fit Saint to guide & to illustrate it. Is the occasion & person
so poetical I am tempted in every line I write to assay rhymes. Well he
brot me these wonderful pictures of the Sequoia the grisly giant

Well you are to know that we love you dearly, & prize your necessity
to that New Country, as we prized the fame & affection which this older
country gave you already, & that we remember you in times of social
gathering & boast your name to each other. — Did not our earth bear this
son? and in p[er]ilous [152] present times we say, He is for us & in [153] an
essential bulwark of the republic, necessary to our glory & safeguard he
stands firm. Long may you reign over it teaching moderating inspiring
I am trying to say to people that I think we are not hurt so much by
malignity as by levity of people [154] And if the Lord wd. vouchsafe us a
serious population capable of public regards, it would not take long to
save us; but the frivolity of these young & grey fops has all the effect of
treachery.

R. W. E.

Rev. Starr King

To Almira Penniman Barlow, Concord, December 3, 1862 [155]

Concord
Wednesday 3 Dec^r

My dear Mrs Barlow,

I am very sorry to learn that General Barlow is ill today. It is
a sad disappointment to all of us — I trust he will quickly mend. Meantime, my wife sends (from her bed just now) her best wishes, & hopes

152. Partly blotted out.

153. Emerson probably intended to delete this as he did several words following
in the MS.

154. Cf. a note on Oct. 15, 1862, and the entry in *Journals*, IX, 449, which also belongs to October.

155. MS owned by Mrs. Pierre Jay; ph. in CUL. The only year in which Wednesday fell on Dec. 3 when Hawthorne could have met Francis Channing Barlow after
the latter had received the title of General, was 1862. Barlow had been made
Brigadier-General on Sept. 19, 1862, after the battle of Antietam, in which he was
severely wounded. The letter is to his mother, Almira Penniman Barlow, of Concord,
as Mr. Robert Shaw Barlow, the general's son, informs me. Cf. Dec. 26, 1863, to Barlow.

that *you* will be able to come down & dine with her & Mr Hawthorne at 2 o'clock, & Mr Bradford [156] if we can keep him.

With great regard,

Mrs Barlow.   R. W. Emerson

To Frederic Henry Hedge, Concord, December 4, 1862 [157]

Concord, 4 Dec? 1862.

Dear Hedge,

What Nemesis made me keep this good pamphlet so long? I, who hastened to find that your weeks of keeping " Arnold " [158] made a month? I read this at once, & with great satisfaction. It is very neat, clear, & honest, with good points made, though air of completeness is a little factitious & Frenchy. He is a little at a loss to find the importance of the Semitic to our literature, when he is driven to eke out " Milton " with " Lamartine & Lemmenais." But I prize the piece, which I have read twice. Conway has got your house.[159] Please order another.

Ever yours,
R. W. Emerson

Dr Hedge.

To Thomas Carlyle, Concord, December 8, 1862

[MS owned by RWEMA; incompletely printed in Ireland, *In Memoriam*, pp. 73–74; much more fully, in *C–E Corr.*, 1883.]

To ——————————, Concord, December 15, 1862

[MS listed and partly quoted in Anderson Auction Co., Jan. 26, 1914; Emerson says he will not be able to meet his correspondent at Miss Peabody's, but adds that it would be a satisfaction to learn something of these interesting Orientals from an instructed eyewitness.]

To John Sullivan Dwight, Concord, December 19, 1862

[MS listed in C. F. Libbie & Co., May 28, 1902; printed in Cooke, *John Sullivan Dwight*, p. 190.]

156. George Bradford had doubtless been at Concord for Thanksgiving.

157. MS owned by RWEMA; ph. in CUL.

158. Perhaps one of Matthew Arnold's essays on translating Homer (*cf.* the letters of June 12 and July 16, 1862).

159. For Conway's brief residence in Concord about Aug., 1862–Apr., 1863, in the house formerly occupied by Barzillai Frost, see *Autobiography*, I, 365–389. *Cf.* also letters of Mar. and Apr., 1863. Apparently Emerson had urged Hedge to buy the Frost house.

To Henry D. Burlingame, Boston, December 24, 1862 [160]

Parker House, Boston —
Dec 24 1862

Dear Sir,

I shall take lodgings at the Delavan House on Friday [161] P. M.
Respectfully,
R. W. Emerson

Mr Burlingame.

P. S. I mean to take the train which leaves Boston at 8.30 A. M.[162]

To John Sullivan Dwight, Concord? December 30, 1862

[MS listed and partly quoted in American Art Association, Apr. 28 and 29,
1924; printed in Cooke, *John Sullivan Dwight,* p. 191. Only the day of the
week is given if Cooke's version is complete, but the full date is obvious.]

To William Emerson, Concord, December 31, 1862,
and January 1, 1863 [163]

Concord
31 Dec[r] 1862

Dear William,

Thanks & hearty returns of love for your letter received yes-
terday. I had one some time ago which spoke of Salome.[164] I waited for
Salome to arrive, then I would reply. It came only ten days ago, I think.
It was good to a surprise. I read it through — highly gratified with the

160. MS owned by Mr. Walter R. Benjamin; ph. in CUL. Henry D. Burlingame
is listed as an attorney in *The Albany Directory,* 1862, where the Delavan House is
described as the largest hotel in the town.

161. For Emerson's offer to lecture at Albany, N. Y., on Friday, Dec. 26, see Nov. 12,
1862. The *Albany Morning Express,* Dec. 25 following, published an announcement,
signed by Burlingame as chairman of the lecture committee, that Emerson would
read " Perpetual Forces " before the Independent Lecture Association the next day.
The spelling of " Friday " in the MS is doubtful.

162. A train left Boston for Albany at this hour on the Boston & Worcester Railroad *(Boston Daily Advertiser,* Dec. 23, 1862) .

163. MS owned by HCL; ph. in CUL.

164. William Emerson, Oct. 18, 1862 (MS owned by Dr. Haven Emerson) , told of
Salome, the dramatic poem, perpetrated by Joseph Converse Heywood. William Emerson promised to send his brother a copy and asked him to read it and, if he thought
it worth while, to write a notice, or cause one to be written, for *The Atlantic.* The
book was, however, merely listed, with other recent publications, in that magazine,
Dec., 1862.

general power & with the taste & culture indicated. The author holds a
little strongly for a poet to the old theology. But Channing carried off
my book before I had done with it & he is the best electrometer or py-
rometer for the poetic flame I know & he gave a good report. I found the
book already named in the newspapers but they will give no right guess
of its merit for a time. I will write you of it again when I see it. . New
Years. The happiest day to you & your house! We are all well and all at
home for Edward came last night. We are all heartily glad of your letter, & with its good aspects of your home. We have not so late news of
Charles, as all desire. Col. Lowell assured me he was on Banks's staff; [165]
but I have never heard that confirmed from you, & counted it premature.
I go today to the musical concert in Boston, where I am to read some
rough verses.[166] But we find no proclamation this morning: must meet
it in town. Hope & health & assured faith forever & ever! Waldo E.

To Edward W. Russell? Concord? 1862

[MS listed and partly quoted in Goodspeed's Book Shop, June, 1931, where it
is dated only as to year, is without the name of the person addressed, and is
described as an unsigned draft. It accepts an invitation to lecture in Chicago.
For the probability that it was to Russell, cf. a note on Jan. 10, 1863, to Edith
Emerson.]

To —————————, Concord? 1862

[Partly quoted by Thomas Wentworth Higginson in " The Personality of Emerson," The Outlook, LXXIV, 222 (May 23, 1903). Higginson says the letter
is to be found in Kennedy's life of Emerson, a work which, so far as I know,
does not exist.]

To John Sullivan Dwight, Concord? December? 31? 1862?

[MS listed and partly quoted in C. F. Libbie & Co., May 28, 1902, where it is
dated simply 1863. But as Emerson tells of " a string of verses, a sort of Boston
Hymn " that he has written, the letter belongs more probably to the last day
of 1862 than to the following day, when he read these verses at the celebration.
It almost certainly follows the letter of Dec. 30, though possibly on the same
day. Cf. Dec. 31, 1862, and Jan. 1, 1863.]

165. Cf. Sept. 29, 1862.
166. The " Boston Hymn." Cf. the letters of Dec. 19 and 30, 1862, and Dec.? 31?
following for Dwight's finally successful efforts to persuade Emerson to read his
verses. The Boston Daily Advertiser, Jan. 2, 1863, reported that the exercises at the
Music Hall in celebration of the Emancipation Proclamation were opened by Emerson's reading of his poem and that the " Egmont " overture followed.

1863

To Salmon Portland Chase, Concord? January? *c.* 2? 1863?

[Trowbridge, pp. 385–390, tells of finding this letter in Whitman's possession and of taking it to Chase, who was glad to keep it as an Emerson autograph but would not listen to its plea in favor of Whitman. Thomas Donaldson, *Walt Whitman the Man,* 1896, p. 156, prints comments from Whitman's diary for Dec. 11, 1863. According to this entry, the letter was carried to Chase on Dec. 10 and had therefore, it seems, been kept by Whitman himself for nearly a year. It is clear from a letter Whitman dated Mar. 19, 1863, that he then had "strong letters of introduction" in his pocket from Emerson to both Chase and Seward and had already seen Sumner several times (Emory Holloway, *Whitman,* 1926, p. 203). And he had asked Emerson for letters to all three of these men as early as Dec., 1862:

"Washington, D. C.
"Monday afternoon, Dec. 29, '62.
"Dear friend,
    "Breaking up a few weeks since, and for good, my New York stagnation — wandering since through camp and battle scenes — I fetch up here in harsh and superb plight — wretchedly poor, excellent well, (my only torment, family matters,) — realizing at last that it is necessary for me to fall for the time in the wise old way, to push my fortune, to be brazen, and get employment, and have an income — determined to do it, (at any rate until I get out of horrible sloughs) I write you, asking you as follows:
    "I design to apply personally direct at headquarters, for some place. I would apply on literary grounds, not political.
    "I wish you would write for me something like the enclosed form of letter, that I can present, opening my interview with the great man. I wish you to write two copies — put the one in an envelope directed to Mr. Seward, Secretary of State — and the other in an envelope directed to Mr. Chase Secretary of the Treasury — and enclose both envelopes in the one I send herewith. So that I can use either one or the other. I wish you also to send me a note of introduction to Charles Sumner.
    "It is pretty certain that, armed in that way, I shall conquer my object. Answer me by next mail, for I am waiting here like ship waiting for the welcome breath of the wind.
"Indeed yours, &c
"Walt Whitman"]

To WILLIAM HENRY SEWARD, CONCORD? JANUARY? *c.* 2? 1863?

[See the preceding note. Trowbridge says the letters he saw were to Chase and Sumner, but as Whitman had seen Sumner several times " anent " his " office hunting " before the end of March, there is the best reason for supposing that he must have delivered, early in the year, any letter directed to him. Presumably, however, Emerson had written the letter to Sumner which Whitman wanted; but I have no satisfactory proof of it. A letter somewhat mysteriously described in *The Complete Writings*, 1902, I, lxxix, as " written eight years later " — apparently eight years later than 1855 — may well be one of the two I have dated Jan.? *c.* 2? 1863? or may have been written to Sumner about the same time. *Cf.* also the " unpublished letter " mentioned *ibid.,* I, xcv. Probably a note to Whitman himself accompanied the introductions for which he had asked.]

To EDITH EMERSON, BOSTON? JANUARY? 3? 1863? [1]

Dear Edith

The copy must be made for Miss Dunkin & the original copy sent to Mrs Stearns at once by mail.[2]

Pray mamma to go down into the cellar & look to the wild cider barrels at once & to have the unpainted barrel drawn off 1/3 of it that the rest may be vinegar. I send her a glass to read newspapers by in a hurry. Papa.

To ROBERTS BROTHERS, CONCORD, JANUARY 4, 1863

[MS listed in Newark Galleries, Dec. 10, 1931; Emerson expresses his admiration for Jean Ingelow's poems. The Boston edition of *Poems*, 1863, was published by Roberts Brothers, perhaps on Emerson's advice.]

1. MS owned by RWEMA; ph. in CUL. The date " 1863 Jan 3rd " has been supplied in another hand and agrees with the slight evidence cited below. On Jan. 7, 1863, Edith Emerson wrote her father that she had received a note from him on Saturday morning (Jan. 3) .

2. It is very probable, I think, that the MS here referred to was that of the " Boston Hymn." Emerson had read this poem on Jan. 1, 1863, at the Music Hall celebration of emancipation and, on the same night, repeated it at the home of George Luther Stearns, in Medford (F. P. Stearns, *The Life,* p. 275) . It is easy to understand why the original should have been given to the wife of the man who had long encouraged Emerson's antislavery activities. Miss " Dunkin," who was to have a copy, may well have been Rebecca Duncan, sister-in-law of the E. G. Dudley to whom Emerson frequently wrote about engagements at the Music Hall. Both these women appear elsewhere as Emerson's correspondents.

To Edith Emerson, Rochester, New York, January 8, 1863 [3]

> Eagle Hotel.
> Rochester, New York.
> [1]Jan. 8. 1863[1]

Dear Edith,

I hoped to find a word from home here, or, at least one from Mr Fields,[4] which should have come, but Mr John Bower [5] says, No. I mean today or tomorrow to send you a business letter. [II]I spent Sunday at Niagara Falls, which you must see with leisure & advantage some time. The great feature that struck me now was its immense plenty. The vast quantity of water that pours over it in five minutes suggests the huge continent from which it draws its supplies. At night I went to bed early in the American House, the only hotel open in winter, and, at 3 o'clock, was waked by the cry of Fire! within the house. I put on my clothes or some of them, & gathered up my properties as many & as fast as I could in the dark, & got down stairs through a cloud of smoke & cinders, and found women clothed in blankets & barefooted in the hall & in the street, & great distress everywhere. The house was burned out thoroughly, before all our eyes, & nothing left but the four walls.[6] All the furniture, & quantities of clothing, & much money of the guests & of the proprietor, were lost. I had left my baggage at the Suspension Bridge, & had with me only my black-bag; but contrived to lose my ticket from Buffalo to Chicago, and some brushes, &c. no insurance. I walked down with another traveller, in the early morning, to the Suspension Bridge,, 2 miles, & there met Mr Reuben N. Rice of Detroit, who insisted on giving me a pass over his road [7] from Detroit to Chicago, which diminishes my loss.[II] I have had a very agreeable visit as always in Toronto.[8] You must not burn up the castle, &, if it kindles, save the little black trunk under your mother's bureau, & all the MSS in the study. Papa

3. MS owned by RWEMA; ph. in CUL. Excerpts I–II are in *Memoirs of Members of the Social Circle in Concord,* 3d series, pp. 147–148. An editorial note in *Journals,* IX, 479, contains a brief quoted passage which is closely related to the present letter but not from it. According to *The Rochester Evening Express,* Jan. 8, 1863, Emerson was to read " Classes of Men " before the Athenæum on that evening.

4. *Cf.* Jan. *c.* 12, 1863.

5. Bower is named in the entry of this date in the MS memorandum book for 1862, 1863, and 1864.

6. *Cf.* the note in *Journals* cited above. Emerson's spelling of " proprietor " in the following sentence is doubtful.

7. *Cf.* Feb. 1, 1854.

8. The MS memorandum book already referred to lists two lectures for Toronto

[Postscript. I enclose a draft for $93.13 which your mother must endorse, & which Mr Cheney will pay Call his attention to the fact that it is a draft on *Boston*.][9]

I found Dr & Mrs Holmes in the cars at Boston (bound for Philadelphia to find the captain again [10] who is sick there,) & had the Doctor all the way to Springfield. who broke his " rule," & talked steadily twenty miles.

To EDITH EMERSON, ROCHESTER, NEW YORK, JANUARY 10, 1863 [11]

Eagle Hotel
Rochester N Y
10 Jan[y]

Dear Edith

I sent you yesterday [12] a draft from Mr Powers,[13] banker, on Boston, for $93.13. You should also receive, within a few days, a letter addressed to me from Canada, containing, say $50.00. From Buffalo or Cleveland [14] I shall probably send you another remittance on Wednesday or Thursday next, and others, later. For the spending of these, I have no doubt you will have direction enough from the creditors at home. Smaller debts pay in full; larger in instalments. I borrowed of the Concord Bank $100. on the understanding that it should be paid within two or three weeks. And I suppose Jonas Melvin [15] will come for the

---

— " Classes of Men," Jan. 5, and " Criticism," Jan. 6. *The Rochester Evening Express* of Jan. 8 following states that Emerson lectured at Toronto on both those days. I am indebted to Mr. Carl F. Klinck for an excerpt from *The Globe,* Toronto, Jan. 7, 1863, containing a friendly account of Emerson's appearance before the Ontario Literary Society on the 6th; according to this paper the subject on that evening was " Talent and Genius."

9. The square brackets, apparently Emerson's own, set off the postscript, which is wedged tightly between the salutation and the beginning of the first paragraph.

10. Oliver Wendell Holmes, Jr., later of the United States Supreme Court, had been wounded at Antietam the preceding September. His father's adventures in search of him after receiving the news of that battle were told in " My Hunt after ' the Captain,' " *The Atlantic,* Dec., 1862, where there was some comment on the nuisance of conversations in the cars.

11. MS owned by RWEMA; ph. in CUL. The year is fixed by evidence noted below.

12. In the letter of Jan. 8, 1863.

13. Daniel W. Powers is listed as a banker in *Boyd's Rochester Directory* for 1863–1864.

14. See the letters of Jan. *c.* 12 and 14, 1863.

15. Jonas Melvin is listed as collector of taxes in *Reports of the Selectmen, and Other Officers, of the Town of Concord,* 1863, p. 2.

Town tax on which you must pay him $50. as soon as you can & $50—
more as soon as you can. But to James Burke I promised to send some
money early, as he took only $6.00 If he remains in the hospital, send
him $15. by Adams

In Boston I paid Warren & Co.[16] $50. and Dr Keep's bill, 8.00. Gilbert
can wait longer. I should like to have $30. paid on B. Hastings's account
as early as possible.

I hope you sent no letter for me to Clyde,[17] for I did not go there, having received a countermand, as has happened to me several times from
that town.

Send me word to care of Mr Peixotte, (or of George Willey Esq.)
Cleveland, of your prosperities what news from James, & how Mike gets
on. The mild weather will be friendly to his charge, and to the whole
household. I must write a note to Mamma presently. But Ellen in a
couple of days I suppose will return & govern you all, I alone escaping
from her tyrannies. At Detroit I am on the 15th R W King at Chicago on
the 16 & 22 care E W Russell at Milwaukee (W. G. Whipple) 19th at
Beloit, 21st H C Dickenson [18] Papa.

Milwaukee *Wisconsin.* I fear I wrote *Michigan* on my Journal
When the Atlantic comes out Ticknor & Fields will send $50.[19]

To Edgar Judge, Rochester? New York, January 10, 1863

[Judge, Montreal, Jan. 13 (or 15?), 1863, acknowledges this letter, accepts Emerson's terms for two lectures ($100), sets Feb. 3 and 5 as the dates, and asks
an immediate answer.]

16. Drygoods merchants, according to *The Boston Directory* for the year commencing July 1, 1862.

17. Clyde is down for Jan. 9 of this year in the MS memorandum book for 1862,
1863, and 1864, where B. F. Peixotto is named in the Cleveland entry of Jan. 14 following. The subject given for Cleveland is " Third Estate in Literature." Willey appears in Jan. 8, 1853, and in later letters.

18. Edward W. Russell, apparently acting as Western manager, had written from
Chicago, Dec. 30, 1862, that Emerson was scheduled to lecture for the Detroit Y. M. A.
on Jan. 15; the Milwaukee Y. M. A., 19; Beloit College, 21; and Chicago Y. M. A., 22.
Russell said the 16th was still unoccupied. He gave the names of persons listed here.
The MS memorandum book for 1862, 1863, and 1864 has the same information as
well as the subjects of the lectures Emerson proposed to read — " Clubs " at Detroit
and Milwaukee, " Perpetual Forces " at Chicago, and " Third Estate in Literature "
at Beloit. For Milwaukee and Chicago, see also Jan. 24, 1863.

19. Doubtless for the " Boston Hymn," which was published in *The Atlantic* for
the following February.

To Edith? Emerson, Buffalo, January *c.* 12, 1863 [20]

> American House
> Buffalo Jan^y

Two memoranda.

1.   I sent home in Edward's bag (did I not?) or, if not, in some parcel from Boston, a package from Ticknor & Fields, containing a Manuscript of Mr Thoreau.[21] That should go to Miss Sophia T.

2.   Please look in a file of of letters on the rosewood bookcase a file exclusively of *Lyceum* correspondence, for a letter inviting me to Meadville Pa.[22] and send me at once the letter to care of E. W Russell [23] Chicago) or, at least the signature of the letter. For, if I go to Pittsburgh, as may be, I can perhaps go to M.

To Edith Emerson, Cleveland, January 14, 1863 [24]

> Cleveland Ohio
> 14 Jan^y
> Angier House.

Dear Edith, Not to send you nothing, I enclose $20.[25] today, which will keep you in hope. Here, this morning, arriving [26] I find no letter. I enclose a memorandum [27] that should have gone before.

> R. W. Emerson.

20. MS owned by RWEMA; ph. in CUL. Evidence cited below shows that the year was 1863. For the day, the *Buffalo Commercial Advertiser*, Jan. 12, 1863, announced that Emerson was already in town and would lecture on the 13th. " The Third Estate in Literature " was reported briefly *ibid.*, Jan. 14. In the letter of Jan. 14, 1863, Emerson apparently refers to this note as the " memorandum that should have gone before."

21. *Cf.* the letters of Jan. 8, 1863, to Edith Emerson and Oct. 19 to Fields.

22. See Jan. 30, 1863, for both Meadville and Pittsburgh.

23. *Cf.* Jan. 10, 1863, to Edith Emerson.

24. MS owned by RWEMA; ph. in CUL. The year 1863, added in pencil, is correct, as the following notes show.

25. In Jan. 24, 1863, Emerson says he has not heard that Edith received the " $20. in a letter sent 14th Jany "

26. Emerson was to read the " Third Estate in Literature " before the Library Association at Cleveland that evening (MS memorandum book for 1862, 1863, and 1864, and Edward W. Russell, Dec. 30, 1862) .

27. Doubtless Jan. *c.* 12, 1863.

To ELBRIDGE G. DUDLEY, INDIANAPOLIS, JANUARY 23, 1863 [28]

Indianapolis, Ind.
23 January 1863

Dear Sir,

I am always disappointing you. I read now with some alarm in my Note Book that I am in some sort due at the Music Hall, 8 February. But my engagement to read two lectures at Pittsburg, Pa. has been necessarily, by the Association there, staved off to 3d & 5th Feb.y [29] so that I cannot come to you till Feb.y [30] 15 or 22d If either of these will be free, you can choose, though it would be the easiest for me to take the last.

Always yours,
R. W. Emerson

E. G. Dudley Esq.
You can send me word to Concord, or if this reaches you in time to write to me at Pittsburg Pa. care of W. H. Kincaid, Esq. I shall know sooner.

To ELLEN EMERSON, INDIANAPOLIS, JANUARY 24, 1863 [31]

Bates House
Indianapolis, Ind
24 Jany 1863

Dear Ellen, I have good letters from you & from your Mother & Edith & Edward at Chicago,[32] night before last, & at Milwaukee,[33] containing much which I was glad to know, &, I doubt not, I have all that you have sent me, including *Clyde*.[34] I have had one or two hitches in my road one

28. MS owned by Goodspeed's Book Shop; ph. in CUL. The story of the visit at Indianapolis is told in the letters of Jan. 24 and 30, 1863.

29. See Jan. 30.

30. The *Boston Evening Transcript* of Saturday, Feb. 14, 1863, announced that Emerson would speak at the Music Hall the following morning. The MS memorandum book for 1862, 1863, and 1864 gives the subject as "Courage."

31. MS owned by RWEMA; ph. in CUL.

32. Emerson was introduced to the Young Men's Association at Bryan Hall on Jan. 22 by the Rev. Robert Collyer; "Perpetual Forces" won the applause of the audience (*Chicago Daily Tribune,* Jan. 23, 1863).

33. The *Daily Milwaukee News,* Jan. 20, 1863, said "Clubs and Conversations," read on the 19th, was one of the poorest lectures Emerson was capable of and suspected him of underrating the capacity of Western audiences. But the *Milwaukee Daily Sentinel* of the 20th declared that the crowd at the Academy of Music to hear the Concordian was a testimony to the good sense of the lecture-going public.

34. See Jan. 10, 1863, to Edith Emerson.

of being forced to postpone Pittsburg, Pa to 3ᵈ & 5ᵗʰ Feb.ʸ ³⁵ a week later than I had meant, and now here another that on arriving last eve. in this town, at great haste & inconvenience from Chicago, there was no hall, & no preparation, & I must wait till Monday night. Mr Russell had delayed a little in his writing to this Committee & there was not time to get their explanation back to him & me. Tis a long day's ride from Chicago. Glad of Edward's peace of mind but tis pathetical that Tom should have difficulties.³⁶ Heartily glad Edward went to the Pres.ᵗ on his account, and he should have made his statement so urgent as settle the fact. The worst of my delays is that I lose the boy at home. Tell Edith that I am glad she retains her post at the Treasury, although it is long time empty. I have not heard that she recᵈ $20. in a letter sent 14ᵗʰ Janʸ I have left with Mr Wiley ³⁷ money to be sent as it is collected, and, I suppose, within two or three days he will send, say $90. to your mother's order. I dare not send a draft I hold for Mr Cheney of 50. until I replenish my purse. If the Toronto letter ³⁸ has not come, it is, no doubt, because Mr Edgar ³⁹ waits till he thinks I am at home. When it comes tho' it will want my endorsement Mr Cheney will no doubt pay it & hold it till I return. Thank Mamma for her letter, & tell her we expect to be preserved, or better. I hope the Milton party was happy.

R. W. Emerson

I shall go to Pittsburg, say, 27ᵗʰ or 28, & stay there. W. H. Kincaid's care.⁴⁰ And expect to return thence immediately leaving on the 6ᵗʰ for home: and I believe I am to be at Gloucester, 11ᵗʰ ⁴¹

To ——————————, INDIANAPOLIS? JANUARY 24? 1863

[Described in Jan. 30, 1863, as a telegram to Erie, Pa.]

35. See Jan. 30 following for Pittsburgh and for a more detailed account of the Indianapolis adventure.

36. Edward had written, Jan. 16, 1863, that he passed his week of examinations safely but that Tom Ward's fate was still undecided.

37. B. B. Wiley, of Chicago, appears in numerous letters.

38. For the lectures at Toronto, see Jan. 8, 1863.

39. Doubtless the J. D. Edgar mentioned in a note on Jan. 29, 1860.

40. In the MS this phrase is set off by an irregular line.

41. According to the MS memorandum book for 1862, 1863, and 1864, the subject for Gloucester, Mass., was " Perpetual Forces." *The Gloucester Telegraph, and News,* Feb. 14, 1863, reported that the lecture of the 11th was " Emerson all over."

To ELLEN EMERSON, PITTSBURGH, JANUARY 30, 1863 [42]

Monongahela House
Pittsburg, Pa.
30 Jan. 1863

Dear Ellen,

Thanks for the excellent history I received last night, by the hands of Mr Kincaid.[43] Only, at the end, it appears that it is too good either to keep or to destroy. What to do? Milton & all its persons shine & glow in your pictures. But Richards, of whom I have never heard, is the hero of the scene.

I did not have good fortune in my trip to Indianapolis [44] for though my engagement there was made months ago yet the day remained to be fixed by the Chicago Committee & they did it so late that when I arrived at I. on Friday eve, there was no preparation for me & the secretary had sent letters to Chicago which never arrived to me stating the impossibilities, &c. Well, I will stay till tomorrow night. On inquiry, the hall, sole hall, is engaged then. — On Monday night, then. " No; on Monday the Union meeting: Not possible is lecture till Tuesday." But, at Chicago, not suspecting difficulty here, I had emptied my pockets, & made it necessary to read here. So I accepted Tuesday, & telegraphed to Erie, whence I had urgent invitation, that I could come there on

42. MS owned by RWEMA; ph. in CUL.

43. *Cf.* Jan. 24, 1863. According to the *Directory of Pittsburgh and Allegheny Cities,* 1864, William H. Kincaid was a clerk. Newspaper advertisements show he served as a member of the lecture committee.

44. *Cf.* Jan. 24, 1863. *The Indianapolis Daily Journal* of Jan. 26, 1863, told of Emerson's plight and threw some light on how he used his enforced leisure: " This distinguished philosopher and author has been in our city since Friday night, waiting an opportunity to deliver a lecture before the Young Men's Christian Association . . . The accidental occupancy of Masonic Hall every night till Tuesday night has caused the delay, which we may hope will not be unprofitable or unpleasing to our distinguished visitor. On Saturday morning he visited the Blind Asylum, where he witnessed the examination of the different classes . . . Mr. Emerson addressed them for a few minutes. . . . At the request of Mr. Churchman . . . he recited a pretty little ballad of Sir Walter Scott's." The same paper for Jan. 28 reported Emerson's lecture of the 27th on " Clubs, or Conversation " and made some interesting, if not very elegant, comments on the lecturer's style: " The delivery simply gets out the idea, and don't try to keep it on its feet afterwards, and the idea takes no pains to shape itself so as to let the delivery have a graceful task of it. He has a fashion of seeming to forget the last word or two, always significant . . . and stumbling upon them unexpectedly with an effect that the most elaborate declamation could not produce. This is manifestly not a trick of the rostrum, but the necessary halting of the speech to let the idea catch up with it."

Wednesday Answer, "not possible on Wednesday." Bad, for to Erie belongs the correspondence with Meadville.[45] However Mr Davis [46] at Ind—— made my visit or imprisonment in dingy hotel & muddy town as tolerable as he could, brought me lawyers & college professors, carried me to hear Gottschalk & Patti [47] (!) The best feature in the city is, that it is laid out on the model of Washington City & its streets are named for the States. I was in Massachusetts St., California St. & others. 30 000, population. On Wednesday hitherward, & arrived Thursday Morning; but am out of reach of Meadville,[48] I find, & have no duty here till Tuesday 3^d & Thursday, 5th [49] Yesterday with Mr Gilman [50] a purser of the Navy, with whom I came here, I visited the Arsenal & afterwards the forge of Knapp, Rudd, & Co [51] to see the casting of a 15 inch cannon, which is the sublime in mechanics. The look into the furnace is like looking at the sun, and, after the eye is a little used to it, you begin to see the white iron thawing into drops & rivulets, like thawing glaciers, until presently you see floating islands, all white, in the white sea. We stayed a couple of hours: at last the ore was ready in the two great furnaces; the great clay spouts, one from each, were heated by burning chips, &c. and the rosy iron brooks rushed out along these channels, say 40 feet long each, into the mould, which is sunk into a perpendicular pit 18 or 20 ft deep Tis a wonderful spectacle, & one comes to look at every one in the crowd of workmen with vast respect.

——

Here has just come into my room your letter of the 25th, containing Edith's letters, & the Antioch one.

I am sorry to find that you have been uneasy in not hearing from me.

45. Apparently Emerson lectured at neither Erie nor Meadville.

46. As Davis brought lawyers, he was probably Edwin A. Davis, of the law firm of Davis & Bowles, listed in *H. H. Dodd & Co.'s Indianapolis City Directory*, 1863.

47. The farewell concerts of L. M. Gottschalk, pianist and composer, and Carlotta Patti, prima donna, were advertised for the Masonic Hall, Jan. 23 and 24 (*The Indianapolis Daily Journal*, Jan. 23 and 24, 1863).

48. *Cf.* Jan. c. 12, 1863.

49. *The Daily Pittsburgh Gazette and Commercial Journal*, Feb. 4, 1863, reported the reading of "Clubs" on the 3d before the Young Men's Mercantile Library Association in a hall the temperature of which was "somewhere between 32° and zero according to our estimate." The same paper, Feb. 5, announced "Classes of Men" for that night.

50. Of the Gilmans who were paymasters at this time, Augustus H. seems the most likely. According to the official *Register of Officers and Agents . . . Thirtieth September, 1863*, he was on special duty at Cairo, Ill.

51. The *Directory of Pittsburgh and Allegheny Cities*, 1862, gives the name as Knap, Rudd & Co.

It is often so inconvenient to write, my stay in each place is usually short & much interrupted, that I confine myself to letters of necessity. I doubted not, the Canada letter would come: so will, if it has not, one from Mr Wiley at Chicago [52] (after the 23ᵈ) containing money, though he may wait several days to receive money due from Ann Arbor [53] & Beloit.[54] You say you will pay Warren [55] $20. I paid him $50. leaving only 8., I think, due.

For Edward, if his needs for a coat were great, he can go to James Tolman, & have one made & charged, though I suppose it will cost more than at MacCullan's.[56]

Edith should have told me what was the subject of Miss Biggs's note. I shall no doubt come home from this place by a very direct course, leaving P. on Friday, & hardly stopping in N. Y., unless compelled: Yet perhaps can not reach home before Monday Morn. I send today $50. to Mr Cheney in a draft on Mechanics Bank N. Y. to pay my debt at the Bank. Edward must look carefully to Mike. Tell the last to be a very good boy, and that I am putting great dependence on him, day by day. I hope Mamma forgives me also for not writing. Love to her & all.

R. W. Emerson

To WILLIAM EMERSON, CONCORD, FEBRUARY 8, 1863 [57]

Concord
Feb. 8, 1863

Dear William,

On coming home last night,[58] Ellen gave me news of you & your house, & of Charles's advance in rank [59] (I hope it is) . I left Pittsburgh in time, I hoped, to dine or at least spend an evening with you, but encountered a snowdrift on the mountains which delayed us for some hours, & I reached New York late at night, slept at the St Denis, & took

52. For letters expected from Toronto and Chicago, see Jan. 24, 1863.

53. The MS memorandum book for 1862, 1863, and 1864 shows that " The Third Estate in Literature " was scheduled for Ann Arbor, Jan. 16, 1863.

54. The *Beloit Journal and Courier,* Jan. 29, 1863, complained that though a lecture by a person of lesser importance could attract a paying audience, Emerson's " The Third Estate in Literature" of Jan. 21 was not a financial success for the Archæan Union.

55. *Cf.* Jan. 10, 1863, to Edith Emerson.

56. Probably Emerson means John McCullum, listed as a tailor in *The Boston Directory,* 1862.

57. MS owned by HCL; ph. in CUL.

58. From the Western lecture tour narrated in earlier letters.

59. For Charles Emerson's war record, see a note on Sept. 29, 1862.

the morning train to Boston, as my sole hope to arrive last night. I grieved to go by you in so savage a way.

I find here at home a letter from Ralph Haskins asking from me a letter in his behalf to Gov Boutwell to solicit an appointment to the stamp office in Boston [60] &c Now I know nothing of R. H. Do you know if he is, or if he is reputed, honest & capable? He tells me, he is trying to get a living as a real-estate-broker in State Street; but that his property in Virginia is irreparably lost by the war. If you can answer these Jeffersonian queries favorably, pray do so at once, & I must wait to answer him. If I go to Boston, I will talk with Jewett, who is good & frank, &, I think, I could gather his impressions. But if I could write the best report of him, his chances must yet be small. Dear love to Susan. I hear the best accounts of the brave boys. Affectionately,

Waldo E.

To George Luther Stearns, Concord, February 18, 1863 [61]

Concord —
Wednesday, 18 Feb. 1863

My dear Sir,

I am promised at Montreal, Canada, on Tuesday & Thursday of next week.[62] But if I were at liberty, an enterprise such as your note suggests [63] is quite foreign to my habits or power. I live solitary in the country, because I have not skill to talk with people, & draw them to my views. Mr Phillips has genius for this task, & I delight in his devotion to it. Nor do I, at this moment, think of the right colleague for him,

60. Haskins, Boston, Feb. 7, 1863. It is not clear whether the letter to Boutwell was written.

61. MS owned by Mr. F. R. Fraprie; ph. in CUL.

62. According to the MS memorandum book for 1862, 1863, and 1864, Emerson was to read " Classes of Men " and " Clubs " at Montreal. The dates Feb. 24, 25, and 26, 1863, are listed; but the 24th is marked as doubtful and the 26th is canceled. The Montreal visit of this winter is recalled in Feb. 8, 1864.

63. Stearns had written, Boston, Feb. 18, 1863, asking Emerson to go with others to Washington the following week and help impress upon Lincoln New England views regarding the conduct of the war; he suggested that Wendell Phillips should make the political statement and that Emerson should be responsible for the proper moral and intellectual impression. If Conway gives his dates correctly, he and others, including Phillips and Stearns, had already called at the White House and had made an opening; and now, it seems, plans were afoot for a final drive (cf. Conway, Autobiography, I, 377 ff., and F. P. Stearns, The Life, 277 ff.) . Emerson did not go on the projected mission, but the letters of this year show his growing interest in political affairs.

to represent the second part you indicate. Bryant in New York; or
Beecher; — in Boston, James F. Clarke were a good man.

Yours faithfully,

R. W. Emerson

Geo. L. Stearns, Esq.

To F. N. Knapp, Concord? February 23? 1863

[Mentioned in Feb. 23, 1863, to Redpath; about Walt Whitman.]

To James Redpath, Concord, February 23, 1863

[MS owned by the New York Historical Society; printed in Donaldson, pp.
143–144.]

To Benjamin B. Wiley, Concord, February 23, 1863 [64]

Concord

Feb 23 1863–

My dear Sir

Your letter containing Mr. Thoreau's letters [65] arrived safely
three days ago: So did your earlier notes, & all the remittances to Mrs.
Emerson or to Edith.[66] I am afraid you have found us a very slow &
ungrateful house, after your many & kindest actions in our behalf. But
I believe my daughters were absent in Boston — as they were for weeks
when your first letters came. Nor can I find them now to recite their own
apologies. The letters of Mr. Thoreau are characteristically excellent, &
shall go presently to his sister,[67] & be kept for you. Your own letter will

64. MS copy, not in Emerson's hand, owned by RWEMA; ph. in CUL. A number
of later letters are to this same friend, who, according to a note in Thoreau, *The
Writings*, VI, 298, had earlier lived in Providence. *John C. W. Bailey's Chicago City
Directory*, 1864, shows he was a member of Wiley Bros. & Co., bankers, in the heart
of the business district.

65. Probably those to Wiley later printed among Thoreau's letters. *Cf.* May 1,
1865. Wiley's interest in Thoreau is mentioned in Jan. 24, 1857.

66. *Cf.* Jan. 30, 1863.

67. Sophia Thoreau took much interest in her brother's letters and especially desired that Emerson, in his edition of 1865, should include as much as possible that
would show the friendly, familiar figure she knew. On Jan. 28, 1865, Ellen Emerson
wrote to her father that Miss Thoreau had called that day, anxious about the proofs,
and "desires that you should know that all kind beginnings and endings of Mr
Thoreau's letters, and little messages to friends, being left out give a too cold idea
of him, agreeing with the popular notion that he wanted affection." Sophia's feeling
seems to have prompted Sanborn's purpose to prepare a new edition, to include particularly "familiar" letters (*cf. The Writings*, VI, xi) .

interest her much, — as it ought. I am to be a traveller again today,[68] & will only say, therefore, what you have probably already found, that the lines, " If this great world of joy & pain." are Wordsworth's, contained in his volume called, " Yarrow Revisited & Other Poems," — a little piece by itself. I fear I doctored the last line of it, for my purposes. My answer to your letters must be still postponed. But I am glad you will come & see me soon.

With great regard
R. W. Emerson —

To Ethan Allen Hitchcock, Concord and Boston, February 28, 1863 [69]

Concord
28 Feb.ʸ 1863

My dear Sir,

I learn with great regret that the name of Brigadier General Barlow of New York originally nominated by the President, after the battle of Antietam,[70] is not returned in the list newly sent to the Senate for confirmation.[71] This omission is deeply lamented by many good persons here to whom General Barlow is known. A man of great natural ability, — from a boy, first among his mates; at Harvard College, first in his class; and in the army, which he entered as a private, so strong was the impression of personal power he made, that he rapidly became Brigadier General, — we have looked on him as one of those valuable officers which the war was creating. I earnestly hope, & I am sure I speak

68. To Montreal, no doubt (cf. Feb. 18, 1863).

69. MS owned by Mr. Robert Shaw Barlow; ph. in CUL. Ethan Allen Hitchcock was Lincoln's military adviser. He had gone to Concord in Aug., 1861, to see Emerson, and again, it seems, in the following year (Hitchcock's diary, Fifty Years, ed. W. A. Croffut, 1909, pp. 432 and 444). Cf. also Nov. 20, 1863.

70. Cf. a note on Dec. 3, 1862.

71. Major General James F. McKinley, the Adjutant General, informs me that, according to the records of the War Department, Francis C. Barlow was given a recess appointment by letter on Sept. 19, 1862, as brigadier general of volunteers in the service of the United States, with rank from Sept. 19, 1862, for distinguished conduct at the battle of Fair Oaks; he accepted the appointment Oct. 4, 1862, subject to confirmation by the Senate at its next session; his nomination was transmitted to the Senate by a message from Lincoln on Dec. 23, 1862, and again on Mar. 9, 1863; on Apr. 4 of the latter year he was duly commissioned, agreeably to nomination and confirmation, with rank from Sept. 19, 1862; and, finally, he acknowledged receipt of the commission on Apr. 25, 1863.

the thought of many informed persons, that his name may yet be brought so prominently before the President, that his service & genius may be secured to the country. His wounds at Antietam, which are slowly healing, & in spite of which the surgeons promise early return to duty, ought to plead strongly in the same interest. May I ask of your goodness to give effect to this statement in the Presidents mind.

With great respect,
R. W. Emerson

Major General Hitchcock

I am happy in finding a few gentlemen near me [72] who add their signatures as concurring in this statement.

R. W Emerson

We heartily concur

J. M Forbes
E. R. Hoar —
Saml G. Ward

I am happy in finding a few gentlemen near me who add their signatures as concurring in this statement.

Horace Gray Jr
Charles Eliot Norton.
J. R. Lowell.
Nathl Hawthorne
O. W. Holmes
E. P. Whipple
Estes Howe
C. R. Lowell, Jr
S. G. Howe.

To James Redpath? Concord? February? c. 28? 1863

[According to Donaldson, p. 144, Emerson, on his return from Montreal, " wrote to or saw " several friends about Whitman and gave Redpath " a letter to show other persons, indorsing Mr. Whitman." Cf. Feb. 23, 1863, to Redpath.]

72. This postscript, on a sheet with the printed caption " Parker House," was evidently written at the Saturday Club. Feb. 28, 1863, was Saturday and the regular meeting would have been on the last Saturday of the month. Of the signers, all were members of the Club except Horace Gray, Jr. (later a member) , and C. R. Lowell, Jr. The letter, which reached Hitchcock, it seems, through Barlow, was later returned to Barlow, his son informs me, with the remark that he ought to keep it on account of the signatures. For Emerson's delay in sending the letter to Barlow in the first place, see Mar.? c. 10? 1863.

To CHARLES SUMNER, CONCORD, MARCH 1, 1863 [73]

Concord
1 March 1863

My dear Sumner,

I learned in town yesterday, that W. T. G. Morton is again besieging Congress with a claim of reward to himself for Dr Jackson's discovery.[74] I trust there is no danger that such a wrong can be done.

Dr Jackson is a skilful chemist, but is no match for this sturdy adversary in the tactics of aggression. He has never made the smallest claim for a reward. But, when another makes a false claim to *his* discovery, he is bound for truth's sake to resist it. Meanwhile, it is certain, that Dr Jackson first of known men made the discovery that sulphuric ether paralyzes the sensations of pain; that he communicated it to Morton, & taught him how to use it; & was himself the advising physician, & solely responsible for the success, when Morton made the first experiment at the Hospital — in 1846. Dr J. had already made the discovery known, as early as 1842, to several persons. —

By various acts & words, Morton, in 1846–7, admitted the discovery to be Dr J.'s I cannot trespass on you now with details — but it is a sad story the injustice with which Dr J. has been treated in this, which should have been his glory — But if now or hereafter it will be of any use, I can furnish good evidence of his just claim, and I think I understand some of the causes of the opposition he has encountered.

Ever yours faithfully,
R. W. Emerson

Hon. Charles Sumner.
U. S. Senate

73. MS owned by RWEMA; ph. in CUL.

74. A petition by Morton praying remuneration as the " original discoverer " of practical anæsthesia and for its use in the army and navy, was presented in the Senate on Jan. 24, 1863, and was referred to the Committee on Military Affairs and the Militia (*Journal of the Senate,* 37th Cong., 3d Sess., p. 144) . This committee submitted a lengthy report which gave the opinion that some compensation was due to Morton but made no recommendation. The appendices contained a narrative of the discovery; an analysis of the testimony of the contestants for the honor; and extracts from the H. R. report of 1849 and from that of 1852, which had been agreed upon but not presented for lack of opportunity. (Senate report 89, 37th Cong., 3d Sess.) For the history of the Morton controversy, see especially a note on Apr. 20 and 21, 1848, and *cf.* Apr. 18, 1864, to Boutwell.

To Edward Waldo Emerson, Concord? March 3, 1863 [75]

Tuesday 3 March

Dear Edward,

If you want a hat, as Edith says, go to Bent & Bush, & ask Mr Rhoades to furnish you one & charge it to me [76]

R. W. E

To Edward Waldo Emerson, Concord, March? 6, 1863? [77]

Friday 6

Dear Edward,

You are coming up tomorrow — I find it necessary to go down in the morning, & shall return in the last train. I am sorry not to dine at home with you. But if your hours permit, you might take our train into Boston at Porters at 9.20 & find me in the last car; and yourself take the 11 o'c train in Boston.[78] But if this crosses your plans, I shall still you at home in the evening. R. W. E

To Thomas Russell, Concord? March c. 8, 1863

[Russell, Boston, Mar. 6 (endorsed 1863), told of a plan to raise funds, at a meeting then set for the 18th, to equip a Negro regiment, the Fifty-fourth, and asked Emerson to make a brief speech on that occasion. Russell, Boston, Mar. 12, 1863, acknowledged " Your note . . . duly rec'd " and hoped Emerson would be there on Mar. 20 (as the date was now given). For Emerson's attendance, see the note on Mar. 24 following.]

To Francis Channing Barlow, Concord? March? c. 10? 1863 [79]

My dear Sir

I send these few lines thus late to you. I was going to send them to Washington, but heard Mr G. L. Stearns say that some joint applica-

75. MS owned by RWEMA; ph. in CUL. The year " '63 " below the date line was probably added by another hand. The full date was endorsed, apparently by Edward.

76. *The Boston Directory*, 1863, lists Bent & Bush, dealers in hats, caps, and furs, and gives Jacob Rhoades at the same address.

77. MS owned by RWEMA; ph. in CUL. Another hand, apparently Edward's, has added " March 1863 " to the date line, and Mar. 6 fell on Friday in 1863. The reference to Porter's Station, Cambridge, also tends to confirm the date, as it indicates a time during Edward's college years.

78. The train leaving Boston for Concord at 11 a.m. is listed in the *Boston Daily Advertiser*, Mar. 6, 1863, where, however, the schedule for Cambridge is not given.

79. MS owned by Mr. Robert Shaw Barlow; ph. in CUL. The inclosure referred

tion was proposed in your behalf,[80] and I suppose you will be consulted
& can add this note to others. I earnestly hope that the country will not
lack your service nor you a great & auspicious fortune.

With kindest regards,

R. W. Emerson

General Barlow.

To WILLIAM EMERSON, CONCORD, MARCH 11, 1863 [81]

Concord

11 March, 1863

Dear William,

Mr Conway came to me this morning to say that he
wished to sell his house in Concord.[82] He is, you know, the editor of the
" Commonwealth " newspaper in Boston, & begins to find it very inconvenient to live here. Then he is now proposing to go in April to England, & there stay till October.[83] And he added, that he had promised
(I so understood him,) Mrs Wm Emerson, that he would let her know
if he should at any time wish to sell the house. I asked him, on what
terms would he sell it? He said, he wished to sell the house *and the
furniture* together, and the real price for both, — for he had no " asking
price," — is $5000. I asked, if he had made any repairs, since he took the
place? " No, none; but the garden, vines, &c were now in perfect order."
He gave $4000. for the house; a very low price, as we all thought: but,
in the depreciation of the currency, I suppose, might well ask 4500. now,
for the same value.

I also remember that he had it on very easy terms of payment, & I
suppose might transfer to the purchaser whatever of the debt is unpaid,

---

to must have been the letter of Feb. 28, 1863. How long the delay was is a matter of
pure conjecture.

80. The General Hitchcock of Feb. 28, 1863, had dined at Stearns's home in April
of the preceding year (F. P. Stearns, *The Life*, pp. 264–265) .

81. MS owned by HCL; ph. in CUL.

82. For Conway's brief residence in Concord, see a note on Nov. 15 and 17? 1862?

83. *The Commonwealth*, Boston, Mar. 27, 1863: " MONCURE D. CONWAY will soon
sail for Europe, and will write exclusively for the Commonwealth. Mr. C. will remain for the most part in England, in constant communication with those who there
advocate the cause of America." The same paper for Apr. 17 following reports that
" M. D. CONWAY, one of the Editors, has sailed for Europe." Conway's decision to go
to England as a propagandist for the Northern cause, his voyage thither, and his
subsequent residence there during many years are recorded at length in his *Autobiography*, I, 388 ff. *et passim*.

on the same terms. If there be any such good will in you as has sometimes been to buy a house here, write me at once what your wishes are
on the matter.

We heard with entire interest Susan's letter to Ellen & Charles's to
Haven. I grieve to hear of William's feebler health. Ellen has sent, I
believe, her reply. I neither like to spare nor to refuse her to Susan.

With dear love to all the house,
Waldo E.

TO PERCIVAL BONNEY, CONCORD? MARCH *c.* 13? 1863

[Bonney, Waterville, Me., Mar. 11, 1863, said Emerson had been elected orator
of the Erosophian Adelphi of Waterville College at their anniversary of Aug.
11 following and asked his lowest terms in an immediate reply. Bonney wrote
again, Mar. 30, 1863, accepting Emerson's terms — " viz $50." In the *General
Catalogue of . . . Colby College,* 1920, Bonney is listed as a graduate in the
class of 1863.]

TO J. H. STEPHENSON, CONCORD? MARCH 24, 1863

[Described in Stephenson, Boston, Mar. 26, 1863, as inclosing $10, Emerson's
subscription to the fund for the Fifty-fourth Regiment; Stephenson also referred to Emerson's remarks made at the recent meeting. The *Boston Daily
Advertiser* of Mar. 21 of this year reports the meeting of the 20th at Chickering Hall in support of Shaw's Negro regiment and mentions Emerson as one
of the speakers — " Quite a large sum was collected, almost every gentleman
present putting down his name for something." *Cf.* the letters of Mar. *c.* 8 and
Sept. 10, 1863.]

TO SEVER AND FRANCIS, CONCORD, MARCH 30, 1863 [84]

Concord,
30 March, 1863

Gentlemen,

You are quite at liberty to use the little poem " The Mountain & the Squirrel," [85] in the way you propose.

Respectfully,
R. W. Emerson

Messieurs Sever & Francis.

84. MS owned by the Public Library, Boston; ph. in CUL.
85. That is, the " Fable," first published many years earlier.

To William R. Emerson, Concord? April 4, 1863

[William R. Emerson, Boston, Apr. 2, 1863, charges, jestingly, that the Concord Emerson has pirated a couple of his pieces, "The Shadow Dance" and "Maggie's Gone." William R. Emerson, Apr. 5, 1863, acknowledged the "note of yesterday"; he explained that he had not sent the verses "Maggie's Gone" but that they were sent by Whipple — Edwin Percy Whipple, no doubt — on Apr. 1 and in the spirit of that day, as appeared from inquiry at the office of the *Transcript*. The *Boston Evening Transcript*, Mar. 17, 1863, published some uninspired verses entitled "The Shadow Dance," inscribed to Maggie Mitchell and signed "W. R. E." Presumably these verses and perhaps "Maggie's Gone," which I have not seen, were printed elsewhere on Apr. 1 or 2 over the same initials differently ordered. For William R. Emerson, see Jan. 1, 1857.]

To Matilda Ashurst Biggs, Concord, April 8, 1863 [86]

Concord —
April 8, 1863

My dear Mrs Biggs,

I send you hearty thanks, — though so late, — for your prized letter, which arrived when I was absent on a long journey in our Western States.[87] I read it with joy on my return. I wished to write instantly, as I ought. But my absence had provided me with a crowd of duties on my coming home, and I waited days & weeks and — But I did not love less [I]the probity & honor[I] which prompted this protest [II]against what appears the governing opinion in England,[II] — nor could I expect less from you. It looks so easy & inevitable to be just & noble when we see good people, that we cannot account for any others. Your beautiful house [88] at Leicester, & the beautiful & excellent people in it, shine in my memory out of such a rearground of years! I wish to see the mother again, & the beautiful children once more. All that I heard of you — in the short interview I had with your father,[89] — or from others — has been happy. [III]I remember that Mr Biggs in Leicester questioned me on the point — why good & cultivated men in America avoided politics (for so he had heard) & let them fall into bad hands? He will find in our calamities today the justification of his warning — Our sky is very dark but the feeling is very general in the Union that bad as the war

86. MS owned by Miss Maude Ashurst Biggs; ph. in CUL. Excerpts I–III are in Conway, *Emerson at Home and Abroad*, pp. 272–273.

87. Recorded in the letters of Jan., 1863.

88. For Emerson's visit there, see Dec. 15, 1847, to Biggs and Jan. 24, 1848.

89. William Henry Ashurst had come to Concord nearly ten years earlier (see Aug. 13, 1853).

is it is far safer & better than the foregoing peace. Our best ground of
hope now is in the healthy sentiment which appears in reasonable people all over the country, accepting sacrifices, but meaning riddance
from slavery, & from Southern domination. I fear this sentiment is not
yet represented by our government or its agents in Europe, but it is
sporadic in the country. Indeed the governments of both England &
America are far in the rear of their best constituencies. in England, as
shown in the resolution with which the government shuts its eyes to
the building of ships of war in your ports to attack the Republic, —
now in this spasm to throw off slavery. This unlooked for attitude of
England is our gravest foreign disadvantage — But I have gone quite
too far into these painful politics whose gloom is only to be relieved by
the largest considerations. I rejoice in so many assurances of sound
heart & clear perception as come to us from excellent persons in England, — among which I rank your letter chiefly; — and the significant
sympathy of the Manchester workmen, which I wish had been better
met.[III] I beg you to present my kindest remembrances to Mr Biggs, &
to the young people of your house though they be 14 or 15 years older
than they are in my memory. I dare hope that when better days soon
come I shall yet see inmate or friend of your house here in mine. May
it be so!

Your affectionate servant,
R. W. Emerson.

To Matilda Ashurst Biggs, Concord, April 9, 1863 [90]

Concord
April 9 1863

My dear Mrs Biggs,

Will you let me make you acquainted with Mr Moncure D.
Conway, a gentleman of great worth & ability, who goes to London on
the invitation of some friends of Freedom & of America there, who
wish justice done to the best public opinion here.[91] Mr Conway is a
native of Virginia, & thoroughly knows the South Country, &, for the
last ten years, has been a resident in the North, which is his true home.
He is a very accomplished person, & has eminent ability as a public
speaker, as well as an intelligent companion.

With great regard,
R. W. Emerson

90. MS owned by Miss Maude Ashurst Biggs; ph. in CUL.
91. *Cf.* a note on Mar. 11, 1863.

To Alexander Ireland, Concord, April 9, 1863 [92]

ᴵConcord

9 April, 1863ᴵ —

My dear Ireland,

ᴵᴵMr Moncure D. Conway, a valued neighbor of mine, and a man full of public & private virtues, goes to England just now, having, as I understand, both inward & outward provocation to defend the cause of America, there.[93] I can assure you, out of much knowledge, that he is very competent to this duty, if it be one. He is a Virginian by birth & breeding; & now for many years a Northerner in residence & in sentiment. He is a man of excellent ability in speaking & writing, and I grudge to spare his usefulness at home even to a contingency so important as the correcting of opinion in England. In making you acquainted with Mr Conway, I charge him to remind you that the first moment of American Peace will be the best time for you to come over & pay us & *me* a long promised visit.ᴵᴵ

With affectionate remembrances, Yours,

A. Ireland, Esq.   R. W. Emerson

To Thomas Carlyle, Concord? April? *c.* 9? 1863

[Conway, *Thomas Carlyle,* p. v, says that, early in 1863, when he first visited England, Emerson gave him a letter of introduction to Carlyle. For the probable date, *cf.* the letters of Apr. 9 to Mrs. Biggs and Ireland.]

To William Edward Forster, Concord, April 16, 1863 [94]

Concord⎱ April 16

Massᵗᵗˢ⎰   1863

My dear Mr Forster,

Will you allow me to make you acquainted with William M. Evarts, Esq. of New York, a gentleman of great worth, & of excellent connection here, who embarks for England tomorrow. Mr Evarts is a lawyer at the head of the New York bar, enjoying entirely the confidence of the Government at Washington,[95] & representing the best side

92. MS owned by Mr. W. T. H. Howe; ph. in CUL. Excerpts I–II are in Ireland, *In Memoriam*, pp. 89–90.

93. *Cf.* a note on Mar. 11, 1863.

94. MS owned by Mr. W. T. H. Howe; ph. in CUL.

95. During this crisis the American minister to England was supplied by his government with a number of special assistants — a " complete cabinet," according to

of politics, in what we call the " Empire City." As he has the wish to communicate with intelligent Englishmen on the public questions, I think at once of you. And the danger of a disaster so vast as war between England & America gives extreme importance to every opportunity of intercourse between good & wise persons of each country.

Thanks for every public word that comes from you. In common with all good men here, — & more than they all if possible — I have rejoiced in your efficient friendship to this country,[96] & to the cause of civilization. Mr Evarts shall thank you & your compatriot champions, & may their number be suddenly multiplied! With most affectionate remembrances,

W. E. Forster, Esq.   R. W. Emerson

To RICHARD MONCKTON MILNES, CONCORD, APRIL 16, 1863 [97]

$$\left. \text{Concord} \atop \text{Mass}^{tts} \right\} \begin{array}{l} \text{16 April} \\ \text{1863.} \end{array}$$

My dear Mr Milnes,

Will you allow me, on the claim of much old kindness of yours, to recall myself to your memory after many years, that I may introduce to your acquaintance William M. Evarts, Esq. of New York. Mr Evarts is a lawyer at the head of the bar of New York, a gentleman enjoying the entire confidence of the Government at Washington, & representing the best side of politics in his own important city. At this moment, with such anxious questions arising between England and America, it seems a necessity to bring the most intelligent persons in both countries into communication.[98] Mr E. is provided, I believe, with many letters, but I

---

the minister himself, who was somewhat annoyed by their interference in what he considered his own business but had, nevertheless, a high opinion of Evarts (*A Cycle of Adams Letters 1861–1865*, ed. Worthington C. Ford, 1920, I, 282 and 297). Evarts later served as attorney general of the United States and as secretary of state.

96. Forster's notable activities in Parliament as a friend of the North are mentioned in T. Wemyss Reid, *Life of the Right Honourable William Edward Forster*, 2d ed., 1888, I, 333–338. Emerson must have become well acquainted with Forster during their days together in Paris (see a note on May 17, 1848).

97. MS owned by the Marquess of Crewe; ph. in CUL.

98. For Evarts and his mission abroad, see especially a note on the letter of the same date to Forster. Emerson's introduction was not written in vain. The Marquess of Crewe informs me that he himself well remembers Evarts, " who became the friend both of my father and of Lord Rosebery." Milnes is mentioned in many earlier letters. He was elevated to the peerage as Baron Houghton a few months after the present letter was written.

think his list incomplete without your name. And I heartily hope that no mischance will prevent Mr Evarts from seeing you.

With affectionate remembrances,

R. W. Emerson

R. M. Milnes, Esq. M. P.

To Edith Emerson, Concord, April? 1863? [99]

Concord
Thursday Morning

Dear Edith,

I think I shall not come down today, & so send you the ticket to the Union Club, which you must give to a good hearer.

Papa

To William Emerson, Concord, May 5, 1863 [100]

Concord
5 May, 1863.

Dear William,

Your despatch by telegraph did not reach me until nearly one o'clock of the next day, namely, Saturday. and by the bad custom of our local offices was dated on the day when received, i. e. May 2^d. I went at once to our Depot-master to inquire the date of the despatch he had received from Waltham or Boston, & he assured me that the date of the original was the same, & " it had left New York *this morning.*" So I told Melvin,[101] the sexton, that the body [102] would not arrive until Monday, and that it should be lodged on its arrival in the receiving tomb, until he could build a vault. But Hannah [103] came to our house at 7 o'clock, *walking,* — disappointed of finding us at the station, — & having lost her way to the house. It was vexing to pity. But we were all

99. MS owned by RWEMA; ph. in CUL. A penciled endorsement gives the conjectural date: " In 1863 (probably April)." Among the Emerson papers is a printed letter from the Union Club of Boston, dated Feb. 21, 1863, which is an invitation to membership.

100. MS owned by HCL; ph. in CUL.

101. The same who appears in May 30, 1859. It is not clear whether he is the Jonas Melvin of Jan. 10, 1863, to Edith Emerson.

102. The *New-York Daily Tribune,* May 4, 1863, records the death of the aunt whose fame is known to all students of Emerson: " On Friday, May 1, at the home of Mr. Augustus Parsons, at Williamsburg, Mary Moody Emerson, daughter of the Rev. William Emerson of Concord, Mass., in the 89th year of her age."

103. Hannah Haskins Parsons; cf. June 1, 1863, to William Emerson. For her dedication, almost from childhood, to the care of Mary Moody Emerson, see a note on Apr. 6, 1826.

so glad to see her, & to know her triumphant in her perfect patience, & that this long task of hers was ended. She was not fatigued by her journey, & interested us by her narrative of all that had occurred. Melvin conveyed the body, that evening, to the cemetery. The next day, Hannah went to church, & Mrs Ripley & Elizabeth R. & Elizabeth Hoar came to see her. Yesterday, Melvin made his vault, on the same line with Mother's, that is, on the border of your lot & mine, and, at 3 o'clock P. M., Mary Emerson Simmons, Elizabeth Hoar, Elizabeth Ripley, Lidian, Ellen, Edith, & I, followed the hearse from the receiving tomb to the grave. It was a pleasant misty day such as Aunt would have chosen, — and the rain waited till we had laid her in the ground an hour. I brought all our friends home with me, telling them I would produce all the memorabilia of the Sibyl, if they desired; They came, but did not ask for memories, and I reserved them. The present is ever too strong for the past, & in so many late years she has been only a wreck, & in all years could so readily be repulsive, that few know or care for her genius. Yet I who cling always to her writings, forget every thing else very fast, though her behaviour, when I saw it, was intolerable. Her genius was the purest and though I have learned to discriminate & drop what a huge alloy of theology & metaphysics, her letters & journals charm me still as thirty years ago, & honor the American air. Tis pity you should not come to Concord to live, for I should make you as intimate with her beauties as Elizabeth Hoar & I are, but they cannot be shown to you except in free & disengaged moods.

Love to Susan, & to William & Haven. No news I trust can come from Charles but good, in these eventful days.

I was to have written you ten days ago, that E. Hoar had heard from Hannah, that Aunt Mary's expenses were 25 dollars per quarter more than her income. I suppose, that means, than her board.

Ellen has never heard from William, to whom she wrote & I sent by express, ten days ago, a " Concord grape," & two or three cuttings of " Sage grape." I hope they arrived. They were addressed, 1 Park Place.[104]

Affectionately, Waldo E.

E. H. says she has 2 or 3 *wills* of Aunt, but thinks you have a later.

104. According to *Trow's New York City Directory*, 1863, William Emerson's law office was at 1 Park Place and his home at 109 W. 22d St. William Emerson, Jr., according to the same authority, had his law office at 937 Broadway and his home at 154 W. 48th St.

To Richard Frederic Fuller, Concord, May 15? 1863 [105]

Concord —
May 16, 1863 —

My dear Sir,

On coming home, I found your note & Book.[106] I thank you for the book, which does honor to your love & care for your brave Brother. In my hasty examination of the chapters, I see ample testimony to his activity in his profession, & to the esteem he enjoyed in society. His death reacts to raise every moment of his life.

For the matter of a notice of the book in the " Atlantic," [107] the only course I ever allow myself, & therefore the only one I can propose to you, is, to send a copy of the work to J. T. Fields, the Editor. Much more than this is doubtless sometimes done, but this I think is all that strict self-respect permits.

I have not forgotten my hope of visiting you, but it has been quite out of question with me in these late weeks. A large farmer has not been more encumbered with his " spring work," than I on my few acres with mine: and tomorrow, or the next day, I am to have a ' new man.' But I am coming, one day, to Wayland.[108]

Your affectionate servant,
R. W. Emerson

To William Emerson, Concord, May 20, 1863 [109]

Concord, 20 May, 1863

Dear William,

Ellen sent your trunk by Mr Adams Concord Express to the " Worcester Depot," in Boston, yesterday morning, to be sent *as freight*

105. MS owned by HCL; ph. in CUL. The envelope still with this letter is addressed to Fuller at Boston and bears a Concord postmark dated May 15, 1863. It seems probable that Emerson wrote " 16 " for " 15."

106. Richard Fuller's *Chaplain Fuller,* a biography of his brother, was announced as for sale in the *Boston Daily Advertiser,* May 9, 1863. The *New-York Daily Tribune* of Dec. 15, 1862, had reported the death, in action, on Dec. 12, of Arthur B. Fuller.

107. Apparently the book was never reviewed in *The Atlantic,* though it was listed among recent American publications received, in the issue for July, 1863.

108. For some years Richard Fuller had had a home at Tower Hill, Wayland, Mass. (see Alfred S. Hudson, *The Annals of Sudbury, Wayland, and Maynard,* 1891, pp. 112 and 188) .

109. MS owned by HCL; ph. in CUL.

according to your direction. Adams took it but said " I have no bills of lading, but I can send it." After he was gone, Ellen consulted your letter again & found that you say " Be sure to have a receipt." [110] This morning I asked Adams he took a receipt No, he said, " I told you I had no bills of lading and they do not give receipts except in that form: But it will go well enough." That is the present bad state of the affair, and not quite all yet. In the garret though it was locked Ellen believed last fall she found it unlocked & could not lock it when closed. I was called & locked it, to Ellen's satisfaction. When it was in Adams's wagon I saw it was unlocked again. What to do? Adams undertook to see that it was faithfully corded before it was " shipped." I wrote on the card nailed to the cover, W E— *109 Twenty Second Street,*
And we trust to be early informed that it arrives safe. I send you herewith Elizabeth Hoar's Will of Aunt Mary.

In regard to Hannah Parsons's statement to Elizabeth about the excess of Aunt's expense over her income,[111] Hannah explains that Aunt owes her nothing, for that she had already money in her hands when these last excesses of expense began: But if Aunt had lived longer at the same rate of expense, she would have been in debt to Hannah. The expenses of Aunt Mary's funeral here are $12. I will bring you Melvin's bill.

I do not know whether I ought to keep or burn an old note of hers to me which Gore Ripley caused to be made, when he came to me for some money for her. But I will find it & show it to you.

I mean to make you a call, 8 or 10 days hence, for I am going to West Point as one of the " Board of Visitors," & the Examination commences on 1 June,[112] which, I suppose, this year, means 2ᵈ June. Still I think I shall spend the Sunday there. So I promise myself to see you at leisure in your new house. With love to Susan, & W. & H., Yours affectionately,

Waldo E

To Thomas Ridgeway Gould, Concord? May? *c.* 26? 1863

[Gould, n.p.; May 25 (endorsed 1863), regrets his absence from home when Emerson and his daughter Edith called that morning, says they saw the bust in

---

110. These directions for the shipment of his wife's trunk from Concord were given by William Emerson in an undated letter which he wrote to Ellen Emerson on the same sheet with his letter of May 10, 1863, to her father (MS owned by Dr. Haven Emerson). The following sentence lost a word between MS pages.

111. See May 5, 1863.

112. See the letters of June 1, 1863.

a bad light, and asks that they come again. Gould, Chaddsford, Pa., June 2, 1863, states that just before he left home he received Emerson's "kind note" and read attentively what was said "about my busts"; he and his wife are disappointed at missing the day in Concord for which Emerson invited them.]

To Lidian Emerson, West Point, New York, June 1, 1863 [113]

Roe's Hotel
West Point
1 June 1863

Dear Lidian,

I arrived here this morning from New York, & am not a little astonished to learn that the Examination instead of a two days' affair, is of sixteen! [114] I have no time or patience for any such term, & shall soon learn how to disengage myself — Meantime I will advise you presently what the probabilities are. Thus far, our Board is only just organized, six only out of the fifteen members being yet arrived. And we are presently to receive the visit of the Commander & his Staff to show us the buildings. I have had the kindliest visit in Twenty Second Street; [115] & have seen Dr Perry in Bond St [116] who promises to heal me speedily again. Tell Ellen that if I do not come home quickly I will at

113. MS owned by RWEMA; ph. in CUL.

114. Edwin M. Stanton, Secretary of War, Washington, May 6, 1863, had officially appointed Emerson a member of the visiting board; and doubtless Emerson wrote his acceptance in a letter I have not found. The "Report of the Board of Visitors of the U. S. Military Academy at West Point for 1863" (H. R. Ex. Doc. 1, 38th Cong., 1st Sess.) contains some pertinent facts (pp. 76 and 79): "The session of the board of visitors commenced on Monday, June 1, and continued from day to day to the 16th of June. The first class was examined in the presence of the whole board. In accordance with usage, two divisions of the board simultaneously examined the other classes in sections.

"Daily sessions of the board were also held for conference and discussion, and special committees were appointed to inquire into the details of the various subjects presented for our consideration. . . . The present board of visitors labored under some embarrassment from the fact that all were inexperienced in the special duties here assigned them. Such, we learn, has been the history of former boards. . . ."

Emerson could have had little to do with the report in general, though he might well have been instrumental, I think, in getting a commendation of the study of ethics inserted (p. 78); and there are extant some brief, informal notes in his hand relating to exercise, bathing, food, and so forth. The report was signed by eighteen, not fifteen, members, including Emerson and the Henry Barnard of Connecticut mentioned in the letter of June 1 to William Emerson.

115. That is, with William Emerson and his family.

116. Trow's New York City Directory, 1863, lists Bela C. Perry, dermatologist, at 49 Bond St.

least reinforce her exchequer. Pray tell Patrick [117] to bolt the bulk head door every night.

With love to all,
W.

To WILLIAM EMERSON, WEST POINT, NEW YORK, JUNE 1, 1863 [118]

Roe's Hotel.
West Point.
1 June, 1863.

Dear William,

I am astonished to find that instead of a two days' examination, it is perhaps of sixteen days. That is quite beyond any patience of mine, and I shall inform myself how & when I must disengage myself. I will take care to send you some note before I return, that you may please learn if Hannah Parsons has come home.[119] I had the finest air sun & mountains all the morning, & now. We have only six members (out of fifteen) of the Board yet arrived, two having preceded me on Saturday night, & Dr Barnard [120] of Connecticut came with me. The Commander & staff are to come to us at 11.30 A. M. But what a ridicule is or appears an examination of 16 days! for any issue that I can learn is to come of it!

Affectionately,
Waldo E

To ELLEN EMERSON, WEST POINT, NEW YORK, JUNE 3, 1863 [121]

Roe's Hotel
West Point
June 3, 1863

Dear Ellen,

It does not yet appear what day I shall find it honest to release myself from this Board,[122] & I am kept pretty well occupied, so

117. Probably the " new man " mentioned in May 15? 1863. He reappears in June 3 following.

118. MS owned by HCL; ph. in CUL.

119. *Cf.* May 5, 1863.

120. See a note on the letter of the same date to Lidian Emerson.

121. MS owned by RWEMA; ph. in CUL.

122. See the letters of June 1, 1863.

that I have no list even of orders for Patrick [123] yet, to send; but you must tell him that he must use all his eyes to see what is most needful to be done, reminding him that James B.[124] has for years taken the whole year's work in his hand, & has foreseen every piece of work in its time. Edith has a key of my closet, & will give him the box of seeds, & Mr C. Stow or Mr Walcott will add any more that he wants. Be sure to put in what melon seed he has which I think he has already at the barn. And it is time for a new planting of sweet corn. 2 *P. M.* I enclose for " government " [125] $5.oo If I must stay longer say till Saturday night or Monday, I must send you a draft. My friends Mr & Mrs Quincy [126] are here — and our Board have just called on General Scott [127] who is here & had called upon the Board. He has you know the stateliest form in America & his behavior belongs to it.

R. W. Emerson

To Benjamin and Susan Morgan Rodman, Concord, June 17, 1863 [128]

Concord
17 June, 1863 —

My dear friends,

I have waited a week since I heard the heavy news from Port Hudson, — fearing to disturb you, — but do not like to wait longer. I believe I have read every syllable which the journals contain of William's heroic behavior & death at the head of his regiment,[129] & with entire sympathy for, &, I fear, too true knowledge of the desolation the tidings will have brought to your house, however consoled by the cordial testimony which the Army sends home of the love & honor which attached to him in life & in death. I had kept up by frequent inquiries some

123. *Cf.* June 1 to Lidian Emerson.

124. Burke, mentioned in many earlier letters.

125. In accordance with the promise in June 1, 1863, to Lidian Emerson.

126. Presumably Josiah Quincy, Emerson's college classmate, and his wife, Mary Miller.

127. Winfield Scott had retired from the army shortly after the opening of the war but lived at West Point.

128. MS owned by Mr. W. Rodman Peabody; ph. in CUL. For the Rodman family, see Charles H. Jones, p. 71.

129. Emerson may have read in the *Boston Daily Advertiser* of June 11, 1863, the news that Lieut.-Col. William L. Rodman had been killed " by a rebel sharpshooter " during the recent Union attack upon Port Hudson, La. The *Record of the Massachusetts Volunteers*, 1870, II, 794, shows that Rodman's death occurred during the attack of May 27, which was repulsed with heavy loss.

knowledge of his whereabouts, & read the New Orleans correspondence with hope of quite happier news. — — But this sacrifice which he has finished, I am sure, could not be a surprise to his thoughts, nor to yours. The soldier & the soldier's father & mother must have rehearsed this dread contingency to themselves quite too often, not to know its face when it arrives. — And yet there can be no sufficient preparation.

His life, so fair & amiable from the childhood which I remember, — his manly form & qualities, promised a solid character & fortune. I dread to think how the change will darken your house, — hitherto the home of every friendly influence.[130] Neither perhaps can any considerations of duty to country & mankind for a long time reconcile to this devastation in the family. And yet who dare say, amid all the greatness the war has called out, in the privatest & obscurest, as well as in eminent persons, that these calamities do not suddenly teach selfrenouncement, & raise us to the force they require. I am sure your son's own devotion will arm you to surrender him.

I think daily that there are crises which demand nations, as well as those which claim the sacrifice of single lives. Ours perhaps is one, — and that one whole generation might well consent to perish, if, by their fall, political liberty & clean & just life could be made sure to the generations that follow. As you suffer, all of us may suffer, before we shall have an honest peace. — I have seen Mrs Anna Lowell, not long since, (whom I believe Mrs Rodman knows,) mother of Capt. James J. Lowell who fell on the peninsula,[131] — and found in her not so much grief, as devotion of herself & all her family to the public service. My kindest remembrances & best thought to both your daughters. Susan at home will miss her brother most, & love him best. —

One of these days, I shall seek an opportunity of learning all you know & think in these hours.

Very affectionately yours,
R. W. Emerson

To Mr & Mrs Rodman.

TO EDITH EMERSON, CONCORD? JULY 15, 1863?[132]

Dear Edith,
          Tell Edward to send me his college bill, or its amount. & Mrs

130. There are many letters from Benjamin Rodman relating to Emerson's visits to the Rodman home in New Bedford.

131. *Cf.* July 16, 1862.

132. MS owned by RWEMA; ph. in CUL. The year 1863 has been supplied in another hand, and the letter clearly belongs to Edward's college years.

Upham's. I enclose Dr Holmes.[133] Glad, you are mending, & presently we must have clear sky again, you happy children three.

15 July.

I will give Adams the zouave [134] tomorrow morn^g to send with the gloves. Tell Ellen that Adams brings answer that *lignum vitae* will cost 1.00 per ball, & boxwood .75, and I will advertise her friend when I have learned the turner's name, which I have forgotten.

To Ellen Emerson, Concord, July 17, 1863 [135]

Dear Ellen We opened this letter to know if Uncle William had been burned out — and I read today in the bulletin that there was an encounter of the rioters in 22^d Street.[136] Tonight we learn that the Seventh Reg^t & other troops have arrived, and I hope this dismal ruin is at an end. You have been peaceful at Newport at least and I looked for a letter this eve. to say that Edith is mending. Perhaps she must wait for weather to go abroad in. Frank Browne [137] is not drafted, nor is George Brooks. Frank Gourgas is Tell Edward that Mrs Conway goes to England in two or three weeks, & so can carry the Hawthorn-Browning message.[138] By all means read Dr Holmes's speech at the Alumni Dinner, & Everett's & Quincy's.[139]

Papa.

Friday night
17 July.

133. If Emerson's date is correct, this could not have been a report of Holmes's address mentioned in July 17, 1863; perhaps it was his Fourth of July oration.

134. Presumably a Zouave jacket, to be sent to Edward at Newport, R. I., by Augustus Adams's express; *cf.* July 17, 1863.

135. MS owned by RWEMA; ph. in CUL. July 17 fell on Friday in 1863, and that year is proved by evidence cited below.

136. There had been serious anti-draft riots in New York during the past week. The police station in 22d St. was burned by a mob on July 15. The Seventh Regiment was called upon to restore order. (*New York Commercial Advertiser,* July 13 ff., 1863.)

137. That is, doubtless, Brown.

138. Conway himself had already gone (see a note on Mar. 11, 1863). The *New York Commercial Advertiser,* Aug. 20, 1863, reported Mrs. Conway and her children as passengers on the "Arabia" from Boston for Liverpool. Whatever the "Hawthorn-Browning" message was, she soon met Browning (Conway, *Autobiography,* II, 18), who "loved to talk of the Hawthornes" (II, 25).

139. The speeches of Holmes, Edward Everett, and President Josiah Quincy at the Harvard alumni dinner of July 16 were briefly reported in the *Boston Daily Advertiser,* July 17, and printed in full, apparently, *ibid.,* July 18, 1863.

I have sent Ida [140] a reply to her questions without waiting for your re-quest. And by this time probably Adams has sent to Édith his double package.[141]

To ELLEN EMERSON, CONCORD, JULY 19, 1863 [142]

Dear Ellen,

Your letter to your Mother wandered to Concord, N. H., so that Edith's wants have been neglected. The address of it was right. If she does not mend when the sun comes out, she must herself consider whether she would like better a ride on Grace's back or to stay a day or two more by the sea, if Mrs Hemenway so advises. I grieve that she should lose the lustre of her holidays. I enclose $3. You are to know — but I believe I already told you of Mrs Conway's voyage.[143] With love to you all three, & my grateful regards to your two hostesses, Mrs Hemen-way & Charlotte, who make you so contented,

Papa —

Sunday Night.
19 July.

To ————————, CONCORD, JULY 30, 1863

[MS listed in Goodspeed's Book Shop, Apr., 1901.]

To WILLIAM EMERSON, CONCORD, AUGUST 3, 1863 [144]

Concord, 3 Augt.
P. M.

Dear William,

A line ought to have gone to you at once on Lidian's hearing from Susan,[145] to say, that you shall come here whenever it suits you best, but I go to Waterville College for *11th instant*,[146] and shall be

140. Perhaps Ida Agassiz. The reply was presumably a letter.
141. *Cf.* July 15, 1863?
142. MS owned by RWEMA; ph. in CUL. Mention of Mrs. Conway's intended voyage shows that the year is 1863, when July 19 fell on Sunday.
143. In July 17, 1863.
144. MS owned by HCL; ph. in CUL. Evidence cited below fixes the year.
145. Susan Haven Emerson to Lidian Emerson, July 30, endorsed 1863 (MS owned by Dr. Haven Emerson), says she and her family hope to visit Concord for a few days in August and wish to know what time would be most convenient for the Concord Emersons.
146. *The Eastern Mail*, Waterville, Me., Aug. 14, 1863, reported that an exception-

at home, I suppose, on the 13th — but you must plan for the best journey, & how to stay longest out of New York, & if you will encamp by our brook for many days it will be best for us. Edward ran up to the top of Mount Washington the other day, but could not see through the clouds, yet enjoyed his journey. We are all interested in Wilky James,[147] who has behaved nobly, and whose father writes the best news of him. I was told yesterday that the Gov! have confided much to Mr Whiting in sending him to London,[148] & fear English war unless he can hinder it. But I must think that England itself must know & do better. Every word from & of your house is good here.

Affectionately,
Waldo E

To ————————, Concord, August 19, 1863

[MS listed in Anderson Galleries, Apr. 25–27, 1916, where the letter is described as inclosing two printed verses.]

To the Library Committee of the Boston Athenæum, Boston, August 29, 1863 [149]

Athenaeum
Aug. 29, 1863.

To the Library Committee.
    I request the privilege of taking from the Library for a short time the Third Volume of " Weale's Journal of Architecture " [150]

Respectfully
R. W. Emerson

---

ally large audience heard Emerson's oration on Aug. 11 at the class-day exercises of Waterville College. The " Office of the Scholar," as the newspaper entitled this oration, appears in *Cent. Ed.*, X, as " The Man of Letters."

147. Susan Haven Emerson to Lidian Emerson, cited above, said she feared Wilkie James was dead or missing. Garth Wilkinson James, adjutant in the 54th Massachusetts Regiment, was severely wounded on the slopes of Ft. Wagner (*The Early Years of the Saturday Club*, p. 328).

148. Mr. E. Wilder Spaulding, assistant to the historical adviser, Department of State, Washington, D. C., informs me that an instruction of July 18, 1863, from Seward, the then Secretary of State, to the American minister in Great Britain refers to William Whiting. Charles Francis Adams to Seward, Aug. 20, 1863, acknowledged " your letter of 18th of July, introducing Mr. Whiting as the successor to the labors of Mr. Evarts " (H. R. Ex. Doc. 1, 38th Cong., 1st Sess., pt. I, p. 395). Whiting, a native of Concord, had become a solicitor of the War Department in 1862.

149. MS owned by the Boston Athenæum; ph. in CUL.

150. *Quarterly Papers on Architecture,* a London periodical of nearly twenty years

To James Thomas Fields, Concord? September? *c.* 1? 1863

[MS listed without date in *Catalogue of Autograph Letters . . . Donated to the Mississippi Valley Sanitary Fair, and to be Sold . . . October 7th and 8th, 1864,* where it is described as to the editor of *The Atlantic,* as accompanying the original MS of " Voluntaries," published in that magazine (in Oct., 1863) , and as donated by Fields. In Sept. 10 following Emerson states that he has already sent the poem to *The Atlantic.*]

To James Thomas Fields, Concord, September 7, 1863 [151]

Concord
7 Sept. 1863

My dear Sir,

Miss Thoreau came to see me, this morning, to consult on the draft of a contract you have sent her, touching the " Excursions." [152] I agreed to see you, on her part; and will endeavor to do so within a few days. I presume there is no need of haste: if there be, I will come to you at once.

Yours ever

R. W. Emerson

Mr Fields.

To Francis George Shaw, Concord, September 10, 1863

[Printed in *Memorial R G S,* 1864, p. 160, where it is followed, on pp. 161–164, by " Voluntaries." Shaw, New York, Sept. 16, 1863, thanked Emerson for " your note & for your copy of the ' Lines ' which express your feeling towards our son & his comrades." The son, Robert Gould Shaw, colonel of the Negro regiment (the Fifty-fourth, mentioned in the notes on the letters of Mar. *c.* 8 and Mar. 24, 1863) , was killed in battle on July 18, 1863. Some thirty years later the memorial by Augustus Saint-Gaudens was unveiled.]

---

earlier, was edited and published by Johan Weale. Copies of the few volumes which appeared seem to have been acquired by the Athenæum in 1847. Beside Emerson's signature on the present letter is a notation by " F. E. P." — doubtless Francis Edward Parker, a trustee of the Athenæum — showing that the request was granted.

151. MS owned by Mr. Howard Eric; ph. in CUL.

152. The MS memorandum book for 1862, 1863, and 1864 has this note under July 30, 1863, but extending across the space for July 31: " Ticknor & Fields contract for Thoreau's new book . . ." Oct. 19, 1863, to Fields, comments upon a contract, perhaps for *Excursions.*

To John Murray Forbes, Concord, September 11, 1863 [153]

Concord —
Sept. 11. 1863

My dear Mr Forbes,

If I were not ailing just at this time, I could not resist your kind message, and should seize the occasion to learn the new English traits which you offer me.[154] I am very curious to know them. William Evarts lately gave me some hints of his: [155] but your experiences are longer & far nearer. And though there is no bright Naushon for me to-day, yet I hope to claim the story of you later.

After talking with Charles Norton about the possibility of aid for the " Commonwealth " newspaper, from the Loyal Pub⁀ Society,[156] I tried to see you, but you were gone westward. I believe the same cause found other advocates — I hope the newspaper will be sustained.

With joy to all your house, that you are safe at home, — if you are not already preparing new flights — & affectionate remembrance to you all,
Yours,
J. M. Forbes, Esq.   R. W. Emerson

To Henry Greenough, Concord? September 15, 1863

[Greenough, Cambridge, Sept. 16, 1863, acknowledges Emerson's " favor of yesterday," says that as soon as he obtains a copy of Horatio Greenough's letter he will return the original, and thanks Emerson for his tribute. Earlier letters relate to the friendship between Emerson and Horatio Greenough.]

To George William Curtis, Concord, October 2, 1863?

[MS listed in Anderson Auction Co., Dec. 15–18, 1914; printed in Adrian H. Joline, *Rambles in Autograph Land*, 1913, pp. 281–282. The letter is apparently undated as to year but mentions Tuesday the 17th and Thursday the 19th

153. MS owned by RWEMA; ph. in CUL.

154. In July, Forbes had returned from England, where he had gone on a special mission for the Secretary of the Navy. Backed by a million pounds of credit, he and W. H. Aspinwall were expected to buy dangerous vessels or otherwise prevent them from being acquired by the Confederates (*Letters and Recollections of John Murray Forbes*, II, 5–48) .

155. *Cf.* the letters of Apr. 16 and Aug. 3, 1863.

156. Norton was in direct charge of the New England Loyal Publication Society, of which Forbes himself was the founder and president. Its purpose was to distribute literature favorable to the Union cause. (See *Letters and Recollections of John Murray Forbes*, I, 324–329; and *Letters of Charles Eliot Norton*, I, 221–223.)

as possible dates for a lecture by Curtis at Concord — the 19th is preferred. Curtis, it is true, lectured there in many different years. But the lyceum nearly always opened in November; and it seems very probable that the reference here is to Curtis's " The Way of Peace," read on Thursday, Nov. 19, 1863 (MS records of the Concord Lyceum, in the Concord Free Public Library). Emerson seems not to have been an officer of the local lyceum then and apparently read a lecture elsewhere on that day; but under that date in the MS memorandum book for 1862, 1863, and 1864 he recorded " G W Curtis."]

To Charles H. Glover, Concord, October 16, 1863

[MS listed and partly quoted in American Art Association, Mar. 10–11, 1924; Emerson apologizes for his delay in returning a stately edition of Confucius and adds that he many years ago knew the substance of this work not only in Marshman (the catalogue has " Marksman ") but in *The Chinese Classical Work,* published at Malacca (*cf.* June 7, 1843). The book Emerson was returning was no doubt James Legge's translation (*cf.* Christy, p. 321).]

To Abel Adams, Concord, October 19, 1863 [157]

Concord
19 October, 1863

My dear friend,

   I assured myself on Saturday that it would clear up at Jamaica Plain when it did with us, — just in time to carry you to the Fitchburg train in season and Ellen went to fetch you — in vain I dont know when I shall be able to show you again such an apple crop as we had piled up in barrels by the barn; and our trees were all in glory. But neither I nor my wife nor my children can release you from the promised visit for this mischance of weather, and next Saturday is still October, & promises a bright sun, and I & we all entreat you & Mrs Adams & Abby to hold yourselves engaged to us for that day. We will not claim you against all accidents, — but if the day permits with any convenience to you all, we shall surely count upon you.

  With love to Mrs A., & Abby, & honor to all your house from all of ours. Yours affectionately

R. W. Emerson

Abel Adams.
Mr Hosmer who called to see you, shall call again on Saturday.

157. MS owned by RWEMA; ph. in CUL.

To James Thomas Fields, Concord, October 19, 1863 [158]

Concord, 19 Oct.
1863

My dear Sir,

[I]I enclose the first form of contract [159] as you requested, with the alterations suggested by Miss Thoreau.[I]

1. The compensation for the engraving is to be struck out as agreed

2. She prefers a term of five years, as in the contract for " Walden," to the term herein proposed.

3. She is sorry to find that her allowance for copyright is to be reduced to 10 cents She would prefer 15. But if you persist in the views expressed in your statement to me, she will acquiesce.

Yours with great regard,
R. W. Emerson

Mr Fields.

To William Emerson, Concord, October 28, 1863 [160]

Concord, Oct. 28, 1863

Dear William,

Ellen, who monopolizes the New York correspondence, is in Boston, so I send you this bill of lading, which Mr Adams only bro't this morn.ᵍ, or it should have gone this morn. You should find, as I suppose she wrote, 7 bbls one of pears, 6 of apples. with their contents all marked with paint on the head. We had, all, our pleasure in the visit of Haven & Charles. I the less, that my working hours are still ostentatiously kept by me, though I rarely accomplish any thing as I would, & so manage to lose both leisure & work. Tis very plain that you & I must be content to be old.[161] Affectionately, Waldo E

158. MS owned by the Henry E. Huntington Library; ph. in CUL. Excerpt I is in *Harper's*, LXVIII, 458 (Feb., 1884) , and in Annie Fields, *Authors and Friends*, p. 69.

159. *Excursions*, mentioned in Sept. 7, 1863, had been published on Oct. 14 (*Boston Daily Advertiser*, Oct. 14, 1863) . Whether this contract related to that book or to one of the other posthumous volumes of Thoreau which were to appear in succeeding years is not quite clear.

160. MS owned by HCL; ph. in CUL. William Emerson, Oct. 30, 1863 (MS owned by Dr. Haven Emerson) , acknowledged the seven barrels and mentioned his sons' visit at Concord.

161. Emerson read " Terminus " to his son in 1866 (*Cent. Ed.*, IX, 489) , but the date of its composition does not seem to be known.

To George Partridge Bradford, Concord, November 11, 1863

[MS owned by RWEMA; ph. in CUL. Printed in *Cent. Ed.,* XI, 613–614, except the date, " 11 Nov.ʳ 1863," and the name " George P. Bradford " at the end of the letter.]

To Ethan Allen Hitchcock, Concord? November 20, 1863

[Partly printed in Hitchcock's diary, *Fifty Years,* ed. Croffut, 1909, p. 457.]

To Julia Ward Howe, Concord? November? *c.* 20? 1863?

[Julia Ward Howe wrote from Chestnut St., Boston, Friday, Nov. 19 (endorsed 1863), that she intended to read some essays on ethical subjects at her home on successive Monday evenings beginning the following Monday and would be glad to have Emerson present at any or all of these readings. In Laura E. Richards and Maud Howe Elliott, I, 291, there is an excerpt from a letter to Mrs. Howe in which Emerson commends her scheme for philosophical readings. The excerpt is there quoted after some account of her readings at Newport in 1868 (*cf.* a note on July 10, 1868) and may belong to that year, but it seems to fit very well into Mrs. Howe's letter cited above; and, according to the Boston directories, the Howes lived on Chestnut St. in 1863 but not in 1868. It should be added that Nov. 19 fell on Thursday, not Friday, in both 1863 and 1868.]

To S. B. Noyes, Concord? November 28, 1863

[Noyes, Mercantile Library (Brooklyn), Nov. 26, 1863, asked whether Emerson could lecture for the Library in December. Noyes, Brooklyn, Dec. 2, 1863, acknowledged Emerson's letter, mentioned the 21st as the date agreed upon, and suggested that the title of the lecture be changed to " American Politics."]

To William Emerson, Concord, December 3, 1863

[WmE List; acknowledged in William Emerson, Dec. 13, 1863 (MS owned by Dr. Haven Emerson) ; apparently told of the finishing of certain tasks and insisted that a first shipment of apples to the New York branch of the family should be accepted as a present.]

To Edith Emerson, Concord? December 5, 1863?[162]

Saturday Morn
5 Dec

Dear Edith,

I enclose $3. for Rosanna's purchase, which, your mother says is 12 yards at 25 cts a yard, also $1. for Ellen.

R. W. E.

The happiest day to your friends & yourselves!

162. MS owned by RWEMA; ph. in CUL. Dec. 5 fell on Saturday in 1863, the year which has been supplied.

To Philip Physick Randolph, Concord? December? *c.* 6? 1863

[Randolph, Boston, Nov. 26, 1863, said he was to be in Boston for a short time and proposed visiting Concord. Randolph wrote, Boston, Dec. 7 following, that he had received Emerson's note and would go to Concord the next day.]

To George E. Tufts, Concord? December? *c.* 12? 1863?

[Tufts, Rawson (N. Y., apparently), Nov. 1, endorsed 1863, gave a long critique on Emerson's writings. Tufts, New York, Dec. 16 (1863?), acknowledged "Your very kind letter" and regretted the impossibility of accepting Emerson's invitation for a visit; Tufts further commented upon his own disillusionment with life and mentioned — what was to have been his literary work — his *Theory of the Relation of Human Actions to the Economy of Nature.* He showed striking independence and vigor, and evidence of Emerson's interest in him is to be found in the letters of Dec. 18 following.]

To William Emerson, Concord, December 16, 1863 [163]

Concord

16 Decr 1863

Dear William,

Thank Mr & Mrs Haven most kindly for their valued invitation; [164] but I had, & still have, from the beginning the design of going to my old perch in the Saint Denis Hotel from whence I can at will descend to breakfast with Mr Haven, if he permit me, or with you. I knew at the first that your house was full, & have only made my errand now in order to talk with a German Doctor [165] who has been commended to Edith. I will endeavor to answer the rest of your letter at your house. Edith doubtless will write, — she is in Boston, — and I think it is settled we shall go by the shore line which leaves Boston at 11. A M on Saturday next.

Affectionately,

Waldo E.

163. MS owned by HCL; ph. in CUL.

164. William Emerson, Dec. 13, 1863 (MS owned by Dr. Haven Emerson), said Mr. and Mrs. Woodward Haven had asked that Emerson stay with them the next time he came to New York.

165. See Dec. 26, 1863, to Edith Emerson.

To William Emerson, Concord, December 18, 1863 [166]

Concord 18 Dec[r]
Friday

Dear William,

I am not sure that I said explicitly that Edith & I mean to leave Boston in the Shore Line railroad tomorrow at 11 A. M. & that I aim at the St Denis & Edith at Twenty Second St on our arrival. I infer from a note of hers just received, that she has not written to Haven of this train. Affectionately

Waldo E.

There is a certain Mr George E Tufts, in N. Y. or in Brooklyn, whom I particularly wish to see.[167] If he should call at your office to ask for me, pray let him be furnished with directions.

To George E. Tufts, Concord? December 18, 1863

[Tufts wrote from New York, Dec. 27 (MS endorsed 1863) : " Your favor of the 18th did not reach me till the time for the lecture was past." He said he was sick and near death at that time but that he was now engaged on a political pamphlet. In an unpublished entry of a notebook dated 1848 but obviously written over a period of years, Emerson recorded his admiration of Tufts, an earlier letter from whom had showed " great talent & character in the writer," and gave a different version of the New York episode: " Later in New York city I learned that he was stopping at a certain house there, &, as I was to lecture in the evening, I sent him my cards & beseeched him to meet me in the Lecture Room. He did not appear, & I went to the house . . . to find him but he was gone, & the Master of the house said that he had refused to go to my lecture because he was not well drest, & had left the city." (Typescript Journals.)]

To Francis Channing Barlow, Concord, December 26, 1863 [168]

Concord, 26 Dec.[r] 1863

My dear Sir,

I found your note on my return from New York,[169] only yes-

166. MS owned by HCL; ph. in CUL. The New-York Daily Tribune, Dec. 21, 1863, announced that Emerson would read " The Fortune of the Republic" that evening before the Mercantile Library Association in Brooklyn.

167. Cf. the letter of this date to Tufts.

168. MS owned by Mrs. Pierre Jay; ph. in CUL. For Barlow, cf. Dec. 3, 1862. It is a curious fact that on Dec. 15, 1863, if the printed official record is correct, Barlow was ordered to proceed at once to Springfield, Ill., and assume command of the depot for drafted men in that place (The War of the Rebellion: a Compilation of the Official Records, 1st series, Vol. LI, 1st part, 1897, p. 1134). Presumably the order was countermanded.

169. For the New York visit, see Dec. 18, 1863, to William Emerson.

terday morning. I had learned first from Edith, who made the discovery, only two days before, that Friday was to be Christmas, & I was properly mortified at the *contretemps*. Had we all persisted in our day, we should have had a philosophic hour, — my wife laid up in blankets, for a few days past, & Ellen & Edward sole cooks, — indispensable Ireland deserting range & pantry on the holiday. Now I offer you the first safe day that I foresee: I pray you to rally your party, & entreat your Mother, Mrs Howe, & Mrs Bell, to come on Thursday, 7th January; [170] convince them that the dangers of the meadows are imaginary, & that we are not worse in January than in December. So I rest in good hope Yours ever,

R. W. Emerson

General Barlow.

To Edith Emerson, Boston, December 26, 1863 [171]

Athenaeum
26 Dec.r

Dear Edith

I was forced to stop all night at Worcester,[172] our Christmas train was so large & slow; — saw Mr Wasson [173] there for an hour. At home I found your Mother still in blankets, Ellen & Edward sole cooks, — Ireland having forsaken range & pantry for the holiday,[174] & Eliza [175] also. But the substitutes created a notable dinner, your Mother descended, & we had our day. Today, I come to my Club, & Professor Wilson of Toronto. who is my guest.[176]

But I write now to say, that I left with the people in the office of the Saint Denis,[177] your knife, & all Dr Shieferdecker's [178] pamphlets for you.

170. They were expected on that day, as the letter of Jan. 6, 1864, shows. Mr. M. A. DeWolfe Howe believes that the Mrs. Howe mentioned may have been either Julia Ward Howe or Alice Howe (Mrs. George Howe) and that Mrs. Bell was almost certainly Helen Choate Bell (Mrs. Joseph Bell).

171. MS owned by RWEMA; ph. in CUL. The year is clearly 1863.

172. On his way home from New York; *cf.* the letter of the same date to Barlow.

173. For David Atwood Wasson, " now of Worcester," *cf.* Dec. 8, 1864.

174. *Cf.* the letter of the same date to Barlow.

175. The reading is doubtful. It is possible that Emerson intended " Elizabeth " but did not quite complete it for lack of room in the margin.

176. As Dec. 26 fell on Saturday in 1863, Emerson doubtless took his guest to the Saturday Club. Daniel, later Sir Daniel, Wilson had become professor of history and English literature in the University of Toronto in 1853 and gained some fame as an archæologist and educational reformer. Earlier letters allude to Emerson's lectures in Toronto.

177. *Cf.* letters of Dec. 16 and 18, 1863.

178. The " German Doctor " of Dec. 16, 1863, appears in *Trow's New York City Directory* for 1863–1864 as Charles C. Schieferdecker, on East 24th St.

I would have separated the pamphlets, if I had had time. The No. 1 of the periodicals contained the Letter of Priessnitz,[179] which you should read. You might omit the pamphlet about Vaccination, and hold the others at command, if the Doctor's practices shall interest you in them. You may say to him, if he wishes to kn[ow][180] that I looked into them, & should have read further, but that I thought they had better be within your reach. I shall write you again presently. The party did not come on Christmas day. I found a note from General B.[181]

Papa.

To James Elliot Cabot, Concord, December 29, 1863 [182]

Concord
29 Dec. 1863

Dear Cabot,

           I have borrowed of Miss Thoreau a volume of her brother's MSS. — taken almost at random from those I have read, — to send you: it will be as good a specimen probably as any. You will find the handwriting hard to read at first, with abbreviations, — *appy* for apparently, *mts* for mountains, &c, but I got through several volumes with ever mounting estimation, though I have postponed further readings for the present. I need not say to you, that Miss Thoreau values these books religiously, and I have assured her they would be perfectly safe in your hands. I am delighted to have you see one, and perhaps you will suggest what can be done with them.[183]

Ever yours,
R. W. Emerson

J. E. Cabot.

179. Vincenz Priessnitz was regarded as the founder of the system of hydropathy.
180. Blotted so that the last two letters are illegible.
181. See the letter of the same date to Barlow.
182. MS owned by Professor Philip Cabot; ph. in CUL.
183. The MS journal of Thoreau yielded several volumes of selections before it was finally published in a very extensive, though not complete, form more than forty years after the date of the present letter.

To Elbridge G. Dudley, Concord, c. 1863? [184]

Concord
Saturday

My dear Sir,

Please tell the chorister that I will read either 44 or 86 of the Hymns. I think I have no other reading.

R. W. E.

184. MS owned by Mr. Oliver R. Barrett; ph. in CUL. Emerson wrote Dudley's name on the back of the sheet, and the note was probably sent by messenger. Apparently this might relate to almost any one of the numerous Sunday lectures which Emerson read before Parker's old congregation in Boston. Other letters to Dudley which I have found fall within the years 1859–1863.

1864

To EDITH EMERSON, BOSTON, JANUARY 6, 1864 [1]

Parker House —
Wednesday, 6 Jan^y

Dear Edith,

You need not go to the Doctor's house, if it looks so ugly. I dont think any thing or body there dare affront a young lady of such determination & rancor, but I wish you first of all to be well, & think you cannot be if you have an uneasy mind. Therefore, assure the Doctor, sweetly tho' peremptorily, that you will not; & I will write him today or tomorow to the like effect, — today, if I have time, — but I cannot be sure.[2] I mean, of course, that you shall go as a day patient, — since you do not fear that, — & stay with Aunt Susan for Angelic protection. I must write, too, to Uncle William with more exactness about keeping you,[3] though he promised everything to you like an Arabian patriarch. Perhaps after longer trial, you may find that the " Institute " is not odious. Tomorrow General Barlow & his friends go to Concord.[4]

Affectionate Papa.

With salutations & hearty thanks to Uncle & Aunt & Haven, for bearing so kindly with such a vixen.

To WILLIAM EMERSON, JR., CONCORD? JANUARY c. 24? 1864

[William Emerson, Jr., Jan. 27, 1864, thanked his uncle for " answering my letter with so special a request to Mr Sumner " and explained that he had now changed his plan and no longer wished a commission from Washington to go south but intended to go to Minnesota on advice of his physician (MS owned by Dr. Haven Emerson).]

1. MS owned by RWEMA; ph. in CUL. The year is obviously 1864, when Jan. 6 fell on Wednesday.
2. Doubtless Emerson duly wrote to Schieferdecker, who appears in other letters of Dec., 1863, and early 1864; but I have no definite proof.
3. It is not clear that Emerson wrote to his brother before Jan. 29.
4. *Cf.* Dec. 26, 1863, to Barlow.

To Charles Sumner, Concord? January c. 24? 1864

[See the preceding note.]

To Edith Emerson, Concord, January 25, 1864 [5]

Concord
25 Jan.ʸ 1864

Dear Edith,

I have just got home from Vermont [6] to hear your Chronicles read by Edward & Ellen, & to congratulate you on their mitigated tone. On the whole, I infer that you find some benefit in the treatment, or from some of the treatment you are trying: and if you can get warm feet & cool head, and good appetite, I hope the whole frame will be sound soon. Your stormy letters keep your family in a highly sympathetic state. I don't know but Edward will call out the Doctor. Dolly herself [7] will charge. But really I am glad that you take the sensible part of exactly keeping the rules, — so to be sure of knowing what the results are. The consolations of 109 W. 22ᵈ [8] Street must be an indemnity for the loss of morning & evening baths in 14ᵗʰ. [9] I wish you will give my love to Haven & thank him for so kindly remembering me in sending the photograph of the Rock Temple in Nubia, which I examine with interest, & have put among my treasures. I will try to find the photograph Mrs Bancroft asks for, & perhaps enclose it herewith, &, at least, the money you ask for. I believe all parties miss your love & wrath here, &, tis quite certain, send you pure love & best wishes, and add kindest wishes to all the New York house.

Papa

To ———————, Concord? January 26, 1864

[MS listed and partly quoted in John Heise, catalogue 69 (1912); Emerson says he is mortified to find himself without voice this morning because of a bad cold.]

5. MS owned by RWEMA; ph. in CUL.
6. The MS memorandum book for 1864 and 1865 gives Jan. 20 to North Bennington, with the subject "Fortune of Republic."
7. Still remembered in family tradition as Emerson's saddle-mare, who, after living to old age in Concord, spent her last years in Naushon Island.
8. William Emerson's home (cf. May 20, 1863).
9. Probably for 24th (cf. a note on Dec. 26, 1863, to Edith Emerson).

To William Emerson, Concord, January 29, 1864[10]

Concord
January 29, 1864

Dear William,

I was glad to hear from you directly, the other day, — and the news that came indirectly, that you had leased the Whiting House,[11] was most welcome. I hope that months & years may show the wisdom of that step. Thanks for certain papers & slips that have also come; & I give you joy on the news from Charles, which really looks like the return of health. And Edith tells us, that Haven is quite himself again.

About Edith, I am not easy. She sends a number of details about her health lately, which, put together, are unfavorable. Abby Adams, who is an excellent sensible person, had inferred from all the Seavers told her, that this hydropathic Dr S. was a very safe, &, probably, in such cases as Edith's, very useful practitioner. And it may be, that, if Edith surrendered herself fully to the treatment, & did not try to combine with it visits, & dinners abroad, & opera! — it might serve her better. But the girl is fastidious, & I dont know but the disgust of staying at the Water cure would be as damaging as these interruptions.[12] And now, at last, she informs us that her mainstay, the bath-maid, is likely to be sick with scarlet fever. I trust, — we all confide, — that Edith has ceased instantly to go there, & will cease until things are right again. But my wish is that you will write me a few lines at once & give me your impression, — yours, & Susan's, and Haven's too, of her appearance & health. Is she losing ground since she arrived in New York? For my confidence has not been strong for a moment in the physician; — expectant merely, — with great willingness to believe that in some cases much may be done by the water-remedies. Ellen was very sanguine that Edith was a proper subject for this treatment, & urged it upon us. Meantime every line of Ediths letters goes show, that, if she does not mend, it is not the fault of her Uncle or Aunt or Haven, for everything is kindliest & best ordered incessantly for

10. MS owned by HCL; ph. in CUL.

11. William Emerson, Feb. 1, 1864, said that as he was very uncertain how much time he could spend in the Whiting house, he did not wish to trouble his brother about it. William wrote again, Apr. 24, 1864, that he would probably start his household goods toward Concord the following day. (Both MSS owned by Dr. Haven Emerson.)

12. William Emerson had written, Jan. 22, 1864: " Edith is still alive, I am happy to say, notwithstanding all the efforts of Dr Schieferdecker to mar her beautiful health " (MS owned by Dr. Haven Emerson) .

her. So I pray you add to all your bounties this expression of your opinion on her case. With dear love to Susan, Your brother Waldo E

I send a Boston paper announcing the death of Anna Jones.[13]

To Henry Sturgis Russell, Concord, February 3, 1864 [14]

Concord

3 February, 1864.

Dear Sir,

Learning that the commissions in the Fifth Mass$_{tts}$ Cavalry are not yet all filled, I beg leave to present to you the claims of Mr Edward Bartlett of this town for such appointment.[15] Mr B. is son of our Dr Josiah Bartlett; he was a private in Company F of the 44th Massachusetts, during its whole term of service. Afterwards, he joined Major Geo. L Stearns, & assisted him in his recruiting of negro soldiers in Tennessee.[16] The resignation of Major Stearns, — who highly valued his services, & had charged him not to seek any other employment, — leaves him now at liberty to re-enter the Army. He is known to me from his childhood for an excellent boy, & a favorite with his mates. He is an intelligent, well-educated, active young man, with hardy habits, & of great endurance. I have confidence that he will approve himself faithful to every duty.

Respectfully,

R. W. Emerson

Colonel H. Russell —

To William Emerson, Concord, February 6, 1864

[WmE List.]

13. On Jan. 18, at the age of 57, according to the *Boston Daily Advertiser*, Jan. 20, 1864. She was once a pupil in the school kept by William Emerson and his brother in Boston (*cf.* letters of Apr. and May, 1860).

14. MS owned by Dr. William B. Bartlett; ph. in CUL. Russell had married Mary, daughter of Emerson's friend J. M. Forbes, in 1863 (*Letters and Recollections of John Murray Forbes*, II, 4) ; he had been lieutenant-colonel of a cavalry regiment and was soon to be colonel of the Fifth Massachusetts Cavalry (*Record of the Massachusetts Volunteers*, I, 668).

15. Edward J. Bartlett was mustered out on June 18, 1863, after his nine months of service as a private in Co. " F," Forty-fourth Massachusetts Infantry; and he was mustered in as a second lieutenant in the Fifth Massachusetts Cavalry on July 5, 1864 (*ibid.*, I, 269 and 767).

16. For Bartlett as a member of Stearns's staff at Nashville, Tenn., see F. P. Stearns, *The Life*, p. 312.

To Edward Everett, Concord, February 8, 1864 [17]

Concord, 8 February,
1864.

Dear Sir,

On my return home from a journey somewhat prolonged, I find a letter from Mr W. S. McLaren & Mr E. Judge, Directors of the Mercantile Library Association in Montreal, requesting my good offices in presenting their petition to you, &, as they add, " urging your compliance with it." I remember, that, being in Montreal, last winter,[18] I offered to assist some of the young men connected with the Association, if I could, by inducing one or two friends of mine, who were named, to accept their invitation. I have no recollection of hearing your name mentioned in reference to lectures. I do not think that then their " presumption soared so high." [19] Now, they send me for transmission the letter which I enclose.

Let me say, in behalf of my rash clients, that they are spirited & excellent young men, who wish to do something for the culture of their city, & who inspire the kindest wishes in those who visit them: and, if it should at any time comport with your convenience & pleasure to visit Montreal, I think, on seeing their good manners & public spirit, you would be tempted to gratify their wishes, at some inconvenience to yourself.[20]

With great respect & regard,
R. W. Emerson

Hon. Edward Everett.

To Wendell Phillips, Concord? February? c. 8? 1864

[Phillips, n.p., Feb., 1864, said he saw no chance of being able to get to Montreal this season, but that if the situation changed, he would write to the persons Emerson named. Cf. Feb. 8, 1864, to Everett. Doubtless Phillips was one of the " friends of mine " there mentioned.]

17. MS owned by the Massachusetts Historical Society; ph. in CUL.

18. See Feb. 18, 1863, and note. In the MS memorandum entry there cited for Montreal, Emerson wrote the names of " McLarin " and Edgar Judge.

19. Slightly altered from Scott's *The Lady of the Lake*, v, 348.

20. Everett replied, Boston, Feb. 11, 1864, that he would like to go to Montreal if he were younger but must save himself for more important occasions.

To Alexander Bliss, Concord? February? *c.* 12? 1864

[See Feb. 18, 1864.]

To Edith Emerson, Concord, February 14, 1864 [21]

Concord —
Sunday Ev.ᵍ 14 Feb. 1864

Dear Edith,

I am sorry that, on the whole, the watercure experiment has not prospered better. It was bad for it, that you should not carry to it a little more hearty good will. You will say that the Doctor & his Hospital did not inspire it. Well, that was bad. But how is it now? In spite of interruptions & in spite of disgusts, you have had, I suppose. enough experience of the treatment to make an opinion that it may help you, or that it will not. If, seriously, you find no promise of benefit in it, I do not wish to spoil the rest of your visit to your Uncle & Aunt, — which so many circumstances strive to make happy, — by this *bête noir* of the " Institute." There is no reason for going on, if you are satisfied that it does not serve you. If it be so, go to the Doctor, & say that your father has new plans for you, & has decided to give up the baths at present, & ask him to give you his account; & ask the same of the Matron. — If, on the contrary, you have any belief, that, on the whole it is worth a longer trial, then persist, & carry to it the cheerfulest good will you can summon. For I hate that my pet should mar her chances by any unnecessary disliking. Edward goes to Newport tomorrow P. M. & will go to N. Y. on Friday or Saturday, and, I suppose, in a week afterwards will be quite ready to bring you home.

I must write at once to your Uncle [22] whose kind letter [23] went fully into details & answered mine, only that I had not I found given him all my facts. I am very happy in the good news from Charles which ought to strengthen Aunt Susan. Your Mother writes I believe at this moment. Good night! Papa.

I enclose $10. which your mother thinks you want for cloth.

21. MS owned by RWEMA; ph. in CUL.
22. Letter of Feb. 15, 1864.
23. In answer to the letter of Jan. 29, 1864, William Emerson wrote on Feb. 1 following in some detail regarding his niece's health. " We don't believe," he said, " that this long-named doctor is doing her any good; but she has such exuberant health that all his treatment fails to do her much harm." (MS owned by Dr. Haven Emerson.)

To WILLIAM EMERSON, CONCORD, FEBRUARY 15, 1864 [24]

Concord
15 February, 1864.

Dear William,

I ought instantly to have thanked you for your careful attention & detailed reply to my letter asking your opinion touching Edith's health,[25] which was very satisfying testimony on the case. I am not physician enough nor has the diagnosis been sufficiently imparted to me here at home that I can make you aware of the real necessity that exists for her medical treatment & which induced us to send her to the Water cure. But there is a morbid condition almost epidemic among young women in & about Boston — they call it *weak back* — which Alice Jackson & both my girls have suffered from in the last two or three years Ellen less Edith more, and for which the Water cure has been found by some patients salutary, as in Miss Sever's [26] case the report of which led us to consult Dr Schieferdekker [27] Edith's fresh colors are not her best symptoms: they often indicate the disease.

I am sorry that she has such a disgust for the Doctor & his Hospital as it is likely to be in the way of such benefit as she might derive. She attended Agassiz's school a year or more,[28] under a pepetual protest on her part, & *therefore* drew the less advantage from it. I have written her last night that she is seriously to consider whether she has found any benefit or hope of benefit from her experience thus far at the Institute. If not, she is at liberty to discontinue it. For I hate, that, with all your & Susan's extreme kindness, & all the abundant means of making her happy, that you & yours, & other friends, secure her in New York, this Bath-house & this Doctor should defeat all & make all powerless, without any certain indemnity from that side. But I wish her to carefully consult her experience of it, before she pronounces. — I wish we could have more comfortable news of W^m. Surely you will not let him depart alone.[29] Better, the frankest dealing with him. I hope he is better than I have heard. Your loving brother

Waldo.

24. MS owned by HCL; ph. in CUL.
25. See a note on Feb. 14, 1864.
26. *Cf.* Jan. 29, 1864, where the spelling differs.
27. Emerson misspelled the name differently in Dec. 26, 1863, to Edith.
28. *Cf.* Oct. 18, 1858, to William.
29. Two letters owned by Dr. Haven Emerson give the last chapter in the life of

To Robert Charles Winthrop, Concord, February 18, 1864 [30]

> Concord
> 18 February, 1864

Dear Sir,

I ought to have acknowledged your note of the instant, sooner, & told you, that I was already in correspondence,[31] on the same subject, with Col. Alexander Bliss, a colleague of Mr Kennedy on the Baltimore Committee.

> Yours, with great regard,
> R. W. Emerson

Hon. R. C. Winthrop.

To Henry Wadsworth Longfellow, Concord, February 24, 1864

[MS owned by the Trustees of the Longfellow House, Cambridge; ph. in CUL. Printed in Samuel Longfellow, *Life*, 1886, II, 402–403, where the name " H. W. Longfellow " is omitted at the end.]

To Edith? Emerson, Concord? February 26, 1864

[Described in Feb. 27, 1864, to Edith Emerson as " a note addressed to you *or* Edward."]

To Edith Emerson, Boston, February 27, 1864 [32]

> Union Club
> Feb. 27, 1864

Dear Edith

Ellen, whom I have just seen arriving from Milton & departing in the 7'c [33] train for Concord, begs me to say to you that you are on

---

William Emerson, Jr. Young William himself wrote, Jan. 27, 1864, that he planned to follow his physician's advice and leave for Minnesota in three weeks or so. But a letter from his father, Feb. 29 following, told of his death on that day and of the plan for burial at Concord.

30. MS owned by Mr. Thomas F. Madigan; ph. in CUL. Kennedy was assisted by Col. Alexander Bliss in preparing *Autograph Leaves of our Country's Authors*, 1864, a volume of facsimiles sold at a fair held in Baltimore for the benefit of wounded soldiers. Presumably Kennedy had applied to Winthrop, his correspondent over a period of many years (Henry T. Tuckerman, *The Life of John Pendleton Kennedy*, 1871, *passim*), for a contribution from Emerson, whose poem " Worship " appears in facsimile on pp. 132–133 of *Autograph Leaves*.

31. Feb.? *c.* 12? 1864.

32. MS owned by RWEMA; ph. in CUL.

33. Hardly legible; this is only a conjectural reading, not fully borne out by such timetables as I have found.

the whole to buy the N. Y. pattern of cloak which suits you, & she will not send the Wilcox (?) I asked her if I should send you money? She said, no, you have enough for that. I sent yesterday in a note addressed to you *or* Edward $10.00, (5. for him, & 5,. for Dr Perry.) If it was too late for him to receive, and if it is not easy for you to bring home the bottle in your trunk, when you come, I will write to the Doctor, & let him send it by Express. — We had your note to Ellen, in letter from Edw.ᵈ, which was opened in its transit through Concord yesterday. Mrs Jackson told me this morning they had just received good news from Alice. Did Ellen tell you that Mrs Mann sent her draft of $550.00 to Washington, the results of the Concord Fair? [34] Ellen could not even lose her spoon on the occasion: it was found yesterday. Give my love to all the loving household who take such kind care of you. R. W. Emerson

To WILLIAM EMERSON, CONCORD, MARCH 11, 1864 [35]

> Concord
> 11 March 1864

Dear William,

I hesitate to put money into a letter again today, against your counsels, & Ediths recent experience. Will you therefore have the goodness to supply her with what money she needs, whereof she will presently send me an account, and I will send you a draft from Mr Cheney or another, for the amount.

I have come tonight from Boston, & just seen her letter. Ellen had told me she had money, but Edith writes she has none. I dined with Dr Frothingham,[36] who was full of kind thoughts about you, & sympathy. Love to you all! Waldo E.

To WILLIAM EMERSON, CONCORD? MARCH 28, 1864

[Described in William Emerson, Apr. 1, 1864 (MS owned by Dr. Haven Emerson) as inclosing a check for $70.]

34. The *Boston Evening Transcript*, Mar. 2, 1864, reported that the Concord fair of Feb. 22 cleared $500 for the colored orphans. " Most of the distinguished people of Concord were present all day. Mr. Emerson spoke for a short time, to explain the object of the Fair, and the claims of the colored people to education, enforcing his statement with an account of the young colored man who took the *double-first* at the Toronto University."

35. MS owned by Mr. Edward Waldo Forbes; ph. in CUL.

36. *Cf.* early letters and Apr. 7, 1864, to Frothingham.

To OLIVER WENDELL HOLMES, CONCORD, MARCH? 31? 1864? [37]

Concord

Thursday, April —

Dear Doctor,

I will come with the greatest pleasure to you on Tuesday. Please make it a point that Lowell come: If the day or hour will not suit him fix one that will & I will come to it,, & will claim my right to come and dine with you on some future day.

Yours faithfully,

R. W. Emerson

Dr O. W. Holmes.

To WILLIAM EMERSON, CONCORD? APRIL 2, 1864

[William Emerson, Apr. 4, 1864 (MS owned by Dr. Haven Emerson), acknowledged this letter; William said that since he could not at once take possession of the Whiting house, he wished Elizabeth Hoar to take charge of the keys.]

To GEORGE BANCROFT, CONCORD? APRIL 6, 1864

[Mentioned in Apr. 7, 1864, to Lowell; dated in Journals, X, 21.]

To WILLIAM CULLEN BRYANT, CONCORD? APRIL 6, 1864

[Also mentioned in Apr. 7, 1864, to Lowell and dated in Journals, X, 21. Bryant at first wrote his acceptance (New York, Apr. 12, 1864) but later changed his mind.]

To EDWARD EVERETT, CONCORD, APRIL 6, 1864 [38]

Concord. 6 April

1864

Dear Sir,

The " Saturday Club," a party of gentlemen, most & perhaps all of whom are individually known to you, — propose to hold their

37. MS owned by the Library of Congress; ph. in CUL. The date is very uncertain, but the most plausible conjecture would seem to be that the projected meeting was for the purpose of discussing plans for the Shakespeare celebration of Apr. 23, 1864, at the Saturday Club. Numerous letters of that month relate to the work of Emerson, Lowell, and Holmes as the committee in charge of the dinner. We know from Apr. 6, 1864, to Ward, that there was a meeting on Tuesday, Apr. 5, " to mature the plan." It seems fairly probable that Emerson's " Thursday, April " was actually Thursday, Mar. 31, and that it was answered by Holmes's letter dated simply Apr. 3:

" Lowell will come on Tuesday.

" So I shall expect you at 21 Charles St at 3 o'clock on that day."

38. MS owned by the Massachusetts Historical Society; ph. in CUL. The names of Lowell and Holmes are, like the rest of the letter, in Emerson's hand.

monthly meeting for April on the 23[d] instant & to invite a few friends of Shakspeare to dine with them.[39] In their behalf we request the honor of your company at dinner at the Revere House at 6 o'clock on that evening.

> R. W. Emerson
> J. R Lowell
> O. W. Holmes — Committee

Hon. Edward Everett.
P. S.

It occurs to me that in asking the honor of your company in hours so precious as the Shakspeare Night, it is but honest to tell you, that we propose a private party, which will not probably exceed forty persons. The Club counts about twenty: Agassiz, Longfellow, Sumner, Hawthorne, Dana,[40] Cabot, S. G. Ward C. Norton, & others are members, Motley when he is here. And, on the coming Night, we hope to enrich ourselves, even to the claims of the hour. I heartily hope that you will find it in your power & pleasure to accede to our request.

> R. W. E.

To Josiah Quincy, Jr., Concord? April 6, 1864

[Mentioned in *Journals*, X, 21, with names of persons invited to the Shakespeare celebration; but perhaps this letter did not relate to the same subject.]

To Franklin Benjamin Sanborn, Concord, April 6, 1864

[MS listed in P. F. Madigan, catalogue 2 (1914), where it is partly quoted and where the year 1863 is supplied, though clearly an error; relates to the Shakespeare celebration by the Saturday Club. *Journals*, X, 21, gives the day as Apr. 7, but that may possibly be only the date of mailing. It is obvious that Emerson's datings in the *Journals* must be regarded as doubtful when there is good evidence in favor of slightly different dates.]

To Samuel Gray Ward, Concord, April 6, 1864

[Printed incompletely in *The Early Years of the Saturday Club*, 1918, pp. 338–339.]

39. Many other letters of this month relate to arrangements for this celebration, and a somewhat detailed account is in *The Early Years of the Saturday Club*, pp. 337–343. The various members of the Club who are named in this and in the following letters are recorded in the same book. Everett replied, Boston, Apr. 13, 1864, that he would come if he did not make a journey that had been proposed. On Apr. 22, however, he definitely declined on account of bad health.

40. Richard Henry Dana, Jr.

To John Albion Andrew, Concord? April 7, 1864

[Mentioned in the letter of the same date to Lowell and in *Journals,* X, 21.]

To Thomas Gold Appleton, Concord? April 7, 1864

[Mentioned in *Journals,* X, 21, and in Apr. 14, 1864. Appleton wrote, Boston, Apr. 19 following, that he would be responsible for any guest assigned him.]

To George Ticknor, Concord? April 7, 1864

[Listed in *Journals,* X, 21, and in Apr. 7 to Lowell.]

To Richard Grant White, Concord? April 7, 1864

[Mentioned *ibid*. White, New York, Apr. 15, 1864, accepted the invitation to the Shakespeare celebration.]

To John Murray Forbes, Concord, April 7, 1864 [41]

Concord
April 7, 1864 —

My dear Sir,

At the last Saturday Club, it was voted that the April meeting shd. be held on the 23ᵈ instant, instead of the 30ᵗʰ, and that we would enlarge the Club for that day by allowing certain gentlemen to join us to keep Shakspeare's festival. But when the arrangement came to a Committee it was thought impracticable for the Club to invite gentlemen to bear their own expenses and it was decided that the Committee should designate twelve or fifteen guests to be invited, & that each Member who was willing should charge himself with the entertainment of one of these. So we proceeded to invite, in the name of the Club, —

Gov. Andrew	Edwᵈ Everett
W. C. Bryant	Geo. Ticknor
George Bancroft	Dr Frothingham
G. C. Verplank	R. H. Dana, Senʳ
Richᵈ Grant White	Dr Asa Gray
G. W. Curtis	Professor Child
Edwin Booth	J. G. Whittier
	J. T. Fields

and we have still more names, if we dared ask more. But we only count with security on 12 or 13 club Members who will accept this duty. But

41. MS owned by Miss Anne Forbes; ph. in CUL.

my word for you at this moment is, first, to show you thus what a Venetian Gov! you have come under, &, next, to pray you to keep this day with us without fail, &, lastly, to take Whittier to be your portion in the affair. I remember you told me, you had tried to bring him, & would bring him some day, to the Club. I shall write him an invitation from the Club,[42] and I entreat you to write him a line yourself, & say how much it is desired.

If our N. Y. guests will come, they will add much splendor; if not, we can fill their places with desired persons. I am very sorry that Ward is to be absent. We have not settled even the place yet, probably the Revere House. Make it certain that you will be here.

> Ever yours affectionately,
> R. W. Emerson

John M. Forbes, Esq.

To James Russell Lowell, Concord, April 7, 1864 [43]

> Concord Thursday
> 7 April

Dear Lowell,

I shall not hasten to be on a Committee of Arrangements again. I think I need four secretaries.

May I ask you to see Agassiz, E. Howe, Dana, Pierce, and make them acquainted with our view of the party & ascertain if they consent If not exactly informed they will invite their own guests, instead of ours.

I have written to Bryant, Bancroft, R. G. White, Everett, Ticknor, Gov. Andrew, Verplank [44] and shall write to Booth, Curtis, Whittier, Fields.[45]

Will you write to R. H. Dana, Senior, to Dr Gray, to Professor Child? I have used all the names of the Committee, as you permitted me.

Norton thinks Wendell Phillips should be invited So do I. Ward wished Martin Brimmer to be his guest. I replied,[46] We have already as-

42. Letter of Apr. 7, 1864, to Whittier.

43. MS owned by HCL; ph. in CUL. The year is obviously 1864.

44. See the letters of Apr. 6, 1864, to Bryant, Bancroft, and Everett and the letters of Apr. 7 to White, Ticknor, and Andrew. Emerson dated the letter to Verplanck Apr. 8.

45. Emerson wrote to Whittier on Apr. 7. He probably also wrote to Edwin Booth, James T. Fields, and George William Curtis on the same day. I have no definite proof, though Apr. 14, 1864, states that Curtis will come.

46. Apr. 6, 1864, to Ward.

signed you a guest, but will consider this name, if there is room. — What of President Hill?

I have written to Forbes [47] about Whittier. Bryant would have been surer, if we had prearranged with Waterston who has hospitable ties with him to send for him.[48]

But here is arrived between these two lines a visiter Dr Hedge and the mail goes — and I will entreat that you will meet me at the Union Club at 4 o'clock on Monday P. M. I will ask Holmes to come there & settle a few things left flying. If that hour does not suit you, will 5 or 6 I shall be in town that day & can the next morn if you are not otherwise to be seen. One thing to be thot of is we have one or two names more than are good. I will hope to see you, if I do not hear otherwise then & there.

Yrs,

J. R. Lowell, Esq.   R. W Emerson

To James Elliot Cabot, Concord, April 7, 1864 [49]

Concord
April 7

Dear Cabot,

You are to know that at the last meeting of the " Saturday Club," it was voted, that the meeting in April should be holden on the 23ᵈ instant, and that the club should be opened on that day by an addition of friends of Shakspeare. Lowell, Holmes, & I were made a committee for the occasion. The conversation contemplated a party, say of fifty, who were to join us on the same foo ing, for that day, as members. But, in the committee, it was believed impracticable for the Club to invite gentlemen to dine with them & bear their own expenses; and it was therefore settled, that the Committee should designate 12 or 15 guests to be invited, & that each member, who is willing, should charge himself with the entertainment of one of these. Cruel is Club-law. We wish you to accept a guest, but he must be one of our choosing. Yet we can only rely on, say, 13 or 14 members, to accept what we impose. We wish first to make these sure, and we must reduce our list of guests proposed. I hope nothing will hinder you from joining us. on the day.

47. Apr. 7, 1864, to Forbes.

48. Bryant's friendship with R. C. Waterston is mentioned in Parke Godwin, *passim.*

49. MS owned by Professor Philip Cabot; ph. in CUL. The year is clearly 1864, the time of the Shakespeare celebration.

Here is the list of guests invited or to be invited. —

Governor Andrew	Mr Everett
W. C. Bryant	Geo Ticknor
Bancroft	Dr Frothingham
Verplank	R. H. Dana
Rich^d. Grant White	Dr Asa Gray
Booth	Whittier
G. W. Curtis	Prof. Child
	J. T. Fields

Our New Yorkers may not come, and we have several desired names. waiting. If any name appear to you indispensable, send it to me Ever yours

R. W. Emerson

J. E. Cabot.

To Nathaniel Langdon Frothingham, Concord? April 7, 1864

[Listed in *Journals*, X, 21. Frothingham accepted, Boston, Apr. 9, 1864.]

To Thomas? Ridgeway? Gould, Concord? April 7, 1864

[Mentioned in *Journals*, X, 21. Apparently no Gould attended the Shakespeare celebration, but if this letter concerned that event, it may have been addressed, I conjecture, to Thomas Ridgeway Gould, the sculptor, who gained some notice as a reader and interpreter of Shakespeare. *Cf.* the letters of May? *c.* 26? 1863, and Mar. *c.* 13, 1865, to Gould.]

To Oliver Wendell Holmes, Concord? April 7, 1864

[Mentioned in *Journals,* X, 21.]

To John Greenleaf Whittier, Concord? April 7, 1864

[Mentioned in *Journals*, X, 21; *cf.* also the letter of the same date to Lowell. Whittier, Amesbury, Mass., Apr. 21, 1864, said he had delayed his answer in the hope of finding it possible to come to the celebration but now found he could not.]

To Gulian Crommelin Verplanck, Concord? April 8? 1864 [50]

Hon. Gulian C. Verplanck

Dear Sir,

The " Saturday Club " in Boston propose to hold their April meeting on the 23^d instant, & to invite a few friends of Shakspeare to

---

50. MS owned by the Folger Shakespeare Library; ph. in CUL. Emerson's date is clearly enough Apr. 8, but, according to Apr. 7, 1864, to Lowell, this letter was writ-

dine with them. In their behalf, we request the honor of your company at dinner on that evening, at 6 o'clock, at the Revere House.

With great regard,
Your obed!. servant,
R. W. Emerson

R W E.
J. R. Lowell.
O. W. Holmes} Committee
   April 8, 1864.
   Concord, Mass^{tts} 51

To Matthew Arnold, Concord? April c. 8? 1864

[Mentioned in *Journals,* X, 23, in an entry of, apparently, Apr. 8 or later, 1864. Arnold replied:

" London,
" June 19th, 1864.

" My dear Sir

" It was a great pleasure to me to receive a letter from you; I look back with great satisfaction to having made your personal acquaintance when you were here some years ago, and I can never forget the refreshing and quickening effect your writings had upon me at a critical time of my life. I wish I could have seen more of M^r. Ward, but he was kind enough to come out one afternoon to me in the country, where I am now staying, so I was more fortunate than one generally is, when one is out of London, in seeing passing guests.

" I think I sent you my last words on translating Homer because of the passage about Clough at the end of them, which I wished you, as a valued friend of his, to see. You must have thought it strange to receive the mere tail of a performance without the commencement; but to say the truth I was thinking of Clough and your interest in him, and not so much of my own lucubrations on Homer, which, however, I am very glad to find you have read with approval. I have just sent you a little book on Middle Class Education which I have published: the matter is of more interest, of course, at home than it can be anywhere else; but I think you will read with interest the account of Lacordaire and the general reflexions on the English Middle Class and its

---

ten before that one. The probable explanation is that a rough draft was written on the 7th and was copied on the 8th. Verplanck explained, Fishkill Landing, N. Y., Apr. 26, 1864, that he had been unable to accept the invitation.

It is of interest to note that, according to the best testimony, the library which now owns the MS of this letter was the outgrowth of an interest in Shakespeare first inspired in Henry Clay Folger by Emerson himself (see Joseph Quincy Adams, *The Folger Shakespeare Library,* 1933, pp. 13–14) , though there may be some doubt as to whether the writing of Emerson's which served as the initial impulse was an address actually delivered at the tercentenary celebration by the Saturday Club (*cf.* a note on Apr. 28, 1864) .

51. Emerson wrote these two words on p. 3, otherwise blank.

tendencies, and you will not be offended by what I have said about America —
indeed I cannot help believing you will agree with it. Thank you for the two
numbers of the Atlantic Monthly; the papers to which you directed my notice
are certainly remarkable, thoughtful and suggestive productions.

"I am always, my dear Sir, with the greatest respect,

"Sincerely yours

"R. W. Emerson Esq.   Matthew Arnold. — "]

To James Elliot Cabot, Concord, April 11, 1864 [52]

Concord, April 11

My dear Cabot,

Your absence on the Shakspeare Day is impossible. Every
thinking creature owes a duty then: and if, in the silence of America,
the poor little Saturday Club said, 'We will at least call half a dozen
poets or poet-lovers together — the self respect of humanity requires it"
— do you think it can spare you from the commemorators? It cannot
and least of all can I. If you think our methods are bad, (and the *modus*
is wide of my wish & proposing,) it is not quite too late, I think, to
modify it; — and, at worst, a dinner is an empty vase, which, however
well or absurdly ornamented, can be filled with mud or wine or dews of
Castalie if not of Hermon. And it is you that are to exert the saving will.
We are to have a meeting tomorrow of Committee at the Union Club.
But I fear this cannot now reach you in time for you to advise us there.

Ever yours,

R. W. Emerson

J. E. Cabot, Esq.

To Charles Sumner, Concord, April 13, 1864 [53]

Concord

13 April, 1864 —

Dear Sumner,

I have received through your careful kindness, lately, in
successive instalments, a huge pile of Public Documents, — some of them
of special value to me, all of them, I doubt not, of value to some of my
neighbors, and I am aiming to carry them to those to whom they best
belong. Eight good volumes go tomorrow to the "Concord Library."
My thanks wait on you always for this persistent thoughtfulness for me.

52. MS owned by Professor Philip Cabot; ph. in CUL. The year is obviously that
of the Shakespeare celebration.

53. MS owned by RWEMA; ph. in CUL.

I write at this moment to ask if there is no day of vacation coming for you before the end of the session? Have you no public or private necessities that will bring you to Massachusetts for 24 hours? The 23ᵈ instant is the Shakspeare jubilee, and our " Saturday Club," at its last meeting appointed its April meeting on the 23ᵈ instead of 30ᵗʰ We have invited Governor Andrew, Bryant, Bancroft, Everett, Dana (Senior) Verplanck, Whittier, & other good men to come, and, except Bancroft, they answer Yes. It is to be at the Revere House at 4 P. M. And even duties to the American State might be remitted for a space in the presence of an interest so cosmical & humane. I am sure the Committee of Foreign Affairs has no foreign affair so commanding as their relation to Shakspeare. — And if you are coming to Boston for a day, we entreat you that it may be then.[54] If impossible, you may yet have a greeting to send? I ask a little officially too as I am Chairman of the Committee with Lowell & Holmes. Strength & success abide with you!

Yours faithfully,

Hon. C. Sumner.   R. W. Emerson

To James Russell Lowell, Concord, April 14, 1864 [55]

Dear Lowell,

Everett & Bryant & Curtis will come.[56] Bancroft will not. Verplanck & White do not reply.[57] Do you know R. G. White's address? I wrote simply " New York." Whittier does not answer. He has a sick sister.[58] But we wait for replies, that we may fill up any vacancies; and it is getting late for invitations. I hope you have favorable replies from Pierce,[59] Agassiz, Dana, — most of all from Longfellow, — and have sped my letter to Appleton.[60] And you have asked Child? & asked Dana Senior? If not, pray do on the instant; and Dr Gray?

Brimmer is invited because Ward had asked him, & will take two

54. Sumner replied, Washington, D. C., Apr. 18, 1864, that he could not be absent from the Senate a single day even for Shakespeare.

55. MS owned by HCL; ph. in CUL.

56. For the replies from Everett and Bryant, see the notes on the letters of Apr. 6, 1864, to them.

57. Verplanck's very tardy reply is mentioned in a note on Apr. 8? 1864. For White's acceptance, see the note on Apr. 7 to him.

58. For Whittier, see Apr. 22? 1864. For the illness and death of Elizabeth Whittier in 1864, see Pickard, II, 479–480.

59. That is, Benjamin Peirce, not Pierce.

60. Written Apr. 7, 1864.

guests if needful. Judge Conway [61] of Kansas has been written to in like manner by Dr S. G. Howe, who will take two guests for his sake. Ward wishes Wm Hunt invited; the rather that he has a picture under his hands of Hamlet,[62] which should grace the Banquet. There is a strong vote for Hillard,[63] & I yield, on the new evidence presented. Wendell Phillips has not yet replied.

I dare not yet write to J. F. Clarke,[64] since, if all now invited or agreed on come, we have no more room. Dr Holmes urges Winthrop,[65] Judge Bigelow,[66] & Dr Bigelow.[67] I shall not vote for Winthrop

I enclose a list of guests against which Holmes made a horizontal mark of approval, & I a perpendicular. You must add the oblique, & send it back to me with what information you have to add.

Ever yours,

R. W. E.

April 14. Evening

P. S. I find in my home list Child's name crossed, & therefore believe I have written to him.[68] I will send Edward E. to him, on Monday Morn.^g.

Whipple & Woodman [69] will accept guests, & Cabot will, and come.

You must write to Rowse and decide upon Booth

Weiss

Hunt

Bigelow

Bigelow

Winthrop

Davis, I suppose, Dr Holmes puts on the footing of Brimmer, Conway, & as you put Rowse that is on the proper peril of the nominator.[70]

61. See Apr. 17, 1864.

62. Cf. Apr. c. 16, 1864, to Hunt. Hunt did not come but sent the picture (Journals, X, 25–26). His vain attempt to paint Emerson and his great admiration of Emerson's writings are mentioned in Helen M. Knowlton, pp. 52–53 and 94. A few years after the Shakespeare celebration, Hunt became a member of the Club (The Early Years, pp. 464–473).

63. See Apr. 19, 1864, to Lowell for George S. Hillard.

64. See Apr. c. 16, 1864, to Clarke.

65. Winthrop came, it seems (The Early Years, p. 339).

66. Doubtless George T. Bigelow, Holmes's college classmate and later chief justice of Massachusetts.

67. Probably Dr. Henry J. Bigelow, Holmes's friend and colleague on the Harvard faculty.

68. I have no proof of this letter.

69. Apparently Emerson had written to Edwin Percy Whipple and Horatio Woodman, but I have no further evidence.

70. Lowell replied, Saturday (Apr. 16, 1864), that if " proper peril " meant paying

To WILLIAM CULLEN BRYANT, CONCORD, APRIL 16, 1864 [71]

Concord, —
April 16, 1864 —

Dear Mr Bryant,

Our committee are very happy in your consent to join us on the 23ᵈ; and we promise to bring you some old as well as younger friends. I write now to say, that the hour fixed for dinner will be earlier than was at first named, and will be at 4 o'clock P. M. at the Revere House.

Yours faithfully,
R. W. Emerson
for the Committee.

W. C. Bryant, Esq.

To JAMES RUSSELL LOWELL, CONCORD? APRIL 16, 1864 [72]

Saturday Mornᵍ

My dear Lowell,

Certainly it is of first importance that Longfellow come, & Mr Greene must be asked if need be. Please to see that duty performed at the fit moment. You send me the best news. I have not a word yet from Verplank or White — none directly from Whittier. I think to write to Curtis today in behalf of White.[73] You do not say that the Danas will come. You were to invite the father.

Ever yours
R. W. Emerson

J. R. Lowell.

---

for Rowse, all right, but that, as for Judge Conway of Kansas, Shakespeare wouldn't have dined with him.

71. MS owned by Mr. Conrad G. Goddard; ph. in CUL. Emerson had sent his first invitation to Bryant ten days earlier. Bryant accepted it but later changed his mind (cf. a note on Apr. 19 following to Lowell).

72. MS owned by HCL; ph. in CUL. This letter, which obviously belongs to a Saturday earlier than the 23d, is a reply to Lowell's letter of " Thursday " stating that Agassiz will take his man; that Longfellow will come if Professor G. W. Greene, who will be his guest at the time, is also invited; that Lowell has written to Curtis, Gray, Weiss, and Rowse and will see Child this afternoon. Lowell's letter must have reached Emerson after he had written the letter of Apr. 14, 1864, to Lowell. Lowell's Thursday must therefore be Apr. 14, and the Saturday of the present letter must be Apr. 16.

73. Apr. 16? 1864, to Curtis. For White's acceptance, see the note on Apr. 7, 1864, to him, and cf. letters of Apr. 17 and 18, 1864. The letter of the 18th to Forbes adds much to the proof of Apr. 16 as the date of the present letter.

To James Freeman Clarke, Concord, April c. 16, 1864

[Mentioned in Apr. 17, 1864. Apr. 14, 1864, shows that Emerson had not then written this letter. Clarke replied, Jamaica Plain, Mass., Apr. 20 following, that he would be present for a part of the evening.]

To George William Curtis, Concord? April 16? 1864

[Emerson wrote to Lowell on Apr. 16 that he thought to write Curtis " today in behalf of White." Curtis, Staten Island, Apr. 19, 1864, acknowledged this note " about White " and promised to " prod him with pen and tongue." Good reasons for asking Curtis to prod White are given in Apr. 14. The letter of the 17th shows that by that time Emerson knew White's intention of coming.]

To William Morris Hunt, Concord? April c. 16, 1864

[Mentioned in letters of Apr. 17 and 19, 1864.]

To James Russell Lowell, Concord, April 17, 1864 [74]

Concord
Sunday night, 17th

Dear Lowell,

I have your note. White accepts.[75] Brimmer accepts. Wendell Phillips refuses with an arrow. You shall please write to Rowse.[76] I am not sure of his exact address. By proper peril [77] I mean that in case the number of guests shall exceed the number of consenting members R is to be charged to you, as in the same case, Brimmer to Ward, Conway to Howe, & Davis [78] to Holmes each of you having said you would rather take two than have your guest left out. I have written to J. F Clarke; & to Hunt, seeing that you also had marked the last favorably. If he accepts I shall ask for his picture. Conway, *Judge* Conway, is a very good kind of man who made the best speech in the last Congress, — though

74. MS owned by HCL; ph. in CUL. The year is obviously 1864.

75. *Cf.* notes on the letters of Apr. 7, 1864, to White and Apr. 18 following to Lowell.

76. Emerson apparently forgot that Lowell had already reported writing to Rowse (see a note on Apr. 16, 1864, to Lowell) .

77. In Apr. 14, 1864.

78. George Thomas Davis, whom Thackeray thought the most agreeable dinner companion he found in the United States (John T. Morse, I, 77) , was Holmes's college classmate. For Davis's presence at the Shakespeare celebration, see *Journals*, X, 25.

it was a mistake in policy,[79] — and is not to be confounded with vulgar men.

Ever yours,
R. W. Emerson

J. R. Lowell, Esq

To George Sewall Boutwell, Concord, April 18, 1864[80]

Concord
18 April 1864

Hon George S. Boutwell,
    My dear Sir,
            I have just heard that Hon. Mr Hooper of the House has presented a Resolution to grant to W. T. G. Morton, $100 000. for the discovery of etherization.[81] The like action has been attempted several times before in Congress,[82] & has hitherto failed. You are probably familiar with the facts, at least in outline. Doctor Charles T. Jackson is known to me as the discoverer. It is on evidence, that, in the outset, Dr Morton who was his pupil, acknowledged his indebtedness to Dr Jackson for the knowledge of this use of sulphuric ether, and used it under his advice. Later, he pretended to the discovery. Some personal feuds & professional jealousies determined the sides which our Boston doctors took, when it was first announed,[83] but, though a few men of mark have continued to sustain Morton's claims, & great numbers have subscribed money to him, I believe the opinion of the largest number of competent judges in Massachusetts has come to the belief in Dr Jackson's inevitable priority. But Dr J is no match in the art of pressing his claim for Dr M.

79. Martin Franklin Conway had been chief justice of the supreme court in Kansas and later served as a member of the House in the 36th and 37th Congresses. Doubtless his speech here referred to was that against the division of Virginia to create West Virginia; Conway had no objection to the new state, if only the application might come in a constitutional way (*The Congressional Globe*, 37th Cong., 3d Sess., pp. 37–38, Dec. 9, 1862).

80. MS owned by HCL; ph. in CUL.

81. The official version was: " *Resolved*, That the Committee of Ways and Means be instructed to inquire into the expediency of reporting a bill to pay the proprietor thereof for the use of anæsthetic agents in the army and navy of the United States " (*Journal of the House of Representatives*, 38th Cong., 1st Sess., Apr. 5, 1864). Apparently nothing came of this.

82. *Cf.* Mar. 1, 1863.

83. The word, like many others, usually not mentioned in the notes, is incompletely written.

Meantime Dr J. has never asked for a reward, public or private. But when the claim is made by Morton he is forced to resist it. In each instance, the claim is sprung on him by surprize, & has been all but carried, I believe, repeatedly. The injustice is in carrying it before an incompetent tribunal, as Congress is. Dr J. would be heartily contented to have it tried before a competent court. Then, that it is attempted to be done without notice to adverse rights. This seems imperative, that if such action is to be in Congress, notice should be given to parties opposed. May I beg your attention to the matter so far as to see that this iniquity is not hurried through, without opportunity of evidence on the other side? I shall, tomorrow, find & send you a copy of the "Minority Report" of the Committee in Congress charged with this matter, in 1849; [84] which, I believe, contains what is most material that Dr Jackson would present. I write hastily on hearing the news, & inadequately. I shall endeavor to write tomorrow to Mr Hooper, [85] who, unfortunately for Dr J., is, I believe, officially in the Mass^{tts} General Hospital, which made & kept a rash opinion on the subject.

> With great regard, Yours,
> R. W. Emerson

To James Elliot Cabot, Concord, April 18, 1864 [86]

> Concord
> Monday, 18th Apr.

My dear Cabot

If it were not such a duty to come, I could heartily thank you for your compliance. [87] But I write now to say, that the hour is 4 o'clock on Saturday, & at the Revere House. Governor Andrew, Bryant, Richd Grant White, Everett, Dana Senior, will come, and others, though Bancroft & Wendell Phillips refuse.

Longfellow comes back too. [88] Whittier has a sister very ill, & I fear will not.

> Yours,
> R. W. Emerson

J. Elliot Cabot, Esq.

84. See a note on Apr. 20 and 21, 1848.

85. Probably this letter to Hooper was written, but I have no further evidence.

86. MS owned by Professor Philip Cabot; ph. in CUL. The year could be only 1864.

87. *Cf.* Apr. 11, 1864.

88. Longfellow had for some time neglected the Club. In Feb. 24, 1864, Emerson had asked him when he would "come back to the Saturdays," which wanted "their ancient lustre."

To JOHN MURRAY FORBES, CONCORD, APRIL 18, 1864

[MS owned by RWEMA; ph. in CUL. Printed in *Letters and Recollections of John Murray Forbes*, II, 87–88.]

To JOHN MURRAY FORBES, CONCORD, APRIL 18, 1864 [89]

Monday Night
18 Apr

My dear Mr Forbes,

I had hardly sent my note, before I found yours,[90] & with great contentment. I was stung by the naming of Charles Spragu whom I cannot forgive myself for overlooking. He has the foremost claims; for he first in Boston wrote elegant verse, & on Shakspeare.[91] I shall, as chairman of the Committee, write to him tonight, presuming the consent of my colleagues, Lowell & Holmes.

We ought to have remembered Halleck, too, when we sent for Verplanck & the New York men. But now I fear it is too late; for each nomination requires a little consultation, as there many desireable guests proposed, and all our invitations are not yet answered. Yet the names you give me shall go in the morning to Lowell & Holmes. Bryant wrote me, that he would come.[92] I hope he is still in the same mind. George Ticknor & Wendell Phillips decline. I am very sorry to lose Ward there; and Hawthorne, I fear, cannot come,[93] but if you will bring Whittier, I can find in the party a fair assortment of virtues.

I shall gladly hear from you what good you found in Washington & New York.

Yours always,
R. W Emerson

J. M. Forbes.

89. MS owned by RWEMA; ph. in CUL. The year is clearly 1864.

90. Forbes, Apr. 17, 1864. The principal contents of this note are mentioned in the present letter and in that of the same date to Lowell. In the following sentence, Sprague's name was written too close to the edge of the leaf.

91. For Emerson's early admiration, see July 27, 1835, to Sprague. As the letter of Apr. 19, 1864, to Lowell shows, Sprague declined the invitation of the Club; but his " Shakspeare Ode," which had been " *Delivered at the Boston Theatre in 1823*," was reprinted in the supplement of the *Boston Evening Transcript* of Apr. 23, the day of the celebration. The same ode, as published, I conjecture, about the time of delivery in the theater, is included in a volume of American pamphlets which bears Emerson's signature and is still in his house, at Concord.

92. See the note on Apr. 6, 1864, to Bryant.

93. *Cf.* Apr. 21 following to Lowell.

To James Russell Lowell, Concord? April 18, 1864 [94]

Apr 18, Monday Night

Dear Lowell,

As soon as I had told you of not hearing from White,[95] his answer came. I am glad of Gray, Dana, & Weiss. I talked over Parsons,[96] lately, with (I think) Dr S. G. H — who thought him very desireable, but liable to become violent over wine, — which put an end to the question. Curtis, I thought I told you, will gladly come. — But Mr Forbes sends me today a name which I think of the first desert, Charles Sprague, and I am mortified to have overlooked it & shall presume your assent & Holmes's & send him an invitation [97] on " my proper peril," to offset your perils. For he it was who first in Boston wrote elegant verses, and behind a bank-counter, and his theme was Shakspeare. I have not heard from Appleton. Forbes also proposes Fitz Green Halleck, & thinks he would come if he should invite Charles W. Eliot,[98] his cousin, to bring him. In the circumstances, I have no interest in this nomination. If you and the Doctor have, you shall invite him. Our list stands now

11 have accepted

$\frac{1}{12}$ Add Conway, since I hear he is in the city

$\frac{5}{17}$ Six or seven more have been invited of whom five may come
Including Sprague, I think we have 18. And on Friday may very easily fill vacancies

Perhaps we add Winthrop & Greene?

I think we may count on the presence of 17 members.

Yours ever

R. W. E.

---

94. MS owned by HCL; ph. in CUL. The year is clear from the contents of the letter.

95. *Cf.* Apr. 16, 1864, to Lowell.

96. Thomas William Parsons.

97. See Apr. 18, 1864, to Sprague. For his verses *cf.* a letter of this date to Forbes.

98. Not the later president of Harvard but the much older Charles Eliot mentioned in James Grant Wilson, *The Life and Letters of Fitz-Greene Halleck*, 1869, p. 574.

To Charles Sprague, Concord? April 18, 1864

[Acknowledged in Sprague, Boston, Apr. 19, 1864. Sprague could not accept. *Cf.* also other letters of Apr. 18.]

To Nathaniel Langdon Frothingham, Concord? April *c.* 18? 1864

[Frothingham, Boston, Apr. 21, 1864, said he was sorry Emerson took the trouble to write about the change of hour.]

To John Murray Forbes, Concord, April 19, 1864 [99]

Concord, 19 April

My dear Mr Forbes

I sent an invitation to *Shakspeare* to William Hunt,[100] a few days ago, by mail to " *Boston.*" I do not know that it is the exact address. If you see him, I wish you would make him come. Better yet, can you not suggest that he should hang the picture of Hamlet, which, Ward told me he was passionately painting, in our hall, to grace the occasion?

Yours,

R. W. Emerson

J. M. Forbes, Esq.

Postscript.

Hunt accepts but the letter may yet go for its request.

To James Russell Lowell, Concord? April 19, 1864 [101]

19 April.

Dear Lowell,

Bryant today sends his regrets,[102] & revokes his acceptance. I feared as much when Forbes wrote how care-worn he found him,

99. MS owned by RWEMA; ph. in CUL. The year is, of course, that of the Shakespeare celebration.

100. Letter of Apr. *c.* 16, 1864, to Hunt.

101. MS owned by HCL; ph. in CUL. The year is obviously 1864.

102. Bryant, New York, Apr. 18, 1864, explained to Emerson that he had duties he could not leave.

stemming the panic.[103] Nothing from Verplanck yet, who may therefore be cancelled. Say 12 have accepted. There remain unheard from

Whittier

Clarke

Hunt

Sprague

Davis ⎫ if the Doctor

Winthrop ⎭ has invited them

Child — of whom you give

      hope —

Greene   if you conclude to

        ask him.

You & the Doctor shall decide on Parsons, & ask him if you think fit. I too am loth to leave him out.

R. W. E.

I am not sure I told you, Hillard comes.

" Very latest "

   Hunt accepts.[104]

   Sprague declines [105]

To Frederic Henry Hedge, Concord? April 20, 1864 [106]

Wednesday

20 Apr

Dear Hedge,

      I trust you are coming,[107] though Bryant, alas! has revoked his acceptance yesterday.[108] And do you know that we changed the hour to *4* o clock P. M. Saturday

Yours always

R. W. E.

To Oliver Wendell Holmes, Concord? April 21, 1864

[Mentioned in the letter of the same date to Lowell. Holmes replied, Boston, Apr. 22, accepting Emerson's proposal for a meeting at three o'clock.]

103. Forbes, Milton, Mass., Apr. 17, 1864: " I saw Mr Bryant yesterday in New York — very busy & care worn, stemming the Panic! " *Cf.* " The Financial Flurry " and other articles on the crisis in *The Evening Post,* Apr. 15–19, 1864.

104. But see a note on Apr. 14, 1864.

105. See the note on Apr. 18, 1864, to Sprague.

106. MS owned by RWEMA; ph. in CUL. Obviously the year is 1864.

107. Hedge came (*Journals,* X, 25) .

108. See Apr. 19, 1864, to Lowell.

To James Russell Lowell, Concord? April 21, 1864 [109]

Thursday Night

Dear Lowell,

I had Appleton's note [110] yesterday, signifying loyal consent, with good hope of Longfellow, & urging Winthrop's invitation.

For the assigning places, I wrote to Holmes, this P. M., praying him to do it. — if he wanted aid, I would meet him at the Revere, at 3 o'c on Saturday. — But doubtless it is safer, as there may be much else to settle, that we should all three meet. If you think 2.30, or an earlier hour better, a note will find me at Parker's on Saturday forenoon.

A note from Mr Everett yesterday: [111] he has postponed his journey to com [112] to the dinner, & now has bronchial affection, & fears he may be prevented. — But is actively treated, & his Doctor has hopes.

I called on Hawthorne, last night, and found him still feeble. [113] He probably will not come; but I shall look in on him tomorrow No word yet from Whittier, though Forbes has written in urgency.

Yours,

R. W. E.

J. R. Lowell, Esq

To James Russell Lowell, Concord? April 22? 1864 [114]

Dear Lowell

Here in the Post Office I have Everetts letter — he cannot come. Holmes says, Child can, if there is room. [115] Let him come, then; if you see good. Tomorrow, I will perhaps ask Calvert. Whittier writes to decline. [116] Let Longfellow come if he has legs & a heart. [117]

Yours,

R. W. E.

109. MS owned by HCL; ph. in CUL. The date is definitely fixed by evidence cited below.

110. T. G. Appleton, Boston, Apr. 19 (1864).

111. Cf. Apr. 22? 1864, for Everett's final decision.

112. The word ran off the paper.

113. Hawthorne died in the following month.

114. MS owned by HCL; ph. in CUL. The date is determined approximately by the reference to Everett's final answer — his letter of Apr. 22, mentioned in the note on Apr. 6, 1864, to him.

115. Holmes, Boston, Apr. 21.

116. In his letter of Apr. 21, mentioned in the note on Apr. 7, 1864, to him.

117. Longfellow came (Journals, X, 25).

To John Murray Forbes, Concord, April? 22? 1864? [118]

Friday P. M

Here in the Post-office, I find your note. I see not how I can come, though you draw me so kindly. The Judge sends a horse down to bring us up at 10. P. M. And I am in such bonds on Monday that I know not how to be in Milton

R W E

Will send Edith note to Cambridge

To James Russell Lowell, Concord, April 28, 1864 [119]

Concord
28 April

Dear Lowell,

As I have no very good opinion of my skill in accounts, I send Dr Holmes's account from the Revere House, with his analysis & distribution of it, back to him, through you, that you may also pass upon it. It looks to me a mild & merciful result. But I am not sure that we all count the responsibilities of Club members in the same way. You alone spoke with Dana & Pierce. Dwight agreed to come, but declined to pay for a guest. Hedge thought he should not come at all, & said nothing of guests therefore. I suppose then these abovenamed are the four whom Holmes counts out. But Dana, though absent, I suppose, pays for himself. And Ward may be charged for himself & a guest.

Dr Holmes should write on Ward's bill, *Approved;* — or he can send

118. MS owned by RWEMA; ph. in CUL. The date Apr. 22, 1864, is given in the endorsement without question. The phrase " Here in the Post-office " seems to link the letter, though not definitely, with the letter to Lowell which was almost certainly written on that day.

119. MS owned by HCL; ph. in CUL. The year of this final comment on the Shakespeare celebration was, of course, 1864. For Emerson's own part in the speech-making of Apr. 23, we are left in doubt. According to Cabot (II, 621–622) , Emerson, who was no impromptu orator, rose to speak, looked about him tranquilly for a minute or two, and then sat down without saying a word. But we have the speech which he prepared, it seems, for this occasion (*Cent. Ed.,* XI, 445–453) ; and there is some reason to believe, as his son pointed out, that it was actually read and that Cabot had forgotten the fact (*cf. The Early Years of the Saturday Club,* p. 342; and see a note on Apr. 8? 1864) . One is tempted, however, to discover pertinent comment in May 7 following to Stearns.

it to me. There were really present 32 persons,[120] and we looked for two more, Hunt & Parsons, — 34; but not 35.

Yes, collect by a collector.

Ever yours,
R. W. Emerson

J. R. Lowell, Esq.

To George Luther Stearns, Concord, May 7, 1864 [121]

Concord
May 7, 1864.

My dear Sir,

Much experience has taught me to be very cautious in making speeches in behalf of any cause to which I have a good will. If the hours of your Emancipation League [122] admit of my being in town, I will try to attend it, but not to speak to it, as I hope for its success.

Yours faithfully,
R. W. Emerson

Mr Geo. L. Stearns.

To Charles Sumner, Concord, May 7, 1864 [123]

Concord —
7 May, 1864 —

Dear Sumner,

I received day before yesterday a letter from a young friend of mine,[124] who is now on General Banks's staff, which is written so ear-

120. This is the number given in Emerson's list in *Journals,* X, 25.

121. MS owned by Mr. F. R. Fraprie; ph. in CUL.

122. The public meeting of the Emancipation League in Boston on May 23 was reported in the *Boston Daily Advertiser* of May 24, 1864. Wendell Phillips was the speaker of the occasion, and he stressed the view that the Lincoln administration, in spite of the emancipation proclamation, considered slavery the only sacred thing in the country.

123. MS owned by RWEMA; ph. in CUL.

124. Charles Emerson, New Orleans, Apr. 20, 1864, praised Gen. Charles P. Stone, who, he explained, had been Banks's chief of staff but was now the victim of unjust persecution, instigated, it was said, by Massachusetts statesmen powerful at Washington. At the end of the letter is such a personal message as Emerson describes. The partial copy here mentioned is still with Emerson's own letter and bears this heading in his hand: " Copy of a letter from an officer on Gen! Banks's staff." Sumner, Washington, D. C., May 11, 1864, simply made it clear that he

nestly in behalf of one of his superior officers, that I have let my daughter copy the whole letter (with the exception of a private message on other matters at the close,) to enclose to you, believing that you will value it as evidence, & may know how to give it a useful direction for the benefit of the public service, & of the officer himself. I know nothing personally of General Stone. I think I first heard of him through some malignant letter written by him to you. But he has since had so great misfortunes, that he is probably a wiser man.

Ever yours affectionately,
R. W. Emerson

Hon. Charles Sumner.

To Thomas Hill? Concord? May c. 8? 1864

[Edward Waldo Emerson, Cambridge, Tuesday, May 10 (1864): "Last night I carried your letter & my petition to the President's office, where the Faculty were in session . . ." This morning, he says, he learned that the petition, like others presented, had been voted down; the president (Hill) advised him to stick quietly to work. Edward wrote again on July 12 following that the news of the day confirmed his decision to enlist and that he expected to join the Acton company shortly.]

To William Emerson, Concord, May 11, 1864

[WmE List.]

To Ticknor and Fields, Concord, May 13, 1864 [125]

Concord
May 13, 1864 —

Messrs Ticknor & Fields.

    Gentlemen,

        I decide to accept your proposition as far as the 1st & 2d series of my " Essays " are concerned, & you shall if you please proceed to print an edition of 3000 copies in " blue & gold " [126] on the terms proposed in your note of May 7th I shall rely on you to carry out in a special contract the further provisions for the more exact protection of my

---

himself had no knowledge of Stone's misfortunes and was in no way responsible for them. Sumner wrote again, June 18 following, to report that, as he had learned from the President himself, Stone was dropped at the order of Gen. Grant.

125. MS owned by the Henry E. Huntington Library; ph. in CUL.

126. Ticknor & Fields announced in the *Boston Daily Advertiser*, Apr. 6, 1865, that their " Blue and Gold " edition of the *Essays*, containing both series in one volume, was published on that day.

copyright, which were suggested in my recent conversation with Mr Fields.

I have been looking over the books with a view to correction, & will send you presently a short list of *errata*.

Respectfully
R. W. Emerson

Messrs Ticknor & Fields.

To Ticknor and Fields, Concord, May 19, 1864 [127]

Concord, 19 May,
1864.

Gentlemen,

I decide to accept your proposition in your note of the 18th instant,[128] and to permit the printing of 2500 copies of " Emerson's Poems," (as they now stand,) in blue & gold, at your expense; for which edition I am to receive ten cents a copy. In the contract which you propose to state the points with exactness, you will have regard to the reporting to me the date & number of copies of each edition. I think, too, that the modification of the Cabinet edition, at $12\frac{1}{2}$ cts., will be important for this neighborhood.

Yours respectfully,
R. W. Emerson

Messrs Ticknor & Fields.

To James Elliot Cabot, Concord, May 25, 1864 [129]

Concord, 25 May —
1864 —

My dear Cabot,

I send you my thanks for the treasure of a book [130] which arrived today, giving wonder & pleasure to yours affectionately,

R. W. Emerson

J. Elliot Cabot. Esq.

127. MS owned by the Henry E. Huntington Library; ph. in CUL.

128. Ticknor & Fields (obviously James T. Fields himself in this case) , Boston, May 18, 1864, offered to bear the expense of stereotyping the *Poems,* as they stood in the old edition, for republication in the " Blue & Gold Series." The publishers would pay the author $250 on an edition of 2500 copies and would pay at the same rate — ten cents a copy — on all future editions. The edition here described was duly published by Ticknor & Fields on Mar. 25, 1865, according to the *Boston Daily Advertiser* of that date.

129. MS owned by Professor Philip Cabot; ph. in CUL.

130. This was, I conjecture, W. Rimmer's *Elements of Design,* first book, Boston, 1864, which contained an " Introductory Note " by Cabot.

To WILLIAM BARTON ROGERS, CONCORD, MAY 25, 1864 [131]

Concord —
May 25, 1864 —

Dear Sir,

Will you please to signify to the Academy my thanks for the honor they have done me in electing me a Fellow,[132] and my acceptance of the same.

Respectfully,
R. W. Emerson.

William B. Rogers, Esq.
Corresponding Secretary of the American Academy of Arts & Sciences.

To WILLIAM EMERSON, CONCORD, MAY 28, 1864

[WmE List.]

To EDWARD WALDO EMERSON, CONCORD? MAY? 1864? [133]

I send Steece.[134] Up to the 24 page he shows mischiefs of standing armies & how they curse Europe. On p. 24, see his Republican Militia.

I withdraw all my objection to the voting. The necessity of being armed is undeniable But all the evils that threaten from voting belong to armies A wise Militia system enrolling every boy, giving him at one period a gymnastic & military drill, then restoring him to civil life, only liable to serve in war, keeps him sound-hearted, & competent to vote. He is domestic. he is adored at home. he reads newspapers The caucus

131. MS owned by the American Academy of Arts and Sciences; I have made a MS copy, which is in CUL. The Philadelphian William Barton Rogers, who had come to Boston by way of Virginia, became the founder and first head of the Massachusetts Institute of Technology.

132. A MS record book of the Academy contains the original nomination of Emerson, with the signatures of James Jackson, O. W. Holmes, James Russell Lowell, Charles Eliot Norton, and Benjamin Peirce and the notation by the secretary showing that the paper was received Nov. 11, 1863. According to the *Proceedings* of the Academy, VI, 238, Emerson was elected at the meeting of Jan. 27, 1864, to be resident fellow in Class III (Moral and Political Sciences), section 4 (Literature and the Fine Arts).

133. MS owned by RWEMA; ph. in CUL. For the date, there is the evidence of the annotation: "Father, May 1864." Mention of Steece apparently shows that the year is not earlier than 1863.

134. Tecumseh Steece, *A Republican Military System*, 1863, favors a small standing army and a large militia.

already knows him, & he will be old enough for the legislature next year. These are the bayonets that think. In the very expansion of Steece's book, I can see that we shall get a Militia in America better than Cromwell's saints — admitting the friendship of the Sacred Phalanx of the Theban [135] & yet elastic to take the dimensions of a Continental Army. Armies are enormously costly, militia will be as much cheaper, & as much more efficient, thro personal virtue & intellect, as steam trains are than stage-coaches; or telegraphing to New Orleans, than sending a courier.[136]

To Charles Eliot Norton, Concord, June 15, 1864?

[MS listed in John Heise Autographs, catalogue 2461, where the date is given as Wednesday, June 15, n. y. According to the summary printed there, Emerson addresses " Dear Norton " and promises to see him and his friends the following afternoon. Until after 1860 Emerson did not, so far as I know, use a less formal salutation than " My dear Sir " in addressing Norton. The only later years in which June 15 fell on Wednesday were 1864, 1870, and 1881. In June, 1870, Norton was in Italy; and 1881 is so late as to be very improbable.]

To Sophia Peabody Hawthorne, Concord, July 11, 1864

[Printed in *The Sunday Herald*, Boston, June 21, 1885, p. 7, and in the *New-York Tribune* of the same date, p. 8; reprinted, only in fragmentary form, in *Memoirs of Members of the Social Circle*, 2d series, 2d part, p. 109 (same page in *Emerson in Concord*), and, completely with the exception of Mrs. Hawthorne's name at the end, in Rose Hawthorne Lathrop, pp. 455–456.]

To Edward Waldo Emerson, Concord, July? 13? 1864?

[MS owned by Mr. Raymond Emerson. The date I have questioned has been supplied, presumably by Edward. The original heading is simply " Wed. Eve." The contents of the letter show that it was written during the Civil War.]

To John Boynton Hill, Concord, July 17, 1864 [137]

Concord. 17 July. 1864

John B. Hill. Esq.

My dear Sir.

Next Wednesday is Commencement.[138] You have, I hope,

135. The Sacred Band; *cf.* Mar. 25, 1847.

136. There is no signature, nor is there any heading or salutation on the extant sheet, and probably no more was written.

137. MS owned by RWEMA; ph. in CUL. This is a copy, not in Emerson's hand, and shows some peculiarities due, no doubt, to the copyist.

138. The next Wednesday was July 20, and the meeting of the class of 1821 at

received a printed circular from the Class. Committee. announcing that the old room at Sanders' next the Episcopal Church, is engaged for a meeting of the Class of 1821, on that day. It is not yet the completed lustrum for which thus far we have been content to wait. Kent, Quincy, Cheney, Upham & one or two others, who have the habit of going to Commencement, have found it a little dreary to go with persistent loyalty & find no contemporaries, & have requested that the attempt may be made to hold henceforth an annual meeting. I who very rarely go, have promised gladly my adhesion, & I doubt not others will be happy to join us. I wish strongly that it may be in your will & power to come. I am sorry to have delayed this note until now, but in thinking of you it occurred late. that possibly your summons might be sent to Bangor & miss you: as I learn that your chief residence is now in your old home.[139] If you can possibly come pray do; & gratify many old friends & with the rest

Your friend & class-mate.
R. W. Emerson.

To Thomas Wentworth Higginson, Concord, July 18, 1864

[MS owned by the Henry E. Huntington Library; ph. in CUL. An incomplete version is printed in *The Outlook*, LXXIV, 222–223 (May 23, 1903); a complete facsimile is in Thomas Wentworth Higginson and Henry Walcott Boynton, *A Reader's History of American Literature*, n. d. (c. 1903), following p. 174.]

To James Elliot Cabot, Concord, July 27, 1864 [140]

Concord
27 July

My dear Cabot,

I see plainly that I shall not probably get as far as to the Club, on Saturday.[141] I am not sure but that I told you I should go. But my brother is to arrive, on Saturday morning, from New York, and

---

its room in Cambridge was duly announced for that day in the *Boston Daily Advertiser* of the same date.

139. Hill's early home was Mason, N. H., the address given in the college catalogues of his student days; and his letters to Emerson in 1869 and later were from that town.

140. MS owned by Professor Philip Cabot; ph. in CUL. Evidence noted below shows that the year is 1864.

141. The last Saturday in July, 1864, was the 30th.

my family are scattered, leaving me almost alone to keep house. As you had professed a good will to come thither, I am the more sorry. But you will keep your social resolutions, I hope, for many months. Since Ward's return, I had a note from Matthew Arnold,[142] in which he qualifies the papers on "Art & Nature," in the "Atlantic,"[143] as "certainly remarkable, thoughtful, & suggestive productions." When he uses his best eyes, he may add a stronger adjective. He sends me, he says, his "French Eton."[144] But it has not yet come to me.

> Yours always,
> R. W. Emerson

J. E. Cabot, Esq.

To JOHN MURRAY FORBES, CONCORD? AUGUST 15, 1864?

[Mentioned in Aug. 17, 1864?]

To JOHN MURRAY FORBES, CONCORD, AUGUST 17, 1864?[145]

> Concord
> Wednesday Eve
> 17 Aug

My dear Sir,

I wrote you by mail, on Monday Morning, addressed, as you bade me, *Wood's Hole,* to say that I would come to you with great pleasure at the Club on Thursday at 5 — And I am vexed that my note should not have arrived. However, since your purpose holds, mine does also —

> Ever yours,
> R. W. Emerson

J. M. Forbes, Esq

142. For Arnold's letter of the preceding month, see the note on Apr. *c.* 8? 1864.

143. The two parts of Cabot's "On the Relation of Art to Nature" appeared in *The Atlantic* for Feb. and Mar., 1864. Emerson had praised this essay to Longfellow in Feb. 24, 1864. *Cf.* also July 13, 1862.

144. *A French Eton; or, Middle Class Education and the State,* 1864.

145. MS owned by RWEMA; ph. in CUL. Another hand has supplied "1864," and Aug. 17 fell on Wednesday in that year. It seems probable that the "Club" was the Union Club, mentioned in other letters of 1863 and 1864.

To WENDELL PHILLIPS, CONCORD, SEPTEMBER 14, 1864 [146]

Concord
14 Sept. 1864

Dear Phillips,

A young English gentleman, Hon. Lyulf Stanley, who has lately taken his degrees at Baliol College, Oxford, and is, if you will permit me to say so, on *our* side in politics, has a strong desire to see you & has taken some pains to that end, in vain. He has promised to come & dine with me next Wednesday 21st instant & I have promised to bring you to meet him if I can. I entreat you to gratify us both, by taking the Fitchburg train at 11 o'c. A. M. on that day, & coming to Concord. He is a well-informed open-minded man has gone to the Potomac &, I think he said, to Chattanooga, and is a fit subject for your impressions. He is not of the Derby Stanleys, but son of Lord Stanley of Alderley. I pray you to put aside all obstacles & come.

Ever yours faithfully,
R. W. Emerson

Wendell Phillips, Esq.

To THOMAS CARLYLE, CONCORD, SEPTEMBER 26, 1864

[MS owned by RWEMA. Brief fragments and a summary were given in Conway, *Thomas Carlyle,* pp. 95–96; the letter was printed incompletely in *Harper's Weekly,* June 10, 1882, p. 358. The version in the *New-York Tribune,* June 7, 1882, seems, in spite of the earlier date, to be reprinted from *Harper's Weekly.* A very incomplete version appeared in Ireland, *In Memoriam,* pp. 74–77. The letter printed in *C–E Corr.,* 1883, apparently from the MS, contains a number of passages not in earlier versions. Presumably the letter of Sept. 23, 1864, in the Bluebook List was a rough draft, which I have not found, of the text sent under date of Sept. 26.]

To EDWIN R. PERKINS, CONCORD, SEPTEMBER, 1864 [147]

Concord Mass^tts

Dear Sir,

It will give me pleasure to come to Cleveland, this season, if I can. I have invitations, which, if they are made good, will bring me

146. MS owned by Mr. Carroll A. Wilson; ph. in CUL. Edward Lyulph Stanley (later fourth Baron Stanley) was at this time a fellow of Balliol. He had written, May 7, 1864, from New York, to say that he had an introduction from Carlyle but would not reach Boston till September. When he came to Concord, on the 21st of that month, he seems to have found not only Phillips, but Agassiz, Channing, and Alcott at Emerson's home (see *Journals,* X, 60) .

147. MS owned by Goodspeed's Book Shop; ph. in CUL. An endorsement gives

into your neighborhood, about the 20ᵗʰ January. If I come to Cleveland,
the Association shall pay me fifty dollars.

Respectfully,

R. W. Emerson.

E. A. Perkins, Esq.
 Chairman.

To Mary Preston Stearns, Concord, October 3, 1864? [148]

Concord

3 October —

Dear Mrs Stearns,

  Mrs Emerson & I mean to keep the day & hour you have set; [149]
but you shall not give yourself the trouble of sending for us. We shall
find our way to the 3 o'clock train in Boston,[150] & come to you by that.
Meantime, I give you joy of the good public news which each day
brings: [151] And may Better show the way to the Best!

Yours faithfully,

R. W. Emerson

Mrs Stearns.

To Paulina Tucker Nash, Concord, October 7, 1864 [152]

Concord

Oct 7 — 1864

Dear Paulina,

  You were a dear good sister for writing that billet to your old
brother who was more delighted than it is wise to own to be called by

---

a complete date but is so badly blotted that only the month and year are definitely
legible. The day may be 6 or 16 or 26. The lecture at Cleveland was finally set for
Jan. 19, 1865, as the letter of that date shows.

 Edwin R. Perkins, assistant cashier of the Commercial National Bank, was corresponding secretary of the Cleveland Library Association, it seems, this year (*Baker's
Cleveland Directory*, 1864, and *Cleveland Leader City Directory*, 1865). Emerson
writes the name correctly in Dec. 19, 1864, to Wiley.

 148. MS owned by Mr. F. R. Fraprie; ph. in CUL. Inconclusive evidence cited
below points to 1864 as the year.

 149. Perhaps Oct. 8, 1864. At any rate, Emerson recorded in *Journals*, X, 71, a
visit to the Stearns home in Medford on that day.

 150. In Oct., 1864, a train on the Boston & Maine Railroad left Boston for Medford at 2:45 p.m. (*Boston Evening Transcript*, Oct. 3, 1864), probably arriving at
the latter place about 3.

 151. If 1864 is, as I think, the year of the letter, the good news would doubtless
be of Sheridan's victories in the Shenandoah Valley during September.

 152. MS owned by RWEMA; ph. in CUL. This is apparently an incomplete

his name & summoned to your new home. I keep the billet near me, & treat it affectionately like a love letter; and though I made no reply, (— for I rarely write a note, or, if I must write, postpone it to the last,) — I fancied that yours needed none, for you would know already that I treasured it. Everything that touches you or your family will always be exceptional to me, quite out of & above the rule I should keep with all others.

To Henry James, Sr., Concord, October 12, 1864

[MS listed, without the year, in Chicago Book & Art Auctions, Apr. 29, 1931; described as an invitation to meet Goldwin Smith at Concord. For the year and for Smith's visit, *cf.* Oct. 16, 1864.]

To Henry James, Sr., Concord, October 16, 1864 [153]

Concord

Sunday Eve., 16 Oct.

My dear James,

I cannot in any manner release you.[154] Goldwin Smith will come on Wednesday; [155] & your great heart & my necessity will not leave you a needle's eyehole of escape. I see not why Mrs James, whose good will to come here gratifies all our household, cannot release herself from her guests for a few hours, & come with you. If that cannot be, she must give us the earliest day of her liberty. But I shall rely on you for Wednesday, & my wife & daughters pray you to bring her if you can.

Ever yours,

R. W. Emerson

Henry James.

To —————, Concord, October 19, 1864

[MS listed in Merwin-Clayton Sales Co., Nov. 20–21, 1905; Emerson details his engagements and fears he must cancel his Western tour.]

---

draft, never sent. The sister of Emerson's first wife appears in a number of earlier letters.

153. MS owned by Mr. Henry James; ph. in CUL. The year is fixed by evidence cited below, and Oct. 16 fell on Sunday in 1864.

154. James must have written, possibly more than once, in reply to the letter of Oct. 12.

155. Matthew Arnold, Llandudno, Carnarvonshire, Aug. 17, 1864, commended Smith, then about to go to America, to Emerson. Some days before the present letter was written, Emerson had been with Smith at Naushon (*Journals*, X, 72). Arnold Haultain, *Goldwin Smith*, n. d., pp. 288–289, tells of Smith's visit to Concord a little later.

To George Bancroft, Concord? October? *c.* 20? 1864

[Mentioned in Oct. 27, 1864; probably there was more than one letter to Bancroft about this time.]

To Charles Eliot Norton, Concord, October 25, 1864 [156]

Concord
Monday, 25 October

My dear Norton,

When Mr Stanley was here,[157] he left with me a copy of Clough's Poems, a duplicate of your London Edition,[158] so that I have not a shadow of a reason for detaining your book another day, & indeed had made it ready for Edward to take to you a week ago. It is a book of worth & pride for his friends, for his University, — one of the watermarks that show to what point the culture of the best class had risen; nay, of pride for England, in showing what a throng of masters she had, wherein so rich & rare a mind was not conspicuous as a leader. But poetry must transcend criticism, must conquer us by divine force, or it remains simply human elegancy & comfort. And Clough, I am sure, who was fulfilled with nobleness, was too dear a lover of the Muse not to acquiesce in the decree which left out his own songs. Who would not rather read Shakspeare & be nobody, than be a poet of renown because there was no Shakspeare? But my boy waits, & I must only crave, as already too often, your forgiveness for not meeting what seemed just expectations. In the hope of soon seeing you, Ever Yours,

Charles E. Norton.   R. W. Emerson

To William Emerson, Concord, October 27, 1864 [159]

Concord
Oct. 27, 1864

Dear William,

I have had a correspondence with Bancroft,[160] lately, about the Bryant festival of the " Century Club "; [161] and it is settled that I am to

156. MS owned by HCL; ph. in CUL. The date is fixed by the evidence cited below.

157. See Sept. 14, 1864.

158. This is apparently a reference to Palgrave's edition, *Poems by Arthur Hugh Clough*, Cambridge and London, 1862. *Cf.* a note on Oct. 30, 1862, for Norton's Boston edition. Palgrave's had reappeared in 1863.

159. MS owned by HCL; ph. in CUL.

160. See Oct.? *c.* 20? 1864.

161. Emerson's speech of Nov. 5, in honor of Bryant, was a graceful and adequate

be his guest whilst I stay in N. Y. — This being agreed, I think I shall go to Philadelphia first, where I wish to pay a short visit,[162] & probably not arrive in N. Y., on my return, until the 5th Nov.ʳ I have not yet informed myself of the necessary points on time tables, & so do not know if I can see you in my first passage through your city, which, I suppose, will be Tuesday morning, — but I shall do so, if the hour permits, & I will send you more exact note of my intentions, perhaps, on Saturday.[163] Ellen has just read me Haven's news of you all.

Affectionately,
Waldo E

To William Emerson, Concord, October 31, 1864[164]

Concord Monday
31 Oct 1864

Dear William,

I believe I was to send you later note[165] of my intentions New-Yorkward. I shall probably leave Boston, if bad weather holds, in the night train, tomorrow, 8:30 P M &, without pause, take the Phila. train in in the morning, and so do not expect to see you until my return to N. Y. In good hope,

Your brother
Waldo.

We were all rejoiced, or all but Ellen, that Charles was safe out of the battle of the 19th.[166] Ellen, I think wishes to make a Major General of him. And I read with great pleasure Dr Griscom's letter to you.

To Bayard Taylor, Concord, October 31, 1864

[MS listed and partly quoted in Merwin-Clayton Sales Co., June 21, 1905; relates to the date of the Bryant festival (*cf.* Oct. 27, 1864). It is apparently the same letter that is listed in American Art Association, Nov. 24–25, 1924.]

---

tribute (printed in *The Bryant Festival at " The Century,"* illustrated ed., 1865, pp. 16–19). Bancroft was president of the association and the first speaker on this occasion.

162. Apparently Emerson read no lectures at this time. It seems probable from a letter of Nov. 16 following that he visited Furness.

163. He delayed writing till Monday, Oct. 31.

164. MS owned by HCL; ph. in CUL.

165. Promised in Oct. 27, 1864.

166. The important battle of Oct. 19 was at Cedar Creek, Va. This was the day of Sheridan's famous ride.

To Richard Randolph, Concord? November? *c.* 10? 1864

[Randolph, Philadelphia, Jan. 10, 1865, said he received a letter, with MSS, about two months since and noted that he and Emerson agreed in regarding life as " an exploring expedition."]

To D. A. Goddard, Concord, November 11, 1864

[MS listed in Anderson Galleries, Dec. 7, 1925, where Goddard's initials are not given; described in Anderson Galleries, June 5–6, 1916, as expressing Emerson's belief that his Boston course would preclude any course at Worcester earlier than the following February and as setting $30 as the fee for each lecture. Perhaps this is the same as the letter of this date listed, without the name of the person addressed, in Thomas F. Madigan's undated autograph bulletin of *c.* May, 1932. The Worcester course beginning Feb. 17, 1865, is mentioned in a note on Dec. 19, 1864, to Wiley. For Goddard, *cf.* Feb. 9, 1865.]

To George Partridge Bradford, Concord, November 16, 1864 [167]

Concord
Nov 16 — 1864

Dear George,

We depend on your company at dinner on Thanksgiving Day but so surely that I have not hastened to send this reminder. [I] give you joy of the Election [168] Seldom in history was so much staked on a popular vote. — I suppose never in history. One hears everywhere anecdotes of late very late remorse overtaking the hardened sinners & just saving them from final reprobation.[I] I saw Mr Tweedie [169] yesterday I think after fifteen years now confirming the good impression I had retained. It is time you should bring your trunks to Concord, & sit down here for good.

Yours affectionately,
R. Waldo E —

George P. Bradford

To Edward Waldo Emerson, Concord, November 16, 1864

[MS owned by Mr. Raymond Emerson.]

---

167. MS owned by RWEMA; ph. in CUL. Excerpt I is in Cabot, II, 609.
168. Lincoln was reëlected on Nov. 8 by 212 electoral votes to 21 for McClellan.
169. I conjecture that this was Edmund Tweedy, the friend of Henry James, Sr. (*cf.* R. B. Perry, I, 31, *et passim*) .

To WILLIAM HENRY FURNESS, CONCORD, NOVEMBER 16, 1864

[MS owned by Mr. Horace Howard Furness Jayne; printed in *Records of a Lifelong Friendship*, pp. 139–140, where it is undated as to year. References to the election and to emancipation in various states show, however, that the year is 1864. *Cf.* also the letter of the same date to Bradford.]

To EDWIN F. SWEET? CONCORD? NOVEMBER? *c.* 16? 1864

[Mentioned in Nov. 17, 1864.]

To ——————————, CONCORD? NOVEMBER? *c.* 16? 1864

[Mentioned in Nov. 17, 1864.]

To ——————————, CONCORD? NOVEMBER? *c.* 16? 1864

[Mentioned in Nov. 17, 1864.]

To EDWIN R. PERKINS, CONCORD, NOVEMBER 17, 1864 [170]

Concord
Nov 17

Dear Sir,

Thanks for your friendly care, which, I fear, has cost you much trouble. Immediately on the arrival of your letter, whose dates I have noted & shall keep, I have written to Fayettevill N. Y. offering the 13 Jan; to Dansville, the 16th; and to Oberlin, the 21st or 23d; as they may see practicable. I have considerably enlarged my contingent list by some western propositions on this & the other side of Chicago, whither I may go before I return home.

Respectfully,
R. W. Emerson

Mr Perkins.

To BENJAMIN B. WILEY, CONCORD, NOVEMBER 18, 1864 [171]

Concord
Nov. 18. 1864

My dear Sir

I have your note & surprising proposition. I fear Chicago is

170. MS owned by CUL; ph. in CUL. For Perkins, of Cleveland, see letters of Sept. and Dec. 19, 1864. In the MS memorandum book for 1865 Fayetteville is entered for Jan. 13 but is canceled. For Dansville and Edwin F. Sweet, the secretary in charge of the lecture there and probably Emerson's correspondent, see Jan. 20 following. Dec. 19, 1864, to Wiley mentions the letter to Oberlin. I have dated the letters to these three towns alike, Nov.? *c.* 16?

171. MS owned by RWEMA; ph. in CUL. This is a copy, not in Emerson's hand.

too busy to come to lectures. But if you wish to try the experiment, I have no objection to the journey. I fear that I cannot promise it before the first of February, as my first day in Boston is the 27ᵗʰ instant, & followed by five Sundays: [172] then I crowd together my more distant engagements, & am not free I think till 25ᵗʰ January.[173] But it would give me much pleasure this project of yours, if it can be. If it drags drop it instantly.

I had, long time ago, your letter in which you sent an enclosure for Mr. Alcott, & for Miss Thoreau. I carried these to them & they were gratefully received. My kind regards to Mr. Collyer,[174] who humors your zeal. The joy of the country [175] rests on us all.

Yours with all kindly wishes,

R. W. Emerson.

To Annie Adams Fields, Concord? November 26, 1864?

[MS listed and partly quoted in American Art Association, Mar. 10–11, 1924, where no year is given; Emerson thanks Mrs. Fields but says he has consented to spend the night at the home of Mrs. Dorr. The year remains entirely conjectural but could, so far as I know, have been 1864, when he lectured in Boston on Nov. 27. For his staying with the Fieldses on the night of the last lecture in the same course, see the note on Dec.? 1864?]

For the extensive course of lectures which Emerson read in Chicago this winter, see Jan. 27, 1865.

172. The six Sunday evening lectures on " American Life," at the Melodeon, under the auspices of the Parker Fraternity, were: " Education," Nov. 27, 1864; " Social Aims," Dec. 4; " Resources," 11; " Table Talk," 18; " Books," 25; " Character," Jan. 1. Each lecture was reported in both the *Boston Post* and the *Boston Daily Advertiser* on the day following its delivery. The first three lectures were recorded at length. Then Emerson made an effort to stop the reporting, as is clear from comments in the papers, and only brief sketches or extracts of the remaining lectures were printed. Meantime *The Commonwealth* had been perhaps the worst offender, publishing what seems to be a complete text of the first lecture in its issue of Dec. 3, and, later, considerable passages from the three following lectures and lesser excerpts from the two concluding ones. It is probable that Emerson wrote to several Boston papers, but I have no proof. *Cf.* also Dec. 16, 1864. A version of the introduction to the first lecture of the course is in *Journals*, X, 82 ff.

173. *Cf.* letters of Jan., 1865.

174. Robert Collyer had become a resident of Chicago in 1859, and by 1870 he was, it is said, the best-known preacher in the Middle West. He received a call, signed, it seems, by Emerson among others, to Parker's old congregation in Boston and finally left Chicago to become pastor of the Church of the Messiah in New York. (*A Memorial of the Rev. Robert Collyer*, 1914; and John Haynes Holmes, *The Life and Letters of Robert Collyer*, 1917.) *Cf.* also a note on Jan. 24, 1863.

175. *Cf.* Nov. 16, 1864, to Bradford.

To John Y. Culyer, Concord, December 6, 1864 [176]

Concord, Mass^tts
6 December, 1864

Dear Sir,

I am sorry that I cannot obey your invitation to read a lecture in Washington. But I have so engaged myself in quite distant directions, that it is for the present for me out of question.

Respectfully,

John Y. Culyer, Esq.   R. W. Emerson

To George William Curtis, Concord? December? c. 6? 1864

[Curtis, New Haven, Conn., Dec. 7, 1864, stated that this note found him there and that he would come to Emerson's house " like a man going home."]

To Charles Sumner, Concord, December 7, 1864 [177]

Concord
7 December 1864

Dear Sumner,

I learn that James Russell Lowell desires to go abroad, & would like to be employed in the public service.[178] I am concerned to hear it; for I think him happily placed now. He is a fortune to the College & might revive things more dead than the " N. A Review " [179] It seems he is out of health, is too hard worked, & holds an estate by his father's will, which is only expensive. I am sorry for the necessity, whatever its cause. But if he wishes to go in the public service, the Government ought to appreciate his great & rare merits. No literary man in the country suggests the presence of so much power as he; with a talent, too, that reaches all classes. Add to this, that he is a person of excellent address, with social & convivial gifts; a man of great spirit, with plenty of

176. MS owned by Mr. Alwin J. Scheuer; ph. in CUL. John Y. Culyer is listed in *Boyd's Washington and Georgetown Directory,* 1865, as a clerk. The spelling " Cuyler " also occurs in the same directory.

177. MS owned by RWEMA; ph. in CUL.

178. It was not until some years later that Lowell received the first of his political appointments.

179. Lowell had been Longfellow's successor at Harvard. He and Norton had taken charge of *The North American Review* with the issue for Jan., 1864 (H. E. Scudder, II, 49-50) .

resistance in him, if need be. His thorough knowledge of the European languages adds to his competency for such duty. His wide popularity as a writer would assure the sanction of the best part of the nation to an important appointment, & would conciliate those to whom he should be sent. I am sorry I did not know this wish of his in time to have had a little conference with you on the point; for there is very much to be said on his behalf. In whatever changes may occur in our representation abroad, if Massachusetts shall have any claims, I trust so old & able a champion for the best policy as Lowell, will be remembered. He is one of those few who are entitled to have all they want.

Ever yours faithfully,

R. W. Emerson

To Charles Sumner, Concord, December 8, 1864 [180]

Concord

8 Dec., 1864

Dear Sumner,

Will you think me a politician, if every day I urge the merits of a new citizen on your notice? Not, I am sure, whilst I have such clients as yesterday,[181] nor yet as today. I believe you have met Rev. David A. Wasson, now of Worcester. He is known to me as a man of superior understanding, and of a broad comprehensive genius, an excellent writer, and, as a preacher, the first choice of the " Fraternity " people after Parker.[182] Of serious papers, he is perhaps the best contributor to the " Atlantic Monthly." [183] He is a social man of agreeable manners. He ought to be a scholar, & stay at home. But he has long been an invalid, & must not be sedentary. He wishes to be a Consul in some healthy port, as his recent experiences by sea & land promise him health, if his vacation from his desk can be prolonged. He is one of those who ought to be gratified, as it is the saving & maturing of a great man. I think it the best inauguration of the new era of the Republic, — to send abroad,

180. MS owned by RWEMA; ph. in CUL.

181. He had recommended Lowell in Dec. 7, 1864.

182. David Atwood Wasson actually became pastor of Parker's old congregation in 1865, but his career as a preacher was unsatisfying, partly because of his ill health.

183. During 1864, according to the index, Wasson contributed no less than five reviews to *The Atlantic*, and he continued to write for that magazine. He is still remembered as a minor figure among the Transcendentalists.

as its political & mercantile functionaries, wise & virtuous men, instead of the vaporers & plotters who have so long misrepresented us.

Yours faithfully,

R. W. Emerson

I have not forgotten the duty you laid on me touching the Academy.[184]

TO HENRY WADSWORTH LONGFELLOW, CONCORD, DECEMBER 12, 1864 [185]

Concord

12 Decr. Monday

Dear Longfellow, —

Sumner left with me an entreaty to send him some counsel what further steps he should take with his Bill for a " National Academy of Literature & Art," which, on his own spontaneity, he has, you know, initiated in Congress.[186] I told him I had not yet any fixed opinion on the matter; had even a doubt of any practical use in it for us in our want of a central city. but promised to talk with those nearly concerned, & report to him. If I were at liberty in these weeks, I should come to you & Lowell at Cambridge with this view. But I am tied to certain days & duties. And it strikes me, that, if you & Lowell & Dana Holmes & Curtis (who is to be in Boston this week) will come, say, next Saturday afternoon to the Union Club, we might in a half hour arrive at the best opinion. I will say 4 o'clock P. M.; though a later hour, if more convenient to you, is alike to me. I hope this proposal may be not inconvenient or disagreeable to you.[187] I will write at once to Lowell, Dana,[188]

184. See letters of Dec. 12 and 19, 1864.

185. MS owned by the Trustees of the Longfellow House, Cambridge; ph. in CUL. The year is clearly 1864, when Dec. 12 fell on Monday.

186. On July 2, 1864, Sumner had introduced in the Senate his bill to incorporate not only the National Academy of Literature and Art but also the National Academy of Moral and Political Sciences. As members of the former, the bill named twenty persons, including Emerson, Bryant, Richard Henry Dana, John Sullivan Dwight, Halleck, Holmes, Longfellow, Lowell, Whittier, Hiram Powers, W. W. Story, Verplanck, and S. Austin Allibone, but not, of course, Whitman or Melville. Each academy was to consist of not more than fifty ordinary members, of whom not more than ten were to be elected in any one year. Each academy was to hold an annual meeting, but there was to be no compensation for any services to the Government. In selecting the names of the academies, Sumner said, he had " followed mainly the usage of France, which is the country which has most excelled in academies of this kind." (*The Congressional Globe*, 1864, pp. 3492–3493; *The Works of Charles Sumner*, 1874, IX, 51 ff.) The bill failed.

187. Longfellow did not come (*cf.* Dec. 19, 1864, to Sumner).

188. Presumably Emerson wrote the same day to R. H. Dana, Sr.; but, though the letter of Dec. 19 to Sumner adds weight to the presumption, it does not prove the case.

& Holmes; Curtis is coming to my house this week.[189] I can change the *venue*, if it is wished, but I am limited just now to Saturday or Monday.

Ever yours,

R. W. Emerson

H. W. Longfellow.

To James Russell Lowell, Concord, December 12, 1864 [190]

Concord

12 Dec Monday

Dear Lowell,

I have just written to Longfellow praying him to join you in giving Sumner the advice he wants about his Bill for a " National Academy of Literature & Art." I propose, that you & L. shall meet Dana, Holmes, Curtis, & me, in Boston, at the Union Club, next Saturday P. M. say at 4 o'c, & talk over the matter for half an hour. I think we might easily agree to advise him to push it or to drop it. Sumner was so urgent with me, at our last Club, that I ought sooner to have seen you. But it is not late. Do come " without fail." Any hour of Saturday or Monday will suit me equally well: but I am limited to those two days. Curtis will be here this week: and I shall write to Holmes & Dana.

I have never thanked you for " Fireside Travels," [191] which I have read with delight; nor have I offered you a poor word of honor to the costly sacrifices of your family.[192] But I am

ever yours,

R. W. Emerson

James Russell Lowell.

P S I have not written to Dana, till I hear from you.

To Oliver Wendell Holmes, Concord? December 12? 1864

[In the letters of Dec. 12, 1864, to Longfellow and Lowell, Emerson said he would write to Holmes about a meeting to discuss the projected academy. Holmes, n. p., Dec. 13 (1864), said he would come to the Union Club for that meeting. *Cf.* also Dec. 19 to Sumner.]

189. See Dec.? *c*. 6? 1864.

190. MS owned by Goodspeed's Book Shop; ph. in CUL. The year is obviously 1864.

191. According to Jacob C. Chamberlain, *A Bibliography of the First Editions . . . of James Russell Lowell*, 1914, *Fireside Travels* had been published in Apr. or May, 1864.

192. Lowell's nephews, officers in the Union army, are mentioned in earlier letters. Emerson's spelling of " sacrifices " is doubtful.

To Louis Agassiz, Concord, December 13, 1864

[MS owned by RWEMA; ph. in CUL. Printed in *Louis Agassiz,* ed. Elizabeth Cary Agassiz, 1885, II, 620–622, where the name " Louis Agassiz " is omitted at the end.]

To James Bradley Thayer, Concord, December 16, 1864 [193]

Concord

16 Dec Friday

My dear Mr Thayer

If you have the ear of the " Daily Advertiser, & can without inconvenience, I wish you would ask the Editor to omit any report of my Lectures. The fault of the reports is doubtless owing to the lecture itself which lacks any method, or any that is easily apprehensible, but it distresses me a little to read them & more that others should. Of course to any general notice I have no objection but much to the rendering of sentences. And I should take it as a great kindness if it were omitted. But it is not worth giving you any trouble. Mr Slack [194] I believe made some such request & told me it was all settled but it is not all ended.

Yours always,

R W Emerson

J. F. Thayer, Esq.

193. MS owned by Professor James B. Thayer; ph. in CUL. Emerson's " J. F." is, I think, an error for " J. B.," though a John F. Thayer is listed in *The Boston Directory,* 1864, as of the 56th Regiment. James B. Thayer is named in the same volume as a counselor. For his marriage to Sophia Bradford Ripley, daughter of Emerson's half uncle, see a note on Apr. 12, 1861. From 1865, he is a fairly active correspondent. In Jan. 6, 1865, he is mentioned as in charge of certain financial affairs for Emerson, and in Aug. 25 of the same year he appears as a contributor to the *Boston Daily Advertiser.* It must have been his connection with that paper which prompted the present letter. For the date, the year 1860 has been supplied on the MS but is certainly wrong. In that year Dec. 16 fell on Sunday, not Friday, and Emerson was not reading a regular course of lectures in Boston. Of the years in which Dec. 16 was Friday, only 1864 fits a Boston lecture course. For that course, see a note on Nov. 18 preceding. The fact that the wholesale reporting ended just before the lecture of Dec. 18 is important evidence of the date of the present letter.

194. Several persons of this name are listed in *The Boston Directory,* 1864.

To Caroline Sturgis Tappan, Concord, December 16? 1864? [195]

Concord
Friday, 16ᵗʰ Dec

Dear Caroline,

We are fully bent on our visit tomorrow, but, as I learn the design, Lidian dines in Concord, goes down at 1.30, &, if the weather permits her marches of duty in the bazaar,[196] will come with me to your tea-table between 5 & 6. If it storms, perhaps she will arrive about 3, but you shall not consider her in your charge till 5. Ever Yours,

R. W. E.

To Charles Sumner, Concord, December 19, 1864 [197]

Concord
19 Decʳ 1864

Dear Sumner,

I tried the other night to engage Longfellow, Lowell, Holmes, & Curtis, to talk over the affair of the "National Academy," with me, at the Union Club.[198] Mr Dana declined to entertain the subject altogether, alleging age as his excuse. To my regret, Longfellow did not come at last; Curtis, too, was unable to come; so that Lowell, Holmes, & I were the whole committee. We agreed that the existence of such a Society was inevitable; that the existence of an Academy of

195. MS owned by Mrs. Gorham Brooks; ph. in CUL. The date offers serious difficulties. The heading is not only incomplete but doubtfully legible: the day is either 16 or 11, but 16 seems the more probable reading. If the letter was written on a Friday, Dec. 16, the possible years are 1842, 1853, 1859, 1864, 1870, and 1881. As there is no superscription on the MS, 1842, when envelopes were not yet in use, may reasonably be disregarded. The hand is too steady for 1881. For 1859, as late as Dec. 14, Emerson believed he might have to be in New York on the 15th or the 17th and so probably had no thought of an engagement nearer home on the 16th; but the present letter seems to refer to an appointment made in advance and adhered to without any question. For 1870, Emerson was presumably busy on December 16 of that year preparing for his New York visit of a few days later. Neither 1853 nor 1864 seems to be open to any such objections. In 1853, however, there was no train leaving Concord at 1:30, as there was in 1859, 1864, and 1870 (*Boston Daily Advertiser,* Dec. 16, 1853, 1859, and 1864; and Dec. 17, 1870).

196. If 1864 was the year, the Orphan Boys' Fair, probably still open on the 16th, might be meant (*cf. Boston Daily Advertiser,* Dec. 12–19, 1864).

197. MS owned by RWEMA; ph. in CUL.

198. *Cf.* the letters of Dec. 12, 1864.

Science [199] would inevitably draw after it the attempt to establish this; and, therefore, it would be prudent to accept the offered form under such good auspices as it now brings from your hands: prudent, — because if the present nominees are not the best, yet, by accepting it, we are likely to defend it from falling into worse. We agreed on the general objects of such a society; as, for the conservation of the English language; a constituted jury to which questions of taste & fitness in literature, might be carried: a jury to sit upon abnormal anomalous pretentions to genius, such as puzzle the public mind now & then. Custodians of sense & elegance — these colleagues are to be, — in literature. They would be the college of experts, to which the Government might sometimes wish to refer questions touching Education, or historic forms or facts. They would perhaps suggest to the Government the establishment of prizes for literary competition. Certain aesthetic & moral advantages did not fail to appear, as the matter was more considered. What recommended to us a cordial sympathy with the proposition, was, the belief shared by us & we believe by the community, that, we are at an important point of national history, & one from which very great expansion of thought & moral & practical activity in all kinds is likely to follow; &, that organizations hitherto sterile may easily hereafter come to be of great scope & utility.

The objections which were raised in our conversation were

1. the obvious one of want of a national centre for an Academy, such as Paris & London furnish in France & in England. We agreed, however, that the only proper centre this Academy could have is Washington, and we found many considerations to fortify this opinion.

2. The want of provision in the Bill for any compensation to the members for their expense pense [200] in attendance on the meetings of the Academy, — which omission, or rather forbiddal, in the Bill, threatens to make full sessions of the Academy impossible, in a country of such geographic distances as ours. An allowance for mileage will probably be found indispensable to its successful operation.

3. We see difficulties in the Union of two classes of such unlike bias & objects as Scholars and Artists, in one Academy; for example, in the first election of officers & of members that may occur, I want Gibbon, & Dwight wants Paganini. But probably we might soon fall on a fair

199. On Mar. 3, 1863, Lincoln had signed a bill creating the National Academy of Sciences (*A History of the First Half-century of the National Academy of Sciences*, 1913, p. 6).

200. This syllable is repeated at the beginning of a page.

proportion of candidates to each, according to the numerical strength of each class. But, really, for all practical purpose, these classes must sit & act as separate sections.

We all agreed that the simple meeting of an Academy under the inspiration of national aims, would tend to quicken the power & ennoble the aims of all the members.

I think this is a fair sketch of the points that appeared in our half hour's conversation. I am sorry to have been so late in getting this little result, but have been unusually occupied since I saw you, & could not well bring together a company which I hoped would be larger. I infer, however, that the heat will rapidly accumulate at future conferences.

Tell me if you wish something more precise.

Ever yours,
R. W. Emerson

Hon. Charles Sumner.

To Benjamin B. Wiley, Concord, December 19, 1864 [201]

Concord.
19 December 1864.

My dear Wiley

  I have notes from Mr. Collyer,[202] who, it seems, is away from home; & from Rev. Mr. Staples,[203] of Milwaukee, on the subject of my lectures at the two cities. I have been & still am a little uncertain as to engagements which Mr. E. R. Perkins [204] of Cleveland, who had charged himself with arrangements for me in that region, & who does not send me the final letter he promised me. I believe I must take the matter strongly in my own hands. I had left to Oberlin the choice between two evenings, in my direct correspondence with it, — namely, 21 or 23 Jan.[205] If they have replied, it has been to Mr. P. I shall now write, they must accept the 21st Then I shall be free to say, I will read at Chicago on the 23rd, 24th & 25th Jan.; & at Milwaukee 2nd, 3rd, & 4th

201. MS owned by RWEMA; ph. in CUL. This is a copy, not in Emerson's hand.

202. *Cf.* Nov. 18, 1864.

203. Carlton Albert Staples, who afterwards achieved some reputation in the East, was at this time pastor of the Unitarian church in Milwaukee.

204. *Cf.* Sept., 1864.

205. Apparently Emerson did not keep either date. *The Lorain County News,* Oberlin, O., Jan. 18, 1865, said there were at present no more lectures scheduled by the local lyceums. *Cf.* a letter of Nov.? *c.* 16? 1864.

Feb͟ʸ.²⁰⁶ Will not this be practicable? & according to the suggestion of
your own & Mr. C's letter? I will write this also tonight to Mr. Staples.
If there be any insuperable difficulty, I shall still have some margin of
time, say, the three or four following days; though it is desirable to me
to be in Worcester, Masstts (where I am to read a course,) on the 7ᵗʰ,²⁰⁷
&, in Lynn, on the 8͟ᵗ͟ʰ. ²⁰⁸ But these two might possibly be staved off a
day or two. I regret to have mislaid Mr. Collyer's late note which is important, but I think would not forbid such a proposition. He speaks
also of other towns: but such extension I must not attempt. I am in good
hope that what I have written may meet your views.

Ever yours

R. W. Emerson —

To Carlton Albert Staples, Concord, December 19, 1864 ²⁰⁹

Concord

19 Decʳ 1864

My dear Sir,

         I have your friendly note with its agreeable invitation

After reading it, & Mr Collyer's & Mr Wiley's from Chicago, I find
that I can come to Chicago, on the 23ᵈ 24ᵗʰ & 25ᵗʰ January; to Milwaukee, on the 26ᵗʰ 27ᵗʰ & 28 January. Then, to Chicago on the 30ᵗʰ
& 31ˢᵗ January and 1ˢᵗ February. Again at Milwaukee, on 2ᵈ, 3ᵈ, & 4ᵗʰ
February. If these days should meet your convenience, and that of
Chicago, it will be to me on both points a very desireable visit. I might
at a pinch control the three or four following days, but I ought, if possible, to be at Worcester Massᵗᵗˢ on the 7ᵗʰ, & at Lynn, on the 8ᵗʰ February. I shall be happy to hear from you that my programme is practicable. I write this evening, to the like effect, to Mr Wiley.

Respectfully,

R. W. Emerson

     206. For lectures at Milwaukee and Chicago, see the letters of Jan. 24 and 27,
1865.

     207. The course of six lectures on "American Life" was postponed. The
Worcester Daily Transcript, Feb. 10–Mar. 25, 1865, announces or reports the follow-
ing lectures: "Education," Feb. 17; "Social Aims," 24; "Resources," Mar. 3; "Table
Talk," 10; "Books," 17; "Character," 24.

     208. Emerson was in Pennsylvania and in New York State on the 8th of February;
and the MS memorandum book for 1865 seems to show also that Lynn was postponed till March.

     209. MS owned by Mrs. Charles J. Staples; ph. in CUL. *Cf.* the letter of the same
date to Wiley.

P. S.

I call my course, as read & to be read in Boston, " American Life," & it stands advertised

1. Education.
2. Social Aims.
3. Resources.
4. Table-Talk.
5. Books.
6. Character.

Of these, I have read the first four, and shall retain these names. Perhaps I shall alter somewhat the names of the two last. A few days will settle the point for one, & a week later for the other. In the last, I hope to treat the present aspects of Religion & Morals: but I think to keep the present title.

To Annie Adams Fields? Concord? December? 1864?

[Partly printed, without place or date or name of person addressed, in *Harper's*, LXVIII, 466 (Feb., 1884), and in Annie Fields, *Authors and Friends*, p. 101. Mention of " our desire to spend the Sunday of my last lecture at your house " seems to connect this letter with the course of 1864–1865, the last lecture of which was given on Sunday, Jan. 1, 1865 (see a note on Nov. 18, 1864). Almost conclusive evidence that this conjecture is correct is to be found in the MS diaries of Annie Fields (now deposited in the library of the Massachusetts Historical Society), where this entry records the same Sunday: " Mr & Mrs Emerson and their children passed the New Year with us. A happy inauguration! "]

1865

To Abel Adams, Concord, January 6, 1865 [1]

Concord, 6 January
1865.

My dear friend,

I believe that you have in your safe a mortgage note of Samuel Coverly, promising to pay $3000 to me, which note, I believe you kindly took charge of, at my request.[2] If you can find it, & will be so good as to send it to James B. Thayer, Esq. 30 Court Street, Boston, you will do me a kindness.

I left home, this morning, with the intention of going out to dine with you: but was held in Dr Keep's chair, instead of one hour, a large part of the day. I was very sorry for it, for I am going West, in a day or two, for several weeks; & I see no room for a visit, before I go. I have heard of Mrs Adams & of Abby where I have been but have seen none of you for long.

For my affairs, I wished to consult you about this mortgage note. It was due at the end of 5 years on the 27th of August last. And Mr Sprague[3] asked if I wished to be paid. I was unprepared for the question And he thought I had better let it remain; saying, that I should so keep all my rights. Mr Thayer tells me, I can make a better investment. But I should have liked to have to have had your opinion.

Ever yours affectionately,
R. W. Emerson

Mr A. Adams.

To James Thomas Fields, Albany, New York, January 13, 1865

[MS owned by the Henry E. Huntington Library; ph. in CUL. Except for the heading, "Delavan House Albany, 13 January 1865," the name and

1. MS owned by RWEMA; ph. in CUL.
2. In Jan. 16, 1860, to Adams.
3. The poet and bank cashier of earlier letters.

salutation, " J. T. Fields, Esq." and " My dear Sir," and the name " Conway " in the third sentence, the entire letter is printed in *Harper's*, LXVIII, 464 (Feb., 1884) , and in Annie Fields, *Authors and Friends*, p. 93.]

To ——————— Perkins? Albany, New York, January 13, 1865

[Printed in *The Boston Herald*, Dec. 28, 1885, p. 4, where the name of the person addressed is omitted; inclosed $10 to repay " Mrs. ——," of whom Emerson had borrowed that amount after losing his purse, probably to a pickpocket, in Fairhaven, Vt. *Cf.* the letter of the same date to Fields. Fairhaven appears under Jan. 11 in the MS memorandum book for 1865. On one of the pages following the diary in this same volume is a record of the payment of $10 to some person at Fairhaven — apparently Mrs. S. G. Perkins, but the name is not clearly legible.]

To Ellen Emerson, Albany, New York, January 13? 1865

[Mentioned in Jan. 19, 1865. Edward Emerson wrote from home, also on Jan. 19, that " we have only heard once (the letter with the check) from you."]

To Ellen Emerson, Cleveland, January 19, 1865 [4]

Cleveland Ohio
19 Jan 1865

Dear Ellen

I enclose a draft on the Revere Bank Boston for $50. payable to your order, which you can carry to Mr Cheney, as you have done, I suppose, with one I sent from you [5] from Albany.[6] On my way here, I have had a day & night or two of car experience which would have been intolerably tedious to you I am sure, had you come with me, tho' I would willingly have you share this good Cleveland day, with the Willeys,[7] with whom I have dined, & where I always like to be. I lost Erie through the dreary delays of the trains: but their committee were

4. MS owned by RWEMA; ph. in CUL.
5. At the beginning of a line.
6. In the letter of Jan. 13? 1865. The *Albany Evening Journal*, Jan. 12, 1865, announced " Social Aims in America " at Tweddle Hall that evening. It is evident from Jan. 13 to Fields that the lecture was postponed or abandoned. The MS memorandum book for this year indicates that the date was changed to the 13th.
7. *Cf.* Jan. 8, 1853. According to the *Cleveland Leader City Directory*, 1865, George Willey, of Willey & Cary, attorneys, was a " perpetual " trustee of the Cleveland Library Association, which sponsored an annual course of lectures. In the evening of Jan. 19 Emerson read " Social Aims in America " before this association (*Cleveland Daily Plain Dealer*, Jan. 19 and 20, 1865) .

here today, & brought your letter, & I have promised to go there on my return say on 6 Feby or 7th.[8] I am urged to stop here & read a second lecture on the 7th In such case I shall probably exchange nights, & be here 6th, at Erie, 7th. I have here your second letter, & am heartily glad of both. I cannot, at this late hour of night, add a word out of the flowery region of finance, but will send you a draft presently: & you must pay Adams [9] & John Clahan (whose day is 20th Jan.^{y}) & Dr Keep, as quickly as you can: Adams, I hope, his full amount, & John as much as you can, of his $35.00 I go to Pittsburg in the morning & thence to Chicago 65000 people live in this handsome city which had only 5 or 6000 I think when I first came to it.[10] The public news is excellent,[11] & I trust your mother yourself & Edith & Edward are stronger day by day.
R W Emerson
Miss Ellen T. Emerson

To WILLIAM EMERSON, PITTSBURGH, JANUARY 20, 1865 [12]

Monongahela House
Pittsburgh Pa
20 January. 1865

Dear William,

Tis too long since I have written this dear old prefix to any letter: and since I have been on this journey I have not had till now the span of time & the petty convenience to say to you that in a town called Dansville [13] of New York some young men bringing me the lecturers fee of fifty dollars in good part made up of bundles of fractional currency because as they said they could not put it into bills unless I would wait over a necessary train I said, " Carry it to the banker here

8. The *Erie Weekly Gazette,* Feb. 9 following, reported that Emerson read " Social Aims in America " on the 7th to one of the largest audiences of the season.

9. Apparently not Abel Adams.

10. So far as I know, Emerson did not visit Cleveland till 1850 (*cf.* May 20, 1850), when the population was about 17,000.

11. The great news of the moment was the capture of Ft. Fisher.

12. MS owned by HCL; ph. in CUL. Emerson read " Social Aims in America " before the Tennyson Club of Pittsburgh on Jan. 20, 1865, according to *The Daily Pittsburgh Gazette* of the 21st.

13. Mrs. Rena S. Kramer informs me that *The Dansville Advertiser* of Jan. 19, 1865, contains an account of " Manners," read in Dansville on the 16th. The reporter wrote an unusually graphic description of Emerson, whose style of oratory he contrasted favorably with that of the popular John B. Gough. The MS memorandum book for this year gives the subject as " Social Aims."

Mr Sweet & ask him to remit the amount in a draft to Wm Emerson Esq in New York." Now if this was done, & if such a draft has come to you will you be good enough to remit it in some shape to the order of Ellen T. E. at Concord to whom also I have not yet announced it though I have sent her other drafts.

I have not had the smoothest roads be sure: More than my usual share of detentions & night riding & arriving late, and mean more fiercely than ever before to stand on my dignity & age, refuse this service, and yet "What are our petty griefs? let me not number mine." [14] With dear love to the present and absent members of your house, ever

Your affectionate brother

Waldo E.

William Emerson, Esq.
    New York

I do not know Mr Sweet's entire name, but he is the banker of Dansville, & his son my "Secretary of Y. Men's Association" is Edwin F. Sweet [15]

To ELLEN? EMERSON, PITTSBURGH, JANUARY 20? 1865

[Ellen Emerson, Jan. 24, 1865: "We received your two letters . . . this morning"; she described them as from Cleveland (with $50) and Pittsburgh.]

To ELLEN EMERSON, MILWAUKEE, JANUARY 24, 1865 [16]

Newhall House
Milwaukee, Wis.
24 Jany 1865
11 P. M.

Dear Ellen, I had today from Chicago your letter & Edith's forwarded to me with all their (especially Edith's) gracious details to my great contentment. I am proud to be papa to such accomplished scribes. I am prospering here very well,[17] with good friends good audience & living

14. Byron, *Childe Harold's Pilgrimage,* IV, cvi.

15. In the MS memorandum book for 1865, E. F. Sweet is named in the Dansville entry of Jan. 16.

16. MS owned by RWEMA; ph. in CUL.

17. The *Milwaukee Daily Sentinel,* Jan. 23, 1865, announced Emerson's lectures on "American Life" to be given as follows: "Education," Jan. 23; "Social Aims," 24; "Resources," 25; "Table Talk," 30; "Books," 31; "Character," Feb. 1. Later notices in the same paper do not give definite proof in every case but leave little room for doubt that the whole series was delivered as planned. The same subjects and dates are given in the MS memorandum book for this year.

in a most comfortable house in very cold weather. Mr Norris son of Mrs Norris [18] (sister of George B Emerson, who last year carried me off to her house for one night) & who now in his sumptuous new house has taken his mother home to him, invited me by telegraph to spend all my time under his roof. I replied with all thanks that it was impossible for I had much work to do, & must be in the Hotel. But today I have dined with him most agreeably, & tonight have read my second lecture. I find Mr Staples [19] an excellent supporter & tomorrow he is to bring to my room a party of my friends some of whom come far to hear the lectures, one 40 miles! I hope I shall have leisure tomorrow to answer the outside letters you have sent me. I cannot send you much money I fear until both courses end, as I shall draw my fees in the lump probably. So, if you come to want, you will need to go to Mr Cheney, & ask him to advance you $50. for a fortnight, on my account. I will venture the experiment of putting $10. into this letter. I shall probably stop at Cleveland & Erie [20] on my return for the 6th & 7th Feb.y & reach Boston on the 9th. With love to Mamma.

R. W. Emerson

To Edith Emerson, Chicago, January 27, 1865 [21]

Tremont House —
Chicago, 27 January.

Dear Edith,

This is almost the first day of any free leisure I have found; for travel & cold weather & the pressure of a lecture every night make the days short. But here, & in Milwaukee,[22] I live in excellent hotels, which is important when the cold is below zero, as it has been for the last three or four days. Julia Lambard Johnson & her husband appeared to me on the platform at Milwaukee, on my last night there, &

18. For Olivia Emerson Norris, see Jan. 7, 1835.
19. Cf. Dec. 19, 1864, to Wiley.
20. See Jan. 19, 1865.
21. MS owned by RWEMA; ph. in CUL. Evidence cited below fixes the year.
22. Emerson had finished half his course in Milwaukee (see Jan. 24, 1865) and was now giving the first half of his Chicago course. The *Chicago Tribune* and *The Chicago Times,* Jan. 27–Feb. 6, 1865, give reports of all the lectures read — the same and in the same order as those listed for Milwaukee in the note on Jan. 24. In Chicago, the dates were Jan. 26, 27, 28; Feb. 2, 3, 4. The comments are generally very favorable; and Robert Collyer, whose Unity Church was Emerson's platform, introduced the final lecture with the statement that " in every particular the course had been a success."

told me her mother was with her, but her house was sick. I shall see them on my return. In this freer day, I have read your letters & all my letters again, Edward's too, which came yesterday. Mr Wiley is incessant in his care of me,[23] & always inquiring after you & Ellen. I doubt he sees few ladies, & he treasures all his memories. "Wished I had charged him to read the letters, before forwarding." Mr Dexter, cousin of Gore Ripley Dexter, a good lawyer here [24] is bent on hospitality, whether I will or not, & I have half promised that, a week hence, on my return, I will spend a couple of days with him. For Miss Waterman,[25] I find there is no letter with the book, (was there none?) so I charged Wiley to find her at the lecture, last night, & bring me to her: but she did not come, or had gone, & I have yet to find her. She keeps school daily, & lives a mile off, so that times & spaces must be considered. Here are 164000 people, & the town growing like young corn. I ought to be at home Thursday 9 February.[26]

R. W. Emerson

I wrote to Ellen, from Milwaukee & Cleveland,[27] letters which she ought to have received. Relieved by Edward's message from Uncle Adams.[28]

To LIDIAN EMERSON, CHICAGO, JANUARY 29, 1865 [29]

Tremont House
Chicago 29 Jan
Sunday Night

Dear Lidian,

Why should you wish to be worried with letters, when you have daughters & son who will relieve you of such irritations? I am sorry to learn that my missives arrive so slowly, but I own I am chiefly concerned lest the valuable ones, as, for example, one from Dansville, *via* W. E.[30] in N. Y., should not arrive at all. Ellen's & Ediths & Edward's

23. *Cf.* Dec. 19, 1864, and Mar. 10, 1865, both to Wiley.

24. Wirt Dexter was a member of the law firm of Walker & Dexter (*Halpin's Eighth Annual Edition Chicago City Directory*, 1865) .

25. *Cf.* Oct. 26, 1859.

26. Feb. 9 fell on Thursday in 1865; *cf.* Jan. 24, 1865, which sets the same date for the arrival in Boston.

27. The letters of Jan. 24 and 19, 1865.

28. Edward had written from Concord, Jan. 19, 1865, that "Uncle" Adams (Abel Adams) was better and had received Emerson's letter.

29. MS owned by RWEMA; ph. in CUL. The year is obviously 1865, when Jan. 29 fell on Sunday.

30. See Jan. 20, 1865.

have duly come, so that I am in possession of the whole Quincy chapter,[31] & therewith your news of Mr Alcott. I am glad that he comes to you; but tis woe to think of poor Concord choked again with " Mr Emison." [32] I do not know but the boys in the street will give me a tin pan concert when I get home. You should have absolutely forbidden it to Mr A., & told him how hateful was honeypie to my weak stomach. We have had bitter winter here, but I have good hotels in both Milwaukee & here, & cannot complain of suffering since I reached this point.

The young men who make the committee here, Wiley & Thompson [33] & others, are heroically faithful to me. If there is no hindrance on the railroads, I shall probably be at home on the 9th Feb.y, — if I shall have to go away on the next day. All the appointments of my wardrobe have proved excellent and I have never unrolled certain mystical bundles in the red bag. I have seen Miss Waterman [34] today. Love to all the children. Yours,

R W E

To Ellen Emerson, Milwaukee, January 31, 1865 [35]

Newhall House
Milwaukee
31 January, 1865

Dear Ellen,

I enclose to you a draft of Marshall & Ilsley [36] of this place on the National Exchange Bank, Boston, for two hundred seventy five dollars, payable to your order; which you must carry to Mr Cheney, who will pay it, & you must pay what debts are due, & keep the remainder for me. I am quite too busy here to add a word for my Milwaukee days

31. Letters from Edith (Jan. 17), Edward (Jan. 19), and Ellen (Jan. 24, 1865) all tell of their visits with the Quincys in Boston — apparently in the home of their father's college classmate Josiah Quincy.

32. The spelling presumably indicates Alcott's pronunciation. Ellen's letter of Jan. 24, cited above, told of Alcott's lecture in Concord on her father. According to the MS records of the Concord Lyceum (owned by the Concord Free Public Library), Alcott gave his " R. Waldo Emerson " on Jan. 11, 1865.

33. Perhaps the John Howland Thompson of earlier letters. His name and address appear on an undated leaf near the end of the MS memorandum book for this year.

34. *Cf.* Jan. 27, 1865.

35. MS owned by RWEMA; ph. in CUL.

36. Listed as bankers in *Edwards' Annual Director to the* . . . *City of Milwaukee, for 1865.*

are the correctors of my MSS. At the Chicago readings I have less work.[37] I doubt not I have all letters up to the 24th, which have come from home. Perhaps I may come back on 8th for 9th as Cleveland is withdrawn

R. W. Emerson

To C. Staples, Milwaukee, February 2, 1865

[MS listed and partly quoted in Charles F. Heartman, July 2, 1930, where the initials of Staples are given as C. E. I conjecture, however, that the person addressed was Carlton Albert Staples of Milwaukee (*cf.* letters of Dec. 19, 1864, and Jan. 24, 1865).]

To D. A. Goddard, Syracuse, New York, February 9, 1865

[A telegram printed in the *Worcester Daily Spy*, Feb. 10, 1865, p. 2. Emerson said his train was delayed and suggested that his lectures be postponed a week. For the lectures, see a note on Dec. 19, 1864, to Wiley.]

To S. Longfellow, Concord, February 20, 1865

[MS listed in C. F. Libbie & Co., Mar. 7, 1919. Presumably the person addressed was Samuel Longfellow, brother of the poet.]

To J. G. King, Concord? March 4, 1865

[Acknowledged in King, Boston, Mar. 6, 1865. King said he had caused subscription papers to be circulated and had published notices in the newspapers that the lectures would be delivered if the tickets were taken. He was almost certainly the John G. King listed as a counselor in *The Boston Directory* for 1864–1865.]

To Abel Adams, Concord, March 6 and *c.* 7? 1865 [38]

Concord

6 March 1865

My dear friend,

I am sure you will be interested to know that my daughter Edith is engaged to William Hathaway Forbes.[39] I found him here, &

---

37. For the lectures at Milwaukee and at Chicago, see the letters of Jan. 24 and 27, 1865.

38. MS owned by RWEMA; ph. in CUL. The last paragraph was clearly written a day or more later than the first.

39. Emerson wrote the same news to a number of other friends (*cf.* other letters of this month). Letters of congratulation from Henry James, Sr., and S. G. Ward (both dated Mar. 9) are probably replies to letters from Emerson which I have not found. Oct. 1, 1865, was his personal invitation to Adams to attend the wedding.

both of them arrived at a perfect understanding, on my return home from Boston on Saturday night. He is still here, & threatens, unless over-ruled, to carry her off with him to Washington in a few days, as his furlough is nearly exhausted.[40] I think Edward who is a devoted friend of William F. takes as much joy in the event as the parties themselves. Edith sends her love to you & " Aunt " Adams, & to " Cousin " Abby, & means to bring Lt. Col. F. to see you, as soon as he is freer. But I myself must come to see you, I hope, very soon.

Ever yours affectionately,
R. W. Emerson

Abel Adams.

Edith has required me to detain this note till today & begs now that her story shall not be repeated till Saturday. as Pauline Shaw & other friends are not yet told.

To William Ellery Channing the Younger, Concord? March 10? 1865

[Written on Mar. 10 or a little earlier; acknowledged in Channing, Concord, Mar. 10, 1865, as received that morning. It was an announcement of Edith Emerson's engagement.]

To Benjamin B. Wiley, Concord, March 10, 1865 [41]

Concord
10 March 1865

My dear Wiley

     I believe I was to report to you my safe arrival home which report was certainly due after all your tender care of me,[42] — yet which report, I fear never came. But the gods & godlike men are for-giving to the penitent. . . . I was . . .[43] surprised on my return from Boston, last Saturday, to find Lieut. Col. Forbes here & that after an acquaintance of four or five years the parties had come to a perfect un-derstanding.[44] This event has brought great joy to this house, for he is

40. For the record of William H. Forbes's service in the Civil War, see a note on Nov. 19, 1861. He was a lieutenant-colonel in the Second Regiment of Cavalry, Massachusetts Volunteers, when he was mustered out on May 15, 1865.

41. MS owned by RWEMA; ph. in CUL. This is a copy, not in Emerson's hand.

42. *Cf.* Jan. 27, 1865.

43. The two omitted passages, containing somewhat less than sixty words, relate to some personal gossip that proved to be unfounded,

44. See Mar. 6 and *c.* 7? 1865.

a noble youth, — & perhaps none takes more delight in it than my boy Edward, who is an old firm friend of his. All this house know your endless good offices to me.

Yours faithfully
R. W. Emerson.

B. B. Wiley.

To Caroline Sturgis Tappan, Concord? March? c. 10? 1865

[An announcement of Edith Emerson's engagement, acknowledged in Caroline Sturgis Tappan, n. p., n. d. *Cf.* other letters of Mar., 1865, on the same subject.]

To Louis Agassiz, Concord, March 11, 1865 [45]

Concord
11 March, 1865

Dear Agassiz,

I learn that your South American expedition,[46] of which you spoke to me, is a fixed fact, & that you are making up your party. If it is not yet complete, it occurs to me to suggest to you the name of a gentleman, who, I think, might be valuable to you, & to whom, I fancy, the offer of a place in it would be welcome. I refer to Edward Hoar, a younger brother of the Judge, — " the Californian," [47] as we call him, he having resided eight years in that country, — at first, practising law, — afterwards, a planter at Santa Barbara. Since his marriage, he has been a farmer in Lincoln, three miles off from here. He is a graduate of Cambridge, a man of character & practical ability, cool & determined, a good man of the woods with a strong taste for wild life. He has a taste for botany &, I believe, some skill in it. He was Thoreau's companion in his tour in the Allegash River district, in Maine. He speaks Spanish, also, which may help him in the South. He has many qualities that would recommend him for such a party. And, though I hear that you go soon, I risk sending you this notice, on the chance

45. MS owned by Mr. George Russell Agassiz; ph. in CUL.

46. The party which sailed with Agassiz from New York on Apr. 1 following did not include Edward Hoar (*A Journey in Brazil. By Professor and Mrs. Louis Agassiz*, 1868, pp. vii–viii) .

47. For Hoar at college and as Californian and as naturalist, *cf.* June 22, 1858? The story of his expedition with Thoreau to Maine is told in " The Allegash and East Branch " (*The Writings*, III, 174–327) and *ibid.*, VI, 315. Hoar's residence on a farm in Lincoln, Mass., and his later years in Sicily and at Concord are mentioned in Moorfield Storey and Edward W. Emerson, *Ebenezer Rockwood Hoar*, 1911, p. 317.

that it may be useful. With confidence in your success & your safe return & speedy,

Yours affectionately,

Louis Agassiz.   R. W. Emerson

To John Murray Forbes, Concord, March 13, 1865 [48]

Concord
March 13, 1865.

My dear friend,

      I cannot allow these young lovers [49] to have all the letters to write or read. If they have the largest stake in their affair, we seniors have a real part, and if an ever diminishing part, we do not value it less. The surprise of Williams visit, when I learned the result, was deeply gratifying to me. In a manly character like his, a tenderness so true & lasting tempers the soldier & endears the man. His manners, so far as I have seen him, are faultless, — manners & speech so modest & sensible, & with such correct opinions, — whilst some turn now & then suggests the soldier quite ready for action. Indeed I found myself measuring him, & very curious to see his behavior with his men, & to watch such a perfect engine at work. You can judge I am rejoiced to give my little country girl into the hands of this brave protector, & shall rest at peace on her account henceforward. I hope she may know how to deserve her felicity. But I confide much in her. She does not please in advance as much as she merits, but can sometimes surprise old friends who tho't they knew her well, with deeper & better traits. She is humble, which is the basis of nobility. But I must not add another word, except to send affectionate salutations to Mrs Forbes, to Alice, to William & Edith & to the juniors also Malcolm & Sarah if they remember me

Yours faithfully,

J. M. Forbes.   R. W. Emerson

To Thomas Ridgeway Gould, Concord? March c. 13, 1865

[Gould, Boston, Mar. 10, 1865, proposes a visit to Concord before he and his wife leave their city residence the first of April. Gould, Mar. 16 following, accepts Mar. 23, the day appointed, he says, by Emerson for the Concord visit. For Gould, cf. May? c. 26? 1863, and a letter of Apr. 7, 1864.]

48. MS owned by RWEMA; ph. in CUL.
49. Cf. Mar. 6 and c. 7? 1865.

To EDWARD WALDO EMERSON, CONCORD, MARCH 20, 1865

[MS owned by Mr. Raymond Emerson.]

To EDWIN PERCY WHIPPLE, CONCORD? MARCH? 25? 1865?

[MS listed and partly quoted in Anderson Galleries, Mar. 31–Apr. 2, 1919, where it is dated simply Saturday noon; Emerson asks to be excused from an engagement because Sam Ward has asked for the same hour. It is at least possible that this follows Whipple's letter, Boston, Mar. 20, 1865, a reminder of the meeting of the Ladies Social Club at his home on Monday, the 27th, with a suggestion that Emerson bring a selection of his verse or prose. But the MS memorandum book for 1865 gives Mar. 27 to Whipple and records: " read ' Adirondac.' "]

To FREDERIC HENRY HEDGE, CONCORD, APRIL 3, 1865 [50]

Concord

3 April, 1865

Dear Hedge,

I have referred my amendment of your proposition to Mrs Ripley & Elizabeth & they consent on the exact condition that you are spend Wednesday night with them, & Thursday to dine with me at 1 o'c. whereof I pray you not to fail.[51] Joy to you, in this joy of the land,[52] & the world!

Yours ever

R W Emerson

To CONRAD? WESSELHOEFT, CONCORD? APRIL? c. 6? 1865

[Mentioned in Apr. 6, 1865, where the first name of the person addressed is not given. Presumably, however, this Dr. Wesselhoeft was the prominent Boston physician.]

To EDWARD WALDO EMERSON, CONCORD, APRIL 6, 1865

[MS owned by Mr. Raymond Emerson. The correct year has been added, apparently by another hand, to Emerson's heading, which dates the letter only Thursday morning. But a reference to a long account of Sheridan's fight that won Richmond as in Tuesday's issue of *The World* (New York, Apr. 4, 1865) fixes day, month, and year.]

50. MS owned by RWEMA; ph. in CUL.
51. Other letters mention the Fast Day dinners of Emerson, Sarah Bradford Ripley, and Hedge.
52. This was the day of the fall of Richmond.

To CAROLINE STURGIS TAPPAN, CONCORD, APRIL 10, 1865 [53]

Concord
Monday, 10 April —

Dear Caroline,

I have your note, & on Saturday night received the stately " Tuscan Sculptors " [54] safely, & with honor due. Thanks for your persistent hospitality, which I gladly accept; — the rather that it gives me a welcome refuge out of some perplexity of invitations.

But what a joyful day is this [55] & proud to Alleghany ranges, Northern Lakes, Missisippi rivers & all lands & men between the two Oceans, between morning & evening stars. Mankind has appeared just now in its best attitude around Mr Lincoln — in these recent experiences — & will aid him to use sanely the immense power with which the hour clothes him.

Ever yours
R. W. Emerson

To ————————, CONCORD? c. APRIL? 1865

[MS listed in Goodspeed's Book Shop, Jan.–Mar., 1922, where it is dated only as to year, is without the name of Emerson's correspondent, and is described as a letter of seven pages concerning Perkins's *Tuscan Sculptors*. If the description is correct, this cannot be the much briefer letter of Apr. 10, 1865, which mentions the receipt of a copy of *Tuscan Sculptors*, but may well be of about the same date and is possibly to the same person. It seems at least equally probable, however, that the present letter is to Rebecca Duncan, as several letters listed in the same lot with it can be shown to be to her.]

To JAMES THOMAS FIELDS, CONCORD, MAY 1, 1865? [56]

Concord
1 May

Dear Sir,

The portfolio contained no picture, only the square drawing paper out of which the oval picture had been cut, — to my great disappointment, when I opened it to an expectant circle! There is ample

53. MS owned by RWEMA; ph. in CUL. This clearly belongs to 1865, and Apr. 10 fell on Monday in that year.

54. Doubtless Charles C. Perkins, *Tuscan Sculptors,* 2 vols., London, 1864. *Cf. c.* Apr.? 1865.

55. On Apr. 9 Grant and Lee had agreed on terms. But on the 15th Lincoln would be dead.

56. MS owned by the Henry F. Huntington Library; ph. in CUL. Comparison

room on this paper to write, below the oval, the whole poem; but did I understand you that I am to use only a part of the space below, because the limits of the book will require to cut off a part of the blank margin? — I write in another house than mine, & have not with me Mrs Fields' note. I will not write till I hear from you.

Ever yours,
R. W. E.

Mr Fields.

To James Thomas Fields, Concord, May 1, 1865 [57]

Concord
May 1
Monday Eve

[1] I send all the Poems of Thoreau which I think ought to go with the Letters.[58] These are the best verses, & no other whole piece quite contents me I think you must be content with a little book, since it is so good I do not like to print either the Prison piece, or the "John Brown," [59] with these clear skyborn letters & poems.[1] I hope to hear from you in the morning concerning the writing on the picture frame.[60]

Mr Fields.   R. W. E.

To John Murray Forbes, Concord, May 2, 1865 [61]

Concord
2 May
Tuesday

My dear Mr Forbes,

I hear that you are or should be in town today. I pray you not to fail to us a visit at this house wherein every soul desires to see you.

---

with the letter of the evening of May 1, 1865, seems to show that the present letter belongs to the same day. Apparently it was planned to include in Thoreau's *Letters to Various Persons* a picture of the author, with some lines in Emerson's hand underneath. But so far as I know, no such frontispiece was actually published.

57. MS owned by the Henry E. Huntington Library; ph. in CUL. Excerpt I is in *Harper's*, LXVIII, 458 (Feb., 1884), and in Annie Fields, *Authors and Friends*, p. 68. Evidence cited below shows that the year is 1865.

58. Thoreau's *Letters to Various Persons*, with Emerson's "Editor's Notice" dated "12 May, 1865," was published by Ticknor & Fields on July 22, 1865, according to the *Boston Evening Transcript* of that date.

59. No such pieces were included. Several of Thoreau's papers on John Brown are to be found in *The Writings*, IV, 409–454.

60. *Cf.* May 1, 1865?

61. MS owned by RWEMA; ph. in CUL. The letter is endorsed 1865; Tuesday

Tomorrow at 11 o'clock, the Fitchburg train will bring you to dinner, & it will take till midnight to hear all that we wish to know. If you cannot come at 11 o'c., then at 4. P. M.[62] If not then, why the next day; but come. With Mrs Emerson's & Ellen's regards, & Edith's filial piety,[63]

Ever yours,
R. W. Emerson

To Bayard Taylor, Concord, May 4, 1865 [64]

Concord
4 May 1865

My dear Sir,

It is one of my many besetting sins — a long procrastination, but I did duly & I believe early receive, and do prize as much as one who is no artist can, your pleasing sketch of Hammerfest.[65] I have thanked you anew every time I have shown it to new spectators, — and they are many, — and I observed that it drew the most praise from the most discerning — A fine sketch has certain advantages over poetry or prose; it is a perpetual ornament, it is seen at a glance or conned at leisure, and, whilst it delights the skilful, bores nobody.

I doubt not you are now at Cedarcroft. I hope the great chestnuts & the oaks, &, above all, the Sequoia, thrive in the great Spring.[66] A thousand years to the last! With very kind remembrances to Mrs Taylor, I remain

Yours, with great regard,
R. W. Emerson

Bayard Taylor, Esq.

---

fell on May 2 in that year; and the last sentence confirms this date. A letter from Forbes dated Milton, Monday, May "2 or 3," with the year 1865 supplied, seems to be an answer to the present letter.

62. Trains leaving Boston for Concord at these hours are advertised in the *Boston Daily Advertiser* of May 1, 1865.

63. Edith Emerson's engagement to William H. Forbes is mentioned in earlier letters.

64. MS owned by Mr. Thomas F. Madigan; ph. in CUL.

65. Probably the same "good drawing which I keep & prize" mentioned in Dec. 12, 1870, to Fields.

66. Taylor had returned to Cedarcroft from New York by about the first of April this year (*Life and Letters of Bayard Taylor*, ed, Marie Hansen-Taylor and H. E. Scudder, 1895, II, 427 and 430). What Emerson says of the trees seems to come from first-hand acquaintance. In Dec. 12, 1870, to Fields, he recalls a visit with Taylor " in Pennsylvania," and Albert H. Smyth, *Bayard Taylor*, n. d. (c. 1896), p. 133, mentions Emerson's visit to Cedarcroft; but I am not certain of the date.

To John Stuart Mill, Concord, May 6, 1865

[MS listed and partly quoted in James Tregaskis & Son, late Mar., 1929. I am uncertain whether it is this letter or a later one which is referred to in Mill, n. p., Aug. 12, 1867, as "the letter I had the pleasure of receiving from you last year," and which conferred on Mill "the privilege of writing to you." It is probable, I think, that Mill had forgotten the exact year of Emerson's letter.]

To James Thomas Fields, Concord? May 15, 1865 [67]

May 15

Dear Sir,

A very small instalment, but we shall send more tomorrow.

In one of the last letters of Thoreau, I allowed the name of the Canadian explorer to read *La Houtan*. It ought to be *La Hontan*.[68]

Yours,

R. W. E.

To Forceythe Willson, Concord? May c. 25, 1865

[Willson, Cambridge, May 26, 1865, acknowledges this "letter inviting me to Concord" and accepts June 6, the date proposed by Emerson. Willson says he has never seen his correspondent but regards him as a great benefactor.]

To ———— Heald, Concord, May 27, 1865 [69]

Concord
May 27 1865

Dear Sir,

In a file quite too large of unanswered letters, I find the envelope which enclosed the envelope of this note, but to my regret I do not find the letter which it contained. I find in the envelope a dollar in fractional currency; but I have lost all recollection of the purpose for which it was sent, & which, no doubt, was stated in the letter. In this plight, I can do nothing but send it back to your own address, with my regrets for my carelessness or misfortune.

Respectfully,

R. W. Emerson

Mr Heald.

67. MS owned by the Library of the University of Pennsylvania; ph. in CUL. The reference to Thoreau's *Letters* fixes the year. *Cf.* May 1, 1865.

68. The name was printed correctly in a letter of June 26, 1861 (*Letters to Various Persons*, 1865, p. 203).

69. MS owned by Goodspeed's Book Shop; ph. in CUL. I have been unable to identify Heald.

To JOHN MURRAY FORBES, CONCORD? MAY 29, 1865? [70]

My dear friend,

Very welcome was your kind note — very sorry am I that you & Mrs Forbes should have waited for us in vain. William Forbes found us & led us home in the morning. You are our good angels all & may we never lose you.

Certainly I shall see you on Saturday at the Club.

With love to your household,

R. W. Emerson

J. M. Forbes, Esq
29 May.

To EDITH EMERSON, CONCORD? MAY, 1865 [71]

Papa hears the foolishest saying of his little girl. She never was quite absurd before. Doesn't she know that papa is as proud as he can go of his new son, & would be glad to keep him in the house every day & all days? If you let him go a day before he must, I shall not forgive you.

To CHARLES ELIOT NORTON, CONCORD, JUNE 7, 1865 [72]

Concord

June 7

My dear Norton,

The letter to the Architects, like all your work in this com-

70. MS owned by RWEMA; ph. in CUL. The year is extremely doubtful. Were it not for the endorsed " 1865? " I should be inclined to place the letter some ten years later on account of the note of old age that is sounded here and because of the somewhat angular handwriting. But it is difficult to judge by either kind of evidence. For the handwriting, it may be explained by the miniature sheet on which Emerson wrote. Perhaps the reference to " William " Forbes instead of " Will " would argue 1865. On the other hand, the fact that May 29 was Monday in that year would tend to make it less plausible. The following Saturday would not have been a regular day for the Saturday Club — if that club is meant.

71. MS owned by RWEMA; ph. in CUL. The penciled note, in Emerson's hand, is followed on the same sheet by this paragraph written by his daughter:

" In May 1865 W. H. F. who was coming up from town almost every day thought he ought not to intrude on the family so often — and told me so — I saw he needed an invitation from Father & told Mother that he did not feel at liberty to come without being assured he was welcome to Father and her as well as to us young people — The next day I received this note

" E. E. F."

72. MS owned by HCL; ph. in CUL. The year 1865, supplied in the date line, fits the evidence noted below.

mittee,[73] appears to me as perfect as the yet unsettled facts we stand upon permit. Tis pity we have not more time or a more accessible constituency. It even looks as if we wanted, besides the Academic Theatre, two halls, one for conversation & organized debate of the Alumni, & the other for dining. But I suppose the Library can serve the first purpose. It will be a question in which hall the Memorials will be placed. The letters you inclose are instructive, Mr Wight's is very good. You shall answer your question as to the compensation for designs, for me; for I do not know our power as a committee, but will assent to your decision. For the numbers " 2000 " for audience, & " 750 " for the dining hall, — they are large, but I think needful, & so with great thankfulness I have signed my name to the paper.

Ever Yours,
R W Emerson

To George William Childs, Concord, June 8, 1865 [74]

Concord
8 June 1865

Dear Sir,

I received last night your note of the 5th instant. I had already a note from you, a few days earlier, which, though much in arrears in my correspondence, I had nearly reached. I am not quite ready to promise even the limited contribution to your Journal which your last note requests. I rarely write, & usually feel that the " Atlantic Monthly " has a first claim to any papers of mine. But will you be good enough to send me one number of the Ledger,[75] = for I am not at all acquainted with it — & perhaps I shall be able to send you a precise answer.

I have to acknowledge a great debt to your kindness in the long time in which you have sent me the " Publishers' Circular," which I always read, with much thankfulness for its French & English correspond-

73. *Cf.* July 12, 1865. It was on May 12 of this year that the Harvard graduates appointed a committee of nine, including Emerson, to consider plans for a memorial for their fellow collegians who had died for the Union (*Final Reports of the Building Committee and of the Treasurer of the Harvard Memorial Fund to the Committee of Fifty*, 1878, p. 4; and *New-York Daily Tribune*, July 26, 1865, pp. 4 and 5) .

74. MS owned by the Haverford College Library; ph. in CUL.

75. Childs had become proprietor of the *Public Ledger* of Philadelphia in Dec., 1864.

ence.[76] Were I a little richer, I should certainly have subscribed for it. I give you my best thanks

Respectfully,
R. W. Emerson

G. W. Childs, Esq

To Sarah Swain Forbes, Concord, June 8, 1865 [77]

Concord
Thursday Night
8 June

My dear Mrs Forbes,

My wife shows me your kind note, & begs me to write a word for her.

Yes, she would gladly join you to sing *Te Deum* for the Peace,[78] & *Te Deum* for your son & her daughter [79] & does day by day magnify Heaven for these benefits, & thinks perhaps she cannot magnify the benefits. But she will not come & see you tomorrow, though she desires much to see you; has explained to me that she is fast tied at home & the faster by the absence of Ellen & Edith. Neither can I go to Milton, an engagement tomorrow holds me in Boston. But there or here we must speedily see you, & we will write at the first hour when we see the way open. With love to all your house from us both. . R W Emerson

To ————————, Concord, June 8, 1865

[MS listed in Anderson Galleries, Mar. 23 and 24, 1926; described there as declining an invitation to speak on the Fourth of July.]

To George Luther Stearns, Concord? June? c. 10? 1865

[Printed without date in *The Life and Public Services of George Luther Stearns,* p. 347; refuses an invitation to speak at a meeting held in Faneuil Hall on June 21, 1865.]

76. Childs's *American Literary Gazette and Publishers' Circular,* as the title ran at this time, had in the past included a column of " Our London Correspondence " and still kept " Our Continental Correspondence " as a regular feature.

77. MS owned by RWEMA; ph. in CUL. This was obviously written in 1865, and June 8 fell on Thursday in that year.

78. The war had formally ended with the President's proclamation of amnesty on May 29.

79. The wedding occurred about four months later (see Oct. 1, 1865) .

To EDITH EMERSON, CONCORD, JUNE 15, 1865 [80]

Concord, 15 June

Dear Edith,

You mean to stay till your absence is felt. Well then you can come now, — today specially, when Mrs Swain [81] & her niece came from Boston to call on you. But Ellen will bring your news tomorrow. Mrs Forbes has played the kindest part in her energetic counsel & introductions to Charles.[82] & Charles likes Mr Brooks very well. I advised him to go & see old Reuben Rice, who could at least give him a field lesson when he is surveying; & today he has made with him his first survey. I send enclosed $4.00 Happiest hours to you.

R. W. E.

To SAMUEL BRADFORD, CONCORD, JUNE 23, 1865 [83]

Concord
Friday 23ᵈ June

Dear Sam,

I grieve to learn that on the only day in all the years when you really propose to come to Concord, I must be in Boston. I have sundry unavoidable duties there tomorrow one with a " Memorial Committee " on as we call it for the College,[84] & can not change the day. But you must sit down here with William [85] & spend Sunday with me. & postpone for once some of your despatches & engagements for a day

Affectionately Yours,
R. W. Emerson

Samˡ Bradford.

80. MS owned by RWEMA; ph. in CUL. The year 1865, added in another hand, is correct, as the letter was clearly written after Edith Emerson's engagement and before her marriage. For her absence from home about this time, cf. June 8, 1865, to Mrs. Forbes.

81. Probably Lydia, wife of W. W. Swain, granduncle of William H. Forbes (cf. *Letters and Recollections of John Murray Forbes,* I, 107). Miss A. R. Anthony confirms this conjecture and gives me the additional information that the niece mentioned was Elizabeth Tyson, grandniece of W. W. Swain.

82. Perhaps Emerson's nephew Charles Emerson.

83. MS owned by RWEMA; ph. in CUL. June 23 fell on Friday in 1865, the year fixed by evidence cited below.

84. Cf. the letters of June 7 and July 12, 1865. Emerson first wrote, " a committee on the Memorial as we call it." In altering the phrase, he failed to cancel " on."

85. William Emerson was apparently a resident of Concord at this time.

To Julia A. Lapham, Concord? June 29, 1865

[Julia Lapham, Milwaukee, July 20, 1865, acknowledges this letter and thanks Emerson for " the little gems " — perhaps holograph copies of some of his verses — for the Soldiers Home Fair. I do not know whether this is the letter of the same date listed in Stan. V. Henkels, Oct. 9, 1914, where the name of the person addressed is not given.]

To Isaac Thomas Hecker, Concord? c. June? 1865?

[Mentioned in July 12, 1865.]

To Caroline Sturgis Tappan, Concord, July 2, 1865 [86]

Concord

2 July

Dear Caroline,

One day last week I was in Poultney, Vermont, attending the " Commencement " of the " Ripley Female College," [87] & saw a very good class of young girls. One of them, named Virginia Tryon, of New York City, appeared to be first Scholar, & to have all the social & literary honors. She told me that she was going the next day to Lenox, I think, to spend the summer. I believe her mother is there, or is to be. I wish, if she comes within your horizon, you will shine on her, & perhaps Ellen & Mary [88] may find her, though older, interesting to them. She is a noble girl, with very pleasing manners. The " College " is Methodistic,[89] but she reads Swedenborg, with her family.

Ever yours,

R. W. Emerson

86. MS owned by Mrs. J. Dellinger Barney; ph. in CUL. The year is fixed by the mention of Emerson's visit to Poultney.

87. The commencement exercises at Ripley Female College are recorded at some length in the *Christian Advocate and Journal*, New York, July 13, 1865. Emerson read " Resources " before the Irving Association on Monday (June 26). On Tuesday evening there was a program by the students, and Virginia G. Tryon's essay on " Feminine Culture " won particular praise. Julia C. R. Dorr, Centre Rutland, Vt., Sept. 26, 1865, tells Emerson she has heard much of him from the college girls and others since his visit to Poultney " last summer "; Ripley Female College, she says, was named for her father. The letter of June 30, 1868, is another echo of the Poultney visit.

88. Daughters of Mrs. Tappan (*cf.* May 15, 1867?). Ellen Sturgis Tappan, born 1849, was married in 1875 to Richard Cowell Dixey (*The New England Historical and Genealogical Register*, LXXXI, 189).

89. Originally, and again in later years, called Troy Conference Academy, the college had a varied history, changing from time to time its relationship to the Methodist Episcopal Church (*A History of the Town of Poultney, Vermont*, 1875, pp. 163–165). The present name is Green Mountain Junior College.

To Mary Preston Stearns, Concord, July 5, 1865

[Printed in A. Bronson Alcott, *Ralph Waldo Emerson,* n. d. (c. 1888), pp. v–vi.]

To James Thomas Fields, Concord, July 12, 1865 [90]

Concord
12 July, 1865

My dear Sir,

I was very sorry to lose your visit & Mrs Fields's on Friday. I called that day at your office. I shall be in town on Friday again & will try to find you as soon as the graduates' meeting [91] is over, say, between 12 & 1 o'c., if you are in town.

I have never thanked you for the valued book of your " Arnold," [92] which you sent me, — which is a treasure, & doubled in value by the additions. Miss Thoreau gives me the best account from you of continued success of " Cape Cod." [93] I have never had a word of reply from Father Hecker to my note.[94] She seemed to think that you had heard from him.

My wife joins me in her regret for the loss of Mrs Fields s visit & yours.

R W Emerson

J. T. Fields, Esq

To James Elliot Cabot, Concord, July 18, 1865 [95]

Concord
18 July, 1865.

Dear Cabot,

I take the liberty to introduce to you Mr W. T. Harris, of Saint Louis, who interests himself so much in Hegel & German Phi-

90. MS owned by the Henry E. Huntington Library; ph. in CUL.

91. A meeting of the graduates of Harvard was held in Boston on the morning of Friday, July 14, to hear the report of the committee appointed to consider the subject of a permanent memorial (*Boston Evening Transcript,* July 14, 1865) . For the memorial committee, *cf.* the letters of June 7 and 23, 1865.

92. The copy of the Boston edition of Matthew Arnold's *Essays in Criticism,* 1865, still in the Emerson library at the Antiquarian House bears the inscription " Mr Emerson from J. T. F. June. 1865." In the same library there is a copy of the London and Cambridge edition, 1865, of this book, the gift of E. Lyulph Stanley in the preceding March.

93. The *Boston Daily Advertiser,* Mar. 25, 1865, had announced that Thoreau's posthumous *Cape Cod* was published by Ticknor & Fields on that day.

94. See *c.* June? 1865? Isaac Hecker is mentioned in earlier letters.

95. MS owned by Professor Philip Cabot; ph. in CUL. The last digit of the year is carelessly made and resembles " 8 " as much perhaps as " 5," but must, I am

losophy, that he ought to meet those who know most about it. I have found him a very intelligent gentleman, a faithful student, and using his own eyes on a pretty wide range of facts. I hope he may be so fortunate as to find you.

Yours faithfully,
R. W. Emerson

J. Elliot Cabot, Esq.

To Frederic Henry Hedge, Concord, July 18, 1865 [96]

Concord
18 July 1865

Dear Hedge,

Will you let me make you acquainted with Mr W. T. Harris, of St Louis, who is already interested in you & your studies, & will be glad to converse with you. You will find him a very good reader of Hegel, & of other of your German friends. I have been much gratified & a little surprised to receive from Missouri so sharpsighted a philosopher.

I take the occasion to say that I know I have owed you for weeks a note which will yet arrive.

Ever yours faithfully,
R. W. Emerson

Dr Hedge.

To Annie Adams Fields, Concord, July 27, 1865

[MS owned by the Henry E. Huntington Library; ph. in CUL. The body of the letter is printed in *Harper's*, LXVIII, 465 (Feb., 1884), and in Annie

---

convinced, be " 5." Harris dates his visits to Alcott in Concord as " July 8, 1865, and again in August " (Sanborn and Harris, II, 593). It seems reasonable to conjecture that Harris returned to Concord to visit Emerson on July 18 and received then the letters of introduction to both Cabot and Hedge. Feb. 1, 1866, to Ellen Emerson, mentions the possibility of going to St. Louis at the request of Harris as if he were known to the family in Concord. Further evidence for 1865 rather than 1868 is the lack here of any reference to *The Journal of Speculative Philosophy,* begun in 1867 (mentioned in June 28, 1867, and elsewhere). For Harris, see Feb. 1, 1866, to Ellen Emerson, and later letters. That he was much interested in Hegel as early as 1865 is clear from Sanborn and Harris, II, 552, and Denton J. Snider, *The St. Louis Movement,* 1920, p. 10. Various letters refer to the philosophical studies of Cabot and of Hedge.

96. MS owned by the Emerson Literary Society of Hamilton College; ph. in CUL. Again the last digit of the date line might be read either " 5 " or " 8." For proof that the actual year was 1865, see the note on the letter of this date to Cabot.

Fields, *Authors and Friends*, p. 97. Both printings omit the heading and salutation — "Concord 27 July, 1865" and "Dear Mrs Fields" — as well as the complimentary close and signature and the inside address — "Yours faith-fully, R. W. Emerson" and "Mrs Annie Fields."]

To Sarah Swain Forbes, Concord, August 17, 1865 [97]

Concord

17 August 1865

My dear Mrs Forbes,

Edith & Edward have come home so intoxicated with Naushon that it makes the staple of all conversation, & I doubt not the stuff of the night's dreams. But I think Mrs E. & I must be contented to see & enjoy it, this summer, through their eyes, — helped by happy memories of each of us. It would not be easy for either of us to leave home so far, and my wife has already arranged a little pet vacation of a few days at Dorchester. I remember the solid splendor of a Naushon day of Gold-win Smith's hunt,[98] & the dramatic discourse in the drawing-room be-tween England & America that followed it. But how the anxieties of the last year have given serenity & sweetness to this, and, I can believe, mended the sunshine of the Happy Island! Thanks always for the kind-est heart with which you are receiving my little girl.

Mrs Emerson sends warmest regards to you & Mr Forbes.

Affectionately

Mrs Forbes.   R. W. Emerson

To James Bradley Thayer, Concord, August 25, 1865 [99]

Concord

25 August

My dear Sir,

Thanks for the Criticism on the "Letters." [100] But I am sorry you do not rate them much higher. I confide that some day, after

97. MS owned by RWEMA; ph. in CUL.

98. *Cf.* a note on Oct. 16, 1864.

99. MS owned by Professor James B. Thayer; ph. in CUL. Evidence noted below shows that the year is 1865.

100. The present letter bears this notation: "Notice of Thoreau's Letters in Da. Advr." This unsigned review of *Letters to Various Persons* in the *Boston Daily Ad-vertiser* of Aug. 24, 1865, stresses Thoreau's dependence on Emerson and praises the master much more than the disciple.

a long vacation in the mountains or pastures, you will. I am sure he is entitled to stand quite alone on his proper merits. There might easily have been a little influence from his neighbors on his first writings: He was not quite out of college, I believe, when I first saw him: [101] but it is long since I, and I think all who knew him, felt that he was the most independent of men in thought & in action. I have more to say, — but my messenger waits

Yours faithfully,
R. W. Emerson

Jas. B. Thayer, Esq.

To E. H. Barlow? Concord, September 15, 1865 [102]

Concord
Sept. 15, 1865

Dear Sir,

You shall, if you please, write the list of subjects thus:

———————

Mr E.s Lectures on American Life.

———————

Lecture I. American Life.
     II. Social Aims.
     III. Resources.
     IV. Table-Talk.
     V. Books, Poetry, Criticism.
     VI. Success.

101. *Cf.* June? *c.* 20? 1837. Presumably Emerson had some first-hand knowledge of Thoreau when he wrote that letter in his behalf.

102. MS owned by RWEMA; ph. in CUL. Apparently an incomplete draft or copy, in Emerson's hand. The course here outlined is much, but not quite, the same as courses given earlier in Boston and elsewhere (*cf.* notes on Nov. 18, 1864, and on the letters of Jan. 24 and 27, 1865). As it exactly corresponds to that advertised for Amherst in the following October (see Oct. 23, 1865), it seems probable that the present letter was addressed to the director of the Amherst lectures. The *Hampshire Express,* Amherst, Oct. 26, 1865, in its account of Emerson's appearances there, says, " Great credit is due to Mr. Barlow for the entertainment he has furnished our citizens this fall." In the first two entries for the Amherst course in the MS memorandum book of this year appears the name " E. H. Barlow."

To James Russell Lowell, Concord, September 17, 1865 [103]

Concord
17 September, 1865.

Dear Lowell,

I send you warm thanks, if late, for the admirable Ode.[104] I shall always be sorry that I did not hear it. The eighth Strophe, with its passion & its vision, was made to be spoken. The technical skill shown throughout is masterly, & yet subordinated by the high thought & sentiment of the piece, which make me glad & proud of it as a national poem. When you shall collect your recent poems in a book, I hope you will drop from this the one or two needless reminders of Tennyson, & I shall affirm with joy, against any possible previous speeches of my own to you, that your eminent success with the comic muse has in no wise hindered you from the command of all the resources of the noble & serious goddess.

Ever yours with great regard,
R. W. Emerson

James Russell Lowell.

To James Bradley Thayer, Concord, September 20, 1865? [105]

Concord
20 Sept

My dear Mr Thayer,

I am sorry not to have gone to the mail on its arrival then I could have gone to see you this morning, or, at least, written: for I suppose your broker believes in Today. I am very much obliged to you for your kind thought & care of me in this matter & if it is not too late shall certainly take your advice. But tomorrow is Cattle-Show in Concord & as I am on one of the Committees I must stay at home.[106]

103. MS owned by HCL; ph. in CUL.

104. Doubtless a copy of the privately printed *Ode Recited at the Commemoration of the Living and Dead Soldiers of Harvard University, July 21, 1865,* Cambridge, 1865, now known under a slightly altered title. Emerson made a speech at the same dinner at which Lowell read his poem, and both speech and poem are mentioned in the account of the occasion printed in the *Boston Daily Advertiser* of July 22, 1865 (the speech is in *Cent. Ed.,* XI). Perhaps Emerson left the dinner early or was unable to hear from where he sat.

105. MS owned by Professor James B. Thayer; ph. in CUL. The year added by another hand than Emerson's seems, in the light of facts noted below, to be correct.

106. The events of the " Middlesex Cattle Show " — officially, it seems, the Mid-

For my certificates of C. B. & Q. stock,[107] I believe they are in your safe — as also my Fort Waynes.[108] I have no recollection of transferring them to my little trunk in Mr Ward's care. But if you have them not I will come & find them on [109] Friday, if necessary; otherwise, on Saturday Meantime, I send you my blank signature, hoping that I send what you mean.

Your affectionate serv.[t].

R. W Emerson

To James Bradley Thayer, Concord, September 26, 1865 [110]

Concord

26 September, '65

My dear Sir,

I am highly gratified with the success of your counsel & action thus far, & much your debtor for it, & pray you to proceed as you propose in all particulars.

Ever yours,

Jas. B. Thayer, Esq.   R. W. Emerson

To Abel Adams, Concord, October 1, 1865 [111]

[I]Concord,

Sunday, 1 October.[I]

My dear friend,

I hoped to have seen you again before this month opened, but have

---

dlesex Agricultural Exhibition — of Sept. 21, 1865, are reported in the *Boston Daily Advertiser* of the following day. According to this account, " Ralph Waldo Emerson spoke of the appointment by the Governor of a commissioner to inquire into the means of replanting the Concord and Merrimack Rivers with fish," and there were other addresses. The date given in *Journals*, X, 112, is an error.

107. *Cf.* Jan. 25, 1866.

108. *Cf.* June 5, 1866. The road was apparently the Pittsburgh, Fort Wayne, & Chicago Railroad, resulting from a consolidation in 1856 (*cf.* Wallace A. Brice, *History of Fort Wayne*, 1868, p. 321) .

109. Badly blotted and so somewhat conjectural.

110. MS owned by Professor James B. Thayer; ph. in CUL. *Cf.* Sept. 20, 1865?

111. MS owned by RWEMA; ph. in CUL. Excerpts I–IV are in Cabot, II, 628–629. The year is obviously 1865, and Oct. 1 fell on Sunday then. Annie Fields recorded in her diary the marriage of William H. Forbes and Edith Emerson on Oct. 3, 1865 (M. A. DeWolfe Howe, *Memories of a Hostess*, n.d. [c. 1922], p. 91) . The *Boston Daily Advertiser* of Oct. 6 following announced that the ceremony was performed " In Concord, Tuesday, 3d inst, by Rev. Mr. Reynolds."

not been able to do so. [II]Edith's note will have given you the day & hour of the wedding, but I add this line to say, that I rely on the presence of you & your family as on my own.[II] I know that Mrs Adams & Abby will not permit any common accident to prevent their kind purpose. I trust Mrs H. Larkin can be spared a few hours from her mother, & will come. [III]And I entreat you not to let any superable obstacle stand in your own way hither. My own family connection has become so small, that I necessarily cling to you who have stood by me like a strong elder brother through nearly or quite forty years. You know all my chances in that time, and Edward's career has depended on you. Tuesday will not be the day I look for, unless you are here.[III] It is, to be sure, but for a short hour or two, — but we have come to think it so serious & important, that I wish it to be right in all particulars, and mainly in the friends.

All of us send to all of you kind regards.

[IV]Yours affectionately,

R. W. Emerson[IV]

Abel Adams.

To Margaret P. Forbes, Concord, October 7, 1865 [112]

Concord

Oct. 7, 1865.

My dear friend,

If I had really believed what I was told, that you had hurt yourself by a fall, I should not have looked for you at Edith's wedding. But I grieved to see that neither Margaret nor Fanny Forbes was there. And I must believe that this malicious accident really befel you, or that you use this color to hide some of your high retirements. In the one case, you should have persisted not to be hurt, — for what can overcome a charmed person against her will? — In the other, you should have mercifully forgone your seclusion, & consented to befriend so gentle a petitioner as as E. But if it be sadly true, that you are suffering from this mischance, — then — but I am sure you are all but well again, & no evil can cling to you. I have reproached myself that I did not come to see you, if it were only on the plea that I was to have assisted at the con-

112. MS owned by Mrs. Gorham Brooks; ph. in CUL. For Edith Emerson's wedding, see Oct. 1, 1865. Margaret P. and Cornelia Frances Forbes, her husband's aunts, appear in other letters. John Weiss was known not only as preacher and author but as lecturer. Presumably the *Hints* were manuscript notes taken in the lecture room.

sultations Whither & how you were to carry your household gods —
Whether to the mountains? Whether to the sea? or over-sea? I know
that I could not have helped you by so much as a suggestion; but I delight to see beautiful behavior, & should have enjoyed every particular
of the debate. You will tell me how it should & must be, & shall thank
me that I have not molested you with one word.

I send you back, with thanks, the *Hints from the Weiss Lectures,*
which I have read with interest, & wished them far fuller than they are;
& have even dared to borrow & keep a sentence. For all that is come &
gone, I doubt not to see you soon, and I send my grief to Miss Fanny
Forbes, that she did not grace our wedding.

Ever yours affectionately;
R. W. Emerson

Miss Margaret P. Forbes.

To C. Staples, Concord, October 12, 1865

[MS listed in Charles F. Heartman, July 2, 1930, where it is said to refer to
Agassiz, Dr. C. T. Jackson, and others. The initials are here given as C. E.,
but I conjecture that the person addressed was Carlton Albert Staples (*cf.*
the note on Feb. 2, 1865).]

To Julia Caroline Ripley Dorr, Concord, October 14, 1865 [113]

Concord
14 October 1865

I am grateful to the kind friend who writes me this frank & engaging
letter,[114] whose good sense & perfect tone gives it the best authority &
claim. I have chanced to be much occupied since I received it, or it
should have an immediate reply. The narrative itself of the letter, &
the verses it encloses, make so strong a showing on the affirmative side,
that to any one but the author of the letter I should confidently give
them as the answer of the oracle to the formal query that is put. In
other words, happy the soul which is thus dissatisfied, hard to please,

113. MS owned by the Abernethy Library, Middlebury College; ph. in CUL. Some
account of Mrs. Dorr's life and of her earlier writings in prose and in verse is to
be found in John S. Hart, *The Female Prose Writers of America,* 5th ed., 1870, p. 447.
After 1870 she published several books. *Cf.* Mar. 6, 1872.

114. *Cf.* a note on July 2, 1865, where the contents of Mrs. Dorr's letter from
Centre Rutland, Vt., Sept. 26, 1865, are partly noted. In the same letter Mrs. Dorr
inclosed some MS poems which she wished Emerson to criticize. One of her poems,
she said, had been refused by *The Atlantic,* though later accepted by *Harper's.* She
still wished to contribute to *The Atlantic.*

& which wishes its friends to be as good as its thought. Of course, though you know better, you are pleased to persist in the conceit that there is some magic in the "Atlantic" or the "Blackwood" Magazine, & the surface finish that passes currently therein. But this will, as it ought, look even comic to you, on another day. And I will rather say to you, that, being as you are, with so much sensibility & power, you should scorn to shine, &, if you have had the protection & lessons of Solitude, should cleave to them as the givers of what is best. Cities & literary society are only to be tasted as contrasts & indicators of the good we have left at home This is my short first answer to your letter, which I make thus abrupt only because I see that there is no end to the fulness of the truth. Meantime, I ask leave to retain for a time the verses you inclosed, with the promise that they shall be faithfully restored.[115] If I shall find presently a little leisure, I shall perhaps add a few words to these.

With great regard,

Mrs Dorr.   R. W. Emerson

To Ellen Emerson, Amherst, Massachusetts, October 23, 1865 [116]

Amherst
Monday 23^d Oct

Dear Ellen,

           Very glad of all your letters & inclosures & of your narrative of the tender commencements of housekeeping at Milton,[117] in

115. Mrs. Dorr, Nov. 22, 1865, thanked Emerson for this letter and invited him to stop at The Maples when he came to lecture at Rutland in the following December (cf. Dec. 10, 1865, to Ellen Emerson). On Sept. 24 (1866?) Mrs. Dorr wrote again, asking Emerson for the return of the MS poems she had sent him "last winter" and recalling the fact that he had remarked "when here" — presumably in Dec., 1865 — that there were two or three words or expressions in the poems that seemed objectionable and that he would point them out.

116. MS owned by RWEMA; ph. in CUL. The year is clearly 1865, when Oct. 23 fell on Monday. The *Hampshire Express*, Amherst, Mass., Oct. 19 and 26, shows that Emerson's course of lectures in that town began on Oct. 17 and ended on the 24th. Further details regarding the course are given by George F. Whicher in the *Amherst Graduates' Quarterly*, XXIII, 288–289 (Aug., 1934). The subjects announced, as Professor Whicher shows, were "American Life," "Social Aims," "Resources," "Table Talk," "Books, Poetry, Criticism," and "Success"; but the *Express* of Oct. 19 reported that the first lecture given was "Social Aims," and this agrees with the evidence of the MS memorandum book for 1865, which indicates that "American Life" was read on the 24th. *Cf.* Sept. 15 of this year.

117. Ellen Emerson had told, in two letters, written, it seems, on Oct. 17 and 19, 1865, of the beginnings of her sister's housekeeping at Milton, Mass.

reading which my sympathies are with all parties. I do not know whether your reference to the " childrens letter " is to Will's invitation which you enclose. Is that the " scare "? or is there another, from which my nerves are yet safe? for I have stood this. I leave Amherst Wednesday morn. at 6.30, & should reach Concord at 1.30 Yesterday I was at Northampton all day,[118] — I think the most beautiful town in the state. Edward King, my poet of 17 years, called on me there, from Springfield — a remarkable boy. I had not yet seen him.[119] Professor Shepard [120] came home on Thursday & I saw him on Friday & I suppose I shall see his mineral cabinet widely famed, today Except him not a professor or tutor in this collegiate town have I seen. Even Judge French,[121] the head of the Agricultural College, who boards in this house, took flight, on my arrival, for Boston, & has not returned. A friendly person, Mrs S. Brown's brother. I am sorry the invitation is for next Sunday,[122] for Saturday night is our School Committee's,[123] & I have meant to come home from the Sat. Club, to it. If John [124] is in a hurry for money (due on the 20th) you can give him some of Mr Thayer's,[125] or draw the cheque I sent you. Tell mamma that my outfit proved sufficient in all important particulars.

Affectionately,

Papa.

118. Emerson apparently thought of the neighboring town of Florence as a part of Northampton. The *Northampton Free Press*, Oct. 27, 1865, reported that he " gave two discourses from the platform of the Free Congregational Society of Florence last Sunday " and was heard with " rapt attention " by his large audience. The paper praises him as a liberal. The subjects, as recorded in the MS memorandum book for this year, were " Immortality " and " Natural Religion."

119. The young poet was a friend of Charles J. Woodbury (see Woodbury's *Talks with Ralph Waldo Emerson*, n. d. [c. 1890], p. 55).

120. Charles Upham Shepard, Emerson's cousin, was a professor at Amherst and had also been connected with Yale (see Mar. 16, 1830) and with a medical college in Charleston, S. C.

121. Henry Flagg French, father of Daniel Chester French, the sculptor, had been a judge some years earlier and was president of the Massachusetts Agricultural College 1865–1866.

122. *Cf.* Oct. 25, 1865, to W. H. Forbes.

123. *Reports of the Selectmen and Other Officers of the Town of Concord, from March 1, 1865, to March 1, 1866*, p. 2, shows that Emerson was at this time a member of the local school committee.

124. Probably the John Clahan of Feb. 1, 1866, to William Emerson, and later letters.

125. It is not clear whether this refers to James Bradley Thayer, Emerson's attorney and relative by marriage.

To John Murray Forbes, Concord? October 25, 1865

[Mentioned in the letter of the same date to W. H. Forbes.]

To William Hathaway Forbes, Concord, October 25, 1865 [126]

Concord

25 October

Wednesday Eve

My dear Will,

I received your note announcing the approach of the island Venison just as I was starting for Amherst. It duly came & I find was received with unanimous admiration of all beholders & partakers. I was not too late on arriving today to have my share in it, and have just written my due acknowledgment to your father for his kind thought.

At Amherst I had your invitation for Sunday, forwarded to me; [127] & since, Ediths " coaxing "; [128] and though I had intended quite another use of Saturday Night, I find there is no use in resisting so much outside & inside pressure as is here applied, and I mean to come to you from our Club on Saturday Evening. Mrs Emerson will probably go out by an earlier train. You must have some huge pot of rose color in your house, out of which Ellen writes all her letters home.

Edith, with my love, will be better pleased that I write to you.

Affectionately yours,

R. W. Emerson

William H. Forbes.

To Laurence? Oliphant, Concord? October c. 26? 1865

[Mentioned in Oct. 27, 1865. Laurence Oliphant had, it seems, recently arrived in this country and was to wait for some months before he could gain admission into Harris's brotherhood (Richard M'Cully, *The Brotherhood of the New Life and Thomas Lake Harris,* 1893, pp. 84–85).]

126. MS owned by RWEMA; ph. in CUL. Oct. 25 fell on Wednesday in 1865, clearly the year of this letter.

127. See Oct. 23, 1865.

128. Edith Emerson Forbes, Milton Hill, Oct. 21, 1865, invited her father and his family to Milton on Saturday to spend Sunday — " I must coax you to come to our house-warming." Emerson's intended " use of Saturday Night " is mentioned in Oct. 23, 1865.

To John Murray Forbes, Concord? October 27, 1865 [129]

Friday, 27 Oct.

My dear Mr Forbes,

No, we never mind company in our balloting. The proposer of the candidate carries his hat about, without disturbing the guests.

I have written to Mr Oliphant [130] to come to the Club, but do not know that he is still in town.

I shall certainly obey you as to the way to Milton.

Yours ever

R. W. Emerson

To —————— Russell, Concord, November 6, 1865 [131]

Concord

6 November

Dear Sir,

I am sorry to be so backward in reply to your note. It came to my house when I was absent for ten days, & all my correspondence is behindhand. I am not much an expert in editions, & have contented myself these forty years with the plain duodecimos of the Isaac Reed Edition, London, 1820: but, when I buy a new one, it will be Richard Grant White's, which has the strong approval of all the good Shakspearians whom I know; & which, you know, is just completed.

Respectfully,

R. W. Emerson

Mr Russell.

129. MS owned by RWEMA; ph. in CUL. The full date is endorsed, and Oct. 27 fell on Friday in 1865.

130. For Oliphant see the note on Oct. c. 26? preceding. For the prospective visit to Milton, cf. Oct. 25, 1865, to W. H. Forbes.

131. MS owned by Goodspeed's Book Shop; ph. in CUL. The year is fixed by the mention of the recent completion of White's edition of *The Works of William Shakespeare,* of which Vol. I, the last to appear, was advertised as to be published in Boston on Aug. 26, 1865, and was received in New York by the end of the same month (*New-York Daily Tribune,* Aug. 21 and 31, 1865). For the ten days' absence referred to, we know that Emerson was at Amherst by Oct. 17 of this year, that he concluded his lectures there on the 24th, and that he returned to Concord on the 25th (see the letters of Oct. 23 and 25, 1865).

Isaac Reed's *The Dramatic Works of William Shakespeare,* here revealed as the text Emerson had used for forty years, had appeared in a number of forms during the late eighteenth and early nineteenth centuries. It was based upon the text of Samuel Johnson and George Steevens. The copy Emerson used was presumably that

To ———————, WILLIAMSTOWN? MASSACHUSETTS?
NOVEMBER? *c.* 10? 1865

[One of the letters mentioned in the first letter of Nov. 11, 1865, to Ellen Emerson as caused by the Governor's unexpected decision regarding the date of Thanksgiving Day.]

To ———————, WILLIAMSTOWN? MASSACHUSETTS?
NOVEMBER? *c.* 10? 1865

[See the preceding note. Probably there were other letters of the sort written about the same time.]

To ELLEN EMERSON, WILLIAMSTOWN, MASSACHUSETTS,
NOVEMBER 11, 1865 [132]

Williamstown
11 Nov.

Dear Ellen,

Governor Andrew has made carnage among Lyceums by conforming to the President's Thanksgiving [133] Tis well he is no longer a candidate, he would lose all our votes. I have had a batch of letters to write [134] to get out of this snarl, & try to weave a new web. I am comfortably placed here among these healthy friendly students. Here it is the " Literary Societies " that sent for me, & the whole body of the students appear to come, and the President & Professors as well.[135] Presi-

still in his library at the Antiquarian House, Concord. It had apparently belonged to his brother Charles, whose signature it bears, with the date July, 1822, as Mrs. Howard W. Kent informs me.

132. MS owned by RWEMA; ph. in CUL. Facts cited below show that the year was 1865.

133. *Cf.* Nov. 17, 1865.

134. See the letters of Nov.? *c.* 10? 1865.

135. A graphic account is given by Charles J. Woodbury, pp. 3-4. According to Woodbury, Emerson was invited by students and arrived unheralded; but soon the college bulletin boards were overflowing with notices, and while some students ran from house to house to announce his lecture, others rang the college and church bells. That night the meeting-house was filled. Next day Emerson agreed to remain, and the engagement of a day was lengthened to a week. The *Adams News and Transcript*, North Adams, Mass., Nov. 9, 1865, said Emerson was delivering his course on " American Life " at Williamstown, the special subjects being " Social Aims," " Resources," " Table Talk," " Culture," " Success," and " American Character." The MS memorandum book for this year gives the first three lectures named, in the same order, for Nov. 7, 8, and 9, and has " Success " for the 10th, " Culture " for the 13th, and " American Life " for the 14th.

dent Hopkins [136] called on me early, & they are all kindly & open. I have all your three letters gladly, say rather, your letter, your scrap, & your envelopes. The landscape is good for the eyes every hour of the day, with its frosty morning mountains, its noon purple glooms, & serious invitations to the feet. I am to go on Monday to Bryants glen, where they say " he wrote his Thanatopsis when in College." [137] I suppose I shall not reach Concord till Wednesday 6.30 P. M. Well for the History Class [138] — Sorry to lose the boy & his friend.

R. W. Emerson

To ELLEN EMERSON, WILLIAMSTOWN, MASSACHUSETTS,
NOVEMBER 11, 1865 [139]

Williamstown
11 Novr Saturday Night

Dear Ellen,

I cannot reach home until Thursday Evening, 6.30 as I have consented to read one lecture more here, or in the next town of North Adams.[140] Excellent is Lillie's first poetic day,[141] and the promise is more agreeable of an Athenian than of a Syrian child. I took a ride with Professor Bascom [142] this afternoon [143] on a road that climbed a high hill in Vermont, (for we pass out of Mass^{tts} in the second mile) & had Bennington at our feet, the Green Mountains all before us, & chief & grand the Adirondac range in New York bounding our western line. At the roadside lay snow 3 or 4 inches deep. Turning round to come home, Graylock, & his very respectable spurs, Hoosac, & Prospect Mountain,

136. Mark Hopkins, president for many years.

137. According to report, Bryant, in his old age, definitely disposed of this tradition (Parke Godwin, I, 89).

138. Ellen Emerson, Nov. 9, 1865, said she had joined Miss Peabody's history class.

139. MS owned by RWEMA; ph. in CUL. The year is clearly 1865, when Nov. 11 fell on Saturday. *Cf.* the earlier letter of this day.

140. The announcement in the *Adams News and Transcript,* Nov. 16, 1865, that " Ralph Waldo Emerson of New York " would lecture on " Table Talk " in the Baptist Church at North Adams " this Wednesday " was apparently belated; it must have referred to a lecture of Wednesday the 15th, which, according to the MS memorandum book for this year, was a combination of " Social Aims " with part of " Table Talk."

141. Ellen wrote on Nov. 9 that she had introduced Lily to *The Lady of the Lake.* Lily was apparently the young " ward " of Ellen's mentioned in Jan. 18, 1866. I am uncertain whether she was the Lily Keyes of whose help with household duties Ellen wrote in a letter of Apr. 24, 1871, remarking, " What a blessing it is to have daughters! " For Edith Davidson as Ellen's " daughter," see a note on Nov. 25, 1865.

142. John Bascom, professor of rhetoric at Williams College from 1855 to 1874, was later president of the University of Wisconsin.

143. The date given in *Journals,* X, 116–117, seems to be an error.

held the eyes till we lost the high mountain behind the lower by our own descents. R. W. E.

To George Partridge Bradford, Concord, November 17, 1865 [144]

Concord
17 Novr 1865

Dear George,

Thanksgiving falls on the 7 Dec.^{r} [145] and all in this house are relying on your presence on that day. I have just been climbing the Berkshire hills [146] & will talk to you of them as against Lake Superior. And am ever Yours,

R. W. Emerson

George P. Bradford.

To William F. Phillips, Concord, November 19, 1865 [147]

Concord
19 November

Dear Sir,

I waited, on receiving your letter, till a friendly gentleman in Detroit, who kindly undertook to arrange my Western engagements in a practicable series,[148] should solve his problems, & still I have not seen where I could interpose a visit to Cincinnati. But my series ends about the 10th February, and, if you find that the 12th or 13th February is free, & is not too late, I might spend a day in your pleasant city then.[149] If you shall accept one of these days, I will send you in good time a subject or subjects of lectures. If I come, the Association shall pay me one hundred dollars.

Respectfully,
R. W. Emerson

W. F. Phillips, Esq.

144. MS owned by RWEMA; ph. in CUL.

145. The *Boston Daily Advertiser*, Nov. 20, 1865, published Governor John A. Andrew's proclamation designating that day.

146. See the letters of Nov. 11, 1865.

147. MS owned by Haverford College Library; ph. in CUL. Evidence cited below shows that the year was 1865.

148. For George Andrews, of Detroit, see Jan. 25, 1866.

149. The entry of Feb. 14 in the MS memorandum book for 1866 has William F. Phillips at Cincinnati. Just below this address but under the same date, Cincinnati is repeated but canceled and other, but doubtful, engagements substituted; yet the letter of Feb. 16, 1866, shows that Emerson went there after all, though he may not have lectured.

To AARON M. POWELL, CONCORD, NOVEMBER 19, 1865 [150]

Concord

19 Novr 1865

Dear Sir,

I am grateful to you for your friendly proposition though my absence when your letter arrived has made my answer late. I have an objection to reading lectures in Brooklyn as in N. Y. that I am not safe from the reporters who I suppose might more affect a course than a lecture: and, as I shall read many lectures in the West, this winter, they should not be already in their N. Y. Tribunes. Perhaps you know how to prevent this annoyance, or perhaps it does not now survive. Then I have no great confidence in the attempt to collect an audience for me in Brooklyn — where I have never met a large company. Still I can come, if it is desired. For the times I should prefer nearly consecutive lectures say Tuesday. Wed. Thursd. & Friday of one week Monday & Tuesday of the next; or three in each week. I might come, say, 18 or 19 Decr No that would interfere with Christmas — say then 13th, & read three, & three on Monday, T. & W. following. If I come I propose to demand sixty dollars each lecture. If I have not by this time convinced you of the utter impracticability of the plan, I shall hear from you again

With thanks &

friendly regards

R W Emerson

A. M. Powell Esq

To JOHN MURRAY FORBES, CONCORD, NOVEMBER 24, 1865 [151]

Concord

24th Nov. Friday

My dear Mr Forbes,

I fear there is no Sunday in Milton for me just now, nor party of beautiful children, nor sight of you & yours & mine also there. I shall

150. MS owned by Friends Historical Library, Swarthmore College; ph. in CUL. The superscription is to Powell, at Brooklyn. For the lectures which Emerson read in the Brooklyn Fraternity Course a few weeks later, see Dec. 13, 1865. The MS memorandum book for this year duly records Powell's name. *Cf.* also Feb. 17, 1867, to Cary.

151. MS owned by RWEMA; ph. in CUL. The complete date is given in an endorsement which is pretty clearly correct, and Nov. 24 fell on Friday in this year. *Cf.* Nov. 25, 1865.

try to find you at the Saturday Club, but must be at home that night without fail.

> Yours Ever,
> R. W. E.

To James Bradley Thayer, Concord, November 24, 1865 [152]

> Concord
> 24 Nov! 1865

My dear Sir,

We all of us in this house depend on you & Sophy to aid us in obeying the Presidents & the Governor's ordinance for the 7th of December — [153]

> Yours affectionately,
> R. W Emerson

To Edith Emerson Forbes, Boston, November 25, 1865 [154]

> Saturday
> Union Club

Dear Edith, O yes, I should like well to come & see my obstinately disappeared child but there is no Sunday now for me but only letters to write: And Monday is a high duty day with the School Committee,[155] & both of my charges are to be examined and you know your railroad is not conforming to the need of early Concord travellers.

I return you all your thanks for your mother's box.[156] Had it been mine, I should have put the note in it you looked for. Ellen cannot come to you today. She has invited Edith D.[157] to spend Sunday with her. She means I believe to go to the Hasty Pudding theatricals,[158] — on

152. MS owned by Professor James B. Thayer; ph. in CUL.

153. *Cf.* Nov. 17, 1865.

154. MS owned by RWEMA; ph. in CUL. The date " November 1865 " has been supplied, and comparison with a letter of Nov. 24, 1865, shows that the Saturday of the present letter must be Nov. 25. The date is further proved by evidence cited below.

155. For Emerson as a member of the school committee, see Oct. 23, 1865.

156. Edith Emerson Forbes, Milton Hill, Nov. 23, 1865, thanks her father for her birthday present, the beautiful box, which, she learns, he chose, and invites him to come and spend Sunday with her.

157. Mr. W. Cameron Forbes informs me that this was Edith Davidson, who was frequently in the Emerson home. In *Memories of a Hostess*, p. 99, she is given the epithet apparently often applied to her in the family — " Ellen's ' daughter.' " On Jan. 30, 1866, Ellen wrote her father: ". . . I had my daughter Edie come up to spend Sunday with me . . ." *Cf.* also the letter of Feb. 1, 3, and 6, 1867.

158. In her letter of Jan. 25, 26, and 27, 1866, Ellen tells her father of the success of a later " Hasty Pudding Bill."

Tuesday is it? — I shall make myself amends another day, for not obeying you now.

Papa.

To ——————————, CONCORD? DECEMBER 6, 1865

[MS listed and partly quoted in C. F. Libbie & Co., Mar. 3–4, 1915; incloses Emerson's subscription " to your paper for the freedmen's school."]

To Anne Charlotte Lynch Botta, Troy, New York, December 10, 1865 [159]

Troy N. Y.
10 December.

Dear Mrs Botta,

¹Your hospitality has an Arabian Memory to keep its kind purpose through such long time.¹ I dare not promise you the incumbrances of so bad a traveller for the possible length of of my New York visit, but it will give me great pleasure to come & spend a day or two with you, & on my arrival in the city, I will come & make a treaty with you how & when. Here, where I read your note, I cannot answer for my wife who I suppose under no circumstances could obey your invitation, but I shall send it to her at once. She will feel all the kindness of it. or who knows but a papa will put his own construction on it, & tell his daughter Ellen, that she may go to represent her mother! At all events, I trust soon to see you, & confer with you on the facts.

Your affectionate servant,
R. W. Emerson

Mrs Anne C. L. Botta.

To Ellen Emerson, West Troy, New York, December 10, 1865 [160]

W. Troy
Sunday Night
10 Dec

Dear Ellen,

       I enclose Mrs Botta's note for your mother to read. I sup-

159. MS owned by the Henry E. Huntington Library; ph. in CUL. Excerpt I is in *Memoirs of Anne C. L. Botta*, ed. V. Botta, 1894, p. 178. For the year and for plans for the New York visit, *cf.* the letter of the same date to Ellen. Emerson recalls his visit to the Botta home in the letter of Dec. 29 following.

160. MS owned by RWEMA; ph. in CUL. Dec. 10 fell on Sunday in 1865, and

pose she will not wish to accept the invitation, which yet is so persistently kind. I have said in my reply, that I shall send it to her, & added, " who knows but that a papa may ask his daughter Ellen to go & represent her mamma? " [161] And I have told her that I should not dare to bring her so heavy a traveller as myself for more than a day or two, & when I come to N. Y. I will call on her & make a treaty of how & when.[162] So that if you want to go, as you talked last week, you can. Our train on Friday was run into by a freight train that had run away without any guide & came tilting down a steep grade, broke up our engine, & lifted it into the air. Engineer & fireman jumped out & saved their lives. Engineer having a bad fall, but I think not seriously hurt. Not a passenger was hurt. We were delayed 5 or 6 hours. At Rutland [163] Miss Barrett claimed to know all about you & sent you kind remembrances.

Papa.

If a Cooperstown [164] letter says, Come on 13th Dec telegraph to me at Coxsackie. Care N. C. Bedell

Thus,

> To N. C. Bedell, Coxsackie
> Tell Mr Emerson to go to Coxsackie on Wednesday.

But I see that my proposition was inconsiderate, &, if they accept it, I shall have to go down to N. Y. from thence; & you must send or bring shirts & MSS. for me, Namely, " Clubs,"

" Classes of Men "

" Republic "

" Perpetual Forces."

which you must search & find.[165]

---

other evidence, cited below, fixes that date. The MS memorandum book for 1865 gives Dec. 11 to West Troy but offers no clear information as to a lecture.

161. See the letter of this date to Mrs. Botta.

162. The preliminary negotiations with Mrs. Botta after Emerson's arrival in New York are narrated in a letter of Dec. 15, 1865.

163. The MS memorandum book for 1865 records " Social Aims " at Rutland, Dec. 8.

164. Mrs. A. V. Harboth informs me that, according to the *Freeman's Journal* of Nov. 17, 1865, the lyceum committee at Cooperstown, N. Y., hoped to add Emerson's name to their program for the season. But there seems to be no further mention of Emerson during the winter; and presumably he did not go to Cooperstown, which is not listed in the MS memorandum book for this year. Coxsackie (" Resources ") is entered in the book under Dec. 12.

165. Two of these lectures were announced for Brooklyn a little later (see Dec. 13, 1865). In the MS this last clause precedes " Perpetual Forces " on the same line.

To ELLEN EMERSON, CONCORD, DECEMBER 13, 1865 [166]

Concord
Wednesday Night
14 Dec

Dear Ellen,

It is one of the taxes of excellence that it is missed when-ever it is gone, & missed badly: And I am at sea if when I am writing home from my journeys you are not there to do the indispensable. And now I grudge you your beautiful visit, which your mother celebrates. Here am I ready to take you to New York & here is by letter Mrs Botta on tiptoe to receive you, — but it is tomorrow night that I should go, & you have not received my letter,[167] & cannot avail or be availed of in the emergency. My design was to go with you to the Saint Denis Hotel, & take rooms, & thence treat with Madame B. en grand seigneur, en grande demoiselle. And now, if you choose to find me there, by using any good opportunity or coming alone in the day-train (Shore line, say) I shall stay till the 23ᵈ & come home on that day. You might, if you liked, come home the day before, with Charles. I am to read other three evenings, I believe, when the first three are done.[168] I enclose the notes.

Affectionately,
Papa

To EDWIN A. STUDWELL, CONCORD, DECEMBER 14, 1865

[MS listed and partly quoted in American Art Association, Nov. 24–25, 1924. Cf. Dec. 15, 1865, to Ellen Emerson.]

To ANNE CHARLOTTE LYNCH BOTTA, NEW YORK, DECEMBER 15, 1865

[Mentioned in the letter of the same date to Ellen Emerson.]

166. MS owned by RWEMA; ph. in CUL. Comparison with the letters of Dec. 10, 1865, fixes the year. But Wednesday was the 13th, not the 14th, of December that year; and evidence cited below shows pretty conclusively that Emerson went down to New York on the 14th, which must have been the "tomorrow" of the present letter.

167. Of Dec. 10, no doubt. The letter of Dec. 29, 1865, shows that Ellen did not go to New York.

168. *The Evening Post*, New York, Dec. 15, 1865, announced Emerson's lectures in the Brooklyn Fraternity Course: "Social Aims," Dec. 15; "Resources," 16; "Books and Culture," 19. According to a general announcement in *The Brooklyn Daily Eagle*, Dec. 22, 1865, Emerson's second course consisted of "Success," Dec. 20; "Classes of Men," 21; and "Clubs," 22. The MS memorandum book for this year agrees with these accounts of both courses.

To Ellen Emerson, New York, December 15, 1865 [169]

St Denis Hotel
Friday Eve. 15 Dec

Dear Ellen,

I ought to have written you this morn^g that you should have word on Saturday night. But all the short day in this long city was used up in necessary visits, & tonight I was at distant Brooklyn,[170] whence I have just come back, escorted by Haven & Charles. In spite of my written disclaimer,[171] I learned that Mr Studwell was expecting me & on going to 37th St. Mrs Botta was out. " But what is your name, Sir? said the girl at the door. I confessed, & she told me there was a letter for me in the library, & Mrs B had expected me last night and that I was to stay till she returned. I read the note which stated that the only terms offered were " Unconditional surrender " & room for all. I wrote [172] that I wd come & argue the case tomorrow at 12. So, if you like to come by Shore line on Monday, there yet is room. And I suppose you may have this line by Monday morn. I shall probably then be at her house 31 West 37th St.[173] & you can come with your trunk there. Fill this cheque with the amount of Rose's claim & of your journey.

[Concord] Bank

. . . .

Edward or Will Forbes might go with you to the train & bespeak the conductor's care to bring to you the baggage commissioner when you approach N. Y. to whom you can give your check, & take his card & the number of your check. Then you could take a Broadway Omnibus marked *Wall St* or *Wall St Ferry*, I think, which carried me to E. 37th But best to bespeak some Christian gentleman's kindness to agree with a hackman & make a bargain for you. No; Telegraph to Charles on starting let Will Forbes do so, & he or I will await you. Whatever letters for me address to care of Charles Emerson.

169. MS owned by RWEMA; ph. in CUL. The year is obviously 1865, when Dec. 15 fell on Friday. The lower third of the second leaf has been torn away, carrying with it most of the word I have printed conjecturally in square brackets. Presumably the missing fragment contained nothing else but the remainder of Emerson's " cheque."

170. For the Brooklyn lecture of this night, see a note on Dec. 13, 1865.

171. See Dec. 14, 1865, probably the letter meant.

172. Dec. 15, 1865, to Mrs. Botta.

173. *Trow's New York City Directory* for 1865–1866 gives this address as the home of Vincenzo Botta, Mrs. Botta's husband.

To James Bradley Thayer, Concord? December 16, 1865

[Bluebook List.]

To Henry James, Sr., Concord, December 25, 1865 [174]

Concord.
Christmas
Monday

My dear James,

I delight to know you will come hither day after tomorrow & I & we all pray you to bring Mrs James & Alice with you.[175] We will treat them as tenderly as our rude country ways permit; & I assure myself you will give us still better speech & communcation for having them at your side.

With all affectionate regards, ever yours,
R W Emerson

I saw Godwin in N. Y.[176]

To H. F. Tarbox? Concord? December? *c.* 26? 1865

[Tarbox, Batavia, N. Y., Dec. 29, 1865, says the secretary of the lyceum has written Emerson accepting his offer to lecture on Feb. 9. For the lecture at Batavia, see a note on Jan. 25, 1866.]

To Edward Atkinson, Concord, December 27, 1865 [177]

Concord, 27 Dec^r

Dear Mr Atkinson,

When I accepted your kind invitation for this afternoon, it had quite slipped my memory that Mr Henry James was coming this

174. MS owned by Mr. Henry James; ph. in CUL. Christmas fell on Monday in 1865, the year fixed by evidence cited below.

175. James replied, Dec. 26 (endorsed 1865 by Emerson in such a way that the " 5 " might easily be read " 8 ") , that his " wife and wean " could not come but that he himself would come Wednesday afternoon and would be glad to hear of Emerson's New York experiences. For James's Concord lecture of Dec. 27 following, see the letter of that date.

176. Parke Godwin, no doubt. The New York visit is mentioned in earlier letters of this month.

177. MS owned by Mr. Lewis M. Isaacs; ph. in CUL. The year is fixed by the reference to James. The MS records of the Concord Lyceum (owned by the Concord Free Public Library) show that James lectured on Dec. 27, 1865 (*cf.* also the

afternoon at almost the same hour to Concord, to read a lecture here this evening, & to be my guest whilst he is in town. I regret the contretemps, as it will deprive me of the deeply interesting communication you had promised me.

With great regard,
Your obedient servant,
R. W. Emerson —

Edward Atkinson, Esq.

To Anne Charlotte Lynch Botta, Concord, December 29, 1865 [178]

[1]Concord
29 Dec[r] 1865

Dear Mrs Botta,

You were such a good angel to me in New York,[179] that I have wished, every hour since I came home, to say to you that I know well how rare such goodness is, & that I prize it at its height. To be sure, I know little or nothing of New York, but I fancy that few people in it use it so well, have so wise possession of it as yourself. I wish I dared believe that in your miles of palaces were many houses & housekeepers as excellent as I knew at 31 West 37th Street. The house is so apt to spoil the tenant, & Society to brain its votary, that sense & simplicity & good will must not be accepted as things of course, but as most exceptional splendors. And my New Year's wish is, that where I found these they will long long shine for the benefit of all beholders, & to the well-being & better & best being of the luminary: and indeed the chief good is the exercise of our powers & affections.[1]

I found Ellen on my return almost contrite that she had not gone to

letter of Dec. 25, 1865). It is true, however, that James frequently lectured in Concord in December and once — in 1864 — on Dec. 28, so that the ever-present possibility of a slight error in Emerson's date line suggests doubt, perhaps negligible in this case. Edward Atkinson, of Brookline, Mass., a friend of J. M. Forbes, later became known as an industrialist and economist (Harold F. Williamson, *Edward Atkinson*, 1934).

178. MS owned by the Henry E. Huntington Library; ph. in CUL. Excerpt I is in *Memoirs of Anne C. L. Botta*, p. 177. An undated fragment written by Mrs. Botta from New York, now filed with her letter of Dec. 2, 1866, to Emerson, but perhaps written about Jan. 1, 1866, mentions flatteries contained in his letter, alludes to his visit at her home and to his projected visit to the West, and brings best wishes for the new year. It is possible, however, that the fragment was written a year later and refers to a letter of Emerson's which I have not found.

179. *Cf.* earlier letters of this month, where Ellen is also mentioned.

you, not the less when I told her what she had lost, but Ellen carries so much sunshine with her, that I can never pity her. One of these days, perhaps next summer, you will let me show her to you here.

You asked me for the photograph of my head — I enclose that of Rowse's drawing,[180] and another, after nature, far less respectable. Please offer my kind regards to your mother, & to Mrs Robinson & to the young Ida & Alice. I venture to send a bit of bookrack to Ida, & a paper knife to Alice, with my best wishes. My wife desires to be remembered to you with special kindness. Your affectionate servant

Mrs A. C. L. Botta.   R. W Emerson

To Edith Emerson Forbes, Concord? 1865? [181]

Dear Edith

      I confess, on recollection, that I had, whilst in your hands, the strongest wish to obey your invitation when on coming out of the crowd I should con it & find what it accurately was. But the persistent claims of Mrs Dudley to whom a week before I had promised allegiance for that hour and Mr Willsons delaying tenacity to tell me something about coming or not coming to Concord before he goes west & which he did not get told at last for your mother had also an urgent message — all these washed out the details of your plan the rather as I supposed Ellen would guide me in the affair. Now I will come tomorrow & if Ellen permits, for the night

Papa

180. *Cf.* the letters of July 19, 1858, and Jan. 14, 1859.

181. MS owned by RWEMA; ph. in CUL. The year 1865 has been supplied by another hand than Emerson's but is somewhat doubtful. Forceythe Willson had written to Emerson from Cambridge, May 26, 1865, accepting his invitation to Concord on June 6; that letter showed that Willson had not yet seen Emerson. The present letter seems to refer to a conversation with him. According to *Journals*, X, 110–111, Emerson called on Willson on Aug. 23, 1865, and took him to the Athenæum and to the Union Club. But the present letter was presumably written after Edith's marriage, when she had a home to which to invite her father. It is quite possible, I think, that this belongs to a later year. According to *Appletons' Cyclopædia of American Biography*, Willson lived in Cambridge from 1864 to 1866; and we know that Emerson dined with him there on May 31 of the latter year, as Longfellow, who was present, recorded (Samuel Longfellow, *Life*, n. d. [c. 1891], III, 75).

1866

To Frank Preston Stearns, Concord, January 2, *c.* 1866 [1]

Concord
2 January

Dear Frank,

I am sorry to have been so remiss in replying, to your note,
& the more sorry when I found that my tardiness had given your friend
the trouble of a long ride to Concord in vain. It happened, that I had
a rather large correspondence at the moment of the holidays, & was
much in arrears with it. Neither can I now give you any favorable word.
I am, in a few days, to set out on a long journey, & shall not be at home,
or not with any leisure, till near the end of February. So we must adjourn any new promises until I see you again, & learn more exactly from
you the claims & wishes of your society. With thanks for your friendly
proposition, I remain Yours, with all kind regards.

R. W. Emerson

Francis Stearns.

To John Murray Forbes, Concord, January 5, 1866 [2]

Concord —
5 January, 1866.

Dear Mr Forbes,

On Tuesday I saw Mr Hubbard,[3] & told him he should make
out the deed of his woodlot in blank, & that I would fill it, as I might

1. MS owned by Mr. F. R. Fraprie; ph. in CUL. As Stearns, the son of Emerson's
earlier correspondents of that name, was born in 1846, he would hardly have acted
as representative of a "society" earlier than 1860. During the years 1860–1882
Emerson's only long journeys in January and February, such as that here described,
were made in 1865, 1866, and 1867. The last of these dates fits the letter least satis-
factorily. In 1866 Stearns would have been twenty years old. The spelling of "regards" and the punctuation following that word are doubtful.

2. MS owned by RWEMA; ph. in CUL.

3. The letter of July 2, 1852, shows that Emerson had long thought of " Ebba
Hubbard's woods" as a fit country estate for some friend — " the stateliest park in

find another purchaser. I told him I was ready to pay half the price, as we had agreed, on the 1 January; the remainder on 1ˢᵗ February. He asked if I was not willing to fix the 20ᵗʰ January for the payment of the whole sum, instead of dividing it? I told him, I thought that would suit the purchaser just as well. So he is to have his deed ready on that day. As I leave home on the 9ᵗʰ,[4] I think, if you are still disposed to buy the land, you had better let Ellen be your agent on that day. Mr Charles Hubbard will bring the deed to her. The [sq]uare [5] measure of the lot is 15¾ acres and 25 rods; at $30. per acre. I shall be delighted to find you a proprietor in Concord.

Ever yours,
R. W. Emerson

J. M. Forbes, Esq

To THOMAS CARLYLE, CONCORD, JANUARY 7, 1866

[MS owned by RWEMA; printed in *C–E Corr.*, 1883, where two brief passages are omitted — one stating that Elizabeth Hoar likes Jane Carlyle's photograph, the other relating to Edith Emerson Forbes's marriage, Ellen Emerson's housekeeping, and Edward's last year in college.]

To FRANCIS BROWN, CONCORD? JANUARY? *c.* 8? 1866?

[Mentioned in Feb. 1, 1866, to Ellen Emerson. Possibly it was written late in 1865 or after Emerson left Concord for the West.]

To ANSON BURLINGAME, CONCORD, JANUARY 9, 1866 [6]

Concord
9 January, 1866 —

Dear Mr Burlingame,

I send back Mr Wade's Translations,[7] with my thanks. I am sorry I had not time to read it all, for it is interesting from the character of the documents, & for the trust-worthiness of the rendering. But I have been, since at home, unusually crowded with

---

Massachusetts." The woodlot here described, which Emerson duly purchased on behalf of Forbes, is mentioned in later letters (see especially Jan. 26? 1866), and, in spite of different ownership, seems to be the same which Emerson had admired in 1852.

4. *Cf.* the letter of that date.

5. The MS is slightly mutilated.

6. MS owned by the Massachusetts Historical Society; ph. in CUL.

7. Thomas Francis Wade, of H. B. M. legation at Peking, was the translator or editor of several Chinese works.

little affairs, not so much that it was New Year's, as because I leave home today on a journey of five or six weeks.[8] Not the least affliction of this fact is that it deprives me of the power to press a proposition that you half-made, out of the goodness of your heart, that you would come & shine on us at Concord. But your failure to come to our Saturday Club, where many good men assembled to meet you, did not strengthen my faith that you would overcome the snowbanks between Cambridge & Concord. I forgive you, for I know the multitude of public & private claims on you, & the shortness of your time: but I am sorry myself to create a perfect excuse for you. And I seriously regret to lose the private opportunity, possibly open to me, of learning more of the great facts you have now before you.[9] With the trust that your highest hopes may be fulfilled both in public & in private regards, I remain Yours,

R. W. Emerson

Hon. Mr Burlingame.

To Sara Hammond Palfrey, Buffalo? January 10, 1866

[Mentioned in the letter of the same date to Ellen Emerson. Ellen told her father, Jan. 13 and 15, 1866, that he was perhaps fortunate in writing to Miss Palfrey before he had read *Herman*. This work was published at Boston pseudonymously with the date 1866 on the title page. Vol. II is still in Emerson's house, at Concord, and bears his signature.]

To William Frederick Poole, Buffalo? January 10, 1866

[Mentioned in the letter of the same date to Ellen Emerson. Poole was librarian of the Boston Athenæum at this time.]

To Ellen Emerson, Buffalo, January 10, 1866 [10]

Buffalo, 10 Jan — 1866

Dear Ellen,

My tardy train did not arrive in Boston till nearly 2 o'c; &, after checking my baggage, I had only time to pay Jordan & Marsh,[11]

8. See the letters of Jan. 10 ff., 1866.

9. Burlingame, who represented the United States at Peking, was on leave in this country from the spring of 1865 to the fall of 1866 and was full of information about China (Frederick W. Williams, *Anson Burlingame and the First Chinese Mission to Foreign Powers*, 1912, p. 56 *et passim*).

10. MS owned by RWEMA; ph. in CUL. Emerson seems to have stopped in Buffalo — as the last paragraph indicates — mainly to write letters; I find no evidence of a lecture.

11. According to *The Boston Directory* for the year beginning July 1, 1866, Jordan, Marsh & Co. were dealers in dry goods.

but not Rogers.[12] I have just written my note to Miss Palfrey: another to Mr Poole, inclosing my assessment to the Athenæum. Do not forget to tell Uncle William this, for I begged him to send there for a certain book he wished for, & quite forgot the new year, & he may have sent, & been refused.

The moment any letter arrives from Richmond, Indiana, take note of its contents, & not only send the letter to me, but repeat its amount in your own later letters, that I may not fail to know it. If Mr Adams [13] has not carried Mr Burlingame's book to City Exchange, let him take it at once. I send tonight, to Boston, the note that should have gone inside.[14]

I shall write a note to Mr Norton [15] & send it by mail, & Edward must put into a clean envelope of some kind the printed sheets of "Character," which you will find, in a yellow envelope, in the *third drawer.*

I stop here today to write letters, & do things which cannot so well be done at Erie,[16] & am serene because I am within 3 or 4 hours of it. I have not yet had time to write to Edith, but shall.[17] Edward told me that he has your Chaucer. Whisk is getting absolved. Leave Rogers [18] alone till I send you his due.

R. W. Emerson

To WILLIAM F. PHILLIPS? BUFFALO? JANUARY? *c.* 10? 1866?

[One of the letters — there must have been others than that of Nov. 19, 1865 — included in Emerson's " much correspondence " about a lecture at Cincinnati (see Jan. 20, 1866) .]

To SAMUEL? GRAY? WARD, LA PORTE? INDIANA? JANUARY 14? 1866

[Mentioned in Jan. 14, 1866.]

12. For Rogers, see Jan. *c.* 16? 1866.
13. Probably Augustus Adams, of the Concord express.
14. The letter of Jan. 9, 1866. Ellen Emerson wrote from Concord, Jan. 13 and 15 following, that Burlingame's book had been sent.
15. I have no further evidence of such a note.
16. See Jan. 14, 1866.
17. Probably the promised letter was written, but I have not found it.
18. *Cf.* Jan. *c.* 16? 1866.

To Ellen Emerson, La Porte, Indiana, January 14, 1866 [19]

Laporte, Ind. 14 Jan
at house of Mr Charles Paine

Dear Ellen,

   I enclose a letter for Mr Ward, in which you must enclose Miss Waterman's [20] letter, & Charles Emerson's card, both of which you will find, either in my upper, or third drawer, — perhaps one in one, one in the other. I am sorry they go so late, but this is my best penitence. I have had good days at Erie [21] & at Oberlin [22] & yesterday on the road fell in with Mr Paine (son of Mrs Hemenway's [23] friend, & Chief Engineer on this Mich. Southern road,) who has kindly brought me to his house, as I am to speak in this town tomorrow night.[24] On Tuesday, I shall be, I trust, for a few hours in Chicago, & can send you thence a business letter.[25]

To ———— Rogers, Chicago? January c. 16? 1866

[Mentioned in Jan. 18, 1866; cf. also Jan. 25 following. Place and day are wholly conjectural. The letter of Jan. 14, 1866, shows Emerson intended to be in Chicago on the 16th.]

19. MS owned by RWEMA; ph. in CUL. The MS memorandum book of 1866 has for Jan. 14: " At house of Charles Paine." Other evidence, cited below, confirms the year.

20. Cf. Oct. 26, 1859.

21. The *Erie Daily Dispatch*, Jan. 11, 1866, announced that Emerson would lecture before the Y. M. C. A. that evening on " Resources " or " Table Talk." Comment in the same paper for the following day did not disclose the subject.

22. Emerson's reading of " Social Manners " (*i.e.*, " Social Aims ") on Jan. 12 was recorded in *The Lorain County News*, Oberlin, O., Jan. 10 and 17, 1866. The local critic was disturbed by unorthodox views — " Mr. Emerson has little sympathy, we suppose, with the faith that is dearest to us of Oberlin. . . . A man of wondrous mind, of most lovable nature, his philosophy fails beside the faith of thousands of illiterate believing souls."

23. Cf. July 19, 1863.

24. The *La Porte Herald* of Jan. 20, 1866, told of the reading of " Social Aims in America " before the La Porte Reading Room and Library Association on the 15th. The estimate of the lecturer as no orator yet a graceful and fluent talker and of the lecture as one of the most valuable of the course was by this time almost the conventional one.

25. The remainder of the half sheet is blank and there is no signature. It seems doubtful whether the promised letter was written from Chicago. Cf. Jan. 18, 1866, for evidence that Wiley attended to sending the money.

To Ellen Emerson, Princeton, Illinois, January 18, 1866 [26]

Princeton, Ill.

18 Jan. 1866

Dear Ellen

Find on my calendar of the Social Circle, (which I believe hangs on the study wall, & certainly there was a duplicate in the Journal (of daily payments & Receipts)) what day is marked for Cyrus Warren. I have changed days with Mr Warren, I believe; though I have a little doubt whether it was not Cyrus Stow. So you must give me his date too. They were both at the meeting at which it was arranged.

There should be no Lockport on the list. It was once there, & afterwards should have been erased. Was it not Laporte? where I was on Monday last, & found your letter.

Good that your young ward [27] has higher minstrelsies in her than even her poets, & can be so magnanimous, — in small frame large heart enclosed: — I have written to Mr Rogers.[28] Yesterday I suppose Mr Wiley [29] forwarded a draft for $200., minus commissions, to you. & in a few days I shall send more. Chandler is to be paid, & Kennard as fast as we can by instalments of $100. at a time. And on 11 Feb. Mr Cheney 350. I shall probably send directly to him.[30]

To Ellen Emerson, Davenport, Iowa, January 20, 1866 [31]

Davenport Iowa

Burtis House

Jan. 20, 1866.

Dear Ellen, I enclose a draft to your order for two hundred & twenty dollars. In this bitter cold town & day I have a warm fire in a comfort-

26. MS owned by RWEMA; ph. in CUL. *The Bureau County Patriot,* Princeton, Ill., Jan. 16, 1866, announced that Emerson would lecture before the Young Men's Association on the following day.

27. Apparently the " Lillie " of the second letter of Nov. 11, 1865.

28. Jan. *c.* 16? 1866.

29. Wiley, of Chicago, was Emerson's correspondent.

30. But Emerson sent to his daughter instead (see Feb. 5? 1866) . There is no signature here, and it is possible, since the half sheet is nearly full, that a part of the letter is lost.

31. MS owned by RWEMA; ph. in CUL. The MS memorandum book for 1866 gives Jan. 19 to Davenport, and the added note " Remitted to the Lyceum " seems to indicate that Emerson returned his fee or agreed to ask none. For his schedule of lectures in Iowa at this time, see Hubert H. Hoeltje's account in *The Iowa Journal of*

able hotel. It seems I shall not go to Cincinnati which is a disappointment after much correspondence.[32] I have not time to add the messages
that I have meant to write. I have not heard from you since Laporte.[33]

Affectionately,

R. W. Emerson

Ellen T Emerson

To Ellen Emerson, Freeport, Illinois, January 25, 1866 [34]

Freeport 25 Jan.ʸ

Dear Ellen,

Your carrier pigeons fly well, & I have had great content
from them at Aurora,[35] Lyons, Dewitt,[36] & today here: [37] Good news too,
all of it substantially, & worth the bringing, and you are an excellent
sustaining & consoling girl. And you judged well that Edith's letter —
all otto of roses — would be a fabulous luxury in an Illinois tavern.
Hold her & Will to the February visit, by all means. With some unavoidable discomforts; like sitting up the whole of night before last in a
railroad station, waiting for the train, — I have had good fortune for
the most part. & met many good people. On the way from Toledo,[38] I
was introduced to Mr Phillips, President of the Michigan Southern
R. R.,[39] who told me, that his first acquaintance with me was when he
had wheeled a barrel of flour to my house from the store of Charles B.
Davis, whose apprentice he was (& next after Phoenix Derby.) [40] He
chiefly remembered the weight of the barrel. Here are three fine days in
succession, and the landscape of this young country needs the best sunshine in winter to make it passable. The institution of these Lyceums is

---

History and Politics, XXV, 241–246 (Apr., 1927). Besides Davenport, there were
Lyons, Dewitt, and Dubuque within a few days.

32. See Nov. 19, 1865, to Phillips, Jan.? *c.* 10? 1866? and Feb. 16, 1866.

33. *Cf.* Jan. 14, 1866.

34. MS owned by RWEMA; ph. in CUL. The year is fixed by evidence cited below.

35. According to the MS memorandum book for this year, " Social Aims " was
to be read at Aurora, Ill., on Jan. 16.

36. For Lyons, Dewitt, and other Iowa towns, see a note on Jan. 20, 1866.

37. The *Freeport Weekly Journal*, Freeport, Ill., Jan. 24, 1866, announced that
Emerson would appear before the Young Men's Lecture Association on the following day.

38. But there seems to have been no lecture at Toledo till later (see Feb. 5? 1866).

39. E. B. Phillips was listed as president in the *Annual Report of the Mich.
Southern & Northern Indiana Railroad Company*, 1866.

40. George Horatio Derby, the humorist, had come to Concord after his school
days at Dedham, Mass.

a stroke of heroism in each town, — desperate if it snows or blows on the appointed evening. Here is America in the making, America in the raw, but it does n't want much to go to lecture, & tis pity to drive it. Yet I saw last night at Dubuque one of the goodliest audiences in a most agreeable hall. In the next town all may be doleful. Everywhere the young committees are most friendly people.

I did not leave you names of correspondents, since of many towns I do not know them — their communication was with George Andrews of Detroit.[41] It is sufficent address anywhere to write, *Care of Young Men's Lecture Committee.* As at present informed, the only safe address, after I leave Batavia,[42] is Indianapolis,[43] as my engagement is not fixed at Harrisburg [44] yet. Tell mamma that I daily prize her works, if I do not use them all. I will write to Abraham Jackson that he shall draw & send you the Mad River & Erie dividend, on 1 February, which should be $60. minus the tax; & Mr Barrett will probably pay you $30., on the 15th Feb.y I hope also that A. Jackson will pay you some Plymouth rents. So you can probably afford your mother $10. for her New Years gift to Frank B.[45] Mr Rogers' 40. is not paid. The tinman I paid 13. & a fraction. I hope you found Tom W.'s [46] blank sealed & stamped letter (I think a 3 cent stamp) in my upper drawer.

My journey thus far has been prosperous in weather & & perfect timekeeping, though I arrive an hour or two before night, at towns with which I have never corresponded, & the whole agreement made months ago between Mr Andrews of Detroit & them. This C. B. & Q. road, on which I have been riding for two or three days, & in which I hold 15 shares, is an excellent one, & praises its managers Mr J. M. F.[47] & the rest. Yesterday, John H. Bryant, a brother of W. C. B. spent an hour

41. *Cf.* Nov. 19, 1865, to Phillips.

42. The *Spirit of the Times,* Batavia, N. Y., Feb. 3, 1866, announced Emerson for Feb. 9.

43. "Social Aims in America" was announced by the Young Men's Mercantile Library Association for Feb. 13 (*The Indianapolis Daily Journal,* Feb. 13, 1866).

44. Harrisburg, Pa., appeared in the MS memorandum book for 1866 under Feb. 15 but was canceled. There seems to be no notice in the Harrisburg papers.

45. Brown, Lidian Emerson's nephew. The "transition state about Christmas" in New England which Longfellow noted in his diary for 1856 (Samuel Longfellow, *Life,* n. d. [c. 1891], II, 324) was not yet ended. New Year's Day still kept the honors at Concord.

46. Tom Ward's, no doubt. It is not clear whether the reference is to a letter from Emerson to young Ward.

47. For J. M. Forbes's part in the making of the C. B. & Q., see Henry Greenleaf Pearson, *An American Railroad Builder,* 1911.

with me, to my great pleasure. He " *squatted* " here 33 or 34 years ago.[48]
is a farmer & a poet, & a better politician than the " Evening Post," of
which he seriously complains. I do not probably arrive at Concord till
the 20 Feb.[y]

R. W. Emerson

To MARY R. WHITTLESEY, FREEPORT? ILLINOIS? JANUARY? *c.* 25? 1866?

[Mary R. Whittlesey, Cleveland, Feb. 3, 1866, tells of the great pleasure she
had felt for three or four days after receiving a letter from Emerson and alludes
to a possible visit from him. The place and date of his letter are conjectural.]

To ELLEN EMERSON, JANESVILLE? WISCONSIN? JANUARY 26? 1866 [49]

Sorry for Edward's ears,[50] glad to believe him at home. I forgot to tell
you that he told me he has your Chaucer.[51] I may send you a business
letter tomorrow, if I find Janesville [52] favorable. After Mr Hubbard
found his plan, I trust all the rest went right. I informed Mr Heywood
that the deed was to run " *to R W E. trustee,*" & Mr F. (who is not
named to any party,) [53] will no doubt have remembered the day (20
Jan.) of payment. You have rec.ᵈ before now two drafts from Chicago [54]
& Rock Island.[55] I must write to Uncle William [56] to thank him for his

48. Parke Godwin gives the date as 1831 (I, 280).

49. MS owned by RWEMA; ph. in CUL. Evidence cited below fixes the year and
shows that the conjectural day is approximately correct.

50. Ellen Emerson had written, Jan. 13 and 15, 1866, that Edward's ears had been
frozen.

51. But this information had been given in the letter of Jan. 10, 1866, to Ellen.

52. The MS memorandum book for 1866 gives Jan. 26 to Janesville, Wis. (" Social
Aims "). Perhaps Emerson could not have sent a draft till the following day, the
" tomorrow " of this letter. Whether he wrote on Jan. 27 I do not know.

53. *Cf.* the letters of Jan. 5 and Feb. 1, 1866, to Ellen Emerson. The deed
from Charles A. Hubbard, of Concord, executor of the will of Cyrus Hubbard, to
" Ralph W. Emerson, Trustee " was signed on Jan. 24, 1866, and recorded on
Feb. 17 following (now in the Registry of Deeds, Middlesex County). It describes a
tract of somewhat more than fifteen acres near Walden Pond. This tract I suppose
to be the same described as " Ebby Hubbard's oaks and pines," which Thoreau
liked to study from Brister's Hill (*The Writings*, IX, 218), but I am not certain.

54. *Cf.* Jan. 14, 1866; the draft from Chicago was probably that sent by Wiley.

55. This indicates, but does not prove, that Emerson himself wrote from Rock
Island. *The Evening Argus*, Jan. 18, 1866, announced " Social Aims in America " for
that evening. The same paper for the 19th praised, though it did not name the lecture.
Emerson must, however, have had some difficulty in capturing his audience unless
the reporter exaggerated the " painful sensation produced by the slamming of doors;
the tramp of heavy feet on the stairs and aisles; the rattling of stoves, and the
thunder produced by the driving of teams on the noisy planks under the hall."

56. Letter of Feb. 1, 1866, to William Emerson.

love & care in writing. My days are very short with continual packing & riding.

R. W. Emerson

To Alfred? T. Goodman, Delavan, Wisconsin, January 28, 1866

[MS listed in American Art Association, May 7–8, 1925, where the place is not given; and in George D. Smith, n. d., where the place is given and the year but no other date. I am uncertain whether this is the same as the letter of Jan. 28, 1866, listed, without the name of either the writer or the place, in Anderson Auction Co., Feb. 1–3, 1905, and there described as relating to a series of lectures in Western cities. The MS memorandum book for 1866 shows that Emerson was scheduled to lecture at Delavan, Wis., on Jan. 27 and gives Goodman — the initials seem to be " E T " but are probably meant for " A. T." — in the canceled entry of Feb. 15 for Harrisburg. Presumably, then, the " letters to Harrisburg & other towns eastward " mentioned in Feb. 1, 1866, to Ellen include this one. They may also include some of which I have no record. For Harrisburg, *cf.* also Jan. 25 preceding. For Goodman and his initials, see Mar. 1 following. Though the first two catalogues cited above have " W. T.," I conjecture that the " W." is an error for " A." The only Goodman in *The Harrisburg City Directory* for 1867–1868 is Alfred T., a reporter.]

To William Emerson, Battle Creek, Michigan, February 1, 1866 [57]

Battle Creek, Mich.
1 February

Dear William,

    Thanks for your letter, & the almost incredible kindness of transcribing Lecky's pages.[58] It ought to be very good to deserve that compliment at your hands. Of course, I was glad to read it, & a page of good sense on pure literature is thrice welcome in these prairies. Lecky is judicious & right, but by no means a finished writer, — wanting compression, — that I wonder a little at the sudden fame of the book. Ellen keeps me advised of news from your house as from ours, & makes my distance less. The newsboy in the trains & the bookshop in the towns have kept me in heart, & the fine weather has made my jour-

57. MS owned by HCL; ph. in CUL. The MS memorandum book for 1866 shows that " Table Talk " was scheduled for Battle Creek, Jan. 31.

58. William Emerson, Concord, Jan. 16, 1866 (MS owned by Dr. Haven Emerson), told of reading the first volume of William E. H. Lecky's *History of the Rise and Influence of the Spirit of Rationalism in Europe* and inclosed a transcript of a passage beginning, in the New York edition of 1866, on p. 111 of Vol. I.

ney more pleasant than heretofore. In every one of these expanding towns is a knot of loving New Englanders who cherish the Lyceum out of love to the Charles & the Merrimac & the Connecticut rivers. I see the first settlers in many of them, who came here 27 or 30 or 33 years ago, and their performance is wonderful, & with an open horizon all around. And yet Landor is right for scholars, — " Who would live in a new country, who can live in an old one? " [59] In all this swarming country, I have hardly seen anybody I ever saw before, but they treat me very kindly, and they are as anxious for the success of radical politics as the Concord people.

I hope all things, health especially, go well under your roof. I never remembered to give John Clahan any instruction about having your 8 cords (was it?) of wood ready at a certain day. But if you give him your wishes on the matter, he will convey them to John Craig, who is the woodcutter.

With love to Susan, Your affectionate
Waldo E

To Ellen Emerson, Jackson, Michigan, February 1, 1866 [60]

1 February
Jackson, Mich

Dear Ellen

You are the best of daughters for minding so well my affairs, & writing such & so many good letters, though they end sometimes so tantalizingly with " But there is no " —. I have no right to complain of any short-comings at least till I answer them. You forgot to insert Mrs Drury's letter, which I am impatient to read. I read with joy that Tom Ward is so near. I have your story of Birdy Cheney's release,[61] &

59. Perhaps an inaccurate quotation from the bellicose *Letter from W. S. Landor to R. W. Emerson.* Landor there agrees with Alfieri (as cited in *English Traits*) that Italy and England are the only countries worth living in (quoted in *Literary Anecdotes of the Nineteenth Century*, ed. Nicoll and Wise, New York, 1896, II, 210). It is hardly probable that Emerson here recalled a passage from conversation which he had not recorded in the *Journals* or in *English Traits*.

60. MS owned by RWEMA; ph. in CUL. The year is obviously 1866. Miss Ruth Foster informs me that Emerson's reading of " Resources " before the Young Men's Association on Feb. 1 is reported in the *Jackson Daily Citizen* of Feb. 3, 1866. The reporter thought the lecture unsuitable for a miscellaneous audience.

61. The *Boston Daily Advertiser*, Jan. 23, 1866, recorded the death of Elizabeth C. Wheeler, daughter of John M. Cheney, in Concord, Jan. 20. Ellen Emerson had written this news in her letter of Jan. 22, where Mrs. Wheeler is called " Birdy."

the second chronicle of Ediths Milton days, as well as your notes of the wedding party at your Aunt's in Boston. My programme for my journey is a little broken up by the derangement of the Cincinnati visit [62] & I have a new letter from thence proposing it anew & if I could recall my letters [63] to Harrisburg & other towns eastward, I should like to go to St Louis according to Mr Harris's proposal.[64] Possibly I may. I have quite forgotten the dates of Edwards vacation, & am glad to learn it had not begun, so I shall see the boy the more.

As soon as Mr Hubbard brings you the deed of the wood lot,[65] carry it to Mr George Heywood, & ask him to please to have it recorded at the Registrar's Office.

I shall not send you any more money immediately, as I must begin to pay my debt at the Concord Bank which now falls due. I sent you $300. by Mr Wiley on the 30th and you must husband that. Glad that Mamma went to the Boston party. Tell her that the West is of her politics, or my West is. You have told me nothing of Mrs Brown's affairs. I had written Frank [66] about her cheque from A. Jackson, &, after I had written, came to me Mrs Bigelows & Mrs Hastings bills These must be considered. R W Emerson

To William Torrey Harris, Ann Arbor, Michigan, February 2, 1866

[MS listed in C. F. Libbie & Co., Dec. 4 and 5, 1902; gives prices and dates for lectures Emerson could read in St. Louis. *Cf.* Feb. 1, 1866, to Ellen Emerson, and the letters of Feb. 20 and 23 following.]

62. *Cf.* Jan. 20, 1866.
63. *Cf.* Jan. 28, 1866.
64. *Cf.* Feb. 2, 1866. The *Tri-weekly Missouri Democrat*, Feb. 16, 1866, told of Alcott's presence in St. Louis " at the instance of a philosophical society recently formally organized here " and as the guest of William T. Harris. " It is not improbable," said the writer, " that Mr. Emerson may also be induced to come to St. Louis in the course of the winter." I have found no definite proof, but it seems likely that Emerson did not visit the famous Philosophical Society till the following year (*cf.* letters of Feb. 13, Apr. 4, and Dec. 17, 1867), though he had met Harris, presumably for the first time, in 1865 (see the letters of July 18, 1865). Alcott had, it seems, visited St. Louis, at Harris's suggestion, as early as the winter of 1858–1859, before the Society had come into being (Sanborn and Harris, II, 552–553).
65. See Jan. 26? 1866.
66. Letter of Jan.? *c.* 8? 1866?

To ELLEN EMERSON, TOLEDO, OHIO, FEBRUARY 5? 1866 [67]

Toledo

Dear Ellen,

I sent you this morning by the hands of Edward Boltwood [68] of Detroit a draft for $300. I should have sent it directly to Mr Cheney as it is to pay what it can on my note to the Bank. But I forgot this at the moment & begged him to address it to you. I shall soon send $50. which will pay the whole note.[69] I found Edward B & his his young wife boarding at the Russell House, where the Prince of Wales & I always stop.[70] Here too was young Concord [71] in the shape of Mr Rice, John Hosmer, James Bartlett & Ripley B. Mr Hurd & others. Mr & (Mrs Armitage) Mrs Lambards daughter) live here, but it was Sunday & I saw them not: but the Concord men I saw, & James B & his wife came to my hotel and I read them the story of the fox hunt. I sat too by General Casey & wife at dinner & talked with him as a venerable soldier. Afterwards I learned that he was younger than I.[72] But Mr George Andrews's [73] representative enriched me with five letters, — from others as well as your own. I am yet to hear from certain correspondents either here or at Cleveland, & shall then decide on the remainder of my journey. I hope not to lose all Edwards vacation, but it will be short for me. I think you must go to Mr Stow & ask him if it is not he who is to exchange Social Circle with me.[74] I hope it is for I have promised Mr

67. MS owned by RWEMA; ph. in CUL. The year is fixed by evidence cited below. The MS memorandum book for 1866 shows that " Social Aims " was scheduled for Detroit, Feb. 3, and for Toledo, Feb. 5; but the *Toledo Daily Blade* of the 5th announced " Table Talk " for that evening. Emerson seems to have spent Sunday, the 4th, in Detroit and to have remained there until the morning of the 5th.

68. *Cf.* the note on June 4, 1855.

69. *Cf.* Jan. 18, 1866.

70. *Cf.* the letters of Jan. 29, Feb. 18, and Feb. 19, 1860. The Prince of Wales, later Edward VII, was at the Russell House in Detroit Sept. 20–21, 1860 (Kinahan Cornwallis, *Royalty in the New World*, 1860, pp. v and 161–162) .

71. *Charles F. Clark's Annual City Directory . . . of the City of Detroit*, 1866, has Reuben N. Rice, general superintendent of the Michigan Central Rail Road; James W. Bartlett, mechanical superintendent of locomotive works; S. Ripley Bartlett, draughtsman, locomotive works; John Hurd, clerk in the Michigan Central Rail Road depot; and William E. Armitage, rector of St. John's Episcopal Church — all of whom were perhaps among the persons Emerson mentioned. For Hosmer, *cf.* Feb. 19, 1860. I am uncertain whether Mrs. Lambard was the Sibyl Farnham Lambard of other letters.

72. Silas Casey, Sr., was born in 1807.

73. *Cf.* Jan. 25, 1866.

74. *Cf.* Jan. 18, 1866.

Warren's night 27 Feb at Hudson N. Y. meaning to make that journey from Rome.[75] But pen & ink refuse to go farther. Affectionately,

R. W. E.

To Edward Waldo Emerson, Columbus, Ohio, February 11, 1866

[MS owned by Mr. Raymond Emerson.]

To Anne Charlotte Lynch Botta, Cincinnati, February 16, 1866

[MS listed and partly quoted in Anderson Galleries, Mar. 29–31, 1916, where the year is not given. Emerson explains that he cannot go home by way of New York, as he had hoped to do, and so must give up his dream of making Mrs. Botta acquainted with Ellen and Edward that month. For a projected lecture at Cincinnati, cf. Nov. 19, 1865, to Phillips, and Jan. 20, 1866. I have found no proof that this lecture was actually given. For Mrs. Botta and her proffered hospitality, see letters of Dec. 10 and later, 1865, and May 28, 1866.]

To William Torrey Harris, Concord, February 20, 1866

[MS listed in C. F. Libbie & Co., Dec. 4 and 5, 1902; described as " concerning a series of lectures in St. Louis."]

To William Torrey Harris, Concord, February 23, 1866

[MS listed in C. F. Libbie & Co., Dec. 4 and 5, 1902; " in regard to a misunderstanding as to lectures in St. Louis," says the catalogue. Cf. Feb. 2, 1866.]

To Alfred? T. Goodman, Concord, March 1, 1866

[MS listed in American Art Association Anderson Galleries, Nov. 17 and 18, 1936, where the correspondent is given as A. T. Goodman and the letter is described as " regarding the forwarding of some mail." It is perhaps the same MS listed in John Heise Autographs, catalogue 2454, where it is described as about letters to Emerson that have been misdirected, and in Stan. V. Henkels, Apr. 26, 1921. Neither Heise nor Henkels names the person addressed. Cf. Jan. 28, 1866.]

To William Hathaway Forbes and Edith Emerson Forbes, Concord, March 9, 1866 [76]

Concord
9 March 1866

Dear Will & Edith,

I am delighted with your letters, proud of you both, & never do

75. Rome is not listed in the MS memorandum book for this year, and I find nothing in the local papers, but Hudson is given for Feb. 27, with " Social Aims " as the subject.

76. MS owned by Mr. William H. Forbes; ph. in CUL.

not think of your happy home. But I am the most unskilful of all visiters, mainly because I am always haunted by a dream of what might be done perhaps this very day on some one of twenty unfinished tasks — &, though the power has not come in twenty days or weeks, I hesitate to budge, lest it should call in the moment I have stepped out. Do not ask me — I shall surely come — not next Sunday, but many a good time thereafter, the day of your " opera " included, & others of quieter joy. It was good what you Edith wrote Ellen, that you " were consoled by her having been in the house, though you did not see her ": so am I by the thought of the peace & honor & hope your house, which I can almost *see*, — contains. And so, with all benedictions on you both, affectionately, Papa.

Little people cannot help remembering the answer which the priest at Delphi made for the great Apollo, when asked if he would assist at Salamis, —

Deus et vocatus et non vocatus aderit.[77]

To Charles Eliot Norton, Concord, March 17, 1866?[78]

Concord, 17 March

My dear Norton,

I sent back yesterday morning to the Printers my corrected revises. At the bottom of the last page, they had written a *caret* for the author's name, and I wrote it. If it is optional to write it or not, I should not. But if you mean considerately to establish a new usage, I shall not resist it.

Ever yours,

R. W. E.

Let me use the opportunity to give you the formal notice that Professor Gurney is to be nominated at the Saturday Club on the 25th April.

77. The incident Emerson had in mind was doubtless that recorded by Thucydides at the end of Book I, chapter cxviii, of his history of the Peloponnesian War and had no connection with the victory of Salamis. I have not found the source of the Latin version apparently quoted. Horace's somewhat similar " Vocatus atque non vocatus audit," in the eighteenth ode of his second book, relates to a very different god.

78. MS owned by Messrs. Colbeck Radford & Co.; ph. in CUL. The question of date is a difficult one. Norton became a member of the Saturday Club in 1860, and Gurney, in 1867. During the period thus limited, Apr. 25 fell on Saturday only in 1863. But presumably the revises here mentioned were of an article for *The North American Review;* and Norton apparently was not connected with that journal till the fall of 1863, and Emerson contributed to it, during 1863–1867, only one article — " Character," printed anonymously in the number for Apr., 1866.

To Edward Waldo Emerson, Concord, March 23, 1866

[MS owned by Mr. Raymond Emerson.]

To Brantz Mayer, Concord, March 25, 1866

[MS listed and partly quoted in C. F. Libbie & Co., Nov. 15–16, 1889; refers to Emerson's Italian visit of 1833, during which he met Mayer.]

To Blanche Smith Clough, Concord, March 30, 1866

[MS owned by Mr. Arthur Clough; ph. in CUL. Printed in *Emerson-Clough Letters.*]

To Annie Adams Fields, Concord, April 10, 1866? [79]

Concord —
Tuesday, 10 April.

Dear Mrs Fields,

I fear it is becoming a fixed idea in the minds of you & your husband to do good to me & mine.[80] My wife does not seem to fear being spoiled, delights in your good offices as you do, &, at this particular moment, answers you, that she will come with the greatest pleasure; — though she has been mostly in her chamber for I know not how many weeks. If she will go, I certainly shall. Ellen must stay at home, as she has invited guests, & Edward, who is at Cambridge, will probably find it necessary to be at Concord on that day.

And so we are heartily your bondsmen & women.

R. W. Emerson

Mrs Annie Fields.

To James Thomas Fields, Concord, April 17, 1866 [81]

Concord
17 April 1866

My dear Sir,

I received last night your note & the surprising six hundred

79. MS owned by the Henry E. Huntington Library; ph. in CUL. During Edward Waldo Emerson's college course, Apr. 10 fell on Tuesday only in 1866, the year of his graduation. The fact that Edith is not mentioned seems to indicate a year later than 1865, when she was married. If 1866 is correct, the party turned out to be larger than Emerson expected, for Annie Fields wrote (MS diaries, on deposit, Massachusetts Historical Society) that after the lecture on Apr. 14 " Mr E. Ellen, Edith & her husband Edward & Mr Longfellow all joined us at dinner."

80. *Cf.* Apr. 17, 1866.

81. MS owned by the Henry E. Huntington Library; ph. in CUL.

dollars it contained. I entreat you to present my first thanks to the Foundress of the Lectureship,[82] for her good suggestion, which you have so ably put into effect. Certainly I never encountered the like task under circumstances half so agreeable.

With all kind regards

R. W. Emerson

James T. Fields, Esq

To Sarah Swain Forbes, Concord, April 22, 1866? [83]

Concord

Sunday Eve, 22 Apr.

My dear Mrs Forbes,

Thanks for your Euphorbia in this its second life. I am often struck with the advantage to mortals of the reflection over the direct ray. Things that have no beauty in themselves acquire it when reflected in the river. This flower, to be sure, in nature is a little burst of glory, yet I have seen it many times and always as a new object, & have to ask its name. But with this bright & faithful portrait, I make a personal & lasting acquaintance with it & shall have a fixed point whereon to hang any related facts I may meet with. I don't wonder at your making it a study, I wonder at your success; & am very well pleased to call the picture mine.

Yours faithfully,

R. W Emerson

Mrs Sarah S. Forbes.

---

82. Emerson's course of six lectures on " Philosophy for the People " was delivered at Chickering's Rooms at noon Saturdays; tickets, at $3, were sold at the bookstore of Ticknor & Fields. These lectures, as announced and reported in the *Boston Evening Transcript,* Apr. 14–May 21, 1866, were as follows: " Seven Meters in Intellect," Apr. 14; " Instinct, Perception and Memory," 21; " Genius, Imagination and Taste," 28; " Common Sense," May 5; fifth lecture (no title given) , 12; sixth lecture (on immortality, but reported without exact title) , 19. The first of the series attracted, said the *Transcript,* one of the most brilliant audiences ever gathered in Boston. Further evidence of the financial success of the course is to be found in May 21, 1866.

83. MS owned by RWEMA; ph. in CUL. Of the years in which Apr. 22 fell on Sunday, only 1866 and 1877 are later than the date of Edith Emerson's marriage. But the year 1860, long before Edith's marriage, is perhaps a possibility. Two notations on the MS record attempts to complete Emerson's date line: " probably about 1870 " and " ?1866 or 1877."

To Oliver Wendell Holmes, Concord, May 7, 1866

[MS listed and partly quoted in John Heise Autographs, catalogue 2464, and, with incomplete date, in Goodspeed's Book Shop, June, 1931. Emerson says the attractive feature of Pennell's plan is its suggestion of a literary fellowship of three countries. Pennell, he thinks, has made a good beginning in America by his desire to engage Holmes and Lowell. Emerson, though he counts himself a poor hand at a magazine, is content to join them if they decide to enter the scheme, and his fancy is piqued by the thought of writing in the same journal with Sainte-Beuve.]

To ————————, Concord, May 8, 1866

[In the other letter of this date, Emerson said he had learned that morning that Stirling was a candidate for a chair in Glasgow University and wished a testimonial. The inclosed note, he said, was to be properly addressed by Stirling if the latter chose to send it. Presumably Stirling supplied the name of some official of the University. Stirling, Edinburgh, May 24, 1866, acknowledged both Emerson's letter to him and the testimonial.]

To James Hutchison Stirling, Concord, May 8, 1866

[Printed in Amelia H. Stirling, p. 176.]

To Abel Adams, Boston, May 9, 1866? [84]

Boston 9 May

My dear friend,

     I saw Mr Hosmer this morning & told him you were still looking for your cow.[85] He said he had not yet found any which he liked to bring you. but, if he does not find one soon, he means to sell you his own cow, which he values much, yet which he could not sell to any person who sells milk. But you must wait for her, as it will be a fortnight before she calves. I encouraged him to persist in his good intention, & told him I should write to you today. I hope we shall have more rain from this South wind, for all our country ponds are low.

     I send salutations to all your household

Affectionately,

R. W. Emerson

Mr Abel Adams.

84. MS owned by RWEMA; ph. in CUL. The full date is given, without question, in an annotation, apparently in Adams's own hand.

85. Edmund Hosmer appears much earlier as an adviser on the same subject (see several letters of Apr., 1853).

To Harrison Gray Otis Blake, Concord, May 14, 1866 [86]

Concord
14 May, 1866 —

My dear Blake,

I have been so preoccupied lately that my correspondence is more than usually in arrears, & I have now two notes of yours on my table. I confess there was somewhat so charming in knowing who & what the incendiaries were who had tried to burn Dodona up, that I could hardly lament the injury for joy at convicting the Angels. So you & you are the rogues! we say, & cannot decide whether to post you on the church-door, or in the N. Y. Herald. But yesterday we took our family walk — my son & daughter & Mr Charles Newcomb [87] & I to Walden & discovered the place & limits of the new fire (for a larger one, as you may have seen, burned there two months ago) & found that yours did not come into my lines proper, but is on land which I hold as trustee for a friend, having bought it at New Year's. [88] I shall in due time communicate the fact & the names of the perpetrators to him, &, it is to be hoped, with all due emphasis on the enormity of the offence, & the high necessity that exists for holding the parties accountable. For the proposition in your new note of lectures in Worcester, I am not very eager to come, as perhaps I should make better use of this first rehearsal by sitting down instantly & siezing & carrying out all the suggestions that come from it into the written page, than to read them too much. But there is good hope on the other side also. I should, however, like to be sure that the Lectures are really desired, & not carried to an audience too much solicited. Then In [89] that case of a supposed unwilling audience, I like to demand a good deal of money, & so settle the question. But I will say that if your friends think that people desire to hear me, and will let me come on two consecutive evenings or days of each week, I will read the six lectures [90] on the terms you have proposed.

Yours faithfully [91]

H. G. O. Blake

86. MS owned by Mr. W. T. H. Howe; ph. in CUL.

87. Newcomb, Providence, May 24, 1866, told how he walked all the way back to Providence in three days.

88. See Jan. 5, 1866.

89. At the beginning of a new page; Emerson apparently forgot that he had already begun his sentence.

90. The letters seem to contain no later reference to such a course.

91. A strip of the MS has been cut away below. To the left, the name " R. W. Emerson " has been supplied, and at the bottom of the page is the notation: " Signature cut out July 9, 1886, for Mrs. Abby Hutchinson Patton."

To THOMAS CARLYLE, CONCORD, MAY 16, 1866

[MS owned by RWEMA; printed in *C–E Corr.,* 1883.]

To FORCEYTHE WILLSON, CONCORD? MAY *c.* 18, 1866

[Willson, Cambridge, May 21 (or just possibly 26), 1866, says he found this letter had already arrived when he reached home Saturday evening (May 19) and proposes that Emerson visit him on the 31st.]

To JAMES THOMAS FIELDS, CONCORD, MAY 21, 1866 [92]

Concord
21 May 1866

My dear Mr Fields,

I received this morning your letter, & the draft for three hundred & forty seven dollars, in addition to the six hundred received before.[93] How the expenses were dwarfed to 26 dollars, I have no arithmetic to explain.

I give due honor to the house of Ticknor & Fields for their generous & successful management of my affair; But I believe myself still more deeply indebted to the House of Mr & Mrs Fields, for the inventing conducting & perfecting it.

And so, ever yours gratefully,

R. W. Emerson

J. T. Fields, Esq

To HARRISON GRAY OTIS BLAKE, CONCORD, MAY 26, 1866

[MS listed in C. F. Libbie & Co., Apr. 26 and 27, 1904; described as "on business matters."]

To ANNE CHARLOTTE LYNCH BOTTA, CONCORD, MAY 28, 1866 [94]

[1]Concord
28 May
1866

Dear Mrs Botta,[1]

Your kind note was welcome to me. No I have not approached your city since I left your house,[95] though I remember I was there con-

92. MS owned by the Henry E. Huntington Library; ph. in CUL.
93. See Apr. 17, 1866.
94. MS owned by the Henry E. Huntington Library; ph. in CUL. Excerpts I–III are in *Memoirs of Anne C. L. Botta,* p. 341.
95. *Cf.* Dec. 29, 1865.

vinced that I was quickly to return. And you may be sure there is no unwillingness in Lidian E., nor in Ellen or in Edward to visit New York & you: but each of these four spinners has a special web to weave, & has not yet found a day when the threads could be left without certainty of tangling. But there are more days & reliefs. I hoped & IIhope that having found so frank & intelligent good will in your house, I may not lose it. I even persuade myself that my next visit will be better than II my first, IIIsince we shall begin at some advance, & who knows but we shall arrive at our best experiences. For I think in the short winter days, — & in New York they are shortest, — we left many good topics untouched, & hardly came into the precincts of those which interest each of us most.III

Still I do not now know when my liberty will send me to New York. But when there is any question your invitation will make the scale preponderate. At present, I fear there is none for the weeks before me.

But meantime perhaps Mr Botta will sail for Boston; then you will come here to meet him: Then you will let me show Concord to you & him. If not so, — still some day you will come hither. Meantime I send you thankful greetings from all this household. Yours affectionately,

R. W Emerson

To Edward Waldo Emerson, Concord? May? 1866? [96]

Yes offer them. The tone musical & the first stanza all right. In the second can't you get out that harsh " arena " by " career " or its equivalent or " lifes armed lists " or " thronged lists " or do something with " barrier "

Up heart & the barrier leap —

or the like?

To ——————, Concord, June 1, 1866

[MS listed in American Art Association, Mar. 3-4, 1926, where it is described as relating to literary matters and mentioning Oliver Wendell Holmes.]

96. MS owned by RWEMA; ph. in CUL. The date " May '66 " has been supplied on the penciled note from Ellen Emerson, which now accompanies Emerson's own unsigned note. Ellen wrote:
" Dear Papa,
        Length & metre being prescribed and the word Sixty six required, Edw has tried for the *class song*, and sends for your criticism. Please return by morning's mail. . . ."
    Ellen's note is written on the back of the sheet containing her brother's two stanzas, in the second of which is the line
        " Into life's arena we leap."

To William Hathaway Forbes, Concord, June 5, 1866 [97]

> Concord
> 5 June Tuesday

Dear Will,

I had not time yesterday to acknowledge your note & its contents which all rightly came. Certainly, be kind enough to keep the receeipt of Mr Denison [98] until he wants it again. And, I doubt not, Mr Thayer will put himself in communication with you, in order to keep proper time with his sale of Ft. Wayne shares.[99] I have fifteen, and, I believe, your father in his counting for me, the other day, counted them all in.

But I grieve to hear of this lame knee, & Ellen today does not mend your report; & finds you quite too kind & polite to allow yourself to get well. You must send at once for your physician, & be savage & selfish to the dismay of all beholders.

> With love to Edith, & with hope of your rapid relief,
> Yours,
> R. W. Emerson

W. H. Forbes.

To James Bradley Thayer, Concord, June 21, 1866 [100]

> Concord
> 21 June, 1866 —

Dear Mr Thayer,

Please pay to the order of William H. Forbes, say, fourteen hundred & sixty five $\frac{25}{100}$ dollars, minus commissions due from the same.

$1465.25 —)   R Waldo Emerson

James B. Thayer, Esq.

97. MS owned by RWEMA; ph. in CUL. This is clearly later than Oct., 1865, when Edith Emerson was married. In later years, June 5 fell on Tuesday only in 1866 and 1877.

98. Probably the John N. Denison of Apr. 4, 1867, to W. H. Forbes. The extra letter in " receipt " may be " c " rather than " e."

99. Emerson's Ft. Wayne shares, in Thayer's safe, are mentioned in Sept. 20, 1865? It seems almost certain that the sum mentioned in June 21 following was realized from the sale of these shares.

100. MS owned by Professor James B. Thayer; ph. in CUL. Presumably Emerson wished his son-in-law to invest the sum mentioned. A notation records: " p^d W. H. F. June 25/66." *Cf.* June 5, 1866.

To Edith Emerson Forbes, Concord? June 30, 1866 [101]

Sat. 30 June

Dear Edith,

I brought away yesterday afternoon thus much of Ellen's letter. The Monadnoc campaign [102] appeared thus far a happy one with only chagrins enough to spice the joy. The mountain I thought, well deserved the devotion it inspires in these young madmen & women: It is great of its kind, its shadow at sunset reaching across the wide champaign actually to the horizon the fixed & floating ornaments of cloud & rainbow, rock-sierra, hills, ponds, & towns, & the climate in which you can see your breath morning & evening, and the terms on which all these are enjoyed by the gay companions, animate & please everybody. The risks too which are not few, warn every one to to make the best & the quickest of it & have not yet done them any harm. I should like well to have stayed long & got used to the work & play. Ellen was happy, & the mistress of the situation. I was repeatedly shown " the throne " they called it, where Will & you sat, when in presence.

I believe that new company goes up today.

Your loving Father,
R W E

To William Bull Wright, Concord? June? 1866

[Wright, Goshen, N. Y., June, 1866, acknowledges this letter and says he values all the suggestions about his poem. *Cf.* Aug. 21, 1866.]

To Rebecca Duncan, Concord? July 1, 1866

[Printed in *Boston Evening Transcript*, July 12, 1897, p. 6, where it is dated " Sunday Eve., 1st July " and is without the name of the person addressed. The Monadnock trip here mentioned occurred in June, 1866 (see June 30, 1866). For Rebecca Duncan as " Theodore Parker's Bettine," see earlier letters.]

101. MS owned by RWEMA; ph. in CUL. The date 1866 is fixed by evidence cited below, and June 30 fell on Saturday in that year.

102. The entry of July 2, 1866, in *Journals* (X, 149–153) shows that Emerson went to Monadnock on June 27 to join Ellen, Edward, Una Hawthorne, and others, and that he remained there on the 28th. I conjecture that he returned home on the 29th.

To Robert Woodward Barnwell, Concord, July 6, 1866 [103]

Concord, Mass^{tts}

6 July 1866

My dear Barnwell,

Will you let an old classmate after nearly half a century claim you thus, in writing you I think for the first time. But I wish you to know that distance, politics, war,[104] even, at last, have not been able to efface in any manner the high affectionate exceptional regard in which I, in common I believe with all your old contemporaries of 1817–21, have firmly held you as our avowed chief,[105] in days when boys, as we then were, give a tender & romantic value to that distinction, which they cannot later give again. We are not — we men of 1821 — a very cohesive Class, — as compared with some of our foregoers & followers, but have managed to keep for a long time a Quinquennial festival at Mrs Saunders' house, in Neyle's chamber,[106] on Commencement Days, at which we collect, I think, an average of fifteen members. At every such meeting Upham tells as far as known the chronicle of the Class & punctually you may well believe all tidings of yourself are eagerly asked & heard. I have ever cherished the hope that such a collective magnet of old love would one day be irresistible, & that you would be drawn to your own. Of late years, of course, this hope was sadly postponed, but only postponed, &, I trust, that the day will yet arrive when, if you do

103. MS owned by Mr. Nathaniel B. Barnwell; ph. in CUL. Emerson addressed the letter to Charleston, S. C., but it was forwarded to Columbia, in the same state.

104. Barnwell, earlier a congressman and senator of the United States, had taken an important part in the government of the Confederate States. He signed the ordinance of secession and was a senator from 1861 to 1865 (*The South Carolina Historical and Genealogical Magazine*, II, 74) . He was, as his grandson, Mr. Nathaniel B. Barnwell, informs me, known as a warm friend of Jefferson Davis, a fact which " makes this letter from Mr. Emerson all the more striking."

105. In *Journals* Emerson recorded, during his senior year, his admiration of Barnwell as an orator and noted that a " great struggle of ambition " was going on between Barnwell and Upham (I, 68) ; and years later he referred to Barnwell as " the first scholar in my class " (V, 166) . The MS *Records of the College Faculty*, IX, 240, Oct. 23, 1820 (in HCL) tells of a petition by Barnwell on behalf of the military company. Josiah Quincy recalled, in 1875, that Barnwell had commanded the Harvard Washington Corps, of which Upham was the " orderly sergeant " (*Proc. of the Mass. Hist. Soc.*, 1st series, XV, 190) . Charles W. Upham himself wrote to Barnwell, Salem, Mass., Feb. 18, 1871: " You are our natural head and chosen leader. Your name and character are dear to us all." (MS owned by Mr. Nathaniel B. Barnwell.)

106. The Harvard catalogue of Oct., 1819, has Emerson's classmate Henry M. Neyle, of Charleston, S. C., at " Mr. Saunders'."

not come to your friends, we shall come & fetch you. I dare not hope we shall win you this year, the time is so near; but this year completes another *lustrum,* &, as we are summoning our men, I use the occasion to say thus much. With oldest kindest regards [107]

Hon R. W. Barnwell.   R. W. Emerson

To David Wood Gorham, Concord, July 6, 1866 [108]

Concord
6 July 1866

My dear Gorham,

You have heard that the " Harvard Memorial " has at last taken shape as an " Alumni Hall," [109] which proves satisfactory to the great majority of Cambridge men: Alumni Hall, with the needed adjuncts of Academic Theatre & Dining Hall, &, in general design & in special arrangements adapted to commemorate the patriotism & sacrifices of our heroes. Meantime, it prospers in favor & in means. Last Saturday, the Committee of Six assured me that they now felt that $220,000 (inclusive of the " Saunders Fund ") were secure. They now call for the contributions of classes, as classes. It happens, I am sorry for it, that neither Lowell nor Reed profess much sympathy with the enterprize, & Upham writes me that his private engagements hinder him from any activity. Still, both he & Reed will contribute. As one of the Committee of Fifty, appointed a year ago,[110] & one of a Sub-committee of that, I promised to

107. Barnwell replied, Columbia, S. C., July 15 following, thanking Emerson for his " affectionate letter of 6th." " I consider it under the circumstances," he wrote, " very good fortune that I have been kept apart from you all: for amid such fierce contests as we have passed through, a nature so impulsive & prone to prejudice as mine continues to be, could not have escaped the influence of feelings hostile to the old associations which bind us together. Now I am thrown at once from the present to the distant past, from age to youth . . ." The war had brought ruin upon him, but he now had a professorship in the University of South Carolina. (From a MS copy.)

108. MS owned by HCL; ph. in CUL. Gorham's reply, presumably to this letter, is mentioned in Oct. 30, 1866.

109. For the genesis of the plan, *cf.* June 7, 1865. The cornerstone was laid on Oct. 6, 1870, and Memorial Hall was ready for use in 1874; it included an auditorium known as the Saunders Theatre (Arthur S. Pier, *The Story of Harvard,* 1913, p. 203) . The hall still remains a conspicuous object at Harvard.

110. *Cf.* the letters of June 7 and July 12, 1865. At a meeting on July 19 a " full report " was presented by " the Committee of Fifty on the Memorial Hall " (*Boston Evening Transcript,* July 19, 1866) .

aid if necessary, our Class Committee in calling the attention of our men of 1821 to the matter.

In looking over the *Catalogu* [111] I count twenty men who, I think, will give each something, — a few who may give much. But it were a pity that our class alone should make no contribution to this important benefit, simply for want of being appealed to. I think it will be easy for the class to pay the one thousand dollars, the sum assessed by the Committee on each class of or near our standing. Like so many others, I have little money to spare, but will strain a point to pay one hundred. If you speak or write to any member, I entreat you to urge his coming to our Quinquennial meeting which *you* will surely attend on the 18th instant,[112] & stir their pure hearts by way of remembrance. And there & then we can do ourselves & the College justice. Ever your affectionate Dr David Gorham.   R. W. Emerson

To John Boynton Hill, Concord, July 6, 1866 [113]

Concord. 6 July. 1866.

My dear Hill. You have heard that the Harvard Memorial has at last taken a shape which proves satisfactory to the great majority of Cantabrigians, as an Alumni Hall, with the needed adjuncts of theatre (i.e. hall for Commencement exercises) dining-hall, & in general design & in special arrangements adapted to commemorate the patriotism & sacrifices of our heroes. This building is of extreme necessity. The parish-church, in which the college has some rights,[114] is no longer suitable, & very soon untenable. In five years the College must give up the public Commencement or hold it in a tent. The new power passing into the Alumni, this year. also requires a Hall; as also do the memoirs of the College. Well, the design prospers in favor & means. The Committee of six assured me on Saturday, that they now feel that $220.000. inclusive

111. There was not room to complete the word in the margin.

112. The secretary of the class of 1821 announced in the *Boston Daily Advertiser* of July 18, 1866, that members would find their room, near the Episcopal Church, open for them that day — commencement day. It was at this commencement that the college gave Emerson the honorary degree of LL.D. and, according to the *Advertiser* of the 19th, officially proclaimed him " jucundissimum poëtam et hominem multarum literarum."

113. MS owned by RWEMA; ph. in CUL. This is a copy, not in Emerson's hand. *Cf.* the letter of the same date to Gorham.

114. The right of the college to use this church at commencement time is set forth in the *Report on the Connection at Various Times Existing between the First Parish in Cambridge and Harvard College,* 1851, pp. 15–16.

of the " Sanders fund," — is secure. Having exhausted the individual
subscriptions they now call on the classes as such. For whatever reason
our Class Committee, Lowell, Upham. & Reed, will not work in the
matter, though Upham & Reed will both contribute money. As one of
the Committee of Fifty appointed a year ago, & one of a sub-committee
of that, I promised to aid our Class-Committee if necessary, in calling
the attention of our men of 1821 to the matter. In looking over the
Catalogus, I count twenty men, who, I think, will give something. — a
few who may give much. But it were a pity, that our Class alone should
make no contribution simply for want of being appealed to. I think it
will be easy for the Class, to pay the one thousand dollars assessed by
the Committee on each Class of or near our standing. I have little
money to spare, but mean to strain a point to give a hundred. If you
speak or write to any member, I entreat you to urge his coming to our
Quinquennial meeting. (which you must surely attend on the 18$\underline{th}$ instant.) & otherwise stir his pure heart by way of remembrance.

With old & kind regards

Yours.

R. W. Emerson.

John. B. Hill. Esq.

To Edith Emerson Forbes, Concord, July 11, 1866 [115]

Concord

11 Evening

[1]My dear Edith,

Happy wife & mother that you are — & not the less surely
that the birth of your babe touches this old house & its people & neighbors with unusual joy. I hope the best gifts & graces of his father &
mother will combine for this blossom, & highest influences hallow &
ripen the firm & perfect fruit. There is nothing in this world so serious
as the advent of a child with all his possibilities to parents with good
minds & hearts. Fair fall the little boy — he has come among good people. I do not grudge to William & you the overflow of fondness & won-

115. MS owned by Mr. William H. Forbes; ph. in CUL. Excerpt I is in Cabot, II,
487–488. The date " 11 July 1866," supplied in another hand, is undoubtedly correct,
as comparison with the letter of the same date to Adams shows. Ralph Emerson
Forbes, Emerson's first grandchild, was born July 10, 1866 (The Ipswich Emersons,
p. 370) . He is mentioned by name in July 24, 1866, to Ellen. A picture of him with
Carlyle, taken some years later, is reproduced as the frontispiece of Journals, X,

der, — & to the boy it is the soft pillow prepared for him — and it is long before he will come to himself, — but I please myself already that his fortunes will be worthy of these great days of his country, that he will not be frivolous, that he will be noble & true, & will know what is sacred.[1] I send affectionate congratulations to William with our joint thanks here for his careful & successful forwarding of the tidings, & to Mrs Forbes for every syllable of her welcome letter.

Your Mother joins me in this writing & sending, & adds after her way but quite sincerely, a text for your reading, which I too find in my bible, Luke, chapter 1. verse 63.

Your loving father,
R. W. Emerson

To Abel Adams, Concord, July 11, 1866 [116]

Concord
11 July
1866

My dear friend,

   I know you & yours will wish to know that William & Edith Forbes have a son [117] born last night of which he & Mrs John Forbes write us most favorable accounts & that Edith is in very comfortable condition. Edward left us this morning for Burlington; [118] & Ellen this noon for Milton. With affectionate regards to Mrs Adams, & Abby, & to Mrs Larkin

Ever yours,
R. W. Emerson

Mr Abel Adams.

I hope the fine shower of Sunday & the cooler weather have mended your own health, of which Edward did not give the best report, on the day of his visit. My wife insists on my adding " her love for the dear good man, & Mrs Adams, & Abby, & is sure of your sympathy."

To Edward Kent, Concord? July? c. 19? 1866

[Mentioned in Sept. 5, 1866.]

116. MS owned by RWEMA; ph. in CUL.
117. See the letter of the same date to Edith Emerson Forbes.
118. For Edward's residence with Charles Elliott Perkins at Burlington, Ia., see July 24, 1866, to Ellen Emerson.

To EDWARD WALDO EMERSON, CONCORD, JULY 24, 1866

[MS owned by Mr. Raymond Emerson.]

To ELLEN EMERSON, CONCORD, JULY 24, 1866 [119]

Concord
Tuesday

Dear Ellen

Here is the answer of Gisela,[120] which appears a little late, but will, no doubt, bring its own explanation. Of course, we cannot wait our turn in reading it till Saturday — you must come sooner — which course, Edith, fond of variety, will urge. We have a good letter from Edward with an account of his good housekeeping *with* Mr Perkins [121] which, of course, you will prefer to read here. Besides, Mr Akers arrived today, & how can we take proper care of him, without you? If you persist in contumacy one or both of you I shall have the expense of sending the letter to Milton. Love to you all, — Wm, Ralph,[122] Ellen, Edith.

R. W. Emerson.

To ELLEN EMERSON, CONCORD, AUGUST 1, 1866 [123]

Concord
1 Aug[t]

Dear Ellen,

Please bring me Mrs Clough's book of " Remains." [124] Also, if you so determine, Edith's order for her deposit in the " Middlesex

119. MS owned by RWEMA; ph. in CUL. The year is clearly 1866, when July 24, the date supplied, apparently by Ellen Emerson, fell on Tuesday.

120. Ellen wrote, Milton, Mass., July 25 and 26, 1866, that she had been looking over her letter from Gisela and had found many references to her father. In Apr. 14, 1867, Emerson mentions Gisela von Arnim Grimm's letter which, he says, though addressed to Ellen, directly concerns him.

121. In Mar. 3, 1867, Emerson tells of his own visit at the home of Charles Elliott Perkins, at Burlington, Ia., and recalls Edward's stay there. Perkins, who was a cousin of J. M. Forbes and had married the latter's niece Edith Forbes, became president of the C. B. & Q. (see *Letters and Recollections of John Murray Forbes,* II, 216–217 *et passim*).

122. *Cf.* July 11, 1866, to Edith Emerson Forbes.

123. MS owned by RWEMA; ph. in CUL. The year " 66," which has been supplied, is doubtless correct.

124. *Letters and Remains of Arthur Hugh Clough.*

Institution for Savings." Edwards will lie still at present. We have your yesterday's note which in spite of the genial illustration does not give the most cheerful account of your patient. But your mother thinks well of her condition on the whole, considering who she is, & who is taking care of her, & whose wife she is, & what she has to take care of.[125] So I commend her & you & all of you including the youngest housemate to the All Good & All Sufficient, not doubting & serene. On Saturday at 5 P. M. we shall find you at the Station.

R W E

To James Thomas Fields, Concord, August 21, 1866 [126]

Concord

21 August, 1866.

James T. Fields, Esq

My dear Sir,

[I]Give me leave to make you acquainted with[I] William B. Wright, Esq. now of Goshen, New York. Mr Wright [II]has written a poem which he now thinks of publishing.[127] It is in my judgment, a serious & original work of great & various merit: with high intellectual power in accosting the questions of modern thought, full of noble sentiment, and especially rich in fancy, & in sensibility to natural beauty.

I remember, that, while reading it, I thought it a welcome proof, & still more a prediction, of American culture. I need not trouble you with any cavils I made on the manuscript I read, as[II] Mr Wright [III]assures me that he has lately revised & improved the original draught. I hope you will like the poem as heartily as I did.[III]

Ever yours faithfully,

R W Emerson

125. Pretty clearly a reference to Ralph Emerson Forbes (*cf.* letters of July 11 and 24, 1866).

126. MS owned by the Henry E. Huntington Library; ph. in CUL. Excerpts I–III are in *Harper's,* LXVIII, 459 (Feb., 1884), and in Annie Fields, *Authors and Friends,* p. 75.

127. For Wright's earlier negotiations with Emerson regarding his poem, see the note on June? 1866. Wright wrote again, Goshen, N. Y., Aug. 26, 1866, apparently in acknowledgment of the present letter and, perhaps, of a letter to him inclosing this. He thanked Emerson for " these last tokens of your Kindness & Goodness." Wright's long poem *Highland Rambles* was published in 1868 at Boston, but not by Ticknor & Fields. The letter of Feb. 25, 1867, seems to refer to Fields's unhesitating refusal of this book.

To Edith Emerson Forbes, Boston, August 25, 1866 [128]

Boston, 25 Aug[t]

Dear Edith,

I am sorry to hear from Ellen that " they " have told you I should come to you today. Whoever " they " are, it was very naughty of them to tell fibs. But I must pay myself for the loss of my visit (for I cannot come for this Sunday,) by spending a day or a night with you, say next Wednesday or Thursday, & I will try to send you word Monday more exactly.[129] Today I expect to see Agassiz whom I have not yet seen,[130] & the Judge [131] & I go home late. I hope the envelope which I am carrying to City Exchange contains Edwards letter. Everything the boy tells is good excepting of his eyes.[132]

The aunt as well as the pictures give good accounts of the boy.[133]

Your loving papa,
R W E

To Edith Emerson Forbes, Concord, August 26, 1866 [134]

Concord
Sunday night

Dear Edith,

Put one potato more in your pot next Thursday,[135] for I mean to dine with you, coming by the 1'o'clock train. Nay, you may add two, for Ellen threatens to join me, if things permit. If Thursday is an engaged day with you, you must send me word. I found Mr Agassiz yesterday very rich with his Brazil experience: [136] — but we both agreed before we had done to brag of our daughters. Then he engaged me to

128. MS owned by RWEMA; ph. in CUL. The year 1866, supplied in another hand than Emerson's, is confirmed by evidence cited below.

129. See Aug. 26, 1866.

130. Agassiz returned to Cambridge from Brazil in Aug., 1866. See Aug. 26 for a report of the visit of the 25th.

131. Presumably Ebenezer Rockwood Hoar.

132. Cf. Nov. 7, 1866, to Edith Emerson Forbes.

133. Apparently Ralph Emerson Forbes, mentioned in several letters of this summer.

134. MS owned by Mr. David C. Forbes; ph. in CUL. The date is fixed by evidence cited below.

135. Cf. Aug. 25, 1866.

136. Ibid.

bring Ellen to Nahant to show us his photographs & other treasures just brought home.[137] Health & happiness to William & Ralph Forbes.[138]

Papa.

To John Boynton Hill, Concord, September 5, 1866 [139]

Concord, 5 September. 1866.

Dear Hill,

I received your letter immediately after its date, & should have replied at once had I not foreseen that I should need probably to write again, as matters should ripen. I regretted seriously your absence at the Class-meeting [140] & when I had your letter on yours also. Bunker, Cheney, Emerson, Gardner, Kent, Lowell, Quincy, Reed, Stetson & Withington were there in person, & Gorham & Upham were represented by their sons. We looked for a still larger meeting but liked this so well that we sat together from 12 o'c till 4, quite neglecting the College Dinner. Late in the Meeting I got a hearing for the question of the Harvard Monument & urged, that in view of the importance of the claim, & also of our fair share of prosperity as a Class we should do our part by a donation. There was little response & a good deal of silence. Gardner was opposed to the design as keeping alive hostile feeling, Lowell because the College wanted money more for other things: Bunker said he was unable to give to it; Kent was ready & willing to assist it. Reed came to the rescue when the matter seemed to be dropt & declared that if the members would subscribe what they could, he would be one of four to complete the sum so that the Class should subscribe $1000. Cheney also signified his willingness to assist. I was then requested by Reed & others to persist in taking charge of the affair. A few days later I received a letter from Barnwell in reply to one I had written to him [141] on Frank Lowells suggestion. Lowell thought it would cheer him to know how strong a kindness the Class had always retained for him, a quite exceptional regard. I consented & wrote a few days before Commencement — we could not expect to see him now, but whenever hereafter he could

137. See the account of this visit in *Journals*, X, 161–162 (Aug. 31, 1866).

138. *Cf.* earlier letters of this summer.

139. MS owned by RWEMA; ph. in CUL. This is a copy, not in Emerson's hand, and with peculiarities that are not his.

140. See the letters of July 6, 1866. The projected Harvard " Monument " — the Memorial Hall — is also mentioned in two letters of that date.

141. July 6, 1866, to Barnwell; Barnwell's reply is cited in a note on that letter.

come, we would convene the Class to meet him. (Lost the half-sheet that followed, but send his letter)

After turning over the matter at home, I decided to write to each member of the class, who, I had reason to think would like to aid the design. I wrote to Kent,[142] who kept me waiting for a time, & now tells me that he has to learn from his man of affairs, whether he shall give $100. or only $50. Reed sends me word that I may put down his name for $100. & if there is need he will add a sum not exceeding $150. to make his gift as large as either Gardner, Lowell, Pratt or Quincy." [143] shall contribute. This is generous & wise, as it adds an inducement to the gentlemen named to make & to increase their gift. But today this is all our basis. B. T. Reed $100. R. W. E. $100. I hope Kent will soon decide for the same sum: then we shall only [144] $700. to raise. In these beginnings what will you do? If you see your way to give to this lasting benefaction, I shall be very glad, & shall of course carry a new motive to all the rest. But less or more, send what you can. I was very glad to get a real letter from you, and as I am getting older, find I value my earlier companions not less but more. — I have had to write even this little letter by scraps, having been driven to the city between the lines, & returned. I hope you will see to it that your neighbors in New-Hampshire are put up to their weighty political duties & go to the polls, to put a check on our mad President.

Please to return the copy of Barnwell's letter that I may send it to Gorham.

Ever your old friend

R. W. Emerson.

TO EDITH EMERSON FORBES, CONCORD, SEPTEMBER? 10? 1866? [145]

Tis pity & shame that you who so tenderly send these faithful letters to console your sister & us ancients sitting here in the Concord rains, with tales of the sea & the boy & all the bright friends around you, should not get your questions answered. But Ellen's pen will not now

142. July? *c.* 19? 1866, to Kent. Presumably Emerson wrote to several other members of the class at about the same time.

143. Probably the copyist omitted an earlier pair of quotation marks.

144. The copyist may have omitted a word from Emerson's MS.

145. MS owned by RWEMA; ph. in CUL. Mention of " the boy " seems to indicate a date earlier than the fall of 1867, when the second child of Edith Emerson Forbes was born. For her stay at Naushon with her son, *cf.* Sept. 12, 1866, where some illness of her husband is also alluded to.

sleep long. I like well to think of Naushon, & so fitly peopled. Be sure tell me in your next sheet that Will's arm is getting well. Papa.

To Sarah Swain Forbes, Concord, September 12, 1866 [146]

Concord

12 September

My dear Mrs Forbes,

No such happiness appears to be reserved for any of us as to see Naushon this September. My wife goes to Plymouth tomorrow,[147] where a fortnight's visit has been long promised. Ellen must keep house the while for me at home, for me whose employments do not less tie me that they are insignifcant.[148] But we are all glad to be reminded of you & Naushon by your kind note. I hope the little guest to whom it is a novelty [149] is pleased with it as his seniors are. Some of us I am sure have counted days & hours until his arrival in Middlesex shall occur. Will, of all men should be entitled to health with his build & habits, & I trust you will heal him [150] entirely in these weeks. All of us send love to all of you.

Affectionately

R. W. Emerson

To Lidian Emerson, Boston, September? 14? 1866 [151]

Boston

Friday Eve

Dear Lidian,

Here is Edith's letter received this morning which Ellen read so hastily that she thought it heroic to send you the same day I have also a note from Mr Collyer of Chicago, dated 11th who apologises

146. MS owned by RWEMA; ph. in CUL. The year 1866, which has been supplied, is confirmed by evidence cited below.

147. Cf. Sept.? 14? 1866.

148. A letter was omitted at the beginning of a line.

149. This seems to refer to the first visit of Ralph Emerson Forbes to Naushon, at a time before he had come to Concord. Apparently his mother, and doubtless he too, visited in Concord in Jan., 1867 (cf. Jan. 22, 1867).

150. Cf. Sept.? 10? 1866?

151. MS owned by RWEMA; ph. in CUL. The date Sept., 1866, has been supplied. The year is confirmed by the mention of Edward Waldo Emerson in the West. The reference to the receipt of a letter dated the 11th and presumably from Chicago suggests that this Friday was Sept. 14 rather than 21 or 28. For Edward's departure for Burlington, Ia., see July 11, 1866, to Adams. Edward returned, according to his own account, in Dec., 1866 (see Cent. Ed., IX, 489). For the day of the present letter, cf. evidence cited below.

for not coming to Concord &c & adds " But next best to my coming to Concord, your son was here Sunday, came to church then to tea & we had ever such a good visit, — only too short — from the bright handsome young fellow. He is in good spirits, & in clover, does not seem a bit homesick so far, likes his place, & I guess is liked. I bid him come here whenever he felt like it," &c. &c. — As no letter came from Edward today, this scrap must stay your stomach. For the rest Concord is well on its feet, & can stand your absence, & mine tonight. Ellen has a tea-party. I believe you know that the Nahant mistake was Ellen's, & not Mrs H.'s Her two girls have accepted an invitation from Edith to Naushon & later Ellen's.

But all these will be trifles to you at Plymouth [152] & with Mr & Mrs Watson [153] to whom give from me very kind remembrances By tomorrow or Monday you will be pretty sure of Ellen's First Chapter of Chronicles. R. W E

To Cyrus Briggs, Concord? September 17, 1866

[Briggs, Augusta (Me.?), Dec. 31, 1866, acknowledges this letter and another from Emerson dated Dec. 26, both about the Harvard memorial.]

To Edward Waldo Emerson, Concord, September 17, 1866

[MS owned by Mr. Raymond Emerson.]

To Nathaniel Wood, Concord? September 17, 1866

[Wood, Fitchburg, Mass., Sept. 18, 1866, acknowledges this letter and agrees, though critical of the college, to contribute to the fund for the memorial.]

To James Thomas Fields, Concord, October 5, 1866 [154]

Concord

Oct. 5, 1866 —

My dear Editor,

[1]I have the more delight in your marked overestimate of my Poem,[155] that I had been vexed with a belief that what skill I had

152. *Cf.* Sept. 12, 1866, which shows that Lidian Emerson expected to go to Plymouth on the 13th.

153. Doubtless Benjamin Marston Watson and Mary Russell Watson, mentioned in earlier letters.

154. MS owned by the Henry E. Huntington Library; ph. in CUL. Excerpt I is in *Harper's*, LXVIII, 461 (Feb., 1884), and in Annie Fields, *Authors and Friends*, p. 82.

155. Perhaps " My Garden," published in *The Atlantic* for Dec., 1866.

in whistling was nearly or quite gone, & that I must henceforth content myself with guttural consonants or dissonants, & not attempt warbling. On the strength of your note, I am working away at my last pages of rhyme.[156] But this has been & is a week of company. Yet I shall do the best I can with the quarters of hours.[I]

Ever yours
R. W. Emerson

J. T. Fields, Esq

To Charles Eliot Norton, Concord, October 7, 1866 [157]

Concord
7 October, 1866.

My dear Norton,

Tis high time that your note, every word of which was welcome to me, should have a precise answer. I am of course gratified by such an invitation [158] from two friends so highly valued by me as yourself & Lowell, and the terms are most generous. I thought I ought to begin the next day on the task. But I have allowed myself to be drawn this one winter more into Western lectures.[159] It happened chiefly from some old promises & later urgencies at St Louis. Add that at other western towns, last winter, I had given half promises for this coming one. And now I regret them because I am trying to make an end of my second collection of poems (so called).

Yet I do not wish to be entirely wanting to a proposition which has something noble in my eyes; and therefore, though I cannot fully meet it, I shall seriously aim to do some part of what you ask. Alas, if it should be July before I arrive at your door! [160]

156. This seems to refer to the MS of *May-day and Other Pieces,* which Ticknor & Fields published on Apr. 29 following (*Boston Daily Advertiser,* Apr. 29, 1867). *Cf.* the letter of Oct. 7, 1866.

157. MS owned by HCL; ph. in CUL.

158. Norton wrote Lowell Oct. 19, 1866, telling of the invitation he had sent Emerson in the name of both editors to contribute regularly to *The North American Review;* Emerson, he said, had written a most pleasant reply, promising to do so " for a year," furnishing his first article for the issue of the following July (*Letters of Charles Eliot Norton,* I, 292–293). Norton thus read a more definite promise into the present letter than Emerson intended to make.

159. *Cf.* letters of Jan. 12 ff., 1867.

160. It was much later that Emerson actually arrived (*cf.* the letters of Aug. 6, 1867, and Jan. 16 and Feb. 5, 1868).

Thanks again for your summons to Berkshire — I must cling to my fens at present. I am glad you have had such a solid season in your hill country & as I learn with such good results, though I have missed you much at the Saturday Club. With kind regards to Mrs Norton,

Yours affectionately,

R. W. Emerson

Charles E. Norton, Esq

To Edgar M. Levy, Concord, October 10, 1866

[MS listed and partly quoted in American Art Association, May 6, 1915, where the person addressed is described simply as the Rev. Mr. Levy; Emerson says he cannot yet fix with certainty the date of his visit to Newark. The *Newark City Directory* for 1866–1867 lists Edgar M. Levy as a minister. For the lecture at Newark, see Dec. 7 following.]

To Octavius Brooks Frothingham, Concord, October 12, 1866

[MS listed and partly quoted in James Tregaskis & Son, Caxton Head catalogue 1019; Emerson says that he has already promised too many lectures and that he is now held fast by printing.]

To Harrison Gray Otis Blake, Concord, October 19, 1866

[MS listed and partly quoted in C. F. Libbie & Co., Apr. 26 and 27, 1904; Emerson finds that " Judge Holmes's book on Shakespeare . . . looks sensible " and says that " Bancroft's new volume makes one ashamed of having ever tired of Washington."]

To John Boynton Hill, Concord, October 30, 1866 [161]

Concord. 30 October. 1866.

Dear Hill.

I send you my best thanks for your excellent letter duly received long since, & not answered because I was then glad to use its purport in writing to our friends.[162] But replies of some of them came slowly. some not at all. Wood wrote [163] bravely that he does not love the College very well, but whether masking his goodwill under some

161. MS owned by RWEMA; ph. in CUL. This is a MS copy, not in Emerson's hand.

162. Presumably Emerson wrote, during July–Oct., 1866, several letters to classmates which I have not found.

163. For Nathaniel Wood's letter, see the note on Sept. 17, 1866, which it answered.

petulance I know not he ended his letter by promising fifty dollars to the fund whenever I should call for it. Only last night Upham wrote me [164] that he will give fifty. Bunker promised me verbally, that, if an expected contingency results favorably he would give fifty. But, he said, it was likely to be decided in a few weeks, — & I fear it has not so fallen. I have been talking with Reed, & he bids me send the little subscription list at once on its travels, get what it can & then bring it to him, & he will try its success in Boston. So I enclose it in this initial state to you. Please to put your name to it, & send it back to me without the delay that I have used. And I will send it to Kent.[165] Gorham wrote me [166] that he was utterly unable this year to subscribe.

Yours affectionately
R. W. Emerson.

To William Hepworth Dixon, Concord, October 30, 1866?

[MS listed, without year, in Sotheby & Co., Apr. 18–19, 1932; Emerson asks Dixon to visit Concord. Dixon, the historian and traveler, was in America in 1866 and again in September, if not later, in 1874. He was at Longfellow's home on Oct. 28, 1866 (Samuel Longfellow, *Life,* n. d. [c. 1891], III, 79); and it is very probable that the present letter was written two days later.]

To Edith Emerson Forbes, Boston, November 7, 1866 [167]

Parker House
7 Nov —

Dear Edith,

Ellen & I could not resist the necessity of peeping into Edwards letter for which we had waited a fortnight although it was guarded by your name. You shall revenge yourself on one to either of us After I reached Cambridge, I discovered that I also had one from the boy, which I had thrust into my pocket as a stranger's letter. He has come back to Burlington, & is making new arrangements for his housekeeping. but with the expectation of going back to the prairie. He is delighted with Mrs Perkins [168] in her house. No eyes yet.[169] But

164. Presumably in answer to a letter from Emerson, but I have no proof.
165. Probably Emerson wrote to Edward Kent later, inclosing the subscription list.
166. In answer, I conjecture, to the letter of July 6, 1866, to him.
167. MS owned by RWEMA; ph. in CUL.
168. *Cf.* July 24, 1866, to Ellen Emerson.
169. *Cf.* Aug. 25, 1866.

Ellen shall send you the letter. Your Mother does not leave her chamber yet but comforts herself that you going to pay her a sudden visit some time.

Papa —

To Edward Waldo Emerson, Boston, November 7, 1866

[MS owned by Mr. Raymond Emerson.]

To George Washburn Smalley, Concord, November 17, *c.* 1866?

[MS listed and partly quoted in Thomas F. Madigan, Jan. 22, 1926; in reply to Smalley, Emerson invited him to Concord on the afternoon of the 17th, the day of the letter, asking him to persuade Mr. Young to come too. The letter was sent, it seems, in care of Wendell Phillips, whose adopted daughter Smalley married in 1862. Smalley had a long career as a correspondent, living abroad for many years; but I conjecture that this letter was most probably written after his return in the fall of 1866 from his service as correspondent during the Austro-Prussian war. He had received his assignment to report that war from John Russell Young, who had only that year been appointed managing editor of the *New-York Tribune*. In his *Anglo-American Memories*, 1911, pp. 51 ff., Smalley tells in detail of his first visit to Emerson, in 1855, and alludes (p. 55) to many later meetings.]

To James Freeman Clarke, Concord, December 3, 1866 [170]

Concord
Monday 3 Dec^r

My dear Sir,

I am very glad to see that you are announced to speak to us on Thursday of this week; and it will add to my content, & that of my family, if you will spend the night with us. . Yours ever

R. W. Emerson

Rev. James F. Clarke.

To Anne Charlotte Lynch Botta, Concord, December 7, 1866

[MS owned by the Yale University Library; printed in *The Journal of English and Germanic Philology*, XXVI, 478–479 (Oct., 1927), where " 1865? " is given as the year. Much of this letter is, however, in answer to Mrs. Botta's dated

170. MS owned by Mr. Walter R. Benjamin; I have made a MS copy, which is in CUL. Dec. 3 fell on Monday in 1866; and the MS records of the Concord Lyceum (owned by the Concord Free Public Library) show that Clarke delivered his lecture " What For " on the following Thursday.

New York, Dec. 2, 1866. She said she saw it reported in the papers that Emerson was about to set forth again to the West and wished to know whether he could not visit her in New York on his way; both she and her husband, who had returned home in August, would be glad to have Emerson and any member of his family he cared to bring; she inclosed a photograph of a bust she was modeling when Emerson was last there; her husband had secured from the Italian government the right to bore for petroleum. Emerson's references to the volume of poems printed but not published, to his intended visit to New York on Dec. 21, and to his lectures promised for Newark and Paterson likewise show the date was 1866. In Oct. 5, 1866, Emerson told Fields he was working away at his " last pages of rhyme." In the MS memorandum book for 1866, Mrs. Botta's name and address are entered under Dec. 21, Newark is down for the 24th, and Paterson, under the 26th, is canceled. The lecture of the 24th was on " Society in America " and was read in a course conducted by the Young Men's Christian Association (*Newark Daily Advertiser,* Dec. 24 and 26, 1866) .]

To John Murray Forbes, Concord, December 17, 1866 [171]

Concord

Dec. 17, Monday

My dear Sir,

I should be heartily glad to come to your house & to see Mr Fox [172] — but I am to go to Salem on Wednesday,[173] at your very hour. Pity me the more Ever Yours,

R. W. Emerson

J. M. Forbes, Esq.

To James Freeman Clarke, Concord, December 18, 1866? [174]

Concord

18 Dec

My dear Sir,

I return you (by this mail) , with thanks, after reading it, Channing's Prize Essay. It is a capital specimen of thorough scholar's work, & the matter cited in it full of interest, — though painful enough, as

171. MS owned by RWEMA; ph. in CUL. Evidence cited below fixes the year as 1866, when Dec. 17 was Monday.

172. Gustavus Vasa Fox had returned from his mission to Russia only a few days earlier. Forbes's interest in him is shown by numerous passages in *Letters and Recollections of John Murray Forbes.*

173. The MS memorandum book for 1866 gives Wednesday, Dec. 19, to Salem, Mass. (" Man of the World ") .

174. MS owned by Mr. James F. Clarke; ph. in CUL. The year, as the following note shows, is almost certainly 1866.

Greek civil history is prone to be. Presently after you left the pamphlet with me, arrived duplicates of the two brochures [175] with a note from William Channing. I do not wonder he is proud of his boy's work.

Ever yours,
R. W. Emerson

J. F. Clarke.

To Sidney Henry Morse, Concord, December 19, 1866? [176]

Concord
19 Dec^r

My dear Sir,

I hope there may come an end to my negatives, but it is not yet. I go to the West on the 2^d January & though my Programme has not yet been accurately finished it threatens now more than two months This is inconvenient to my further plans & I shall try to reduce it. But it looks as if I could not securely promise any aid till late in March. When I see the list, which a secretary at Chicago is now authorized to make, I will send you more accurate word. If I am not too late for your course, I will try to take a part in it.

With great regard
R. W. Emerson

Rev. S. H. Morse —

To Cyrus Briggs, Concord? December 26, 1866

[Briggs, Augusta (Me.?), Dec. 31, 1866, acknowledges Emerson's letters of Sept. 17 and Dec. 26. The second letter, he notes, inclosed one from their classmate Barnwell and urged something for the Harvard memorial — " you say ' the contribution of only a stone or rafter will be acceptable.' " Briggs therefore contributes his mite.]

175. Doubtless *Instinct. A Prize Essay Read in the Theatre, Oxford, June 21, 1865,* Oxford, 1865, and *The Greek Orators Considered as Historical Authorities. The Arnold Prize Essay for 1866,* Oxford, 1866. Both were by Francis Allston Channing, son of Emerson's friend William Henry Channing. According to O. B. Frothingham, *Memoir of William Henry Channing,* p. 343, the second essay received the prize on Mar. 6, 1866.

176. MS owned by the Rosenbach Company; ph. in CUL. What is said of the prospective Western lecture tour fits the letters of more than two months following. A slight delay in starting is partly explained in Dec. 28, 1866. For Emerson's " secretary at Chicago," *cf.* the letters of Dec. 28, 1866, and Jan. 22 and Feb. 12 (second letter), 1867. Probably the lecture mentioned in Mar. 31, 1867, was the contribution to Morse's course conditionally promised in the present letter.

To Edith Emerson Forbes, Concord, December 28, 1866 [177]

> Concord
> Dec 28, Friday

Dear Edith,

I had intended to come to Milton on Saturday evening from our Club [178] as you & Mr Forbes, I learn, had proposed to me. But I have now a letter from my Chicago correspondent [179] that makes it unnecessary for me to leave Boston till the 4th Jan[y],[180] so that I shall not be forced to leave Milton in any haste on Wednesday morning; and, as I want a good deal of time for my home affairs, I find it prudent & necessary to come back hither tomorrow night from Boston. So I pray you to make my apologies to your husband & to your father, for my slower appearance on the Hill.[181] Edward is unfolding his plans [182] with excellent cheer to himself his sister & me, in these hours, & the days are very short. With love to you & all yours, specially to Ralph, Affectionately,

> R. W. E.

To Harrison Gray Otis Blake, Concord, December 31, 1866

[MS listed and partly quoted in C. F. Libbie & Co., Apr. 26 and 27, 1904; Emerson says that if he is to " stay for the affliction of a photographer " perhaps he had better " stay over a train in the morning."]

177. MS owned by RWEMA; ph. in CUL. For the date, 1866 is the only year in which Dec. 28 fell on Friday that fits the evidence cited below. The lecture tour of Jan.–Feb., 1867, was the last to the Middle West which Emerson began in January; and the mention of Ralph Emerson Forbes makes it certain that the present letter was not earlier than 1866.

178. The Saturday Club, no doubt.

179. For Edwin Lee Brown, see especially a note on the second letter of Feb. 12, 1867.

180. An earlier date is mentioned in Dec. 19, 1866? and Jan. 4, 1867, seems to show that there was a further delay.

181. Milton Hill.

182. Cf. Feb. 17, 1867, to Lidian Emerson.

1867

To Louis Prang, Concord? January? 1? 1867?

[In Feb. 18, 1867, Emerson tells Prang: "I received on or before New Year's Day the elegant parcel of colored prints you were so good as to send me, and wrote immediately a note to you, which I am sorry to find by your letter just forwarded to me from home, was never sent."]

To William Hathaway Forbes, Concord, January 4, 1867 [1]

Concord
Friday Eve 4 Jan

Dear Will,

I had rather at this time by much go to Milton than to Chicago; but must set forth in that line on Monday, & need all the Sunday at home. With love to all your house, from oldest to youngest, Yours

R. W. E.

To Benjamin Tyler Reed, Concord? January c. 6, 1867

[Mentioned in Jan. 12, 1867; presumably about the Harvard memorial.]

To Edward Waldo Emerson, *en route* to Buffalo, January c. 10, 1867

[Mentioned in the letters of Jan. 12 and 13, 1867. Ellen Emerson, Jan. 12, 1867, says, "Your note to Edward came yesterday," and adds that they were sorry to hear "of the snow-drift and Batavia."]

---

1. MS owned by RWEMA; ph. in CUL. Jan. 4 fell on Friday in 1867, the year which has been supplied on the MS. The day for starting westward mentioned in Dec. 28, 1866, seems to have been slightly changed for the second time. The following letters show a part of the geography of the tour of this winter. In the MS memorandum book for 1867 Batavia ("Resources") has been changed from the 8th to the 9th of January. The letter of Jan. 13 shows that Emerson had lectured as far west as Cleveland on the 10th of this month.

To Ellen Emerson, Jamestown, New York, January 12, 1867 [2]

Jamestown, N. Y.

12 Jany Saturday

Dear Ellen,

I hoped I might find a word from you here but I suppose Monday & Tuesday's Town halls [3] have left you no leisure. I wish to hear that my letter went safely to Mr B. T. Reed concerning which I wrote to Edward in the trains but I believe, it was only mailed at Buffalo. I was to say also that not a scrap of all the miscellaneous letters halfsheets & scraps I left about the study must be burned. Several notes one especially — from Mrs G. T Winthrop in England, I meant to take with me If you can find hers inclose it to me Send me good news· of all the house I inclose a draft for $170 which Mr Cheney will pay to your order. My road thus far is not as skilfully laid out as in the last year as my distances are wasteful of time. I wish it may be better after Chicago. You found, I hope, my programme as I put it into the end of the " Journal."

R. W. E

Care of Lecture Committee

Pontiac	Mich	21 Jan [4]
Battle Creek	do	23
Chicago	Ill	24

care B. B. Wiley [5]

To Ellen Emerson, Jamestown, New York, January 13, 1867 [6]

Jamestown N Y

13 Jan

Dear Ellen

Directly after I had put my note (inclosing a draft) to you

2. MS owned by RWEMA; ph. in CUL. The year is clearly 1867. The *Jamestown Journal* of Jan. 11 announced " The Man of the World " for that evening and stressed the lecturer's " enigmatical " style by printing a few lines from " Brahma." The same paper for Jan. 18 following called the lecture Emersonian, brilliant, inconsistent. The audience was " the best probably ever drawn together in Jamestown on any occasion." But Emerson was no orator. " We dismiss him," said the critic, " with the desire to *hear* him no more; but to *read* him, ever." The subject as recorded for Jamestown in the MS memorandum book for this year was " Social Aims."

3. For Ellen Emerson's " Town Hall sociables," *cf.* the letters of Jan. 13 and Feb. 5, 1867.

4. This engagement was canceled (see Jan. 18, 1867).

5. See Jan. 22, 1867, for both Chicago and Battle Creek. I have found no notice of the lecture presumably delivered at the latter place.

6. MS owned by RWEMA; ph. in CUL. The year is obviously 1867.

yesterday afternoon, into the mail, came your welcome note & its in-
closures All is right & good that you tell me & I am delighted with the
success of your " Sociable," as it makes their sequel sure. One thing you
do not say that Edward put my letter to Mr Reed into the mail, but
E. will presently have had my note from Buffalo about it. My lecture
here on Friday night [7] allows me to remain here in a good hotel till
tomorrow, when I go to Fredonia.[8] Tell Mamma that I find all I want
in my trunk & bags — or if I do not, it is not her fault or yours. At
Cleveland [9] the actor Murdoch read to me " Sheridan's Ride," in Mr
Willey's parlor [10] I had heard wonders of his reading, & he reads with
great skill & force, but, as usual, with the *surplusage* of actors. Probably
it would sound far better in a hall. He had never heard of The " Old
Sergeant." [11] I did not pay Alden & B and will answer the letters you
inclose.[12] R W E

To CHARLES HURD? ADRIAN? MICHIGAN? JANUARY *c.* 16? 1867

[In Jan. 18, 1867: " I have written to Pontiac . . ." The canceled entry of Jan.
21 in the MS memorandum book of this year names Hurd as the representative of the Students' Lecture Association at Pontiac.]

To ELLEN EMERSON, ADRIAN, MICHIGAN, JANUARY 18, 1867 [18]

Adrian, Mich.
Friday Night
Lawrence House

Dear Ellen,

I am here for the last three days, the engagement at Pontiac

7. See a note on Jan. 12, 1867, for the lecture of Friday, the 11th.

8. Emerson read " American Resources " instead of " The Man of the World,"
the subject originally announced, before the Young Men's Association on Jan. 14
(*The Fredonia Censor,* Jan. 9 and 23, 1867) .

9. *The Cleveland Daily Plain Dealer,* Jan. 11, 1867, reported the reading of " The
Man of the World " before the Library Association on the 10th.

10. James E. Murdoch turned from the stage to the lecture platform in his later
years. " Sheridan's Ride " must have been Thomas Buchanan Read's poem. George
Willey is mentioned in earlier letters.

11. Two editions, 1866 and 1867, of Forceythe Willson's *The Old Sergeant* are
still in the Emerson library at the Antiquarian House. For the author, *cf.* the note
on 1865?

12. Probably Emerson wrote, in reply, letters I have not found.

13. MS owned by RWEMA; ph. in CUL. This letter, on which the date Jan. 18,
1867, has been supplied, was acknowledged in Ellen Emerson's dated Jan. 24, 1866,
but clearly written in 1867, as received " last night." The MS memorandum book
for this year gives Jan. 16 to Adrian (" Social Aims ") .

having been broken by Pontiac,[14] as they wrote me; and so I have no letters since Jamestown.[15] I have written to Pontiac [16] to forward your letters, — if they come, — to Chicago. I have been comfortably housed in this hotel & was glad that the rest came in a lump instead of scraps. I was thankful to Uncle William for his brave goodness to Mr Vincent, & glad of the success of your Town-Hall party.[17] You might have added a word or two from Dr Farnsworth's letter,[18] since it was to be sent away. Did it need any answer from me? I have nothing to tell you or to send you for a few days yet. But make me sure that Mr Reed's letters [19] reached their mark. R W E

TO ELLEN EMERSON, DETROIT, JANUARY 22, 1867 [20]

Russell House
Detroit
22 Jan

Dear Ellen

Here on the way from Saginaw [21] to Battle Creek [22] I acknowledge a good letter & its enclosures of Gov Kent's & Dr Farnsworth's, Charles's & Mr Cary's; & Reed's.[23] All welcome & chiefly greeted the arrival of his Papa & Mamma with Scrap.[24] I have not yet sent the original etching his surprised head to Harpers Weekly. I send you David Preston & Co's draft on Importers' & Traders' National Bank

14. *The Pontiac Gazette*, Jan. 11, 1867, announced " Courage " for the Students' Lecture Association on the 21st of that month, but the same paper for Jan. 18 explained that an elocutionist had been substituted for Emerson.

15. See the letters of Jan. 12 and 13, 1867.

16. Letter of Jan. *c.* 16? 1867.

17. *Cf.* other letters of this month.

18. Doubtless from Dr. Ralph Farnsworth, who, like Reed, was a classmate of Emerson. I conjecture that the correspondence with these persons concerned the Harvard memorial mentioned in earlier letters.

19. *Cf.* Jan. 12, 1867.

20. MS owned by RWEMA; ph. in CUL. The year is clearly 1867.

21. Ellen Emerson, Jan. 25, 1867, acknowledged her father's " Detroit letter " with it hundred dollars and observed that he did go to " E. Saginaw " after all. In the MS memorandum book for this year East Saginaw has been shifted from the 18th to the 21st of January.

22. Battle Creek was down for Jan. 23 (see the letter of Jan. 12, 1867) . It appears so in the MS memorandum book but has been canceled there.

23. For Farnsworth and Reed, see Jan. 18, 1867. Charles is doubtless Charles Emerson. A letter of Feb. 17 following is to Edward Cary.

24. This and the following imperfect sentence are not entirely clear but seem to relate to a picture or pictures of W. H. and Edith Emerson Forbes and young Ralph Emerson Forbes, who was apparently the " Scrap " referred to.

N. Y.[25] for a hundred dollars. My gains have not been rapid, as my secretary [26] has scattered the lectures thinly, only two in the last week — & whilst he assesses each Lyceum 75. I had answered the early letters of the committees usually naming 50.[27] When I arrive, they all put the question " Under which King, Bezonian? " [28] & show me my carefully saved letter. Of course I must honor my own signature. John Clahan should be paid at once to the 20ᵗʰ $35., & add $5.00, telling him that I gave him no new year's present, & this therefore can go to diminish his increased rent. From Chicago,[29] perhaps, I can send you 100. more. I hope by this time Mr Abraham Jackson has sent in his account & his rents which will make you easy for the time. Remember Augustus Adams, — & B. Hastings ($30. I think still due Mr G. M. Brooks for him) and Jabez Reynolds meat bill. And as soon as we get through the imperative bills, Jordan, Marsh, & Co. &c it will be time to think of some notes which Mr Cheney holds at the Bank against me, not however due till about 10. Feb.ʸ Before this time, you have had Edith's visit out, & another sociable, & one more comes tonight.

R. W. E.

To Edward? Waldo? Emerson, Chicago, January 24, 1867

[Acknowledged in Edward's letter of Feb. 2, 1867, and described as " with your programme " of lecture appointments to Feb. 14; also referred to by place and date in two other family letters of February of this year. Ellen may have been the person addressed (cf. Feb. 15, 1867) .]

To Ellen Emerson, Faribault, Minnesota, January 31, 1867 [30]

Faribault Minn
Jan 31 1867

Dear Ellen,

I am sorry to have left you so long without knowledge of my route So I miss all my letters that should have preceded me here. Nor

25. D. Preston & Co., bankers, duly appear in *Charles F. Clark's Annual City Directory . . . of the City of Detroit,* 1867; and the Importers' & Traders' is listed as a national bank in *Trow's New York City Directory* published the same year.

26. Several letters refer to Edwin Lee Brown as the manager of Emerson's Western tour of this winter. *Cf.* especially the second letter of Feb. 12, 1867.

27. This seems to refer to a number of letters I have not seen.

28. From Shakespeare's *II Henry IV,* V, iii.

29. *The Chicago Times,* Jan. 25, 1867, reports the reading of " The Man of the World " at the Unity Church on the 24th. According to this account, Robert Collyer, pastor of the church, announced that Emerson would return on Mar. 4 to deliver his lecture on " Eloquence."

30. MS owned by RWEMA; ph. in CUL. Hubert H. Hoeltje, " Ralph Waldo

have I had opportunity to send you any notes for many days. But I am in a good new country with plenty of robust people who take kind care of me & my visit to Madison [31] to LaCrosse,[32] to Winona where I drank tea with Mr Loring [33] & Sue & after lecture spent another hour with them & their friends had these & other alleviations. Still it is a little pathetic to see this affectionate gentle Susie L. born to be delicate & petted removed into this rough yeomanly lair of the Giants. I shall try to write you a little more at leisure, for I have been three times interrupted in this note & perhaps tell you my adventures I send you a draft for $280. on Plumer & Co 173 State St. Boston & hope to send you more soon & when you have paid your pressing debts, begin to pay notes at Concord Bk. R. W. Emerson

To ELLEN EMERSON, ST. PAUL, FEBRUARY 1; MINNEAPOLIS, FEBRUARY 3; AND FOND DU LAC, WISCONSIN, FEBRUARY 6, 1867 [34]

St Paul, 1 Feb. 1867

Dear Ellen,

At Faribault, I found Ingersoll Wyer,[35] son of my cousin Hannah Ladd

---

Emerson in Minnesota," *Minnesota History*, XI, 145–159, gives the schedule of Emerson's only lecture tour in this state as recorded in local papers: Jan. 30, 1867, Winona, " The Man of the World "; Jan. 31, Faribault, " American Culture "; Feb. 1, St. Paul, " The Man of the World "; Feb. 2 and 3, Minneapolis (no subjects noted). These dates and places correspond, except for Feb. 3, with those in the MS memorandum book for this year, where, however, the title for the 31st is " Social Aims," and for the 2d, " Man of the World." Emerson leaves Feb. 3, Sunday, unrecorded.

31. On Jan. 26 Emerson read " Society " before the Madison Institute and on Sunday, the 27th, he delivered a discourse on " Immortality of the Soul " at the Unitarian Church. No public notice of his appearance at the church had been given, and few people were aware that he was expected there; but the lecture of Saturday drew, it was said, the best audience, and was the best lecture, of the season. On the following Monday, Emerson visited the Capitol, the State Historical Society, and the University, and left at noon for La Crosse. (*Wisconsin State Journal*, Madison, Jan. 28, 1867.)

32. In the MS memorandum book for this year La Crosse has both Jan. 28 and 29 (" Social Aims "), but the earlier date is canceled. Miss Lilly M. E. Borresen informs me that the *La Crosse Daily Democrat*, Jan. 26 and 29, 1867, announced Emerson for both the 28th and 29th; " Society in America " was the subject for the latter date. The same paper for Jan. 24 had warned the citizens against Emerson as a freethinker.

33. For David Loring, formerly of Concord, see a note on July 28, 1837.

34. MS owned by RWEMA; ph. in CUL. For the lectures in Minnesota, see a note on Jan. 31, 1867.

35. For the members of the Wyer family, see especially a note on the letter of *c.* 1824. *Cf.* also Mar. 18, 1859.

Wyer, who introduced me to his sister Sarah, a fine girl, who almost restored her mother's youth to me. They had come over from Northfield,
where they live, to invite me to come & see them on my way next day to
St Paul. I could not promise this, but they undertook to bring their
mother to the station at the hour when I should arrive there and she
actually came, as good & almost as handsome as in her youth. The elder
sister too, Elizabeth, who teaches drawing,[36] — for I found a scholar of
hers, a New York boy, with me in my car. I entreated the son & the
daughters to come to Concord without fail, when they go to Mass[tts]: —
they are as good as Cousin Charlotte. I should tell you also that I rode
with young Faribault, grandson of the founder of the town F.,[37] a little
way out of the village, to see a little village of eight Sioux *tepis,* (conical
tents)

Here in a wild piece of timber were the Aborigines The warriors,
they said, had been removed to Nebraska, or elsewhere, but the old
Chief Opie or Opequa, & his family occupied one, & old women & young
men & girls (& twice I mistook girls for young men) & their dogs, the
others.[38] Led by Faribault we lifted the skin curtain, & entered one &
another. Supper was all ready on a board on the ground in one, — the
family all asquat on the earth, not looking at it, what I took for young
men smoking their pipe. They said nothing, but looked cheerfully
enough at Faribault who spoke Indian to them. In one tent we heard
singing as we approached, but were silent on our entrance. I begged him
to ask them to sing again, & the two girls got their book, — Indian
psalms, — & sung very sweetly. I am sorry to say that the light was not
birch-bark nor pine-knot, but a kerosene lamp: but the fire in the middle of the tent was Monadnoc boughs. I inquired whether I could see
such another Indian picture between that spot & Boston, & was assured
I could not.

36. *Cf.* the letter of Mar. 31, 1870.

37. Jean Baptiste Faribault, the noted French-Canadian fur trader, had died in
1860; his son, Alexander, who lived till 1882, was the founder of the town (*Collections
of the Minnesota Historical Society,* III, 168–179, and XIV, 216).

38. Such of the Sautel Sioux as could be rounded up had been transferred from
Minnesota to Dakota and later — in 1866 — to Nebraska (*Report on Indian Affairs,*
1868, pp. 264 ff.). In June of 1865 a special commissioner had written from the town
of Faribault that Alexander Faribault had donated the use of some thirty acres for
that season and that there were then " twelve families of these Indians here, com-
prising sixty-five souls . . . living in tents on the land of Mr. Faribault " (*Report
of the Commissioner of Indian Affairs,* 1866, p. 235). A Sioux chieftain Taopi, described as civilized and as distinguished by his friendship for the white men, is
recommended (*ibid.,* pp. 236 and 238) for a reward, but I am uncertain whether
this was Emerson's " Opie."

Old Faribault was a French trader here & married an Indian wife, his son too married an Indian wife so that young Faribault my guide is three quarters Indian But he was educated in Montreal & was as handsome & as accurately dressed & did the honors as gracefully with his fine horses & cutter as any youth from New York could be or do.

Minneapolis Feb. 3.

I went to Winona & drank tea with Mr Loring & Susan, but I remember that I have told you this.[39] From F. then to St Paul, proud new thriving town 12 to 15000 people with a great many handsome buildings many fine houses the capital of the state was introduced to Governor Marshall who carried me into the Senate Chamber & House & I listened a short time to the debates. The Governor a Swedenborgian, &, tell Mamma we discussed the Baron.[40] Thence to Minneapolis a town of greatest promise in all the Northwest; said to be of admirable climate, — all Mayday while I was there, — the Falls of St Anthony being the waterpower, & all behind & around it a land of wheat & lumber. If Edward wishes to come out west, let him come here. It is the house, St Paul being only the front door. I came in the train with C. C Washburn,[41] Member of Congress from Wisconsin, & dined with his brother W. D. Washburn, on Sunday. They two are the principal owners & workers of the waterpower. At my hotel my cousin Phebe Chamberlin sent her son to me to invite me to come & see her, which I did on Sunday morning, & saw the whole family.[42] Mr C. carried me to his house. I had a pleasant visit Mrs C is Mrs S. M. Haskins's sister. Cousin Phebe I had not seen for 30 years, & we talked over Hannah & Charlotte & I did not fail to tell her what kind memories Lois C. had left with us.

R. W. Emerson

6 Feb. Fond du Lac. I have just received your letter of 28 Jan^y & all its contents. It was excellent, — your Sunday School meeting — which I

39. In Jan. 31, 1867.

40. The famous scientist and religious teacher took the name Swedenborg on his elevation to the peerage.

41. This builder of a flour mill at Minneapolis was more than once a member of Congress and later became governor of Wisconsin. His brother, with whom Emerson dined, was likewise both industrial promoter and politician; many years later he reached the United States Senate.

42. Emerson's cousin Phebe Ripley Haskins, daughter of his paternal aunt Rebecca Emerson and his maternal uncle Robert Haskins, had married John Chamberlain. The Mr. and Mrs. "C." mentioned were, I conjecture, Phebe Chamberlain's son and daughter-in-law. Samuel Moody Haskins was a brother of Phebe Chamberlain, Hannah Haskins Parsons, and Charlotte Haskins Cleveland. I do not know whether "Lois C." was a Chamberlain or Cleveland, but the name was common in the Cleveland family.

must read again, — & all your news interesting. I was puzzled for a time about the two Edith's in E. F. E.'s [43] letter. Cousin Abraham's lapse of memory was a stroke of humor.[44] I have sent you a letter [45] this morn by mail.

To ELLEN EMERSON, FOND DU LAC, WISCONSIN, FEBRUARY 5, 1867 [46]

> Fond du Lac
> Wis.
> 5 Feb.ʸ 1867

Dear Ellen

I sent you from Faribault a draft for $180 [47] which I hope arrived safely. I enclose now one drawn by the " First National Bank " of Minnesota, on Ninth National Bk., New York, for $160.00

Thanks for your letters, which have reached me now in two parcels through Mr Wiley who plainly delights in playing the part of good angel to me. You should not come quite to the ground, when money does not arrive quite in time; but should ask Mr Cheney to let you draw for a few days, giving him your note; — that is, when you know that the money is on its way. But I think Abraham Jackson must have brought you money before this time.[48] I shall send more soon, & as quickly as you can you must pay Mr Cheney amounts convenient to you on my notes. R. W. Emerson

The Babe's [49] letter was lovely, or the Babe is, & the Babe's mother that sent it. The letters have no word of Edwards eyes.? Keep me along with the history of the Town Hall sociables,[50] & with Aunt Elizabeth's Hours of Homer.[51]

43. Just possibly a slip for E. E. F. — Edith Emerson Forbes. The second Edith was doubtless Edith Davidson, the child whom Ellen Emerson called her daughter. See a note on Nov. 25, 1865.

44. Abraham Jackson appears in many letters in connection with Emerson's business affairs, which he handled badly for many years and, at times, dishonestly (cf. the letters of Aug. 3, 11, and 16, 1869).

45. Presumably the letter of Feb. 5, 1867.

46. MS owned by RWEMA; ph. in CUL. The MS memorandum book for 1867 gives Feb. 6 to Fond du Lac (" Social Aims ").

47. Inclosed in Jan. 31, 1867, where the sum is given as $280; the larger sum is also named in the first letter of Feb. 12, 1867.

48. Cf. a note on the letter of Feb. 1, 3, and 6, 1867.

49. Ralph Emerson Forbes.

50. Earlier letters of this year mention the " sociables " sponsored by Ellen Emerson.

51. Edward Waldo Emerson, Jan. 30, 1867, told of going every week with Ellen to " Aunt Lizzy's " (Elizabeth Hoar's) for a reading in the Odyssey.

To Edwin Lee Brown, Fond du Lac? Wisconsin? February? *c.* 5? 1867

[See the note on Feb.? *c.* 13? following. Both place and date are highly conjectural.]

To Benjamin B. Wiley, Fond du Lac, Wisconsin, February 6, 1867 [52]

Lewis Hotel.
Fond du Lac. Wis.
6 February 1867

My dear Wiley,

       I have thanked you heartily many times, if silently, for so many good offices, & still more for the silent goodwill which inspired them. Thanks again lately for cheering my journey with these letters forwarded duly & arriving surely.

[I]Such a citizen of the world as you are should look once at these northern towns which perhaps I have seen under the perhaps too smiling face of the mildest best winter weather, which[I] is perhaps [II]exceptional though the people almost to a man extol their climate. Minneapolis would strongly attract me, if I were a young man, — more than St. Paul, — & this town is a wonderful growth & shines like a dream, seen this morn, from the top of Amory Hall.[II] I am glad you like Anquetil Du Perron, & I transcribe my translation of his letter. From Concord I can send you the original.[53] But I have to bracket, in reading one clause. Continue to befriend me prays

Yours. R. W. Emerson —

To Benjamin B. Wiley, Fond du Lac, Wisconsin, February 6, 1867 [54]

Fond du Lac.
6 Feb. 1867.

My dear Sir

       I wrote this morning, & now it occurs that Ellen Emerson has

52. MS owned by RWEMA; ph. in CUL. This is a copy, not in Emerson's hand. Presumably it is the MS actually sent that is listed and partly quoted in John Heise Autographs, catalogue 2463. Excerpts I–II are in *Memoirs of Members of the Social Circle in Concord*, 2d series, 2d part, p. 181 (same page in *Emerson in Concord*).

53. The catalogue cited above lists, with this letter, the four pages of the MS translation mentioned, "incorporating," according to the description, "the full preface of Anquetil Duperron." For Emerson's early readings in this French Orientalist, see Christy, p. 302.

54. MS owned by RWEMA; ph. in CUL. This is a copy and is not in Emerson's hand.

by some miscarriage never received my programme *after* Chicago, & so still sends to your care. Mr. Brown [55] sent me while at home only the list as far as C.; so that Ellen had no guide beyond, except your name, which she knew was a sure card. I sent her, when I remembered this, the new list I had received,[56] which the snow blockade may have detained. I shall send her a new one, in spite of the pleasure which I know it gives you to help unskilful travellers. Only I hope you will keep account of the double & treble postages you will have to bear. Perhaps only, Rev. Mr. Brooks of Hamilton College, at Madison N. Y.[57] is I learn from Mrs. Carr at Wisconsin University, Madison Wis.[58] the second Thoreau, who, she thinks is fit to edit the " Field Notes " of the first. Him I have not yet seen.

Yours R. W. Emerson.

To Ellen Emerson, Lacon, Illinois, February 12, 1867 [59]

Lacon Ill.
Feb 12 1867

Dear Ellen,

Last night a welcome letter from you at Milton & at Janesville [60] the day before a pacquet from Mother Edward & you. But I am uneasy that you had not heard from me nor yet on 4th Feb. I have only time at this instant — my bearer just going to the village, — to say that I sent you from Faribault, 31 Jan. a letter containing a draft for $280. to my best belief; then I think from Minneapolis 4th or 5th letter [61] & draft for 160. & yesterday from Chicago draft for 300. & no letter.[62] If these have not arrived write at once to me & I will write to the drawers of the missing drafts. Lovely letters came & I will answer presently to-day to some points

R. W. Emerson

55. *Cf.* especially the second letter of Feb. 12 following.

56. It is not clear whether this was sent in some letter I have not found.

57. The information about Brooks is confused and I have not identified him. At any rate he did not edit Thoreau's journals.

58. Ezra Carr was at this time professor of chemistry and natural history (*Catalogue of the University of Wisconsin,* 1867). He and his wife turn up later in California (see May 20 and 22, 1871).

59. MS owned by RWEMA; ph. in CUL. According to the MS memorandum book for this year, " The Man of the World " was the subject at Lacon on Feb. 11.

60. Emerson read " The Man of the World " before the Y. M. A. on Feb. 9; and on Sunday, the 10th, he spoke at All Souls Church on the immortality of the soul (*The Janesville Gazette,* Feb. 11, 1867).

61. Dated from Fond du Lac, Wis., Feb. 5, 1867.

62. *Cf.* Feb. 13, 1867.

To Ellen Emerson, Lacon, Illinois, February 12, 1867 [63]

[64] Tis excellent to have Edward at home, & I wish he may stay there as long as he can. I lose the best opportunity now that he has no eyes [65] of inflicting on him never so many old darling passages of Bacon Burke & Milton & other Olympians. Here is an errand for him which I have many times forgot to set down. Rev. Samuel Johnson [66] of Lynn was to leave at the Office of the " Radical," Bromfield St. Boston a book I lent Mr S. Dr Roer's Translation of one of the Upanishads. Tis a book I value highly, one of Henry Thoreau's bequests,[67] & I fear it has been lying months, at some risk. It is at an up-stairs book-store. I wrote you a letter this morning giving you a list of the drafts I have sent. and if they have not arrived, — since Detroit, — one from Faribault; one from St Pauls mailed at Fond du Lac; one from Chicago, you are to send me quickest word. Since 1 Feb. there is a little money due me from Mad-River-bond, but, as I hope you have my letters before this, it does not seem worth while to send an attorney-power for this. Your Mother asks if Mrs Brown can borrow money at the Bank, &c. I suppose not easily If she only needs a little you must advance it, if you can. I wish you would find on some page in the " Journal " a list of payments from which you deduced not long since the amount of balance I owed her; & then find the payments since recorded, which may show that we are still in her debt. It does not yet appear how soon I can come home. I

63. MS owned by RWEMA; ph. in CUL. The date is fixed by comparison with the letter of the same morning here referred to and by evidence cited below.

64. At the top of the portion of the MS now owned by RWEMA is this note, which seems to be in Ellen Emerson's hand: " Gave A B J. the first sheet of this letter." " A B J." was undoubtedly Ellen's cousin Alice Bridge Jackson (cf. notes on Aug. 19, 1853, and Feb. 17, 1867, to Lidian Emerson) , and the sheet given to her must have contained Emerson's comment on her engagement to Lieut. Arthur, for Ellen wrote, Lexington, Mass., Feb. 18, and Concord, Feb. 19, 1867, in acknowledging his " second letter from Lacon," that she was glad he did like Arthur and that she would show the letter to Alice.

65. Edward's difficulty with his eyes is mentioned in several letters of this winter.

66. For Johnson as a contributor to The Radical, see June 19, 1867? He was at this time and for many years pastor of an independent church at Lynn, Mass., and he was to gain some note as a writer on Oriental religions. Presumably " Mr S." is an error for " Mr J."

67. The copy of Bibliotheca Indica, XV, a translation by Dr. E. Roër, Calcutta, 1853, still in the Emerson library at the Antiquarian House bears the inscriptions: " Henry D. Thoreau from Thomas Cholmondeley " and " R. W. Emerson from Henry D. Thoreau." Cf. Journals, IX, 419–420. Ellen Emerson wrote, Feb. 18 and 19, that if she had time in Boston she would get the Upanishad.

have not yet received the last items of my programme from Mr Brown.[68]
I hope to crowd them up.

R. W. Emerson

[69] Your letter of the Sunday School meeting was charming & did high
honor to all parties. What a true humanity the Judge [70] hides under his
every-day-coat of common sense & criticism! He is Elizabeth Hoar's
brother. You do not get so far as to tell me whether Aunt Elizabeth ac-
ceded to the wish that she should take part in the school.

My conditions are so unfavorable for writing that Mamma & Edward
& Edith & even Ralph, whose letter [71] adorns my file, must forgive me
that I send only bulletins through you in acknowledgment of all these
good letters I have at Janesville [72] & here.

To Ellen Emerson, Washington, Iowa, February 13, 1867 [73]

Washington Iowa

13 Feb.

Dear Ellen,

I hoped for a letter in Peoria [74] to say that you had at last
received my letters & drafts, after my Detroit one: but Mr Coy had none
for me I directed Mr Coy to send you a draft to your order for $75.

---

68. Brown's initials are given in Feb. 24 following. Edwin Lee Brown appears
in *Halpin's . . . Chicago City Directory*, 1865, as a member of Brown Brothers &
Adams Machine Graining Co. He is referred to in several earlier letters of 1866–1867
as Emerson's Western manager. G. L. Torbert, corresponding secretary of the Associated Western Literary Societies, writing from Dubuque, Ia., June 23, 1867, mentioned him as an unfriendly rival. Torbert won the duel, and Brown himself wrote,
Chicago, Sept. 19, 1867, that he was closing his bureau and handing over all his
data on lecture courses to Torbert. *Cf.* a note on Nov. 13, 1867.

69. What follows is on a separate sheet dated, perhaps by Ellen, Feb. 12, 1867.
It is possible that it belongs to the first letter of this date.

70. Ebenezer Rockwood Hoar.

71. *Cf.* Feb. 5, 1867.

72. *Cf.* the first letter of this date.

73. MS owned by RWEMA; ph. in CUL. For the lectures at Washington, Ia.,
and other towns in that state mentioned below, see Hubert H. Hoeltje's account in
The Iowa Journal of History and Politics, XXV, 248–261. The lecture at Washington
is there set down for Feb. 14 and the dates for the other towns are the same Emerson
gives.

74. According to the *Peoria Daily Transcript*, Feb. 5 and 13, 1867, Emerson read
" The Daily Life of American Society " before the Library Association on Feb. 12.
After being introduced by E. W. Coy, he began with some remarks about his travels
in Illinois, about the growth of the West, and about Chicago in particular. His
lecture won great applause.

which I trust you will receive in a day or two after that which Mr Drake of the Tremont House Chicago was to forward to you for 300.[75]

Yesterday I wrote you from Lacon, I believe, two letters And this scrap goes only by way of certificate or rather duplicate of these certificates of life & health. We have made in this country a sudden transition from snow to mud: The brooks are grown to rivers, & threaten the integrity of bridges & roads. I cannot give you yet exact note of my remaining lectures, as Mr Brown is to try to crowd them up: but Chicago, 4 March,[76] is a sure date, & St Louis 6th [77]

Keokuk Iowa 28 Feb

Des Moines Ia 1 March

Independence Ia 19 Feb

Cedar Falls, Ia.\ 20 Feb

Quincy Ill. 26 Feb.[78]

Bloomington, Ill. 5 March [79]

When Edward can carry $3. (I believe it is) to Mr Rhoades (Bent & Bush) [80] for my soft hat, he must do so I was heartily glad of his writing except for the thought of eyes. R. W. Emerson

To EDWIN LEE BROWN, WASHINGTON? IOWA? FEBRUARY? c. 13? 1867

[Referred to in Feb. 17 following to Lidian Emerson as " my last note." This reference implies an earlier but probably recent letter to Brown, which I have

75. Cf. the first letter of Feb. 12, 1867. John B. Drake belonged to the firm of Gage & Drake, owners of the Tremont House (cf. Halpin's . . . Chicago City Directory, 1865, and the letter of Feb. 15, 1867).

76. The Chicago Tribune, Mar. 5, 1867, has a brief report of " Eloquence," read on the 4th under the auspices of the Unity Church Fraternity. Robert Collyer, pastor of Unity Church, introduced Emerson, who, he said, desired that the lecture be reported only briefly if at all and that the anecdotes and personal allusions should be omitted. According to the MS Autobiography this lecture was new, though the title was old.

77. The Daily Missouri Democrat, Mar. 6, 1867, announced that Emerson would lecture on " American Culture" that night in the Public School Library course. Cf. the letter of Mar. 6? 1867; and for the lecture on " Inspiration " before the Philosophical Society, see a note on Apr. 4 following to James.

78. Miss Helen B. Osborn informs me that the Quincy Herald of Feb. 28, 1867, commented on the lecture of the 26th (" The Man of the World ") under the caption " Another Bore."

79. The same lecture given at Quincy was repeated at Bloomington before the Ladies' Library Association on Mar. 5; and The Daily Pantagraph, of the latter town, printed in its issue of Mar. 8, 1867, an attempt at satire on " Ralph Cold-Dough Simmerson " by " Boswell."

80. The Boston Directory, 1867, lists Jacob Rhoades at the same address with Bent & Bush, dealers in hats, caps, and furs.

dated Feb.? *c. 5*? Doubtless there were still earlier letters to him, of which, however, I have no proof (*cf.* especially Dec. 28, 1866) .]

To WILLIAM HATHAWAY FORBES, DUBUQUE, IOWA,
FEBRUARY 15, 1867 [81]

Dubuque, Ia.
15 Feb^y '67

Dear Will,

I had today, in leaving Washington,[82] Ia. a letter from Ellen, announcing with natural enough uneasiness, that she has no letter from me since 24 January. Perhaps it is only because the snows have blocked the mails in the last weeks. But perhaps some of my letters are lost, &, as I have sent several drafts to her address, they should be looked after. May I then give you the trouble to look after one or two of them? At Faribault, Minnesota, I bought a draft for say, $280. of Mr J. W. Griggs, of the Banking House of W. H. Dike, & Co. drawn on a Mr Plumer of State Street Boston.[83] I cannot find my memorandum containing Mr Plumer's full name. But I understood Mr Griggs, who is Dike's partner & brother-in law, to say that he was a member of the Board of Trade. And I cannot doubt that it was all right. I spent a pleasant evening at Mr Griggs' house. It was to be paid to the order of Ellen T. Emerson, & I enclosed it in a letter to her, on the 31 January.[84] As I do not find my memorandum, it is possible, that it was $180. & not 280., but I believe it the larger amount. At St Paul, Minn. on the 2 Feby I bought a draft for $160. from First National Bank, Minnesota, (Thompson & Brothers) (payable to my own order,) on *Ninth National Bank New York.* I endorsed it, adding, *Pay to Ellen T. Emerson,* & enclosed that also in a letter to her, which I mailed either at St Paul, or more probably at Fond du Lac, Wisconsin, either on the 2^d or the 3^d February.[85] Now if you see how to make any inquiry after these two papers, it will be a great favor to us both, as I fear Ellen is very hungry for them. On the 11 Feb. I paid

81. MS owned by RWEMA; ph. in CUL.

82. For the lecture at Washington, Ia., see Feb. 13, 1867. I have no proof of a lecture at Dubuque.

83. Both John Williams Griggs and William Hammond Dike were New Englanders who had settled in Faribault some years earlier (*Collections of the Minnesota Historical Society,* XIV, 177 and 279) . Plumer (Avery) & Co. duly appear in *The Boston Directory,* 1866.

84. The letter, at least, arrived safely, as it is extant.

85. Actually in Feb. 5, 1867, dated from Fond du Lac.

Drake of Gage & Drake proprietors of Tremont House Chicago, $300.[86] to be sent to her order but I know not on what Bank drawn. Forgive me for giving you this trouble but I know not how to help myself so well. Affectionately,

W. H. Forbes.   R. W. Emerson.

To Ellen Emerson, Davenport, Iowa, February 16, 1867 [87]

> Davenport, Ia.
> Saturday, 16 Feb.
> 1867

Dear Ellen,

As my letter from Faribault, Minn., with a draft, was mailed 31 January, it does seem extraordinary that it should not have reached you by the 9 Feb.ʸ I had your letters addressed to Washington, Ia. yesterday. & sent a letter today to W. H. F. with particulars, begging to inquire of Mr Plumer in Boston on whom the order was drawn. I have been trying this morning to find Mr Holmes to give him particulars about his daughter,[88] but he lives out of town has no office in town & perhaps I shall not be able to find him as I must probably leave D. presently after dinner. Yet Mr Bennett [89] thinks perhaps he can carry me to him. If, as is possible, I shall find that I can safely stay here tomorrow, I shall go to his house. I have written you several letters & sent you four drafts; which you, it seems, have not received. They or some of them will doubtless arrive. Meantime, you must show this to Mr Cheney & borrow money of the Bank for your wants. I hope before this hour Mrs Ripley is out of danger.[90] I have your mother's & Edwards letters & Prang's.[91] I cannot send you an order for Mad River Bonds' interest about $57. because the coupons are locked up by my key at Mr Ward's office.

R. W. Emerson

To ————— Holmes, Davenport? Iowa? February 16? 1867

[Mentioned in Feb. 17, 1867, to Lidian Emerson. For the probable place and date, cf. Feb. 16.]

86. See the first letter of Feb. 12, 1867, and that of the following day.
87. MS owned by RWEMA; ph. in CUL.
88. Clara Holmes is mentioned in Feb. 24, 1867.
89. Possibly H. W. Bennett, "speaker" of the Associated Congress, a literary association (*Davenport City Directory*, 1866, p. 140). But I have no proof that Emerson lectured in Davenport at this time.
90. But she died a few months later (see the letters of July? 31? and Aug. 1, 1867).
91. See Feb. 18, 1867.

To Edward Cary, Port Byron, Illinois, February 17, 1867 [92]

Port Byron, Ill.
17 February, 1867

Dear Sir,

I fear I have behaved very badly touching the kind propositions of Mr Powell [93] & yourself. It has chanced I think that two letters
on the matter of lectures came to me when I was so entirely unable to
give any definite answer, that I postponed all answer; and that is a dangerous neglect for a traveller, whose correspondence brings him every
day new conundrums. I suppose that the practical negative has settled
itself already, at all events it has become pretty clear to me that I shall
not be able to go to Brooklyn in March which I think was the last proposition. I designed to end my Western tour with February, but my agent
has so committed me to engagements in March that I am much embar-
rassed how to combine them with some imperative duties at home. I am
sorry, as it would on many accounts have been very agreeable to me to
have come to you. Hoping your forgiveness, I remain Yours,

R. W. Emerson

Edward Cary, Esq.
    Brooklyn, N. Y.

To Lidian Emerson, Port Byron, Illinois, February 17, 1867 [94]

Port Byron, Ill.
17 February

Dear Lidian,

Be sure the letter came, with its pleasant tidings of Alice
Jackson,[95] & its mixed narrative of the Boston visit, & was duly noted &
honored. I knew you would not look for any letter from me, who can

92. MS owned by Mr. Owen D. Young; ph. in CUL. The person addressed was
doubtless Edward Cary, well known as the editor of *The Brooklyn Union.*

93. Probably Aaron M. Powell, who presided at a lecture delivered by Elizabeth
Cady Stanton on the 19th of this month in the Brooklyn Fraternity series (*The
Brooklyn Union,* Feb. 20, 1867) . *Cf.* Nov. 19, 1865, to him.

94. MS owned by RWEMA; ph. in CUL. The year is clear from the evidence
noted below.

95. Lidian Emerson had written, Feb. 1, 1867, that her brother Charles Jackson's
oldest daughter was to be married to Lieut. Arthur of the army, and Ellen had
written the news in her letter of the same date. Emerson had sent his own comments to Ellen, in the second letter of Feb. 12, 1867. Later Alice Bridge Jackson appears as the wife of William Arthur, a lieutenant (*cf.* July 23, 1868) . According to
the *Genealogy of the John Bridge Family,* p. 323, the wedding occurred June 6, 1867.

best crowd the little I like to write into Ellen's address. Here I have been to church stranded for the day on the shore of the Missisippee River — to go up, perhaps tonight, to Dubuque & Independence Ia.[96] I see across the river the town of Leclaire, & the river rose yesterday 14 inches in 24 hours, & rises still, though last night was colder, but the ice yet does not run. It does not yet appear when I can come home, as Mr Brown's [97] reply to my last note has not come It is a grief to me to lose Edwards presence at home this winter as the chances are against its being repeated soon. And yet, why not? if the plantation at Quincy [98] prospers, the next winter he should be nearly as much at leisure as this, & I invite him to stay with me — I who do not mean to travel westward again. Tell Ellen that finding it impossible to see Mrs Holmes I wrote her a note giving the substance of her information about her daughter,[99] &, whilst confiding it to the landlord of the hotel, a gentleman informed me, that Mr & Mrs Holmes had gone to Boston in the morning, *yesterday,* on news of their daughter's illness. My letter however will go to their house & be opened. I hope before now you have a heap of letters from me, long held back by the snow. If still they do not come, better Edward telegraph to me that fact,, say, at Burlington,[100] where I shall no doubt be one day about 23, 24, or 25.th

And so I remain Yours —

R. W. Emerson

To Louis Prang, Freeport, Illinois, February 18, 1867

[Printed in the *Boston Daily Advertiser,* Nov. 23, 1867, second page of supplement. This repeats, presumably, at least part of the contents of the letter of Jan.? 1? 1867? thanking Prang for a parcel of colored prints and is one of twenty-seven letters to him which are printed together in an advertisement headed " Chromo-Lithography. Letters from Poets, Painters, Authors and Journalists." These letters range in date from Dec., 1866, to Nov., 1867, and show that Prang was surprisingly successful in collecting testimonials from

96. He was to lecture at Independence two days later (see Feb. 13, 1867) .

97. See a note on the second letter of Feb. 12, 1867; and *cf.* Feb.? *c.* 13?

98. An autobiographical outline shows, Mr. Raymond Emerson informs me, that during a period of doubtful health in 1867–1870, his father was employed in a vineyard owned by W. H. Forbes. The story of the vineyard is preserved in family tradition, and the hill it occupied at Quincy, Mass., is still known as Forbes Hill. Several contemporary letters relate to the early stages of the enterprise. Edward himself had written his father on Jan. 30, 1867, from Concord and on Feb. 3 from Milton of the preparations he and his brother-in-law were making.

99. *Cf.* Feb. 24, 1867.

100. So far as I know, Emerson did not expect to lecture in Burlington, Ia.

noted persons. There are letters here from John G. Whittier, James Parton, Wendell Phillips, Harriet Beecher Stowe, John Neal, Bayard Taylor, Henry Wadsworth Longfellow, George William Curtis, Edward Everett Hale, Edmund Clarence Stedman, Thomas Wentworth Higginson, Thomas Bailey Aldrich, Louisa M. Alcott, William Dean Howells, and others. The Silesian immigrant had become a great man among lithographers and publishers.]

To Ellen Emerson, Chicago, February 23, 1867 [101]

>Tremont House
>Chicago 23 Feb^y
>1867

Dear Ellen,

I have today the two happy parcels of letters from Edward & you bringing Ediths & Carlyle's.[102] I can only acknowledge them now, & enclose a draft on the " Nat. Hide & Leather Bank," [103] Boston, for $240. &, if time serves, this eve or tomorrow may write a few lines to you all blessed ones.

>R. W. Emerson

To Ellen Emerson, Chicago, February 24, 1867 [104]

>Tremont House
>Chicago
>24 Feb

Dear Ellen,

I cannot find any escape, — after talking again with this most deserving of agents, Mr E. L. Brown,[105] — from his elongated programme reaching to 19 March, which I enclose. It is very awkward, as my Poems are promised for 1 April,[106] that I should be eleven hundred miles & more from the printers, & with so many *errata* that I am bound to correct. I shall have to pray Mr Fields [107] to postpone a little, now that he has postponed so much. For often as I have looked never so wishfully at the *proofs,* which I carry in my trunk, the capricious Muse invariably

101. MS owned by RWEMA; ph. in CUL.

102. Probably his letter of Jan. 27, 1867, in *C–E Corr.*

103. This bank is duly listed in *The Boston Directory,* 1867.

104. MS owned by RWEMA; ph. in CUL. Evidence cited below fixes the year.

105. See a note on the second letter of Feb. 12, 1867.

106. The volume was actually published on the 29th of that month (see a note on May 10, 1867) .

107. See Mar. 6, 1867.

replies, " Not at home: no Sir, I do not live on railway wheels: Snatch your dinner, but not me."

Interrupted, have no time to write. Heard today an excellent sermon from Mr Collyer.[108] Drank tea tonight with Mr Arnold late a member of Congress, who has written the Life of Lincoln [109] & has a very agreeable family. The young Fays came to see me today & give a good account of themselves. And I answer none of your treasured letters, Edith, & Edward, & Ellen, but want the remainder of Ellen's story of the " Sociable " & of Clara Holmes whom you left sick.[110] R. W. Emerson

I wrote yesterday, & enclosed a draft on Hide & Leather Bk. Boston.

To Seneca M. Dorr, Chicago, February 25, 1867 [111]

Tremont House
Chicago, 25 Feb.ʸ 1867

My dear Sir,

Your letter, dated I think weeks ago, was forwarded to me by my son from Concord, but shared more than the delays by the snow-storms on account of my own erratic tour; &, though I had it some days ago, I have not been until now in condition to bring up the arrears of my correspondence. Neither is it a letter quite easy to answer. The book-sellers appear to have made up their minds to refuse to print all new poetry except at the sole risk of the author. I have not been able to induce my friend Mr Fields to insert in the " Atlantic " some poems intrusted to me by several writers, each of which poems I read with pleasure, & thought better than poems which are printed there. And last summer, I sent him MS volume from a new poet in New York [112] which I thought to have extraordinary claims, — but which he did not hesitate to decline. I have not fared much better with my own private venture. At his own instance long ago, I began in the autumn to collect my own scattered verses not hitherto published in a book, & added of quite unpublished verses about half the volume & when it was all in type about

108. Robert Collyer appears in various earlier letters and notes.

109. Isaac Newton Arnold was elected to Congress in 1860. He wrote *The History of Abraham Lincoln, and the Overthrow of Slavery,* 1866.

110. During Feb. 9–19 Ellen Emerson wrote her father three letters telling of her visits to Clara Holmes, ill at Lexington, Mass.

111. MS owned by the Abernethy Library, Middlebury College; ph. in CUL. For Julia Caroline Ripley Dorr, Seneca M. Dorr's wife, and for Emerson's interest in her poetry, see Oct. 14, 1865.

112. I conjecture that this was the MS mentioned in Aug. 21, 1866.

the 1 December. he said he was sorry but it would be madness to print it for New Year's for all his western correspondents had written to him, " Send us no new book, least of all poetry." So it was put aside, with the chance of better times in April.[113] I have quite ceased therefore to recommend to him any new adventure in this kind. And he is the only publisher with whom I have any particular acquaintance, — I may almost say, any acquaintance at all. But he, like other booksellers, may easily mistake. In fact they were all agreeably surprised by the large & facile sale that all the new books, including poetry, found last Christmas: It was quite as large as in former years. In these circumstances, I know not what to advise. In regard to the terms to be made, I have a very limited experience. Phillips & Sampson published for me, for many years. In each instance, I paid for the printing, & owned the stereotype plates. They took all the books, &, on the issuing of each edition of any book, that is, in advance, paid me 20 per cent on the retail price of all they printed. Of course, they issued, after the first edition, small editions, say 250 copies, or only so many copies as they judged would easily sell.

Ticknor & Fields, after the dissolution of Phillips & Co, took my books [114] on the same contract. Where the author does not choose to own his plates, they pay a less rate; in the case of Mr Thoreau's books,[115] they pay I think 12 per cent, more often 10.

I beg you to say to Mrs Dorr, with my affectionate regards, that I think she will yet sympathize with me in a kind of surly pleasure that I find in these resistances which it is good practice to overcome & establish our right to find our predestined readers in spite of the bookseller.

With great regard

S. M. Dorr, Esq   R W Emerson

P. S. I add a few lines which I might say to a publisher.

I have read with much interest a number of Mrs Dorr's Poems. They are written with an elegance which shows much practice & easy command of lyric metres & expression; but much more than that, with great tenderness & humanity. It is long since I have seen them, but a poem, which, I think, was entitled " Outgrown," [116] was a favorable example of her truth to life & living characters. And I think all the pieces I read

113. *Cf.* Feb. 24, 1867.

114. *Cf.* letters of Oct., 1859.

115. *Cf.* the letters of Sept. 7 and Oct. 19, 1863, to Fields.

116. For the publication of this poem and for Emerson's preference for it, see Mar. 6, 1872.

had the warmth & vivacity which belong to poems growing out of the writer's personal observation & experience, — a merit which good readers are sure to appreciate.

R. W. Emerson

Concord [117] 1867

To Ellen? Emerson, Chicago, March 3, 1867

[Printed, according to Hoeltje, in *The Burlington Gazette,* Nov. 9, 1907; partly reprinted in *Annals of Iowa,* 3d series, VIII, 372–373 (Apr., 1908), in what seems to be a very corrupt text, and, again, much more fully, by Hoeltje in *The Iowa Journal of History and Politics,* XXV, 261–262 (Apr., 1927). This letter, telling of a visit to the home of Charles Elliott Perkins, also mentions a telegram Emerson wished to send to Perkins from Chicago on Mar. 3 but could not send at that time and may not have written. Ellen Emerson, Mar. 8 and 9, 1867, acknowledged her father's "Burlington letter" and told of her brother's great satisfaction in reading the good opinion of the Perkins family. For Edward's stay with the Perkinses at Burlington, Ia., see letters of July 24 and Nov. 7, 1866.]

To James Thomas Fields, St. Louis, March 6, 1867

[MS listed in Anderson Galleries, May 3–4, 1926, where it is described as relating to corrections to be made in *May-day.* This is almost certainly the letter incompletely published in *Harper's,* LXVIII, 461 (Feb., 1884), and in Annie Fields, *Authors and Friends,* p. 83. Presumably it is also the same letter described in Thomas F. Madigan, 1927, as from St. Louis (date not given), about Emerson's "travels and engagements, and an urgent request for the finishing of a forthcoming book."]

To Ellen? Emerson, St. Louis, March 6? 1867

[Ellen Emerson, Mar. 11, 1867, says her father forgot to endorse the check for $100 which he sent from St. Louis. For the date, *cf.* the letters of Feb. 13 and Mar. 6, 1867.]

To Sidney Henry Morse, Lawrence? Kansas? March? 9? 1867

[Mentioned in Mar. 31, 1867; pretty clearly the letter inclosed in Mar. 9, 1867.]

To Edward Waldo Emerson, Lawrence, Kansas, March 9, 1867

[MS owned by Mr. Raymond Emerson. In spite of the February date line, the month was obviously March; and the MS memorandum book for 1867 gives Mar. 9 to Lawrence ("Man of the World"). Mr. Nyle H. Miller informs me

117. Presumably these "few lines which I might say to a publisher" were actually written at Chicago.

that the *Kansas Daily Tribune,* of Lawrence, Mar. 10, 1867, duly reports this lecture of the preceding day and also announces that Emerson is to speak at the Unitarian Church on the morning of the 10th.]

To James Thomas Fields, Concord, March 23, 1867?

[MS listed and partly quoted in Maggs Bros., Christmas, 1916, where no year is given; Emerson says he finds at the last moment that he cannot go to town this afternoon. If the postponed trip to town was in connection with the publication of some book of Emerson's, the year could have been almost any one from 1860 to 1870. On Mar. 23, 1867, Emerson had probably just reached home from the West (*cf.* Mar. 26 of that year) and was much concerned about his new volume of poems, which was to be published on the 29th of April following (see a note on May 10 of this year).]

To Frederic Henry Hedge, Concord, March 26, 1867 [118]

Concord
Tuesday March 26

My dear Hedge,

I gladly urge an invitation, which I believe Mrs Sophy Thayer has already given as my proxy, that you will dine with me, — you & Mrs Hedge, on Thursday Fast Day, 4 April. So shall you keep that best custom [119] of good will & good deed to Concord, & see our suffering friend Mrs Ripley, & gratify your warm friends in this house. I have only come home two days ago, or three is it? [120] &, I regret to say, have not yet seen Mrs R., partly that I have had to run directly to Bos-

118. MS owned by RWEMA; ph. in CUL. The only year after the marriage of Sophia Ripley Thayer (Apr. 24, 1861) and before the death of her mother, Sarah Bradford Ripley (July 26, 1867) in which Mar. 26 fell on Tuesday was 1867, and this year exactly fits the facts given here. The marriage of the daughter is mentioned in earlier letters and the death of Mrs. Ripley in the letters of July? 31? and Aug. 1, 1867.

119. A number of letters of other years refer to the custom which Emerson, Hedge, and Mrs. Ripley used to observe together. Hedge's old friendship for Mrs. Ripley is recorded in his reminiscence of her which Elizabeth Hoar included in her chapter of *Worthy Women,* pp. 155–157.

120. Emerson wrote in Feb. 24, 1867, that his lecture schedule in the West, as then outlined, extended to Mar. 19. By Mar. 6, it seems, the end was set for the 20th or 21st. The MS memorandum book for 1867 gives Mar. 22 to Pittsburgh, but without a subject. Apparently the actual date for that town was earlier. Miss Florence Spofford informs me that *The Pittsburgh Commercial* of Mar. 19, 1867, formally announced "The Man of the World" for that evening as the last lecture in the Mercantile Library Course but on the next day confused matters by referring informally to Emerson's lecture of "this evening" and had nothing more about Emerson the rest of the week.

ton, & partly that I doubt a little — from the reporters — that Mary Simmons [121] likes to have me see her as she has been & is still very feeble.

Ever yours affectionately,
R. W. Emerson

Dr F. H. Hedge

To SIDNEY HENRY MORSE, CONCORD, MARCH 31, 1867 [122]

Concord
Sunday night, 31 March.

My dear Sir,

On returning home last night,[123] I found your note. I am much gratified to learn that speed is not important in your Course, & I will hold myself ready for the first Sunday Eve in May, if you shall so please, or the second [124] at your choice. It would not be easy to me to come much earlier, as I have competing engagements.

I have to correct a blunder of mine in the note introducing Guerrier [125] I told you I had a personal acquaintance with him But on my return home on talking with my son I discovered that I had confounded his personality with that of another young gentleman who visited me one evening last Autumn, & that I had never met young Guerrier, & only knew him through my son's good report.[126] But I am glad to learn that you have been able to give him a trial, & I confide that no inconvenience will grow out of my misconception.

With great regard
R. W. Emerson

Rev S. H. Morse

121. Mrs. Ripley's daughter, mentioned in earlier letters.

122. MS owned by Captain Frank Lester Pleadwell; ph. in CUL. The year is fixed by evidence noted below, and Mar. 31 fell on Sunday in 1867. For Morse and his journal, *The Radical*, see Gohdes, pp. 214 ff., and *The Poets of Transcendentalism*, pp. 319–320.

123. From Maine; see letters of Apr. 4, 1867, to the Forbeses.

124. Emerson lectured in the " Radical " course at Boston, Sunday, May 12, on " The Rule of Life " (*Daily Evening Traveller*, May 13, 1867) . I conjecture that Morse was in charge of this course. He certainly delivered one of the lectures in it (*The Commonwealth*, Apr. 13, 1867) ; and Emerson wrote in his MS memorandum book for 1867, under date of Apr. 14: " ' Radical ' Lecture in Boston S. H. Morse."

125. Mar.? 9? 1867.

126. Edward Waldo Emerson, Milton, Mass., Feb. 3, 1867, praised a young Englishman, George P. Guerrier, whom he had first known in Burlington, Ia., and who, he said, was selling books on commission for Ticknor & Fields but wished to obtain a place on *The Radical* under Morse. Edward had promised to try to get a letter of recommendation from his father to aid Guerrier.

To —————————, Concord? *c.* March? 1867?

[MS listed and partly quoted in Goodspeed's Book Shop, Feb., 1919, where neither the date nor the name of the person addressed is given; Emerson says he finds all of " Adirondac " (presumably " The Adirondacs ") but ten lines or so, which will come tomorrow. This poem was published in *May-day,* which was ready to print by early April of 1867 (see Apr. 2, 1867, to Ticknor & Fields). The present letter may have been written to the publishers or the printers.]

To Frederic Henry Hedge, Concord, April 2, 1867 [127]

Concord
Tuesday 2 April

My dear Hedge,

I am sorry to say that I must ask you to defer your visit to Concord & me. I woke up yesterday morning to a disagreeable & bad-looking affection in my face,[128] which has increased today, & which Dr Bartlett calls erisypelas, & promises me more of it, & proposes to shut me up. I am vexed the more for its unseasonableness, as I was very glad that you could & would come, and I believed there was much to tell as well as to hear. On one account the time was less propitious to your visit now, inasmuch as, such is Mrs Ripley's state, that I doubt if you could see her. I was there on Sunday afternoon, & was not permitted. She is in a very weak & nervous state, & sees no one but Mrs Simmons.

I have not seen you since the shock of your daughter's death [129] to your heart & happiness. Some circumstances made me very sensible of the calamity, & my children gave it all their sympathy. We go with firmness enough when we go at ripe time, but see with pain the order broken.

You are to bear in mind that we are only to change the date but that you will owe me the visit. Affectionately,

F. H. Hedge.   R W Emerson

To Ticknor and Fields, Concord, April 2, 1867

[MS listed and partly quoted in Ritter-Hopson Galleries, Mar. 16, 1933; Emerson gives his consent to the printing of *May-day* and incloses " a few errata

127. MS owned by RWEMA; ph. in CUL. The letter pretty clearly follows that of Mar. 26, 1867; and Apr. 2 fell on Tuesday in that year.

128. In Apr. 4, 1867, to W. H. Forbes, Emerson says that, " two days ago," he was ailing " with a bandaged head."

129. According to Lucy T. Poor to Louise Bradley, May 10, 1933 (MS in my possession), Hedge's daughter Ellen Elizabeth married Walter S. Poor about 1865 and they went to live in the South, where, after a year, she died.

to be at once corrected on the plates." Earlier letters seem to show that the book had long since been put into type and that Emerson had been for some time at work on the proofs. For publication, on Apr. 29, see the letter of May 10, 1867, to Cabot.]

To William Hathaway Forbes, Concord, April 4, 1867 [130]

Concord
4 April 1867

Dear Will,

I ought to have acknowledged, two days ago, the receipt of Mr Denison's [131] draft, kindly collected & forwarded by you, for three hundred & fifty dollars, less government tax, from Burlington & Missouri R R Company. I was ailing that day & the next with a bandaged head,[132] or should have been more prompt. On my return from a journey on some accounts very pleasant — and if you should ever pass through Brunswick, you should go into Upjohn's Chapel,[133] — I found my house a good deal emptied. and shall have to indemnify myself by coming to yours.

R. W. E.

W. H. Forbes.

To Edith Emerson Forbes, Concord, April 4, 1867 [134]

Concord
Fast Day Eve.

Dear Edith,

I missed you sadly when I came home from Brunswick,[135] having been haunted by an obscure hope that you were still at Concord.

130. MS owned by RWEMA; ph. in CUL.

131. John N. Denison was treasurer of the Burlington & Missouri Rail Road (*The Boston Directory*, 1867). An account of the development of this road as a feeder to the C. B. & Q. is given in H. G. Pearson, pp. 84–87.

132. *Cf.* Apr. 2, 1867, to Hedge.

133. I am indebted to Professor Herbert Ross Brown for an account of the Bowdoin College Chapel and for newspaper notices of Emerson's lecture in Brunswick. The chapel, a Romanesque building of undressed granite, was designed by Richard Upjohn, of New York, and erected in the decade 1845–1855. For the lecture, the *Brunswick Telegraph* of Mar. 22, 1867, announced that Emerson would appear on the 27th of that month, under the auspices of the class of '67. According to *The Daily Sentinel and Times* of Bath, Me., for Mar. 27, the Brunswick lecture was to be " The Man of the World."

134. MS owned by RWEMA; ph. in CUL. Evidence cited below shows that the year 1867, which has been supplied, is correct.

135. *Cf.* the letter of the same date to W. H. Forbes.

I mean now to find a way of coming to your house at short periods, & *so* keeping my children around me. As we drive it, tis rarely & casually that friends meet who have yet a high esteem for each other. In the same house or in the same room, one or both may be so diverted by their own work, or by other persons, that they two do not once fairly converse. Well, we acquiesce in this as instinctive & best for both, provided we can only now & then secure one full radiant gaze, or a pair of cordial words. Tis plain that in general we are ever on the hunt for comparative strangers, but later we discover that we may find some of our best friends in our own blood. You are a very good girl, & have been nobly true, & all the more because so quiet, to your own convictions. I like to say this because it is the glory of character to be thus, without hearing of it, or expecting to hear, & yet the observer wants to say, Thanks & Persist. — I remember you every day with joy in your husband & his large power & promise, &, in spite of my inveterated cloister ways, do not despair of those fireside sessions which have always floated before me, though ever a little out of reach. Health & joy to the little boy,[136] whose photograph delights me.

R. W. E.

To Henry James, Sr., Concord, April 4, 1867 [137]

Concord, 4 April.

My dear James,

I am too glad to get your note [138] to cavil at its brave superlative; indeed, I am long used to know you as the only Occidental who has mastered all the grace of the Persian pen. And who would not run the risk of being ridiculously plucked presently by some ill natured real-

136. Ralph Emerson Forbes, mentioned in earlier letters of 1866 and 1867.

137. MS owned by RWEMA; ph. in CUL. The year offers some difficulty but is fixed, I believe, by evidence cited below.

138. James, Cambridge, Apr. 2, n. y., says he has heard Emerson is home from the West. "It was very nice of you," he adds, "to cohabit with those St. Louis chickens, and make them lay the eggs over which the Commonwealth keeps up such a clucking . . ." *The Commonwealth* later printed several favorable notices of Harris's journal, but James had probably noticed the account, cited below, of Emerson's recent lecture before the young philosophers. For *The Journal of Speculative Philosophy*, begun by Harris in this same year, see June 28, 1867, and later letters. That James's note of Apr. 2, which was obviously his first gesture toward Concord since Emerson's return from the West, could not belong to 1868 is clear from James to his son William, Mar. 18 of that year, which reports that Emerson is interested in William's letters and that James is to take these letters to Concord on Mar. 21 (see R. B. Perry, I, 96).

ist, for the pleasure of being once covered over with such superb
plumes? Besides, I must believe that your diluvial good-nature indicates a sea of health. And it is on this base, that I have steadily dis-
credited all your own & some of your neighbors' dirges concerning your
maladies or malaisances. A spring that overflows all the other wells will
not be the first to run dry. And perhaps you have achieved Plato's
charm, " making secure from harm until another period." [139]

It was a true gratification to see Harris at St Louis amidst the German
Atheists, & to share his pleasure in that, though he had begun alone, he
now counted I think nineteen young men as spiritual or affirmative philosophers, & could rely on them as active propagandists.[140] They did not
wish to see or hear me at all, but that I should see & hear them, — which
was the easiest duty & the greatest relief. I am sorry that you could not
gratify them, as they much desired, by a visit. You would have met
them as they wished to be met, & as I could not. Thank your boy Harry
from me for his good stories.[141] I prize all your boys, and Alice, & send
sympathetic regards to Mrs James. Yours ever, R. W. Emerson

To William James, Concord? April c. 7, 1867

[William James wrote from Cambridge, Apr. 6, 1867, asking Emerson for an introduction to Herman Grimm, whom he hoped to see in Germany the follow-

139. This phrase from Plato's *Phaedrus* — it may be found in slightly different
form in Jowett's translation (*The Dialogues,* New York, 3d ed., 1892, I, 454) — appeared on the first page of " Quotation and Originality " in *The North American
Review* for Apr., 1868. But the essay was, it seems, substantially the same as a lecture
of years earlier (*cf. Cent. Ed.,* VIII, 398) .

140. Harris, who must have met Emerson in 1865 (see letters of July 18 of that
year) , was one of the founders of the St. Louis Philosophical Society in Jan., 1866
(Denton J. Snider, pp. 7 and 10–11) . Alcott arrived on the scene early, and Harris
tried — probably without success, I think — to bring Emerson there, presumably
for a meeting in February or March of the first year (see Feb. 1, 1866, to Ellen
Emerson) . About a year later Emerson lectured in St. Louis in the Public School
Library course (see a note on Feb. 13, 1867) , and, on his return from engagements
further west, read " Inspiration " for Harris and his men. According to the MS
memorandum book for this year, the date of this latter reading was Mar. 12. *The
Commonwealth* of Mar. 30, 1867, printed a report from St. Louis dated Mar. 20 — an
" imperfect abstract of Emerson's lecture here before the Philosophical Society, and
some fragments of the conversation which followed." The letter of Dec. 16? 1867,
seems to show that Emerson again saw Harris in St. Louis at that time. But the second
Western trip of 1867 was completed by early January of 1868, so that James's reference
in a letter dated Apr. 2 would hardly apply to it.

141. The future novelist had begun to publish stories as early as Mar., 1865, and
put forth a few more in 1866 and 1867 (LeRoy Phillips, *A Bibliography of the
Writings of Henry James,* 1930, p. 132) .

ing winter. After his arrival abroad James wrote to Grimm (MS owned by the
Goethe- und Schiller-Archiv) :

> " Christian Strasse, 6 III
> " Dresden, Sachsen
> " May 21. '67

" Dear Sir

 " About 6 weeks ago, a fortnight before I left Boston, I wrote to Mr.
Emerson to ask for a letter of introduction to you, as I thought it very probable
I might spend next winter in Berlin, and I was desirous of the honor of your
acquaintance. He wrote me in a day or two that he would send me a letter to
you as soon as he had finished some book wh. he was reading and of wh. he
wished to speak to you. I sailed before his letter arrived, but my Father has
just sent it after me. It is sealed and I suppose it contains something more than
an introduction, so I send it to you without delay. I shall probably pass the most
of the summer here in Dresden trying to arm myself with enough German for
the next winter's University Campaign. When I reach Berlin, one of my earliest
acts will be to call upon you, and in the meanwhile I remain

> " With great respect
> " Yours truly
> " Wm. James

" To
 " Mr. Hermann Grimm
  " Berlin."]

To Herman Grimm, Concord, April 14, 1867

[MS owned by the Goethe- und Schiller-Archiv. Printed in *The Atlantic*, XCI,
477 (Apr., 1903) , and in *Correspondence between Ralph Waldo Emerson and
Herman Grimm*, pp. 67–68. This introduces William James and was probably
inclosed in a letter to the future psychologist or to his father. *Cf.* the note on
Apr. *c.* 7, 1867.]

To Sarah Louise Blatchley, Concord, April 22, 1867 [142]

Concord

22 April, 1867.

I am sorry that my hoped for visit to Vassar College should encumber
you with so long a correspondence. If you will let me write Friday

142. MS owned by Vassar College Library; ph. in CUL. Sarah Louise Blatchley
is listed as a senior in the *Third Annual Catalogue of . . . Vassar College . . .
1867–68*. In the back of the MS memorandum book for 1867, Emerson wrote
" S L Blakeley Poughkeepsie," apparently an error; and under May 17 he noted
" Poughkeepsie Vassar College Man of the World." The mention of " so long a correspondence " seems to imply that he had written at least one earlier letter to Vassar
of which I have no further evidence.

May 17th instead of May *10th* as your note proposes, I shall keep the day. It happens that I have an important engagement on the 12th May,[143] which will keep me at home on the 10th & 11th.

Unless I hear from you to the contrary, I shall presume your consent to an arrangement for the 17th.

Respectfully

S. L. Blatchley —
R. W. Emerson

    Chairman.

To the Trustees of Cornell University, Concord, April 23, 1867

[In *Testimonials,* privately printed, Boston, 1879, p. 32. This letter recommends Francis Ellingwood Abbot as a candidate for the chair of intellectual philosophy at Cornell. For Abbot, who did not become a member of the Cornell faculty but, within a few years, founded and conducted *The Index,* a radical paper, see Gohdes, pp. 233 ff.]

To James Thomas Fields, Concord? *c.* April? 1867?[144]

Monday

My dear Sir

    Mrs E. Forbes is bent on giving her counsel on the form & coat of the Poems & will call on you at a little before 3 o'clock today — I am sorry to propose so questionable an hour, but the train arrives at 2.30 & she will come here immediately. I am going to the Parker House. Ever yours

R W Emerso

To George Washburn Smalley, Concord, May 8, 1867[145]

Concord
8 May

Dear Mr Smalley,

I am greatly obliged by your kind thought, & brave proposal. I have begged Mr Fields to strain your good nature so far as pray you to protect

---

143. See a note on Mar. 31, 1867.

144. MS owned by the Henry E. Huntington Library; ph. in CUL. I conjecture that the volume alluded to was *May-day and Other Pieces,* published Apr. 29, 1867 (*cf.* May 10 following to Cabot). The signature was crowded into the corner of the sheet. Mrs. E. Forbes was Edith Emerson Forbes, whose interest in this book is confirmed by Ellen Emerson's letter of Apr. 29th to her cousin Haven Emerson.

145. MS owned by Thomas F. Madigan, Inc.; ph. in CUL. The year is fixed by

a few copies of my " May-day," which should go in advance to friends, —
a few having already gone, — & some others can follow at more leisure.

Your note finds me in the preparation at short warning of a paper to
be read presently that requires all my attention, or I should have a word
to add in regard to your new visit, which yet I hope will be still more
successful to yourself & to the public than your last.

With grateful regards,
R. W. Emerson

G. W. Smalley, Esq.

I take the liberty to send you a copy of my little book in which I have
written your name.

To James Bradley Thayer, Concord, May 9, 1867 [146]

Concord
9 May 1867

My dear Mr Thayer,

My search has proved as yet unavailing to find the Judge [147] in
proper time & place to put to him so grave a question as that I carried,
so I am forced for the present to content myself with the stenciled
stamp on the box, which carries the mysterious legend, " J. P. Whiton,[148]
21 Broad Street." Boston. & the price, I believe was $1.31

But you must not expect to find in them any hint of the fine brown
aromatics you sent me from Egypt,[149] — for so your messenger said, —
& which I burn a little oftener than I deserve to.

Ever yours,
R. W. Emerson

J. B. Thayer, Esq.

---

the reference to *May-day*. For Smalley, *cf.* Nov. 17, *c.* 1866? The present letter was
written to him about the time of his departure for England to establish the European
office of his newspaper. The lecture which was " to be read presently " was presumably
the same promised in Mar. 31 preceding.

146. MS owned by Professor James B. Thayer; ph. in CUL.

147. Probably Ebenezer Rockwood Hoar.

148. *The Boston Directory* for the year commencing July 1, 1867, lists John P.
Whiton, a dealer in cigars and tobacco. Thayer, Boston, May 6, 1867, had thanked
Emerson for *May-day* and had asked where he could obtain the " Spanish cheviots "
which he had tried, it seems, at Concord.

149. *Cf.* Mar. 3, 1869, to Thayer.

To James Elliot Cabot, Concord, May 10, 1867 [150]

Concord

10 May

My dear Cabot,

      I am delighted with the hope of seeing you & Dr Wyman here, & promise you all the " expert " advice the village can supply.[151] Next week is broken for me, & I am to be away two or three days. But in the week after, I shall be steadily at home. Will Wednesday 22^d, suit your convenience? If not, Thursday, or Friday, are alike to me. And the 11 o'clock A M train will be the best for the design.

      Thanks for your friendliest note. I read with amazement the word " Damsels " which slipped into the new text,[152] I know not how. " Daughters " was right & shall be.

Ever yours

R. W. Emerson

J. E. Cabot, Esq.

To Octavius Brooks Frothingham, Concord, May 10, 1867

[MS listed in Rains Galleries, Nov. 22, 1934; Emerson promises " to attend a meeting organized by Frothingham."]

To Caroline Sturgis Tappan, Concord, May 15, 1867? [153]

Concord

Wednesday, 15 May

Dear Caroline,

      I tried hard yesterday to reach your house with Ellen, as I had

---

150. MS owned by Professor Philip Cabot; ph. in CUL. The year is obvious. Cabot, Brookline, Mass., May 6, 1867, thanked Emerson for *May-day*. He asked why " damsels " had replaced " daughters " in " Days," one of his old favorites. For " Terminus," he thought that " nobler verses surely never saw the light on this side of the world " but pleaded " to the jurisdiction of that God — at least as far as philosophy is concerned." " Wyman and I," he added, " talk of coming to Concord to look up the shell-heap that Thoreau told me of — left by the Indians "; and he asked what day they should come, provided Emerson did not think the expedition sacrilegious.

151. An exploration by Dr. Jeffries Wyman and Cabot of the Indian shells on a cliff above the river at Concord is mentioned in *The Early Years of the Saturday Club*, p. 427.

152. *May-day and Other Pieces* was published on Apr. 29 (*Boston Daily Advertiser*, Apr. 29, 1867). In both American and English editions, the word " Damsels " had replaced the " Daughters " of the original version printed in *The Atlantic* for Nov., 1857. But the form Emerson desired reappeared in later editions.

153. MS owned by Mrs. Gorham Brooks; ph. in CUL. Of the years in which

arranged with her, but she was at Milton, & did not arrive, & I was forced to come away at an early hour by affairs at home. Ellen's design was to entreat you, & Ellen & Mary to come & spend a pair of days with us, next week, say Tuesday & Wednesday, & so relieve her of her returning dream that you will not come or let your children come to the poor little town. And this desire of hers I heartily second. To this I wish to add the question — Will you have room for me at your house next Monday to spend the night? &, if so, will you not write a note to Lidian, expressly inviting her to come with me? She may not be able to come, but I think she would be seriously gratified to come, if she is able, & were directly asked. And I write all this happily to you, for what is the use of a noble friend, if you cannot deal frankly with her?

Yours always,
R. W. Emerson

Mrs Caroline Tappan

over.

I have called Ellen to council about the days of next week, — & she reminds me that the only reason why her invitation of your household to ours was not weeks ago, — was my own social impossibilities in the times when a lecture was to be prepared; [154] but she trusts as I trust that you do not mean to take your flight to the hills until the end of May. And so we cling to the purpose of bringing you home with us next Tuesday afternoon. Ellen reminds me that her mother joined her heartily in this request.

To James Thomas Fields, Concord, May 19, 1867 [155]

Concord
19 May
Sunday Eve

My dear Fields,

Is it not possible & is it not easy to bind one set of my books, [omitting " Conduct of Life " & " Mayday,"] say in the style of that set of Hawthorne put up in boxes, or in the style of the red or the brown " Mayday," & to be ready within a week?? If this can easily be done,

---

May 15 fell on Wednesday, 1867, 1872, and 1878 are late enough for the reference to Milton; but Edith Emerson Forbes was abroad in May of 1872 (see Apr. 30 of that year).

154. Perhaps a reference to the lecture of May 12, 1867 (*cf.* Apr. 22 preceding).

155. MS owned by the Henry E. Huntington Library; ph. in CUL. The only year in which May 19 fell on Sunday after the publication of *May-day* and before Fields's retirement was 1867.

I am told it would be a well received gift to a young person whom I wish to oblige.

I send to Mrs Fields the white copy that was promised, & enclose the autograph quatrain you asked for.

Ever yours,

R. W. E.

For the binding of the books, there may be the same lettering as usual, only leaving off " Emersons Works " & the stamping of the sides;

To George Bancroft, Concord? May *c.* 20, 1867

[Bancroft, New York, May 17, 1867, acknowledged *May-day;* a sheet containing some queries about certain poems is now with Bancroft's letter and was presumably inclosed in it. Bancroft, May 24 following, said he was stupid in failing to understand the meaning of certain lines.]

To George William Childs, Concord, June 15, 1867

[Printed in *The Public Ledger Building, Philadelphia: with an Account of the Proceedings Connected with its Opening June 20, 1867,* 1868, p. 140; Emerson regrets that he cannot be present at the inauguration of the building.]

To Samuel Johnson, Concord, June 19, 1867? [156]

Concord

19 June

My dear Sir,

Yes, if you shall ask me, I shall like very well to come. I am very much your debtor lately, when I read in the Radical your shining chapter on the genius of America.[157] I hoped to find you at Mr Sargent's the other day.[158] We wanted one or two mediaevals between the Juniors & the Seniors.

Ever yours,

Samuel Johnson.   R. W. Emerson

156. MS owned by Mr. Thomas F. Madigan; ph. in CUL. The conjectural year is based on the information given below about Johnson's article. For Johnson, *cf.* the second letter of Feb. 12, 1867.

157. The reference is, I think, either to Johnson's " American Religion," in *The Radical* for Jan., 1867, or, much more probably, to his " The Spiritual Promise of America," in the same magazine for April of that year. For Emerson's special interest in such topics about this time, *cf.* his " Remarks at the Meeting for Organizing the Free Religious Association, Boston," May 30, 1867, in *Cent. Ed.,* XI. Johnson, however, continued to contribute to *The Radical,* and the question of date remains.

158. Pretty clearly a reference to a meeting of the Radical Club at the home of

To WILLIAM TORREY HARRIS, CONCORD, JUNE 28, 1867 [159]

Concord, 28 June, 1867.

My dear Sir,

I have both numbers of the Journal of Philosophy,[160] besides the advance sheets you were so good as to send me of No 2. It is a brave undertaking, & I shall think better than ever of my countrymen if they shall sustain it. I mean that you shall make me acquainted in it with the true value & performance of Hegel, who, at first sight is not engaging nor at second sight satisfying. But his immense fame cannot be mistaken, and I shall read & wait. At present I am glad to find the more attractive levels of the criticism on Raffaelle & Beethoven; & of the Lycidas.

I entreat your pardon for retaining so long, — & yet a little longer — the valuable manuscript letters you trusted me with. It has happened that I have passed from task to task, since I came home from the west,[161] & have not had a day of wild leisure. — I enclose $2., for the Journal.

With high regard, yours,

R. W. Emerson

W. T. Harris.

To JAMES RUSSELL LOWELL, CONCORD, JULY 14, 1867? [162]

Concord

July 14. Eve

Dear Lowell,

I wish much to have Henry James elected a member of the Phi Beta Kappa. I do not think he was ever nominated. Perhaps I shall

John T. Sargent, 13 Chestnut St., Boston. The Club originated in the spring of 1867, and Emerson was the chief speaker at what seems to have been the first meeting, that of May, 1867. The record of that meeting in *Sketches and Reminiscences of the Radical Club*, ed. Mary Fiske Sargent (Mrs. John T. Sargent), 1880, pp. 3–20, does not mention Johnson.

159. MS owned by Miss Edith Davidson Harris; ph. in CUL.

160. Both Nos. 1 and 2 of *The Journal of Speculative Philosophy* gave much space to Hegel, in whom the members of the St. Louis Philosophical Society were chiefly interested. Harris's " Notes on Raphael's ' Transfiguration ' " appeared in the first number. A part of his " Music as a Form of Art," in the second number, concerned Beethoven. Anna C. Brackett's " Notes on Milton's Lycidas " was also in the second number.

161. See notes on Apr. 4, 1867, to James.

162. MS owned by HCL; ph. in CUL. Henry James, Sr., was elected an honorary

not arrive in Cambridge, on Thursday, in time for the business meeting; & perhaps, if I should, there may be rules or preliminaries I know not of, that would prevent his election in season for that day's dinner. In this doubt, may I beg you, if you have no objection to the nomination, & if there be no obstructing rule, to take order that his name be balloted for in just season? And you [163]

To Charles Franklin Dunbar, Concord, July 17, 1867 [164]

Concord 17 July

Dear Sir,

Agreeably to my promise to Mr Thayer I send you a note of the divisions of my address to the Phi Beta K I am sorry to send you so little when you asked so early but I had not thought of such a contingence & could not get the frame even to stand until a late hour.

Respectfully,

R. W. Emerson

Mr Dunbar.

To Edwin Lee Brown, Concord? July 25, 1867

[Acknowledged in Brown, Chicago, Sept. 19, 1867. See a note on the second letter of Feb. 12, 1867.]

To James Thomas Fields, Concord, July 25, 1867?

[MS listed and partly quoted in American Art Association, Mar. 10–11, 1924, and listed there again, Dec. 2–3, 1926. No year is given, but Emerson says that, as for "Domestic Life," he sees no grave objection, though he means to put it

---

member of the Harvard chapter of Phi Beta Kappa in 1872. In that year, however, the annual meeting occurred on June 27, as reported in the *Boston Daily Advertiser* of the 29th, and Lowell sailed for Europe on July 9 (H. E. Scudder, II, 150). The latest preceding year in which the annual meeting occurred on the Thursday following July 14 was 1867, when the day was the 18th. The business meeting was held on that morning at nine o'clock, when new members were admitted and Lowell was elected president; at the principal meeting, later in the day, the orator was Emerson himself. An account of both meetings, with the oration, appeared in the *Boston Daily Advertiser*, July 19, 1867. It is a significant fact that Lowell had been at least partly responsible for Emerson's appearance on this occasion, for he had written from Cambridge, May 4, 1867, urging Emerson to be the speaker.

163. The remainder of the MS is missing.

164. MS owned by Mr. Carroll A. Wilson; ph. in CUL. The year is obviously 1867. Dunbar was at this time editor of the *Boston Daily Advertiser*. The report of the second Phi Beta Kappa address in that paper is mentioned in a note on July 14, 1867? For James Bradley Thayer's connection with the same paper, *cf.* Aug. 25, 1865.

into his slow volume of essays or miscellanies. The brief " Domestic Life " contributed to *The Atlantic Almanac,* 1868, was, I conjecture, the result of Fields's request. Doubtless the volume of essays or miscellanies referred to was *Society and Solitude,* which duly included the lecture " Domestic Life " but which was not published till 1870.]

To Edith Emerson Forbes, Concord, July 31, 1867 [165]

Concord
1 August

Dear Edith,

Ellen prays me to write you word that your letter to Mamma & your letter to herself were heartily welcomed & exhausted. She fully meant to write you back, but is in her bed, now for the third day, with some slow fever, which Dr Bartlett will not pronounce either short or long, & which I wish she may jump out of as Ralph out of his diseases, taking a nap & waking up well. But she was well for two of Haven & Susan T.'s days, & gave her high approval to the last.[166] She is certainly a well behaved young lady, with a good face, & makes an impression of good sense & worth.

We could so heartily have wished a different close to Mrs Ripley's life — but, as there was no hope, her death was a relief. Gore had stayed a week after he had fixed his departure, & all the family were together. The company at the funeral were all friends from near & far, Dr Hedge officiating.

I fear that Ellen's ailing will postpone or break up her Monadnoc plans as the nearest days were now the most practicable for it.

I went to Jamaica Plain yesterday, but Mrs Adams was gone to her brother's, at Boston.[167] I found Abby & her own sister Mrs Merchant at home, & stayed to dine. I believe it is you — you & not Edward — whom Ellen charged me to tell, that his visit here on Sunday & Monday gave her great comfort.[168]

---

165. MS owned by RWEMA; ph. in CUL. The reference to the death of Mrs. Ripley, on July 26, 1867, fixes the year (see a note on Aug. 1, 1867). The present letter is certainly later than her funeral but seems to precede the other letter which Emerson dated Aug. 1, and to his date line another hand has added " or 31 July 1867." Comparison with the following letter to Edward shows that July 31 is correct.

166. For the marriage of Susan Tompkins and Emerson's nephew, see May 21, 1868, to William Emerson.

167. It is barely possible that the word is " Bolton."

168. Abel Adams had died on July 9 of this year (see a note on Sept. 22 following).

On further inquiry, Ellen says, your letter did arrive on Saturday night, & was a noble writing. We thought the accounts of Will highly favorable, & send to him love & a balloon of kisses to Ralph; & love & joy to all your household. R. W. Emerson

To Edward Waldo Emerson, Concord? July 31, 1867

[MS owned by Mr. Raymond Emerson.]

To Edith Emerson Forbes, Concord, August 1, 1867 [169]

1 August

Dear Edith,

Ellen is comfortable today, & better, she says, than she expected to be. The Doctor would not say that she was better this morning. Lucy Jackson & Edith [170] are still here, & Charles at Uncle W.'s [171] You must send a line to Ellen, when you cannot send a letter, for she thinks always of you

R. W. E.

Mamma says Ellen appears much better today, & helps herself more

I send you by mail the Advertiser containing my Sketch of Mrs Ripley.

To Edith Emerson Forbes, Concord, August 5, 1867 [172]

Concord
Monday Aug 4

Dear Edith,

Ellen is better today & the Doctor is markedly satisfied with her as the dangerous symptoms are disappearing & it now seems he thought her sickness dangerous & does not think it much that she may

169. MS owned by RWEMA; ph. in CUL. The year is fixed by the reference to Sarah Bradford Ripley. She died on July 26, 1867; and Emerson's sketch of her, which appeared in the *Boston Daily Advertiser* of July 31 following, was reprinted in *Worthy Women*, pp. 223–225.

170. Probably Edith Davidson (*cf.* Nov. 25, 1865, and the letter of Feb. 1, 3, and 6, 1867).

171. Earlier letters show that William Emerson had for some time been a resident of Concord.

172. MS owned by RWEMA; ph. in CUL. The year 1867, added in another hand, exactly fits the facts mentioned here and in the preceding letters; but Monday was Aug. 5, not 4, in that year.

be a good while in getting well. Ellen & I who did not think her endangered are not so easily contented. She has no appetite & no strength, & must keep her bed & wait. She was of course very glad to have Edward here yesterday who is a capital nurse. Yesterday came John Jackson & Miss Hubbard & we were glad to have Edward Lucy J & Edie [173] here to entertain them. She appears to be a good child amiable & contented But this note was only to tell you of Ellen

R. W. E.

Ellen sends dear love & thanks Will for his beautiful peaches, which, I believe, she must not eat, poor child. She is charmed with the image of Ralph walking,[174] & clucking to his horse made of boots.

To Charles Eliot Norton, Concord, August 6, 1867 [175]

Concord
6 August, 1867.

My dear Norton,

You make me happy to hear the new joy & strength of your house in the birth of your son.[176]

I did not write yesterday & hesitate at writing now, because I have not a clear answer ready to your request respecting the North American. I looked over my projected materials — but they did not satisfy me — at least made the usual reply of materials, — "A little more time, if you please." Not to go into those distressing experiences, I will only say that I have not forgotten my consent to your proposition, & the proposition still pleases me well, & that I confide in my power, though postponing & interrupted, — still to make the word good.[177] I depended much on seeing you at Phi Beta, — as Lowell did also; though I now see well why you could not be there. I fancied I never saw a house so good in quality. It was a *saving* audience, to hear everything, & pardon everything.[178] I give joy to all your household on the new event & in these good days. R W Emerson

Charles E. Norton.

173. *Cf.* the Edith mentioned in Aug. 1, 1867.

174. Ralph Emerson Forbes was about thirteen months of age; *cf.* the letters of July 11, 1866.

175. MS owned by HCL; ph. in CUL.

176. Rupert (see *Letters of Charles Eliot Norton*, II, 71).

177. See Oct. 7, 1866.

178. Emerson was the orator (see a note on July 14, 1867?).

I have a letter this week from Mrs Clough, to the same purport as your note some time ago,[179] & shall write to her.[180]

To Edith Emerson Forbes, Concord, August 11, 1867 [181]

Sunday Eve, 11 Aug^t

Dear Edith,

We are so well pleased with the Chronicles of Naushon which duly come day by day, that we are quite willing to send you news of Ellen, at least ever since she made up her mind to be better. Today she has migrated to her own chamber, & there received company, Aunt Elizabeth; & Charles E.; Lily Keyes, & more. Dr Bartlett called this morning, but I doubt if he will come again. We did not fail to urge Elizabeth Hoar to go to the Elizabeth Islands,[182] but she pleaded her impossibilities. Edward you have already, who will fill one of Mrs Forbes's many chairs, & it will be strange indeed if in this week one is left empty. Ellen says, she will write her own letter tomorrow, but that you are to know that Charles was delighted with your charade, & the Storer girls [183] with Ralph's climbing the stairs.

Your loving Papa,

R. W. E.

To Edith Emerson Forbes, Concord, August 15, 1867 [184]

Concord 15 Aug^t

Dear Edith,

I am sorry to find that you were not answered aright. Ellen with whom I talked seriously of the best plan for her was so convinced that she must stay at home, & found so many obstructions to your

179. Norton, Cambridge, May 22, and Ashfield, Mass., May 26, 1867, acknowledged *May-day* and had much to say about Clough. Having obtained permission of Mrs. Clough, he meant to write, during the summer, a paper based on *Letters and Remains* (1865). He wished Emerson would fulfil Mrs. Clough's request and write out memories of her husband and permit them to be included in the projected paper. It is probable that Emerson had replied to Norton's request in an earlier letter, which, however, I have not found. Norton's long article on the *Letters and Remains* duly appeared in *The North American Review* for the following October but seems to contain no hint of help from Emerson.

180. Presumably he wrote her on this subject, but I have seen no such letter.

181. MS owned by RWEMA; ph. in CUL. For the year, *cf.* the letters of July? 31? and Aug. 1 and 5, 1867. Aug. 11 fell on Sunday in 1867.

182. Naushon is one of the Elizabeth Islands.

183. Nieces, I conjecture, of Elizabeth Hoar, whose sister, Sarah Hoar Storer, is mentioned in earlier letters. *Cf.* Aug. 15, 1867.

184. MS owned by RWEMA; ph. in CUL. The year 1867, added to Emerson's date line, fits the evidence of earlier letters of this month.

project of her visit, that I was about to write you to that effect. But
Ellen thought that her letter, which she had already sent, would make
all clear to you, and I forbore to write. Now it seems, you waited for
letter & telegraph & in vain. Of this, I am sorry; but Ellen is mending
fast, &, this morning, came down stairs to breakfast with Mr Sam Ward;
then to bed, again, & now, later, came down to dinner. She has lost
flesh, poor thing, but is excellently hungry & cheerful, & Charles E. &
all her young things, Lily K. & Florry, Martha Pierce, Mary Fay & I
suppose more, yes Lizzie S; [185] — & let me not forget Aunt Lizzie — come
& cheer her. and so her will is not to be resisted, being believed wise.[186]

To John Murray Forbes, Concord, September 6, 1867 [187]

Concord, Sept. 6, 1867

My dear friend,

I am heartily sorry that a long promised visit to Northampton [188] is irrevocably fixed for tomorrow, & will cost me two or three
days., so that I cannot as, were it otherwise, I should, make a swift
course to the Happy Islands.[189]

Ever your affectionate

J. M. Forbes, Esq.   R W Emerson

To Charles Eliot Norton, Northampton, Massachusetts, September 9, 1867 [190]

Northampton

9 September

My dear Norton,

I would gladly go to Ashfield [191] at your bidding, &, indeed
was already plotting such a visit for a half day, when your note came

185. Storer? *Cf.* Aug. 11, 1867.

186. Here the extant part of the letter ends without a signature, and perhaps
there was no more.

187. MS owned by Lord Russell; ph. in CUL.

188. See Sept. 9, 1867.

189. The Elizabeth Islands.

190. MS owned by HCL; ph. in CUL. The *Hampshire Gazette*, Northampton,
Mass., Sept. 3, 1867, announced that Emerson would lecture in Agricultural Hall
on the morning of the 8th and for the Free Congregational Society at the neighboring
town of Florence that afternoon. According to the MS memorandum book for this
year, the subjects were " Truth " and " Success."

191. In 1864 Norton had begun to spend his summers at Ashfield, Mass. (*Letters
of Charles Eliot Norton*, I, 269–270). This village is perhaps twenty-five miles from
Pittsfield.

to me: but, on inquiry, I find your town so inaccessible & so inexcessible for a speeding traveller, that the journey is out of question for me who must be in Pittsfield tomorrow.[192]

Meantime I am glad to take your measures & distances in the hope to conquer them another day, & to hear, as I do again, the best accounts of the town as well as of the great hearted inhabitants. But is it not almost time to return to Cambridge?

Ever yours affectionately,
R. W. Emerson

Charles E. Norton.

To F. G. Wheeler? Concord? September? c. 15? 1867?

[S. H. Morse, n. p., n. d., said he had a note from Wheeler at Stamford, Conn., apparently indicating that Emerson was to consider himself engaged for one of the nights mentioned " in your note " — in November. Morse was not certain whether Wheeler himself wished to write this news to Emerson. Morse further suggested that he be permitted to print in *The Radical* the lecture Emerson read " here " on Monday. The date of Emerson's " note " cannot be determined on such unsatisfactory evidence. But Morse's journal, *The Radical*, was published from Sept., 1865, to June, 1872. On Monday, Sept. 16, 1867, Emerson read " The Preacher " at John T. Sargent's in Boston (Cabot, II, 797) , no doubt for the Radical Club. The MS memorandum book for 1868 lists " Social Aims " for Stamford under Feb. 11, and it seems possible that this was the lecture which, after some delay, resulted from the negotiations carried on by Wheeler and Morse. On a flyleaf of the MS memorandum book for 1867 Emerson wrote: " F. G. Wheeler, Stamford, Ct." E. B. Huntington, *History of Stamford*, 1868, p. 478, mentions Frederick G. Wheeler.]

To Abby Adams, Concord, September 22, 1867 [193]

Concord —
September 22, 1867.

Mrs Abel Adams,

My dear friend,

I received, two days ago, a note from Mr Ingersoll Bowditch,[194] announcing that he was or would presently be ready to pay me the bequest which Mr Adams had given me in his Will, and also

---

192. Emerson was to read " The Man of the World " under the auspices of the Berkshire County Medical Association at the Baptist Church on Sept. 10 (*The Pittsfield Sun*, Sept. 5, 1867) .

193. MS owned by RWEMA; ph. in CUL.

194. J. Ingersoll Bowditch is listed in *The Boston Directory*, 1867.

those which he has given to each of my children.[195] If I had been sure that you were at home, I should have instantly come to your house, to say to you, for myself & for them, how much I rejoice in these proofs of his persistent kindness & care for me & mine. He intimated, at one of the last times when I saw him, such a purpose. I told him that his great goodness in charging himself with Edward's education at Cambridge,[196] should have relieved him of any further care of my interests; for that was a solid & enduring benefit, that had made him very dear to us all; and, besides, I had given him, first & last, a good deal of trouble, in his counsels & anxieties about my different pieces of property which he had looked after with the same faithfulness & final success he brought to his own. But he has chosen to carry his loving purpose into full effect, as his habit was. We can not love him better than we did, but it is certain that in this house, when the ear heareth of him then it shall bless him.[197] My debts to him, however, are much older than these I have named; for, from the first day when I saw him in 1828,[198] until you left Boston for Brookline,[199] your house was always one of my homes, & long my only home.[200] His hospitality would make any house beautiful, but he had also a talent for making abundance of comfort wherever he was, & seeing that his guests shared it. He seemed so built for long life & useful power, that it is painful to me that he should not fill his full term; — more sad, that disease should have clouded his last years. But perhaps our own eyes, — yours and mine, — shall soon see through these shadows.

Edith has been spending a fortnight with us, & has just gone home with her husband & child. Ellen & Edward are at Naushon, for a few days more. I do not yet know whether you are travelling, or at home. As soon as I have passed the 1 October, which is a task-day for me,[201]

195. The *Boston Daily Advertiser* of July 9, 1867, reports the death of Abel Adams, in West Roxbury, July 7, in his seventy-fifth year. His will (MS Norfolk County probate records, CXVIII, 72) includes this item: " To my much respected friend Ralph Waldo Emerson I give the sum of two thousand dollars, and the further sum of one thousand dollars to each of his children Ellen Emerson, Edith Emerson and Edward Emerson."

196. See July 8, 1861.

197. The source is *Job*, 29:11.

198. *Cf.* a note on June 30, 1828.

199. The names West Roxbury, Jamaica Plain, and Brookline are, it is not surprising to find, somewhat confused in various passages of the letters.

200. *Cf.* Mar. 6, 1829, and later letters.

201. The *Boston Daily Advertiser,* Oct. 1, 1867, announced that Emerson would deliver a new lecture on " Eloquence " in the Parker Fraternity course that evening.

I mean to come & see for myself how it is with you & your household. My wife, who admired your husband, is fully sensible of this new mark of his hand to her children & to me. She sends you her blessing & her sympathy. Kindest remembrance to Abby, & to Mrs Larkin. Affectionately yours,

R. W. Emerson

To George F. Tinker, Concord, September 24, 1867 [202]

Concord, Sept. 24
1867

Dear Sir,

I will try to come to New London on Wednesday, Eve. 27th November.[203] I shall endeavor, within a few days, to make this certain, & will write you, if I find any serious obstruction. You shall not give any trouble about sending a fee in advance.

Respectfully,
R. W. Emerson

G. F. Tinker, Esq.

If you wish to announce a subject for me at once, you shall call it, " The Man of the World ": If not to be advertised now, I may probably wish to name another subject a few weeks hence.

To Edith Emerson Forbes, Concord, October 2, 1867 [204]

Concord —

Dear Edith,

I enclose my cheque on the Atlantic Bank for one thousand dollars, which I received for you yesterday from Mr Bowditch, as executor of Mr Adams's will.[205] You shall send me a receipt when you have drawn it.

Affectionately,
R. W. Emerson

2 October, 1867.

202. MS owned by Goodspeed's Book Shop; ph. in CUL. I am indebted to Dr. Charles Perley Tinker for information about his father, George F. Tinker, who left his place as a teacher in an academy at Marlow, N. H., to come to New London, Conn.; became a provision merchant; was later mayor of New London and, afterwards, a member of the Connecticut House of Representatives; and conducted for many years the long-lived Citizens' Course of Lectures and Entertainments.

203. See Oct. 24, 1867.

204. MS owned by RWEMA; ph. in CUL.

205. Cf. Sept. 22, 1867.

To Charles Eliot Norton, Concord, October 12, 1867 [206]

Concord
October 12 1867

My dear Norton,

You load me with benefits, and, if I had been a little younger, your leading & light would have made a good Italian of me. Yet not a page you have written is quite lost on me! & the new matter in this Book [207] (as well as the splendor which so flatters the eye,) is full of interest. What a dazzling scrap of history is that preamble you have cited from Cicognara! [208] it is an honor to the planet. In season or out of season we must all read Dante now & in the last weeks I have been peeping again many times. The prodigies are all in the Commedia, but the humanity still in the Vita Nuova.

I have just got a new note from you, but it would be inconsistent for such a procrastinator to answer it before tomorrow.[209]

Ever affectionately & gratefully
R. W. Emerson

Charles E. Norton.

To Charles Eliot Norton, Concord, October 15, 1867 [210]

Concord
15 October

My dear Norton,

I must not be wholly wanting to you, &, though, of late, I write no new & find little good in old manuscripts, I shall try to keep

206. MS owned by HCL; ph. in CUL.

207. *The New Life of Dante Alighieri Translated by Charles Eliot Norton* had been published by Ticknor & Fields on Sept. 26 of this year in a volume described in the *Boston Daily Advertiser* of that date as uniform with Longfellow's translation of the *Divina commedia*. The copy alluded to in the present letter is still in the Emerson House, at Concord, and bears Norton's inscription of Sept. 25, 1867. A portion of the work, Norton explains on p. 109, had appeared in 1859, first in *The Atlantic* and then in the form of a book (see Jan. 2, 1860, to Norton).

208. On pp. 104–105 Norton quotes from Leopoldo Cicognara, *Storia della scultura*, the proud Florentine decree directing the rebuilding of the church of Santa Reparata " with such supreme and lavish magnificence that neither the industry nor the capacity of man shall be able to devise anything more grand or more beautiful."

209. Probably he waited till Oct. 15.

210. MS owned by HCL; ph. in CUL. There is no reason to doubt that the year 1867, supplied presumably by Norton himself, is correct. This would, then, be the intended letter mentioned in Oct. 12, 1867.

your November first, or, more securely, an early day of that month.[211] I shall gladly see Ashfield, but, if you will remember your club days, trust to meet you much sooner.

Ever yours,

R. W. Emerson

Charles E. Norton

To RICHARD HENRY DANA, JR., CONCORD, OCTOBER 16, 1867? [212]

Concord

October 16

My dear Mr Dana,

I am very sorry to lose the pleasure of dining with you & of meeting M. de Broglie,[213] tomorrow, but I am suffering from an absurd boil on the face, which makes my youth & beauty quite unpresentable.

Yours, with great regard,

R. W. Emerson

Richard H. Dana Jr. Esq.

To THOMAS GOLD APPLETON, CONCORD, OCTOBER 18, 1867?

[MS listed in American Art Association, Feb. 12–13, 1923, where it is dated only Friday, Oct. 18, and is described as accepting an invitation. After 1848, by which time Emerson knew Appleton well (cf. the letter of June 28, 29, and 30 of that year), Oct. 18 fell on Friday in 1850, 1861, 1867, 1872, and 1878. There seems to be no further substantial evidence.]

To GEORGE F. TINKER, CONCORD, OCTOBER 24, 1867 [214]

Concord —

October 24 1867

Dear Sir,

It was very heedless in me to have forgotten, when I fixed my day for New London,[215] that it was pretty sure to be the day before Thanksgiving, & therefore probably less convenient to many families

211. Cf. Oct. 7, 1866, Aug. 6, 1867, and Jan. 16 and Feb. 5, 1868.

212. MS owned by the Richard H. Dana Estate; ph. in CUL.

213. Charles Francis Adams, II, 340, seems to show that Dana had at least met the Prince (later the Duc) de Broglie before seeing him at Washington, D. C., in Nov., 1867.

214. MS owned by Goodspeed's Book Shop; ph. in CUL.

215. In Sept. 24, 1867, Emerson had tentatively set Nov. 27 for a lecture at New London, Conn. Nov. 28 was Thanksgiving Day, as the Boston Daily Advertiser of that date shows.

in your city as well as to myself who must not fail to keep my Thanksgiving at home. I believe that the time-tables of your railroad allow me to return to Boston by night-train, arriving in Boston at 6 A. M.; and that this time-table will remain the same till 1 December. If this be not so, I shall wish to propose to you on all accounts a change of the day, say to Monday 25 November, or to another day mutually convenient. For the subject of my Lecture, I incline still to adhere to that already named, — " The Man of the World." I shall not fail to take the train you have indicated, 11.15 [216] A. M.[217]

Respectfully,
R. W. Emerson

G. F. Tinker, Esq.

To Charles Eliot Norton, Boston, October 31, 1867 [218]

Boston
31 Oct

Dear Norton,

Lady Amberley expressed to Mr Alcott on Tuesday a wish to attend the meeting of the Religions Club,[219] which should hold its next meeting at Mr Sargent's house in Chestnut Street. But that meeting was appointed for 18th Nov.r a day too late for herself & Lord A. to be present. Mr Alcott wrote to Mr Sargent proposing to hold the meeting on the 9th & asked me to certify myself by seeing Sargent today that it could be so settled. I find on inquiry that Mr S. & his family will then be out of town but will gladly receive the Club, or, as they think would be better (on account of some believed inconveniences to the Club,) a party for conversation containing several members of the Club & some others, — say on the 14th November, when they shall be at home again. But I

216. There are several possible readings; it may be that Emerson first wrote " 16 " and tried to change it to " 10."

217. Dr. Charles Perley Tinker informs me that he often heard his father tell of a lecture Emerson gave at New London about 1867. The day and subject here suggested are confirmed by the MS memorandum book for this year.

218. MS owned by Lord Russell; ph. in CUL. The year is fixed by several letters of Nov., 1867, in which the Amberleys are mentioned. John Stuart Mill, Blackheath Park, Kent, Aug. 12, 1867, introduced Amberley to Emerson. Kate Amberley wrote from Montreal, Oct. 23 of the same year, saying that she and her husband thought of stopping at Concord the 26th or 27th, on their way to Boston; and Journals, X, 222, records their visit of that month.

219. Emerson seems to use this name for the Radical Club. The Club and Sargent are mentioned in a note on June 19, 1867?

did not take care to learn of our guests on what day they leave Boston, & perhaps the 14ᵗʰ is too late for them. Will you be so good as to ascertain from them whether the 14ᵗʰ is a practicable day, — the 14ᵗʰ at 10 A. M? If not, Mrs Bartol assures me that Dr Bartol & herself will gladly open their house for such meeting on the 9ᵗʰ as already proposed. And if you will send me word of the answer I will communicate it to all concerned.[220] Forgive me for troubling you thus, but it could not be avoided Ever yours,

C. E. Norton, Esq.   R. W. Emerson

To George L. Torbert, Concord? *c.* October? 1867

[Mentioned in Nov. 13, 1867. It is barely possible that this was the letter of " Nov. 1867 " listed and partly quoted in C. F. Libbie & Co., Dec. 3, 1906, asking that the title of a lecture be advertised as " Eloquence."]

To Katharine Stanley Russell, Viscountess Amberley, Concord? November 4? 1867

[Mentioned in the letter of Nov. 4, 1867, to Bartol; sent on that day and probably written then.]

To Cyrus Augustus Bartol, Concord, November 4, 1867 [221]

Concord

4 Novʳ

Dear Bartol,

Do not believe I have forgotten my promise to send you word about the *Conversation*. My note to Norton to obtain the consent of Lady Amberley to the arrangement for the 9ᵗʰ or for the 14ᵗʰ instant has no answer up to this time. Only on Saturday night, I learned, that Norton gave up his dinner-party on account of Governor Andrew's death.[222] On Saturday I learned that Lady A. is still Mr Forbes's guest at Milton,[223] & I have sent a line to her today to learn her will: — rather, to learn what day she leaves Boston; & according to her answer, when it comes, I will report.

Ever yours,

R. W. Emerson

220. A few letters on this subject follow, but Emerson probably wrote others.

221. MS owned by Mr. Harry F. Marks; ph. in CUL. The year is fixed by the references to the death of Andrew and to the " *Conversation* " for the Amberleys.

222. John Albion Andrew, the war governor of Massachusetts, died on Oct. 30, 1867.

223. *Cf.* Nov. 10 following to Sarah Swain Forbes.

To John T. Sargent, Concord? November 4, 1867

[Printed incompletely in *Sketches and Reminiscences of the Radical Club*, pp. 21–22. The date is given only as "Monday Eve," but comparison with the letter of Nov. 4, 1867, to Bartol shows that this was written later on the same day.]

To Amos Bronson Alcott, Concord? November 6, 1867 [224]

Wednesday, 6th
Nov.

My dear Sir,

Mr Sargent & Mr Bartol have agreed that it is best that the meeting should be at Bartol's 17 Chestnut Street, on the 14th, & desire that you & I should invite the party.[225]

R. W. E.

To Sarah Swain Forbes, Concord, November 10, 1867 [226]

Concord
Sunday Evening
10 Nov.r

Dear Mrs Forbes,

Mr Alcott is to hold a " conversation " at *Dr Bartol's house,* 17 Chestnut Street, on Thursday next, at 10 o'clock A. M. at which your guests, Lord & Lady Amberley, are to be present. I hope it will be in your power & good will to be present also, & aiding. Phillips, Wasson, Weiss, & I hope Norton, & other men, & Mrs George Russell,[227] Miss

224. MS owned by Mr. F. W. Pratt; ph. in CUL. The year is fixed by comparison with other letters of early Nov., 1867. The heading is set off by a short line, which I have not reproduced.

225. Alcott pasted this note in his diary and below it wrote two groups of names — the first of persons to whom, as he indicated, he was to write notes of invitation —
" And Emerson invites
" Mrs Josiah Quincy   Mrs Howe
Mr & Mrs J. P. Quincy Mrs Russell
Mr & Mrs J. F. Fields. Mrs Parkman
Charles E. Norton   Miss Russell "
Alcott's " J. F." Fields was, of course, J. T. Fields. Whether Emerson wrote all the invitations listed for him is not clear, but he wrote some not set down for him, including one to Sanborn, who is named in Alcott's much longer list.

226. MS owned by RWEMA; ph. in CUL. Nov. 10 fell on Sunday in 1867, clearly the year of this letter, as other letters of the same month show.

227. *The Boston Directory,* 1867, lists Mrs. George R. Russell, 1 Louisburg Square.

Hoar & other ladies, will probably be there. Come if you can, & you shall speak or forbear, — especially the first, — according to Quaker rule.

Your affectionate serv!

R. W. Emerson

Mrs Forbes.

To CHARLES ELIOT NORTON, CONCORD, NOVEMBER 10, 1867 [228]

Concord
Nov 10

Dear Norton,

I neglected, I believe, in loading you with a message to the Amberleys,[229] the other day, to pray you to come in person to the " Conversation." It is to be at Dr Bartol's, on the 14ᵗʰ at 10 A. M. As it is not the Club day, it is to be wholly independent of the Club: but Wasson, Weiss, J. P. Quincy, & others are invited & some excellent women. I wish it may be in your power & good will to come. The conversation, I suppose, will take a religious direction.

With affectionate regard,

R. W. Emerson

Charles E. Norton.

To CAROLINE? HALL? PARKMAN, CONCORD, NOVEMBER 12, 1867

[MS listed in Anderson Galleries, May 3–4, 1926; described there as an invitation to " Mrs. Parkman " to attend a conversation at Bartol's. I conjecture that this was the Mrs. Francis Parkman who appears in 1867 in *Memories of a Hostess*, p. 35. *Cf.* Jan. 3, 1869, to W. H. Forbes. Caroline Hall Parkman, widow of the Boston preacher Francis Parkman and mother of the historian of the same name, died at Jamaica Plain, Mass., in 1871 (*The New-England Historical & Genealogical Register*, XXV, 400).]

To FRANKLIN BENJAMIN SANBORN, CONCORD? NOVEMBER 12, 1867 [230]

Tuesday Night
12 Novʳ

Dear Sir,

If Mr Alcott has not asked you, let me ask you to give your presence & aid to a conversation which is to be at Dr Bartol's house,

228. MS owned by HCL; ph. in CUL. The year is obviously 1867. See especially the note on Nov. 12 to Sanborn.
229. In Oct. 31, 1867.
230. MS owned by Mr. Gabriel Wells; ph. in CUL. The year is clearly 1867,

Chestnut Street, on Thursday, at 10 A. M. The Amberleys are to be present & probably Weiss, Wasson, Norton, Phillips, & others. The conversation will probably take a religious direction. It will be a great favor to the party, if you can come.

R W Emerson

Mr Sanborn.

To Edward Waldo Emerson, Concord? November 13? 1867

[Edward Waldo Emerson to Lord Amberley (MS owned by Lord Russell) :

" Parker House Nov 13$\frac{th}{''}$ 1867

" My dear Lord Amberly

" I have this evening received a note from my father asking me to tell you that he will meet you and Lady Amberly at the house of Dr Bartol, No 13 Chestnut St where the Conversation is to be held at ten o'clock on Thursday morning and will present you to Dr Bartol.

" Truly yours
" Edward Waldo Emerson

" Viscount Amberly
    " Parker House "]

To Samuel H. Emery, Jr., Concord, November 13, 1867 [231]

Concord
November 13th

My dear Sir,

I received long ago your letter, — nay, I am twice in debt to you, & you have no reply hitherto. My correspondence is always in arrears, nor does it seem to me quite my own fault: but it were long to state the palliations.

Your suggestions, both of coming to Quincy, & specially of the parlor audience, are entirely agreeable to me, & I wrote immediately to Mr Torbett,[232] the secretary at Dubuque, that he must, if possible, put

---

when Nov. 12 fell on Tuesday. Higginson gives in his *Letters and Journals*, 1921, p. 227, a lively picture of the conversation of the 14th: Alcott, seated at the end of two long parlors at Bartol's, was flanked by the Amberleys, in armchairs. Weiss read an essay, and Alcott, Emerson, Lucretia Mott, Bartol, Hedge, Wasson, Samuel Longfellow, and Higginson talked about religion and science. Further detail is given in *Sketches and Reminiscences of the Radical Club*, pp. 21–25.

231. MS owned by Mrs. Alfred S. Ellis; ph. in CUL. The year is fixed by evidence cited below. *The Directory; History and Statistics of the City of Quincy*, 1864, lists Samuel H. Emery as pastor of the First Congregational Church and Samuel H. Emery, Jr., as a bookkeeper.

232. Letter of *c*. Oct.? 1867. George L. Torbert appears in the *Dubuque City Directory*, 1868, as an agent for real estate and insurance. For his activity as corre-

Quincy into my tour.[233] The chosen company & the form of conversation please me, & I shall readily consent to any mitigation of Mr Torbett's tariff that you shall find necessary.

It is possible that he has already corresponded with you; but I have yet no word from him, though the time I gave him, at his request, of my readiness to leave home is approaching.

With great regard,
R. W. Emerson

S. H. Emery, Jr.

To Charles Eliot Norton, Concord, November 15, 1867 [234]

Concord
15 Nov[r] 1867

My dear Norton,

Allow me to make you acquainted with my friend Mr Philip P. Randolph [235] of Philadelphia, who tells me that he proposes to spend a short time in Cambridge. Mr R. is a reading & thinking man, with great tenacity of purpose, & carrying ever in his mind a certain sense that he must be useful to his fellow creatures. Long ago when I first knew him, I think he leaned to socialism. In the war, he was a working member of the Union League, in Phil[a]; & now, he is nourishing in his heart a sublime hope of moral power to be unfolded, whereof today's *zymosis* of the sciences is only an omen. Yet I remember to have heard with surprise in Phila. that he was the best chess-player in the city: & I doubt not he has other virtues that I do not know, for he abounds in silence. But he is to me for many years, though I seldom see him, a most interesting & attractive person. He is the grandson of the celebrated Dr Physic,[236] whose name he bears. I hope you may have opportunity to converse with & know him. But I think it best to seal my letter. Ever yours,

R. W. Emerson

C. E. Norton, Esq.

---

sponding secretary of the Associated Western Literary Societies, see a note on the second letter of Feb. 12, 1867.

233. Apparently Torbert did not do so (see Nov. 29, 1867).

234. MS owned by HCL; ph. in CUL.

235. For Philip Physick Randolph, see especially the note on July *c.* 20? 1851. He had been for years Emerson's occasional correspondent. His death, less than two years after the present letter, is recorded in Richard Randolph, Philadelphia, May 5, 1869.

236. That is, Physick, known as the father of American surgery.

To Edith Emerson Forbes, Boston, November 22, 1867 [237]

Parker House
Friday, 22 Nov[r]

Dear Edith,

Ellen assured me that I could go & see you, & spend a couple of hours without harm to my town engagements. I am mortified for the Old Colony Company, that they would not make her words true. I long to see you & the children [238] beautiful, but must not try to explain the obstructions, which are quite too real, & yet all grow out of my fagging writing. Ellen rolled up a snarl of ribbons & what seem homoeopathic merchandise, which I was to have brought you, with discriminating messages which I cannot remember. But I rejoice to hear that you & the babes are well & bettering day by day. I should come out to see you today, but must go home to receive Mr Phillips (who lectures tonight) in Edward's room.[239] Farewell, good happy Edith! and many joyous birthdays [240] to you! R. W. E.

To Samuel H. Emery, Jr., Concord, November 29, 1867 [241]

Concord
Nov 29 1867

My dear Sir,

Just now at the eleventh hour when I am to leave home on Monday for Buffalo [242] Mr Torbett the Dubuque secretary sends me the list of engagements he has made up, — those I sent him, & those he has added, & there is no Quincy among them,[243] though Jacksonville [244]

237. MS owned by RWEMA; ph. in CUL. Evidence cited below shows that the year was 1867, when Nov. 22 fell on Friday.

238. Ralph Emerson Forbes is mentioned in earlier letters. His sister Edith was born on Oct. 28 of this year, according to *The Ipswich Emersons*, p. 370.

239. Wendell Phillips lectured, Nov. 22, 1867, on "The Times" (MS records of the Concord Lyceum, in the Concord Free Public Library). Edward Waldo Emerson had been made a curator of the Lyceum for this season (*ibid.*, entry of Sept. 14, 1867).

240. The letters of Nov. 22, 1841, record her birth on that day.

241. MS owned by Mrs. Alfred S. Ellis; ph. in CUL.

242. Emerson read "Eloquence" before the Young Men's Association on Dec. 3. St. James Hall was filled, even to the gallery stairs, and some persons were compelled to stand. "Possessed of a clear, pleasant voice, and speaking in a mild conversational way," the lecturer "never fails to hold the attention." (*Buffalo Commercial Advertiser*, Dec. 3 and 4, 1867.)

243. *Cf.* Nov. 13, 1867.

244. See Dec. 15, 1867.

& Galesburg [245] & perhaps other approaching points are down. Whether he has overlooked my note containing a special request in regard to Quincy, or whether he has heard from you & replied to you, I know not, but it is too late for me to ask anew his attention to it, or to make room for it in this list. I am sorry it is so, & the 18 or 19 engagements are so immediately consecutive, as to allow of no insertions. I shall carry the old invitation in my mind, & if any contingency shall make any opening to Quincy, I shall at once communicate with you.

With great regard
Yours,
R. W. Emerson

S. H. Emery, Esq.

To Josiah Phillips Quincy, Boston, December 2, 1867 [246]

Union Club
Dec 2, Monday —

My dear Sir,

  I am sorry to leave home, as I do today for a few weeks, without having been able to bring yourself & my friend Mr P. P. Randolph together, as I had hoped to do at my house. I have been absent from home whilst he has been at Cambridge. But I have so strong an impression that you would both be interested in each other, that I cannot help hoping that it may be in your power to call on him at Cambridge, where he is at present staying (with Mrs Wyatt, corner of Broadway & Quincy Streets) that I venture to urge it. Perhaps you will show him this note, as a card of introduction, that I may have a share in your meeting.

  I am doubly sorry that you should come to my house, next Wednesday, without my being able to draw the full benefit of your visit.

With affectionate regard
R. W. Emerson

Josiah P Quincy, Esq.

245. I have not found any newspapers for Galesburg, Ill., for this period; but according to the MS memorandum book for 1867, "Social Aims" was read there on Dec. 21. For the "note" mentioned in the following sentence, see c. Oct.? 1867.

246. MS owned by Mr. M. A. DeWolfe Howe; ph. in CUL. Randolph's proposed visit to Cambridge is mentioned in Nov. 15, 1867; and Emerson's plan to leave home on Monday, Dec. 2, for a lecture tour of several weeks is noted in the letter of Nov. 29 of the same year.

To LIDIAN EMERSON, ERIE, PENNSYLVANIA, DECEMBER 5, 1867 [247]

Erie
December 5 1867

Dear Lidian,

I send tomorrow, written by another hand, a letter [248] to Ellen, &, as it occurs to me that she may be at Milton, I write now only to say that if she is absent you must open it & take charge of it until she comes home, instead letting it wander away to Lower Mills. Thus far I have had a pleasant enough journey, & fall daily among kindly people, though I am more than usually mindful of the stars in the East. At Cleveland,[249] I was introduced to General Sherman at the house of his brother, Judge Sherman,[250] & had some few minutes' conversation with the great soldier, a handsome, eager, easily talking man. Tonight a card was sent up to me of Mr Abel A. Adams, & I went down to see him, & found it was a brother of Abby A. who is a young merchant settled here, & he has promised to come & see me tomorrow morning, when I shall have more leisure. Dear love to the children, & keep Ellen as the apple of your eye. Not room for another word tonight from your

R. W. E.

To GEORGE L. TORBERT? CHICAGO? DECEMBER 7, 1867

[The telegram mentioned in Dec. 8, 1867.]

247. MS owned by RWEMA; ph. in CUL.

248. Andrew Caughey's (cf. Dec. 8, 1867). Miss Sarah A. Reed informs me that she recalls Emerson's visit at the home of her brother-in-law Andrew Caughey, president of the association before which the lecture was given, though she does not remember the date. Emerson, she remembers, talked about the death of Hawthorne, which had occurred in 1864. The *Erie Business Directory*, 1867, lists A. H. Caughey, of Caughey & McCreary, as well as A. A. Adams, dealer in shoes. This was not Emerson's first visit to Erie.

249. *The Cleveland Daily Plain Dealer*, Dec. 4, 1867, announced that Emerson would read " Eloquence " before the Cleveland Library Association that evening.

250. Charles T. Sherman, oldest brother of General William T. Sherman, is listed in the *Cleveland Leader Annual City Directory*, 1867, as a judge of the U. S. Court.

To Ellen Emerson, Chicago, December 8, 1867 [251]

Tremont House
Chicago Sunday
8 Dec[r]

Dear Ellen,

If I had known that I should spend Sunday here, no doubt I should have found a letter. Our train from Painesville [252] yesterday arrived a half hour too late to make connection with that for Dubuque; so I had to telegraph thither, last night, that I could not go to Manchester, for no train goes in that direction till tomorrow morn, & that not in season to reach it. I shall now go to Mendota,[253] Ill. on Wednesday. I am not very sorry to stop for a pair of days, & not at all sorry that the stop is here. I hope you had a letter yesterday — no, will have one on Monday morning, if at home, from Mr Caughey of Erie.[254] He was to send you $250. which will enable you to pay Walcott & H. $60. & Hudson for coal, say $100.

I hope you had a good evening with Dickens, & you must read to Mamma the report of it in the N. Y. Tribune,[255] — a pair of columns

251. MS owned by RWEMA; ph. in CUL. Dec. 8 fell on Sunday in 1867, the year fixed by evidence cited below.

252. Emerson lectured on "American Culture" before the Y. M. C. A. on Dec. 6. A local observer reported the disappointment of the audience as the lecturer culled "here and there a pithy sentence or quaint illustration from a mass of manuscript that seemed quite embarrassing to him, judging from the frequency with which he turned his pile of paper first one way and then the other." He said a few things excellently, but "he utterly failed to interest his audience and realize in their thought and feeling their beautiful ideal of the transcendental lecturer — Ralph Waldo Emerson." (*Painesville Telegraph*, Dec. 12, 1867.)

253. Dec. 15 following shows that Mendota was also dropped.

254. *Cf.* a note on Dec. 5, 1867.

255. Edward Waldo Emerson, Dec. 6, 1867, told of the "Dickens Expedition"; the excellent seats beside those of Lowell, Longfellow, Fields, and their families; and the excellent reading of *A Christmas Carol*. The *New-York Tribune*, Dec. 3, 1867, printed a humorous account of Dickens's reading at Boston on the previous day — the first reading of his second American tour — and of the excitement of the Bostonians. Nearly all the celebrities, said the reporter, were present, and he added: "Emerson's face I could not catch. Concord is far away, and snow storms no joke to travel in." Emerson, who was no great admirer of Dickens, happened, as we know, to be farther away than Concord; but he had already seen something of the novelist. He had dined with him at Fields's home on Nov. 21 (*Memories of a Hostess*, p. 141). According to Annie Fields, Emerson heard the first reading of "Dr. Marigold" in Boston (*Authors and Friends,* p. 74); but this statement seems at least doubtful, unless the reading referred to was a private one in advance of the first open to the public.

which will be pretty sure to be in the Weekly T. Did he actually caper?
— for so it reads. I shall probably do my errand to Miss Waterman [256]
today — whose christened name I cannot recall, — & Mr Collyer's card
I have already found under my door. My faithful Wiley has not yet discovered my arrival. Ralph's charming ambrotype I find safe in my
pocketbook & send my love to his father & mother. I do not yet fix Edward in my memory as surely at home, yet shall write to him as there.[257]
Tell mamma that I have not yet explored far enough in my trunk to
know all that is there but hitherto discover no omissions

R. W. Emerson

I hope Edward will make a personal visit to the woods where John [258]
is chopping & use his own eyes there as well as his recollection of my
three oak trees which mark the spot.

To George L. Torbert? Chicago? December c. 8? 1867

[Described in Dec. 15, 1867, as to " the Dubuque man." Torbert, of Dubuque,
Ia., manager of Emerson's Western tour of this year, appears in several letters.
I conjecture that the present letter followed closely upon the telegram of
Dec. 7, 1867.]

To Ellen Emerson, Mattoon, Illinois, December 15, 1867 [259]

Mattoon
15 Dec^r
Sunday Evening

Dear Ellen,

     Not a word from home since I left it. You are always so
vigilant for me, that I am sure there are letters for me lodged some-

---

Probably he did not actually hear Dickens read till late in the following February, on
an occasion also recorded by Mrs. Fields (*Memories,* pp. 157–158).

256. Doubtless the teacher mentioned, but not fully named, in earlier letters.

257. So far as I know, he did not write to Edward till Dec. 16 or 17.

258. Perhaps the John Clahan of other letters.

259. MS owned by RWEMA; ph. in CUL. The year is clearly 1867, when Dec. 15
fell on Sunday. G. L. Douthit, a Congregational pastor, wrote from Shelbyville, Ill.,
Nov. 29, 1880, recalling Emerson's lecture at Mattoon on a Saturday " some twelve
years ago " and his reading of " Immortality " to Douthit's congregation the following day. On the Saturday afternoon before the lecture Douthit had, he remembered, found Emerson at the hotel, reading Grimm's life of Michelangelo. The MS
memorandum book for 1867 gives the dates for Mattoon as Dec. 14 (" Success ") and
15 (" Immortality ").

where, but I have asked in vain of each committee, at Lincoln,[260] Jacksonville,[261] then of the Dubuque man by letter,[262] & here. Tomorrow, then, I shall find them at St Louis.[263] From Saint Louis I shall send you, no doubt, a letter with a draft, as I did already from Erie, through Caughey, which I hope safely arrived. You know I did not go either to Manchester or Mendota.[264] We have not had your great snow storm; only a small one at Jacksonville. My journey has been easy enough, & in this town all the accidents have been unusually agreeable. This town is only eleven years old, & holds 4000 people.

Tell mamma I did not mean to leave home without seeing to the repairs of her south window, which must have become troublesome before now. Tell Edward, if it is not attended to already, to go to Silas Hosmer, who has served Uncle William so well, & who is the man for jobs. I wish hereafter to employ Hobson for important things, but this is too little for him to begin with. Yet it should be thoroughly done.

Tell Edward also that I could not find a MS. wrapped in newspaper & marked " Originality & Quotation," which I believed of course was in my trunk. Let him find it in the study & guard it. It is the paper I have been working on for Mr Norton,[265] & was to have finished, if possible, on this journey. I wish good news of you all & of Aunt Susan, — Ralph [266] comes out of my pocketbook, & has not exhausted his power to please, but tells me no new word of his mother & sister & sire.

R. W. Emerson

To Edward Waldo Emerson, St. Louis, December 16? 1867 [267]

Southern Hotel
St Louis
17 Dec. Evening

Dear Edward, I am delighted to get your letter & its enclosures, on arriving here this afternoon. It is the first news I have had from you all, &

260. I have found no papers for Lincoln, Ill., for this period; but according to the MS memorandum book for 1867, " Social Aims " was read there on Dec. 12.

261. According to a local paper, Emerson's address before the Sigma Pi Society on Dec. 13 was fascinating and the delivery much better than had been expected, but a " terrific " snowstorm made the audience small (*Daily Jacksonville Journal*, Dec. 13 and 14, 1867).

262. Dec. *c*. 8? 1867.

263. See Dec. 16? 1867.

264. Mentioned in Dec. 8, 1867.

265. *Cf.* Oct. 15, 1867.

266. The " ambrotype " of him is mentioned in Dec. 8, 1867.

267. MS owned by Mr. Raymond Emerson; ph. in CUL. The year is obvious.

it appears that you have sent me something else already, which I have not, — you name a letter from Mr Holmes,[268] & I suppose there must be one from the unfailing Ellen somewhere. Of course I wished to know of your Evening with Dickens,[269] & that there were no disasters, & some pleasure. Then of Quincy; [270] and how the Lyceum prospers, under admirable management.[271] You have not, I think, seen St Louis. 'Tis a noble town as seen in the approach — from the Illinois side, and it has a superb house for travellers, this Southern. And it has singular & surprising lights in this little Philosophical Society of Mr Harris & his men, who edit the Philosophical journal,[272] all whose three Numbers are contained in one of my pamphlet boxes, which were my last New Year's present, if any metaphysician should descend upon the house. Tell me, when you write again, whither the lost letters were directed, that I [273] may straightly inquire for them. I did not arrive in time today to send you any draft, but shall tomorrow; &, on the 20th instant, pay John [274] $40., though 35. is the old rule for this month. The Milton letter was welcome, & also the card of Carlyle.[275] Tell Mr Alcott, if he does not already know it, that the Englishman Davidson [276] is already well placed here, & much valued. And get Mr Silas Hosmer for your mother's window.

R. W. Emerson

According to the *Daily Missouri Democrat* of Dec. 17, 1867, Emerson read " Success " to a spell-bound audience assembled under the auspices of the Public School Library Society on Dec. 16. If, as he says, he arrived " this afternoon," the date of the letter can hardly be later than the 16th. On Dec. 20, 1867, Edward wrote from Concord, acknowledging " Your letter written from St Louis on Monday 16th I suppose, though dated 17th by you."

268. Perhaps the Holmes of Feb. 17, 1867, to Lidian Emerson.

269. Edward's comment on the Dickens reading is mentioned in a note on Dec. 8, 1867.

270. The MS records of the Concord Lyceum (in the Concord Free Public Library) show that Josiah P. Quincy, of Boston, lectured Dec. 4, 1867, on " Defects of our Public Schools." Edward had mentioned this lecture in his letter of Dec. 6, and Ellen, in hers of the 9th.

271. Edward was one of the curators of the Concord Lyceum (*cf.* Nov. 22, 1867) .

272. For both society and journal, see earlier letters of this year.

273. This word may have been inserted by another hand.

274. *Cf.* Dec. 8, 1867.

275. I have found neither.

276. Doubtless this was the Thomas Davidson mentioned in Mar. 3, 1870, and described by Denton J. Snider, p. 33, as a " lively and ingenious Scotchman." According to Frederic Boase, *Modern English Biography,* 1912, Davidson, born in Scotland, was master in several English schools, went to Boston in 1867, and became a teacher in St. Louis the same year.

To Ellen Emerson, St. Louis, December 17, 1867 [277]

St Louis
Dec 17, 1867

Dear Ellen,

I enclose a draft of Allen, Copp, & Nisbet,[278] Bankers here, on Spencer, Vila, & Co. Boston,[279] for $300. payable to your order. This should serve to pay debts of the moment, & furnish a fund to meet the first bills of the new year. I still hope to be at home on the 1st Jan [280] but may be detained.

R. W. Emerson.

I go to Alton today.[281]

To Edward Waldo Emerson, Des Moines, Iowa, December 19? 1867

[MS owned by Mr. Raymond Emerson. Printed incompletely in Cabot, II, 569. The same fragment in *Journals*, X, 223, bears the date Dec. 17. No date is included in Emerson's heading, but month and year are clear from the contents. For the day of the month, the MS memorandum book records " Success " at Des Moines, Dec. 19. Edward wrote, Dec. 24, 1867, that "the letter from Des Moines " had arrived that morning.]

To Edward Waldo Emerson, Chicago, December 22, 1867

[MS owned by Mr. Raymond Emerson. Mr. L. Hubbard Shattuck informs me that *The Chicago Republican* of Dec. 24, 1867, reports the reading of " Country Life " before the Young Men's Association on the 23d.]

To Edward Waldo Emerson and Ellen Emerson, Cleveland,
December 28, 1867

[MS owned by Mr. Raymond Emerson.]

277. MS owned by RWEMA; ph. in CUL.
278. Duly listed in *Edwards' Annual Director . . . in the City of St. Louis* for 1867.
279. Listed in *The Boston Directory* for the year commencing July 1, 1867.
280. He arrived at Milton, Mass., on Jan. 2 (see Jan. 7, 1868).
281. Edward wrote, Dec. 24, 1867, acknowledging a letter " from Alton enclosing the $300.00 check." It is probable, however, that he referred to the present letter, which may well have been mailed at Alton. The MS memorandum book for 1867 gives Dec. 17 to that town (" Social Aims ").